CORRECTION SYMBOLS IN ALPHABETICAL ORDER

Boldface numbers and letters refer to chapters and sections of the handbook.

ab	Faulty abbreviation, **28**
ad	Misuse of adjective or adverb, **9**
agr	Error in agreement, **8**
ap	Apostrophe needed or misused, **23**
appr	Inappropriate diction, **31a**
awk	Awkward construction
bib	Error in bibliography form, **35d-2**
ca	Error in case form, **6**
cap	Use capital letter, **26**
cit	Missing source citation or error in form of citation, **36i**
coh	Coherence lacking, **1h-3, 3b**
con	Be more concise, **31c**
coord	Coordination needed or faulty, **16a**
cs	Comma splice, **11a–b**
d	Error in diction, **31**
dev	Inadequate development, **1, 3c**
div	Incorrect word division, **30**
dm	Dangling modifier, **14f**
emph	Emphasis lacking or faulty, **18**
exact	Inexact word, **31b**
fn	Error in footnote form, **36i-2**
frag	Sentence fragment, **10**
fs	Fused sentence, **11c**
gl/gr	See Glossary of Grammatical Terms, p. 731
gl/us	See Glossary of Usage, p. 713
gr	Error in grammar, **5–9**
hyph	Error in use of hyphen, **34d**
inc	Incomplete construction, **15c–e**
ital	Italicize (underline), **27**
k	Awkward construction
lc	Use lowercase letter, **26f**
log	Faulty logic, **4b-4**
mixed	Mixed construction, **15a–b**
mm	Misplaced modifier, **14a–e**
mng	Meaning unclear
ms	Error in manuscript form, **App. A**

no cap	Unnecessary capital letter, **26f**
no ∧	Comma not needed, **21j**
no ¶	No new paragraph needed, **3**
num	Error in use of numbers
p	Error in punctuation
. ? !	Period, question mark, exclamation point
∧	Comma, **21**
;	Semicolon, **22**
∨	Apostrophe, **23**
" "	Quotation marks, **24**
: — ( ) [ ] . . . /	Colon, dash, parentheses, brackets, ellipsis mark, slash, **25**
par, ¶	Start new paragraph, **3**
¶ coh	Paragraph not coherent, **3b**
¶ dev	Paragraph not developed, **3c**
¶ un	Paragraph not unified, **3a**
pass	Ineffective passive voice, **7h, 18d**
ref	Error in pronoun reference, **12**
rep	Unnecessary repetition, **31c-2**
rev	Revise or proofread, **2**
shift	Inconsistency, **13**
sp	Misspelled word, **34**
spec	Be more specific, **3c, 4e**
sub	Subordination needed or faulty, **16b**
t	Error in verb tense, **7e–f**
t seq	Error in tense sequence, **7f**
trans	Transition needed, **3b-6, 3e**
var	Vary sentence structure, **19**
vb	Error in verb form, **7a–d**
w	Wordy, **31c**
ww	Wrong word, **31b-1**
//	Faulty parallelism, **17**
#	Separate with a space
⌢	Close up the space
⸜	Delete
∿	Transpose letters or words
x	Obvious error
∧	Something missing, **15e**
??	Manuscript illegible or meaning unclear

The Little, Brown Handbook

Instructor's Annotated Edition

FOURTH EDITION

The Little, Brown Handbook

H. RAMSEY FOWLER
Memphis State University

JANE E. AARON
Parsons School of Design/
The New School for Social Research

Instructor's Annotated Edition

ROBERT A. SCHWEGLER
University of Rhode Island

SCOTT, FORESMAN AND COMPANY
Glenview, Illinois • Boston • London

Instructors using *The Little, Brown
Handbook, Fourth Edition*, by H. Ramsey
Fowler and Jane E. Aaron as a class text
are permitted to duplicate portions of the
instructor's material, pages IAE-1–IAE-55.

ISBN 0-673-49691-0

 2 3 4 5 6 7 8 9 10—RRC—94 93 92 91 90

Printed in the United States of America

Contents

The Little, Brown Handbook

Instructor's Annotated Edition

Designing and Teaching Composition Courses: Four Essays

Teaching Writing: Process and Beyond

Most writing instructors would agree that helping students become aware of various strategies for discovering, planning, drafting, and revising is central to composition courses. This emphasis on the *how* of writing is the legacy of two decades of careful research on the composing process of novice and professional writers. Concurrently, it is a reaction against teaching that places inordinate emphasis on the form of the essay at the expense of ideas, audience, self-discovery, and self-expression.

Yet even those who argue strongly for process-oriented instruction have admitted possible pitfalls, especially the way a composing process can become for students (and even instructors) a rigid formula difficult to adapt to varying audiences and purposes for writing. Moreover, studies of the social contexts for writing and programs of writing across the curriculum have both contributed to a renewed interest in forms of expression and led to greater understanding of readers' expectations and needs.

While most composition instructors accept the key assumptions of the process approach, they also want to emphasize flexibility in the composing process and to pay attention to the forms of writing. As the introductory chapters and the marginal comments in this *Annotated Instructor's Edition of The Little, Brown Handbook* make plain, *The Little, Brown Handbook, 4th edition*, is designed to alert students to the processes and also to the forms of written expression. The blending of flexibility with firm, concrete advice that characterizes the handbook is highlighted in the *Annotated Instructor's Edition*, to enable beginning and experienced instructors to draw on the text's resources in designing and teaching a composition course.

It would be foolish to suggest that all composition instructors who emphasize the composing process are in agreement over specific teaching strategies—or that they ought to be. Two teachers who share a belief in the importance of revision or who encourage students to discover ideas and information through freewriting may also disagree strongly about the purposes for writing: one emphasizing personal discovery and self-expression, the other concentrating on social texts such as argument and academic discourse. Nonetheless, it is possible to identify some generally agreed-upon elements of a process paradigm. Behind this paradigm lie case studies of skilled and unskilled writers (Emig, 1971; Perl; Sommers, 1980), cognitive models of the composing process (Flower and Hayes), arguments about the primacy of personal discourse and its relationship to expository and persuasive discourse (Britton, Moffett), and process-oriented teaching strategies (Murray, Sommers, 1982). Our process paradigm is based upon the following assumptions:

Writing consists of a variety of activities including developing (exploring, gathering, focusing, organizing); drafting (finding and expressing meaning, establishing relationships); and revising (rethinking, rewriting, editing, proofreading).

The activities that make up the writing process are recursive, not fixed in order. For example, revising often includes the discovery of fresh insights, and the drafting of one part of a paper may occur at the same time the writer is gathering materials for another part.

Writing often is a process of discovering ideas, arriving at knowledge of the self, and selecting effective ways to present concepts and information.

Knowledge of the conventions of expression and of stylistic options is an important part of the writer's repertoire, but a premature striving for correctness and for grace and clarity often can impede the free flow of ideas and the discovery of appropriate form. Thus, activities like editing and proofreading, which pay considerable attention to style, grammar, and mechanics, are generally best left until relatively late in the composing of an essay.

Skilled writers (in contrast to unskilled writers) are characterized by the range of strategies they know and employ in developing, drafting, and revising—strategies that can be both taught and learned.

Effective writing is the product of interaction among the three elements of the writing situation: author, subject, and audience.

These assumptions shape the advice offered throughout *The Little, Brown Handbook*, not only in discussions of the writing process and the whole paper (Part I), but also in treatments of the research paper and writing in the disciplines (Part VIII), and in the treatment of strategies for clear and effective sentences (Parts III and IV). Even the discussions of grammatical sentences (Part II), punctuation (Part V), and mechanics (Part VI) mix firm and relatively conservative advice with an awareness of the demands of various audiences and of the difference between an early draft and a final, carefully edited draft.

At the same time, however, discussions in the handbook point out that different writing situations may call for different composing processes and that the knowledge of forms for expression—the *what* of writing—is an important companion to an awareness of the *how*. In this, the handbook agrees with the work of such theorists and teachers as Maxine Hairston, James Reither, Patricia Bizzell, Richard Coe, and Arthur Applebee. These writers share a belief that the process paradigm needs to be augmented by (1) an awareness of the ways the writing process varies according to the writer's purpose and the social context, (2) a recognition of the important roles knowledge of form and convention can play in guiding the composing process, and (3) an acknowledgment of the extent to which communities of readers and writers are bound together by specific expectations governing the form and content of discourse.

While the outlines of a post-process approach to writing instruction are still a matter of considerable debate, several areas of broad agreement have emerged, and these are reflected in the current edition of *The Little, Brown Handbook*.

As Maxine Hairston points out in "Different Products, Different Processes: A Theory About Writing," writing situations may call for contrasting composing processes and varying sorts of knowledge. Some tasks such as technical reports or routine memoranda may be conventional in form and draw on knowledge the writer has already mastered, but at the same time they may pose stylistic challenges in adapting to the needs and attitudes of a particular audience. Other kinds of prose, such as much scholarly writing and nonroutine professional or personal writing, may require originality in content and expression and require extensive discovery and revision.

The handbook recognizes that the processes of composing are "strategies that writers employ for particular purposes" (Applebee, 106) and emphasizes this perspective in the initial treatment of composing in Chapters 1 and 2. The discussions of specialized forms of writing, in turn, highlight strategies appropriate to the tasks: argument (Chapter 4); the research paper (Chapters 36 and 37); writing in academic disciplines (Chapter 38); writing essay exams, business letters, and memoranda (Chapters 39 and 40).

In discussions of paragraphing (Chapter 3), critical thinking and writing (Chapter 4), the research paper (Chapters 36 and 37), writing in the disciplines (Chapter 38), and of essay exams and business writing (Chapters 39 and 40), the handbook alerts students to a variety of commonly used rhetorical patterns. The emphasis throughout is on seeing the forms as the shared expectations of readers and writers and on using them to guide the discovery and expression of ideas, not on constraining creativity.

The treatment of disciplinary conventions of thought and expression in Chapter 38 may be particularly interesting and useful for both instructors and students because of what it reveals about both the social and generative roles of rhetorical form in academic settings.

Ultimately, however, the roles that form plays in composing will depend on the willingness of instructors and students to regard rhetorical patterns as flexible frameworks rather than as rigid formulas—as essential parts of a creative composing process.

Resources for Teaching Writing

Applebee, Arthur N. "Problems in Process Approaches: Toward a Reconceptualization of Process Instruction." In *The Teaching of Writing*. Chicago: National Society for the Study of Education, 1986. 95–113.

Beach, Richard, and Lillian S. Bridwell, eds. *New Directions in Composition Research*. New York: Guilford, 1984.

Bizzell, Patricia. "College Composition: Initiation into the Academic Discourse Community." *Curriculum Inquiry* 12 (1982): 191–207.

Britton, James, et al. *The Development of Writing Abilities (11–18)*. London: Macmillan, 1975.

Coe, Richard M. "An Apology for Form; or, Who Took the Form Out of the Process?" *College English* 49 (1987): 13–28.

Cooper, Charles R., and Lee Odell, eds. *Research on Composing: Points of Departure*. Urbana: NCTE, 1978.

D'Angelo, Frank J. *A Conceptual Theory of Rhetoric*. Cambridge, MA: Winthrop, 1975.

Emig, Janet. *The Composing Processes of Twelfth Graders*. Urbana: NCTE, 1971.

————. *The Web of Meaning*. Upper Montclair: Boynton/Cook, 1983.

Faigley, Lester. "Competing Theories of Process: A Critique and a Proposal." *College English* 48 (1986): 527–42.

Flower, Linda, and John R. Hayes. "A Cognitive Process Theory of Writing." *College Composition and Communication* 32 (1981): 365–87.

Hairston, Maxine. "Different Products, Different Processes: A Theory About Writing," *College Composition and Communication* 37 (1986): 442–52.

Knoblauch, C. H., and Lil Brannon. *Rhetorical Traditions and the Teaching of Writing.* Upper Montclair: Boynton/Cook, 1984.

Moffett, James. *Teaching the Universe of Discourse.* Boston: Houghton Mifflin, 1968.

Murray, Donald M. *A Writer Teaches Writing,* 2nd ed. Boston: Houghton Mifflin, 1985.

Perl, Sondra. "The Composing Process of Unskilled College Writers." *College Composition and Communication* 31 (1980): 389–401.

Perelman, Les. "The Context of Classroom Writing," *College English* 48 (1986): 471–9.

Reither, James A. "Writing and Knowing: Toward Redefining the Writing Process." *College English* 47 (1985): 620–8.

Rose, Mike. "Rigid Rules, Inflexible Plans, and the Stifling of Language: A Cognitivist Analysis of Writer's Block." *College Composition and Communication* 31 (1980): 389–401.

Sommers, Nancy. "Responding to Student Writing." *College Composition and Communication* (1982): 148–56.

————. "Revision Strategies of Student Writers and Experienced Adult Writers." *College Composition and Communication* 31 (1980): 378–88.

The Handbook In Composition Courses

At the center of a composition course should be the students' writing. Their acts of discovery or sharing and the time spent in drafting, revising, responding, and editing should form the essential structure of the course. Yet despite the centrality of students and their work, instructors play an important part in effective composition courses, and textbooks can, too, as long as they are aids and do not dominate a course.

The Little, Brown Handbook can be a valuable resource for teaching composition, partly because of its flexibility. There are almost as many ways to organize a composition course as there are skills involved in successful writing or different kinds of reading and writing. Writing is a complex act, drawing together many skills, including the ability to discover and organize ideas, the ability to reach a compromise between the aims of personal expression and the needs of an audience, and the ability to produce acceptable sentences and paragraphs. The kinds of texts with which students are generally expected to be familiar—as readers and writers—are likewise complex and diverse: persuasive, informative, expressive, and academic texts. As a result, a composition instructor faces a wide range of options in deciding how to structure a course and what to emphasize. This section suggests possible uses of *The Little, Brown Handbook* with a variety of organizations and emphases.

Organizing a Composition Course

Organizing a composition course means choosing to emphasize those aspects of writing or kinds of texts that the instructor (or the department) considers most important and that meet students' needs. At the same time, it means figuring out a way to include in the course the other aspects and kinds of writing. In recent years, composition teaching has followed several general patterns for organizing a course, including emphasis on patterns of expression and thought, on the writing process, on content and ideas, on genres of nonfiction, and on academic writing (writing across the curriculum). Each approach can be successful if it meets the needs of a particular group of students and if the instructor pays some attention to all aspects of composing, not merely those emphasized in the design of the course. In addition, each approach can be enriched by *The Little, Brown Handbook*.

Emphasis on Patterns of Expression and Thought

Many instructors believe that a composition course ought to give students a chance to understand and practice basic patterns of expression and thought. Courses may vary widely, however, in the patterns they emphasize: rhetorical and logical patterns (classification, comparison-contrast, deduction), general essay structures (thesis and support, general to specific), types of essays (informative, argumentative), patterns of paragraph development, and sentence patterns. Such courses have in common two assumptions about the way students learn to write: first, that by understanding and mastering the elements of a finished essay, students will be able to improve their writing; and second, that patterns of expression can act as patterns of thought, in that they help a writer to understand, shape, and communicate experience.

The first assumption predominates in what might be called *skills courses*, often designed to serve developmental students or students who have difficulty writing whole essays. Skills courses focus on developing sentence and paragraph skills, moving to the whole essay only after students have mastered different kinds of paragraphs. Instructors who choose this approach generally argue that the basic sentence pattern of subject + assertion and the standard paragraph pattern of subject + assertion + support are simply smaller versions of the thesis + support pattern of whole essays and the assertion + support pattern of thought characteristic of much expository writing, particularly in academic settings. Thus, skills courses not only try to break the task of academic writing into manageable units but also help introduce patterns of thought essential to success in college courses.

In organizing a skills course, you might begin with a unit on sentence structure, drawing on Chapters 5–9 of the handbook ("Grammatical Sentences"), and you might stress an understanding of phrases, clauses, basic sentence types, and verb forms and tenses. Along with this, or beginning later in the semester if appropriate, you might require paragraph-length writing and make use of the extensive discussion in Chapter 3 ("Composing Paragraphs"). Paragraph-length writing can continue through the semester, accompanied by work in Chapters 10–15 ("Clear Sentences") and 16–19 ("Effective Sentences"). Starting with paragraphs as early as possible can give students a sense of accomplishment and a chance to put into practice what they are learning in the sentence units. Chapters on punctuation, mechanics, diction, and usage can be assigned whenever they meet the needs of the class or of individual students.

Although an effective skills course can focus on sentence, paragraph, and essay patterns, it also needs to pay attention to the writing process and to audience (Chapters 1, 2, and 4 in the handbook). Students who have trouble mastering the basic forms of expression are also likely to underestimate the importance of planning and revising and to have difficulty shaping their writing to the needs of an audience. These matters need to be covered and reinforced throughout the course, perhaps through assignments that require planning, drafting, and revising and also create realistic audiences and situations for students to address in their writing.

The other assumption behind this emphasis on patterns of expression and thought—that patterns of expression can also be ways of viewing experience—leads to *rhetorically oriented* courses. Instructors who teach this sort of course often survey basic essay types (narration, description, exposition, and argument), patterns of development (classification, analysis, comparison-contrast), or specific essay types (particularly forms of argument and exposition). Yet they may also introduce the patterns of development as a means of probing subjects and developing and organizing essays. Regardless of their approach, these instructors share the belief that students who have understood these patterns and practiced them in their writing will be able to make use of them in a variety of writing tasks. Most of these instructors would also agree that each pattern of development directs attention to a different aspect of a subject. In this way, patterns of expression can be seen as shaping the way we think about a subject and as affecting a reader's attitudes.

If you wish to give your course a rhetorical orientation, you may want to begin with Chapters 1–4 of the handbook ("The Whole Paper and Paragraphs") as a way of showing students how to develop, write, revise, and edit an essay and to adapt it to an audience. Later in the course, you may want to return to this material to remind students how important are the stages of the writing process, particularly planning and revising. You can also point out that Chapters 1 and 3 treat the rhetorical patterns as answers to questions about aspects of a topic, as well as ways of organizing and developing essays and paragraphs. The main portion of the course might consist of a review of essay types or patterns of essay and paragraph development (Chapters 1–3) with assignments that give students a chance to use the forms. The chapters on coordination and subordination, parallelism, sentence emphasis, and variety (Chapters 16–19, "Effective Sentences") can be introduced later in the course to add variety and style to students' writing. The chapters on common sentence errors, punctuation, mechanics, diction, and usage can be assigned according to the needs of individuals or of the class and may also be used for reference. The course might culminate in a research paper (Chapters 35–37) or with memos and essay questions (Chapter 39).

Instructors of rhetorically oriented courses often rely on a reader or rhetoric to provide examples of essay types and patterns of development. The risk in a rhetorically oriented course is that students will come to regard the various forms as ends in themselves and ignore the role they play in viewing experience and in shaping communication to an audience or situation. For this reason, many instructors emphasize throughout the course the process of exploring subjects and revising the plan for an essay, and they try to create specific audiences and situations for students to address in their writing.

Emphasis on the Writing Process

Many instructors believe that a composition course should emphasize the process of writing rather than the forms writing can take. This approach assumes that by helping students respond to writing situations with a full awareness of the importance of each activity in the writing process—discovering, focusing, planning, drafting, revising, and editing—and by giving them a chance to adapt the process to the demands of different kinds of writing, we enable them to respond effectively to future writing tasks. A *process-oriented* course does not ignore the forms of expression but instead presents them as strategies best learned in the context of a particular writing task. It also assumes that matters of grammar, punctuation, and mechanics are learned most readily when they are necessary for effective communication in an essay.

In organizing a course that emphasizes the writing process, you might begin by having students look over the discussion of the process in the handbook (Chapters 1 and 2, "Developing an Essay" and "Drafting and Revising the Essay"). You will, of course, have to briefly review the writing process as part of each assignment, both to remind students that each of the elements of composing is important and to show how the kinds of planning and revising a writer must do will vary slightly depending on the subject, the aim of the writing task, and the audience for the essay. You may wish to start the course with personal writing because it turns attention inward and often makes students aware of how their minds operate as they write. When you move to more public kinds of writing, however, Chapter 4 ("Convincing Your Readers") will help alert students to the need to take their readers into account as they shape what they have to say and decide how to say it.

The assignments in a process-oriented course should stress planning and revising in all writing tasks. They should also suggest writing strategies that students can use to deal with a subject and meet the needs of a reader. If the assigned essay requires particular attention to paragraphing—a persuasive paper, for example—then students might be required to look at Chapter 3 ("Composing Paragraphs"). Chapters 16–19 ("Effective Sentences") will also help introduce students to useful strategies, and Chapters 35–38 ("Research Writing") and 39 ("Practical Writing") can be good resources when students are asked to write academic papers or memos directed at a business or professional audience. Coverage of matters of grammar, punctuation, diction, and usage will depend on the needs of the class and of individual students.

Since many problems in student writing can be traced to a lack of effective planning or revising, a composition course that emphasizes process can have a significant effect on student writing. But students need to be aware that word choice, sentence structure, paragraph development, and essay organization also contribute to the effectiveness of writing. Therefore, a course that emphasizes the writing process needs to introduce students to the options and to their usefulness in communicating the writer's purpose to an audience.

Emphasis on Content and Ideas

Courses that emphasize ideas and essay content—often called *thematic courses*—generally rest on the beliefs that the best kind of writing grows out of a strong need to communicate and that students are most likely to have a desire to communicate when they are exposed to significant ideas and issues. The ideas and issues around which such a course is built may be personal—family life, education, or social relationships—or they may be matters of public policy—the environment, pornography, or the American legal system. The sources for the content of the course may be an anthology, a lecture series, films, or the students' own research and experiences. Since instructors who teach such courses generally consider a piece of writing important for what the writer has to say, they cover the forms of writing and the writing process primarily to help students communicate ideas and feelings clearly and effectively. If you choose to emphasize the content of essays in your composition course, you may wish to begin by introducing students to the writing process and the basic forms of the essay with Chapters 1–4 ("The Whole Paper and Paragraphs"). These chapters suggest ways students can develop their ideas and organize them into paragraphs and whole essays. As students struggle to express their ideas, you may wish to assign Chapters 31–34 ("Effective Words") to help them communicate more precisely and Chapters 16–19 ("Effective Sentences") to help them add variety, clarity, and style to their writing. Chapters on punctuation, mechanics, grammar, and usage can be assigned to the class or to individual students according to need. If students are required to use research in their writing, Chapters 35–37 ("Research Writing") will be helpful.

Emphasis on Genres of Nonfiction

Some instructors may view emphasis on patterns like comparison-contrast and cause-effect as strategies for whole essays because the patterns do not represent widely used types of writing and because most good writing combines patterns to suit its purposes. Many of these instructors would point out that while writers employ comparison-contrast in evaluating a product or performance and use cause-effect in analyzing a problem, the patterns that actually guide their composing are genres of nonfiction: the evaluation and the problem analysis. Nonfiction genres like evaluation, autobiography, problem-solution, explanation, issue analysis, the proposal, and the position paper grow out of the practices of many writers and the demands of common writing situations; they represent, moreover, the expectations that readers use as guides when they encounter a text. The genres of nonfiction are not fixed forms, of course, any more than the genres of literature are. Yet they are a valuable part of any writer's knowledge and can offer students fresh perspectives on a topic or a social situation, particularly one that requires students to take the role of knower or persuader.

Courses emphasizing the genres of nonfiction generally provide students with examples in the form of readings or ask students to locate and identify different kinds of writing on their own. Chapter 4 of the handbook ("Critical Thinking and Writing"), particularly 4a ("Summarizing") and 4c ("Understanding the Construction of Arguments"), can help students develop analytical skills important for examining and constructing different kinds of writing. The attention paid to audience and the needs of readers in Chapters 1 and 2 should also be of help in developing the skills and awareness necessary to understanding the range and uses of different kinds of nonfiction. Much nonfiction is based on research, and the extensive treatment of research papers in the handbook (Chapters 35–37) introduces students to some of the many different kinds of writing with sources. In addition, Chapter 38 ("Writing in the Disciplines") looks at the many forms of academic writing.

The attention to form in courses of this kind needs to be balanced with an attention to process, particularly to revision. The advice given on using the handbook in process-oriented courses (p. IAE-7) is appropriate here, as are the many resources the handbook offers for achieving correctness and variety in writing.

Emphasis on Academic Writing

Chapter 38 of the handbook, "Writing in the Disciplines," covers much of the territory appropriate for a course emphasizing *writing-across-the-curriculum*. Such a course may ask students to write papers in each of the areas covered by the chapter—the humanities, the social sciences, and the natural and applied sciences—and may ask students to become acquainted with the research tools in each area (also discussed in detail in Chapter 38). The treatment of the writing process in Chapters 1 and 2, of paragraphing in Chapter 3, of critical thinking and writing in Chapter 4, and of the varieties of sentence structure in Chapters 16–19 can also be important elements of a course built around the varieties of academic writing.

In many writing-across-the-curriculum programs, however, writing instruction is part of content courses, employed both as a tool for learning and as a way of sharing knowledge in forms appropriate to a discipline. Because it is designed as a reference tool and therefore does not impose a particular design on a course, the handbook can be a useful resource for content courses emphasizing writing. It provides discussions of the writing process and of research and documentation in specific disciplines as well as resources for editing style, grammar, and mechanics. Whatever the particular uses of writing in a course, the handbook's advice about the process of writing (Chapters 1 and 2) is likely to prove valuable.

Using the Handbook with Other Texts

Although the handbook can be used as the only text in a course, many instructors also adopt a reader, a rhetoric, or a workbook like *The Little, Brown Workbook*. Each kind of text enables you to emphasize different elements of the course and also provides activities to help students develop their writing.

With a Reader

Readers are generally of three kinds: rhetorical, thematic, and cross-curricular. Rhetorical readers illustrate the different aims and patterns of writing with selections by professional authors and sometimes by students. Readers of this type frequently begin with writing patterns that students find most accessible—narration, description, exemplification—and move on to patterns that students find more difficult to use—classification, comparison-contrast, inductive and deductive argument. Many readers provide extensive introductions to the rhetorical patterns, discussing their uses in writing and the aspects of a subject that they focus on. Some recent rhetorical readers go beyond the basic rhetorical patterns to discuss common forms of nonfiction writing—such as the problem-solution report, the personal essay, the evaluation, and the proposal—that combine the basic patterns in a number of ways. Rhetorical readers, as well as some thematic readers with rhetorical indices, can be sources for model essays that illustrate, among other things, patterns of development, essay and paragraph strategies, variety in tone, and sentence emphasis and variety. The questions accompanying the essays in most rhetorical readers direct students' attention to the most important features of the models and suggest ways students can incorporate such features in their own writing.

Thematic readers present writings that illustrate and explore a number of themes, such as the stages of personal growth or family relationships, or topics of general interest, such as capital punishment or the impact of technology. The writings may include fiction or poetry as well as essays. If the main purpose for using the reader is to provide subject matter for essays, a thematic reader may be preferable because, as a rule, readers of this type provide several perspectives on a subject and more background information to get class discussion started and give students material to use in their writing.

Some readers are both rhetorical and thematic in organization and coverage, providing a table of contents for each emphasis. Both types of readers can be used to generate class discussion and topics for student writing. Some readers even provide questions to stimulate discussion and include lists of possible topics for papers.

Cross-curricular readers typically provide examples of writing in a variety of disciplines and cover a range of topics. Some include essays directed to general readers as well as specialists. Others focus on the kinds of writing expected from students or professionals in a discipline. While the primary aim of readers of this type is to provide models of academic and professional prose, some also arrange readings in thematic clusters designed to encourage discussion and suggest subjects for students to pursue in their own writing. It is important for an instructor to choose a reader whose essays are intrinsically interesting to students or are arranged in intriguing clusters, because a purely formal approach to models of academic writing is likely to prove boring to most students, even those planning to study one or more of the disciplines represented in the sections.

Instructors who adopt a reader typically make discussion of its essays a major activity in the course, yet they also tend to make significant use of a handbook. If the reader chosen for a course does not provide a rhetorical framework for students' essays or a thorough coverage of writing and reasoning processes, instructors using *The Little, Brown Handbook* may wish to direct students to the coverage of these matters in Chapters 1, 2, and 4. The handbook provides explanations and examples of other matters frequently not covered in readers, such as paragraphing (Chapter 3); sentence structure, grammar, and style (Chapters 5–19); diction and usage (Chapter 31 and Glossary of Usage); the research paper (Chapters 35–37); and writing in the disciplines (Chapter 38). In addition, the handbook can be used as a reference guide for punctuation and mechanics, as an aid in marking student papers, and as a guide for revision. Some instructors who use a reader like to devote one period each week to subjects covered in the handbook; others like to set aside part of each day.

With a Rhetoric

Rhetorics cover many of the same topics as handbooks—discovering, planning, drafting, revising, rhetorical patterns, and paragraphing—but do so in greater depth, at the same time giving much less coverage to grammar, punctuation, mechanics, and usage. A rhetoric usually embodies a particular perspective toward writing and the teaching of writing—a theoretical bias, perhaps, or an emphasis on thesis-and-support essays, personal writing, academic writing, argumentation, critical thinking, or tone and style. Since a rhetoric thus helps determine the emphasis within a course, it provides less flexibility for the teacher than the handbook does, especially if the rhetoric has been chosen by a department rather than by the instructor.

Because rhetorics provide full coverage in some areas at the expense of others, instructors frequently adopt a handbook as a supplement. Used in this way, *The Little, Brown Handbook* can provide treatment of sentence style (Chapters 16–19), the research paper (Chapter 35–37), and writing in the disciplines (Chapter 38) for rhetorics that give only brief attention to these matters. It can also provide discussion and exercises for sentence structure and grammar (Chapters 5–15), punctuation and mechanics (Chapters 20–30), and diction and usage (Chapter 31 and Glossary of Usage). The discussions of paragraphs, the essay, and the writing process (Chapters 1–3) can supplement the material in a rhetoric and provide useful exercises.

When the handbook is used with a rhetoric, instructors often assign its chapters and exercises along with those in the rhetoric, and they devote class time to discussing both texts and reviewing the exercises. They also use the handbook as a reference for students, as an aid to grading papers, and as a guide for revision.

With the Handbook's Ancillary Publications

When combined with its ancillary publications—*The Little, Brown Workbook,* Fourth Edition; *Diagnostic Tests of Standard Written English to Accompany The Little, Brown Handbook; The Little, Brown Handbook Software Program;* a portable correction chart; and this *Instructor's Annotated Edition*—the handbook is the center of an instructional package that will meet the needs of many classes. The diagnostic tests provide a way for instructors to determine their students' needs at the beginning of a course and to design the course accordingly. Because the tests are keyed to the sections of the handbook, instructors can decide what chapters in the text need most emphasis. (The tests can also be used to place students in different courses or levels within a composition program.)

The Little, Brown Workbook is designed to give students more extensive practice with fundamentals than the handbook alone can provide. Since each section of the workbook includes a brief, simplified version of the discussion in the handbook, the workbook can be used on its own. Yet because each section corresponds to the treatment of the same subject in the handbook, the workbook can be a source of individual and class activities to complement the primary text. Answers for exercises in the handbook and the workbook are published as separate booklets that instructors can order, free, for their students.

The marginal notes in this *Instructor's Annotated Edition* describe many activities for class discussion, small-group work, and individual preparation, each keyed to a particular section of the handbook. The essay "Using Collaborative Learning with *The Little, Brown Handbook* on pages IAE-34–IAE-55 of the *Instructor's Annotated Edition* discusses how the handbook may be used in courses emphasizing collaborative learning and includes advice on adapting particular handbook exercises for small-group work.

Sentence Combining with the Handbook

During the past decade, extensive research has shown that having students work with the elements of sentences—manipulating, combining, and altering—leads not only to a greater understanding of sentence structure but also to a greater command of options for expression. Best of all, students who practice sentence combining develop a willingness to use the structures emphasized in the exercises, and their writing begins to display the flexible, expressive syntax characteristic of mature writing.

The handbook contains several kinds of sentence-combining exercises. Some ask students to combine two short (kernel) sentences so that the new sentence displays the grammatical or stylistic feature being emphasized in a chapter. Others ask students to combine sentences to produce a longer sentence following the pattern illustrated by a model sentence. And still others ask students to combine sentences to form a paragraph.

Sentence-combining exercises can be assigned at any point in the semester; however, they are most likely to have a positive effect on students' writing when they are part of an ongoing program of sentence combining. Regular work on sentence combining each week for an entire semester can be even more effective than an intense two- to three-week session of sentence combining.

Students can begin a sentence-combining program by working with simple exercises like those in Chapter 5 ("Understanding Sentence Grammar"). Though some of the exercises in that chapter may seem a bit basic for many classes, the ones dealing with appositives and absolutes will acquaint students with features they have probably used little in past writing. From the basic exercises, students can move on to those which introduce relatively complex sentence strategies, and they can conclude their work with paragraph-length exercises. The list below suggests a sequence for a sentence-combining program and identifies chapters in the handbook that contain appropriate exercises. If you decide to make sentence combining a substantial part of your composition course, you may want to supplement the exercises in the text by making up your own. Doing so will undoubtedly be necessary if your students discover that they like discussing and comparing the results of the exercises in class and want to spend a good deal of time on the activity.

A Sequence for Sentence Combining

Chapter 5, "Understanding Sentence Grammar," Exercises 9, 11, 13, 14, 16, 17, 18, 22

Chapter 6, "Case of Nouns and Pronouns," Exercise 4

Chapter 11, "Comma Splices and Fused Sentences," Exercise 3

Chapter 14, "Misplaced and Dangling Modifiers," Exercise 6

Chapter 21, "The Comma," Exercises 2, 4, 6

Chapter 22, "The Semicolon," Exercises 2, 4, 6, 8

Chapter 16, "Using Coordination and Subordination," Exercises 1, 3, 4, 7

Chapter 17, "Using Parallelism," Exercise 3

Chapter 18, "Emphasizing Main Ideas," Exercises 2 and 4

Chapter 19, "Achieving Variety," Exercises 1, 2, 3

Chapter 3, " Composing Paragraphs," Exercises 3 and 10

Chapter 5 introduces students to basic sentence structures, and Chapters 14 and 21 introduce modifying clauses and phrases along with their primary focus on grammar and punctuation. Chapters 21 and 22 present strategies of coordination as well as of punctuation, and Chapters 16 and 17 introduce progressively more sophisticated sentence strategies. In Chapters 18 and 19 students encounter sentence patterns characteristic of mature writing, and in Chapter 3 they get a chance to combine all the strategies in paragraphs.

Tutoring with the Handbook

Writing centers and tutoring programs can make good use of the handbook and its entire package. The handbook provides explanations and exercises for students, of course, but it can also perform several other valuable functions. It can help resolve conflicts over points of grammar and usage by being a primary reference, the final arbiter in debates. It can be a training manual for new tutors, providing simple and clear explanations of problems they will encounter every day. And it can be a reference for students who are working on a paper in the writing center without direct supervision by a tutor.

The *Diagnostic Tests of Standard Written English to Accompany The Little, Brown Handbook* can be used to screen students as they come to the center, identifying their writing problems and helping the tutor choose appropriate instructional materials. *The Little, Brown Workbook* can provide the "raw material" of tutoring—sample sentences, exercises, and brief explanations—to be used in discussion with the student or for independent work. The workbook can be particularly effective for tutoring if students are taking composition courses that use the handbook, because the language, rules, and exercises encountered in tutoring will be consistent with those encountered in the classroom.

Evaluating and Responding to Student Writing

Nothing we do as composition teachers—not lecturing, setting up peer critique groups, leading discussions, or preparing activities—has as much potential for helping students improve their writing as do our efforts to respond as sensitive and thorough readers. Moreover, as readers we can play several roles, some of them simultaneously. We can respond to a work in progress, acting as editors and critics with suggestions for revision or as ordinary readers whose reactions students can take into account as they shape the final product. Or we can be judges of a finished work, justifying a grade (as evaluators) or pointing out strengths and weaknesses (as teachers), encouraging students to build on one and avoid the other.

Yet evaluating student papers can be time-consuming: Instructors often report spending fifteen to twenty minutes on each paper, making marginal notes, writing summary comments, and deciding on a grade. Many set aside hours of office time for individual conferences. To help make the job of marking papers a bit easier and quicker, *The Little, Brown Handbook* provides a number of aids: a list of correction symbols keyed to discussions in the text, a number-and-letter correction code that refers students to appropriate sections of the handbook, and a thorough index and glossary of grammatical terms directing students to explanations of terms used in an instructor's written comments.

The Roles of Response

It takes more than an efficient correction system to bring about improvement in writing, however. How we respond and when are most important. In addition, the correction system we choose needs to be consistent with our purposes for responding and the roles we play as readers.

Responses directed toward a paper in progress often need to pay as much attention to the way the writer approaches the task as to the evolving text. On the one hand, it makes little sense to comment on detailed matters of punctuation in a draft full of helter-skelter ideas, thereby drawing attention away from advice about strategies the writer can employ to develop focus and discover purpose. On the other hand, helpful comments on agreement or mechanics coming at later stages in the writing of an essay can enable students to understand the importance of editing and can provide knowledge for later use.

Responses to a paper in progress ought to focus to a considerable extent on the writer's behaviors. Novice writers generally need to pay as much attention to learning how to discover ideas or draft an entire paper as to using topic sentences and effective patterns of paragraph development. Much of the advice in the handbook, especially in Chapters 1 and 2, is directed toward strategies for writing. Other discussions, such as the treatment of paragraphs in Chapter 3, pay more attention to the specific features of essays, though they do not ignore the process of composition.

Response to a final draft ought to provide a clear evaluation and the justification for it yet at the same time look toward future efforts. Student writers need to recognize and consolidate their successes; they need as well to understand what steps they can take in later essays. The essentially supportive tone of explanations in the handbook can help create this kind of understanding even when comments or the number-and-letter codes are used to identify outright errors.

In commenting on drafts of an essay, we can assume the role of a general reader, noting points of interest or confusion, expressing an interest in more information or requesting stronger support, sharing feelings of pleasure and surprise— but always recognizing that at this point a paper belongs primarily to the writer, not yet to the reader. When a draft of an essay has a clear purpose and structure, however, we can read as editors or critics, identifying particular options for paragraphing or expression the writer might consider during revision or suggesting areas of grammar and style that need attention.

When as evaluators we comment on a graded final draft, we need to provide a clear justification for the judgment in terms of (1) the paper's success in achieving its goals, (2) the requirements set by the assignment, or (3) the standards established for the course. At the same time, our comments can convey our responses as teachers, helping students develop images of themselves as writers, with an understanding both of their strengths and of the skills they need to develop. Comments that refer students to a particular section of the handbook, perhaps to specific sets of exercises, can provide a bridge to future writing efforts.

Three Methods for Commenting on Papers

Composition instructors have developed innovative and useful ways of evaluating student writing, including conferences, tape-recorded commentary, and peer evaluation. The handbook can be a useful aid for all these approaches, particularly peer evaluation (see "Using Collaborative Learning with the Handbook," pp. IAE-34–IAE-55). Many teachers, however, still prefer to respond to student essays through marginal and summary comments. These responses take three general forms: a correction code, correction symbols, and written comments. Each method has advantages and disadvantages, and most teachers choose to combine them to draw on the strengths of each.

To use the correction code, an instructor simply writes in the margin of a paper the number and letter of the section of the handbook a student should consult for help with a particular problem or error, for example, 8b (pronoun and antecedent agreement), 11a (comma splice), or 1d (problem with thesis). The code for each section of the handbook is listed inside the back cover; after a short time, most instructors find they have memorized the codes for common problems and seldom have to consult the list.

Here is a section of a student paper marked using the correction code:

Parents have become more lenient with regard to television watching. For example, allowing their children to watch car- (10)

(B3) toon in the early morning before school. As soon as they come (31c)

(21b) home from school they sit before the set again, completely in- (34a)

(31b) grossed with a soap opera or a talk show. Some parents ac-

tually allow their children to watch television while they are (12a)

at the supper table. Of course, the latter part of the eve-

(14c) ning, the prime time, is solely set aside for the purpose of

watching a special show or a favorite series. In some ways,

parents are using the television as a substitute for personal

communication with the child. The days then, remain a never (21c)

ending chain of program after program. (34d)

When students get their graded papers back, they need only turn to the back of the handbook to understand what the instructor's notations mean and then refer to the appropriate section of the text for a full explanation (the code for each section appears in colored boxes at the sides of the pages). Students, too, quickly learn to recognize the notations for common errors and problems.

Correction symbols work in much the same way as the number-and-letter code. An instructor locates the appropriate symbol in the list inside the front cover of the handbook (e.g., *dev, log, agr, coh*) and writes it in the margin of the essay, often drawing a line to indicate the location and extent of the problem. Students reverse the procedure, looking up symbols on the list, which also gives the name of the problem and a reference to the appropriate section of the text: for example, *dm*—Dangling modifier, 14g. Here is the passage from above marked in this way:

Parents have become more lenient with regard to television

watching. For example, allowing their children to watch car- *frag*

toon in the (early morning before school.) As soon as they come *rep*

P home from school, they sit before the set again, completely in- *sp*

grossed with a soap opera or a talk show. Some parents ac- *ww*

tually allow their children to watch television while they are *ref*

at the supper table. Of course, the latter part of the eve-

ning, the prime time, is solely set aside for the purpose of *mm*

watching a special show or a favorite series. In some ways,

parents are using the television as a substitute for personal

P communication with the child. The days, then, remain a never *hyph*

ending chain of program after program.

Because correction symbols are easier to remember than the number-and-letter code, both students and teachers can spend less time turning away from a paper to consult the list of symbols than they might do with the code. Yet symbols are less specific than the code; *shift*, for instance, covers a variety of problems—13a (person and number), 13b (tense and mood), 13c (subject and voice), and 13d (indirect and direct discourse). Moreover, instead of being able to turn directly from the paper to a discussion in the handbook, students may need to consult the list of symbols to find the appropriate section of the text. The symbols, however, also appear in the colored boxes in the margins of the pages.

Although using a correction code or correction symbols can be an efficient way to grade papers, most instructors prefer to give their comments a more personal touch than numbers and letters or symbols alone can offer. Moreover, while the need to have the handbook at hand to understand the instructor's comments may be an advantage for some students, others—perhaps those who need help the most—may put off reviewing their papers or ignore the job entirely because of the effort involved. If you choose to use the code or symbols, you should remember also that there is nothing in either system to let students know they have done a good job on a passage or to encourage them to do a thorough job of looking up explanations in the handbook. To praise good work and make sure students turn to the handbook for help, you will have to rely on written or oral comments. You may also wish to require students to do exercises in the text and hand them in.

Although written comments take a good deal more time than symbols or the correction code, they allow the instructor to address specific problems in an essay, not just indicate a general type of problem. For example, even though the symbol *mng* ("meaning unclear") may be an accurate response, the following written comment tells the student writer a good deal more about the need to communicate clearly with an audience: "I've read this several times and I still can't figure out which side you agree with on this issue—or if you are just trying to avoid taking a stand." In addition, written comments give the teacher a chance to praise successful passages and respond to interesting ideas.

Written comments can be specific and helpful, but they are seldom as detailed as explanations in the handbook. Most instructors therefore combine grading systems by using written comments to praise a paper's strengths and including references to relevant sections of the handbook in their notations on serious problems—for example, "This passage is hard to follow because of the loose way you use *that* and *which*. See 12c." Without such a reference, the student who wants more help than the comment gives may have to look elsewhere, a procedure that will work only if the student already knows something about the problem or if the instructor has used a term that also appears in the Glossary of Grammatical Terms or the index. By combining the correction code with written comments, however, an instructor can provide the necessary guidance.

Another reason for combining methods of grading is that a system may be better suited to some kinds of problems than to others. For example, most instructors prefer writing *21a* in the margin rather than "You need a comma before *and* connecting main clauses"—particularly if the error occurs again and again in an essay. And // is more direct and can be just as effective as the comment "You need to make the elements in this sentence parallel." Yet when brevity is less important, when a symbol doesn't say enough, or when the problem is peculiar to an essay and no reference to the handbook is possible or desirable, a written comment is appropriate.

Pat Lucas's final essay in Chapter 2 of the handbook (pp. 68–70) illustrates how an instructor may combine code, symbols, and written comments. Here, in addition, is a selection from a student paper showing all three methods:

One cause of student stress, and probably the most common, is academic pressures. College academics create so much stress on a student that every college campus in America should be required to have free psychiatric counseling available. The pressure on a student from his or her workload is incredible. The pressure just doesn't occur during mid-terms and finals but occurs all semester, also. The constant pressure to do well and to keep from falling behind is always present.

Parent and peer pressure also increases the amount of stress a student must indure, parents and friends are always

[Marginal handwritten annotations:]
pressure?
This sounds like a conclusion. It might work better below. You might decide to combine the paragraphs, too.

|| (17a) {
reminding ∧the student of the importance of academic success.   Parents bring up the importance of academic success not only for reasons of achievement *no comma* ○ but also reminding the student of who is paying the tuition.
} *good point*

Whether you rely on a single method or a combination of methods to mark students' papers, it is usually important to provide students with a comment at the end of their papers to explain the grade and to tie together the marginal commentary, emphasizing the key points. This is also a good place to assign exercises in the handbook and to remind students what they need to do in future essays. The discussion "Evaluating Essays for a Grade" later in this section contains several examples of summary comments.

Making Sure Students Understand Your Comments

Having chosen a method for commenting on papers, you need to make sure that your students understand the system; unless they do, the time you spend grading papers will be largely wasted. Perhaps the most common reason students fail to understand our comments is that they do not understand the symbols or terms we use. If you were to ask a class what a fused sentence is, some students might answer in this vein: "a sentence where everything seems to run together and gets confused or awkward." Terms like *reference, development*, and *parallelism* are also likely to draw puzzled or incorrect responses, though a few students might be able to give general explanations. Asking students the meaning of common symbols like *pass, cs, dm*, and // will produce similar results.

Telling students to look up correction marks on the front or back endpapers of the handbook can help, as can alerting them to the Glossary of Grammatical Terms or handing out a list of terms you plan to use in written comments. A lot of students, however, are likely to put off learning the symbols or terms until they absolutely have to, perhaps several papers into the semester, when they realize how much help they need to improve their writing.

A more effective way to alert students to the need to understand your correction system and at the same time to find out how much they already know is to quiz them on the terms or symbols you will be using. Here are some sample questions:

What is parallelism? Give an example.
Define "fused sentence" and give an example.
What does each of these symbols mean: *frag, dm, ww, t*, and //?

The misconceptions that surface from such a quiz can be an aid to instruction. For example, students who think fused sentences are "long sentences where everthing seems to run together" are likely to respond to criticism of fused sentences in their work by writing short, choppy sentences. The teacher who has spotted the potential misunderstanding can point out in class discussion that fused sentences are caused by a failure to recognize sentence boundaries and to punctuate them correctly, not by the length or complexity of sentences. Comments on papers can also be expanded in an appropriate manner: "There are a lot of fused sentences in this paper. Make sure you know what a fused sentence is by reading section 11c in the handbook and by doing Exercises 2 and 3."

Another good way to help students understand your comments is to discuss a graded paper with them. As noted earlier, Chapter 2 of the handbook (pp. 68–70) contains an example of a marked paper that you may wish to use as the basis of class discussion. In addition, the paragraphs presented earlier in this section contain many errors of the kind likely to turn up on student papers. The paragraphs can be distributed in class with either or both of the marking systems or with some other system you prefer. If you choose to distribute the paragraphs without markings, you can ask the students to work with you in identifying errors and choosing appropriate symbols or comments.

Focused, Positive Commentary

Two ways to avoid the problem of unfocused commentary are to make selective comments and to make comments that establish priorities for future writing. Selective commentary assumes that errors vary in importance depending on the particular assignment, the goals of the course, or the student's progress. On a narrative or descriptive paper, for example, selective commentary might focus on the presence or absence of vivid, concrete detail. In grading an argumentative essay, however, an instructor might pay primary attention to thesis, adequate support, and transitions. If class discussion has placed considerable emphasis on avoiding fragments and comma splices and has paid relatively little attention to reference problems, the instructor's commentary might take note only of the most serious reference problems, those which are particularly confusing or irritating. Of course, after the class has discussed pronoun reference, the instructor would begin paying considerable attention to it when marking papers.

Other assumptions behind selective commentary are that it is difficult for students (and the rest of us) to pay attention to more than one major job at a time and that students who are having the most trouble with their writing may also have trouble understanding elements that have not been reviewed in class. A or B students with only a few minor marks on their papers—*ref, sp, ww*—can be expected to profit from looking up all the problem areas on their own in the handbook. But weaker students with ten or fifteen serious errors—*frag, agr, log, shift, coh, dev*—need the combined assistance of lecture, small-group discussion, and readings and exercises in the handbook. They will need time to come to grips with the many different problems in their writing.

In addition, students who see a host of grammar, punctuation, and usage errors marked on a paper may assume that these are the most important problems in their writing and may pay less attention to matters such as thesis, development, and organization. Or, having corrected sentence-level problems, they may be unwilling to undertake large-scale revision that would require throwing out the very sentences they have just worked so hard to fix.

Yet one might argue that students have to learn to pay attention to all the problems in their writing and that to ignore some errors in a student's paper, whatever the reason, may be to send a misleading signal. Even instructors who find selective commentary useful may find it hard to refrain from making numerous notations on some papers, feeling that it is their responsibility to alert students to serious problems in communication. For these instructors the solution may be to establish priorities for the way students are to understand and respond to the comments. A system of priorities allows the instructor to point out all the different problem areas in a paper while at the same time directing a student's attention to the most important kinds of problems.

Perhaps the easiest way to establish priorities is to use the summary comment to identify the most serious problems (and strengths, too) and to suggest concrete steps for solving the problems through revision or in future papers. Here are two examples of such comments:

> . . . The most serious problem in this essay is the lack of development in the paragraphs. You need many more extended examples to support your point about the role of computers at all levels of education. But the many comma splices in the paper are also an important problem because they are so distracting to a reader. I have taken note of comma splices in determining the grade; work on avoiding them in your next paper because they will count even more heavily in the grade. The other problems noted in the margins— 14g, etc.—occur less consistently and do not interfere as much with the reader's perception of your meaning and enjoyment of your essay. Look them up in the handbook, however, and watch for them as you proofread your next essay.

> Your topic and your point of view on it are very intriguing. But the lack of concrete detail at the places I have noted weakens the essay. Work to add detail as you revise. The problems in logic in the fourth paragraph are significant and need to be dealt with if you decide to retain the preceding paragraph (see 4d-3 in the handbook). After you have completed these more substantial revisions, look for problems in pronoun reference, which make many of your sentences confusing. (Do Exercises 1 and 2 in Chapter 12 of the handbook.) Check on the other problems pointed out in the body of the paper, and be sure to correct the spelling errors before you hand in the revised essay for a final grade.

Many instructors read student essays twice, the first time to identify general strengths and weaknesses, the second time to make comments praising successful passages and indicating areas that need more work. Other instructors decide ahead of time which elements of the assignment or course are most important and try to restrict their comments to these. But though the latter procedure saves a bit of time, it will not be successful unless both the instructor and the students understand the aims for the assignment and the grading standards in the course. Making the goals of the course clear is a good procedure because it provides a firm basis for evaluation.

Evaluating Essays for a Grade

A grade can carry several messages: it can describe the overall quality of a paper; it can indicate how close the essay comes to achieving the goals for writing set forth in the course; and it can help tell a student writer what elements to work on in the next assignment. But unless grading standards are clear, the grades we assign will have little value for teaching beyond establishing a final grade for the course.

To help establish clear evaluation standards, many instructors discuss grading criteria with students and distribute sample papers, either already graded or to be graded in class. Another method is to attach to each paper a comment sheet reflecting the goals for the assignment. Preparing a comment sheet for each assignment can be taxing, however, and so many instructors prepare a sheet that can be used for all assignments. Here are two samples, each of which uses different grading criteria:

These are the areas in which your paper is

strong		weak
	thesis	
	development	
	paragraphs	
	sentences	
	grammar	
	word choice	
	punctuation	
	style	

Comment/grade:

Thesis:

Organization:

Development

Grammar and
punctuation:

Style:

Comment/grade:

If you do not like to use comment sheets, you may prefer to hand out grading criteria at the beginning of the course. Sometimes a department or program provides its own set of criteria for grading papers; if your does not, you may wish to adapt for your own use the following set that reflects the major areas of emphasis in the handbook:

A (superior). An *A* paper meets the standards in all these areas and excels in one or more of them:

The *paper as a whole* presents a fresh subject or main idea or treats it in an interesting or original manner, displaying unusual insight. The paper has a clear pattern appropriate to the audience. The *paragraphs* are fully developed with detail that supports the main idea; sentences within the paragraphs are clearly linked, forming an appropriate pattern; transitions are effective. *Sentences* are varied and imaginative in style, concise and creative in wording. The paper contains few errors in *grammar and punctuation* or errors only in sophisticated matters, and few *spelling* errors.

B (strong). A *B* paper meets the standards in all these areas:

The *paper as a whole* presents an interesting subject or main idea and approaches it in a consistent and careful manner, displaying good insight, though without the freshness or originality characteristic of the *A* paper. The pattern of the essay is appropriate to its purpose, and the writing makes use of consistent rhetorical strategies and a tone appropriate to the audience. *Paragraphs* are, with only a few exceptions, adequately developed and generally successful in supporting the main idea; transitions are clear, and sentences within the paragraphs are, for the most part, clearly related. *Sentences* are clear and correct in structure and style and are not excessively wordy. Word choice is usually appropriate. *Grammar, punctuation, and spelling* follow accepted conventions, except for a few minor errors.

C (adequate). A *C* paper is seriously deficient in one of these areas:

The *paper as a whole* presents a clearly defined subject or main idea, but the treatment may be trivial, uninteresting, or too general and the insight adequate but not marked by independent thought. The plan and purpose are clear but inconsistently or incompletely carried out; tone may be inconsistent. Some *paragraphs* may lack adequate supporting detail or may be only loosely linked to the main idea. Sentences within paragraphs may be only loosely related, and some transitions may be missing. *Sentences* are generally correct in structure but may be excessively wordy, vague, or, at times, even incorrect. Style and word choice may be flat, inconsistent, or not entirely appropriate to the audience. The paper may display isolated serious errors in *grammar and punctuation* or frequent minor errors that do not interfere substantially with meaning or that do not greatly distract the reader; the paper may contain occasional *misspellings*.

D (weak). A *D* paper is seriously deficient in any one of these areas:

The *paper as a whole* presents a poorly defined or inconsistently treated subject or central idea and displays little insight. The plan and purpose are not treated consistently. The tone is inappropriate to the audience.

Paragraphs contain little supporting detail. Sentences within paragraphs are often unrelated to the main idea, and transitions are lacking. *Sentences* are frequently incorrect in structure, vague, wordy, and distracting. Style and word choice are inappropriate, incorrect, or inconsistent. The paper may contain serious and distracting errors in *grammar and punctuation* as well as numerous irritating minor errors and frequent *misspellings*.

F (unacceptable/no credit). An *F* paper is unacceptable in any one of these areas:

The *paper as a whole* does not have a clear subject or main idea and has no apparent purpose or plan; *or* the subject and main idea are defined and treated in a way that clearly does not meet the requirements of the assignment. *Paragraphs* are not related to the main idea; sentences within paragraphs are unrelated, and transitions are missing. *Sentences* are so faulty in structure and style that the essay is not readable. Frequent serious errors in *grammar, punctuation, and spelling* indicate an inability to handle the written conventions; there are excessive minor errors or misspellings.

These criteria need to be adapted to the level of students in a particular course or institution and to the goals set for the course. For example, admirable organization or style may differ markedly for a student in a two-year technical program and a student in a four-year school that stresses the arts and humanities. The following samples of graded papers attempt to put into practice the grading techniques suggested in this section. (The papers are preceded by the instructors' assignments.) Because of the wide variations one can expect between schools and courses, ranges of quality rather than specific grades are suggested: good, average, and weak. Keep in mind that these are merely samples and that the best grading procedures are those which reflect the personality of the teacher as a sensitive and thorough reader.

Good

[Assignment: Write an essay in which you try to give your readers a fresh look at a subject, perhaps by choosing one they probably have not paid much attention to in the past. You may wish to present examples, look at causes and effects, classify, or compare and contrast. Remember that the detail you use to develop your essay and make your point will help determine the essay's effectiveness.]

```
                    Winter in New England

     So you were raised in Miami and now you are moving to New

England.  You say you are excited about the move, but do you

know how your life will change here?  Living in a cold climate

like New England's influences how you spend your money, what
```

good opening paragraph

you do with your time, and how you feel about yourself and others.

The most obvious effect of the winter cold is financial, as you'll quickly learn. Even though you wear only casual clothes, you'll need a new wardrobe: a collection of sweaters and flannel shirts; a very warm coat; and a pair of boots suitable for deep snow, glassy ice, messy slush, and rain. You have probably heard enough about our heating bills up here, so I won't go into that financial effect of the cold. But you may not know what this climate will do to your car. You'll have to "winterize" it, which means putting antifreeze in the radiator and <u>who knows what else</u>. Inevitably, more than once your winterized car will refuse to start in the cold weather, so you'll have to fork over money for road service or towing. But that inconvenience and cost does not compare to the agony of watching your car disintegrate over a few years from the salt laid down on the roads to melt ice.

Explaining this a bit more would make your point even more effective.

Yes, this really is agony.

Even if you are prepared for the financial costs of living in the North, you will probably be startled by how the cold climate affects your activities. Winter here is hibernating time. The outdoors is something to be passed through as quickly as possible on your way from one heated place to another. In winter you resign yourself to huddling around the radiator (if you have paid the heating bill). With all your money going toward self-defense from

the cold, boredom can be a problem, so you may find yourself cooking soups, playing games, or <u>imprinting</u> on the

This is an interesting use of the word.

television. Actually, you may end up relishing your free
time, no matter how boring or frustrating, when you experience the great winter activity--battling ice and snow.
If it's a wet winter, count on spending a few hours minimum every week shoveling snow from driveways and sidewalks, scraping ice and snow off your car, and (most fun
of all) pushing your car or someone else's out of icy
snowbanks.

Ugh! (but these are good details)

The strangest effect of life in the cold is the way
it influences your attitudes. After a hot, humid summer
the crisp, dry air of autumn at first fills you with energy and cheerfulness. But, as the air becomes downright
chilly and the tree branches become bare, you will sense

true— good insight into human nature

yourself and others dying a little each day. Gradually
you find it necessary to don heavy, constricting clothing;
you avoid any contact with the depressing out-of-doors;
you begin to shiver inside your own home, for turning on
the heat for the first time since last winter is an <u>admis-</u>
<u>sion of death</u> that everyone puts off. But inevitably win-

good phrase

ter comes, in full force. Your face feels tight, and you
see your expression mirrored in the thin-lipped scowls of
the people you pass quickly on the street. Your posture
is hunched, elbows squeezed to the waist, and your mood is

excellent detail

similarly withdrawn. Except for the Christmas/Chanukah
frenzy, you will spend the next four months in a gray mood
that matches the dominant color of the sky.

So you won't be discouraged from coming north at all,
I've held the saving grace of winter for last. It ends.
And when the punishment finally stops, you understand that
you had to go through it to experience the sheer elation
of spring. So come ahead and do not fear. Bad as it is,
winter is worth the intense joy of its leaving.

Fine paper. Your thesis is clear and you develop each part of it with effective detail. The third set of effects you discuss, the effect on feelings, is particularly insightful. And the last paragraph ties the whole essay together nicely.

Average

[Assignment: Write an essay in which you use classification to help readers
understand a complicated topic or to highlight the characteristics of groups
of people, ideas, objects, or events in such a way that you shed fresh light on
the subject. Remember that the details you use to develop your essay will
help determine its effectiveness.]

The Second Half of Sleeping: Waking

The human being, it is estimated, sleeps away one
third of his or her life. Much research on this topic *21j*
has been done in sleep clinics throughout the world. A
more fasinating aspect of the sleeping process has been   *the thesis*
virtually ignored: waking up. The ways in which people   *is clear,*
but not
wake up can, however, be narrowed down and described in   *very*
interesting
four main groups.

The Last-Minute Riser is often seen stumbling through the quad, five minutes into class time, with wet hair and still wearing pajamas.   *17a*   The actual waking process is an extremely painful one.   The last-minute riser has mathe-   *hyph* matically calculated the number of minutes it takes to get ready in the morning.   He is awakened by the piercing screech of the alarm clock at the predetermined moment,   *good* and again five minutes later, and five minutes after that. Alarm clock manufacturers have installed "snooze buttons" on alarm clocks for people falling into this category.

hyph The last-minute riser realizes with a mixture of shock and teror *sp* that he has slept well into the alloted *sp* getting-ready time.   He begins an emotional display of a person in *w* panic, *no comma* as he rushes to and fro throughout the room *w* in an effort to make up for lost time.   This person never has time for breakfast and must deal with an array of stomach- *hyph* gurgling noises that last through his first three classes. Persons fitting this description have been known to change in and out of majors so as to avoid required morn- *true!* ing classes.

The Early Birds are in direct contrast to the last- *hyph* minute riser.   Early birds are easy to spot, they are the people who look bright-eyed, and cheerfully well-rested; *22e*   *¶* *dev* the people who eagerly answer questions during an eight o'clock class.   They make a point to skip to the cafeteria

6S

every morning to eat an elaborate meal. Then the early

bird is fully alert and anxious to begin the day.

¶
dev

The Zombie is a living testimonial to the theory that

we are fully alert only one minute of each hour. The zom-

bie is not aware of her alarm clock when it buzzes, but

she manages to shut it off anyway. A zombie usually awak-

ens halfway through lunch. Although this is a daily oc-

curence, she is nonetheless always bewildered at finding

that she is not asleep in bed as she imagined.

true

The Complainer does not enjoy waking up, as is well

known by anyone he lives with. He finds it soothing to

know that although he is unhappily awake, so, too, is any-

one within listening range. The complainer allows his

alarm clock to beep continuously for twenty minutes. He

does not hear this; everyone else in his dorm does. When

he does respond, the alarm clock is hurled across his   dm

room. It lands with a blood-curdling crash. The com-

plainer is ready to get up. He shocks the room to life by

                                              ww (while?)
turning on every light and blaring his stereo. When at-

tempting to get ready, the complainer is unable to find

any of his belongings. He finds it necessary to awaken
                              no commas necessary
his roommate several times and make him aware of the di-

lemma. After slamming shut any drawer within reach, he

stomps to the cafeteria. The cafeteria is often visited   good
                                                           phrase
by complainers, as it supplies an inexhaustible supply of

subjects to grieve over. It is best to avoid the com-

plainer until noontime.

In college life, a person is forced to deal with oth-

ers every hour of the day: the hours when others are

asleep, awake, and especially the hours in between.

Awareness of the ways different people wake up is neces-

sary if one is to survive the first half of every day.

This essay is often quite funny, but the paragraphs
on "The Early Birds" and "The Zombie" need more
development. You might add details like these in
the paragraphs describing the other catagories. The
thesis is clear, but it is not very interesting. You
might try to indicate what the readers will learn
from your essay -- you do this effectively in the
last paragraph. Watch out for the sentence and
punctuation problems. Look up the appropriate
sections in the Handbook.

Weak

[Assignment: Write a narrative about an event in your life that had an important impact on you or that you remember vividly because of the insight it gave you into yourself and other people. Remember to choose details carefully because they will make your narrative vivid and effective.]

The First Day

It was a beautiful day in late August, kind of warm

and very nervewracking for me. Because I was embarking on

the most important day in my life, the beginning of my   (10a)

college experience.   The day began with its normal rituals

and everything appeared to be fine until I arrived at the college. Suddenly I found myself asking, what am I doing here? Am I really ready for this. I wanted to cry, but I pushed back the tears and plunged onward. Before I knew it, I was pushed ~~sp~~ amoungst the hustle and bustle of the first day.

good — I must have looked like a child whoe [whose] teddy bear was taken from him.

Being as how I was ~~sp~~ truely frightened I ~~sp~~ desparately tried to find my first class and with the ~~sp~~ aide of a few older students I successfully found my place.

After that things got easier, but not ~~sp~~ to. The hardest part was yet to come. The adjustment to new and different people. The biggest difficulty was starting a conversation. Most of the time you say nothing for the fear of sounding dumb. The first time beginning to talk to someone, my voice cracks and I must have turned scarlet red, but I never stuck around to find out. I ducked out quicly and found the nearest (lady's) room.

good detail *find out what?* *ladies' (ladies is plural)*

The strange thing about college is its proffessors. ~~sp~~ Each has (its) own technique but the same basics. On the first day ~~they~~ each tell you what ~~they~~ expect during the semester and then ~~they~~ hand you a forty page syllabus of work to be done in fifteen weeks. I had (another) who when (every time) she spoke sounded like she was having her hand for dinner.

a professor is a "he" or a "she" *one — s* *he or she — s* *too much exaggeration here* *one professor* *use the singular here* *This ¶ doesn't fit with the thesis.*

24a *3c* *10d* *13a* *dm* *31c*

People asked me what I thought about my first <u>year</u> in

school.   My response is simply, "It was different".

You didn't really cover this much territory in the essay.

This is a good topic for an essay, but you need to spend more time describing specific incidents so that your readers can share and understand your experience. The second and third paragraphs, for example, are far too short. They ought to be combined and developed with concrete details.

The fourth paragraph also needs to contain specific incidents — — you would be better off concentrating on the first day and describing the events in detail. The paragraph about professors doesn't seem to fit in with the rest of the essay because it covers a different topic.

When you revise, try to focus the essays more clearly on the first day and pay attention to the marginal comments.

Evaluating for Revision

In recent years the process of revision has come to be viewed as increasingly important in composition instruction. Instructors who make revision a regular part of their composition classes argue that writers should be judged not (or not only) on the early version of an essay but on what they are able to make of the essay after they have had a chance to revise it and, perhaps, to take into account the comments of readers.

Composition instructors have, of course, long viewed revision as an important process for student writers to learn. What is new is the extent to which revision is being made a regular part of instruction, an emphasis reflected in the extensive treatment of both revision and editing in Chapter 2 of the handbook. Furthermore, many instructors have begun structuring their classes around collaborative learning groups that provide audiences for papers in progress and advice for revision. The section "Using Collaborative Learning with the Handbook," which follows this discussion, contains suggestions for sheets to help students analyze their peers' work.

The distinction made in Chapter 2 of the handbook between revision and editing is important for instructors to keep in mind when responding to a student paper in progress. For essays whose perspective, form, and content are well enough developed to require only editing, your role may be simply to call attention to errors or to suggest ways to polish sentences and paragraphs. Many of the techniques already discussed for commenting on papers can be used to aid editing, particularly those which refer students to sections of the handbook for advice on improving a passage or correcting a problem. In addition, you may wish to refer students to the editing checklist in Chapter 2 (p. 64).

Evaluation for revision, however, is more likely to suggest extensive changes in a paper, often encouraging the writer to adopt a different perspective on a topic.

An instructor commenting on a draft might suggest, for example, that the essay could be more interesting or useful if the writer shifted from arguing about recent government regulations controlling the disposal of dangerous substances to examining the effects of toxic wastes or discussing the costs to industry of completely safe disposal procedures. Since revision may and often should involve substantial changes in the direction of an essay, you should be wary, however, of comments that impose your view of what a paper should do or how it should be accomplished. Instead, try to identify a problem clearly and offer some possible solutions but at the same time leave the student writers free to make their own choices. Comments like "your thesis statement needs to focus more sharply on the specific government toxic-waste regulations to which you object" may be helpful in cases where the student's intentions and the direction of a paper are quite clear. But when a writer is still struggling with subject and intention, such statements may limit the process of revision rather than encourage it. A comment like the following, however, leaves the eventual direction of the essay up to the student:

> I'm not sure which specific regulations you object to most. Is this a place in the essay where you want to focus your concerns sharply for readers? From the detailed evidence you present later about the struggles of small businesses to pay for state-of-the-art pollution equipment, I suspect that one of your main purposes is to have readers understand the hard times these ordinary people are facing. What do you care most about in this subject, and what do you most want your audience to understand and feel?

In commenting on papers for revision, you should, of course, call attention to any serious errors. At the same time, however, keep in mind this maxim: "Don't spend time improving a sentence that ought to be dropped from the paper." Remember, too, that awkward and confused sentences are often signs of confusion about the overall direction of an essay, and problems at the sentence level may disappear as the writer resolves the larger problems. Thus comments on errors are most effective when they place the errors in a larger context, as in this comment:

> You shift pronouns often in this passage, sometimes addressing the reader as "you," sometimes using "one" or "we." I think the root of the problem is that you are not sure of your relation to your readers. Since you are talking about a situation that you face along with most readers, you might choose "we" and stick to it.

In addition, most students need more than advice about what sections of a paper need to be revised; they need advice about the process of revision itself. By focusing your comments on how to go about revising rather than solely on the direction of possible changes, you can avoid doing the students' work for them and can instead help them develop an effective writing/revising process. Instead of simply telling a student to add more detail to an essay discussing the social effects of unemployment, you might say:

> Imagine that you are the father of five children and that your wife is a homemaker. You have just lost your job. Write for five minutes about how your being home all day, depressed because you are out of work, might upset the normal life of your family. When you are done, look over what you have written for details and examples you can use in your paper.

Advice of this sort not only helps a student revise the paper at hand but also shows the student ways to revise future papers.

Conferences

Conferences are worthwhile alternatives to written responses. While some instructors choose to rely solely on them, others use them as supplements to provide a fresh perspective for student writers. They give an instructor a chance to respond to essays as a sensitive reader, with opinions and feelings, words of encouragement, and suggested corrections—all of which are generally hard to convey in the margins of papers. Conferences also require students to contribute by commenting on their own papers, explaining why they made certain choices, and indicating how they want to revise an essay or how they plan to change their approach in the next assignment. In a conference you may find that your judgment of a paper or of the source and seriousness of a writing problem changes when you hear what the student writer was trying to accomplish.

Remember, however, that conferences ought to provide an opportunity for students to talk about their papers. Try to resist the temptation to use the conference as a lecture period. Whenever possible, make your advice come in response to a student's questions or comments. And make your comments direct and relatively personal so that the student can understand better how a reader reacts to an essay, not just how a teacher grades a student paper.

Resources for Evaluation and Response

Brannon, Lil, and C. H. Knoblauch. "On Students' Rights to Their Own Texts: A Model of Teacher Response." *College Composition and Communication* 33 (1982): 157–66.

Cooper, Charles R., and Lee Odell, eds. *Evaluating Writing: Describing, Measuring, Judging.* Urbana: NCTE, 1977.

Dietrich, Julia C. "Explaining One's Rhetorical Choices." *College Composition and Communication* 29 (1978): 195–96.

Ford, James E., and Gregory Larkin. "The Portfolio System: An End to Backsliding Writing Standards." *College English* 39 (1978): 950–55.

Freedman, Sarah Warshauer. *Response to Student Writing.* Urbana: NCTE, 1987.

————, and Melanie Sperling. "Teacher Student Interaction in the Writing Conference: Response and Teaching." In *The Aquisition of Written Language: Response and Revision.* Ed. Sarah Warshauer Freedman. Norwood: Ablex, 1985.

Gere, Ann Ruggles, and Robert Stevens. "The Language of Writing Groups: How Oral Response Shapes Revision." In *The Acquisition of Written Language: Response and Revision.* Ed. Sarah Warshauer Freedman. Norwood: Ablex, 1985. 85–105.

Hillocks, George. "The Interaction of Instruction, Teacher Comment, and Revision in Teaching the Composing Process." *Research in the Teaching of English* 16 (1982): 261–78.

Johnston, Brian. "Non-Judgmental Responses to Students' Writing." *English Journal* 71 (1982): 50–53.

Knoblauch, C. H., and Lil Brannon. "Teacher Commentary on Student Writing: The State of the Art." *Freshman English News* 10 (1981): 1–4.

McDonald, W. U. Jr., "The Revising Process and the Marking of Student Papers." *College Composition and Communication* 29 (1978): 167–70.

Miller, Linda P. "A Conference Methodolgy for Freshman Composition." *Teaching English in the Two-Year College* 7 (1980): 23–26.

Olsen, Gary A. "Beyond Evaluation: The Recorded Response to Essays." *Teaching English in the Two-Year College* 8 (1982): 121–23.

Purves, Alan. "The Teacher as Reader: An Anatomy." *College English* 46 (1984): 259–65.

Schiff, Peter. "Responding to Writing: Peer Critiques, Teacher-Student Conferences, and Essay Evaluations." In *Language Connections: Writing and Reading Across the Curriculum.* Urbana: NCTE, 1982. 153–65.

Sommers, Nancy. "Responding to Student Writing." *College Composition and Communication* 33: 148–56.

Stanford, Gene, Ed. *How to Handle the Paper Load.* Urbana: NCTE, 1978. (Includes Neil Ellman, "Structuring Peer Evaluation for Greater Student Independence"; David A. England, "Objectives for Our Own Composing Processes—When We Respond to Students"; Mary Louise Foster and Patricia Markey Naranjo, "Peer Evaluation: One Approach"; Isabel Hawley, "Critique Groups for Composition Classes"; Muriel Harris, "The Overgraded Paper: Another Case of More Is Less"; Sheila Ann Lisman, "The Best of All Possible Worlds: Where X Replaces AWK"; Thomas Newkirk, "Read the Papers in Class"; Audrey J. Roth, "Editorial Groups"; Linda Shadiow, "Eureka! Moments and Reflection Questions"; and R. Baird Shuman, "How to Grade Student Writing" and "Writing Roulette: Taking a Chance on Not Grading.")

Using Collaborative Learning with the Handbook
by Tori Haring-Smith, Brown University

Within the past few years, writing instructors have been rediscovering the value of collaborative learning, in which students work together to solve problems, do exercises, and evaluate one another's work. Some instructors ask students to work in groups only occasionally, and others design their entire writing courses around group work. Whether you use collaborative learning and peer criticism regularly or would like to try just a few collaborative exercises in your course, you will find that it is easy to use this teaching method with *The Little, Brown Handbook.* This discussion will define collaborative learning, offer suggestions for designing collaborative exercises, and suggest ways to guide students in peer criticism.

What Is Collaborative Learning?

Collaborative learning is a general phrase used to describe any of a number of different kinds of activities in which students work together as active co-laborers, rather than passive learners. Most exercises that can be done individually or as a class can also be completed in small groups. You can ask students to collaborate when they analyze an essay, correct a set of flawed sentences, identify parts of speech or rhetorical strategies, or revise a piece of prose. Small-group interaction gives all students a chance to participate, and it exposes students to each other's opinions. In this kind of collaborative learning, students negotiate among themselves to reach an answer that they all can accept.

Another form of collaborative learning is peer criticism, in which students comment on each other's writing. For this exercise, students can exchange papers in small groups of three or four, or they can work in pairs. You may ask students to summarize a classmate's essay or provide feedback on their partners' thesis, organization, style, or grammar. You may even ask them to provide counterarguments or additional support for their partners' essays.

The instructor plays an important role in both collaborative classroom exercises and peer criticism. Even though these are student-centered activities, the instructor must shape them carefully by designing a sheet of questions or instructions to guide the students' work. In this way, the instructor controls the learning activity, even though the students carry it out. (There are sample instruction sheets at the end of this discussion.)

What Are the Benefits of Collaborative Learning?

Instructors who use collaborative learning have found that it has numerous benefits. Students involved in collaborative activities take an active role in their own education. Rather than sitting silently at the back of the room, students work in small groups where they can participate and hear reactions to their ideas. They get the kind of individualized attention that is rare in these times of increasing class size.

Moreover, as they work in groups, students learn to cooperate in order to learn, rather than competing against one another for the best grades or the instructor's approval. In this way, collaborative learning is very similar to the way people learn when they are outside school. Peer interaction teaches students the skills they will need to work on projects with colleagues and to accept criticism of their work.

This teaching strategy also reminds students that language and writing are social products. They experience firsthand the ways in which groups of people develop standards for writing and the ways in which these standards are enforced. As they negotiate among themselves, students learn to exercise independent judgment. They see how others make decisions, they practice defending their ideas, and they learn to compromise or shift their positions as necessary.

Peer criticism also provides students with valuable feedback during the writing process. Although most instructors recognize the benefits of commenting on early drafts of student work, few have time to do so. Even though they may want to intervene while students are writing in order to see what strategies they are using, most instructors can comment only on final drafts. Even when instructors do have the time to comment on students' drafts, their comments are usually interpreted as demands for specific revisions. It is very hard for an instructor who must hand out grades to convince students that comments made on a rough draft are merely suggestions. Too often, students will follow an instructor's suggestions slavishly, without thinking about why the instructor has made these suggestions. But they will consider and question suggestions that come from a fellow student.

Finally, students involved in peer criticism are exposed to a variety of points of view on their writing. They can see how different audiences with different backgrounds and interests react to their prose. It is far too easy for students to dismiss an instructor's judgments, because so many students believe that English instructors have a special set of standards not shared by the rest of the world. If an English instructor comments that a paragraph is unclear, students can assume that such a comment arises from that instructor's unusual sensitivity to language. If students must revise on the basis of the instructor's comments, they may follow these suggestions to the letter. But they may still discount them as too "picky."

However, if their peers, other students just like themselves, say that their writing is unclear, they are more likely to listen and to consider the criticism carefully. Of course, students can dismiss each other's comments as uninformed, but after a few collaborative exercises, they come to trust and respect each other. Through peer criticism, students can see the importance of writing to communicate an idea, not just to demonstrate competence.

Using the Handbook to Design Collaborative Activities

Many of the exercises in *The Little, Brown Handbook* are suitable for collaborative learning. The wide variety of types of exercises and levels of difficulty will make it fairly easy for you to select exercises that will not bore your students or be too difficult for them.

The exercises are also well suited for use during class time, when it is easier for groups of students to meet. Because the exercises are so clearly focused (usually they deal with only one aspect of writing at a time), they will not take long for a group to complete. Groups can work through an exercise, and then have time to compare their answers with those of other groups before the class is dismissed. The exercises at all levels offer students enough freedom to consider the merits of alternative solutions, but most do not ask students to write from scratch—a very difficult task for a group to accomplish. It is reasonable to ask groups to revise short passages of prose or even to create sentences and paragraphs from ideas, phrases, and sentences given to them. But in order to create whole compositions, students would need to spend large amounts of time outside of class working in groups. (This kind of collaborative writing is a very useful exercise, especially for students in technical and scientific fields, but it is not closely related to the work students will do with the handbook.)

To avoid limiting the ways in which students and instructors use the handbook, none of the exercise instructions specify that the work should be completed in groups. The instructions are always explicit, however, and you can easily adapt them for group work. In many cases, you simply need to direct students to complete the exercise in groups. Just be sure that one student in the group takes notes as its members work so that the group can reconstruct its discussion if necessary.

In some cases, however, an exercise will be more suitable for collaborative learning if you make one of the following changes.

1. If the exercise asks students to choose among alternatives, then add the requirement that students defend their choice. For example, if students are directed to combine sentences in one of several ways, ask them to discuss why they chose a particular combination. In this way, students within the group will have a chance

to explain not only what they would write but also why. This kind of discussion helps students understand the strategies that lie behind successful writing.

2. If an exercise informs students that there is more than one correct answer, ask students working in groups to find as many correct answers as possible. This activity keeps everyone in the group thinking, even after one answer has been found, and it allows students to discuss the differences among the answers. In Chapter 11, for example, students are asked to fix fused sentences in several ways. If students try to fix these sentences in as many ways as possible, the class can discuss the different effects of the various solutions. This procedure also gives students a chance to discover how creative they can be within the confines of correctness.

3. If an exercise directs students to revise their own work, ask them to exchange papers and provide each other with peer criticism.

Although almost any exercise in the book could be adapted for collaborative work, some are more suitable than others. Those kinds of exercises throughout the handbook which will work best in groups are the following.

1. *Exercises requiring students to use judgment.* Because collaborative learning allows students to practice making judgments individually and in a group, any exercise that asks students to select among possible correct answers and defend their choice is suitable for group work. Exercise 2 in Chapter 4, for example, asks students to determine if statements are generalizations or evidence, and Exercise 1 in Chapter 16 asks students to judge which method of coordinating ideas within a sentence is most effective. Exercises asking students to correct features of a text may also require judgment if, as is the case with fragments, some occurrences of the feature are more appropriate and acceptable than others. These kinds of exercises reinforce the important concept that writing involves making choices at all levels, from topic selection to style.

2. *Exercises in critical reading.* Because writers need to become critics of their own work, they need practice in critical reading. When students read alone, they discover only their own reactions to a text. But any good writer must learn to anticipate the reactions of many different kinds of audiences. When a group of students reads and analyzes a passage, each student can see the passage from a variety of different perspectives.

3. *Difficult exercises in identification.* Of course, you must decide what "difficult" means for your students. But if you can determine the kinds of discriminations that are difficult for your students to see, then you can select exercises for group work that cover those features of prose. For example, if students find it difficult to understand why some modifiers are misplaced, then this is an appropriate exercise for group work. If these kinds of identification exercises were done with the entire class, students who could not see the problem with a flawed sentence, much less understand how the new, correct sentence was different, would be afraid to stop the momentum of the class to inquire. But in the supportive atmosphere of a small group of other, equally confused peers, students are more apt to ask for an explanation.

4. *Exercises in sentence combining.* Because students can combine sentences in a number of correct ways, such exercises give students a chance to see how different styles can change meaning and affect readers.

5. *Exercises in revision*. Group revision is another chance for students to discuss the relative effectiveness of various organizations, tones, and styles. Whether students work together to revise sentences, outlines, paragraphs, or whole essays (such as Pat Lucas's in Chapter 2 of the handbook), they will have a chance to see different revising strategies at work. Some revision exercises that focus on certain specific flawed features in sample sentences may not be challenging enough for all students, but when students must revise paragraphs containing several different kinds of errors, they will find it helpful to have several pairs of eyes searching for the errors.

6. *Exercises that invite group invention or brainstorming*. Although most of the exercises in Chapter 1 are designed to guide an individual through the process of writing a paper, most can be altered to take advantage of sharing ideas early in the writing process.

7. *Exercises in controlled composition*. Although it is difficult for groups of students to write compositions from scratch, they can compose paragraphs from sets of sentences (as in Chapter 3, Exercise 3). But in exercises like 13 in Chapter 1, students should probably work in groups to discuss persona and then do the actual writing on their own.

Kinds of exercises that are not appropriate for group work include private kinds of writing (e.g., journals in Chapter 1, Exercise 1) and exercises designed to lead an individual writer through an extended writing assignment (many of those in Chapters 1–2 and 35). Exercises in which there is only one correct answer (identifying parts of speech or choosing from a pair of possible answers) are also inappropriate because they offer little chance for group members to exchange opinions, and they invite one bright student to dominate the group.

Of course, you will want to mix group work with individual exercises and work with the entire class, but, as you can see, you have many opportunities to use the handbook as the basis for collaborative learning. To identify quickly those exercises which are easily adapted for group work, refer to the index below.

Chapter 1: Exercises, 5, 6, 7, 8, 12, 13, 15, 16, 18, 19
Chapter 2: Exercises 1, 3, 4, 5, 6, 7, 8
Chapter 3: Exercises 1, 2, 3, 5, 6, 7, 8, 10, 12, 13, 15, 18, 19, 20
Chapter 4: Exercises 1, 2, 3, 4, 5, 6, 8, 9, 10, 12, 13, 14
Chapter 5: Exercises 3, 9, 11, 13, 14, 16, 17, 18, 22
Chapter 6: Exercises 4, 5
Chapter 7: Exercises 5, 6, 8, 9
Chapter 8: Exercises 1, 2, 3, 4
Chapter 9: Exercises 2, 4, 5
Chapter 10: Exercises 1, 2, 3, 4, 6
Chapter 11: Exercises 1, 2, 3, 4
Chapter 12: Exercises 1, 2, 3
Chapter 13: Exercises 1, 2, 3, 4, 5
Chapter 14: Exercises 1, 4, 5, 6, 7
Chapter 15: Exercises 1, 2
Chapter 16: Exercises 1, 2, 3, 4, 5, 6, 7
Chapter 17: Exercises 1, 3, 4
Chapter 18: Exercises 2, 3, 4, 5, 6
Chapter 19: Exercises 1, 3, 5
Chapter 20: Exercise 4

Chapter 21: Exercises 3, 4, 5, 6, 12, 13, 14
Chapter 22: Exercises 2, 4, 6, 8, 9, 10
Chapter 23: Exercise 6
Chapter 24: Exercises 4,5
Chapter 25: Exercise 5
Exercise for Chapters 20–25 (following Chapter 25)
Chapter 31: Exercises 1, 3, 4, 5, 7, 8, 9, 10, 11, 12, 13
Chapter 35: Exercises 1, 7, 10, 12

Preparing Students to Work in Groups

You may be hesitant to use collaborative learning because it seems unstructured. This is not the case. Collaborative learning is just as structured as traditional methods of learning—but it is structured in a different way. You direct the students' learning not by controlling discussion but by carefully preparing students to work collaboratively as they confront questions and problems in writing.

Designing Instructions for Group Work

Be sure that students know what they are to do. If you are using one of your own exercises, be sure that you have written out the directions clearly and that each student has a copy of them. If you are using an exercise from the handbook, be sure that every student knows which exercise it is and how you may have adapted it. If you have made significant changes in the exercise, you should probably write them out for students. In your instructions, be sure to indicate how much time you want students to spend on the exercise, or, if it is a long exercise, how much time they should spend on each part of it. This kind of guidance helps groups know how long to discuss points of contention. Be sure to allow enough time for groups to report to one another or for the entire class to discuss an exercise. Although some exercises may take the entire class period for groups to complete, it is preferable for groups to discuss an exercise and report during the same class period. It is difficult to sustain a conversation with a two-day or even a twenty-four-hour hiatus.

The instructions that you give students should explain both the tasks they must accomplish and the reasons for doing the exercise. If students cannot understand the goal of an exercise, they will be less able to tell when they are on the right track. In these written instructions, you may also want to remind students that their task is to cooperate, not compete. Students are so accustomed to battling with each other to speak and to gain the instructor's attention that they need to be reminded constantly how to work together as allies rather than rivals.

Helping Students Learn to Work in Groups

Because your students will probably not have had much experience in collaborative learning, you will need to help them learn how to work effectively. Be sure that the groups you establish are small enough for every student to feel involved. Usually groups of three to five students work best. For some exercises, you may want to put students with similar strengths together, but in general you do not need to worry about whether the students in a given group are at the same or at different levels. Good writers will help other good writers polish their prose, and they will help poor writers with fundamental concerns like logic and organization.

Poor writers will be glad to discover that they are not the only members in a class who have trouble writing, and they will help each other by being aware of the special problems they share. You may be surprised to know that these less talented students will also be able to help more experienced writers by providing honest readers' reactions. They will be able to tell good students, who are frequently more successful in writing to the instructor than to a lay reader, how their prose sounds to a "real" reader. Some students who have had a great deal of trouble writing may also be surprised to see how well their classmates can write. Although this discovery can make some writers feel inadequate, most will be heartened to know that it is possible for students to write well.

Although you need not worry too much about placing students of different abilities in the same group, you should try to vary the ways in which students are grouped. Because students should be exposed to as many points of view as possible during the semester, they should not always work in the same small group. To ensure that the composition of the collaborative groups changes from exercise to exercise, you may want to control the assignment of students to groups.

Once groups are established, students should decide upon a note taker for the group. Try to be sure that this position rotates among group members so that everyone gets a chance to participate fully in the conversation. Groups will also need to have a spokesperson to report the outcome of their deliberation. If this person is different from the secretary, more students will feel responsible for the group's performance.

When students are working in small groups, you may find that the noise level in the classroom is higher than normal, but you will also know that this noise means students are talking and learning. If you design collaborative activities carefully, students will remain "on task." But if you are worried, you can move from group to group to be sure that students are talking usefully. Try not to hover over groups, watching them closely. Remember, one advantage of collaborative learning is that students have a chance to work outside the usual lines of evaluation within a classroom. When collaborative learning works well, students should lose their fear of seeming ignorant to others in their group, and they should be more willing to ask questions and to take intellectual risks. If you move from group to group as if you are "grading" them, students will perform for you and not work with each other. Once instructors are comfortable with collaborative learning, they find that they can leave groups of students alone and do their own work while the students collaborate.

If you have not used collaborative learning, you may worry about students' arriving at the wrong answer and then having it reinforced by other students. What do you do if a group of four students agrees that a particular sentence is not a fragment when it really is one? What if students decide that they prefer slang to standard English? You will discover that students working in a group rarely reach a consensus that is completely wrong. Usually some student in the group will dissent or, if one group of students arrives at the wrong answer, other groups will set them right.

But if students insist that their wrong answer is right, you have a good opportunity to teach them about language as social convention. Explore their answer with them and have them articulate why they feel so strongly about their opinion. Then explain to them why the users of standard written English have agreed upon a different convention. Tell students that if they want to be considered proficient writers by the users of standard written English, then they must conform to the standards set by that community. In this way, you can teach students the conventions of good writing but also reinforce the idea that these are, after all, just conventions.

Preparing Students to Provide Peer Criticism

You need to prepare students to comment on each other's writing just as carefully as you prepare them to do collaborative exercises in groups. Sometimes students may comment directly on a photocopy of a writer's paper; at other times, they will write on a reader response sheet like those at the end of this chapter. You will probably be designing a set of instructions for each peer criticism exercise, but you will also need to let students practice this new way of responding to each other's work. Students rarely receive careful peer criticism of their work. Some may ask their friends or roommates to read over a paper and give them a general response, but this kind of evaluation usually amounts to simple proofreading or is not very detailed (after all, the students want to remain friends). Because students do not know what serious peer evaluation is, they need to study several models and to practice on sample essays before they go to work on each other's papers.

Teaching Students How to Be Peer Critics

Before your students comment on each other's work, and then periodically throughout the semester, you will want to spend a class period or two discussing what they will be doing. Be sure that they really understand how their role differs from yours as the instructor and grader. If you do not explain to them that they will be responding as readers rather than as judges, they may imitate the worst kinds of "teacherly" comments as they criticize each other's work. When they confuse a reader's responses with an instructor's judgments, students reveal that they do not really understand the purpose of peer criticism. If they consider it a substitute for the instructor's comments, they will imitate an instructor and may well wonder why they are being assigned to do the instructor's duty. If, however, they realize that their peer criticism provides a different kind of response from that which they would expect from an instructor—the response of an interested reader rather than an omnipotent judge—then they will better understand the kinds of comments that are appropriate for them to make.

In class a few days before the peer criticism exercise, you might ask students to comment on a sample student paper. (Since you will probably want to have students engage in peer criticism when they are concerned with paragraphs or the whole essay, you might have them critique the first draft of Pat Lucas's paper in Chapter 2 or another student essay from your files.) After students have evaluated the paper and written responses to it, you should go over the paper and their comments in class. You may even want to comment on the paper yourself (playing your role as an instructor) in order to show them how their comments differ. For instance, you might comment, "This paper is poorly organized," whereas a helpful peer, knowing that the paper will be revised, might say, "I'm confused. How does this paragraph relate to the paragraph before it?" Students will see that they frequently respond with questions, indicating the difficulties that they have reading the paper, whereas they expect instructors to respond with statements, because instructors judge against a set of standards.

In addition to discussing sample papers in class, you will want to collect the students' written comments (either on the paper or on reader response sheets) so that you can comment on each of them individually. In this way, students who are silent during the class discussion will still receive feedback on their comments.

Be sure that students know how educated readers respond to others' writing. At first, students may suspect that you have a hidden agenda, and so they may praise each other's work in order to convince you that their friends are really competent writers. Or they may think that, despite what you say, you really want them to demonstrate their knowledge of writing by finding every single error in their classmates' papers. With constant reminders from you and with practice, these misconceptions can be overcome.

Students should practice giving specific criticism rather than vague comments. Instead of saying, "I don't agree with your idea," peer readers should point out where and how they disagree. One peer reader might say, "I don't agree with your definition of religion—it doesn't seem like an addiction to me." Whether applied to content, organization, or mechanics, this kind of detailed feedback will be most helpful to the author in the revision process. Giving the author vague impressions like "I felt good here—this reminded me of my own childhood" may establish a friendly, "readerly" tone, but it won't help the writer evaluate the essay or revise it.

Although students should be encouraged to give authors detailed feedback, they must learn to focus their comments. If they respond to every feature of the writer's text, the writer won't know where to begin revising it—the author will simply stare at the sea of ink and wonder which problems interfered most with the reader's comprehension and enjoyment of the material. You can help readers focus their responses by asking specific questions on reader response sheets like those at the end of this chapter, or you can let the readers select which features of the text they want to emphasize. But in either case, readers must learn to perform triage on the paper, addressing the most important elements of the paper first and taking on other features of the text if there is time.

Of course, students may not know which features of the text deserve the most attention. If left on their own, many students will choose to comment primarily on the grammar and mechanics of their peers' work. These subjects are "safe" because judgments about them seem more "objective" than judgments about tone, organization, and logic. But most instructors want their students to stress the larger elements of an essay, even if this means that style is not discussed at all. If peer critics concentrate first on sentences and later on paragraphs, they may find themselves making inconsistent recommendations. They may suggest, for example, that a writer revise a sentence in a paragraph that later turns out to be a digression. Since the writer will be omitting that irrelevant paragraph, the sentence problem probably does not deserve comment.

One way to encourage students to focus on larger elements of the essay is to remind them that peer evaluators usually help their partners revise, not edit. (The distinction between these two activities is explained in Chapter 2 of the handbook.) Sometimes it may be appropriate for peer readers to help the writer by revising some sample sentences from the essay, but readers should be warned against taking control of the text and revising it for the writer. Remind them that the paper remains the property of the author, and all that readers can do is respond and suggest, not revise.

You will probably find that students also have difficulty giving positive comments, even though positive feedback is sometimes the most valuable. Be sure to have students address the strengths of any paper they read. If they think of the papers they read as drafts rather than final versions, they may be less judgmental and more encouraging. Even if an introduction is boring now, taking one idea from it and building a new introduction might be just what the writer needs to do. If so, the "poor" introduction can be seen as an introduction with potential.

Setting Up and Overseeing Groups

Once students have a good introduction to peer criticism, they are ready to comment on each others' work. This activity can take place during class time or as homework. You may ask students to exchange papers within groups of three so that each student reads the work of the other two in the group. With this arrangement, students will get more than one set of responses and will be able to practice evaluating two different papers in the same exercise. What they see in one paper may help them comment on the other. But, of course, commenting on two papers takes more time than commenting on just one.

For this reason, the most common arrangement is for students to exchange papers in pairs. As with collaborative classroom exercises, you need not worry much about assigning students in pairs. Whomever they work with, students will learn from their peers' comments. You will want to be sure, however, that students group themselves in different pairs as the semester proceeds so that they benefit from a variety of readers' opinions.

In addition to commenting in writing on each other's essays, students should talk together about their papers. The written comments are a record that will help the author remember the reader's comments and allow the instructor to evaluate the work of the peer evaluators. But the oral comments may actually be the most valuable kind of feedback for the writer. When writer and reader talk together, they can question each other's responses and judgments. In this way, they learn not only how each reacted to the other's paper, but also why each responded that way. These conversations will also help students learn which of their comments are most helpful to the writer. Face-to-face conferences remind students that writing is communicating. It is not an act like competitive diving, in which you perform, someone responds by judging you, and it's over. In writing, one person performs, another responds, the first reacts to that response, the other responds, and so on.

Another form of oral conferencing is the group critique wherein a writer reads aloud and then readers respond while the writer listens. In such a forum it is important that the writer listen carefully to the readers' responses before "answering" them. If writers interrupt or appear defensive, they may discourage their readers from commenting fully. Like any other kind of peer evaluation, these group conferences need to be carefully directed by the instructor, who should create a sheet of directions to focus the peers' discussion.

After students have received their peer evaluation(s), they should be required to revise their essays. Peer criticism should be part of the writing process, not an evaluation of the final product. As they revise the papers, writers will need to study readers' comments carefully and find a way to respond to them. Be sure students understand that after considering a reader's responses, they may accept or reject them. Although many people may become involved in the production of a single writer's essay, the final responsibility for that essay belongs solely to the writer.

Preparing Guidelines

For each peer evaluation exercise, you will want to provide written guidelines for the reader. (The sample forms referred to below are appended to this discussion.) Although some of the same questions may appear on every instruction sheet (requests for positive comments, for example), you can tailor the directions so that peer critics focus their attention either on particular aspects of the essay assignment (e.g., depth of analysis in a critical book review) or on a certain feature of writing (e.g., paragraphing). (See Forms F and G.) Although students may want to refer to the handbook if they are concentrating on a skill like paragraphing, they should avoid using the symbols or error-correction codes, since those imply the strong voice of the judge, not the helpful suggestions of a peer reader.

If students will be commenting directly on each other's papers, you will need to give them a set of questions to answer in order to ensure that they consider the entire paper carefully. Form A at the end of this discussion provides some very general guidelines, but these procedures could be focused to suit any given class and its specific needs.

As you design a series of reader response sheets to use over the course of a semester, you will want to begin by requesting relatively straightforward critiques, and then move the students on to more sophisticated kinds of responses. At first, direct the students just to describe the writer's paper: What is its main idea? What evidence is offered in support of that idea? This kind of student response requires little training beyond the ability to distinguish between description and evaluation, but it is frequently the most useful way for writers to find out if their messages are being received loud and clear. Writers and readers must reach a fundamental understanding about what an essay says (or intends to say) before they can evaluate its success in fulfilling its objective. For this reason, every peer evaluation should begin with a summary of the paper's content. (See Form B.)

Later in the semester, your reader response sheets can direct students to evaluate the writer's paper as well as summarize it. Students at this level can comment on the organization, logic, paragraphing, style, diction, or grammar of the paper, but they should not take sides or argue with the writer about the content of the essay. At this stage, students need to know how to respond as careful peer critics, but they do not need to entangle themselves in the writer's argument. (See Form C.)

By the end of the semester, your students may be ready to comment on the content as well as the expression of a writer's work. To construct this kind of criticism, students need to be comfortable in their role as readers rather than judges, and they need to be proficient at limiting the number of their comments and focusing them. In this type of peer critique, students respond as "real" readers who argue with the writer's statements, question his or her evidence, provide additional support, or raise counterarguments, as well as noticing the quality of the writer's organization and style. (See Form D.)

Because this kind of peer critique may lead the reader and writer to debate an issue, you may want to allow writers to respond formally to their readers. In fact, some instructors suggest that this kind of sophisticated peer evaluation be done in two rounds: the writer writes and the reader responds; then the writer answers and the reader responds again before the writer revises the paper for the last time. Students undertaking this kind of critical reading should be reminded that their first job as a peer evaluator is to summarize the writer's argument. Only when the writer and reader understand how each views the essay can they begin to discuss the merits of the essay's content. (See Form E.)

Some classes may not be able to reach this stage, but even those who practice only descriptive responses to their peers' work will be providing valuable feedback to the writer and learning valuable critical-reading skills themselves. When students practice this kind of peer criticism regularly, they learn from one another and they come to internalize their "editor," the voice inside their heads that tells them when an idea is irrelevant or a sentence incomplete.

Combining Self-Evaluation and Peer Criticism

Sometimes you may want to give writers a chance to direct some of the peer critics' comments. Allowing writers to construct part of the reader response sheet for a given assignment may make the process of peer criticism more efficient. (See Form C, for example.) This extension of the conversation between writer and reader will also help emphasize that writing is an act of communication.

Another way of involving writers early in the process of peer evaluation is to have them fill out self-evaluation sheets, which can then be used either by peer readers or by an instructor. Knowing what strengths and weaknesses the writers see in their essays can help readers respond more efficiently. They do not have to waste time telling writers what those writers already know—that their transitions are rough, for example. Instead, readers can acknowledge where they agree with the writers' assessments and then spend more time discussing areas where the reader and writer disagree. If the two agree completely about the strengths and weaknesses of an essay, then they can move immediately to considering how to revise it.

Constructing a self-evaluation sheet is much like creating a reader response form. Be sure writers discuss the strengths as well as the weak points in the essay, and help them focus first on large elements and then on smaller elements of writing. Form H provides a sample self-evaluation sheet.

Students will also need some guidance in responding to criticism. You can refer them first to Chapter 2 of the handbook, but you will also want to discuss this valuable skill with the class as a whole. It is important for writers to share with one another the joys and frustrations of having their work evaluated. Writers must learn how to curb their anger if a reader disagrees with them, and they should practice separating themselves from their writing.

Give writers as many practical tips as possible. You will want to help students learn to question readers carefully in order to understand all the readers' comments. If writers are extremely sensitive about their prose, you can suggest that they pretend to be discussing and revising someone else's work instead of their own. You can also suggest that when writers want to experiment with following or rejecting readers' comments as they revise, they can photocopy their papers in order to retain the original version while they cut and paste or scratch out and scribble in words on the photocopy. Sometimes it is easier to accept a reader's suggestions if the writer feels that the pristine, original version still exists. It is always difficult to accept a reader's criticism of our writing—whether we are professional writers or novices. But if our students play the role of writer and reader simultaneously, they will be more apt to remember that the reader is simply trying to help them.

When you first experiment with collaborative learning, you may be surprised to find that some students do not want to participate. They may find it difficult to adjust to this new method of learning. Usually, though, it does not take long for these students to overcome their initial fears about exposing themselves to peer criticism, and they soon discover that while students' comments may differ from yours, they are equally valuable.

Sample Reader Response Forms

On the following pages are some samples of the instruction sheets used to guide peer critiques. You can use these samples as models when you create your own forms to suit your particular course objectives, or you can simply duplicate the forms and use them intact.

Form A
General Guidelines for Peer Readers
Commenting Directly on a Writer's Work

Author: Reader:

As a reader, you are going to comment directly on a photocopy of a classmate's paper. Read the paper through carefully before making any comments. Then follow the guidelines below. If the writer has submitted a self-evaluation sheet, read it *after* answering question 1.

1. Consider the thesis, purpose, and audience for the paper. Are they indicated clearly? Are they consistent? If not, ask the writer questions to help clarify these essential elements of writing.

2. Skim the paper to see how it is organized. Are there any breaks in the organization? If so, try to explain why you feel that a gap exists. Whenever possible, phrase your comments as questions, not judgments. If you think that the organization needs to be revised significantly, skip to question 7 after answering this question.

3. Now go back and look at each paragraph. Is it unified, coherent, and developed? If not, ask the writer a question to help focus or complete the paragraph.

4. Are the paragraphs connected to one another smoothly and logically? If there are any logical gaps between the paragraphs, ask the writer how one paragraph is linked to the next. If you think that most of the paragraphs need to be revised significantly, skip to question 7 after answering this question.

5. Now look at sentences. Do any sentences confuse you? If so, try to describe your confusion or ask the writer a question about the sentence.

6. Are there any mechanical or grammatical problems in the paper? If so, point them out to the writer, but do not correct them.

7. Decide what the paper's two most important strengths are. Point these out to the writer.

Form B
Reader Response Sheet
for a Descriptive Critique

Author: Reader:

Answer the questions below, being as specific as possible.

1. Read the first paragraph and then pause. Write down what you expect will be the topic, purpose, and audience of the paper.

2. Now finish reading the paper. Were your expectations for the paper's topic, purpose, and audience fulfilled? If not, what do you now think the topic, purpose, and audience are?

3. What do you think the main idea, or thesis, of the paper is?

4. What sort of evidence is used to develop or support this main idea?

5. Summarize the paper, devoting one sentence to each paragraph.

Form C
Reader Response Sheet
for an Evaluative Critique

Author: Reader:

Answer the questions below, being as specific as possible. If the author has included a self-evaluation sheet, do not read it until you have answered questions 1
through 6.

1. Read the first paragraph and then pause. Write down what you expect will be
the topic, purpose, and audience of the paper.

2. Now finish reading the paper. Were your expectations for the paper's topic, purpose, and audience fulfilled? If not, what do you now think the topic, purpose, and
audience are?

3. What do you think the main idea, or thesis, of the paper is?

4. What sort of evidence is used to develop or support this main idea?

5. Summarize the paper, devoting one sentence to each paragraph.

6. What did you like best about the paper?

7. Did anything in the paper surprise you?

8. What two features of the paper most need improvement?

9. Please respond to the author's questions on the back of this sheet.

_____

To the author: Before giving this sheet to your reader, list below the three questions that you would like your reader to answer about this paper.

Form D
Reader Response Sheet for a Thorough Critique

Author: Reader:

Answer the questions below, being as specific as possible. If the author has included a self-evaluation sheet, do not read it until you have answered questions 1 through 3.

1. Read the first paragraph and then pause. Write down what you expect will be the topic, purpose, and audience of the paper.

2. Now finish reading the paper. Were your expectations for the paper's topic, purpose, and audience fulfilled? If not, what do you now think the topic, purpose, and audience are?

3. Summarize the paper, devoting one sentence to each paragraph.

4. What do you think the main idea, or thesis, of paper is? Do you agree with this thesis? Why or why not? What is your position on this topic?

5. What sort of evidence is used to develop or support this main idea? Is this evidence appropriate? Is there sufficient evidence? If not, what sort of evidence should the writer consider?

6. Does the author take into account different points of view about thesis of the paper? Does the author consider counterarguments?

7. Are there any counterarguments that the author does not consider, but should?

8. What did you like best about this paper?

9. What two features of the paper most need improvement?

10. Please respond to the author's questions on the back of this sheet.

To the author: Before giving this sheet to your reader, list below the three questions that you would like your reader to answer about this paper.

Form E
Author's and Reader's Responses
in the Second Round of a Thorough Critique

Author: Reader:

Author's section. Please attach a revision of your original paper to this form and answer the following questions.

1. What do you think is your reader's point of view on this subject? Do you share that point of view?

2. What assumptions does your reader make about the topic? Do you agree with these assumptions? Why or why not?

3. What two comments by the reader were the most useful? Why were they helpful?

4. What are the two most important changes that you have made in this revision?

5. What do you like best about the essay?

6. What two questions would you like your reader to answer about this revision?

Reader's section. Please respond to the questions below.

1. Please summarize the author's revision, devoting one sentence to each paragraph.

2. How do you think that the author has improved the essay?

3. Has the author changed your feeling about the topic?

4. What is the strongest argument against the revised essay?

5. What two features most need improvement?

6. Respond to the author's questions.

Form F
Reader Response Sheet for an Essay Assignment
Stressing Paragraphing (Handbook, Chapter 3)

Author: Reader:

Answer the questions below, being as specific as possible. If the author has included a self-evaluation sheet, do not read it until you have answered questions 1 through 6.

1. Read the first paragraph and then pause. Write down what you expect will be the topic, purpose, and audience of the paper.

2. Now finish reading the paper. Were your expectations for the paper's topic, purpose, and audience fulfilled? If not, what do you now think the topic, purpose, and audience are?

3. What do you think the main idea, or thesis, of the paper is?

4. What sort of evidence is used to develop or support this main idea?

5. Next, number the paragraphs. Are the author's paragraphs unified, coherent, and developed? If so, note them. Also indicate any that confuse you, and explain why.

6. Do the paragraphs follow a logical order? List each pair of neighboring paragraphs and describe how the argument does or does not flow from the first to the second.

7. What did you like best about the paper?

8. What two features of the paper most need improvement?

Form G
Reader Response Sheet for an Essay Assignment
Stressing Clear and Effective Sentences
(Handbook, Parts III and IV)

Author: Reader:

Answer the questions below, being as specific as possible. If the author has included a self-evaluation sheet, do not read it until you have answered questions 1
through 4.

1. Read the first paragraph and then pause. Write down what you expect will be
the topic, purpose, and audience of the paper.

2. Now finish reading the paper. Were your expectations for the paper's topic, purpose, and audience fulfilled? If not, what do you now think the topic, purpose, and
audience are?

3. What do you think the main idea, or thesis, of the paper is?

4. What sort of evidence is used to develop or support this main idea?

5. Were the author's sentences easy to read? Number the sentences and indicate
below any that you thought were confusing. Next to the sentence numbers, try to
explain why the sentences were confusing.

Sentence number   Problem

6. Did you notice any grammatical problems in the author's sentences? If so, list
the sentence number and the grammatical problem below.

Sentence number   Problem

7. Describe the most common sentence structure found in the author's paper. Does
the author vary sentence structure? If so, describe two instances in which sentence
variety was especially effective. If not, suggest places where sentences need to be
varied.

8. What did you like best about the paper?

9. What two features of the paper most need improvement?

Form H
Self-Evaluation Sheet to Accompany an
Essay for Peer Response or Instructor's Evaluation

Author:

In order to help your instructor or peer reader evaluate this essay, you should explain where you are in the writing process. Be as specific as possible in answering the following questions.

1. What are you trying to say in this paper? What is your main idea?

2. Who might be interested in reading this paper?

3. What do you like best in the paper?

4. What do you like least in the paper?

5. What would you work on if you had twenty-four hours more to spend on the project?

6. What three questions would you like to ask your reader? How can your reader help you develop the paper further?

Resources for Collaborative Learning and Peer Criticism

Bruffee, Kenneth. "Collaborative Learning and the 'Conversation of Mankind.'" *College English* 46 (1984): 635–52.

————. *A Short Course in Writing.* 3rd ed. Boston: Little, 1985.

Clark, Beverly Lyon. *Talking About Writing: A Guide for Tutor and Teacher Conferences.* Ann Arbor: U of Michigan P, 1985.

Fox, Len. "What to Do When Grammar Exercises No Longer Help: Group Proofreading." *College Composition and Communication* 32 (1981): 332–33.

Fraser, Scott C., et al. "Two, Three, or Four Heads Are Better Than One: Modification of College Performance by Peer Monitoring." *Journal of Educational Psychology* 69 (1977–78): 101–8.

Gebhardt, Richard. "Team Work and Feedback: Broadening the Base of Collaborative Writing." *College English* 42 (1980): 69–74.

George, Diana. "Working with Peer Groups in the Composition Classroom." *College Composition and Communication* 35 (1984): 320–26.

Gere, Anne Ruggles. *Writing Groups: History, Theory, and Implications.* Carbondale: Southern Illinois UP, 1987.

————, and Robert D. Abbott. "Talking About Writing: The Language of Writing Groups." *Research in the Teaching of English* 19 (1985): 362–86.

————, and Ralph Stevens. "The Language of Writing Groups: How Oral Response Shapes Revision." In *The Acquisition of Written Language: Response and Revision.* Ed. Sarah Warshauer Freedman. Norwood: Ablex, 1985. 85–105.

Hawkins, Thom. *Group Inquiry Techniques for Teaching Writing.* Urbana: NCTE, 1976.

Kail, Harvey. "Collaborative Learning in Context: The Problem with Peer Tutoring." *College English* 45 (1983): 817–23.

Schuster, Charles. "The Un-Assignment: Writing Groups for Advanced Expository Writers." *Freshman English News* 13 (Winter 1984): 433–46.

Salmon, Phillida, and Hilary Claire. *Classroom Collaboration.* London: Routledge, 1984.

Trimbur, John. "Collaborative Learning and Teaching Writing." In *Perspectives on Research and Scholarship in Composition.* Ed. Ben W. McClelland and Timothy R. Donovan. New York: MLA, 1985, 87–109.

FOURTH EDITION

The Little, Brown Handbook

H. RAMSEY FOWLER
Memphis State University

JANE E. AARON
Parsons School of Design/
The New School for Social Research

SCOTT, FORESMAN AND COMPANY
Glenview, Illinois • Boston • London

LIBRARY OF CONGRESS
Library of Congress Cataloging-in-Publication Data

Fowler, H. Ramsey (Henry Ramsey)
    The Little, Brown handbook / H. Ramsey Fowler, Jane E. Aaron. —
4th ed.
      p.   cm.
      Includes index.
      ISBN 0-673-39859-5
      1. English language—Grammar—1950-   2. English language-
-Rhetoric. I. Aaron, Jane E. II. Little, Brown and Company.
College Division. III. Title.
PE1112.F64 1989
808'.042—dc 19   88-21142
                                                       CIP

   2 3 4 5 6 7 8 9 10—RRC—94 93 92 91 90

Printed in the United States of America

Photograph, page 16: Balthazar Korab, Ltd.

We would like to thank the following authors and publishers for permission to quote from their works.

Bonnie Angelo, from "Those Good Ole Boys," *Time,* 27 September 1976. Copyright 1976 Time Inc. All rights reserved. Reprinted by permission from *Time.*

Peter Bogdanovich, excerpted from "Bogie in Excelsis," *Pieces of Time.* © 1973 by Peter Bogdanovich. Used by permission of Arbor House Publishing Company and the author.

Daniel J. Boorstin, from *The Discoverers.* Copyright 1983. Reprinted by permission of Random House, Inc.

Lynn M. Buller, from "The Encyclopedia Game" in Saul D. Feldman and Gerald W. Thielbar, eds., *Life Style: Diversity in American Society.* Copyright © 1972 by Little, Brown and Company (Inc.). Reprinted by permission.

Arthur L. Campa, from "Angelo vs. Chicano: Why?" *Western Review,* 1972. Reprinted by permission of Mrs. Arthur L. Campa.

Bruce Catton, "Grant and Lee: A study in Contrasts" from *The American Story,* Earl Schenck Miers, editor. Copyright U.S. Historical Society. Reprinted with permission.

David L. Chandler, from "Air Bags—Life Saving and Unavailable," Sci/Tech, *The Boston Globe,* March 1985. Reprinted courtesy of *The Boston Globe.*

Arthur C. Clarke, from "The Star of the Magi," copyright © 1972 by Arthur C. Clarke. Reprinted by permission of the author and the author's agent, Scott Meredith Literary Agency, Inc., 845 Third Avenue, New York, New York 10022.

Definition of *conjecture* and synonym study for *real.* Copyright © 1985 by Houghton Mifflin Company. Reprinted by permission from *The American Heritage Dictionary, Second College Edition.*

Definition of *reckon.* By permission. From *Webster's Ninth New Collegiate Dictionary* © 1988 by Merriam-Webster Inc., publisher of the Merriam-Webster Dictionaries.

(continued on page 748)

Preface for Instructors

The changes in this fourth edition of *The Little, Brown Handbook* are paradoxically both few and numerous. The book continues to serve a dual function as both a text for composition classes and a reference for writers, distinguished by its comprehensiveness, clarity, accessibility, and an organization that places the writing process up front. But within this context myriad revisions and additions keep pace with changes in the teaching and learning of composition. The most significant of these alterations make the handbook even more convenient as a reference, introduce critical thinking and academic writing, and expand and refine the discussions of the writing process and the research paper.

Undoubtedly the most conspicuous change in the fourth edition is the brightened design, conceived to be functional as well as handsome. Headings are easier to find and read; exercises are more distinct; and crucial material is more accessible in eighty-three boxes either shaded or bordered in gold. These boxes extend a popular feature of the previous edition, the two-page guide to punctuation (pp. 360–61 in this edition). New this time are four summary/index charts that pull together all the book's information on nouns, pronouns, verbs and verbals, and modifiers (pp. 201–06); a comprehensive guide to handling quotations (pp. 414–15); and seventy-seven other summaries, indexes, diagrams, and checklists encompassing everything from the writing situation to patterns of parallelism to the uses of the comma. Intended for quick reference, these boxes supplement rather than replace more detailed text discussions, providing students with two levels of explanation.

Throughout the handbook, new chapters and sections respond to a changing composition curriculum and the changing needs of students. Chapter 4, formerly devoted mainly to persuasive writing, has been broadened to encompass critical thinking, reading, and writing. It emphasizes writing summaries as an aid to analysis, discusses inference and other aspects of reasoning, and explains how to read as well as how to write an argument. Chapter 38, all new, treats writing in the disciplines, introducing students to the demands and rewards of academic writing and outlining the methods, goals, and concerns of the humanities (with an emphasis on literature), the social sciences, and the natural and applied sciences. The chapter provides four sample papers (including literary analyses both with and without secondary sources), complete models and explanations of the documentation style in psychology (APA), and highlights of a style commonly used in the sciences (CBE).

Instructors concerned with the writing process will appreciate the expansions in Chapters 1 and 2, especially in invention (including clustering), audience, organization (including tree diagrams, drafting, and writing a title. As before, examples in these chapters come from the work-in-progress of several students, including one student's complete first, revised, edited, and final drafts. A new Appendix B on word processing adapts the process outlined in Chapters 1 and 2 as the context for specific, practical advice on using a computer to write and revise.

The material on the research paper is also much strengthened. Although it continues to treat research writing as a process, it is divided into three chapters (35–37) for easier access to bibliographic models and other practical information. New sections advise students on planning and scheduling a long-term research project and on conducting interviews as primary research. Boxes frame such reference aids as a model schedule, indexes to the book's bibliographic and parenthetical-reference forms, and a list of verbs for introducing quotations. The discussion of paraphrasing and summarizing is fuller and is now followed by the former appendix on avoiding plagiarism, with a new exercise. A new student paper on women in management illustrates all stages of research writing and appears in final form with extensive facing-page annotations. As before, an analytical paper on the editing of the Declaration of Independence is also included.

These substantial revisions in the handbook are complemented by innumerable smaller adjustments. Among the other additions are a treatment of narrative and descriptive paragraphs (3c-2), guidance on double negatives (9f), a discussion of sexist and other biased language (31a-8), and detailed instructions for typing punctuation (Appendix A). Editing has affected nearly every page, producing tighter explanations and clearer examples. The exercises in all the chapters that typically receive the hardest use—case, verbs, fragments, commas, and the like—now consist entirely of connected discourse on subjects as diverse as computerized music and humor in business. As before, paragraph-format exercises conclude most chapters.

Supplements

The changes in the fourth edition have their equal in an extensive package of supplements. Robert A. Schwegler, University of Rhode Island, has transformed his helpful instructor's manual into the *Instructor's Annotated Edition of The Little, Brown Handbook.* A new essay on contemporary approaches to teaching writing joins chapters on designing a composition course, evaluating student writing, and collaborative learning. Further, the manual and handbook have now been combined in a large format so that chapter notes, bibliographical references, activities, and answers to exercises are printed alongside relevant text. Donna Gorrell, University of Wisconsin at Milwaukee, has prepared a fourth edition of *The Little, Brown Workbook* that parallels the handbook in organization while providing varied exercises for students who need additional help with the writing process, grammar, or usage. New with this edition is word-processing software with extensive documentation: *PFS:Write* for the Apple and *PFS:Professional Write* for the IBM and compatibles, accompanied by the text/workbook *Composing with PFS:Write/PFS:Professional Write*, by Rosalie Hewitt and Vicky T. Miller, Northern Illinois University; and *MacWrite* for the Macintosh, accompanied by *MacWrite and the Writing Process*, by Mark Coleman, State University of New York at Potsdam.

Other supplements in this large package are an answer key to the handbook, available to students at an instructor's option; a student manual for peer evaluation; a collection of essays; a collection of student research papers; videotapes of the PBS television series *The Story of English*, with an accompanying study guide; a compilation of ideas for teaching writing; a set of transparency masters drawn from the handbook; a poster-size correction chart; a competency profile test bank; two sample CLAST tests; and diagnostic tests keyed to the handbook. Information on any of the supplements may be obtained from the publisher.

Acknowledgments

Dozens of instructors contributed thoughtful, detailed, and constructive comments based on their classroom experiences with students and with handbooks. We thank Christopher Baker, Lamar University; James E. Barcus, Baylor University; Glynn Baugher, Frostburg State University; Lynn Beene, University of New Mexico; Ethel L. Bonds, Virginia Western Community College; John Briggs, University of California, Riverside; Sally J. Bright, Tulsa Junior College; Harry M. Brown, Midwestern State University; Sara L. Brown, Tulsa Junior College; Wayne A. Buchman, Rose State College; Betsy R. Burke, Columbus State Community College; Santi Buscemi, Middlesex County College; Sylvia Cara-Monica, Clark County Community College; Barbara Carr, Stephen F. Austin State University; Margaret L. Carter, Bradley University; Betty Clement, Paris Junior College; Suzanne Clepper, Tarrant County Junior College; Paul Cohen, Southwest Texas State University; Mark Coleman, State University of New York, Potsdam; Thomas A. Copeland, Youngstown State University; Pat Coward, Bowling Green State University; Richard Cox, Abilene Christian University; Mary Ann Dazey, Mississippi State University; John T. Dever, Thomas Nelson Community College; Norbert Elliot, East Texas State University; G. Dale Gleason, Hutchinson Community College; Craig M. Goad, Northwest Missouri State University; D. Wayne Gunn, Texas A & I University; Iris Rose Hart, Santa Fe Community College; Milton Hawkins, Del Mar College; Vicki L. Hill, Southern Methodist University; Con Hood, Southwestern Oklahoma State University; Maurice Hunt, Baylor University; Vanessa Furse Jackson, Bowling Green State University; Judy Kaplow, William Rainey Harper Community College;

Helen E. Kaufmann, Parkland College; Philip M. Keith, St. Cloud State University; Joanne Little, Pima Community College; Daniel T. Lochman, Southwest Texas State University; Larry R. Long, Harding University; Helen M. Loschky, Lincoln University; Helen Maloney, Tidewater Community College; Michael Meyer, University of Connecticut; Sandra Nagy, Arizona State University; Christopher O'Hearn, Los Angeles Harbor College; Blakeney J. Richard, Texas A & I University; Brad Rogharr, Weber State College; Robert Ross, Southern Methodist University; Bea Sandlin, Scottsdale Community College; Adeline Skillman, Essex County College; John F. Slater, University of Wyoming; Barbara Sloan, Santa Fe Community College; Louise Z. Smith, University of Massachusetts, Boston; M. Clare Sweeney, Arizona State University; Marc E. Tappmeyer, Southwest Baptist University; Richard F. Thompson, Northern Virginia Community College; Noel Toups, Nicholls State University; William J. Vande Kopple, Calvin College; George Van Devender, Hardin-Simmons University; Sue Fisher Vaughn, University of Rhode Island; and Laura W. Zlogar, University of Wisconsin at River Falls.

We extend special appreciation to several instructors who contributed text as well as ideas to the fourth edition: Kathleen S. Cain, Merrimack College; Mary E. McGann, Rhode Island College; Leonard J. Rosen, Bentley College; and William Van Pelt, University of Wisconsin at Milwaukee. Special thanks also to Andrew Christensen for insightful suggestions and to those responsible for producing this handsome edition: the book editor, Andrea Cava; the copyeditor, Roberta H. Winston; the designer, Patricia Girvin Dunbar; the artist, Lyrl Ahern; and the editorial assistants, Dorothy Paschal and Susan McIntyre. As in previous editions, we again happily acknowledge a great debt to Robert A. Schwegler, University of Rhode Island, and Richard S. Beal, professor emeritus at Boston University, for their advice and support.

As author of this annotated edition, I extend thanks to former graduate student Daryl Sanchez, who helped research and prepare many annotations. I also thank my wife, Nancy Newman Schwegler, and my sons, Brian and Christopher Schwegler, for being there for me.

Preface for Students: Using This Book

A handbook is a comprehensive reference guide to the essential information in a field or discipline, whether it is stamp collecting, home maintenance, or chemistry. *The Little, Brown Handbook* is no exception. A basic resource for English composition, grammar, and usage, it can serve you as a text and reference book for writing not only in a composition course but also in other courses and outside college. Mastery of the principles and conventions discussed in this book will not by itself make you a good writer; for that, you need to care about your work at every level from conceiving a topic to spelling words. But learning how to use the handbook and then referring to it as the need arises will give you the means to say *what* you want in the *way* you want. The following pages tell you about the book's organizaton and store of information, the ways of locating that information, and the standard of usage recommended.

The handbook's organization and coverage

An overview of the handbook's contents appears inside the back cover. The first four chapters discuss larger elements of composition—the essay and the paragraph. Chapters 1 and 2 describe and illustrate the writing process, from choosing a topic through considering an audience and generating and organizing ideas to revision. Chapter 3 treats composing and revising paragraphs. And Chapter 4 discusses critical thinking and writing, including how to read and write an argument. The principles discussed in these chapters are basic to everything that follows in the handbook, so you may want to read and digest them even if they are not assigned.

You may also want to read Chapter 5, which presents the system of English grammar. Though much of the material will be familiar to you, the chapter will repay your attention because it shows that the grammar of English is more than just a hodgepodge of rules, and it provides background for the fourteen chapters that follow. After Chapter 5 (beginning p. 201), are four charts that summarize the information in these later chapters about nouns, pronouns, verbs and verbals, and modifiers. Then each chapter treats a principle or convention of grammatical correctness (Chapters 6 to 9), clarity (Chapters 10 to 15), or effectiveness (Chapters 16 to 19). Your instructor may discuss some or all of these chapters in class or may suggest that you consult specific chapters when you encounter problems.

Chapters 20 to 25 of the handbook describe the current conventions of punctuation. Punctuation is also discussed in earlier chapters, but these separate chapters bring together all the conventions for each mark. Preceding Chapter 20, on pages 360–61, is a chart showing the rules and options for the marks that cause the most confusion, even for experienced writers. If you aren't sure how to punctuate a sentence you are working on, this chart can suggest the alternatives. Another chart, in Chapter 24 (pp. 414–15), shows all your options when you are quoting others, including what punctuation to use and where to put it. Chapters 26 to 30 present the conventions of mechanics—capitalization, abbreviations, italics (or underlining), numbers, and word division. Whether or not you are assigned these chapters, you should think of them as resources to consult continually for advice on specific questions.

Chapters 31 to 34 deal with words. Chapter 31, which discusses the principles guiding effective word choice, is intended to help you express your meaning exactly and concisely. Chapter 32 introduces the features and uses of any desk dictionary. Chapters 33 and 34 suggest ways in which you can develop your vocabulary and master the complexities of English spelling.

The last chapters of the handbook treat specific kinds of writing. Chapters 35–37 trace the process of writing and documenting a research paper for which you consult books and periodicals on some issue or question. Chapter 38 discusses writing in the various academic disciplines, such as literature, psychology, and biology. Chapter 39 provides specific advice on writing essay examinations for college courses. And Chapter 40 explains and illustrates basic business writing: the letter of complaint or request, the job application and résumé, and the memorandum.

The handbook concludes with two appendixes, two glossaries, and an index. Appendix A describes a widely accepted standard for preparing a manuscript. Appendix B offers practical advice on writing and revising with a word processor. The Glossary of Usage provides brief notes on troublesome or confusing words and expressions that plague writers at all levels of experience. The Glossary of Grammatical Terms defines all the specialized words that appear in the handbook as well as a few others. And finally, the index contains an entry for every principle, convention, and term discussed in the book as well as many specific words and phrases that you may need to look up.

Throughout the handbook gold boxes contain information that is especially important or that writers tend to seek often, such as a checklist for revising a paper (p. 58) or the uses and misuses of the apostrophe (p. 407). Like the charts described above, these boxes can be used for quick reference. Further explanation can generally be found in the adjacent text.

Finding information in the handbook

The Little, Brown Handbook provides a wealth of specific information—what form of a verb to use, how to express an idea concisely, whether to punctuate with a comma or a semicolon, whether to capitalize a word, how to arrange the title page of a paper, and so on. The handbook also provides many ways of locating such information quickly. When you seek information on your own, you can check the guide to useful lists and summaries inside the front cover; you can refer to the table of contents inside the back cover or immediately after this preface; or you can refer to the index. The table of contents shows all the book's parts, chapters, and main sections within chapters. The sections are labeled with letters (*a*, *b*, and so on). These letters and the corresponding chapter numbers (for instance, 9d or 12a) also appear before the appropriate convention or guideline in the text itself, and they are printed in colored boxes on the sides of the pages. Thus you can find a section heading in the contents and thumb the book until you arrive at its number and letter on the side of the page. If you are uncertain of what to look for and need a more detailed guide to the book's contents, consult the index.

Your instructor may mark your papers using heading numbers and letters, symbols, or written comments. Pages 68–70 show a student essay marked in all three ways. If your instructor marks your paper with, say, 10a, you can refer to the contents to learn that you have made an error involving a sentence fragment. If you need further information to correct the error, you can then refer to the text by finding the appropriate page number or by locating 10a in a colored box on the side of the page, as described above. If your instructor uses a symbol such as *frag* to mark your paper, you can find out how to correct the error by referring to the alphabetical list of symbols inside the front cover. Using this guide, you would be directed by the symbol *frag* to Chapter 10 on sentence fragments. The symbols also appear in the colored boxes at the sides of the pages. The best way to find specific handbook sections from your instructor's written comments is to consult the index. Look up the term used by your instructor and scan the subentries under it until you find one that seems to describe the error you have made. Then turn to the page number given.

The handbook's recommended usage

The Little, Brown Handbook describes and recommends the conventions of standard written English—the written language common to business and the professions. Written English is more conservative than spoken English in matters of grammar and usage, and a great many words, phrases, and constructions that are widely spoken remain unaccepted in careful writing.

When clear distinctions exist between the language of conversation and that of careful writing, the handbook provides examples of each and labels them *spoken* and *written*. When usage in writing itself varies with the level of formality intended, the handbook labels examples *formal* and *informal*. When usage is mixed or currently changing, the handbook recommends that you choose the more conservative usage because it will be acceptable to all readers.

If you follow the guidelines discussed in this handbook, your writing will be clearer and more demanding of serious attention than it might otherwise have been. Remember, however, that adhering to established conventions is but a means to the real achievement and reward of writing: communicating your message effectively.

Contents

Glossaries

Index   **750**

The Whole Paper and Paragraphs

Why write? Many students are likely to have this question in mind when they first open *The Little, Brown Handbook* or even when they first register for a composition course or sit listening to the instructor on the first day of the class.

This chapter begins by addressing the question directly and recognizing the difficulties faced by all writers—experienced or inexperienced. Next, the chapter alerts students to the various elements of the writing situation and the writing process and discusses ways to discover subjects and purposes for writing. The concluding sections explore flexible strategies for developing and grouping ideas, considering an audience, focusing on a thesis, and creating a plan for the initial draft. Student Pat Lucas's essay-in-progress runs throughout this chapter and the next as a source of concrete examples.

The exploratory strategies discussed include freewriting, journals, observation, clustering, reading, brainstorming, and systematic questioning. The strategies for developing and planning include tree diagrams, thesis sentences, patterns of development, and outlines (both scratch and informal). Two special features of this chapter are the attention paid to the role of audience in each of the various activities of composing and the list of "Questions About Audience" (p. 27) that highlight the extended discussion of readers' expectations in the latter part of the chapter (lf.).

Though Chapter 1 looks at activities typical of the early stages of composing and Chapter 2 treats drafting and revising, the text does not endorse a strictly linear view of the composing process. Instead, both chapters emphasize the writer's many options and the flexibility of the composing process. They point out that writing is a way of thinking and discovering: that in the middle of drafting an essay a writer may recognize the need to develop new supporting ideas, to make major changes in the organization, or to shift the purpose of the essay and modify the thesis.

CHAPTER 1

Developing an Essay

"Writing is easy," said the late sportswriter Red Smith. "All you have to do is sit down at the typewriter and open a vein." This wry comment may seem negative: Smith clearly found writing demanding. But the humor tells another story as well—that writing, for all its demands, gives something back. Whatever your experience with writing, you probably can appreciate Smith's point about its difficulties. You may, however, be less certain of its rewards.

Obviously, one reward of writing is that it will help you get through college and into a good job. The better you write, the better student and worker you'll be. But Red Smith did not bleed at his typewriter primarily for money; there are easier ways to earn a salary. Like most writers, he wrote for the challenge and the satisfaction of learning and communicating. For you, throughout college and beyond, writing will be a principal means of mastering ideas, managing information, demonstrating your abilities, and persuading others to agree with you. But more than that: if you let it, writing will also be an exciting way to explore the world and yourself and to share your discoveries with others.

Part of gaining rewards as a writer is learning the skills to express yourself clearly and interestingly, skills covered throughout this book. But you can also learn from other writers—from the comments of classmates and teachers on your work, from the reading you do for information and stimulation, and (a particular concern of Chapters 1 and 2) from an understanding of how other writers work. You'll know you're really working at writing if now and then you experience some of Red Smith's pain; but the insight and control you earn in exchange will more than make up for it.

1a The writing situation and the writing process

All writing occurs in a context that simultaneously limits and clarifies the writer's choices. Most obviously, context includes the nature of the assignment, the assigned length, and the deadline. But context can also be seen as the **writing situation,** neatly captured in this analogy by the writer and composer Virgil Thomson: "It's like Spanish boys playing bullfight. It takes one to be the matador, one to be the bull, and one to stand by and shout 'Olé!' " In the writing situation, the writer (the matador) aims to communicate something about a subject (the bull) to a particular audience of readers (the one standing by). The three elements interact continuously throughout the development, drafting, and revision of a piece of writing, with the writer balancing his or her view, the demands of the subject, and the needs, interests, and expectations of the audience. As we will see throughout this chapter, the nature of the elements and their relative importance change with each new writing task, but the elements are always present. Asking for each task what your subject is, who your audience is, and how you want to present yourself and your subject to that audience can help you define and make choices.

Sometimes the writing situation is clearly defined from the start. Imagine, for instance, that you are assigned a report on an experiment in your physics course, a report expected to show your instructor that you have mastered scientific observation and the principles studied in the course. In this case, your subject, your audience and its expectations, and the way you should present yourself are predefined for you by the assignment. For other writing tasks, however, the writing situation may be left to you to define. Suppose, for instance, that your composition instructor asks you to write an essay relating a significant learning experience. You will have to determine what experience to relate as well as how you want to present yourself and your experience, and you may be required to select your audience and determine its needs and expectations.

THE WRITING SITUATION

Writer ⟶ Subject ⟶ Audience

The student essay-in-progress shows how Pat Lucas responds to another writer's ideas about modern buildings with an example from her own experience. Through it the chapters provide concrete illustration of the principles and strategies discussed in the text. And in describing Lucas's successes, false starts, and frequent revisions, the chapter offers students a model for understanding their own composing processes.

AT EASE

Students often bring their apprehensions about writing (and writing instructors) with them to class. To create a positive atmosphere for your course, you may wish to establish a setting in which students feel at ease about acknowledging and sharing their apprehensions. One way to do this is to ask them to *list* what they dislike (and like) about writing without worrying about the form or correctness of entries in their lists. Voluntary sharing of the entries can help reduce the isolation many students feel and help you (and them) set priorities for instruction.

RESOURCES AND IDEAS

R. Baird Shuman, "Basics in Composition: Fluency First," *Teaching the Basics—Really!* ed. Ouida Clapp (Urbana: NCTE, 1977): 43–46. Shuman presents activities to overcome students' fears of writing and to help them get started.

RESOURCES AND IDEAS
The Writing Situation

Linda S. Flower and John R. Hayes, "The Cognition of Discovery: Defining a Rhetorical Problem," *College Composition and Communication* 31 (1980): 21–32. This article reports on a detailed study of how good writers and poor writers conceive of writing tasks as they begin to compose.

Ken David, "The Circle Game: A Heuristic for Discovering Rhetorical Situations," *College Composition and Communication* 29 (1978): 285–87. David suggests giving students roles to play in social situations and challenging them to develop writing tasks appropriate to the situations.

David Tedlock, "The Case Approach to Composition," *College Composition and Communication* 32 (1981): 253–62. Tedlock argues for the use of cases—detailed, self-contained descriptions of a writing situation—as a basis for assignments and instructions.

The Writing Process

Linda Flower and John R. Hayes, "A Cognitive Process Theory of Writing," *College Composition and Communication* 32 (1981): 365–87. This article contains what is probably the best known and most widely accepted discussion of the elements and goals of the writing process, though the model it presents is admittedly theoretical rather than practical.

Nancy MacKenzie, "Teaching the Composing Process: A Three-Part Project," *The Writing Instructor* 1 (1982): 103–111. MacKenzie describes an in-class exercise, a diary assignment, and a process paper designed to direct "students' attention to the strengths and weaknesses of their own composing processes."

Understanding the writing situation is an important part of the **writing process**—the term for all the activities, mental and physical, that go into writing what eventually becomes a finished piece of work. Even for experienced writers, the process is usually messy, which is one reason that it is sometimes painful. Though we get a sense of ease and orderliness from, say, a well-crafted magazine article, we can safely assume that the writer had to work hard to achieve it, suffering frustration when ideas would not come, struggling to express half-formed thoughts, shaping and reshaping the same paragraph to make a point convincingly.

While engaged in the writing process, a writer continually alternates between a wide and a narrow focus—opening up the mind to take in new information and then closing in on a single idea to shape and refine it, seeking the general picture and then filling in the specific details. This alternating pattern continues through a sequence of overlapping stages: *developing* or *planning*, the stage of exploring ideas, gathering information, developing a central theme, and organizing material; *drafting*, the stage of expressing and connecting ideas; and *revising*, the stage of rethinking and improving the structure, content, and style.

Aside from the widening and narrowing of focus and the rough division into stages, there is no *one* writing process: no two

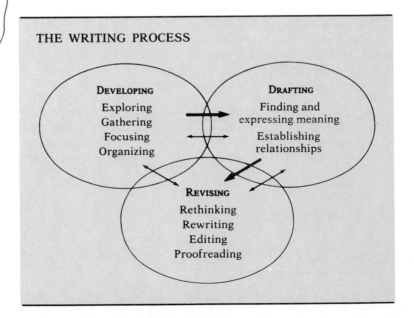

THE WRITING PROCESS

writers proceed in the same way, and even an individual writer adapts his or her process to the task at hand. Still, most experienced writers rely on a bundle of procedures that have consistently helped them with the activities involved in writing: finding a topic (section 1b), defining a purpose and identifying an audience (1c), developing ideas (1d), shaping ideas (1e), considering the audience (1f), developing a thesis (1g), organizing (1h), and drafting, revising, and editing (Chapter 2). As you encounter difficulties with any of these activities in the course of writing, you can experiment with the procedures suggested until you find one or more that work for you. With experience, as you complete a variety of assignments and try a variety of procedures, you will develop your own basic writing process.

Periodically in this chapter and the next you will see examples of how one student worked from an assignment to a finished essay by drawing on some of the procedures discussed. Occasionally, examples of other students' work will also be introduced to illustrate other approaches. These students' writing situations are not yours, and their solutions to writing problems may not work for you. But following their progress should supplement what you learn on your own about the difficulties and the rewards of writing.

EXERCISE 1

Recall several writing experiences that you have had in the past —a letter you had difficulty with, an essay you enjoyed, an all-nighter spent happily or miserably on a term paper, and so on. What do these experiences reveal to you about writing, particularly your successes and problems with it? For instance:

> Do you like to experiment with language?
> Do you prefer writing to specific assignments rather than general ones?
> Are some kinds of writing easier than others?
> Do you have trouble getting ideas or expressing them?
> Do you worry about grammar and spelling?
> Do your readers usually understand what you mean?

Write these thoughts down as the first entry in a continuing journal or log in which you track your new experiences as a writer. As you complete writing assignments for your composition course and other courses, keep adding to the journal, noting especially which procedures seem most helpful to you. Your aim is to discover your feelings about writing so that you can develop a dependable writing process of your own.

ANSWERS: EXERCISE 1
Individual response.

1b   Discovering and limiting a subject

Many writers (including experienced ones) encounter their first stumbling block in finding a subject to write about or in finding a way to make an assigned subject their own. Sometimes an appropriate subject or a unique angle may come to you with little effort; but when it does not, you can try one of the approaches discussed in this section.

TECHNIQUES FOR DISCOVERING A SUBJECT

1. Pursue your interests and experiences (1b-1).
2. Keep a journal (1b-2).
3. Observe your surroundings (1b-3).
4. Read (1b-4).
5. Freewrite (1b-5).
(See also p. 15, "Techniques for developing a topic.")

RESOURCES AND IDEAS

D. Gordon Rohman, "Pre-writing: The State of Discovery in the Writing Process," *College Composition and Communication* 16 (1965): 106–12. Rohman describes a program of invention based on techniques of self-analysis and meditation.

Raymond J. Rodrigues, "Folklife: An Unlimited Writing Source," *On Righting Writing*, ed. Ouida H. Clapp (Urbana: NCTE, 1975), 37–39. This selection offers a list of family and community traditions that students can explore as sources for essays.

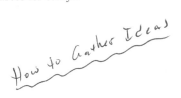

How to Gather Ideas

1   Pursuing your interests and experiences

To discover an essay subject when one is not assigned, review your own experiences, interests, and curiosities. Look for a subject you already know something about or have been wondering about, such as some issue at your school or in your town. Recall something you have discussed with others recently: perhaps an event in your family's history or a change in relations between men and women. Consider what you have read or have seen at the movies or on television: for instance, a shocking book, a violent or funny movie, a television commercial. Run your mind over the reading and class discussions in your courses to discover an idea or situation that intrigues you or that you can apply to your own experience—perhaps a social issue such as homelessness or a psychological issue such as diagnosis of depression. Think about things that make you especially happy, such as a hobby, or especially angry, such as the behavior of your neighbors. Examine your own or others' dislikes and preferences to identify any that you would like to understand better. The goal here is to think of a subject that sparks your imagination and gets your mind working. If you care about your subject, then writing will be more interesting for you, and what you write will be more likely to interest readers.

If you are assigned a general subject, as often happens in college courses, then your goal is to discover your special interests within the boundaries of the assignment. For instance, if you are assigned a comparison-and-contrast essay on two people you know, then you will need to think of two people—friends, relatives, teachers—whose similarities or differences you find striking. If you are assigned a history essay on, say, Abraham Lincoln as President, then you will need to review the reading you have done for the course and your notes from lectures and discussions to find an aspect of that subject that you'd like to know more about—perhaps Lincoln's economic policies or his weaknesses as President.

2 Keeping a journal

Many writers record their thoughts and observations in a **journal,** a diary that is concerned more with ideas than with day-to-day events. *Journal* comes from the Latin for "daily," and many journal keepers do write faithfully every day; others make entries less regularly, when the mood strikes or an insight occurs or they have a problem to work out. Journal keepers often become dependent on the process for the writing practice it gives them and the concentrated thought it encourages. Usually for the same reasons, teachers of writing and other subjects sometimes require students to keep journals.

Whether you keep a journal on your own or by request, it can provide many ideas for writing. When you need to invent an essay topic or find a way into an assigned topic, review your journal entries for observations and connections you may have forgotten or been unaware of. A thought you recorded months ago about a chemistry experiment may be just what you need for direction on a research paper. Two distant entries about arguments with your brother may suggest a psychology paper on sibling relations.

3 Observing your surroundings

Sometimes you can find a good subject by looking around you, not in the half-conscious way most of us move from place to place in our daily lives but deliberately, all senses alert. On a bus, for instance, are there certain types of passengers? What seems to be on the driver's mind? On campus, which buildings stand out? Are bicycle riders and pedestrians at peace with each other? At a movie, do the viewers seem well suited to the film? Does one type of viewer eat popcorn?

To get the most from observation, you should have a tablet

JOURNALS

Ask students to keep a journal for ten days to two weeks, writing for ten to fifteen minutes a day. Encourage them to record past or present experiences and feelings or to explore ideas and opinions. To make sure the journals contain different kinds of writing, ask students to devote a certain number of entries to specific tasks, such as describing a scene, exploring feelings about a controversial topic, or creating a character sketch of a friend. The journal entries can later be developed into formal essays. Journals can also be used to record responses to essays and literary works or to develop reactions to newspaper articles and television programs. When used in this way, journals can be a preparation for critical, argumentative, or expository essays.

This activity can be combined with Exercise 1, which asks students to record their experiences as writers.

RESOURCES AND IDEAS

Toby Fulwiler, ed., *The Journal Book* (Portsmouth: Boynton/Cook Heinemann, 1987). The essays in this collection decribe the uses of journals for discovering and exploring ideas and as an important strategy for writing and learning in various subject areas.

Fred D. White, "Releasing the Self: Teaching Journal-Writing to Freshmen," *The Writing Instructor* 1 (1982): 147–54. White offers practical advice on the use of journals: kinds of journals and entries, professional samples, exercises, and a summary of supporting research.

Sharon Whitehill, "Using the Journal for Discovery: Two Devices," *College Composition and Communication* 38 (1987): 472–74. Whitehill argues that journal assignments calling for lists and for imaginary dialogues can help generate ideas and alleviate writing blocks, and she provides detailed examples of each strategy.

**dev
1b**

ACTIVITIES THAT SUGGEST TOPICS AND IDEAS

1. Ask students to take a notebook with them to some place likely to be filled with activity and vivid sense impressions—a laundromat, the center of the campus, a busy restaurant. They can record their impressions of the scene in the notebook, later turning those impressions into a structured description, or use the material in some other form of writing.

2. Ask students to look at a variety of magazines and to bring in a list of the topics covered in the articles. These topics may in turn suggest topics for student essays. The exercise can be extended by asking students to summarize the contents of one or more of the articles and to indicate how the content might appeal to a particular audience.

3. Check with your audiovisual center on a film rental service for short films that deal with values or controversies. The films or the ensuing discussions can become the basis of student papers.

4. Set up class presentations or debates on an issue in order to provide information and sharpen the focus for papers dealing with the issue or related topics.

RESOURCES AND IDEAS

Kris Lackey, "Amongst the Awful Subtexts: Scholes, the *Daily Planet*, and Freshman Composition," *College Composition and Communication* 38 (1987): 88–93. In this thought-provoking piece, Lackey suggests encouraging and enabling students to tease out the binary oppositions in texts as a way of discovering various subtexts that suggest topics for students' own writing.

PLACES TO WRITE

To help students discover interesting topics and ideas through freewriting, you might give them some places to begin. For essays focusing on events:

sports, contests, camping, accidents, storms, childhood experiences, giving a speech, getting lost in a department store, robberies, fires.

and pen or pencil handy for notes and sketches. If you have a camera, you may find that the lens sees things your unaided eyes do not notice. (When observing or photographing people, though, keep some distance, take photographs quickly, and avoid staring. Otherwise, your subjects will feel uneasy.) Back at your desk, study your notes, sketches, or photographs for oddities or patterns that you'd like to explore further.

4   **Reading**

Even when your assignment does not require reading, you can mine newspapers, magazines, and books for writing subjects. People often read passively, absorbing content like blotters, not interacting with it. To read for ideas, you will need to be more active, probing text and illustrations with your mind, nurturing any sparks they set off. Perhaps an article on a jazz trumpeter reminds you of your own experiences playing the trumpet. Or perhaps an editorial on financing public colleges makes you wonder how primary and secondary schools are financed. In either case you have the seed of a subject.

If your general subject is assigned—say, public art or corporate public relations—then your reading will obviously be focused on material that deals with the subject. (Chapter 35 includes lists of general references and periodical indexes in most subjects. See 35c.) An article on changes in public art may raise interesting questions about how corporations are using art. A book on public relations may suggest looking at corporate annual reports as tools of public relations.

NOTE: Whenever you use the information or ideas of others in your writing, you must acknowledge your sources in order to avoid the serious offense of plagiarism. (See 36d.) If a writer's ideas merely suggest a direction for you, you need not acknowledge the source. But if you actually present any of those ideas in your final paper, then you must also acknowledge where they came from. (See 36h and 36i for how to acknowledge sources.)

5   **Freewriting**

Another way to find a subject is to write your way into it: write without stopping for a certain amount of time (say, ten minutes) or to a certain length (say, one page). The goal of this **freewriting** is to bypass the part of your mind that doesn't want to write or can't think of anything to write and to let words themselves suggest other words. *What* you write is not important; that you *keep* writing is. Don't stop, even if that means repeating the same words until new words come. Don't go back to reread, don't censor ideas that seem dumb or repetitious, and above all don't stop to edit: grammar, punctuation, spelling, and the like are irrelevant at this stage.

In the physical act of freewriting, you may gain access to ideas you were unaware of. Here is an example of freewriting done to come up with a subject for writing.

> Write to write. Seems pretty obvious, also weird. What to gain by writing? never anything before. Writing seems always— always—Getting corrected for trying too hard to please the teacher, getting corrected for not trying hard enuf. Frustration, nail biting, sometimes getting carried away making sentences to tell stories, not even true stories, *esp.* not true stories, *that* feels like creating something. Writing just pulls the story out of me. The story lets me be someone else, gives me a disguise.

In this rough sample the student has broken through his resistance to writing to realize that he enjoys fiction writing for the sense of creation and disguise it gives him. He seems to have learned something about himself and to have given himself a general subject at the same time. (For a discussion and example of freewriting done to discover ideas when you already have a subject, see pp. 15–16.)

6 **Limiting the subject**

An assigned subject or one you find by a method described above is likely to be quite general—say, summer jobs, federal aid to colleges, two friends, Lincoln's weaknesses as President, corporations and art. You could begin developing such a subject right away, generating the ideas and details that will eventually form the substance of the essay. But sooner or later you might run into trouble because these subjects are too broad to be covered thoroughly and interestingly in the few pages often specified in college writing assignments.

It takes experience and often some actual drafting to gauge whether a subject is too broad for the space and time allowed. You need to be able to provide ample specific information—facts, examples, sensory details, and so on—to support the subject fully so that readers understand and appreciate what you have to say. For example, Abraham Lincoln is justly considered one of the greatest American Presidents, but he was not perfect: others who were also brilliant and able found fault with him, and he did make mistakes. A careful examination of all his weaknesses as President, including

For writing about a scene or character:

> outdoors—woods, seashore, mountains, fields, city streets, parks
> indoors—dorm rooms, laundromats
> scenes—family gatherings, football games, funerals, a snowy morning
> people—parents, grandparents, uncles, aunts, childhood friends, people in a public place, teachers, unpleasant people, cartoon characters

For informative or explanatory writing:

> hobbies, jobs, investments, fields of study, recent scientific discoveries, places to visit, ways to save money, fishing, gardening, study habits, car repairing, canoeing, audio equipment, magazines

For persuasive writing:

> campus issues, environmental concerns, automobile or airline safety, support for education, cost of medical care, regulation of new drugs, specialized education versus liberal arts education, rights of minorities and women, gun control, divorce and child rearing, school prayer, censorship, proposals to improve campus or local services, ways of dealing with a social problem

RESOURCES AND IDEAS

Mark Reynolds, "Make Free Writing More Productive," *College Composition and Communication* 39 (1988): 81–82. Reynolds offers twenty "questions, activities, and guidelines" for drawing useful ideas and promising topics from the often jumbled material provided by freewriting.

Gayle B. Price, "A Case for a Modern Commonplace Book," *College Composition and Communication* 31 (1980): 175–82. This article reviews freewriting and other techniques for helping students generate ideas and tells how students can use a notebook to record ideas.

dev
1b

RESOURCES AND IDEAS

Richard M. Coe, "If Not to Narrow, Then How to Focus: Two Techniques for Focusing," *College Composition and Communication* 31 (1981): 272–77. Coe describes ways to get students to focus on a particular aspect of a topic as an alternative to the usual approach of narrowing a topic.

the pros and cons of each accusation, could conceivably take a whole book. An essay of, say, six pages would have to deal with a much smaller area, a specific weakness. The examples below illustrate how this and other broad subjects can be scaled down to one of several manageable **topics**—limited, specific essay subjects.

BROAD SUBJECTS	SPECIFIC TOPICS
Lincoln's weaknesses as President	Lincoln's most significant error as commander-in-chief of the Union army Lincoln's delay in emancipating the slaves Lincoln's difficulties in controlling his cabinet
Summer jobs	Kinds of summer jobs for unskilled workers How to find a summer job What a summer job can teach
Federal aid to college students	Which students should be entitled to federal aid Kinds of federal aid available to college students Why the federal government should (or should not) aid college students
Two friends	How _____ and _____ are alike despite their differences Why _____ and _____ don't like each other The different roles of _____ and _____ as friends

The specific topics above are just a few of the possible approaches to the corresponding broad subjects, and they suggest the problems that might result from trying to cover the full range of ideas implied by any of the subjects. The much narrower area defined by each specific topic could, however, be covered both clearly and interestingly in a limited space. (The essay on pp. 72–73 illustrates how a student developed the specific topic of what a summer job can teach into a focused and reasonably well-detailed essay.)

You may find that you need to do some planning and writing, exploring different facets of the general subject and pursuing your specific interests, before you hit on the best topic. And the topic you select may require further narrowing or may shift subtly or even dramatically as you move through the writing process. Still, the earlier you can narrow your subject to a specific topic, the more focused your subsequent work will be, so it's worthwhile to push yourself soon after you have your subject to limit its scope.

EXERCISE 2

Use one or more of the techniques discussed in the preceding section to come up with three or four subjects for writing. Or take three or four of the following general subjects and use one or more techniques to make them your own.

1. immigration
2. the environment
3. city or town politics
4. working
5. college sports
6. college courses
7. success
8. science

ANSWERS: EXERCISE 2

Individual response.

EXERCISE 3

Narrow each of the broad subjects from Exercise 2 to one or more specific topics suitable for a brief essay of two or three pages (500 to 750 words). What aspect of the subject interests you most? What aspect can you discuss most effectively, using enough specific information to convey your perspective to your readers?

ANSWERS: EXERCISE 3

Individual response.

EXERCISE 4

For each of the following general subjects, provide at least one specific topic that interests you and that you think you could cover well in a brief essay of two or three pages.

1. music, dance, painting, drama, or some other art form
2. automobile safety
3. relations between parents and children
4. relations between the sexes
5. travel

SAMPLE ANSWERS: EXERCISE 4

1. The influences of the Rolling Stones on rock music.
   The distinctions between classical ballet and modern ballet in classical style.
2. Driving defensively versus driving offensively.
   How to drive in a rainstorm.
3. What children learn from their peers that they can't learn from their parents.
   Parental discipline as an expression of love.
4. Why male children should play with dolls.
   Why female children should play competitive sports.
5. Long-distance bicycle touring.
   The advantages of traveling on back roads instead of on highways.

1c Defining a purpose and identifying an audience

Purpose

A writer's **purpose** is his or her chief reason for communicating something about a topic to a particular audience. *Purpose* thus includes all three elements of the writing situation: writer, topic, and audience. It ties together both the specific context in which the writer is working and the goal the writer hopes to achieve.

IDENTIFYING PURPOSE

Use paragraphs drawn from magazine articles, essays in a reader, or student papers as the basis for class discussion of the purposes of writing. You may ask students to compare the aims of individual paragraphs with the overall purpose of the essay from which they are taken and to decide what role the paragraphs play within the essay.

THE PURPOSES FOR WRITING

1. To entertain readers
2. To express yourself
3. To explain something to readers (exposition)
4. To persuade readers to accept or act on your opinion (argumentation)

Most writing you do will have one of four main purposes. Occasionally, you will *entertain* readers or *express yourself*—your feelings or beliefs—to readers. More often you will *explain* something to readers or *persuade* readers to respect and accept, and sometimes even act on, your opinion. These purposes often overlap in a single essay, but usually one predominates. That dominant purpose will demand an emphasis on one of the three elements of the writing situation. When you write mainly to express yourself, for instance, *you* predominate. In contrast, when you write mainly to persuade or entertain readers, *they* predominate. And when you write mainly to explain, the *topic* predominates. Always, though, the other two elements also help determine what and how you write.

Most college and business writing has the primary purpose of explaining or persuading. Writing that is mainly explanatory is often called **exposition** (from a Latin word meaning "to explain or set forth"). Almost any topic is suitable for exposition, from how to pitch a knuckle ball to why you want to major in business to the implications of a new discovery in computer science. It is the kind of writing encountered most often in newspapers, magazines, and textbooks; and it is the kind of writing this book concentrates on. (Expository essays appear on pp. 68–70 and 74). Writing that is primarily persuasive is often called **argumentation.** A newspaper editorial favoring city council reform, a magazine article urging mandatory seatbelt use, student papers recommending more required courses or upholding legalized abortion—all these are argumentative essays. (Chapter 4 discusses argumentation in some detail and provides an illustrative essay.)

Often a writing assignment will specify or imply your purpose: when assigned a report on a physics experiment, for instance, you know the purpose is to explain; when assigned an editorial presenting a case for or against expanding your school's health facilities, you know the purpose is to persuade. If the assignment leaves your purpose up to you, then try to define it soon after you have your topic, to give yourself some direction. You may not be successful: sometimes writers do not discover their purpose until

RESOURCES AND IDEAS

James L. Kinneavy, *A Theory of Discourse* (Englewood Cliffs: Prentice, 1971). Kinneavy classifies discourse according to purpose and emphasis. Expressive discourse emphasizes the writer or speaker; persuasive discourse focuses on the audience; referential discourse focuses on the object and may be informative, scientific, or exploratory; and literary discourse emphasizes the text.

C. H. Knoblauch, "Intentionality in the Writing Process: A Case Study," *College Composition and Communication* 31 (1980): 153–59. Knoblauch argues that (1) the purposes used to classify finished works differ from "operational" purposes that guide the act of writing and (2) the teaching of composition needs to pay attention to the shifting, tentative purposes that guide writing.

they begin drafting. Or you may find that your initial sense of purpose changes as you move through the writing process. Nonetheless, if you are able to define a purpose early, it can set a preliminary course for you to follow and help you recognize changes in your thinking when they occur.

Audience

While you are defining your purpose for writing, you may also be identifying who your readers will be and why they will be reading your work. As discussed above, the two are closely linked, with purpose establishing a certain relation of writer to topic and audience. Like purpose, audience is often specified or implied in a writing assignment: when you write an editorial for the student newspaper favoring expansion of the college health facilities, your audience is fellow students, who will be reading the paper for information of general and personal interest; when you write a report on a physics experiment, your audience is your physics instructor, who will be reading to evaluate your competence and see if you need help. If no particular audience is specified or implied, then, as with purpose, you are free to decide whom you want to address: your classmates? your boss? those who drive cars?

This sense of your readers tells you something about how you need to treat your topic: for example, your fellow students will expect you to treat the subject of health facilities nontechnically and to outline the benefits of the proposed expansion for them. A sense of audience can also help you discover ideas about your topic by making your purpose more concrete. The realization that you want to address an essay on bicycle riding to car drivers could direct you to a persuasive purpose and ideas about drivers' carelessness toward riders.

In the earliest stages of the writing process, many writers find it inhibiting to think much more specifically than this about the traits and views of their audience. Most of the discovery activities covered in the previous section and the next one will work best when you concentrate on pulling ideas out of yourself and expanding your mental horizons rather than on people "out there." It is important to give your audience detailed consideration, but we will postpone the guidelines for doing so until later in the writing process (see 1f).

EXERCISE 5

For each of the following topics, suggest both a likely purpose for an essay on the topic (entertainment, self-expression, explana-

RESOURCES AND IDEAS

Dean R. Baldwin, "Introducing Rhetoric in Remedial Writing Courses," *College Composition and Communication* 29 (1978): 392–94. Baldwin suggests that prewriting sheets can help students identify an occasion, audience, and purpose for their writing.

Russell C. Long, "Writer-Audience Relationships: Analysis or Invention?" *College Composition and Communication* 31 (1980): 221–26. Long describes the kinds of strategies student writers must develop to create in their minds the potential audiences for their writing.

SAMPLE ANSWERS: EXERCISE 5

1. Purpose: persuasion. Audience: college students.
2. Purpose: explanation. Audience: people who prefer easy-listening music.
3. Purpose: self-expression. Audience: all of us (with places of our own for comparison).
4. Purpose: entertainment. Audience: people planning a family vacation.
5. Purpose: explanation. Audience: women (or men) who know little about automobiles.

SAMPLE ANSWERS: EXERCISE 6

1. The joys of playing guitar (self-expression; busy people looking for a hobby).
   A klutz tries to master the guitar (entertainment; people without musical training).
   How to buy a guitar (explanation; teenagers).
   Guitar music should be outlawed (persuasion; parents).

2. A lonely Saturday night on campus (self-expression; college students).
   Saturday night at Lupo's Club (entertainment; lonely college students).
   What's wrong with Saturday-night television (explanation; *TV Guide* readers).
   Why the school should sponsor Saturday-night dances (persuasion; school teachers and administrators).

3. What working does for me besides pay the bills (self-expression; fellow students or workers).
   Baby-sitting for a monster (entertainment; parents of young children).
   How to prepare for a job interview (explanation; college students).
   Why working students should not have to pay income tax (persuasion; legislators).

4. My favorite situation-comedy character (self-expression; TV viewers).
   A ludicrous soap-opera subplot (entertainment; people who seldom watch daytime TV).
   The differences between two popular crime dramas (explanation; avid TV viewers).
   Why the federal government should support cultural programming on television (persuasion; voting public).

5. A seat belt saved my life (self-expression; people with children).
   Riding shotgun in a demolition derby (entertainment; drivers).
   Road safety for the tractor-trailer driver (explanation; people who do much highway driving).

tion, persuasion) and a possible audience to which the essay could be addressed.

1. why a foreign language should be required in college
2. four kinds of rock music
3. the place where I feel most relaxed
4. a vacation that was a comedy of errors
5. how to find a trusty automobile mechanic

EXERCISE 6

For each of the following general subjects, write down four specific topics, each one suitable for a brief essay written with a different purpose (entertainment, self-expression, explanation, persuasion). For each topic and purpose, give an audience that might be interested in such an essay.

> *Example:*
> General subject: sports
> Topics: (1) Football training as torture (entertainment; students who don't play football). (2) Learning by losing (self-expression; composition classmates). (3) How to avoid injury during weight training (explanation; fellow weight trainers). (4) Why the school should build a new athletic facility (persuasion; college administrators).

1. music
2. Saturday night
3. work
4. television
5. driving

EXERCISE 7

To begin developing a brief essay of your own, select a topic that has particular interest for you. (The topic may come from your answers to Exercise 3 or 4 on p. 11 or to Exercise 6.) Define a purpose for your essay, and decide what kind of essay will best suit your topic and purpose.

1d   Developing the topic

As you limit a subject, define a purpose, and identify the audience for writing, you make choices and, at least temporarily, close options. To develop the topic—to generate the ideas and information that will help you achieve your purpose—you open up again within a narrower field. You probe the topic to discover implications, possibilities, and relations not considered before.

Sometimes ideas will tumble forth on paper, especially if

your topic is very familiar or personal. But when they do not, you may need a technique for freeing them. Anything that gets your mind working is appropriate: if you like to make drawings or take pictures, for instance, then try it. The following pages describe varied strategies that writers find helpful, some of which follow from the strategies for finding a subject (see 1b). Whatever strategy or strategies you use, do your work in writing, not just in your head. Not only will your ideas be retrievable, but the act of writing will aid your concentration and lead you to fresh, sometimes surprising, insights.

Why the 55 mph speed limit should be abolished (persuasion; legislators).

ANSWERS: EXERCISE 7

Individual response.

RESOURCES AND IDEAS

Linda S. Flower and John R. Hayes, "Problem-Solving Strategies and the Writing Process," *College English* 39 (1977): 442–48. Flower and Hayes describe techniques for discovering and developing ideas, including cue words, nutshelling, idea trees, role playing, and brainstorming.

TECHNIQUES FOR DEVELOPING A TOPIC

1. Freewrite with a focus (1d-1).
2. Make a list, or brainstorm (1d-2).
3. Cluster (1d-3).
4. Read with a focus (1d-4).
5. Ask the journalist's questions (1d-5).
6. Use the patterns of development (1d-6).
(See also p. 6, "Techniques for discovering a subject.")

---

1 **Focused freewriting**

In **focused freewriting** you start with your topic and write without stopping for, say, fifteen minutes or one full page. As with freewriting for a subject (see 1b-5), you push to bypass mental blocks and self-consciousness, not debating what to say or editing what you've written. With focused freewriting, though, you let the physical act of writing take you into and around your subject.

An example of focused freewriting can be found in the work of a student, Pat Lucas, whose writing process we will follow in this chapter and the next. In a composition course, Lucas and her classmates read and discussed an essay titled "Hard Architecture" by Robert Sommer. Their instructor then gave them the following assignment: "Sommer contrasts 'hard architecture,' which he finds inhumane and oppressive, with 'soft architecture,' which he finds sensitive and stimulating. Write an essay of 500–750 words in which you respond to one or more of Sommer's ideas by drawing on your own observations of one or more buildings." For Lucas, narrowing the broad subject of the assignment to a specific topic presented little problem, for Sommer's comments on hard architecture immediately made her think of a building called the Renaissance Center in her hometown of Detroit, Michigan. (The

RESOURCES AND IDEAS

Peter Elbow, *Writing Without Teachers* (New York: Oxford UP, 1973). Elbow discusses freewriting and other techniques for tapping imagination and creativity during the writing process.

Michael G. Southwell, "Free Writing in Composition Classes," *College English* 38 (1977): 676–81. This article shows how freewriting can be used to encourage fluent writing and to provide material that can be used for working on basic skills or as a preparation for more formal papers.

The Renaissance Center in Detroit

photograph of the Renaissance Center above will help you follow Lucas's thinking.) After deciding to address her classmates and explain something about the Renaissance Center in the context of Sommer's ideas, Lucas tried freewriting for ten minutes to generate ideas:

> Sommer says hard architecture is oppressive & inhumane—also really hard—concrete, metal, etc. Nothing people can hurt, buildings that resist humans—don't like humans. Don't like humans. Turn hard surfaces to them—like a cruel person, hard-hearted Hannah, insensitive—insensitive. Hard building = insensitive person??? Thinks only of itself/himself, no concern for others, blind to others. Ren. Center insensitive? Not concerned with people—not people outside. Shuts off people. Concrete walls, tall, dark towers. Towers shut people out, protect what's inside, say don't bother me. Go away. Ren. Center = cold, insensitive person?

With this freewriting, Lucas generated several promising ideas, especially the distillation of Sommer's ideas to the word *insensitive*, the application of that word to the Renaissance Center, and the parallels between an insensitive building and an insensitive person. As we'll see on pages 20–22, she pursued these ideas further using another discovery technique.

2   **Making a list**

Like focused freewriting, list making requires opening yourself to everything that seems even remotely connected to your topic, without concern for order or repetition or form of expression. You can let your topic percolate for a day or more, recording thoughts on it whenever they occur. (For this approach to work, you need to keep a notebook and pen or pencil with you at all times.) Or, in a method more akin to freewriting, you can **brainstorm** about the topic—that is, focus intently on the topic for a fixed amount of time (say, fifteen minutes), pushing yourself to list every idea and detail that comes to mind. Like freewriting, brainstorming requires turning off your internal editor so that you keep moving ahead instead of looping back over what you have already written to correct it.

A list of ideas and details made while brainstorming might look something like the one following. The student's topic is what a summer job can teach—one of the specific topics derived earlier from the general subject of summer jobs.

> summer work teaches—
>> how to look busy while doing nothing
>> how to avoid the sun in summer
>> seriously: discipline, budgeting money, value of money
> which job? Burger King cashier? baby sitter? mail-room clerk?
> mail room: how to sort mail into boxes: this is learning??
> how to survive getting fired—humiliation, outrage
> Mrs. King! the mail-room queen as learning experience
> the shock of getting fired: what to tell parents, friends?
> Mrs. K was so rigid—dumb procedures
> initials instead of names on the mail boxes—confusion!
> Mrs. K's anger, resentment: the disadvantages of being smarter
>> than your boss
> the odd thing about working in an office: a world with its own
>> rules for how to act
> what Mr. D said about the pecking order—big chick (Mrs. K)
>> pecks on little chick (me)
> probably lots of Mrs. Ks in offices all over—offices are all barn-
>> yards
> Mrs. K a sad person, really—just trying to hold on to her job,
>> preserve her self-esteem
> a job can beat you down—destroy self-esteem, make you desper-
>> ate enough to be mean to other people
> how to preserve/gain self-esteem from work??
> Mrs. K had to call me names to protect herself—I forced her into
>> a corner
> if I'd known about the pecking order, I would have been less
>> show-offy, not so arrogant

This informal list jumps around quite a bit, but toward the end the student focuses on what she learned about office politics from working as a mail-room clerk. Thus list making helps her both refine her topic and discover what she thinks about it.

dev
1d

RESOURCES AND IDEAS

Gabriele Lusser Rico, *Writing the Natural Way* (Los Angeles: Tarcher, 1983). Rico draws on research about brain functions as the basis for advice about strategies—especially clustering—that encourage creativity in expression.

RESOURCES AND IDEAS

Robert A. Schwegler, *Patterns in Action*, 2nd ed. (Glenview: Scott, 1988). In the opening chapter the author describes four processes in the act of reading—responding, understanding, analyzing, and evaluating—and discusses the use of reading logs as a bridge between reading and writing.

3   Clustering

A technique similar to freewriting and list making is **clustering.** As developed by the writer and teacher Gabriele Lusser Rico, clustering also draws on free association and rapid, unedited work but combines writing and nonlinear drawing. When clustering, you radiate outward from a center point, your topic. When an idea occurs, you pursue its implications in a branching structure until they seem exhausted. Then you do the same with other ideas, staying open to possibilities and connections, continuously branching out or drawing arrows.

The example of clustering on the next page shows how a student used the technique for ten minutes to expand on the topic of creative writing as a means of disguise, an idea he arrived at through freewriting (see p. 9). Though the student ventured into several dead ends, he also came to the interesting possibility (lower right) that the fiction writer is like a god who forgives himself by creating characters that represent his good and bad qualities. With such a start, the student next began a draft of his paper. If he had felt the need to develop ideas further, he could have tried another diagram or another strategy such as focused freewriting.

4   Focused reading

Reading magazines, newspapers, and books can help you find or narrow a subject for writing (see 1b-4), and it can help you develop your topic. Unless the topic draws exclusively on your own observations and experiences, reading can introduce you to ideas you hadn't considered or can help you expand on what you already know. Often, of course, an assignment will require reading: to respond to Sommer's essay on architecture, for instance, Pat Lucas must carefully digest what Sommer has written; and essays on literary works as well as research papers demand reading. But even when reading is not required by the assignment, it can help you develop a topic by providing opinions, facts, and examples and by stimulating your own thinking. (See 35c for techniques of library research that you can use to locate readings on your topic.)

When you read to discover information or to respond to the author's ideas, do so with a pen or pencil in hand and (unless the material is yours to mark up) with a pad of paper by your side. Then you will be able to keep notes on what you read and—more important—on what the reading makes *you* think. Writing while reading leads you to participate actively in the process, not just passively. (See also Chapter 4 on reading critically.)

Nice Point!

NOTE: To avoid the serious offense of plagiarism, you must ac-

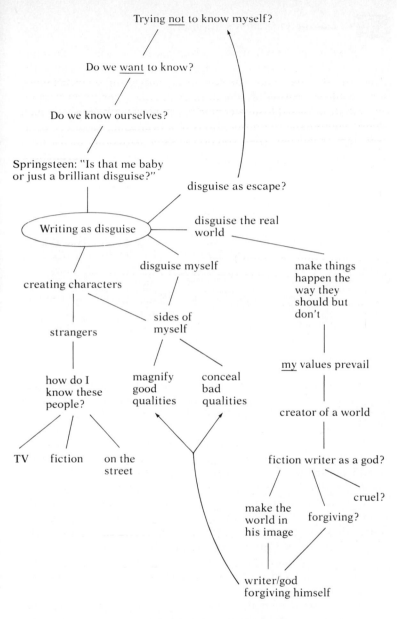

knowledge all ideas and information that you borrow from others'
writings and present in your final paper. See 36d on how to avoid
plagiarism, and see 36h and 36i on how to acknowledge sources.

RESOURCES AND IDEAS

Charles W. Kneupper, "Revising the Tagmemic Heuristic: Theoretical and Pedagogical Considerations," *College Composition and Communication* 31 (1980): 160–68. Kneupper offers a simplified version of the powerful question system introduced by Young, Becker, and Pike in their text *Rhetoric: Discovery and Change* (New York: Harcourt, 1970).

Eugene Washington, "WH-Questions in Teaching Composition," *College Composition and Communication* 28 (1977): 54–56. Washington suggests using what, why, where, and how questions to increase density of information in essays and clarify structure.

USING QUESTIONS AND PATTERNS

To help students discover the power of sets of questions or the patterns of development for exploring topics, begin by giving them a list of general subjects—music, sports, guns, the environment—and then ask them to explore each, looking for limited aspects that might make good topics for essays. Do not encourage students to use either the questions or the patterns in probing the topics. Class discussion can focus on how to limit the topics and can indicate how an audience might respond to them.

Following the discussion, ask students to explore the same topics using either the journalist's questions (1d.4) or the patterns of development as described in 1d.5. Ask students to direct their attention to as many different aspects of the topic as they can and at the same time to suggest ways of developing it and organizing an essay around it. Discussion should focus on differences between the "guided" and "unguided" approaches to developing a topic.

5 Using the journalist's questions

Asking yourself a set of questions about your topic—and writing out the answers—can help you look at the topic objectively and see fresh possibilities in it. Asking questions can also provide some structure to the development of ideas.

One such set of questions is that posed by a journalist with a story to report:

Who was involved?
What happened and what were the results?
When did it happen?
Where did it happen?
Why did it happen?
How did it happen?

These questions can also be useful in probing an essay topic, especially if your purpose is to entertain or to explain by telling a story from your experience or from history or by examining causes and effects. (See also pp. 22 and 43.) For instance, the student writing about a summer job as a mail-room clerk could use the journalist's questions to isolate the important people involved, the main events and their order, and the possible causes of the events. Similarly, if you decided to explain the dynamics of a single-parent, single-child family, the questions would lead you to consider the characteristics of the two people, the ways they interact, and the possible causes and effects of their style of interaction.

6 Using the patterns of development

Also useful for probing a topic and at the same time providing some structure for developing ideas is a set of questions derived from the **patterns of development.** These patterns—such as narration, illustration, definition, and comparison and contrast—are ways we think about and understand a vast range of subjects, from our own daily experiences to the most complex scientific theories, and they also serve as strategies for writing about these subjects. As you will see later in this chapter and then in Chapter 3, the patterns of development can provide an organization for an essay (see pp. 41–43) and a means of introducing information in a paragraph (see pp. 101–10, where the patterns are illustrated with paragraph-length examples). Here, Pat Lucas's further work on her essay about the Renaissance Center in Detroit will show how the patterns can open up the possibilities in a topic.

How did it happen? In **narration** the writer develops the topic as a story, with events usually arranged chronologically (as they occurred in time): for instance, an exciting hockey game, or the steps leading to a war. Pat Lucas thought narration would be most useful if she needed to provide background information on how the Renaissance Center evolved. (Another student's narrative essay appears on pp. 72–73.)

How does it look, sound, feel, smell, taste? This question opens up the possibilities of **description,** the use of sensory details to give a clear impression of a person, place, or thing: a friend, a favorite room, a building. Thinking of the Renaissance Center, Pat Lucas realized that she could rely heavily on description to portray and characterize the building.

How can it be illustrated or supported? The pattern of **illustration or support** suggests development with one or more examples of the topic (one couple's efforts to adopt a child, say, or three television soap operas) or with the reasons for believing or doing something (three reasons for majoring in English, four reasons for driving defensively). When Pat Lucas asked this question, she quickly saw that her freewriting (p. 16) suggested using the Renaissance Center as an example to illustrate and thus extend Sommer's comments on hard architecture.

What is it? What does it encompass, and what does it exclude? These questions lead to development by **definition:** specifying what the topic is and is not to give a precise sense of its meaning. For Pat Lucas the questions suggested an essay defining hard architecture, perhaps using the Renaissance Center as an example in the definition. But since definition was the thrust of Sommer's essay, she decided to use it only for a brief summary of Sommer's ideas.

What are its parts or characteristics? Or what groups or categories can it be sorted into? These questions derive from the related patterns of **division** and **classification**—dividing a singular subject such as a short story into its parts (characters, setting, plot, and so on) or classifying a plural subject such as automobiles into groups or classes (subcompact, compact, and so on). When Pat Lucas considered these questions, she concluded that while developing her essay primarily as an illustration, she might also divide the building into its parts to show how each part illustrated some characteristic of hard architecture.

How is it like, or different from, other things? The pattern of **comparison and contrast** suggests development by pointing out the similarities and differences between ideas, objects, people, places, and so on: the differences between two similar computer systems, for instance, or the similarities between two political candidates from different parties. For Pat Lucas this question opened up an approach to her topic that her freewriting had not: she could compare the Renaissance Center, as an example of hard architecture,

RESOURCES AND IDEAS

Frank J. D'Angelo, *A Conceptual Theory of Rhetoric* (Cambridge: Winthrop, 1975). D'Angelo argues that rhetorical patterns of organization (e.g., analysis, classification, and description) are also patterns of thought and invention and can be used to probe experience as part of the composing process. See also D'Angelo's "Topoi and Form in Composition," *The Territory of Language,* ed. Donald A. McQuade (Carbondale: Southern Illinois UP, 1986), 114–22.

with another Detroit building illustrating soft architecture. To ex-plore this approach, she spent some time making lists of the fea-tures of the two buildings in relation to Sommer's ideas. (Another student's comparison-and-contrast essay appears on p. 74.)

Is it comparable to something that is in a different class but more familiar? This question leads to **analogy,** an extended com-parison of unlike subjects. Analogy is often used to explain a topic that may be unfamiliar to readers (for instance, the structure of a government) by reference to a familiar topic (the structure of a family). Pat Lucas's freewriting had begun to develop an analogy between an insensitive building and an insensitive person, and this question led her further along that track. She anticipated that readers who had never seen the Renaissance Center might better understand her feelings if she drew parallels with her own experi-ences of people.

What are its causes or its effects? With the pattern of **cause-and-effect analysis,** the writer explains why something happened or what its consequences were or will be, or both: the causes of ce-rebral palsy, the effects of a Supreme Court decision, the causes *and* effects of a gradual change in the climate. In asking this ques-tion, Pat Lucas foresaw that her essay on the Renaissance Center would attempt to explain the effects of the building on an observer, but otherwise cause-and-effect analysis did not seem useful.

How does it work or how do you do it? This question prompts a **process analysis**—an explanation of how the topic occurs natu-rally or how it is accomplished: the growth of a plant, the making of a robot, the writing of an essay. Of all the pattern questions, this is the one in which Pat Lucas saw the least potential. A narrative of how the Renaissance Center evolved might include stages in a pro-cess (such as the workings of city government), but Lucas aban-doned this approach because she lacked enough information and interest to pursue it.

As the examples of Pat Lucas's thinking indicate, more than one of these questions are likely to seem promising, and several may in fact play a role in the development of an essay. After con-sidering each question, Lucas determined that her essay would pri-marily illustrate Sommer's ideas on hard architecture with the single example of the Renaissance Center. But she also expected to divide the building into its parts, describe it, and develop an anal-ogy between the insensitive building and an insensitive person. Thus an essay developed by example seemed likely to contain parts developed by other patterns—a very common occurrence. Even when you are assigned an essay in a specific pattern, other patterns will almost inevitably prove useful to develop certain ideas or to organize certain categories of information. (For further discussion of how the patterns may combine in an essay, see 3e, pp. 121–23.)

EXERCISE 8

Experiment with freewriting (p. 15), brainstorming (p. 17), or clustering (p. 18) on the topic you chose in Exercise 7 (p. 14) for your essay-in-progress; or start anew with one of the following topics. Write or draw for at least ten minutes without stopping to edit. When you finish, examine what you have written for ideas and relationships that could help you develop the topic.

1. a shopping mall or other center or building
2. a restaurant
3. borrowing (or lending) money
4. prejudice in my home-town
5. the college grading system
6. pigeons
7. a country music singer
8. a television show
9. a brother or a sister
10. an awkward or embar-rassing moment
11. a radio personality
12. basketball strategies
13. shyness
14. parties
15. patriotism

ANSWERS: EXERCISE 8

Individual response.

dev

1e

EXERCISE 9

Continuing from the preceding exercise, generate further ideas on the topic by writing answers to each of the questions derived from the patterns of development (pp. 20–22). Give the closest consideration to the questions that seem most promising. Which pattern might you use for the overall development of your essay, and which other patterns might you use to introduce or organize ideas within the overall pattern?

ANSWERS: EXERCISE 9

Individual response.

EXERCISE 10

If you feel that the topic from Exercises 8 and 9 should be developed further, try reading about it or asking the journalist's questions (p. 20). Subsequent exercises leading you through the writing process will be based on the ideas you generate in Exercises 8–10.

ANSWERS: EXERCISE 10

Individual response.

1e   **Grouping ideas**

After developing ideas about your topic, you may need to organize the ideas to see what you have. This procedure is not the same as organizing the essay itself, although the relationships and patterns you discover in your ideas may prove useful later (see 1h, p. 38). Rather, at this point in your thinking and writing you apply order to ideas so that connections, distinctions, hierarchies, overlaps, and gaps will become apparent. Grouping ideas helps you control and understand your topic. It helps you see your central theme and how specific ideas fit into it.

To group ideas, you need to distinguish between general and specific ideas and to see the connections between ideas. **General and specific** refer to the number of instances or objects included in a group signified by a word. *Plant*, for example, is general because it encompasses all kinds of plants; *rose* is specific because it refers to a certain kind of plant. But *general* and *specific* are actually relative terms—that is, something is one or the other only in relation to something else. Thus *plant* is general in relation to *rose*, but it is specific in relation to the broader category of *life form*. And *rose* is specific in relation to *plant*, but it is general in relation to the smaller category of *American Beauty rose*, which is itself general in relation to the singular category of *Uncle Dan's prize-winning American Beauty rose*.

When you group your ideas, subordinate the more specific ideas to the more general ones. At the same time, respect the meaning of your ideas so that your hierarchies are not jumbled—so that you don't end up with *rose* subordinated to the more general category of *animal*.

One technique for sorting ideas is the tree diagram in which ideas and details branch out in increasing specificity. On the next page is a tree diagram prepared from the earlier list of ideas on a summer job (p. 17), which helped the student focus on what she learned about office politics. Each main part of the four-part diagram represents a different general idea about the summer-job experience. Notice that the diagram helped the student to drop irrelevant ideas from her earlier list. In addition, the structure of the diagram showed where she needed more details (such as effects of the office pecking order).

Some writers use a simple list with two or three indentions— a kind of rough outline—to accomplish the same purpose. Pat Lucas prepared such a list from her notes on the Renaissance Center:

Sommer's "hard architecture"
  denies "trust and respect" among human beings
  "used by one group to exclude or oppress another"
  "impervious, impersonal," "inorganic"
  uses hard, human-proof materials (metal, concrete)
Ren. Center exterior
  round tower surrounded by octagonal towers
  the most visible feature of the city—calls attention to itself
  dark surfaces shield activities inside
  armor-like surfaces of octagons
  reflecting surface and round tower
  high concrete wall at street level
  wall is a barrier, like a prison wall
  no apparent entrance to building for pedestrians

RESOURCES AND IDEAS

Linda S. Flower and John R. Hayes, "Problem-Solving Strategies and the Writing Process," *College English* 39 (1977): 442–48. The authors discuss idea trees as well as other techniques for discovering and developing ideas.

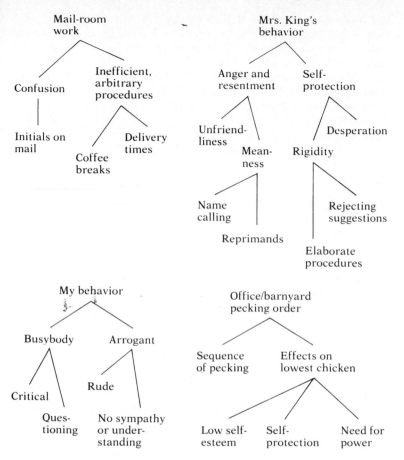

messages: Keep out, don't bother me
    from a distance, the building stands apart from rest of city
    much larger than other buildings, nothing like their design
Ren. Center interior
    confusion of walkways, escalators—like a maze
    glitter of metal, water, light
    fancy restaurants, stores, hotel
insensitive building = insensitive person
    cold exterior—hard surfaces
    shuts out outsiders/others
    concerned only with itself/himself
"soft" Detroit buildings
    pleasing decoration—varied detailing of windows and walls
    open, inviting entrances at street level
    lobbies welcome visitors, give sense of order and calm

In forming these groups of ideas and details, Lucas isolated several approaches to her topic: the ideas in Sommer's essay that she wanted to illustrate with the Renaissance Center; the parts of the building (exterior and interior); the analogy between an insensitive building and an insensitive person; and the contrasting appearance of "soft" buildings. The groups led her to see that the exterior of the building was her main interest because it best illustrated Sommer's ideas and the analogy she developed from them. The details of the interior did not fit as well into the theme of insensitivity. And the comparison with other buildings seemed both underdeveloped and potentially distracting from her main interest, the Renaissance Center. Thus, by grouping her ideas, Lucas discovered how she wanted to focus her essay, and with that focus she could make early decisions about what *not* to cover.

ANSWERS: EXERCISE 11

Individual response.

EXERCISE 11

For your essay-in-progress, use a tree diagram or a list to group the ideas you generated in Exercises 8, 9, and 10 (p. 23) into general categories. Delete, add, or modify ideas as necessary to reflect your thinking at this new stage.

1f   Considering the audience

As we saw earlier, the basic purpose of all essay writing is to *communicate ideas and information to readers*. Readers are your audience. If they do not understand what they read or do not react the way you want, then you may be at fault. The chances are good that you have not considered carefully enough what the audience must be told in order to understand and to react appropriately.

You will probably consider your audience to some extent from the start of the writing process—when, for an obvious example, you decide not to write on macroeconomic theory for your music history teacher—and a sense of your audience can help you refine your purpose, as we saw in 1c. But at some point while you are developing an essay, it's important to make your readers your primary concern.

As you know from your own experience as a reader, anyone who begins a text has needs and expectations. Readers require clarity and a certain interest—qualities that prove the writer's commitment to make reading easier. Readers also require a clear structure, a certain kind and amount of information, and a sense of who the writer is. Many academic disciplines prescribe some of

---

QUESTIONS ABOUT AUDIENCE

1. Why are readers going to read my writing? Will they expect information, opinion, entertainment, self-expression, or some combination?
2. What do I want readers to know or do after reading my work, and how should I make that clear to them?
3. What characteristic(s) do readers share? For instance:

   age or sex
   occupation: students, part-time workers, professional colleagues, etc.
   social or economic role: adult children, car buyers, potential employers, etc.
   economic or educational background
   political, religious, or moral beliefs and values
   hobbies or activities

4. How will the characteristic(s) of readers influence their attitudes toward my topic?
5. What do readers already know and *not* know about my topic? How much do I have to tell them?
6. If my topic involves specialized language, how much should I use and define?
7. What ideas, arguments, or information might surprise readers? excite them? offend them? How should I handle these points?
8. What misconceptions might readers have of my topic or my approach to the topic? How can I dispel these misconceptions?
9. What role and tone should I assume? What role do I want readers to play?

---

these needs and expectations; thus Chapter 38 discusses the special concerns of writing in the arts and humanities, social sciences, and natural applied sciences. But even in these fields, the writer must make many choices based on audience. In other areas where the conventions of structure and presentation are vaguer, the choices are even more numerous. The box above contains questions that can help you define and make these choices.

 Using specific information

When you write, you use specific information to gain and keep the attention of your readers and to guide them to accept your conclusions or opinions. This information may be concrete details,

RESOURCES AND IDEAS

Fred R. Pfister and Joan Petrick, "A Heuristic Model for Creating a Writer's Audience," *College Composition and Communication* 31 (1980): 213–20. The authors describe questions writers can ask to probe the nature of a potential audience and the relationship among the audience, the subject, the writer, and possible forms of expression.

Walter J. Ong, S. J., "The Writer's Audience Is Always a Fiction," *PMLA* 90 (1975): 9–21. Ong argues that writers must construct audiences in their imaginations as an essential part of the act of writing and that readers must play the role defined for them by the writer's act of imagination.

AUDIENCE INVENTORY

Ask students to choose a possible topic for an essay and to list the kinds of people who might be interested in the topic. Tell students that if they wish they may employ the "Questions About Audience" on p. 27. (In theory, the lists might be very long. In practice, students soon run out of ideas but not until they have begun to visualize the audience for their essays.) To extend the exercise, ask students what part of the potential audience they would most like to address or what kinds of people would be most interested in the topic. Then ask them to list either (1) what the restricted audience probably already knows about the topic and what it needs to know or (2) what its attitudes are and what kinds of arguments will be needed to change them.

Excellent illustration of "voice"

facts, examples, or any other evidence that makes your ideas clear or supports your assertions. And your selection of information must suit what you know of the background of your audience: its familiarity with your topic, its biases, and its special interests.

Consider the student who needs money. He writes two letters, one to his parents and another to his school's Office of Student Aid. First he writes to his parents:

> Well, I did it again. Only two weeks into a new semester, and I'm broke already. But you know I needed a sweater, and besides, book prices have just skyrocketed and I've got this Constitutional History course that almost broke the bank all by itself ($70.00 for books!). Oh, and I've met this really great girl (more later). So anyway, I'm pretty low on cash right now and am going to need another $50.00 to make it through the rest of the month. This should be the last time I have to ask for money, though. Starting next week I'm going to work part-time at a restaurant—doing some short-order cooking and general kinds of work—so if you want your money back . . .

Then he writes to the Office of Student Aid:

> I am writing to request a short-term loan of $50.00 for bill consolidation and for other personal reasons. Starting in ten days, I will be employed for ten hours per week, as a cook, at Better-Burgers, 315 North Main Street. Thus I will be able to repay the loan easily within the required three-month limit. I understand that if I fail to make any payment . . .

The two letters make the same request, but they contain very different information. In the first letter the student chooses details that he believes his parents will relate to: he's "broke already" and not, apparently, for the first time; he needed new clothes; he's serious enough about his studies to pay large sums for his books; he has a new girl friend; he's not specific about his job. In the second letter he chooses details that will reassure the administrators of student aid: he omits any mention of his purchases, his girl friend, or other personal details; he explains where he will be working and for precisely how many hours each week; he stresses the certainty of repayment; he proves he knows the regulations—the "three-month limit" and the penalties for nonpayment. If, by accident, the student mailed the second letter to his parents, they might be mystified or amused. And if he mailed the first letter to the Office of Student Aid, the recipients might deny his request.

The questions in the box on the previous page lead you to analyze both the general orientation of your readers and their specific position on your topic, and that analysis can help you decide how best to approach them. For instance, Pat Lucas determined that while her readers (her classmates) resembled her in age, education, and other general characteristics, they might not share her interest in how architecture affects people. In addition, since Lucas attended a college in the East, she could not expect her classmates to be familiar with a building in Detroit or with the feelings the building aroused in her. Thus she would not have to overcome any biases of readers toward the building, but neither could she draw on what they already knew about it. She realized that she must try to relate her interests and experiences to those of her readers, and she must describe the Renaissance Center in enough detail to create a clear picture in readers' minds.

If Lucas's audience had been quite different—for instance, residents of Detroit—then her approach would have differed. Detroit residents would not require as much detail about the appearance of the building, but some of them might be expected to like the Renaissance Center or at least to find it unobjectionable. Thus Lucas would have planned to deal directly with their preconceptions in order to overcome them—perhaps by acknowledging that the building is striking before explaining how it is insensitive.

2   **Deciding on an appropriate role and tone**

Besides deciding what information your audience needs, you should also consider how you want to present yourself and your topic to readers—that is, how you want them to perceive both you and your attitude toward your topic. One way to make this decision is to think of yourself, as writer, playing a role in relation to the reader. The possible roles are many and varied, including, for instance, storyteller, portrait painter, lecturer, guide, reporter, advocate, and inspirer. The choice of a role for yourself will depend partly on your purpose—on whether you intend primarily to express yourself, entertain, explain, or persuade—and partly on how you feel about your topic and expect your readers to feel about it. As you write your essay, the role you choose will help determine *what* you say and also the *way* you say it—your **tone.** Tone in writing is like tone of voice in speaking: words and sentence structures on the page convey some of the same information about attitude as pitch and volume in the voice.

Conceived broadly, tone may be informal or formal, as illustrated by the two requests for money opposite. In the first letter, the student's tone is informal, personal. His sentences are typical of conversation: loose and full of the second-person pronoun *you,*

DISCOVERING SOMEONE ELSE'S AUDIENCE

Distribute to your class an article from a special-interest magazine, a newspaper feature or editorial, or another brief essay whose appeal to a particular audience students will be able to recognize fairly easily. Ask students to read the essay and then to write down the characteristics and attitudes of the intended audience as they think the author viewed it. Ask them also to identify the tone of the essay and to decide whether or not it is appropriate to the subject, the intended audience, and the publication in which the essay appeared. Tell them to be ready to point out what evidence in the essay they used to identify the intended audience and the tone.

contractions (*I've, I'm*), and casual expressions like *really, pretty, so anyway*. His paragraph is loosely structured, introducing subjects like the new girl friend as they occur to him and burying the most important point, the request for money, in the middle. The student's purpose is as much to entertain his parents as to persuade them to lend him money. He plays the role of a still scatterbrained but always lovable and almost responsible son—a role he expects his parents to appreciate. In contrast, the second letter is written in a much more formal tone. The student's words (*bill consolidation, employed, per week, this*) are formal and serious. He avoids *you* and contractions. His carefully constructed sentences (*Thus I will be able to repay the loan easily within the required three-month limit*) would sound stiff in most conversation. The paragraph is tightly structured. The student's purpose is strictly to persuade the school administrators to lend him money, and he assumes the role— serious, responsible adult—that he believes his readers expect.

As these examples suggest, different roles and tones are appropriate for different topics, purposes, and audiences. You have the widest range of choice when your purpose is entertainment or self-expression and when you can assume your audience is sympathetic. Then your attitude toward your topic may lead you to play any role from comedian to tragic figure, adopting any tone from teasing to solemn. For other purposes, one or more elements of the writing situation, in addition to your own attitude, are likely to narrow your choices. In business reports and memos, for instance, clarity and conciseness take precedence over self-expression, and formality of tone tends to increase with the rank and number of readers being addressed.

When Pat Lucas considered an appropriate role and tone for her essay on the Renaissance Center, she referred to her purpose of explaining how the building illustrated Sommer's ideas about hard architecture. Since her readers would not be familiar with the building, that purpose suggested the role of a guide, showing readers how the parts of the building contributed to an overall impression. Lucas realized, though, that she felt too strongly about the building to write impersonally or objectively about it. She disliked the building and she wanted her readers to share her attitude. Thus Lucas decided that the role of critical guide, "speaking" in a slightly disapproving tone, was most appropriate for her.

Most writing you do for your college courses will demand an academic role and tone. You will be expected to present yourself as a serious and competent student of the subject you are writing in, one who possesses at least a basic understanding of the discipline's research methods, vocabulary, and principles and who can write clearly. Befitting such a role, the tone of most academic writing is somewhat formal and impersonal. Here, for instance, is a passage from a student's psychology paper:

> One technique for heightening the emotional appeal of advertisements is "color engineering." Adding color to an advertisement or product can increase sales despite the fact that the color serves no practical purpose. For example, until the 1920s fountain pens were made of hard black rubber. When colored pens were introduced, sales rose dramatically.

Such straightforward writing allows considerable room for you to express your attitudes by your choice of words and sentence structures. Consider the effect of small changes in the second sentence above:

> New color in an advertisement or product can boost sales even when the color serves no other use.

The brisker tone and the idea of the writer it conveys still fall within the range of academic writing. As you gain experience with such writing, you will develop the flexibility to write in your own voice while also respecting the conventions of the various disciplines.

EXACTLY!

3   **Writing for a general audience—or for your instructor**

What do you do when you are not writing exclusively for your parents or the Office of Student Aid—when, in other words, you don't know much about your audience? From compositions assigned to be written "for your classmates" to bulletins inviting film-society subscriptions, much of the writing you do will be for a **general audience**—"general" because it includes people of diverse backgrounds and interests. General audiences read newspapers and magazines such as *Time* and *Newsweek*. These readers are skeptical and easily distracted, but they are also curious and thoughtful. They may not share all your interests, but they can understand and appreciate anything you write, as long as it is specific, clear, honest, and fresh. They will expect you to explain any specialized terms you use and to support any assertions you make with ample details, examples, and reasons. Further, they will expect you to present yourself as thoughtful and competent, the master of your information and a careful writer. An appropriate tone may range from lighthearted to grave, depending on the topic and writing situation; but a moderate and assured tone midway between the extremes of informality and formality will almost always work.

Of course, much of your college writing may have only one reader besides you: the instructor of the course you are writing for. In a composition course your instructor is likely to read your work as representative of a general audience and respond to it in the additional role of helpful critic (see 2e). That means you should not assume specialized interest in or knowledge of your topic, nor should you expect the patience and tolerance of a doting parent who fills in what his or her child can't or won't express. If something about your topic would need to be said to a classmate or a reader of your local newspaper, say it clearly and carefully.

As discussed in the previous section, most writing for the academic disciplines such as literature, psychology, management, and chemistry is not really addressed to a general audience but to a specialized audience of practitioners of the discipline, represented by your instructor. If you are writing a paper on the economic background of the War of 1812 for an American history course, you may assume your instructor's familiarity with the key events, players, and published interpretations. Your job is to show your own command of them and their relevance to your topic while assuming an appropriate academic role and tone and, as you would for any reader, being specific, clear, and concise.

ANSWERS: EXERCISE 12

1. Author's role: humorous guide. Attitude toward subject: disparaging yet indulgent. Intended audience: readers who share the same attitude (i.e., not the "good ole boys" being discussed).

2. Author's role: educator. Attitude toward subject: objective. Intended audience: readers interested in the details of how air bags work.

SAMPLE ANSWERS: EXERCISE 13

1. *For elementary school students:* physical effects in simple terms; statistics in simple figures; difficulty of quitting once addicted; importance of resisting peer pressure.
   Role: combined teacher and parent. Tone: warm, slightly admonitory.
   For adult smokers: graphic depiction of physical effects; detailed statistics; influence on children; effect on smoker's appearance, odor, breath.
   Role: combined friend and lecturer. Tone: no-nonsense.

2. *For someone who is on welfare:* help for children; possibility that government support will lead to self-support; need for bureaucracy to manage system; need for periodic checks to protect against cheating by a few recipients.
   Role: caring observer. Tone: sympathetic.

EXERCISE 12

Analyze the content and tone of each paragraph below. What do the writer's choice of information and selection of words and sentence structures indicate about his or her role, attitude toward the subject, and intended audience?

1.   It is Friday night at any of ten thousand watering holes of the small towns and crossroads hamlets of the South. The room is a cacophony of the ping-pong-dingdingding of the pinball machine, the pop-fizz of another round of Pabst, the refrain of *Red Necks, White Socks, and Blue Ribbon Beer* on the juke box, the insolent roar of a souped-up engine outside and, above it all, the sound of easy laughter. The good ole boys have gathered for their fraternal ritual—the aimless diversion that they have elevated into a life-style.   —BONNIE ANGELO, "Those Good Ole Boys"

2.   All air bags [in automobiles] work in essentially the same way. First, a sensor detects a sudden decrease in speed and triggers the device. The sensitivity of the sensor is such that no normal driving situation, such as abruptly slamming on the brakes at highway speeds or hitting another car while parking, will trigger it: an impact equivalent to hitting a wall at a speed of at least 12 miles an hour is required to set it off. Then a powdered chemical, sodium azide, is electrically ignited, and produces a quick

burst of nitrogen gas to inflate a fabric bag. Nitrogen is a harm-less gas that constitutes 78 percent of the air we breathe, but so-dium azide can be poisonous and is therefore carefully sealed in the air-bag cannister until used. The bag can inflate fully within 1/25th of a second, then deflates again within seconds.
                                                  —DAVID L. CHANDLER, "Air Bags—Life-Saving
                                                                                          and Unavailable"

EXERCISE 13

To practice considering an audience, choose one of the following topics and ask the questions on pages 27–28 for each audience specified. Decide on four points you would make, the role you would assume, and the tone you would adopt for each audience. Then write a paragraph for each based on your decisions.

1. the effects of smoking: for elementary school students and for adult smokers
2. your opinion of welfare: for someone who is on welfare and for someone who is not and who opposes it
3. the advantages of a summer camp: for a prospective camper and for his or her parents
4. why your neighbors should remove the wrecked truck from their yard: for your neighbors and for your town zoning board
5. the beauty of a snowfall: for someone who has never experi-enced snow and for someone who hates it

EXERCISE 14

Continuing from the groups of ideas that you prepared in Exer-cise 11 (p. 26), use the questions on page 27 to determine as much as you can about the probable readers of your essay-in-progress. Evaluate your groups of ideas to ensure that they include the specific information your readers need. Decide what role you want to assume and what tone may best convey your attitude to-ward your topic.

Good definition of "thesis."

1g Developing the thesis

Most essays are focused on and controlled by a single main idea that the writer wants to communicate to readers—a central point to which all the general statements and specific information of the essay relate. This main idea, called the **thesis,** encompasses the writer's attitude toward the topic and purpose in writing.

Sometimes your thesis may be apparent to you very early in the writing process: you may have chosen your topic in the first place because you had an idea about it that you wanted to com-

For someone who opposes welfare: need to provide for people who can't work; need to provide for children; low cost relative to other budget expenditures; low incidence of cheating.
Role: fellow citizen. Tone: reasonable, appealing to shared values.

3. *For the camper:* chance to get out of the dirty city; opportunity to swim and hike; chance to meet other children; chance to get away from parents.
Role: guide and conspirator. Tone: light, cheerful.
For the parents: low cost; expert staff; constructive experience; opportunity to be free of the child.
Role: salesperson. Tone: sincere, re-sponsible.

4. *For your neighbors:* angry feelings of neighborhood residents; dangers to children and pets; lowered property values; threat of petition to zoning board.
Role: peer. Tone: direct, a bit angry.
For the zoning board: violation of zon-ing regulations; length of time the wrecked truck has been present; num-ber of unsuccessful appeals to neigh-bors; dangers to children and pets.
Role: plaintiff. Tone: serious, reason-able.

5. *For someone who has never experienced snow:* the air during snowfall; how snow accumulates on the ground; ap-pearance after snowfall of trees, build-ings, and so on; muffled sounds after snowfall.
Role: landscape painter. Tone: serene.
For someone who hates snow: interrup-tion by heavy snow of boring routine; cheering effect of snowfall on children; peace and quiet of city during and after snowfall; snow's protection of plants against cold.
Role: friend. Tone: cheerful.

ANSWERS: EXERCISE 14
Individual response.

tempt, sometimes over one or more drafts of the essay. But the thinking required can help you discover potentially serious problems, such as that you're trying to write about three ideas, not one.

Pat Lucas went through a common procedure in writing and revising her thesis sentence on the Renaissance Center. First she turned her topic into an assertion:

> The Renaissance Center in Detroit is an example of hard architecture.

This sentence reflected Lucas's intention to explain her understanding of Sommer's term "hard architecture" using the example of the Renaissance Center. However, it conveyed nothing specific about the term and the building and none of Lucas's attitudes toward them. The word *insensitive* was absent, even though it had figured prominently in Lucas's thinking almost from the beginning. When she recognized this omission, she rewrote the sentence:

> Hard architecture is insensitive, and the Renaissance Center in Detroit is an excellent example of it.

This sentence was better, but Lucas still needed to link the two parts of the sentence by saying *why* the Renaissance Center is an excellent example. She tried again:

> The Renaissance Center in Detroit is an excellent example of hard, insensitive architecture because it shows a lack of concern for the people of the city.

With this sentence Lucas felt she had drafted an assertion that encompassed all her ideas and supporting details and that conveyed her attitude toward the Renaissance Center. Though she knew the sentence might require further revision, she felt it was adequate to help her for the time being.

When you are writing and revising your thesis sentence, check to be sure it fulfills the following requirements.

REQUIREMENTS OF THE THESIS SENTENCE

1. Does it make an *assertion* about your topic?
2. Does it convey your *purpose*, your *opinion*, and your *attitude*?
3. Is it *limited* to an assertion of only one idea?
4. Is the assertion *specific*?
5. Is the sentence *unified* in that the parts relate to each other?

Here are other examples of thesis sentences revised to meet these requirements:

SUPPLYING AN OMITTED THESIS STATEMENT

Ask students to read their papers to the class or to a peer group, deliberately leaving out the thesis statement. Ask the other students to supply a thesis for the essay. If the original thesis and the one supplied by the students match, fine. If not, the thesis a student has chosen may be inappropriate for the paper and the discussion that follows can suggest possible revisions.

ASKING READERS TO AGREE ON THE THESIS

Ask students to read an essay from a collection or a fellow student's paper and then to state its thesis in their own words. If students are working in groups, ask the group members whether they can agree on the thesis. Next have the students try to identify a thesis statement in the essay. If the essay has an explicit thesis statement, ask if they consider it effective or if the thesis statement they produced would be more effective. If the thesis is implicit, ask students whether or not the essay would benefit from an explicit thesis statement.

dev

1g

ORIGINAL

People should not go on fad diets. [A vague statement that needs limiting with one or more reasons: what's wrong with fad diets?]

Televised sports are different from live sports. [A general statement that needs to be made more specific: how are they different, and why is the difference significant?]

Seat belts can save lives, but now car makers may be required to install air bags. [Not unified: how do the two parts of the sentence relate to each other?]

REVISED

Fad diets can be dangerous when they deprive the body of essential nutrients or rely on excessive quantities of potentially harmful foods.

Although television cannot transmit all the excitement of being in a crowd during a game, its close-ups and slow-motion replays more than compensate.

If drivers more often used life-saving seat belts, the car makers might not be required to install air bags.

Good Exercise

EXERCISE 15

Evaluate the following thesis sentences, considering whether each one is sufficiently limited, specific, and unified. Rewrite the sentences as necessary to meet these goals.

1. Traveling on a tight budget can be educational.
2. Aggression usually leads to violence, injury, and even death, and we should use it constructively.
3. Gun control is essential.
4. One evening of a radio talk show amply illustrates both the appeal of such shows and their silliness.
5. Good manners make our society work.
6. City people are different from country people.
7. Television is a useful baby sitter and an escape for people who do not want to think about their own problems.
8. I liked American history in high school, but I do not like it in college.
9. We are encouraged to choose a career in college, but people change jobs frequently.
10. Drunken drivers, whose perception, coordination, and reaction time are impaired, should receive mandatory suspensions of their licenses.

EXERCISE 16

Write limited, specific, and unified thesis sentences for three of the following topics. Each of your sentences should convey the purpose given in parentheses and your own attitude.

ANSWERS: EXERCISE 15

1. The sentence needs to be more specific, saying why traveling on a tight budget can be educational.
   Possible revision: Traveling on a tight budget provides an opportunity to learn about people and their customs.
2. The sentence lacks unity because the two halves do not seem to relate to each other.
   Possible revision: We should channel our natural feelings of aggression toward constructive rather than destructive ends.
3. Both halves of the sentence need to be more specific: What kind of gun control? essential for what end?
   Possible revision: To curb the rising rate of murder with handguns, restrictions on the sale of handguns should be legislated and strictly enforced.
4. Good thesis sentence: limited, specific, and unified.
5. Both *good manners* and *make our society work* need to be more specific.
   Possible revision: Courtesy between people makes human interaction smoother and more efficient.
6. *Different* needs limiting.
   Possible revision: City people are different from country people in their attitudes toward strangers, politicians, and money.
7. The sentence lacks unity because the first half is positive but not very specific, while the second half is negative and specific. Making the first half more specific and the second half positive would unify the sentence.
   Possible revision: Television is both a useful baby sitter for children, offering them education and entertainment, and a good escape for adults, providing them with relief from their own problems.
8. The sentence is a flat statement of personal preference that provides no preview of reasons for the preference.

Possible revision: Although I liked American history in high school because the teacher focused on social trends and events, I do not like it in college because the teacher focuses on political events and personalities.

9. The sentence lacks unity because the two halves do not clearly relate to each other.

Possible revision: Because a person should delay a career decision until he or she has worked in several jobs, students should not be encouraged to choose a career while they are in college.

10 The sentence lacks unity because the clause *whose . . . impaired* is not directly related to the opinion being stated.

Possible revision: Drivers who have demonstrated bad judgment and lack of control by operating a car under the influence of alcohol should receive mandatory suspension of their licenses.

SAMPLE ANSWERS: EXERCISE 16

1. If more students majored in business, U.S. corporations would be run more efficiently.
2. Helping my friend overcome drug dependency taught me how to be patient and consistent in my dealings with others.
3. Cable television provides a worthwhile community service and should, like other community services, be delivered by the government at no charge.
4. Everyone should live for a while in an old building, for old walls and floors provide an essential sense of continuity with the past.
5. The sounds of the city at midnight conjure up a dual image of people having fun and people in trouble.
6. To care for a plant, one must understand and fulfill its special needs for sunlight, water, and nutrition.

1. why (or why not) major in business (*persuasion*)
2. a frustrating experience (*self-expression*)
3. why cable television should be free (*persuasion*)
4. how an old house or apartment is better than a new one (or vice versa) (*explanation*)
5. the sounds of the city or country (*self-expression or entertainment*)
6. how to care for a plant (*explanation*)
7. why students attend college (*explanation*)
8. how a rumor spreads (*explanation*)
9. why divorce laws should be tougher (or looser) (*persuasion*)
10. a disliked person (*explanation*)

EXERCISE 17

Continuing from Exercise 14 (p. 33), write a limited, specific, and unified thesis sentence for your essay-in-progress.

1h Organizing the essay

An effective essay has a recognizable shape—an arrangement of parts that guides readers, helping them see how ideas and details relate to each other and contribute to the whole. If readers can't see a clear order in your material or how each new idea or piece of information develops your thesis, they will have difficulty understanding you and they may mistrust what you say.

Writers sometimes let an effective organization emerge over one or more drafts. But many writers find that organizing ideas to some extent before drafting can provide a helpful sense of direction, as a map can help a driver negotiate a half-familiar system of roads. If you feel uncertain about the course your essay should follow or have a complicated topic with many parts, devising a shape for your material can clarify your options.

1 Arranging the parts of an essay

Most essays share a basic shape consisting of an introduction, a body, and a conclusion. The introduction draws readers into the world of the essay, stating the topic and often the thesis sentence. It makes a commitment that the rest of the essay delivers on. The conclusion generally gives readers something to take away from the essay—a summary of ideas, for instance, or a suggested course of action. (Both introductory and concluding paragraphs are discussed with other special kinds of paragraphs in 3d, pp. 115–19.) The body of the essay is its center, the part offering ideas and supporting details, examples, and reasons to develop the thesis and thus fulfill the commitment of the introduction. In an essay of two or three pages, the body may contain three to five substantial paragraphs, each presenting and supporting a part of the thesis.

The organization of the body of your essay will depend on your topic, your purpose, and your sense of what your readers need and expect from you. In almost any writing situation, at least one of the organizing schemes listed below will be appropriate. These schemes are so familiar that readers expect them and look for them. Thus the schemes both help you arrange your material and help readers follow you.

SCHEMES FOR ORGANIZING IDEAS IN AN ESSAY

1. Space
2. Time
3. Emphasis

General to specific   Decreasing familiarity
Specific to general   Increasing complexity
Increasing importance (climactic)

4. Pattern of development

Narration   Comparison and contrast
Description   Analogy
Illustration or support   Cause-and-effect analysis
Definition   Process analysis
Division and classification

Organizing by space or time

Two organizational schemes—spatial and chronological—grow naturally out of the topic. A **spatial organization** is especially appropriate for expository essays that describe a place, an object, or a person. Following the way people normally survey something, you move through space from a chosen starting point to other features of the subject. Describing a friend, for instance, you might begin with his shoes and move upward or begin with his face and move downward. If, instead, you moved from hands to face to shoes to arms, your arrangement might be less effective because your readers would have to work harder to stay with you. The following thesis sentence suggests that the writer might move in space from one end of the street to the other.

7. Most students seem to attend college for one of three reasons: to prepare for a career, to enhance social life, or to delay the decisions of adulthood.
8. Tracing the rumor of Mr. Petrieka's secret sin revealed a laughable series of misunderstood conversations.
9. As long as they do not have children, married people should be able to divorce easily so that they can seek happier, more stable relationships elsewhere.
10. For the two months I stayed with my ex-roommate, his slothfulness, rudeness, and deceit caused me constant pain.

ANSWERS: EXERCISE 17

Individual response.

RESOURCES AND IDEAS

Lance Wilcox, "Time Lines in the Composing of Narratives: A Graphic Aid to Organization," *The Writing Instructor* 6 (1987): 162–73. Wilcox describes in detail the use of time lines to help develop and organize narrative essays.

Neil Berman, "Language, Process, and Tinkertoys," *College Composition and Communication* 26 (1975): 390–92. Berman offers concrete exercises to teach process analysis as a form of writing.

Terry Dean, "Causal, Not Casual: An Advance Organizer for Cause-and-Effect Compositions," *Structuring for Success in the English Classroom*, ed. Candy Carter (Urbana: NCTE, 1982), 92–97. Dean describes exercises to make students aware of causal relationships and to provide a basis for writing.

George D. Haich, "If the Reader Never Saw One, How Would You Describe It?" *College Composition and Communication* 26 (1975): 298–300. The author suggests having students describe an object the class has not seen so that the class can begin to understand what information and strategies are necessary for effective description.

Richard L. Larson, "Towards a Linear Rhetoric of the Essay," *College Composition and Communication* 22 (1971): 140–46. Larson proposes teaching students to shape their essays by planning a linear sequence of moves or stages rather than a hierarchical structure.

Leonard A. Podis, "Teaching Arrangement: Defining a More Practical Approach," *College Composition and Communication* 31 (1980): 197–204. Podis describes a teaching sequence designed to make students aware of the basic principles of organization, and he reviews some standard patterns of arrangement useful for academic and professional writing.

Judith G. Stitzel, "Is There a Box on the Board? An Exercise in Classification," *On Righting Writing*, ed. Ouida H. Clapp (Urbana: NCTE, 1975), 87–93. The author outlines classroom activities providing an awareness of how the mind organizes perceptions, ideas, and experience.

> The main street of my neighborhood contains enough variety to make almost any city dweller feel at home.

To illustrate variety, the writer can provide details of the shops, apartment buildings, and people encountered along the street.

A **chronological organization** reports events as they occurred in time, usually from first to last. This pattern, like spatial organization, corresponds to readers' own experiences and expectations. It suits expository essays in which you recount a historical or more recent sequence of events or explain a process from beginning to end (for instance, how to run a marathon). And it suits the retelling of more personal stories for the purpose of self-expression or entertainment. In an essay developed from the following thesis sentence, the author would probably proceed chronologically through the event, emphasizing the difficulties and the effects they had on his friends.

> The surest way to lose good friends is to enlist their help in a move from one fourth-floor walkup to another.

A chronological organization structures the essay on pages 72–73. This is the essay on a summer job for which we earlier saw a list of ideas (p. 17) and a tree diagram (p. 25).

Organizing for emphasis

Several other organizational schemes do not so much grow out of the topic as they are imposed on it to aid readers' understanding and achieve a desired emphasis. Two of these depend on the distinction between the general and the specific as discussed on page 24. The **general-to-specific scheme** is common in expository and argumentative essays that start with a general discussion of the main points and then proceed to specific examples, facts, or other evidence. The following thesis sentences forecast expository and argumentative essays with general-to-specific organizations:

> In families consisting of a single parent and a single child, the boundaries between parent and child often disappear so that the two interact as siblings or as a married couple.

> If it hopes to win the technological race, the United States must make higher education possible for any student who qualifies academically.

Following from the first sentence, the body of the essay might first discuss generally the dynamics of the families in question and then provide specific examples of the two forms of interaction. Following the second sentence, the body of the essay might first elaborate on the basic argument and then provide the supporting data.

In some expository or argumentative essays, a **specific-to-general scheme** can arouse readers' interest in specific examples or other evidence, letting the evidence build to more general ideas. The following thesis sentence could be developed in this way.

> Most of us are unaware of the public relations campaigns directed at us, but they can significantly affect the way we think and live.

The writer might devote most of the essay to a single specific example of a public relations campaign, showing how it influenced people without their knowledge. Then he could explain more generally how the example typifies public relations campaigns.

The other ways of organizing for emphasis draw on different principles for arranging material. In a **climactic organization,** ideas unfold in order of increasing drama or importance to a climax. For example, the following thesis sentence lists three effects of strip-mining in order of their increasing severity, and the essay would cover them in the same order.

> Strip-mining should be tightly controlled in this region to reduce its pollution of water resources, its permanent destruction of the land, and its devastating effects on people's lives.

As this example suggests, the climactic organization aids argumentation by leaving readers with the most important point freshest in their minds. In exposition such an arrangement can create suspense and thus hold readers' attention.

Expository essays can also be arranged in variations of the climactic pattern. An essay on learning to play the guitar might proceed from **most familiar to least familiar,** that is, from simply plucking strings and sliding the hand up and down the instrument's neck, which most people have seen, to the less familiar styles of picking and chording. Similarly, an essay on various computer languages might proceed from **simplest to most complex,** so that the explanation of each language provides a basis for readers to understand the more difficult one following.

Using a pattern of development

Each of the patterns of development discussed as a discovery strategy on pages 20–22 also suggests at least one overall structure for an essay. If you have been assigned or have chosen a pattern as a way to develop your essay, it can help you arrange your material, almost always in combination with one of the organizational schemes already discussed. (See 3c, pp. 101–10, for paragraph-length examples of each pattern.)

In **narration** the arrangement is almost always chronological, with events arranged as they occurred in time. When writing a narrative, you will probably want to manipulate the sequence of events for emphasis or interest, extending some significant events to minute-by-minute replays, collapsing less significant events to mere summary. (See the narrative essay on pp. 72–73 for an example.) In addition, you may want to alter the sequence, using flashbacks to recall earlier events or forecasting later events.

For **description** of a person, place, or thing, the organization is usually spatial, beginning at one point and surveying others in an orderly way such as near to far or top to bottom. Pat Lucas's essay on the Renaissance Center (final draft on pp. 68–70) illustrates a near-to-far spatial arrangement, first giving an overview of the structure and then viewing it from increasing distances.

Using **illustration or support,** you list examples or reasons, or you expand on a single example. You can arrange the individual examples or reasons or the details of the single example in the way that seems most appropriate. For instance, you might arrange several examples in climactic order for an essay arguing that the children's television program *Sesame Street* displays subtle sexism. Or you might arrange a single example chronologically for an essay explaining how one episode of the local evening news illustrates a tendency to downplay serious news in favor of trivial stories.

Using **definition** to specify the precise meaning of a word, object, or concept, you will usually differentiate the topic from other things in its class and then fill in the special characteristics of the topic itself. In an essay defining *soap opera*, for instance, you might first differentiate the soap opera from other television dramas (other members of its class) and then extend the definition with examples of the distinguishing features, arranged in the way most appropriate for emphasis.

Division (separating something into its parts) and **classification** (sorting many things into groups or classes) lead you to list and detail the parts or classes of your topic, which you further arrange for maximum emphasis. In a division essay pointing out the unvarying format of local evening news shows, you might cover the most obvious regular segments first (headline news, weather, sports) and then turn to the less obvious regular segments (police-and-fire story and human-struggle story). In a classification essay sorting soap opera characters into groups, you might arrange the groups in order of increasing complexity—say, from consistently evil characters to consistently wholesome characters to good-hearted but weak characters whose behavior is inconsistent.

In **comparison and contrast** and **analogy,** similar patterns specifying the similarities and differences between topics, you usually follow one of two basic organizational schemes: (1) you discuss each topic separately, covering all the pertinent features of one and then all the pertinent features of the other; or (2) you discuss the topics side by side, comparing them feature for feature. A comparison of the attitudes toward defense spending revealed by the network news programs might follow the first scheme, with each network being examined separately. (See the essay titled "The Obsolete Hero" on p. 74 for an example of a comparison organized in this way.) The second scheme might work for an analogy between wild cards in poker and goodhearted but weak characters in soap operas, showing how both cause sudden realignments among players. Both topics would be examined under each comparable feature. In either scheme, the specific features can be arranged in any order that achieves the desired emphasis.

The pattern of **cause-and-effect analysis** also usually leads you to one of two organizations, depending on whether you are examining why something happened or what its consequences were or will be: (1) you first explain an effect and then examine its causes; or (2) you first explain a cause or causes and then examine the actual or possible effects. The first scheme would suit an essay explaining why television game shows are popular; the second scheme would suit an essay arguing that television news makes viewers impatient for quick solutions to complex problems. The causes or effects themselves may be arranged in order of their occurrence (chronologically) or of their importance or complexity.

The final pattern, **process analysis,** is almost always organized chronologically, as the steps in the process actually occur. In a process essay explaining how to improve one's chances of winning a television game show, for instance, you would present the sequence of steps involved in preparing for the show and playing the game on the air.

2   Outlining

When you have chosen an overall organization for your essay, you may find it helpful to work it out in an outline, a blueprint showing what you will cover and where. Some writers rarely use an outline, and some use one primarily during revision to check the underlying structure of a draft (see p. 57). But writers who do use some form of preliminary outline during planning find that it helps them see potential problems—flaws in organization, gaps or overlaps in coverage, unwanted digressions—and then helps guide the actual drafting. (For these reasons, writing teachers often encourage or require students to experiment with outlining.)

Any of the several kinds of outlines discussed below can be

useful. Keep in mind, though, that while the thought you give an outline can be very productive, you may not be able to anticipate changes that drafting will demand. Think of the outline as an aid, not a taskmaster.

Using a scratch or informal outline

For many essays, especially those with a fairly straightforward structure, a simple listing of ideas and perhaps their support may provide adequate direction for your writing. A **scratch outline** lists the key points of the paper in the order they will be covered. Here is Pat Lucas's scratch outline for her essay on the Renaissance Center.

THESIS SENTENCE

The Renaissance Center in Detroit is an excellent example of hard, insensitive architecture because it shows a lack of concern for the people of the city.

SCRATCH OUTLINE

Analogy between insensitive building and person
Parts of Ren. Center—towers and base
Relation of Ren. Center to pedestrians
Relation of Ren. Center to rest of city

Lucas put more into this outline than its simplicity might indicate. From her rough groups of ideas (pp. 24–25), she followed through on her earlier decision to omit discussion of the building's interior and other Detroit buildings. Thinking of her readers' needs, she also moved her analogy to the beginning of the essay, where she believed it would do more to explain her attitude. And for the clearest possible depiction of the building, she sorted its many features into three main groups (the last three points in the outline). With this much thought, such a scratch outline may be all you need to begin drafting. Sometimes, though, it may prove too skimpy a guide, and you may want to use it as a preliminary to a more detailed outline. Indeed, Pat Lucas used her scratch outline as a base for a detailed formal outline that gave her an even surer sense of direction (see p. 46).

An **informal outline** is usually more detailed than a scratch outline, including key points and the evidence for them. As we saw on pages 39–40, the thesis of the essay about a neighborhood street suggests a spatial organization. In an informal outline the writer set up topic headings that would correspond to separate paragraphs of her essay, and she added the features of the street.

RESOURCES AND IDEAS

Karla F. C. Holloway, "Teaching Composition Through Outlining," *Teaching the Basics—Really!"* ed. Ouida Clapp (Urbana: NCTE, 1977), 36–39. Holloway suggests using outlines as a critical tool to teach writing.

THESIS SENTENCE

The main street of my neighborhood contains enough variety to make almost any city dweller feel at home.

INFORMAL OUTLINE

The beginning of the street
    high-rise condominium occupied by well-to-do people
    ground floor of building: an art gallery
    across the street: a delicatessen
    above the delicatessen: a tailor's shop, a camera-repair
        shop, a lawyer's office
The middle of the street
    four-story brick apartment buildings on both sides
    at ground level: an Italian bakery and a Spanish bodega
    people sitting on steps
    children playing ball on sidewalks
The end of the street
    a halfway house for drug addicts
    a boarding house for retired men
    a discount drugstore
    an expensive department store
    a wine shop
    another high-rise condominium

Using a tree diagram

In addition to its use for grouping ideas, the branching tree diagram described and illustrated on pages 24–25 can be a helpful preliminary and guide to drafting. You isolate your main ideas as if for a scratch outline and, under them, array supporting points and then details. If you have already used such a diagram for grouping ideas, then a revision or extension of it may serve you at this later stage. Or you can begin one now. In either case, the diagram can serve the functions of any detailed outline: provide a map and warn of gaps, overlaps, and digressions. Further, because the tree diagram can be supplemented and extended almost indefinitely, it is easy to alter for new ideas and arrangements discovered during drafting and revision.

Using a formal outline

For complex topics requiring complex arrangements of ideas and support, you may want or be required to construct a **formal outline,** either before you began drafting or afterward, as a check on what you have done (see p. 57). More rigidly arranged and more detailed than a scratch or informal outline, a formal outline not only lays out main ideas and their support but also shows the relative importance of all the essay's elements and how they connect with each other.

On the basis of her scratch outline (p. 44), Pat Lucas prepared this formal outline for her essay on the Renaissance Center:

THESIS SENTENCE

The Renaissance Center in Detroit is an excellent example of hard, insensitive architecture because it shows a lack of concern for the people of the city.

FORMAL OUTLINE

   I. Analogy between insensitive building and insensitive person
      A. Cold exterior and hard surfaces
      B. Concern only with self
  II. The parts of the Renaissance Center
      A. The five towers
         1. Fortress-like appearance
         2. Dark shapes turning in on themselves
      B. The base
         1. High concrete wall at street level
         2. Lack of apparent entrance for pedestrians
 III. The Renaissance Center as a whole
      A. Building set apart from city
      B. Scale and architecture unrelated to city

In this formal outline Lucas refined her thinking even further, seeing the building first in its parts (section II) and then as a whole (section III) and arranging her evidence carefully under each point. Though she knew her outline might change as she drafted and revised her essay, she was satisfied that it solved some problems and would provide a course for her to follow until new issues arose.

Lucas's outline illustrates not only the potential value of outlining but also several principles of outlining that can help ensure completeness, balance, and clear relationships. (These principles largely depend on distinguishing between the general and the specific. See p. 24.)

1. So that the outline both clarifies the order of ideas and details and indicates their relative importance, all its parts are systematically indented and numbered or lettered: Roman numerals (I, II, III) for primary divisions of the essay; indented capital letters (A, B) for secondary divisions; further indented Arabic numerals (1, 2) for principal supporting examples. A level of detail below the Arabic numbers would be indented further still and labeled with small letters (a, b). Each succeeding level contains more specific information that the one before it.

2. The outline divides the material into several groups. An uninterrupted listing of ideas like the one following would in-

---

PRINCIPLES OF THE FORMAL OUTLINE

1. Labels and indentions indicate order and relative importance.
2. Sections and subsections reflect logical relationships.
3. Topics of equal generality appear in parallel headings.
4. Each subdivision has at least two parts.
5. Headings are expressed in parallel grammatical form.
6. The introduction and conclusion may be omitted (though not, of course, from the essay).

---

dicate a need for tighter, more logical relationships among ideas. (Compare this example with Parts II and III of Lucas's actual outline.)

II. The Renaissance Center
    A. Fortress-like appearance
    B. Dark shapes turning in on themselves
    C. High concrete wall at street level
    D. Lack of apparent entrance for pedestrians
    E. Building set apart from city
    F. Scale and architecture unrelated to city

3. Within each part of the outline, distinct topics of equal generality appear in parallel headings (with the same indention and numbering or lettering). In the following example points B and C are more specific than point A, not equally general, so they should be subheadings 1 and 2 under it.

    A. The five towers
    B. Fortress-like appearance
    C. Dark shapes turning in on themselves

4. All subdivided headings in the outline break into at least two parts because a topic cannot logically be divided into only one part. The following example violates this principle.

    B. Scale unrelated to city
       1. Architecture in an unrelated style

Any single subdivision should be combined with the heading above it (as the example is in part IIIB of Lucas's outline), matched with another subdivision that is missing, or rechecked for its relevance to the heading that precedes it.

5. All headings are expressed in parallel grammatical form. Lucas's is a topic outline, in which each heading consists of a noun plus modifiers. In a sentence outline all headings are expressed as full sentences (see 36e and pp. 608–09 for discussion and an example). Compare the mixture of forms at the top of the next page with section IIA of Lucas's actual outline.

PURPOSE OUTLINES

Some students have trouble maintaining unity of purpose and coherent organization even after they have outlined an essay because the outline describes the content of the essay but does not indicate the function of each part. To help students overcome this problem, ask them to add a statement of purpose to each major section of their outlines and to indicate how the section will carry out the purpose of the paper, as in this example:

> In this section I plan to explain how much money industries lose by failing to treat industrial waste to recover precious metals like chromium, gold, silver, and platinum. This will be the second of the three little-known costs of pollution that my thesis statement promises the paper will discuss.

Statements of purpose can alert students to potential problems in the organization or unity of an essay, and they can provide instructors with a quick way to spot the problems. Some instructors even ask students to submit "purpose outlines" in place of formal outlines:

> In this section of the paper, I plan to show that there is a real need for this university to provide more funds for the library. To support my point, I plan to explore three serious effects of underfunding—lack of basic reference materials, lack of staff to shelve books properly and check for missing volumes, and poor maintenance of the library building.

SAMPLE ANSWERS: EXERCISE 18

1. A block party, seen from above: the activity and bright colors of the scene as a whole; gatherings of people on the doorsteps lining the street; children playing games in the street; in the center, people buzzing around the barbecues where food is being prepared.
2. First, an objective view of those left behind; second, a gradual fading of the earthly world; third, an expanding

   A. The five towers
     1. Fortress-like
     2. Dark shapes turn in on themselves.

6. The outline covers only the body of the essay, omitting the introduction and the conclusion. The beginning and the ending are important in the essay itself, but you need not include them in the outline unless you are required to do so or anticipate special problems with their organization.

3   Checking for unity and coherence

In conceiving your organization, devising and checking your outline, and writing your essay, you should be aware of two qualities of effective writing that relate to organization: unity and coherence. An essay has **unity** if all its parts support the thesis sentence and relate to each other. It has **coherence** if readers can see the relations and move easily from one thought to the next. A unified and coherent outline will not necessarily guide you to a unified and coherent essay. Much depends on how you specify connections in sentences and paragraphs, and the very process of specifying connections may lead you to see different relations and arrangements from those suggested by the outline. Still, checking your outline for unity and coherence will help you spot and solve obvious problems and thus perhaps avoid unnecessary distractions during drafting.

To check your outline for unity, ask whether each primary division is relevant to the thesis sentence and whether, within major sections of the outline, each example or detail supports the main idea of that section. Don't be too hard on your information at this stage: you may find a way to use an apparently wayward idea or example while drafting. But do cut anything that is clearly irrelevant and likely to sidetrack you during drafting.

To check your outline for coherence, ask whether your arrangement of material suits both your purpose and your readers' needs and whether readers are likely to recognize the shape of your material. You may see a clear need to rearrange parts of your outline, as Pat Lucas did when she moved her analogy to the beginning of her scratch outline (see p. 44).

The unity and coherence of an essay begin in its paragraphs, so the two are treated in greater detail in Chapter 3 (see 3a and 3b).

EXERCISE 18

Choose three of the following topics and list four to six specific points for each one. Then arrange the ideas using the organizational scheme given in parentheses, unless a different scheme seems more appropriate for your material.

1. a festive or depressing place (*spatial*)
2. my view of what happens after death (*chronological or climactic*)
3. why parking facilities for commuting students should be expanded (*specific to general*)
4. ways to release frustration or tension (*illustration*)
5. the meaning of success or failure (*definition*)
6. the parts of a religious service, a ten-speed bicycle, a camera, or a baseball (*division*)
7. kinds of self-help books, students on campus, joggers, part-time jobs, or teachers (*classification*)
8. the differences or similarities between two television sitcoms, grandparents, newspapers, magazines, or cars (*comparison and contrast*)
9. the causes or effects of an accident, quitting smoking, playing a sport, or cheating (*cause-and-effect analysis*)
10. how to make a great dessert, take a photograph, make a triple play in baseball, train a dog, or study for an examination (*process analysis*)

EXERCISE 19

Revise the following outline so that it adheres to the principles of the formal outline given on pages 46–48. Use the thesis sentence as a guide to appropriate divisions in the outline.

THESIS SENTENCE

Strip-mining should be tightly controlled in this region to reduce its pollution of water resources, its permanent destruction of the land, and its devastating effects on people's lives.

FORMAL OUTLINE

I. Effects of strip-mining in this region
  A. Causes of water pollution
    1. Soil acids are leached by rainwater.
    2. Run-off of acids into streams
  B. Disappearance of fish
  C. Poisoning of water supply
  D. Appearance of hills caused by mining
    1. Scarring
    2. Vegetation is destroyed.
  E. Erosion of the land
    1. Topsoil removed
    2. Mud slides are very common.
  F. Elimination of people's forms of recreation
  G. Health problems
    1. Polluted water causes illness.

bright light from above; fourth, a brilliant, peaceful, eternal presence.

3. The occasional class missed because of inadequate parking; the frequent need to walk long distances from the remote lots; the common difficulty of wasting time hunting for a parking space; the unfairness to all commuting students in comparison with resident students.
4. Swimming laps, dancing, listening to loud music, attending movies, fighting with your roommate.
5. Failure: a personal, not societal, judgment; an opportunity lost because of inattention, laziness, or confused priorities; a prerequisite to success.
6. Parts of a ten-speed bicycle: frame, handlebars, seat, wheels, brakes, derailleur, gear shift, and cables.
7. Kinds of students: partiers, scholars, leaders, followers, wallflowers.
8. Two newspapers, serious paper versus tabloid: political versus human-interest news; liberal versus conservative bias; sedate versus loud design; no gimmicks versus frequent promotional games.
9. Causes of cheating: pressure from parents, pressure from peers, lack of self-confidence, laziness, immorality.
10. Making a triple play in baseball: the basic play, with players on first and second (second baseman or shortstop catches a line drive, steps to second base, throws to first baseman); other plays.

ANSWERS: EXERCISE 19

Possible revision (changes underlined):
I. Effects of strip-mining in this region
  A. Pollution of water resources
    1. Causes
      a. Leaching of soil acids by rainwater
      b. Run-off of acids into streams
    2. Results
      a. Disappearance of fish
      b. Poisoning of water supply

dev

1h

B. Destruction of the land
  1. Appearance of hills
    a. Scarring
    b. Destruction of vegetation
  2. Erosion
    a. Removal of topsoil
    b. Frequent mud slides
  3. Elimination of people's forms of recreation
C. Devastation of people's lives
  1. Illness from water pollution
  2. Destruction of farmland and homes
    a. Acid soil
    b. Mud slides
    c. Inadequate compensation
II. Possible controls on strip-mining
  A. Regulation of mining techniques
    1. Limitations on erosion
    2. Limitations on pollution
  B. Mandatory replacement of topsoil and restoration of vegetation
  C. Compensation for destruction of farmland and homes
    1. Cash payments
    2. Rebuilding

ANSWERS: EXERCISE 20

Individual response.

H. Destruction of people's farmland and homes
  1. Acid soil
  2. Mud slides
I. Inadequate compensation for destruction of farmland and homes
II. Possible controls on strip-mining
  A. Regulate mining techniques.
    1. To limit erosion
    2. Limitations on pollution
  B. Mining companies should be required to replace topsoil.
    1. Restore vegetation to prevent erosion
  C. Compensation for destruction of farmland and homes
    1. Cash payments
    2. Rebuilding

EXERCISE 20

Continuing from Exercise 17 (p. 38), choose an appropriate organization for your essay-in-progress. Then, to discover whether and to what extent an outline can help you plan and draft an essay, prepare a tree diagram or a scratch, informal, or formal outline, as specified by your instructor.

CHAPTER 2

Drafting and Revising the Essay

The separation of drafting and revising from the planning activities discussed in Chapter 1 is somewhat artificial because the stages almost always overlap during the writing process. But gradually for some writers, more distinctly for others, the primary goal shifts during the writing process from gathering and shaping information to forming connected sentences and paragraphs in a draft and then restructuring and rewriting the draft.

2a Writing the first draft

Just as they vary in every other part of the writing process, writers vary in the way they draft. At one extreme is the writer who essentially drafts and revises at the same time, getting each unit of thought right before going on to the next. At the other extreme is the writer who plunges on until ideas are exhausted, rarely or never stopping to reread and rewrite. Neither of these styles is preferable, nor is any style between the extremes, except as it suits the writer. But all effective drafting styles share a common characteristic: the writers do not transcribe fully formed, coherent, and polished thoughts into words but strive to find and convey their meaning through the act of writing.

Because of its uncertainties, drafting can be off-putting. Many experienced writers as well as inexperienced ones find elaborate ways of avoiding the blank page or screen: arranging shelves, changing typewriter ribbons, washing hairbrushes, napping, lunching with friends. Such procrastination may actually help you if you let ideas for writing simmer at the same time. At some point,

HIGHLIGHTS

This chapter continues the exploration, begun in Chapter 1, of writing as a flexible process and looks in detail at strategies for drafting, revising, editing, and proofreading. The journey from initial draft to finished essay may involve many decisions and changes of direction for which there are no firm rules. To alert student writers to the options available to them, the chapter provides lists of strategies for drafting an essay and checklists for revising and editing. It also provides concrete advice for the stages of composing that many writers find the most difficult: getting started and completing the initial draft.

Students who view revising as an expendable stage in the writing process may benefit from following, draft by draft, the development of Pat Lucas's essay (begun in Chapter 1) on the Renaissance Center. Like most initial efforts, Lucas's early draft can benefit from revisions in organization, content, tone, and approach to clarify the essay's purpose and the relationships among its ideas and also to make it easier for readers to share Lucas's perspective. The revised draft, in turn, needs editing for clarity, style, and correction of errors in grammar, usage, punctuation, and spelling—changes that appear in the final version of the essay, along with the instructor's corrections and comments.

Teachers who draw on the handbook in correcting and commenting on student papers may wish to direct students' attention to the instructor's corrections on Pat Lucas's full essay (pp. 68–70); these corrections use a combination of the number-and-letter codes, symbols, and written comments. To familiarize students with use of the handbook, you can assign Exercise 7,

rev
2a

which asks them to revise Lucas's essay by making use of the instructor's comments. The two additional student papers at the end of the chapter (Exercise 9) are also appropriate for class discussion and criticism. All three papers can provide material for small-group discussion and evaluation, and the section on benefiting from criticism (2e) can help students learn to work effectively in peer critique groups.

OVERCOMING WRITING BLOCKS

Many students have a hard time writing first drafts because they try to get everything right the first time. They end up writing sentences and then crossing out what they have written so often that they have no time left to revise their thoughts in a second draft. Sometimes the pressure of perfection is so great that students become blocked writers, unable to finish even a single draft before the deadline. Here are four ways to help students get started and to help them develop flexibility and self-confidence in their approach to the task:

   1. Show them copies of your own first and final drafts to indicate that you were not afraid to make mistakes in the initial draft because you had a chance to correct them in the later versions.

   2. Give students a time limit for the first draft, perhaps an hour and a half or two hours, depending on the length of the assignment. Require them to hand in the draft with the final paper so that you can see how they approached the task of writing.

   3. Have students start writing in class, where you can encourage them to get ideas down on paper before they try to perfect the wording.

   4. Require students to spend some time either jotting down ideas and phrases or freewriting so that they will be loosened up before tackling the initial draft.

RESOURCES AND IDEAS

Mike Rose, *Writer's Block: The Cognitive Dimension* (Carbondale: Southern Illinois UP, 1983). The case studies of stu-

though, enough is enough: the deadline looms; you've got to get started. If the blankness still stares back at you, then try one of the following techniques for unblocking.

WAYS TO START DRAFTING

  1. Read over what you've already written—notes, outlines, and so on—and immediately start your draft with whatever comes to mind.
  2. Freewrite. (See 1d-1.)
  3. Write scribbles or type nonsense until usable words start coming.
  4. Pretend you're writing to a friend about your topic.
  5. Conjure up an image that represents your topic—a physical object, a facial expression, two people arguing over something, a giant machine gouging the earth for a mine, whatever. Describe that image.
  6. Skip the opening and start in the middle. Or write the conclusion.
  7. Write a paragraph on what you think your essay will be about when you finish it.
  8. Using your outline, divide your essay into chunks—say, one for the introduction, another for the first example or reason, and so on. Start writing the chunk that seems most eager to be written, the one you understand best or feel most strongly about.

    You should find some momentum once you've started writing. Then, unless you already have a different drafting style that works for you, try to be as fluid as possible. A degree of spontaneity will allow your attitudes toward your topic to surface naturally in your sentences. And, more important, it will make you receptive to ideas and relationships you have not seen before. Your thesis sentence and an outline can help keep you moving by reminding you of your planned purpose, organization, and content; but they should not constrain you from exploring new ideas or even developing a new thesis if that is where your writing leads you. If you feel hampered by your preliminary materials, put them aside until you need them or use them to check your draft when you've finished it.

    To keep a draft flowing, skip over sticky spots. If you can't find the right word, leave a blank. If an idea suddenly pops up out of nowhere but doesn't seem to fit where you are in the draft, jot it down on a separate sheet of paper or write it in anyway and underline or bracket it for later attention. Periodically, you will probably need to stop and reread portions of your draft to see where you are and to recapture momentum. If this rereading turns up serious problems, you may need to resolve them before continuing or at least make marginal notes about them. But resist being too self-critical or wondering what your readers will think: there is occasion enough for that in revision. Also resist the urge to improve style, word choice, grammar, punctuation, spelling, and the like. These are not unimportant matters, but you should save them for a later draft, after you have resolved larger issues of purpose, content, and structure. Tinkering with them during the first draft may distract you from the more important issues, and the time and energy spent may be wasted because substantial additions, cuts, and rearrangements often remove old flaws and introduce new ones.

To accommodate these later changes, write or type your first draft only on one side of the paper, leave wide margins, and double- or triple-space all lines. Then you will find it easy to change words or whole sentences and to cut the draft apart and rearrange it without tedious recopying or retyping.

For a brief essay, a first draft written fairly fluidly is likely to take at least an hour or two. Set aside the time, and work in a place where you are not likely to be interrupted. If interruptions are unavoidable, as they probably will be for longer essays, jot a note before leaving the draft about what you expect to do next. Then when you return you can pick up where you left off.

Pat Lucas's first draft of her essay on the Renaissance Center appears below. She retyped the completed draft in order to have a clean copy for revision.

**rev
2a**

dent writers that Rose discusses demonstrate that blocked writers often follow rigid, absolute rules about the forms and process of writing, whereas fluent writers use flexible, enabling strategies.

Lynn Z. Bloom, "Research on Writing Blocks, Writing Anxiety, and Writing Apprehension," *Research in Composition and Rhetoric*, ed. Michael G. Moran and Ronald F. Lunsford (Westport: Greenwood, 1984), 71–91. Bloom surveys research on the fears and blocks that many writers encounter and examines strategies, similar to those presented in this chapter, for overcoming the difficulties.

First draft

Title?

Robert Sommer says that hard architecture is

opressive and impersonal.   In short, it is insensitive.

An excellent example of hard, insensitive architecture

is the Renaissance Center in Detroit because it shows a

lack of concern for the people of the city.

An insensitive building is like an insensitive

person.   Both present a cold forbidding face to the

world.   Or they turn away completely to only show their backs.   Neither shows caring or concern for their sur-roundings--for the people around them.   They do not care how they affect people.   They shut people out and show no sympathy for their feelings.

The Renaissance Center has two main parts, both of them seem deliberately intended to remind people out-side that they are insignificant as far as the builders of the building or the people inside it are concerned. The five towers look fortress-like, four tall octagonal ones surround an even taller round one in the middle and thin round elevator shafts climb up the outsides of all the towers.   The towers seem to turn in on themselves in an exclusive way whether they are round or octagons. The dark reflecting glass of the central tower reflects light. The glass of the surrounding towers is even darker, and they are covered in silver metal strips as if their wearing armor.   The fortress-like appearance of the towers, plus their reflecting or armor-like sur-faces and their darkness seem to protect the priviledged people inside from the rest of the world as if everyone outside was dirty or dangerous.

The Renaissance Center is clearly not intended to attract pedestrians from the city, only cars from else-where.   All the highways and streets seem to lead right

into the Center's parking garage.   Obviously, the
builders wanted to attract people from outside the city
and make it possible for them to get directly into the
Renaissance Center without the risk of getting lost in
the "dangerous" city or contamanating themselves by
contact with its depraved residents.   The pedestrian
from the city has a hard time even getting near the
building, since its on the other side of a many-lane
highway.   Once across this barrier, a new one presents
itself in the form of the hugh concrete base of the
building.   This base forms a high wall at street level
which has no signs or shop windows to direct pedestrian,
or attract them.   It is not even easy to find a door into
the building.   It tells anyone passing by to keep out and
further reminds them of their insignificance.

The Renaissance Center is by far the most noticable
feature on the horizon.   It stands apart from the rest of
the skyline of downtown Detroit, on the banks of the
river.   It is much higher and bulkier than any Detroit
building, and its design is also much different.   It
seems to say that its no part of old, rundown Detroit or
of the people who live there.

The irony is that the Renaissance Center was conceived as a way to give new life to a depressed city.   In
1977 when the Renaissance Center was completed, the cen-

ter of Detroit was dying of poverty and neglect.   Just about anyone with any money had long since fled to the suburbs and they rarely returned even for visits.   The remaining residents were mostly poor, and crime was a problem.

    The problem is that the Renaissance Center has done little to change all this.   Sure, more shoppers and conventioners come to the city now but the city they come to is the Renaissance Center, not Detroit.   The old city and its residents are still mostly ignored by this insensitive building.

ANSWERS: EXERCISE 1

Some significant differences between Lucas's outline and her first draft:

In paragraph 3 she has added details about the surfaces of the towers, relating the details to other points (planned in the outline) about the towers' fortress-like self-protectiveness.

In paragraph 4 she has developed the description of the building's base into a contrast between the access of drivers and that of pedestrians.

In paragraphs 6 and 7 she has added material on the irony of the building's promise versus its actual effect.

ANSWERS: EXERCISE 2

Individual response.

RESOURCES AND IDEAS

Linda Flower, "Writer-Based Prose: A Cognitive Basis for Problems in Writing," *College English* 41 (1979): 19–37. Flower argues that writers must learn to transform what they have to say from the form in which they came to understand it (writer-based prose) to the form in which readers can understand it (reader-based prose).

EXERCISE 1

Compare Lucas's draft with the last step in her planning (her formal outline) on page 46. Where has the act of drafting led her to rearrange her information, add or delete material, or explore new ideas?

EXERCISE 2

Prepare a draft of the essay you began in Chapter 1. Use your thesis sentence (Exercise 17, p. 38) and your outline (Exercise 20, p. 50) as guides, but don't be unduly constrained by them. Concentrate on opening up options, not on closing them down.

2b   Revising the first draft

Revision literally means "re-seeing"—looking anew at ideas and details, their relationships and arrangement, the degree to which they work or don't work for the thesis. While drafting, you have been focused inwardly, concentrating on pulling your topic out of yourself. In revising, you look out to your readers, trying to anticipate how they will see your work. You examine your draft as a pole-vaulter or dancer would examine a videotape of his or her performance, or as you might examine a photograph of yourself.

Obtaining the needed distance for revision can be difficult, even for experienced writers. Here are three techniques that may help you:

1. Take a break after finishing the draft to pursue some other activity. A few hours may be enough; a whole night or day is preferable. The break will clear your mind, relax you, and give you some objectivity.
2. Ask someone to read and react to your draft. Many writing instructors ask their students to submit their first drafts so that the instructors and, often, the other members of the class can serve as an actual audience to help guide revision. (See also 2e on benefiting from criticism.)
3. Outline your draft. A formal outline, especially, with its careful structure and many possible levels of detail, can show where organization is illogical or support is skimpy. (See 1h-2 for a discussion of outlining.)

Strictly speaking, revision includes editing—refining the manner of expression to improve clarity or style or to correct errors. In this chapter, though, revision and editing are treated separately to stress their differences: in revision you deal with the underlying meaning and structure of your essay; in editing you deal with its surface. Often it is tempting to skip the fundamental work of revision and move directly to editing the first draft. But the resulting essay, though perhaps superficially correct, may not show you at your best and may be flawed in ways that will negatively affect readers' responses. You can avoid the temptation to substitute editing for revision and prevent them from interfering with each other by making at least two separate drafts beyond the first: a revised one and then an edited one (p. 63).

Set aside at least as much time to revise your essay as you took to draft it. Plan on going through the draft several times to answer the questions in the checklist on the next page and to resolve any problems. (If you need additional information on any of the topics in the checklist, refer to the handbook sections given in parentheses.) Note that the checklist can also help you if you have been asked to comment on another writer's draft.

A note on titling your essay

One operation that could fall either with revision or with editing—could in fact occur at any time during the writing process—is titling your essay. Sometimes a title may be obvious as soon as your topic is clear to you. At other times you may find yourself straining for a title when everything else is finished to

REVISING ACTIVITIES

Here are a few revising activities for students working on their own or in groups:

Making out an inventory. After students have written an initial draft, ask them to complete a brief version of the audience inventory described in Chapter 1 (page 27). Their completed inventory can help guide the choices they make during revision. Students may wish to share drafts and inventories with other students.

Using dialogue. For narrative writing, ask students to circle every use of "He said that" and "She thought that" or similar phrases in their own or someone else's paper. Then ask them to consider replacing the indirect discourse with dialogue and direct quotations to make the writing more vivid and realistic.

Using the senses. For narrative and descriptive writing, ask students to check how many of the senses they have drawn on; then ask them to consider making use of the other senses.

Adding other arguments. For argumentative essays, have students list all the arguments they could use but have not yet included in the paper; they may wish to turn to other students for advice about including these arguments.

Soliciting class suggestions. For argumentative essays, ask students to summarize their theses and supporting arguments for their classmates. Then ask the other students to suggest more supporting arguments and opposing arguments the writer might consider during revision.

Answering more questions. For expository essays, ask students to answer these questions for their own or someone else's paper: What five things do you know about this topic that are not included in the draft? Which ones could be put into the essay without harming its unity or coherence? What three things are readers most likely to find interesting, useful, or surprising about this topic? Could these three things be given more emphasis without disrupting the organization or clarity of the essay?

RESOURCES AND IDEAS

Peter Elbow, *Writing with Power: Techniques for Mastering the Writing Process.* New York: Oxford UP, 1981. Elbow's book offers detailed, practical, and often innovative advice on drafting, revising, shaping for an audience, and making use of feedback, including several chapters on revising ("Quick Revising," "Thorough Revising," "Revising with Feedback," and "Cut and Paste Revising and the Collage").

Nancy Sommers, "Revising Strategies of Student Writers and Experienced Adult Writers," *College Composition and Communication* 31 (1980): 378–88. According to Sommers, students see revision as changes in small units—words and sentences. Experienced writers see it as a recursive process directed at larger units of the text and the meaning it conveys.

P. C. Wason, "Specific Thoughts on the Writing Process," *Cognitive Processes in Writing*, ed. Lee W. Gregg and Erwin R. Steinberg (Hillsdale: Erlbaum, 1980), 129–37. Wason argues that multiple drafts are often necessary because writing consists of two processes hard to undertake at the same time: saying (or discovering) something and saying it correctly.

RESOURCES AND IDEAS

Mike Rose, "Writing Around Rules," in *Patterns in Action*, 2nd ed., ed. Robert A. Schwegler (Glenview: Scott, 1988), 473–80. As an illustration of the kinds of rules that block writing and the kinds of strategies that enable it, Rose tells of the difficulties he encountered in titling a poem.

RESOURCES AND IDEAS

Peer editing and collaborative learning have become regular features of many composition courses over the past decade, and these approaches are particularly well suited to drafting and revising activities. The essay "Using Collaborative Learning with the

---

CHECKLIST FOR REVISION

1. Does the body of the essay carry out the purpose and central idea expressed by the thesis sentence (1c, 1g)? Is the reason for writing apparent, not only in the thesis sentence but throughout the essay (1f)? If the body of the essay does not carry out the thesis sentence, is the problem more with the thesis sentence (because it does not reflect a new and better direction in the draft) or with the body (because it wanders)?
2. Are there adequate details, examples, or reasons to support each of the ideas (1d)? Will (or do) readers need more information at any point to understand the meaning or appreciate the point of view (1f)?
3. Is the essay unified (1h-3)? Does each paragraph and sentence relate clearly to the thesis sentence?
4. Is the essay coherent (1h-3)? Are the relationships within and among its parts apparent? Will (or can) readers see the shape of the essay, its overall organization?
5. Does the tone of the writing convey a clear and appropriate attitude toward the topic and convey the role assumed (1g-2)? Is the tone appropriate for the purpose and audience? Is it consistent throughout the essay?
6. Is each paragraph in the body unified (3a), coherent (3b), and well developed (3c)?
7. Does the title state or hint at the essay's scope and approach (see previous page)? Will (or does) the introduction engage and focus readers' attention (3c-1)? Will (or does) the conclusion provide readers with a sense of completion (3c-2)?

---

your satisfaction. If you haven't considered a title before, though, the revision stage is a good time to do so because attempting to sum up your essay in a phrase can focus your attention sharply on your topic, purpose, and audience.

Here are some suggestions for titling an essay:

1. A **descriptive title** is almost always appropriate and is often expected for academic writing. It announces the topic clearly, accurately, and as briefly as possible. For Pat Lucas's essay, "The Renaissance Center as Hard Architecture" would be such a title. Other examples: "Images of Lost Identity in *North by Northwest*"; "An Experiment in Small-Group Dynamics"; "Why Lincoln Delayed Emancipating the Slaves."
2. A **suggestive title**—the kind often found in popular magazines—may be appropriate for more informal writing. The title Lucas finally chose, "Towering Insensitivity," conveys her attitude and her main concern but not her precise

topic, thereby pulling readers into the essay to learn more. A source for such a title may be a familiar phrase (as in Lucas's title), a fresh image, or a significant expression from the essay itself.

3. A title tells readers how big the topic is. For Pat Lucas's essay, the title "Hard Architecture" or "Insensitivity" would be deceptively broad, whereas "Access to the Renaissance Center" or "Do Not Enter" would be deceptively narrow.
4. A title should not restate the assignment or the thesis sentence, as in "Why the Renaissance Center Illustrates Robert Sommer's Ideas on Hard Architecture."

For more information on essay titles, see 12c-4 (avoiding reference to the title in the opening of the paper), 26b (capitalizing words in a title), and Appendix A2-d (the format of a title in the final paper).

When Pat Lucas returned to her first draft after half a day, questions like those in the revision checklist revealed several problems. Though she felt that the purpose and main idea expressed in her thesis sentence had held up well throughout the draft, she was aware of giving little consideration to her readers' needs. Lucas had earlier decided that an audience of her classmates might not share her attitudes toward architecture and probably would know nothing of the Renaissance Center. Yet, as happens to most writers in the press of drafting, Lucas's own need to get her ideas down had taken precedence over her sense of her readers' needs.

In revising her draft, Lucas made many changes directly on the copy, but she also inserted a rewritten introduction and a new second paragraph, and she changed the position of one paragraph. Her revision begins on the next page. The principal changes are explained below and keyed to the revision by numbers.

1. With a suggestive title, Lucas hoped to signal her feelings and engage readers without giving the whole essay away.
2. Lucas rewrote and expanded the previous abrupt introduction to grab readers' attention and show them how her concerns related to their experiences.
3. Lucas wove a shortened version of her analogy into the revised introduction. She felt the previous longer version (second paragraph of draft) interrupted the flow from the introduction to the first descriptive paragraph.
4. In a new paragraph Lucas described the building in detail so that readers would have a clear mental picture of it. The addition allowed her to cut some description from later paragraphs.

rev

2b

Handbook" at the beginning of this annotated edition offers detailed advice about designing collaborative activities and preparing students to work in groups. It also provides sample reader response forms, which you may wish to copy and use in your class.

Much has been written recently about collaborative learning and peer writing groups. Two recent selections, however, offer good starting points for someone interested in examining both the opportunities offered by this approach and the controversies that it has created:

John Trimbur, "Collaborative Learning and Teaching Writing," *Perspectives on Research and Scholarship in Composition*, ed. Ben W. McClelland and Timothy R. Donovan (New York: MLA, 1985), 87–109. Trimbur offers a compact survey of the history and theories behind collaborative learning and raises important questions about the roles of response and evaluation in a student- (rather than teacher-) centered classroom.

Anne Ruggles Gere, *Writing Groups: History, Theory, and Implications* (Carbondale: Southern Illinois UP, 1987). Gere reviews the history, theory, and practice of writing groups and collaborative learning; she also provides a useful annotated bibliography of research and pedagogy.

RESOURCES AND IDEAS

Even though you encourage students to revise and offer them detailed advice about what and when to revise, you may still find that their revisions are limited to superficial changes. Part of the problem may be that students have not yet become good enough readers of their own texts to identify features that might be altered or dropped and to identify places where something might be added. Here are some resources for helping students to become active readers and writers, aware of what they have written and how it might be changed:

James P. Beck, "Asking Students to Annotate Their Own Papers," *College Composition and Communication* 38 (1982): 322–23. Beck asks students to identify specific techniques they have used in their writing (including features of structure, detail, argument, and style) and to evaluate how well they have used those techniques.

Richard M. Coe and Kris D. Gutierrez, "Using Problem-Solving Procedures and Process Analysis to Help Students with Writing Problems," *College Composition and Communication* 32 (1981): 262–71. Coe and Gutierrez offer assignments and activities designed to make students aware of how they go about writing, to help them understand their strengths and weaknesses as writers, and to give them greater control over their composing processes.

Douglas R. Butturff and Nancy I. Sommers, "Placing Revision in a Reinvented Rhetorical Tradition," *Reinventing the Rhetorical Tradition*, ed. Aviva Freedman and Ian Pringle (Conway: L & S Books, 1980), 99–104. The authors argue that the comments instructors make on papers should help students learn writing procedures that will enable them to make effective revisions.

5. Lucas reversed two paragraphs to achieve a clearer movement in space: from close up to middle distance (paragraph being moved) to farthest distance. She also began each paragraph with a phrase indicating the observer's position ("From close up," "Seen from a somewhat greater distance," "From afar").

6. Lucas judged that her tone in several spots was too hostile to help readers identify with her feelings. She cut these passages.

7. The discussion of auto access to the building was irrelevant to the pedestrian's experience—the main point of the paragraph—so Lucas cut the digression.

8. Lucas had not planned her conclusion on the irony of the building's intended and actual effect on Detroit, but she found it worked well. It would work better, she thought, if the two paragraphs were condensed into one tight paragraph.

Revised first draft

~~Title?~~ Towering Insensitivity 1

Everyone knows what its like walking below modern skyscrapers. 2 The skyscrapers may seem beautiful at first, or even awesome, but as they get familiar they begin to seem boring in their sameness or their gigantic bulk seems overwelming. The essay by Sommer entitled "Hard Architecture" gives some idea of why modern skyscrapers affect a person in this particular way. Sommer says that many modern structures are opressive and impersonal, the builders seem to care little for the people who must use them or live with them. Like an 3 insensitive person, a building can also be insensitive - cold, remote and uncaring. An excellent example of insensitive architecture is the Renaissance Center in Detroit because it shows a lack of concern for the people of the city.

The Renaissance Center consists of five towers sitting on a massive concrete base that rises two stories from the street. Four of the 4 towers are octagonal and covered in strips of silver metal over dark glass. The fifth tower is taller than the others and round and completely covered in glass. Thin round elevator shafts climb up the outsides of all the towers. The four octagonal towers surround the round one. The Center stands apart from Detroit's older downtown area on the banks of the Detroit river. Visible from miles around, the most noticable thing in the city skyline.

Seen from a somewhat greater distance, the five towers also
~~The Renaissance Center has two main parts, both of~~   5
send messages to outsiders.
~~them seem deliberately intended to remind people out-~~   6

~~side that they are insignificant as far as the builders~~

~~of the building or the people inside it are concerned.~~

The ~~five~~ towers look fortress-like, *with the* four ~~tall~~ octagonal
appearing to guard the   *central*
ones surround an even taller round one ~~in the middle and~~

~~thin round elevator shafts climb up the outsides of all~~

~~the towers.~~   The towers seem to turn in on themselves in

an exclusive way ~~whether they are round or octagons.~~

The dark ~~reflecting~~ glass of the central tower reflects *all*
black and silver stripped exterior of the
light. The ~~glass of the surrounding towers is even~~
outer towers makes them look like
~~darker, and they are covered in silver metal strips as if~~

their wearing armor.   ~~The fortress-like appearance of~~

~~the towers, plus their reflecting or armor-like sur-~~

~~faces and their darkness seem to protect the priviledged~~

~~people inside from the rest of the world as if everyone~~   6

~~outside was dirty or dangerous.~~

put on next page

From close up   *seems deliberately*
The Renaissance Center ~~is clearly not~~ intended to
remind anyone outside of their insignificance.
~~attract pedestrians from the city, only cars from else-~~   7

~~where.   All the highways and streets seem to lead right~~

~~into the Center's parking garage.   Obviously, the~~

~~builders wanted to attract people from outside the city~~

~~and make it possible for them to get directly into the~~

~~Renaissance Center without the risk of getting lost in~~

~~the "dangerous" city or contamanating themselves by~~

next page

contact with its depraved residents.   The pedestrian   6

A person trying
~~from the city has a hard time even getting near the~~
to approach the building on foot from the city must cross
~~building, since its on the other side of~~ a many-lane
Then once at the foot of the building they are
highway.   ~~Once across this barrier, a new one presents~~
confronted by a new barrier,   *wall of the*
~~itself in the form of~~ the ~~hugh~~ concrete base ~~of the~~
It rises two stories from the
~~building.~~ This base forms a high wall at street ~~level~~
It contains
~~which has~~ no signs or shop windows to direct *the* pedestrian,
                                  does   *have an obvious*   *for the*
or attract ~~them.~~ It ~~is not even~~ ~~easy to find~~ a door ~~into~~
pedestrian to enter by; *delivers a clear message to anyone who*
~~the building.~~ It ~~tells anyone passing by to keep out and~~
is foolish enough or so poor that they must travel on foot
~~further reminds them of their insignificance.~~ *"keep out. Do not enter."*

From afar   *seems insensitive*
The Renaissance Center ~~is by far the most no-~~
not just to the residents of Detroit but also their city.
~~ticeable feature on the horizon.~~   It stands apart from

the rest of the skyline of downtown Detroit/. ~~on the banks~~

~~of the river.~~   It is much higher and bulkier than any De-
does not show even a slight resemblance to the designs of
the city's older buildings
troit building, and ~~its design is also much different.~~
The Renaissance Center clearly wants to say that
~~It seems to say that~~ its no part of old, rundown Detroit

or of the people who live there.

The irony is that the Renaissance Center was   8

conceived as a way to give new life to a depressed
the victim of poverty and neglect. Since
city/, ~~In 1977 when~~ the ~~Renaissance~~ Center was com-
in 1977, it did succeed in attracting business people,
pleted/, ~~the center of Detroit was dying of poverty~~
conventioners, tourists, and shoppers.
~~and neglect.   Just about anyone with any money had~~

~~long since fled to the suburbs and they rarely re-~~

~~turned even for visits.   The remaining residents~~

~~were mostly poor, and crime was a problem.~~

insert from previous page

next page

~~The problem is that the Renaissance Center has done little to change all this.~~ ~~Sure, more shoppers and con-~~ ~~ventioners come to the city now~~ ß *these people* but ~~the city they~~ come to ~~is~~ the Renaissance Center, not ^*to* Detroit. *The builders did* ~~The old city~~ *not care about involving the old city,* ~~and its residents~~ ~~are still mostly ignored by this in-~~ *in their own rebirth, and they built a new city to shut* ~~sensitive building.~~ *out the old.*

EXERCISE 3

Compare Lucas's revised draft with her first draft on pages 53–56. Based on the discussion of her intentions for revision (pp. 59–60), can you see the reasons for most of Lucas's changes? Do you think she identified and solved all the significant problems in her first draft? If not, where would you suggest further revisions, and why?

EXERCISE 4

Revise your own first draft from Exercise 2 (p. 56). Use the checklist for revision on page 58 as a guide. Concentrate on purpose, content, and organization, leaving smaller problems for the next draft.

ANSWERS: EXERCISE 3
Answers will vary.

ANSWERS: EXERCISE 4
Individual response.

2c   Editing the second draft

Editing for style, sense, and correctness may come second to more fundamental revision, but it is far from unimportant. A carefully developed, interesting essay will still affect readers negatively if the writer appears oblivious to or careless about awkwardness, repetition, incorrect grammar, misleading punctuation, misused or misspelled words, and similar problems.

When you have revised your first draft, recopy, retype, or print out the revision so that you can read it easily and have plenty of room for changes. Then as you read the new draft, try to imagine yourself encountering it for the first time, as a reader will. The responses of a friend or relative can help you gain this perspective, as can the comments of your writing instructor and classmates if you share your work in class. Or you can read the draft aloud, perhaps into a tape recorder, listening for awkward rhythms, repetitive sentence patterns, and missing or clumsy transitions. When reading aloud or silently, be careful to read what you actually see on the page, not what you may have intended to write but didn't.

In your editing, work for clarity and a smooth movement among sentences as well as for correctness. Use the questions in the following checklist to guide your editing. (As in the earlier revision checklist, chapter numbers in parentheses indicate where you can look in the handbook for more information.) Note that the checklist may also serve as a guide if you are commenting on another writer's paper.

CHECKLIST FOR EDITING

1. Are the sentences grammatical? Do they avoid errors in case (6), verb form (7), agreement (8), and adjectives and adverbs (9)?
2. Are the sentences clear? Do they avoid sentence fragments (10), comma splices and fused sentences (11), errors in pronoun reference (12), shifts (13), misplaced or dangling modifiers (14), and mixed or incomplete constructions (15)?
3. Are the sentences effective? Do they use subordination and coordination (16) and parallelism (17) appropriately? Are they emphatic (18) and varied (19)?
4. Is the use of commas, semicolons, colons, periods, and other punctuation correct (20–25)?
5. Are the sentences mechanically correct in the use of capitals, italics, abbreviations, numbers, and hyphens (26–30)?
6. Does diction conform to standard usage (31a)? Are the denotations and connotations of words clear and appropriate, and does the writing avoid triteness (31b)? Is the writing concise (31c)?
7. Are the words spelled correctly (34)?

In response to these questions and her own sense of clarity and effectiveness, Pat Lucas edited the second draft of her essay as follows.

Edited second draft

Towering Insensitivity

~~Everyone knows what it's like~~ walking below modern
anyone who has spent any time in a city knows the feeling of

skyscrapers. The skyscrapers may seem beautiful at

first, ~~or~~ even awesome, but as they get familiar they be-
and

1 Reprinted in Marcia Stubbs and Sylvan Barnet, eds., The Little, Brown reader, 5th ed. (Boston: Scott, 1989) 187-201.

gin to seem boring in their sameness or their gigantic
bulk seems overwhelming. The essay by Robert Sommer entitled
"Hard Architecture"[1] gives some idea of why modern skyscrapers affect a person in this particular way. Sommer
says that many modern structures are oppressive and impersonal, the builders seem to care little for the peo-
ple who must use them or live with them as permanent features of their environment. ~~Like an insensitive person, a building can also be insensitive--~~
A hard building is thus insensitive in the same way a person can be insensitive:
cold, remote, and uncaring. An excellent example of insensitive architecture is the Renaissance Center in Detroit because it shows a lack of concern for the people
of the city.

The Renaissance Center is a cluster ~~consists~~ of five towers
sitting on a massive concrete base ~~that rises two stories from the street~~. Four of the towers are octagonal
and are covered in strips of silver metal over dark glass.
They surround an even ~~The fifth tower is~~ taller tower that is ~~than the others and~~ round and
completely covered in glass. Thin round elevator
shafts climb up the outsides of all five ~~the~~ towers. ~~The four
octagonal towers surround the round one~~. The Center
stands apart from Detroit's older downtown area, along ~~on the~~
banks of the Detroit river. It is Visible from miles around,
the most noticeable feature of ~~thing in~~ the city skyline.

From close up, the Renaissance Center seems deliberately intended to remind anyone outside of their insignifi-

in the grand designs of the builders.

cance. A person trying to approach the building on foot

from the city must cross a ~~many-lane~~ *multilane* highway.   Then once

at the ~~foot~~ *bottom* of the building ~~they are~~ *the pedestrian is* confronted with a

new barrier, the concrete wall of the base.   ~~This wall~~ *It*

rises two stories from the street.   It contains no signs

or shop windows to direct or attract the pedestrian; it

does not even have an obvious door for the pedestrian to

enter by. It delivers a clear message to any one ~~who is~~

foolish ~~enough~~ or ~~so~~ poor ~~that they must travel~~ *enough to be traveling* on foot:

"Keep out. Do not enter. "

Seen from a somewhat greater distance, the five

towers also send messages to outsiders.   The towers ~~look~~ *are*

fortress-like, with the four ~~octagonal~~ *outer* ones appearing

to guard the ~~round~~ central one.   The towers seem to turn

in on themselves in an exclusive way.   The dark *bronze* glass of

the central tower reflects all light.   The black and

silver stripped exterior of the outer towers makes them

look like ~~their~~ *they are* wearing armor.

From afar, the Renaissance Center seems insensi-

tive not just to the residents of Detroit but also their

city. ~~It~~ *The Center* stands apart from the rest of the *downtown* skyline. ~~of~~

~~downtown Detroit.~~   It is much ~~higher and bulkier~~ *larger, both in height and bulk,* than any

other Detroit building; and does not ~~show~~ *echo* even ~~a~~ slight*ly* ~~resem-~~

~~blance to~~ the designs of the city's older *stone and brick* buildings.   The

Renaissance Center clearly wants to say that its no part

of old, rundown Detroit or of the people who live there.

The irony is that the Renaissance Center was con-

ceived as a way to give new life to a depressed ~~city~~ *city* ~~by the~~

neglect and

~~victim of~~ poverty ~~and neglect~~   Since the Center was

has   *ed*

completed in 1977, it ~~did~~ succeed in attracting business

e

people, conventioners, tourists, and shoppers.   But

these people come to the Renaissance Center, not to De-

Apparently,

troit. The builders did not care about involving the

so

old city and its residents in their own rebirth, and they

constructed   insensitive

~~built~~ a new city to shut out the old.

EXERCISE 5

Use the checklist for editing (p. 64) and your own sense of your essay's needs to edit the revised draft you prepared in Exercise 4 (p. 63).

ANSWERS: EXERCISE 5

Individual response.

2d   Proofreading and submitting the final draft

After editing your essay, recopy, retype, or print it once more for submission to your instructor. Follow the guidelines in Appendix A or the wishes of your instructor for an appropriate manuscript form. Be sure to proofread the final essay several times to spot and correct errors. To increase the accuracy of your proofreading, you may need to experiment with ways to keep yourself from relaxing into the rhythm of your prose. Try reading the paper aloud and very slowly, distinctly pronouncing exactly what you see. Or try placing a ruler under each line as you read it. Or try reading the essay backward, beginning with the last sentence and moving toward the beginning, examining each sentence as a separate unit. This last technique will help keep the content of your writing from distracting you in your search for errors.

Pat Lucas's final essay, along with her instructor's comments, appears below. The instructor points out the strengths he sees in the essay as well as the flaws remaining in it. He uses a combination of written comments, correction symbols (from inside the front cover of this handbook), and correction codes (from inside the back cover).

RESOURCES AND IDEAS

Jeanette Harris, "Proofreading: A Reading/Writing Skill," *College Composition and Communication* 38 (December 1987): 464–66. Harris argues that proofreading is a reading skill, a process of looking at each word and punctuation mark rather than of paying attention to the meaning of the text; and she suggests teaching students strategies like those outlined in this chapter—using a pointer (finger, pencil), reading aloud, reading in reverse order, and letting time elapse between writing and proofreading—in order to develop the specialized skill of proofreading.

Final draft with instructor's comments

Towering Insensitivity

Anyone who has spent any time in a city knows the
feeling of walking below modern skyscrapers. The skyscrapers may seem beautiful and even awesome at first,
but as they get familiar they begin to seem <u>boring in</u>
<u>their sameness</u> or <u>their gigantic bulk seems overwhelm-</u>

// <u>ing</u>. The essay by Robert Sommer entitled "Hard
Architecture"[1] gives some idea of why modern skyscrapers
affect a person this way. Sommer says that many
structures are oppressive and impersonal⌢ the builders   CS
seem to care little for the people who must use(them) or
live with(them) as permanent features of (their) environment. A hard building is thus insensitive in the same way
a person can be insensitive: cold, remote, uncaring. An
excellent example of insensitive architecture is the
Renaissance Center in Detroit because it shows a lack of
concern for the people of the city.

*Ref
(could be
clearer what
these pronouns
refer to)*

Good analogy.
*An It's
yours, not
Sommer's,
right? You
need
to make that
clearer.*

The Renaissance Center is a cluster of five towers
sitting on a massive concrete base. Four of the towers
are octagonal and are covered in strips of silver metal
over dark glass. They surround an even taller tower
that is round and completely covered in glass. Thin

[1] Reprinted in Marcia Stubbs and Sylvan Barnet,
eds., <u>The Little, Brown Reader</u>, 5th ed. (Boston: Scott,
1989) 187-201.

round elevator shafts climb up the outsides of all five

towers.   The Center stands apart from Detroit's older

downtown area, along the banks of the Detroit (r)iver.   It *26d*

is visible from miles around, the most noti(cab)le feature *sp*

of the city skyline.

From close up, the Renaissance Center seems delib-

erately intended to remind <u>anyone</u> outside of <u>their</u> in- *8b*

significance in the grand designs of the builders.   A

person trying to approach the building on foot from the

city must cross a multilane highway.   Then once at the

bottom of the building the pedestrian is confronted with

a new barrier, the concrete wall of the base.   <u>It</u> rises two *More varied*

sentences

stories from the street.   <u>It</u> contains no signs or shop *would make*

this ¶

windows to direct or attract the pedestrian.   <u>It</u> does *more*

readable –

not even have an obvious door for the pedestrian to enter *see 19b*

by.   <u>It</u> delivers a clear message to anyone foolish or poor

enough to be traveling on foot: "Keep out. Do not enter."

Seen from a somewhat greater distance, the five

towers also send messages to outsiders.   The towers are

fortress-like, with the four outer ones appearing to

guard the central one.   The towers seem to turn in on

themselves <u>in an exclusive way.</u>   The dark bronze glass *meaning?*

of the central tower <u>reflects all light.</u>   The black and *significance*

of this

detail for

silver-stripped exterior of the outer towers makes them *your*

thesis?

see *as if*

16c look (like) they are wearing armor. *This ¶ is not as well*

developed as the others. See 3c.

From afar, the Renaissance Center seems insensi-

rev
2d

ANSWERS: EXERCISE 6

The Renaissance Center in Detroit originally contained 340,000 square feet of stores, but many retailers have left because business has not been good. Some storefronts stand empty, and others have been converted into offices. The empty and converted storefronts and the unpopulated walkways mirror the city outside. Instead of reviving the city as it was intended to do, the Center has lost over $200 million itself since its construction.

ANSWERS: EXERCISE 7

Possible revisions of Lucas's essay:

Paragraph 1

Sentence 2: ". . . boring in their sameness or overwhelming in their gigantic bulk."

Sentence 4: ". . . many modern structures are oppressive and impersonal; the builders seem to care little for the people who must use the structures or live with them as permanent features of their environment."

Sentence 5: "Extending Sommer's ideas, one can see a hard building as insensitive in the same way a person may be insensitive: cold, remote, uncaring."

Paragraph 2

Sentence 4: "Detroit River"
Sentence 5: "noticeable"

Paragraph 3

Sentence 1: ". . . deliberately intended to remind all those outside of their insignificance . . ."

Sentences 4–7: "Rising two stories from the street, the wall contains no signs or shop windows. . . . Nor does it have an obvious door for the pedestrian to enter by. The wall delivers a clear message. . . ."

tive not just to the residents of Detroit but also their

// city. The Center stands apart from the rest of the downtown skyline. It is much larger, both in height and

// bulk, than any other Detroit building. And it does not echo even slightly the designs of the city's older stone and brick buildings. The Renaissance Center clearly

wants to say that its no part of old, rundown Detroit or ~hyph~

of the people who live there.

The irony is that the Renaissance Center was conceived as a way to give new life to a city depressed by neglect and poverty. Since the Center was completed in 1977, it has succeeded in attracting business people, conventioneers, tourists, and shoppers. But these people come to the Renaissance Center, not to Detroit. Apparently, the builders did not care about involving the old *very effective conclusion*

city and its residents in their own rebirth, and so they

21f (comma)

constructed a new insensitive city to shut out the old.

Your example of the Renaissance Center extends Sommer's ideas very effectively. His essay obviously touched a nerve in you, and you convey your impressions well. I like your second paragraph and your spatial organization: they give me a clear sense of what the building looks like.

In revising, see what you can do to develop and clarify the details of the fourth ¶. Also correct the errors noted. Reading Chapter 17 on parallelism could help you avoid faulty parallelism (¶s 1, 5) in your future work.

EXERCISE 6

Proofread the following passage, using any of the techniques discussed on p. 67 to bring errors into the foreground. There are ten errors in the passage: missing and misspelled words, typographical errors, and the like. If you are in doubt about any spellings, consult a dictionary.

The Renaisance Center in Detroit orignally contained 340,000 square feet stores, but many retailers have left becuase business has not been good. Some storefronts stand empty, and other have been converted into offices. The empty and converted storefronts an the unpopulatd walkways mirror the city outside Instead of reviving city as it was intended to do, the Center has lost over $200 million itself since its construction.

EXERCISE 7

To become familiar with the symbols and codes of this handbook, revise Lucas's essay wherever her instructor has used a symbol or code to mark a problem.

EXERCISE 8

Prepare the final draft of the essay you have been working on throughout Chapters 1 and 2. Proofread carefully and correct all errors before submitting your essay for review.

2e Benefiting from criticism

Almost all the writing you do in college will generate responses from an instructor. In writing courses you may submit early drafts as well as your final paper, and your readers may include your classmates as well as your instructor. In any case your readers will act as counselors and editors to help you see both virtues and flaws in your work and to sharpen your awareness of readers' needs. Listen closely to what they say, and try not to become defensive. Repeated practice in working from ideas to essay, along with information on the writing process offered by your instructor and classmates, can help you become a more efficient writer. Attentive responses to the comments of critical readers can help you become a more capable writer.

To increase the benefit from readers' comments, always consider them seriously and, if they seem appropriate, revise your work in response to them, whether or not you are required to do so. Consult your instructor, a classmate, or the appropriate sections of the handbook if you need additional help. (See "Using This Book," p. vii, for a guide to the handbook.) In addition, keep track of problems that recur in your work so that you can give them special attention in revisions and new essays. In this way your learning on one assignment will inform your work on the next one.

One device for tracking recurring problems is a chart like the

rev
2e

Paragraph 4

Sentence 3: "The towers seem to turn in on themselves, <u>excluding everything outside, protecting everything inside. This self-protectiveness is conveyed in the surfaces of the towers as well.</u> The dark bronze glass of the central tower reflects all light<u>, creating a shield that seems to deny intrusion from outside.</u> The black and silver-stripped exterior of the outer towers makes them look <u>as if</u> they are wearing armor."

Paragraph 5

Sentence 1: ". . . seems insensitive not just to the residents of Detroit but also <u>to</u> their city."
Sentence 3: "It is much larger, both in height and <u>in</u> bulk, than any other Detroit building."
Sentence 5: "it<u>'</u>s"; "run<u>-</u>down"

Paragraph 6

Sentence 5: "a new_, insensitive city"

ANSWERS: EXERCISE 8

Individual response.

RESOURCES AND IDEAS

Criticism that is given in a helpful and careful manner is perhaps the easiest kind of criticism to benefit from. The essay "Using Collaborative Learning with the Handbook" at the beginning of this annotated edition contains a detailed section on "Preparing Students to Provide Peer Criticism." You may wish to draw on this discussion as a way of helping your students learn how to benefit from criticism and learn how to offer their classmates advice that can lead to real improvements in expression.

one on the next page, with a vertical column for each assignment (or draft) and a horizontal row for each of the weaknesses that others and you yourself note on your essays. The handbook section is noted for each problem, and check marks in the boxes indicate how often the problem occurred in each essay.

	Assignment			
Problems	1	2	3	4
not enough details for readers (1f)	✓	✓		✓
unity—wanders away from thesis (1h)	✓			
parallelism (17)	✓✓	✓	✓	
agreement (8a)	✓		✓	✓
comma splice (11)	✓✓	✓	✓	

The chart also provides a convenient place to keep track of words you misspell so that you can master their spellings.

ANSWERS: EXERCISE 9

The numbers below match the question numbers in the exercise instruction. (Note that the ways of linking paragraphs in both essays are analyzed in the answer to Chapter 3, Exercise 19.)

"Working in the Barnyard"

1. The writer's purpose is primarily self-expression but also explanation.

2. The thesis sentence (the last sentence of paragraph 1) clearly and specifically states the writer's topic (a work experience) and perspective on that topic (learning something valuable).

3. The essay's organization is clearly chronological. The writer adheres to the organization throughout, providing ample signals to help the reader follow the narrative (for example, *Last May*, *then*, *as soon as I arrived*).

4. This otherwise competent essay is

EXERCISE 9

Carefully read the student essays below, and answer the following questions about each one. (1) What is the writer's purpose? (2) How well does the thesis sentence convey the purpose? What assertion does the thesis sentence make? How specific is the sentence? How well does it preview the writer's ideas and organization? (3) What organization does the writer use? Is it clear throughout the essay? (4) What details, examples, and reasons does the writer use to support his or her ideas? Where is supporting evidence skimpy? (5) Who do you think constitutes the writer's intended audience? What role does the writer seem to be assuming? What does the tone reveal about the writer's attitude toward the topic? (6) How successful is the writer in making you care about the topic and his or her views of it?

Working in the Barnyard

Until two months ago I thought summer jobs occupied time and helped pay the next year's tuition but otherwise provided no useful training. Then I took a temporary job in a large government agency. Two months there taught me a very valuable lesson about how people work together.

Last May I was hired by the personnel department of the agency to fill in for vacationing workers in the mail room. I had seven coworkers and a boss, Mrs. King. Our job was to sort the huge morning and afternoon mail shipments into four hundred slots, one for every employee in the agency. Then we delivered the sorted mail out of grocery carts that we wheeled from office to office along assigned corridors, picking up outgoing mail as we went along. Each mail delivery took an entire half-day to sort and deliver.

My troubles began almost as as soon as I arrived. Hundreds of pieces of mail were dumped on a shallow table against a wall of mail slots. I was horrified to see that the slots were labeled not with people's names but with their initials—whereas the incoming letters, of course, contained full names. Without thinking, I asked why this was a good idea, only to receive a sharp glance from Mrs. King. So I repeated the question. This time Mrs. King told me not to question what I didn't understand. It was the first of many such exchanges, and I hadn't been on the job a half-hour.

I mastered the initials and the sorting and delivery procedures after about a week. But the longer I worked at the job, the more I saw how inefficient all the procedures were, from delivery routes to times for coffee breaks. When I asked Mrs. King about the procedures, however, she always reacted the same way: it was none of my business.

I pestered Mrs. King more and more over the next seven weeks, but my efforts were fruitless, even counterproductive. Mrs. King began calling me snide names. Then she began picking on my work and singling me out for reprimands, even though I did my best and worked faster than most of the others.

Two months after I had started work, the personnel manager called me in and fired me. I objected, of course, calling up all the deficiencies I had seen in Mrs. King and her systems. The manager interrupted to ask if I had ever heard of the barnyard pecking order: the top chicken pecks on the one below it, the second pecks on the third, and so on all the way down the line to the lowliest chicken, whose life is a constant misery. Mrs. King, the manager said, was that lowliest chicken at the bottom of the pecking order in the agency's management. With little education, she had spent her entire adult life building up her small domain, and she had to protect it from everyone, especially the people who worked for her. The arbitrariness of her systems was an assertion of her power, for no one should doubt for a moment that she ruled her little roost.

I had a month before school began again to think about my adventure. At first it irritated me that I should be humiliated while Mrs. King continued on as before. But eventually I saw how arrogant, and how unsympathetic, my behavior had been. In my next job, I'll learn the pecking order before I become a crusader, *if* I do.

marred by omissions of concrete details and examples that would give the reader a sense of actually sharing the experience instead of rushing through it. Paragraph 2: What did Mrs. King look like? How huge were the mail shipments? Paragraph 3: What were some of the actual words spoken by the writer and Mrs. King? Paragraph 4: What was inefficient about delivery routes and times for coffee breaks? What exactly did Mrs. King do or say in reacting to the writer's questions? Paragraph 5: In what specific ways did the writer pester Mrs. King? How were the efforts fruitless? How counterproductive? What snide names did Mrs. King use? How did she pick on the writer's work? What reprimands did she issue?

5. The writer seems to conceive of her readers as other inexperienced workers like herself. She assumes the role of a confider, sharing a difficult experience. Her tone is straightforward yet strangely subdued when she tells of Mrs. King's tyranny. We sense from the beginning that the writer was humbled by her experience, and the last paragraph is genuinely humble in tone.

6. Answers will vary.

"The Obsolete Hero"

1. The writer's purpose is explanation.

2. The thesis sentence (last sentence of paragraph 1) specifies the topic, forecasts the explanatory purpose and comparison-and-contrast organization, and captures the writer's regretful attitude toward the changes he discusses.

3. The writer uses one of the standard comparison-and-contrast organizational schemes, discussing all of one subject (cowboys before the taming of the West) and then all of the other (modern cowboys). (As a result, the essay is also chronological.) To link the two parts of the essay and clarify the contrast, the writer covers points of comparison in roughly the same order and, in the second part (paragraph 4), refers frequently to the earlier material (e.g., *instead of trusting to nature; lean less on survival skills*).

4. Unlike "Working in the Barnyard," this essay contains adequate details and examples to help readers share the writer's attitude toward his topic. Particularly effective in sharpening the contrast are the contrasting details in paragraphs 3 and 4 (e.g., *men who had the stamina to ride in the saddle all day for weeks and sleep on the ground at night* versus *He sleeps in a bed at night and rides to the range in a Jeep or pickup truck*).

5. The writer's use of *we, our,* and *us* reveals that he believes his readers will share his sense of loss at the demise of the legendary cowboy. Apparently, though, he does not expect readers to be familiar with the causes of the change, for he gives the historical background. His role is part reporter, part disappointed romantic. His tone is animated yet nostalgic, especially in paragraph 3.

6. Answers will vary.

The Obsolete Hero

Most Americans admire the cowboy as a symbol of our nation's pioneering spirit. The cowboy represents the values of a young country expanding its frontiers across the untamed West: rugged courage, physical strength and skill, and stubborn independence. In our century the West has been tamed, however, and the cowboy's role has changed. The hero who used to ride the range is obsolete in an era when cattle are carefully bred, fed, inoculated, and shipped instead of herded to market.

The kind of cowboy we see in television westerns originated from the Spanish conquistadors, who brought horses and cattle to the New World. Let loose to graze, the cattle gradually multiplied into huge herds. When easterners began flooding westward in the mid-1800s, the demand for beef grew, and so did the need for cowboys to track down the cattle and drive them to market.

As the railroads moved westward after the Civil War, it became possible to ship beef not only locally but to the large cities back East. Vast trail drives grew up in which cattle from several ranches at once were herded from Texas northward to railhead cow towns such as Abilene, Wichita, and Dodge City. Supervising these drives were men who had the stamina to ride in the saddle all day for weeks and sleep on the ground at night. Their meals, cooked over an open fire, consisted of whatever could be caught on the way or carried in a chuck wagon without spoiling. The cowboys had to know how to rope a runaway cow, tie a calf's feet for branding, pull a stray out of a bog, shoot a rattlesnake from the back of a galloping horse, find food and water in unfamiliar territory, and break and ride wild mustangs.

As civilization spread across the West, ranchers began fencing in their land and breeding cattle instead of trusting to nature. Trail drives dwindled as the range was divided into private property and the railroads provided closer outlets for beef. As a result of these changes, today's cowboys lean less on survival skills and more on agriculture and veterinary medicine. They learn to build and mend fences and to drill wells and grease windmills, which provide cattle with water and irrigate the land for a dependable feed supply. Though horses remain important, the modern cowboy typically trains his ponies from colthood instead of busting wild broncos. He sleeps in a bed at night and rides to the range in a Jeep or pickup truck. His midday meals are delivered fresh and hot by truck. Even the cattle he tends are trucked between ranges. When the cowboy needs to search the brush for strays, he can do it in a helicopter. Many of the colorful skills that used to be essential, such as riding a bucking horse and twirling a lasso, now show up mainly in rodeos.

Today our national focus has shifted from geographic frontiers to the frontiers of space and high technology. But many of us, in our hearts, still dream of being as hardy, self-sufficient, and free as that obsolete hero of the Wild West, the cowboy.

CHAPTER 3

Composing Paragraphs

Whatever our purpose in writing and whatever our subject, we normally write in **paragraphs,** groups of related sentences set off by a beginning indention. In the process of composing paragraphs and revising them, we work toward two complementary goals: to give full expression to our ideas and to help readers follow and appreciate our train of thought. For the writer, paragraphing provides a way to break down complex ideas into manageable parts, discuss each part separately and completely, and relate each part to the central theme or thesis of the essay. For readers, paragraphing focuses attention on one idea at a time and provides the mixture of general statements and specific information needed to understand meaning.

The following paragraph provides a fairly simple illustration of how the paragraph aids the writer and the reader.

> Some people really like chili, apparently, but nobody can agree how the stuff should be made. C. V. Wood, twice winner at Terlingua, uses flank steak, pork chops, chicken, and green chilis. My friend Hughes Rudd of CBS News, who imported five hundred pounds of chili powder into Russia as a condition of accepting employment as Moscow correspondent, favors coarse-ground beef. Isadore Bleckman, the cameraman I must live with on the road, insists upon one-inch cubes of stew beef and puts garlic in his chili, an Illinois affectation. An Indian of my acquaintance, Mr. Fulton Batisse, who eats chili for breakfast when he can, uses buffalo meat and plays an Indian drum while it's cooking. I ask you.
>
> —CHARLES KURALT, *Dateline America*

The thesis of the essay in which this paragraph appears is that a Texas chili championship gives undue attention to an unpleasant food. Kuralt begins the paragraph with a general statement that

HIGHLIGHTS

Many of the choices writers make in composing paragraphs are similar to those they make in composing whole essays, especially in expository and argumentative writing. Studying the basic features of paragraphs—generalizations supported by details, examples, reasons, or other kinds of specific information—and composing paragraphs that employ these features can be a good way for many students to develop their writing skills.

The pattern of the typical paragraph, consisting of a statement of a topic or opinion followed by concrete comment on it, illustrates an essential essay pattern within a length and degree of complexity that students can manage. Moreover, just as the sentences in a paragraph must be related in ways that are immediately clear to a reader, so the paragraphs within an essay must move clearly from one to another. Thus by examining and constructing well-made paragraphs, students can become more confident and accomplished in managing multiparagraph papers. This, at least, is the assumption behind this chapter of the handbook.

Of course, not all paragraphs in professional writing conform in length, structure, or purpose to the models provided in this chapter. Paragraphs in narrative and descriptive writing, dialogue paragraphs, introductory and concluding paragraphs, and paragraphs for emphasis or transition all frequently differ in some way from the standard pattern, differences noted and discussed in this chapter. Nonetheless, helping students master the so-called standard paragraph can be a good way to help them learn better.

75

RESOURCES AND IDEAS

Paragraphing strategies and the features of paragraphing have been a subject of considerable debate, particularly over the past two decades. According to Michael Moran, scholars have taken two views of paragraphing:

> One argues that the paragraph is a unit—either logical, rhetorical, linguistic, psychological, or a combination of them—that possesses an internal structure that can be described using a finite set of rules. The other view argues that the paragraph is a stretch of discourse that owes its existence to the larger requirements of the whole piece of prose. In this view, the paragraph does not exist as a separate entity but as a flexible and convenient method of marking some stage in a larger organic process. ("The English Paragraph," *Research in Rhetoric and Composition: A Bibliographic Sourcebook*, ed. Michael G. Moran and Ronald F. Lunsford [Westport: Greenwood, 1984], 425.)

Though this chapter blends the two points of view, it takes what might be called a fairly traditional approach to paragraphing, at least in light of the research reviewed by Arthur A. Stern, who concludes that the paragraph is not necessarily a logical pattern with a clear topic sentence but is instead a flexible rhetorical structure that can serve a variety of purposes ("When Is a Paragraph?" *College Composition and Communication* 27 [1976]: 253–57).

But more recent scholarship suggests the importance of topic sentences and patterns of paragraph coherence, at least in academic writing and other forms of expository and argumentative prose. The following articles are worth investigating:

Randall Popken, "A Study of Topic Sentence Use in Academic Writing," *Written Communication* 4 (1987): 209–28.

William J. Vande Koppel, "Something Old, Something New: Functional Sentence Perspective," *Research in the Teaching of English* 17 (1983): 85–99.

relates to his thesis. That statement leads him directly to four examples—four pieces of evidence for his claim that people disagree over how to make chili (sentences 2–5). He keeps himself focused on his general statement by tying each example back to it with the word *chili* and by starting each example sentence with a name or another identification of a chili maker. At the same time he helps us, his readers, by stating what his paragraph will be about and sticking to that idea, by letting us know that sentences 2–5 serve a similar function, and by giving us plenty of specific details in those sentences so that we can appreciate his point of view.

Kuralt's paragraph illustrates three characteristics of most effective paragraphs.

QUALITIES OF EFFECTIVE PARAGRAPHS

1. **Unity:** the paragraph adheres to one idea. (See 3a.)
2. **Coherence:** the parts of the paragraph relate clearly to each other. (See 3b.)
3. **Development:** the idea of the paragraph is well supported with specific evidence such as details, facts, examples, and reasons. (See 3c.)

These are three qualities of an effective essay as well (see 1f and 1h), but it is mainly through paragraphs that they are achieved. Thus they are the subjects of the first three sections of this chapter. A fourth section, 3d, treats introductions, conclusions, and other kinds of paragraphs that serve special functions in essays. And a final section, 3e, discusses how paragraphs work together in the whole essay.

3a Maintaining paragraph unity

Since readers expect a paragraph to explore one idea, they will be alert for that idea and will patiently follow its development. In other words, they will seek and appreciate paragraph **unity,** clear identification and clear elaboration of one idea and of that idea only. If readers' attention is not rewarded and they must shift their focus from one idea to another and perhaps back again, their confusion or frustration will impede their understanding and acceptance of the writer's meaning.

In an essay the thesis sentence often announces the main idea as a commitment to readers (see 1g). In a paragraph a **topic sentence** often alerts readers to the essence of the paragraph by stating the central idea and expressing the writer's attitude toward it. Like the thesis sentence, the topic sentence is a commitment to readers, and the rest of the paragraph delivers on that commitment. In Kuralt's paragraph on chili the topic sentence or commitment is sentence 1: the author states generally that people disagree about how to make chili. The next four sentences fulfill the commitment with specific examples of chili concoctions. The last sentence (*I ask you*) invites us to consider the examples with amusement, as the writer does.

In the body of an essay each paragraph is likely to treat one part of the essay's thesis sentence; the topic sentences simply elaborate on parts of the thesis. A topic sentence will not, of course, guarantee a unified paragraph, any more than a thesis sentence guarantees a unified essay. The next several sections explain how to write unified paragraphs controlled by strong topic sentences.

1   Focusing on the central idea

Kuralt's paragraph on chili works because it follows through on the topic sentence. The sentences after the topic sentence do not stray off to other subjects, such as the other food preferences of the people mentioned or of the writer himself. Instead, each one helps us better understand the writer's central idea.

The following paragraph, in contrast, begins to lose its way in sentence 5.

> Professional wrestling satisfies viewers' needs for heroic struggle. The confrontation between men like Carl "Cowboy" Coyote and Boris "Tsar" Ivanov—each one costumed to reflect his nickname—may seem absurd, not heroic. But the absurdity removes the contest from reality, so that the wrestlers are like characters in a fairy tale who symbolize good (the American hero) and evil (the Russian menace). We know the action is all (or mostly all) staged, yet that unreality increases the symbolism of the contest. There is also staged action in TV crime shows. The action *seems* real, so we begin to care about who wins or loses. The shootings and other violence usually do not offend us but seem justified and even necessary. Of course, crime shows are even more violent than professional wrestling.   1 2 3 4 5 6 7 8

By the end of this paragraph, the author seems to have forgotten his commitment (stated in sentence 1) to show how professional wrestling satisfies viewers' needs for heroic struggle. At sentence 5 he becomes distracted by the staged action in TV crime shows, returning to wrestling only weakly in the last sentence.

Linda K. Shamoon and Robert A. Schwegler, "Sociologists Reading Student Texts: Expectations and Perceptions," *The Writing Instructor* 7 (1988): 71–81.

¶ un
3a

HIGHLIGHTS

This section of the chapter (3a) addresses the need for a paragraph to focus on a topic and to make the focus clear to the reader through an explicit statement in the form of a topic sentence. It introduces the basic form of the expository paragraph—topic sentence; optional sentence of clarification or limitation; illustrations and details—and indicates how this pattern can be varied to suit a writer's purpose and to fit within the context created by the surrounding paragraphs.

The concept of a clearly stated and variously placed topic sentence that controls the shape of a paragraph is, of course, an oversimplification. But it appears to help students a great deal to think of the paragraph as a unit dominated and controlled by an expressly stated generalization. Students can see the topic sentence as a commitment they make to the reader, with the rest of the paragraph following through on the commitment. Seeing the obvious parallel between the paragraph's topic sentence and the essay's thesis statement is also helpful to many students. Finally, of course, stating a central point in a single sentence and marshalling support for it enables students to see more clearly what is required for unity.

The exercises for this section ask students to identify the central idea in unified paragraphs, to revise paragraphs, to build a paragraph by combining and revising kernel sentences, and to write their own paragraphs. These exercises can be easily adapted to small-group work; in coming to understand how others view paragraphs, students may more readily understand the influence of paragraph structure and unity on readers.

RESOURCES AND IDEAS

Harvey S. Wiener, "The Single Narrative Paragraph and College Remediation," *College English* 33 (1972): 660–69. Wiener suggests using paragraph-length narrative themes to help students develop both paragraph and essay skills.

RESOURCES AND IDEAS

A. L. Becker, "A Tagmemic Approach to Paragraph Analysis, *College Composition and Communication* 16 (1965): 237–42. Becker observes that expository paragraphs generally follow a variation of one of two patterns: topic-restriction-illustration (TRI) or problem-solution (PS).

CREATING UNIFIED PARAGRAPHS

Give the class five topic sentences on different subjects and ask each student to choose one and write a unified paragraph based on it. Then split the class into groups and ask students to read their paragraphs aloud to the groups. Ask the students in each group to discuss the unity of the paragraphs and to compare the methods of development among the paragraphs.

COLORING PARAGRAPHS

Bring in copies of sample paragraphs and felt-tipped pens or pencils in three colors. Split the class into groups and ask each group to underline topic sentences in one color, sentences of limitation in another, and examples and details in the third. Students should then be able to discover the arrangement of each paragraph, the placement of the topic sentence, and the way the parts fit together to form a unified whole.

The writer might have kept on track and produced a more unified paragraph if he had been more careful to relate every sentence both to the sentence before it and to the central idea of the topic sentence. In sentences 2–4 the writer does establish these relationships, discussing the absurdity and symbolism of wrestling. In sentence 5, however, when he shifts to TV crime shows, the writer leaves behind both the central idea and the more specific notions of absurdity and symbolism. From then on he loses his thread and, in the process, his readers.

Compare the disunified paragraph with the following revision, noting especially how the writer uses the new sentences 5–7 to develop his explanation.

> Professional wrestling satisfies viewers' needs for heroic 1 struggle. The confrontation between men like Carl "Cowboy" 2 Coyote and Boris "Tsar" Ivanov—each one costumed to reflect his nickname—may seem absurd, not heroic. But the ab- 3 surdity removes the contest from reality, so that the wrestlers are like characters in a fairy tale who symbolize good (the American hero) and evil (the Russian menace). We know the 4 action is all (or mostly all) staged, yet that unreality increases the symbolism of the contest. Watching the Cowboy and the 5 Tsar grab, twist, and hurl each other, we are watching good struggle against evil and freedom struggle against repression. It becomes important who wins or loses, so that every ham- 6 merlock has significance. Such a struggle—ending, of course, 7 with the Cowboy victorious—renews our faith in the rightness of the world.   —A STUDENT

Depending on his purpose, the writer may develop the deleted comparison with TV crime shows in a separate paragraph, or he may omit it altogether.

Writers often follow the central idea in the topic sentence with a **clarifying or limiting sentence.** Such a sentence can help the writer maintain unity by providing a sharper, clearer focus for the paragraph; and it can help the reader by providing a more precise sense of the writer's idea. In the following paragraph, for instance, sentence 2 clarifies and limits what the writer means in her topic sentence (sentence 1) about the inconsistent attitude toward computer intelligence.

> Another inconsistency in *2001: A Space Odyssey* is the at- 1 titude toward computer intelligence. The filmmakers appar- 2 ently could not decide whether they wanted to present the shipboard computer, HAL, as self-governed and therefore dangerous or as human-governed and therefore controllable. In his name, the fact that he is a *he* (not an *it*), his soft, slightly 3 menacing voice, and his control over the spaceship, HAL seems human and more than human, with a mind of his own.

When he starts murdering crew members, the filmmakers 4
seem to be saying that computer intelligence can be danger-
ously independent: the nightmare of the appliance taking
vengeance on its users. Yet eventually the one surviving crew 5
member disconnects HAL's circuits to make him harmless.
Then the message seems to be that HAL is, after all, just a ma- 6
chine under human control. In the end, it is not clear whether 7
the filmmakers fear artificial intelligence or not.

—A STUDENT

2   Placing the topic sentence

The topic sentence of a paragraph (along with any limiting or
clarifying sentence) and its supporting details may be arranged
variously depending on how the writer wants to direct readers' attention and on how complex the central idea is. The most common
positions for the topic sentence are discussed below.

Topic sentence at the beginning

In the most familiar arrangement—illustrated by all the paragraphs examined so far—the topic sentence comes first, then
sometimes a clarifying or limiting sentence, then the supporting
information. This arrangement can help the writer maintain paragraph unity because the topic sentence provides a guide for selecting details in the rest of the paragraph. For readers the topic-
first model establishes an initial context in which all the following
details can be understood. Look again at the paragraphs on pages
75 and 78 to see how easily we readers relate each detail or example back to the point made in the first sentence.

The topic-first model is common not only in expository paragraphs, such as those above, but also in argumentative paragraphs, such as the one below. Here the author first states his opinion and then provides the information to support it.

For almost 30 years now, America has been systemati- 1
cally destroying the centers of her cities. In the name of urban 2
renewal, we have declared choice parcels of downtown real
estate to be slums and then forced their rightful owners—
often stable but poor families and small businesses—to move
away. We have sent bulldozers in at taxpayers' expense to 3
flatten the old housing, and then we have given the cleared
land away at bargain prices to the operators of parking ga-
rages, overpriced hospitals, and chain hotels, to the develop-
ers of high-rise bank buildings and luxury housing.

—FRED POWLEDGE, "Let's Bulldoze the Suburbs"

SEEING PARAGRAPHS

Visually, students may find it easier to understand topic sentence placement and
paragraph arrangement by using these diagrams as guides:

Topic sentence at
    the beginning: △

Topic sentence at the
    beginning and in
    the middle: △ △

Topic sentence at
    the end: ▽

Topic sentence at
    the beginning
    and the end:

Topic sentence following transitional sentence

In many paragraphs the opening sentence serves as a transition or bridge for the preceding paragraph, simultaneously pointing back to the previous idea and forward to a new one. The topic sentence is then often the second sentence, with the remaining sentences providing the support. In the following paragraph, for example, the first, transitional sentence refers to the assertion in the author's preceding paragraph that science is taught as if it does not undergo change. Sentence 2 is the topic sentence.

> And, of course, it [science] is not like this at all. In real [1,2] life, every field of science is incomplete, and most of them— whatever the record of accomplishment during the last 200 years—are still in their very earliest stages. In the fields I [3] know best, among the life sciences, it is required that the most expert and sophisticated minds be capable of changing course—often with a great lurch—every few years. In some [4] branches of biology the mind-changing is occurring with accelerating velocity. Next week's issue of any scientific journal [5] can turn a whole field upside down, shaking out any number of immutable ideas and installing new bodies of dogma. This [6] is an almost everyday event in physics, in chemistry, in materials reserach, in neurobiology, in genetics, in immunology.
> —LEWIS THOMAS, "The Art of Teaching Science"

If a writer is making a significant change in direction, the transition from a preceding paragraph may require more than one sentence or even a separate short paragraph (see 3d-3). Even for very slight changes, however, writers frequently use words or phrases to link paragraphs so that readers see the progression of ideas. For instance, in the paragraph on computer intelligence (p. 78) the word *another* creates a bridge from the preceding paragraph. Brief links like this one are discussed in more detail in the next section (see 3b-3 and 3b-6).

Topic sentence at the beginning and in the middle

When the central idea of a paragraph requires fairly extensive support or breaks naturally into two parts, the topic sentence may be divided between the beginning and middle of the paragraph, with each part developed separately. Often the two parts compare two subjects or, as in the following paragraph, examine different sides of an issue.

> So far the only bright side [to nuclear war] I can come up [1] with—at least the only one I can sanely recommend—is the certainty that, in a nuclear war, the perpetrators will also die.

In fact, since they are no doubt somewhat better prepared for   2
it than we are, the likelihood is that they will die more slowly,
and with a more agonizingly clear awareness of what's happened, than the rest of us. But even this prospect gives me   3
only cold comfort. I have never understood those bereaved   4
parents who, as is occasionally reported to us, find it in their
hearts to rejoice at the execution of their child's killer. The   5
thought of the Pentagon brass stumbling in terror through a
darkened bunker or of the Kremlin leadership preparing to
wash down their cyanide pills with shots of Stolichnaya does
not, I am afraid, begin to compensate.

> —Barbara Ehrenreich, "Finding the 'Bright Side'
> to Nuclear War"

In this paragraph sentences 1 and 3 together form the central idea
of the paragraph: the one bright side of nuclear war is not very
comforting. In this case the paragraph is simple enough not to need
an opening statement of the whole idea to tie the parts together. In
more complex paragraphs, however, the opening sentence may
state the entire idea briefly before it is divided. Such an opening
sentence can keep the paragraph from breaking in half and also
help the writer ensure that the two parts are, in fact, closely related.

Topic sentence at the end

In some paragraphs the central idea may be stated at the end,
after supporting sentences have made a case for the general statement. Since this model leads the reader to a conclusion by presenting all the evidence first, it can prove effective in argumentation. And because the point of the paragraph is withheld until the
end, this model can be dramatic in exposition as well. For example, all the details in the following paragraph about the comedian
Steve Martin lead up to and support the idea stated in sentence 12.

When Martin comes onstage, he may do, say, just what   1
Red Skelton used to do, but he gets us laughing at the fact
that we're laughing at such dumb jokes. Martin simulates   2
being a comedian, and so, in a way, we simulate being the comedian's audience. Martin makes old routines work by letting   3
us know that they're old and then doing them immaculately.
For him, comedy is *all* timing. He's almost a comedy robot.   4,5
Onstage, he puts across the idea that he's going to do some   6
cornball routine, and then when he does it it has quotation
marks around it, and that's what makes it hilarious. He does   7
the routine straight, yet he's totally facetious. He lets us know   8
that we're seeing silliness in quotes. There he is, spruced up   9
and dapper in a three-piece white suit; even his handsome-

ness is made facetious. Steve Martin is all persona. That's   10,11
what's dizzying about him—and a little ghoulish. He and   12
some of the other comics of his generation make the *idea* of
doing comedy funny.   —Pauline Kael, "Silliness"

Expressing the central idea at the end of the paragraph does
not eliminate the need to unify the paragraph. The idea in the topic
sentence must still govern the selection of all the preceding details.

Topic sentence at the beginning and the end

Sometimes the central idea may be stated at the beginning of
the paragraph and then restated at the end. Generally, the first sentence provides a context for the supporting information, and the
last sentence provides a new twist based on that information. For
example:

> Portraits of America as the confident, unworried "happy   1
> republic" have never been entirely accurate. The dour Puri-   2
> tans who started it all had bleak views about man's limita-
> tions as a social creature. The Founding Fathers, from Jeffer-   3
> son through Adams, committed treason and waged war, and
> came away with a melancholy understanding that practical
> idealism involves the sacrifice of some ideals. Pre–Civil War   4
> America was uneasily aware that the yeoman's republic was a
> vanishing ideal, and post–Civil War America faced industrial-
> ization and urbanization with the painfully fresh knowledge
> that worthy social objectives may require suffering on a large
> scale. With the late nineteenth century came populism   5
> founded on the suspicion that the mass of Americans were ex-
> ploited by "interests." Then came the progressives, with their   6
> political historians proclaiming that the thralldom of the
> masses was the result of the sly Founders who had drafted an
> antidemocratic constitution. Pessimism is as American as ap-   7
> ple pie—frozen apple pie with a slice of processed cheese.
>   —George F. Will, *Statecraft as Soulcraft*

This model, like the previous one, will not work if the writer
tries to make the last sentence rescue a disunified paragraph. To be
effective, the final statement must reflect some development in the
sentences preceding it.

Central idea not stated

Occasionally, a paragraph's central idea will be stated in the
previous paragraph or will be so obvious that it need not be stated
at all. The following paragraph, from an essay on the actor Hum-
phrey Bogart, has no explicit topic sentence.

> Usually he wore the trench coat unbuttoned, just tied 1
> with the belt, and a slouch hat, rarely tilted. Sometimes it 2
> was a captain's cap and a yachting jacket. Almost always his 3
> trousers were held up by a cowboy belt. You know the kind: 4
> one an Easterner waiting for a plane out of Phoenix buys just
> as a joke and then takes a liking to. Occasionally, he'd hitch 5
> up his slacks with it, and he often jabbed his thumbs behind
> it, his hands ready for a fight or a dame.
> —PETER BOGDANOVICH, "Bogie in Excelsis"

The effectiveness of this paragraph rests on the power of details to
describe Bogart. Thus a stated central idea—such as "Bogart's
character could be seen in the details of his clothing"—not only
would weaken the paragraph but would contradict its intention.
Nonetheless, the central idea is clearly implied.

Paragraphs in descriptive writing (like the one above) and in
narrative writing (relating a sequence of events) often lack stated
topic sentences. But producing a paragraph without a topic sentence does not release the writer from the need to unify the paragraph. Each paragraph should have a central idea, and its details
should develop that idea.

EXERCISE 1

What is the central idea of each paragraph below? In what sentence or sentences is it expressed?

1.   To most strangers they [the Los Angeles freeways] sug- 1
gest chaos, or at least purgatory, and there can certainly be
more soothing notices than the one on the Santa Ana Freeway
which announces MERGING BUSES AHEAD. There comes a mo- 2
ment, though, when something clicks in one's own mechanism, and suddenly one grasps the rhythm of the freeway system, masters its tribal or ritual forms, and discovers it to be
not a disruptive element at all, but a kind of computer key to
the use of Los Angeles. One is processed by the freeways. Ele- 3,4
vated as they generally are above the flat and centerless ex-
panse of the city, they provide a navigational aid, into which
one locks oneself for guidance. Everything is clearer then. 5
There are the mountains, to the north and east. There is the 6,7
glimmering ocean. The civic landmarks of L.A., such as they 8
are, display themselves conveniently for you. The pattern of 9
the place unfolds until, properly briefed by the experience, the
time comes for you to unlock from the system, undo your
safety belt, and take the right-hand lane into the everyday life
below.   —JAN MORRIS, "The Know-How City"

2.   Advocates of the rights of animals have sabotaged re- 1
search laboratories that experiment with animals, physically
prevented seal hunters from killing seals, freed caged animals

ANSWERS: EXERCISE 1

1. The central idea is in sentence 2: the
   Los Angeles freeway system is "a kind
   of computer key to the use of Los Angeles."
2. The central idea is in sentence 3: anti-
   vivisectionists are defending the rights
   of animals in varied ways.
3. The central idea is in sentence 1: scientists know something about the song
   of the humpback whale.

from commercial fur farms, harassed whaling vessels, released animals from zoos, and hindered hunters in their search for prey. In search of public support for their point of view, they have taken advertisements and distributed printed fliers and vivid photographs that give graphic examples of how animals are sometimes inhumanely treated. Such acts represent the philosophy of a growing number of people in this and other countries who believe nonhuman animals are sentient creatures that can feel pain, are aware of their plight, and, like humans, have certain rights.

—BAYARD WEBSTER, ''Should Vivisection Be Abolished?''

3. Though they do not know why the humpback whale sings, scientists do know something about the song itself. They have measured the length of a whale's song: from a few minutes to over half an hour. They have recorded and studied the variety and complex arrangements of low moans, high squeaks, and sliding squeals that make up the song. And they have learned that each whale sings in its own unique pattern.

—A STUDENT

ANSWERS: EXERCISE 2

1. The topic sentence is sentence 1. Unrelated are sentences 4 and 7.
2. The topic sentence is sentence 1, clarified in sentence 2. Unrelated are sentences 5, 6, and 7.

EXERCISE 2

The following paragraphs contain ideas or details that do not support their central ideas. Identify the topic sentence in each paragraph and delete the unrelated material.

1. In the southern part of the state, some people still live much as they did a century ago. They use coal- or wood-burning stoves for heating and cooking. Their homes do not have electricity or indoor bathrooms or running water. The towns can't afford to put in sewers or power lines, because they don't receive adequate funding from the state and federal governments. Beside most homes there is a garden where fresh vegetables are gathered for canning. Small pastures nearby support livestock, including cattle, pigs, horses, and chickens. Most of the people have cars or trucks, but the vehicles are old and beat-up from traveling on unpaved roads.

2. Most people don't realize how difficult it is to work and go to school at the same time. If you want to make good grades but need to pay your own way, the burdens are tremendous. I work in an office sixteen hours a week. Each term I have to work out a tight schedule that will let me take the courses I want and still be at work when I'm needed. I like the job. The people there are pleasant, and they are eager to help me learn. In the end my job will be good training for the kind of managerial position I hope to have some day, because I'm gaining useful experience in office procedures and working with people. It's hard for me to have a job and go to school, but when I graduate both will make me more employable.

EXERCISE 3

Develop the following topic sentence into a unified paragraph by using the relevant information in the statements below it. Delete each statement that does not relate directly to the topic, and then rewrite and combine sentences as appropriate.

TOPIC SENTENCE

Mozart's accomplishments in music seem remarkable even today.

Wolfgang Amadeus Mozart was born in 1756 in Salzburg, Austria.
He began composing music at the age of five.
He lived most of his life in Salzburg and Vienna.
His first concert tour of Europe was at the age of six.
On his first tour he played harpsichord, organ, and violin.
He published numerous compositions before reaching adolescence.
He married in 1782.
Mozart and his wife were both poor managers of money.
They were plagued by debts.
Mozart composed over six hundred musical compositions.
His most notable works are his operas, symphonies, quartets, and piano concertos.
He died at the age of thirty-five.

EXERCISE 4

Develop three of the following topic sentences into detailed and unified paragraphs.
1. Fans of country music (or rock music, classical music, jazz) come in [number] varieties.
2. My high school was an ugly (or attractive or homely or whatever) building.
3. Words can hurt as much as sticks and stones.
4. Professional sports have (or have not) been helped by extending the regular season with championship play-offs.
5. Working for good grades can interfere with learning.

3b Achieving paragraph coherence

A paragraph is unified if it holds together—if all its details and examples support the central idea. A paragraph is **coherent** if readers can see *how* the paragraph holds together without having to puzzle out the writer's reasons for adding each new sentence. Each time readers must pause and reread to see how sentences relate to each other, they lose both comprehension and patience.

¶ coh
3b

ANSWERS: EXERCISE 3

Delete statements not pertaining to Mozart's accomplishments: when he was born, where he lived, when he married, his debts. Possible paragraph:

> Mozart's accomplishments in music seem remarkable even today. At the age of six he made his first concert tour of Europe, playing harpsichord, organ, and violin. He had begun composing music at the age of five, and by adolescence he had published numerous musical compositions. When he died at thirty-five, his work included over six hundred compositions, most notably operas, symphonies, quartets, and piano concertos.

ANSWERS: EXERCISE 4

Individual response.

HIGHLIGHTS

This section of the chapter (3b) deals with paragraph coherence, addressing it from the reader's perspective as well as the writer's. Students are shown how the devices they use to achieve paragraph coherence help readers to follow the arguments or information being presented.

The discussion emphasizes the need to

maintain a clear organizational pattern as one of the principal ways to ensure coherence, and it presents examples of two basic ways of organizing paragraphs: organizing by space or time and organizing for emphasis. Students who have difficulty organizing their own writing can usually see the pattern of organization in a well-made paragraph.

Following the discussion of patterns, the section takes up and illustrates other methods of achieving coherence: parallelism; careful use of pronouns; consistency in person, tense, and number; repetition of words; and transitional expressions. Analysis of paragraphs can help students understand these explicit and implicit means by which individual sentences are held together so that the reader follows effortlessly the flow of ideas and information.

As in the preceding section, the exercises move from analysis to revision to production and are useful in small-group activities as well as individual work.

Coherent paragraphs convey relations in many ways, and we will look at each one in detail. First, however, we will examine what makes a paragraph, like the following one, incoherent.

> The ancient Egyptians were masters of preserving dead people's bodies by making mummies of them. Mummies several thousand years old have been discovered nearly intact. The skin, hair, teeth, finger- and toenails, and facial features of the mummies were evident. It is possible to diagnose the diseases they suffered in life, such as smallpox, arthritis, and nutritional deficiencies. The process was remarkably effective. Sometimes apparent were the fatal afflictions of the dead people: a middle-aged king died from a blow on the head, and polio killed a child king. Mummification consisted of removing the internal organs, applying natural preservatives inside and out, and then wrapping the body in layers of bandages.

This paragraph seems to be unified: it sticks to the topic of mummification throughout. But the paragraph is hard to read. It jumps back and forth between specific details about features, diseases, and causes of death (sentences 3, 4, 6) and general statements about mummies' intactness (sentence 2), the effectiveness of the process (sentence 5), and the process itself (sentence 7). All the sentences seem disconnected from each other, so that the paragraph lurches instead of gliding from point to point.

The paragraph as it was actually written is much clearer.

> The ancient Egyptians were masters of preserving dead people's bodies by making mummies of them. Basically, mummification consisted of removing the internal organs, applying natural preservatives inside and out, and then wrapping the body in layers of bandages. And the process was remarkably effective. Indeed, mummies several thousand years old have been discovered nearly intact. Their skin, hair, teeth, finger- and toenails, and facial features are still evident. Their diseases in life, such as smallpox, arthritis, and nutritional deficiencies, are still diagnosable. Even their fatal afflictions are still apparent: a middle-aged king died from a blow on the head; a child king died from polio.   —A STUDENT

This paragraph contains the same information and the same number of sentences as the previous one, but now we have no difficulty moving from one sentence to the next, seeing the writer's intentions, understanding the writer's meaning. The initial broad assertion (the topic sentence) is the same, but now the writer responds to the expectations it creates with two more specific statements: first (in sentence 2) he defines the process of making mummies; then (in sentence 3) he notes why the Egyptians were masters of the process (because the process was remarkably effective). Sentence 3 automatically leads us to expect an explanation of how the process was effective, and in sentence 4 the writer proceeds to tell us: ancient mummies have been discovered nearly intact. "How intact?" we want to know. And again the writer responds to our expectation: we can make out features (sentence 5), diseases (sentence 6), and even fatal afflictions (sentence 7).

The writer has thus responded to our expectations for content, and he has arranged his sentences in a familiar, general-to-specific organization. In addition, he has linked sentences effectively, so that each either grows out of or aligns with the one before. Here is the paragraph marked up to show these connections.

CENTRAL IDEA

The ancient Egyptians were masters of preserving dead 1
people's bodies by making mummies of them. Basically, 2
mummification consisted of removing the internal organs,
applying natural preservatives inside and out, and then wrap-
ping the body in layers of bandages. And the process was 3
remarkably effective. Indeed, mummies several thousand 4
years old have been discovered nearly intact. Their skin, hair, 5
teeth, finger- and toenails, and facial features are still evident.
Their diseases in life, such as smallpox, arthritis, and nutri- 6
tional deficiencies, are still diagnosable. Even their fatal af- 7
flictions are still apparent: a middle-aged king died from a
blow on the head; a child king died from polio.

EXPLANATION

EXPLANATION

SPECIFIC EXAMPLES

Circled and connected words repeat or restate key terms or concepts. Boxed words link sentences and clarify relationships. Underlined and connected phrases are in parallel grammatical form to reflect their parallel content.

Though some of the connections in this paragraph may have been added in revision, the writer probably attended to them while drafting as well. Not only superficial coherence but also an underlying clarity of relationships can be achieved by tying each sentence to the one before—generalizing from it, clarifying it, qualifying it, adding to it, illustrating it. As we saw just above, each

PARAGRAPH PATTERNS I

Give students a topic sentence and a set of assertions, facts, and details in undeveloped form. Tell them to use the material to write a coherent paragraph, following one of the patterns described in the handbook: spatial, chronological, general-to-specific, specific-to-general, climactic, most familiar to least familiar, or simplest to most complex. Students can manipulate the material however they wish to achieve an effect that is appropriate to the pattern. You may also want to ask for several paragraphs, each using the same content but a different pattern.

sentence in a paragraph creates an expectation of some sort in the mind of the reader, a question such as "How was a mummy made?" or "How intact are the mummies?" or "What's another example?" When the writer recognizes these expectations and tries to fulfill them, readers are likely to understand relationships without struggle.

The next pages discuss organization, parallelism, repetition and restatement, use of pronouns, consistency, and transitional expressions—all techniques used together to achieve coherence while both drafting and revising.

PARAGRAPH PATTERNS II

As a quiz or an in-class exercise, ask students to write a paragraph following one of the basic organizational schemes discussed in 3b-1. Leave the subject and content of the paragraph up to the individual student. If they wish, students may make up information, as long as they keep it plausible.

1   Organizing the paragraph

The paragraphs on mummies illustrate an essential element of coherence: information must be arranged in an order that readers can follow easily and that corresponds to their expectations. The common organizations for paragraphs correspond to those for entire essays (see 1h-1). Here we will examine the arrangements by space, by time, and for emphasis. The patterns of development, each suggesting its own arrangement, will be examined in the next section (p. 101).

Organizing by space or time

A paragraph organized **spatially** focuses readers' attention on one point and scans a person, object, or scene from that point. The movement may be from top to bottom, from side to side, from a farther point to a closer one, or from a closer point to a farther one. Donald Hall follows the last pattern in the following paragraph.

Cinematography!

> Across the yard, between the cow barn and the road, was ₁
> a bigger garden which was bright with phlox and zinnias and
> petunias. Beyond was a pasture where the color changed as ₂
> the wild flowers moved through the seasons: yellow and orange paint brushes at first, then wild blue lupines and white
> Queen Anne's lace, and finally the goldenrod of August. Mount ₃
> Kearsarge loomed over the pasture in the blue distance,
> shaped like a cone with a flattened point on top. We sat on the ₄
> porch and looked at garden, field, and mountain.
> —Donald Hall, *String Too Short to Be Saved*

Since a spatial organization parallels the way people actually look at a place for the first time, it conforms to readers' expectations. The spatial relationships can be further clarified with explicit signals, such as Hall's *Across* and *between* (sentence 1), *beyond* (2), and *over* (3). The writer may place a topic sentence at the beginning of the paragraph, may (like Hall) pull the scene together at the end, or may omit a topic sentence and let the details speak for themselves.

Another familiar way of organizing the elements of a paragraph is **chronologically**—that is, in order of their occurrence in time. In a chronological paragraph, as in experience, the earliest events come first, followed by more recent ones.

> There is no warning at all—only a steady rising intensity 1
> of the sun's light. Within minutes the change is noticeable; 2
> within an hour, the nearer worlds are burning. The star is ex- 3
> panding like a balloon, blasting off shells of gas at a million
> miles an hour as it blows its outer layers into space. Within a 4
> day, it is shining with such supernal brilliance that it gives off
> more light than all the other suns in the Universe combined. If 5
> it had planets, they are now no more than flecks of flame in
> the still-expanding shells of fire. The conflagration will burn 6
> for weeks before the dying star collapses back into quiescence.
> —ARTHUR C. CLARKE, "The Star of the Magi"

Like spatial paragraphs, chronological paragraphs can be almost automatically coherent because readers are familiar with progressions of events. The writer can help readers by signaling the order of events and the time that separates them, as Clarke does with the phrases and words *Within minutes* and *within an hour* (sentence 2), *Within a day* (4), *now* and *still* (5), and *before* (6). Like Clarke's, a chronological paragraph may lack a topic sentence when the idea governing the sequence is otherwise clear.

Organizing for emphasis

Whereas the spatial or chronological organization is almost dictated by the content of the paragraph, other organizational schemes are imposed on paragraphs to achieve a certain emphasis. These imposed organizations are also familiar to readers.

In the **general-to-specific** scheme the topic sentence generally comes first and then the following sentences become increasingly specific. The paragraph on mummies (p. 87) illustrates this organization: each sentence is either more specific than the one before it or at the same level of generality. The following paragraph is a more straightforward illustration.

> Perhaps the simplest fact about sleep is that individual 1
> needs for it vary widely. Most adults sleep between seven and 2
> nine hours, but occasionally people turn up who need twelve
> hours or so, while some rare types can get by on three or four.
> Rarest of all are those legendary types who require almost no 3
> sleep at all; respected researchers have recently studied three

such people. One of them—a healthy, happy woman in her 4
seventies—sleeps about an hour every two or three days. The 5
other two are men in early middle age, who get by on a few
minutes a night. One of them complains about the daily fif- 6
teen minutes or so he's forced to "waste" in sleeping.
—LAWRENCE A. MAYER, "The Confounding Enemy of Sleep"

After the general statement of his topic sentence, the author moves from common and less common sleep patterns (sentence 2) to the rarest pattern (sentence 3) and (in the remaining sentences) to particular people.

In the **specific-to-general** organization the elements of the paragraph build to a general conclusion. Such is the pattern of the next paragraph.

It's disconcerting that so many college women, when 1
asked how their children will be cared for if they themselves
work, refer with vague confidence to "the day care center" as
though there were some great amorphous kiddie watcher out
there that the state provides. But such places, adequately 2
funded, well run, and available to all, are still scarce in this
country, particularly for middle-class women. And figures 3
show that when she takes time off for family-connected reasons (births, child care), a woman's chances for career advancement plummet. In a job market that's steadily tighten- 4
ing and getting more competitive, these obstacles bode the
kind of danger ahead that can shatter not only professions,
but egos. A hard reality is that there's not much more support 5
for our daughters who have family-plus-career goals than
there was for us; there's simply a great deal more self- and
societal pressure.　　—JUDITH WAX, *Starting in the Middle*

The author first states a common belief (sentence 1) and two reasons why it is a misconception (sentences 2 and 3). Then she explains the implications, first specifically (sentence 4) and then generally (sentence 5). The last sentence is the topic sentence of the paragraph.

When the details of a paragraph vary in significance, they can be arranged in a **climactic** order, from least to most important or dramatic. The following paragraph builds to a climax, saving the most dramatic example for last.

Nature has put many strange tongues into the heads of 1
her creatures. There is the frog's tongue, rooted at the front of 2
the mouth so it can be protruded an extra distance for nab-
bing prey. There is the gecko lizard's tongue, so long and agile 3
that the lizard uses it to wash its eyes. But the ultimate 4

EXTRA EXAMPLES

The following examples illustrate the specific-to-general pattern in a sentence and may be extended to short sample paragraphs:

(specific)　　good study habits
(specific) + consistent effort
(specific) + curiosity
(general) = good grades

Good study habits, consistent effort, and intellectual curiosity will result in good grades.

(specific)　　seeds
(specific) + soil
(specific) + sunlight
(specific) + water
(general) = good vegetable crop

A combination of fresh seeds, well-balanced soil, and adequate sunlight and water results in a good vegetable crop.

DRAMATIC EXAMPLES

Climactic order is a form of structuring that moves from least to most important. To help explain this strategy you may wish to draw examples from drama, particularly from the structure of tragedy. *Othello* provides an obvious example of structuring that moves from least dramatic/tension-filled to most dramatic/tension-filled.

Least dramatic—Othello marries Desdemona

More dramatic—Othello suspects Desdemona of infidelity

lingual whopper has been achieved in the anteater. The ant-   5
eater's head, long as it is, is not long enough to contain the
tremendous tongue which licks deep into anthills. Its tongue   6
is not rooted in the mouth or throat: it is fastened to the
breastbone.   —ALAN DEVOE, "Nature's Utmost"

Similar to the organizations discussed so far are those which
arrange details according to readers' likely understanding of them.
In discussing the virtues of public television, for instance, you
might proceed from **most familiar to least familiar,** from a well-
known program your readers have probably seen to less well-
known programs they may not have seen. Or in defending the right
of government employees to strike, you might arrange your reasons from **simplest to most complex,** from the employees' need to
be able to redress grievances to more subtle consequences for
employer-employee relations.

More dramatic—Desdemona defends her chastity and argues for her life

Most dramatic (climax)—Othello kills Desdemona and then realizes that she has been faithful to him

¶ coh
3b

| 2 | **Using parallel structures** |

" This is why I mail you for pointless word repetitions. Because it can be effective! "

Another way to achieve coherence, although not necessarily
in every paragraph, is through **parallelism**—the use of similar
grammatical structures for similar elements of meaning within a
sentence or among sentences. (See Chapter 17 for a detailed discussion of parallelism.) Parallel structures help tie together the
last three sentences in the paragraph on mummies (p. 87). In the
following paragraph the parallel structures of *It is the* and *Democracy is the* link all sentences after the first one; and parallelism also
appears within many of the sentences (for instance, *hole in the
stuffed shirt* and *dent in the top hat* in sentence 4). The author, writing during World War II, was responding to a request from the
Writer's War Board for a statement on the meaning of democracy.

Surely the Board knows what democracy is. It is the line   1,2
that forms on the right. It is the don't in Don't Shove. It is the   3,4
hole in the stuffed shirt through which the sawdust slowly
trickles; it is the dent in the high hat. Democracy is the recur-   5
rent suspicion that more than half of the people are right
more than half of the time. It is the feeling of privacy in the   6
voting booths, the feeling of communion in the libraries, the
feeling of vitality everywhere. Democracy is the score at the   7
beginning of the ninth. It is an idea which hasn't been dis-   8
proved yet, a song the words of which have not gone bad. It's   9
the mustard on the hot dog and the cream in the rationed coffee. Democracy is a request from a War Board, in the middle   10
of a morning in the middle of a war, wanting to know what
democracy is.   —E. B. WHITE, *The Wild Flag*

RESOURCES AND IDEAS

Anita Brostoff, "Coherence: 'Next to' Is Not 'Connected to,' " *College Composition and Communication* 32 (1981): 278–94. Brostoff discusses the causes of lack of coherence in writing and describes a program for helping students achieve coherence.

Francis Christensen, "A Generative Rhetoric of the Paragraph," in *Notes Toward a New Rhetoric: Nine Essays for Teachers,* 2nd ed., ed. Francis Christensen and Bonniejean Christensen (New York: Harper, 1978), 74–103. Christensen views paragraphs as a series of statements on differing levels of generality, often moving from the more general toward the specific.

W. Ross Winterowd, "The Grammar of Coherence," *College English* 31 (1971): 828–35. This article describes the kinds of relations that link sentence to sentence and paragraph to paragraph.

¶ coh

3b

YEAH—YEAH—YEAH!

To recognize the power of repetition, students need only turn to rock music. Have them begin by listing the titles of popular songs whose lyrics they know by heart. Then ask them to identify words and phrases that they remember best from the songs or that they learned first. Chances are that they will identify the chorus because it is the element of the song most often repeated. You might point out that choruses help unify songs. Students may also note that the considerable amount of repetition in many songs makes them easy to remember and helps create a unified effect. This exercise may also be used to point out the difference between effective use of repetition and overuse.

3   **Repeating or restating words and word groups**

Since every unified paragraph has only one topic, that topic is bound to recur in many of the sentences. In fact, repeating or restating key words or word groups is an important means of achieving paragraph coherence and of reminding your readers what the topic is. In the following paragraph, also by E. B. White, the repetition of *poets/poet* and *clearer/clear* ties the sentences together and stresses the important words of the paragraph.

> "I wish poets could be clearer," shouted my wife angrily 1
> from the next room. Hers is a universal longing. We would all 2,3
> like it if the bards would make themselves plain, or we think
> we would. The poets, however, are not easily diverted from 4
> their high mysterious ways. A poet dares be just so clear and 5
> no clearer; he approaches lucid ground warily, like a mariner
> who is determined not to scrape his bottom on anything solid.
> A poet's pleasure is to withhold a little of his meaning, to in- 6
> tensify by mystification. He unzips the veil from beauty, but 7
> does not remove it. A poet utterly clear is a trifle glaring. 8
> —E. B. WHITE, "Poetry"

White's paragraph also includes some restatements of his key words: *bards* for *poets* and *plain* and *lucid* for *clear*. Such restatements or **synonyms**—words with similar meaning—figure prominently in the following paragraph.

> Since the industrial revolution work has been rearranged 1
> and much of the satisfaction has been rationalized out. Very 2
> few workers have a chance to set their own task. Jobs have 3
> been divided and subdivided so that each person performs a
> single operation upon a continuous flow of parts or papers. In- 4
> creasingly the worker is denied not only the chance to set his
> own task but even the task chance to finish the task someone else
> sets for him. The jobs are so fragmented that few workers can 5
> feel they are helping to make a car or to issue an insurance
> policy. They are merely repeating the same few motions, the 6
> same simple calculations over and over throughout a lifetime
> of labor.   —BARBARA GARSON, *All the Livelong Day*

The writer's repetitions and restatements both bind her sentences together and ensure that readers perceive her central idea, the segmenting of workers' jobs. *Work* (sentence 1) becomes a *task* (2, 4), *jobs* (3, 5), *labor* (6). *Workers* and *the worker* (2, 4, 5) become *each person* (3), *him* (4), *they* (5, 6). The work has been *rearranged* (1), *divided and subdivided* (3), *fragmented* (5). It consists of *a single operation* (3), *the same few motions, the same simple calculations* (6).

Though planned repetition can be effective, careless or excessive repetition weakens prose. See 31c.

4   **Using pronouns**

The previous examples illustrate yet another device for achieving paragraph coherence, the use of pronouns like *it*, *him*, *his*, and *they*. **Pronouns** refer to and function as nouns (see 5a-2) and thus can help relate sentences to each other. In the following paragraph the pronouns *he*, *him*, and *his* indicate that the patient is still the subject while enabling the writer to avoid repeating *the patient* or *the patients*.

> The experience is a familiar one to many emergency-room medics. A patient who has been pronounced dead and unexpectedly recovers later describes what happened to him during those moments—sometimes hours—when his body exhibited no signs of life. According to one repeated account, the patient feels himself rushing through a long, dark tunnel while noise rings in his ears. Suddenly, he finds himself outside his own body looking down with curious detachment at a medical team's efforts to resuscitate him. He hears what is said, notes what is happening but cannot communicate with anyone. Soon, his attention is drawn to other presences in the room—spirits of dead relatives or friends—who communicate with him nonverbally. Gradually he is drawn to a vague "being of light." This being invites him to evaluate his life and shows him highlights of his past in panoramic vision. The patient longs to stay with the being of light but is reluctantly drawn back into his physical body and recovers.
> —Kenneth L. Woodward, "Life After Death?"

The pronouns in this paragraph give it coherence, in part because they refer clearly to a noun. The opposite effect will occur if the reader cannot tell exactly what noun a pronoun is meant to refer to (see Chapter 12).

5   **Being consistent**

Being consistent is the most subtle way to achieve paragraph coherence because readers are aware of consistency only when it is absent. Consistency (or the lack of it) occurs primarily in the person and number of nouns and pronouns and in the tense of verbs (see Chapter 13). Although some shifts will be necessary because of meaning, inappropriate shifts will interfere with a reader's ability to follow the development of ideas. The writers of the following paragraphs destroy coherence by shifting person, number, and tense, respectively.

HE'S ON SECOND

To illustrate the importance of clear pronoun reference in paragraphs, try to locate a recording or transcript of the famous Abbott and Costello skit "Who's on First." While humorous, this skit demonstrates the frustration a reader can feel when encountering a series of pronouns with unclear antecedents.

¶ coh
3b

¶ coh
3b

SHIFTS IN PERSON

An enjoyable form of exercise is modern dance. If *one* [1,2]
wants to stay in shape, *you* will find that dance tones and
strengthens most muscles. The leaping and stretching *you* do [3]
also improves *a person's* balance and poise. And *I* found that [4]
my posture improved after only a few months of dancing.

SHIFTS IN NUMBER

Politics is not the activity for everyone. It requires quick- [1,2]
ness and patience at the same time. *A politician* must like [3]
speaking to large groups of people and fielding questions
without having time to think of the answers. *Politicians* must [4]
also be willing to compromise with the people *they* represent.
And no matter how good *a politician* is, *they* must give up on [5]
becoming popular with all constituents. It isn't possible. [6]

SHIFTS IN TENSE

I *am developing* an interest in filmmaking. I *tried* to take [1,2]
courses that relate to camera work or theater, and I *have read*
books about the technical and artistic sides of movies. Though [3]
I *would have liked* to get a job on a movie set right away, *I will*
probably *continue* my formal education and training in filmmaking after college. There simply *aren't* enough jobs avail- [4]
able for all those who *wanted* to be in films but *have* no direct
experience.

RESOURCES AND IDEAS

Two new frameworks for describing patterns of coherence and development in
paragraphs have recently been proposed.
Both draw on current linguistic and rhetorical theory and are somewhat technical, yet
they have considerable (if as yet undeveloped) potential for instruction. Both are
worth a close look.

Robin Bell Markels, *A New Perspective on
Cohesion in Expository Paragraphs* (Carbondale: Southern Illinois UP, 1984).

Richard M. Coe, *Toward a Grammar of
Passages* (Carbondale: Southern Illinois
UP, 1988).

READING ALOUD

Often students can spot a lack of transitions
in their own writing if they read their papers aloud. If you ask students to read one
another's papers aloud, the student writers
will often be able to recognize missing or
unclear transitions at those points where
the readers stumble over a passage or have
to stop to puzzle out the meaning.

---

6   **Using transitional expressions**

In addition to the methods for achieving coherence discussed
above, writers also rely on specific words and word groups to connect sentences whose relationships may not be instantly clear to
readers. Sometimes the omission of these words or word groups
will make an otherwise coherent paragraph choppy and hard to
follow, as the next paragraph shows.

Medical science has succeeded in identifying the hun- [1]
dreds of viruses that can cause the common cold. It has dis- [2]
covered the most effective means of prevention. One person [3]
transmits the cold viruses to another most often by hand. An
infected person covers his mouth to cough. He picks up the [4,5]
telephone. His daughter picks up the telephone. She rubs her [6,7]
eyes. She has a cold. It spreads. To avoid colds, people should [8,9,10]
wash their hands often and keep their hands away from their
faces.

This paragraph is unified and fundamentally coherent because the sentences do seem related to each other. However, it is

choppy to read, and we can only guess at the precise relationships spelled out by the italicized words below:

> Medical science has *thus* succeeded in identifying the 1
> hundreds of viruses that can cause the common cold. It has 2
> *also* discovered the most effective means of prevention. One 3
> person transmits the cold viruses to another most often by
> hand. *For instance*, an infected person covers his mouth to 4
> cough. *Then* he picks up the telephone. *Half an hour later*, his 5,6
> daughter picks up the *same* telephone. *Immediately afterward*, 7
> she rubs her eyes. *Within a few days, she, too*, has a cold. *And* 8,9
> *thus* it spreads. To avoid colds, *therefore*, people should wash 10
> their hands often and keep their hands away from their faces.
> —A STUDENT

Now the paragraph is smoother and clearer because the writer added connections that tell us precisely what to make of each sentence.

The linking words and word groups are called **transitional expressions.** They state relationships clearly and thus enhance paragraph coherence. The following is a partial list of transitional expressions, arranged by the functions they perform.

TRANSITIONAL EXPRESSIONS

TOO ADD OR SHOW SEQUENCE

again, also, and, and then, besides, equally important, finally, first, further, furthermore, in addition, in the first place, last, moreover, next, second, still, too

TO COMPARE

also, in the same way, likewise, similarly

TO CONTRAST

although, and yet, but, but at the same time, despite, even so, even though, for all that, however, in contrast, in spite of, nevertheless, notwithstanding, on the contrary, on the other hand, regardless, still, though, yet

TO GIVE EXAMPLES OR INTENSIFY

after all, an illustration of, even, for example, for instance, indeed, in fact, it is true, of course, specifically, that is, to illustrate, truly

TO INDICATE PLACE

above, adjacent to, below, elsewhere, farther on, here, near, nearby, on the other side, opposite to, there, to the east, to the left

(continued)

PARAGRAPH SCRAMBLES

These activities are suitable for students working individually; when assigned for work in small groups, however, the activities are likely to encourage considerable discussion and discovery.

1. Take a good paragraph, by either a student or a professional, and rearrange the sentences. Then ask students to unscramble the sentences and make a clear, coherent paragraph. This exercise will make students aware of the flow of a coherent paragraph and will alert them to the number of examples and details found in a well-developed paragraph.

2. Choose a paragraph that lacks coherence and rearrange the sentences. Tell students to unscramble the sentences to form a coherent paragraph. Indicate that students are free to add any transitions, sentences, illustrations, or details they feel are necessary to make the paragraph both coherent and well developed. Students will quickly spot any coherence problems in the original paragraph, and unless the topic of the paragraph is quite unusual, they will be able to add any necessary content.

> **TRANSITIONAL EXPRESSIONS** (*continued*)
>
> **To indicate time**
>
> after a while, afterward, as long as, as soon as, at last, at length, at that time, before, earlier, formerly, immediately, in the meantime, in the past, lately, later, meanwhile, now, presently, shortly, simultaneously, since, so far, soon, subsequently, then, thereafter, until, until now, when
>
> **To repeat, summarize, or conclude**
>
> all in all, altogether, as has been said, in brief, in conclusion, in other words, in particular, in short, in simpler terms, in summary, on the whole, that is, therefore, to put it differently, to summarize
>
> **To show cause or effect**
>
> accordingly, as a result, because, consequently, for this purpose, hence, otherwise, since, then, therefore, thereupon, thus, to this end, with this object

(For a discussion of transitional sentences and paragraphs, see pp. 80 and 119, respectively.)

7   **Combining devices to achieve coherence**

The devices we have examined for achieving coherence rarely appear in isolation in effective paragraphs. As any example in this chapter shows, writers usually combine sensible organization, parallelism, repetition, pronouns, consistency, and transitional expressions to help readers follow the development of ideas. And the devices also figure, naturally, in the whole essay (see 3e).

ANSWERS: EXERCISE 5

1. General-to-specific.
2. Chronological.
3. Spatial.
4. Climactic.

EXERCISE 5

Which of the organizational schemes discussed on pages 88–91 has been used in each of the following paragraphs?

1.   The losing animal in a struggle saves itself from destruction by an act of submission, an act usually recognized and accepted by the winner. In some cases, for instance, the loser presents to its rival a vulnerable part of its body such as the top of the head or the fleshy part of the neck. The central nervous system of the winner recognizes the "meaning" of the presentation, and the instinct to kill is inhibited. Typical of this natural pattern is the behavior of two wolves in combat.

As soon as one of the animals realizes it cannot win, it offers 5 its vulnerable throat to the stronger wolf; instead of taking advantage of the opportunity, the victor relents, even though an instant earlier it had appeared frantic to reach the now proffered jugular vein.

—RENÉ DUBOS, "Territoriality and Dominance"

2.   On August 18, 1951, the St. Louis Browns baseball team 1 cracked a joke and forever changed the rules of professional baseball. On that day the Browns were playing the Detroit Ti- 2 gers. In the first inning the St. Louis manager sent to the plate 3 Eddie Gaedel, a man less than four feet tall. Detroit's pitcher 4 at first did not throw to Gaedel, but the small man held his stance, his child's bat cocked. When the pitcher finally let one 5 fly, the ball sailed over Gaedel's head. The pitcher tried again, 6 and again the ball flew over Gaedel's head. The third pitch, 7 too, was high, and so was the fourth. The pitcher simply could 8 not lower his throws to Gaedel's strike zone. Gaedel walked to 9 first base, where he was replaced by a pinch runner who later scored. Within twenty-four hours baseball had a new rule: no 10 midgets would ever again play professional ball.

—A STUDENT

3.   One must descend to the basement and move along a con- 1 fusing mazelike hall to reach it. Twice the passage seems to 2 lead against a blank wall; then at last one enters the brightly lighted auditorium. And here, finally, are the social workers 3 at the reception desks; and there, waiting upon the benches rowed beneath the pipes carrying warmth and water to the floors above, are the patients. One sees white-jacketed psychi- 4 atrists carrying charts appear and vanish behind screens that form the improvised interviewing cubicles. All is an atmo- 5 sphere of hurried efficiency; and the concerned faces of the pa- tients are brightened by the friendly smiles and low-pitched voices of the expert workers. One has entered the Lafargue 6 Psychiatric Clinic.   —RALPH ELLISON, *Shadow and Act*

4.   There are three reasons, quite apart from scientific con- 1 siderations, that mankind needs to travel in space. The first 2 reason is the need for garbage disposal: we need to transfer in- dustrial processes into space, so that the earth may remain a green and pleasant place for our grandchildren to live in. The 3 second reason is the need to escape material impoverishment: the resources of this planet are finite, and we shall not forego forever the abundant solar energy and minerals and living space that are spread out all around us. The third reason is 4 our spiritual need for an open frontier: the ultimate purpose of space travel is to bring to humanity not only scientific dis- coveries and an occasional spectacular show on television but a real expansion of our spirit.

—FREEMAN DYSON, "Disturbing the Universe"

ANSWERS: EXERCISE 6

1. The coherent order would be 1, 2, 5, 3, 6, 4.
2. The coherent order would be 1, 2, 5, 7, 6, 4, 3, 8.

ANSWERS: EXERCISE 7

1. Parallelism in sentences 2, 6, 7, 8: something clicks . . . one grasps . . . masters; There are the mountains . . . There is the glimmering ocean; The civic landmarks . . . display themselves . . . the pattern of the place unfolds; unlock . . . undo . . . take. Repetition and restatement: freeway(s) (1, 2, 3); system (2, 8); key, navigational aid (2, 4); locks, unlock (4, 8). Pronouns: primarily it for system, they for freeways. Transitional expressions: though, suddenly (2); then (5).

2. Parallelism in all three sentences: sabotaged . . . prevented . . . freed . . . harassed . . . released . . . hindered (1); taken . . . distributed (2); can feel . . . are aware . . . have (3). Repetition and restatement: animals (throughout); Advocates of the rights of animals and growing number of people (1, 3); rights (1, 3); inhumanely treated and pain (2, 3). Pronouns: primarily they for advocates. Transitional expression: Such (3).

3. Parallelism in sentences 2, 3, 4: They have measured . . . recorded and studied . . . learned. Repetition: whale, sings, song throughout. Pronoun: they for scientists throughout. Transitional expression: And (4).

4. Parallelism within many sentences and in sentences 7–10: The side pockets . . . bulged . . . one pocket always contained . . . His breast pocket contained; screwdrivers, pliers [etc.] . . . drill bits, gimlets [etc.]. Repetition and restatement: mouth, lips (1, 2, 3, 6); puckers, puckered (3, 4); pucker, smile, both expressions (3, 4, 5); pocket(s) (1, 6, 7, 9, 10). Pronouns: primarily he and his. Transitional expressions: After (4); In addition (9).

EXERCISE 6

After the topic sentence (sentence 1), the sentences in each student paragraph below have been deliberately scrambled to make the paragraph incoherent. Using the topic sentence and other clues as guides, rearrange the sentences in each paragraph to form a well-organized, coherent unit.

1.   We hear complaints about the Postal Service all the time, 1 but we should not forget what it does *right*. The total volume 2 of mail delivered by the Postal Service each year makes up more than half the total delivered in all the world. Its 70,000 3 employees handle 90,000,000,000 pieces of mail each year. And when was the last time they failed to deliver yours? In 4,5 fact, on any given day the Postal Service delivers almost as much mail as the rest of the world combined. That means 6 over 1,250,000 pieces per employee and over 400 pieces per man, woman, and child in the country.

2.   A single visit to New York City will tell you why the city 1 is both loved and hated by so many people. Whether you ar- 2 rive by car, bus, train, plane, or boat, the skyline will take your breath away. And the streets seem so dirty: cans and 3 bags and newspapers lie in the gutters and on the sidewalks or sometimes fly across your path. Even the people who do 4 speak English won't smile or say "Excuse me" or give you good directions. The thrill will only be heightened when you 5 walk down the skyscraper canyons, look in the shop windows, go to the theater or a museum, stroll in the neighborhoods where no one speaks English. You start to notice the noise of 6 traffic and get annoyed at the crowds. But all is not perfect— 7 far from it. After a few days, when your reactions balance out, 8 you have the same love-hate feelings as everyone else.

EXERCISE 7

Study the paragraphs in Exercise 1 (pp. 83–84) for the authors' use of various devices to achieve paragraph coherence. Look especially for parallel structures and ideas, repetition and restatement, pronouns, and transitional expressions.

EXERCISE 8   *Good*

The paragraph below is incoherent because of inconsistencies in person, number, or tense. Identify the inconsistencies and revise the paragraph to give it coherence.

I rebel against the idea of males always being the sole 1 family provider. For me to be happy, I needed to feel useful, 2 and so I work to support myself and my daughter. I did not 3 feel that it is wrong for one to be a housewife while a man supports your household, but that way is not for me. I enjoy the 4

business world, and I have been pleased with my job. Work- 5
ing, I make enough now to support the two of us, and I know
that when I graduate, I will be able to earn even more. I can 6
do very well as my own provider.

EXERCISE 9

Transitional expressions have been removed from the following
paragraph at the numbered blanks. Fill in each blank with an appropriate transitional expression (1) to contrast, (2) to intensify,
and (3) to show effect. Consult the list on pages 95–96 if necessary.

     All over the country people are swimming, jogging,
weight-lifting, dancing, walking, playing tennis—doing anything to keep fit. __(1)__ this school has consistently refused to
construct and equip a fitness center. The school has __(2)__ refused to open existing athletic facilities to all students, not just
those playing organized sports. __(3)__ students have no place to
exercise except in their rooms and on dangerous public roads.

EXERCISE 10

Write a coherent paragraph from the following information,
combining and rewriting sentences as necessary. First, begin the
paragraph with the topic sentence given and arrange the supporting sentences in a climactic order. Then combine and rewrite the supporting sentences, helping the reader see connections by introducing parallelism, repetition and restatement,
pronouns, consistency, and transitional expressions.

TOPIC SENTENCE

Hypnosis is far superior to drugs for relieving tension.

SUPPORTING INFORMATION

Hypnosis has none of the dangerous side effects of the drugs that
    relieve tension.
Tension-relieving drugs can cause weight loss or gain, illness, or
    even death.
Hypnosis is nonaddicting.
Most of the drugs that relieve tension do foster addiction.
Tension-relieving drugs are expensive.
Hypnosis is inexpensive even for people who have not mastered
    self-hypnosis.

EXERCISE 11

Develop three of the following topic sentences into coherent
paragraphs. Organize your information by space, by time, or for

---

¶ coh
3b

ANSWERS: EXERCISE 8

Inconsistency in number: <u>males</u> and <u>pro-vider</u> (sentence 1). Inconsistency in tense:
<u>needed</u> and <u>work</u> (2); <u>did</u> and <u>is</u> (3); <u>enjoy</u>
and <u>have been</u> (4). Inconsistency in person:
<u>one</u> and <u>your</u> (3). Possible revision:

    I rebel against the idea of <u>the male</u> al-
ways being the sole family provider. For
me to be happy, I (need) to feel useful, and
so I work to support myself and my
daughter. I <u>do</u> not feel that it is wrong
for one (or <u>a woman</u>) to be a housewife
while a man supports <u>one</u> (or <u>her</u>), but
that way is not for me. I enjoy the business world, and I <u>am</u> pleased with my
job. Working, I make enough now to support the two of us, and I know that when
I graduate, I will be able to earn even
more. I can do very well as my own provider.

POSSIBLE ANSWERS: EXERCISE 9

  1. *Yet, However, Even so,* or *Nevertheless*
  2. *even, also,* or *further*
  3. *As a result, Consequently,* or *Therefore*

ANSWERS: EXERCISE 10

Possible paragraph:

    Hypnosis is far superior to drugs for re-
lieving tension. It is inexpensive even for
people who have not mastered self-
hypnosis, whereas drugs are expensive.
It is nonaddictive, whereas drugs foster
addiction. And most important, hypnosis
has none of the dangerous side effects of
drugs, such as weight loss or gain, illness, or even death.

ANSWERS: EXERCISE 11

Individual response.

_____ is probably my closest friend in this world.

~~sees~~ Looks?

Walks?

Talks?

Smiles?

Laughs?

emphasis, as seems most appropriate. Use parallelism, repetition and restatement, pronouns, consistency, and transitional expressions to link sentences.

1. Of all my courses, _____ is the one that I think will serve me best throughout life.
2. The movie (or book) had an exciting plot.
3. Although we Americans face many problems, the one we should concentrate on solving first is _____.
4. The most dramatic building in town is the _____.
5. Children should not have to worry about the future.

HIGHLIGHTS

This section (3c) looks at ways to convey the central idea of a paragraph fully and convincingly to the reader. Developing paragraphs and essays fully is often difficult for students. One of the important differences between casual conversation and formal writing is the degree to which ideas must be concretely developed in writing. Because students are more experienced in conversation than in writing, they find generalizations much easier to come by than the details, examples, and reasons to support them.

All of us must grapple with the student essay or single paragraph that is largely a succession of generalizations without support or explanation. Part of the solution to such problem paragraphs is to make students aware of readers as a special kind of audience for ideas. Another part is to make them aware of different strategies for developing paragraphs or essays.

The ways to develop ideas are infinite, of course, but this section focuses on a limited number. The initial emphasis falls on the use of details, examples, and reasons, which are essential to any more specific method of development. Then follow the standard methods or patterns of development, each introduced by questions students can ask about an idea, event, or object to uncover concrete information useful for developing a paragraph.

You may wish to ask students to spend time in class or in groups working with

3c Developing the paragraph

A paragraph may be both unified and coherent but still be skimpy, unconvincing, or otherwise inadequate. The following paragraph is unified and coherent: it adheres to the topic of bad television commercials, and the relations among sentences are apparent. But it is not an effective paragraph.

> Despite complaints from viewers, television commercials 1
> aren't getting any more realistic. Their makers still present 2
> idealized people in unreal situations. And the advertisers also 3
> persist in showing a version of male-female relationships that
> can't exist in more than two households. What do the adver- 4
> tisers know about us, or about how we see ourselves, that
> makes them continue to plunge millions of dollars into these
> kinds of commercials?

Sentences 2 and 3 create expectations in our minds: we anticipate that the writer will give examples of commercials showing idealized people and unrealistic male-female relationships. But our expectations are disappointed because the paragraph lacks **development**, completeness. It does not provide enough information for us to evaluate the writer's assertion in sentence 1.

A well-developed paragraph always provides the specific information that readers need and expect in order to understand you and to stay interested in what you say. Often you may develop and arrange this information according to a particular pattern that is determined by your topic and what you want to say about it.

1 Using specific information

If they are sound, the general statements you make in any writing will be based on what you have experienced, observed, read, and thought. Readers will assume as much and will expect you to provide the evidence for your statements. <u>They need details, examples, and reasons — the heart of paragraph development — to understand and appreciate your meaning.</u>

Here is the actual version of the paragraph discussed above. Notice how the added descriptions of commercials (in italics) turn a sketchy paragraph into an interesting and convincing one.

> Despite complaints from viewers, television commercials 1
> aren't getting any more realistic. Their makers still present 2
> idealized people in unreal situations. *Friendly shopkeepers* 3
> *stock only their favorite brand of toothpaste or coffee or soup. A* 4
> *mother cleans and buffs her kitchen floor to a mirror finish so*
> *her baby can play on it. A rosy-cheeked pregnant woman uses* 5
> *two babies, two packaged diapers neatly dissected, and two ink*
> *blotters to demonstrate one diaper's superior absorbency to her*
> *equally rosy-cheeked and pregnant friend.* The advertisers also 6
> persist in showing a version of male-female relationships that
> can't exist in more than two households. *The wife panics be-* 7
> *cause a meddlesome neighbor points out that her husband's*
> *shirt is dirty. Or she fears for her marriage because her finicky* 8
> *husband doesn't like her coffee.* What do the advertisers know 9
> about us, or about how we see ourselves, that makes them
> continue to plunge millions of dollars into these kinds of com-
> mercials?   —A STUDENT

<u>In this paragraph the writer has recognized that sentences 2 and 6 create expectations for supporting examples, and she has duly responded to these expectations.</u> Whereas the general statements merely *tell* us about the commercials, the detailed examples *show* them to us.

---

2 Using a pattern of development

Sometimes you may have difficulty developing an idea, or you may not see the most effective way to shape the information you have. Then you can use one of the patterns of paragraph development that correspond to patterns of essay development discussed on pages 20–22 and 41–43. Experienced writers use these patterns all the time, often unconsciously. Inexperienced writers can ask themselves a series of questions about an idea that will suggest how to develop it and how to organize the supporting information.

How did it happen?

Asking how something happened leads to **narration**, the retelling of a sequence of events, usually in the order of their occur-

¶ dev

3c

sample topics to discover how the methods of development can be used to probe a topic and how the questions reveal different aspects of a topic. This discussion may help students see how the process of development can be an act of discovery. You will probably want to stress, however, that the methods of development covered in the handbook are not the only ones writers can use and that most paragraphs use more than a single method.

The exercises for this section range from analyzing paragraphs to producing them, and whether used in groups or by students working individually, they encourage students to treat the patterns of development as different ways of viewing a topic.

RESOURCES AND IDEAS

Carol Cohan, "Writing Effective Paragraphs," *College Composition and Communication* 27 (1976): 363–65. Cohan suggests encouraging paragraph development by treating topic sentences as questions to be answered by the paragraph that follows.

rence (that is, chronologically). The paragraph by Arthur C. Clarke on page 89 narrates the stages of a star's death. Here is another narrative paragraph in which events occupy not weeks but moments. The author's larger concern is contemporary language such as "sharing feelings" that reduces complex human interactions to formulas.

> Years ago, my husband and I rented a summer place in which we found ourselves surrounded by a tightly knit community that seemed to be speaking some common and slightly alien language. One night, at a party, one of these neighbors complained about the Moonie encampment around the corner and my husband—whose unconscious must surely have known what his conscious mind was slower to suspect—said that the Moonies weren't half so bad as . . . and he mentioned an especially strident human-potential group then receiving a good deal of publicity and notoriety. As a hush fell over the room, it dawned on us that the language we'd been puzzling over all summer was the language of that same group. No one breathed until at last our host turned to my husband and said, "Thank you for sharing that with us."
>
> —Francine Prose, "Therapy Clichés"

As this paragraph illustrates, a narrative usually does not correspond to real time but collapses transitional or background events (as in sentence 1) and then expands the events of particular interest (2–4). In addition, writers often rearrange events, as when they simulate the workings of memory by briefly flashing back to an earlier time.

How does it look, sound, feel, smell, taste?

Detailing the sensory qualities of a person, place, or thing is the act of **description.** You use concrete and specific words to evoke in readers your own experience of the subject. Some description is **subjective:** the writer filters the subject through his or her biases and emotions. In Donald Hall's subjective description on page 88, the *bright* garden and the mountain that *loomed in the blue distance* indicate Hall's feelings about these physical features of his environment. Similarly, in Pauline Kael's description of Steve Martin (pp. 81–82), such words and phrases as *comedy robot*, *hilarious*, and *spruced up and dapper* convey Kael's interpretation of what she sees and hears.

In contrast to subjective description, journalists and scientists often favor description that is **objective**, conveying the subject without bias or emotion. As the following example from a psychology paper illustrates, the writer of objective description tries to record all relevant sensory data as specifically as possible without interpretation.

> The two toddlers, both boys, sat together for half an hour in a ten-foot-square room with yellow walls (one with a two-way mirror for observation) and a brown carpet. The room was unfurnished except for two small chairs and about two dozen toys. The boys' interaction was generally tense. They often struggled physically and verbally over several toys, especially a large red beach ball and a small wooden fire engine. The larger of the two boys often pushed the smaller away or pried his hands from the desired object. This larger boy never spoke, but he did make grunting sounds when he was engaging the other. In turn, the smaller boy twice uttered piercing screams of "No!" and once shouted "Stop that!" When he was left alone, he hummed and muttered to himself.
> —A STUDENT

How can it be illustrated or supported?

Some ideas can be developed simply by **illustration or support**—supplying detailed examples or reasons. The writer of the paragraph on television commercials (p. 101) developed her idea with several specific examples of each general statement. You can also supply a single extended example, as the author of the following paragraph does to illustrate his assertion (sentence 1) about cultural differences in the ways people communicate.

> One of my earliest discoveries in the field of intercultural communication was that the position of the bodies of people in conversation varies with the culture. Even so, it used to puzzle me that a special Arab friend seemed unable to walk and talk at the same time. After years in the United States, he could not bring himself to stroll along, facing forward while talking. Our progress would be arrested while he edged ahead, cutting slightly in front of me and turning sideways so we could see each other. Once in this position, he would stop. His behavior was explained when I learned that for the Arabs to view the other person peripherally is regarded as impolite, and to sit or stand back-to-back is considered very rude. You must be involved when interacting with Arabs who are friends.   —EDWARD T. HALL, *The Hidden Dimension*

The details of this example are arranged in a rough chronological sequence. In a paragraph containing several examples, a climactic organization is often effective; see the paragraph by Alan Devoe on pages 90–91 for an example.

Sometimes you can develop a paragraph by providing your reasons for stating a general idea. Such is the method used in the following paragraph.

It is time to defend the welfare state—taxes, bureau- 1
crats, rules and regulations—the whole thing. Not only be- 2
cause it actually helps people who need help and subsidizes
and enables a range of socially valuable activities: it does all
that, and all that has to be done. There is another, and ulti- 3
mately a more important, reason for defending the welfare
state. It expresses a certain civil spirit, a sense of mutuality, a 4
commitment to justice. Without that sense, no society can 5
survive for long as a decent place to live—not for the needy,
and not for anyone else.

—MICHAEL WALZER, "The Community"

Sentences 2, 4, and 5 provide reasons for the general assertion in
sentence 1. As is often the case in such paragraphs, the reasons are
arranged in a climactic order. (For another example, see the paragraph by Freeman Dyson in Exercise 5, p. 97.)

What is it? What does it encompass, and what does it exclude?

Asking "What is it?" leads to development by **definition**—
saying what something is and is not, specifying the characteristics
that distinguish it from the other members of its class. You can
easily define concrete, noncontroversial terms in a single sentence:
A knife is a cutting instrument (its class) *with a sharp blade set in a
handle* (the characteristics that set it off from, say, scissors or a ra-
zor blade). But defining a complicated, abstract, or controversial
topic often requires extended explanation (see 4d-2), and you may
need to devote a whole paragraph or even an essay to it. Such a definition may provide examples to identify the subject's characteristics. It may also involve other methods of development discussed
below, such as division (separating things into their parts), classification (combining things into groups), or comparison and contrast.

Here is a paragraph developed by definition. It is from an
essay asserting that "quality in product and effort has become a
vanishing element of current civilization."

In the hope of possibly reducing the hail of censure which 1
is certain to greet this essay (I am thinking of going to Alaska
or possibly Patagonia in the week it is published), let me say
that quality, as I understand it, means investment of the best
skill and effort possible to produce the finest and most admirable result possible. Its presence or absence in some degree 2
characterizes every man-made object, service, skilled or
unskilled labor—laying bricks, painting a picture, ironing
shirts, practicing medicine, shoemaking, scholarship, writing

a book. You do it well or you do it half-well. Materials are 3,4
sound and durable or they are sleazy; method is painstaking
or whatever is easiest. Quality is achieving or reaching for the 5
highest standard as against being satisfied with the sloppy or
fraudulent. It is honesty of purpose as against catering to 6
cheap or sensational sentiment. It does not allow compromise 7
with the second-rate.

—BARBARA TUCHMAN, "The Decline of Quality"

To explain just what she means by *quality*—the key word of her
essay—the author first provides a general definition (sentence 1)
and then refines it with examples of the range of activities in which
quality may figure (2), followed by a list of the characteristics that
distinguish quality from nonquality (3–7). In this paragraph the
sentences after the first move roughly from specific to general, but
an arrangement by increasing specificity, importance, or complexity often works in definition as well.

What are its parts or characteristics? Or what groups or categories can it be sorted into?

Separating a single thing into its parts is the activity of **division** (also called **analysis**). Using division, you might examine a family by dividing it into its individual members—mother, father, daughter, son. Grouping many things according to their similarities is the activity of **classification.** Using classification to describe families, you might examine family structures in various cultures—matriarchal, patriarchal, nuclear, extended, and so on. Division and classification are so closely related that writers often combine them in developing an idea, a paragraph, or an essay. Thus in describing the family you might first classify the types and then divide each type into the separate roles of the individual family members.

In the following paragraph the writer divides a small portion of a daily newspaper into its parts, giving the technical name for each part.

A typical daily newspaper compresses considerable infor- 1
mation into the top of the first page, above the headlines. The 2
most prominent feature of this space, the newspaper's name,
is called the *logo* or *nameplate.* Under the logo and set off by 3
rules is a line of small type called the *folio line,* which contains the date of the issue, the volume and issue numbers,
copyright information, and the price. To the right of the logo 4
is a block of small type called a *weather ear,* a summary of the
day's forecast. And above the logo is a *skyline,* a kind of ad- 5
vertisement in which the paper's editors highlight a special
feature of the issue.

—A STUDENT

EXTRA EXAMPLES

Division: Face

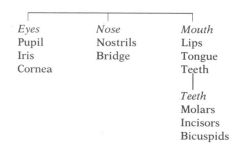

Eyes	*Nose*	*Mouth*
Pupil	Nostrils	Lips
Iris	Bridge	Tongue
Cornea		Teeth

Teeth
Molars
Incisors
Bicuspids

EXTRA EXAMPLES

Classification:

Great Dane, Terrier	Siamese, Tabby
DOGS	CATS

Morgan, Arabian	Guernsey, Holstein
HORSES	COWS

QUADRUPEDS

MAMMALS

¶ dev
3c

Division always begins with a single object or concept; in the preceding paragraph it is a segment of a newspaper's front page. The task is then to identify and explain the distinct elements that constitute the object or concept. The elements might be arranged spatially, as they are above, or in order of importance or complexity.

In the following paragraph the writer classifies parents.

> In my experience, the parents who hire daytime sitters 1
> for their school-age children tend to fall into one of three
> groups. The first group includes parents who work and want 2
> someone to be at home when the children return from school. 3
> These parents are looking for an extension of themselves,
> someone who will give the care they would give if they were
> at home. The second group includes parents who may be 4
> home all day themselves but are too disorganized or too fraz-
> zled by their children's demands to handle child care alone.
> They are looking for an organizer and helpmate. The third 5,6
> and final group includes parents who do not want to be both-
> ered by their children, whether they are home all day or not.
> Unlike the parents in the first two groups, who care for their 7
> children whenever and however they can, these parents are
> looking for a permanent substitute for themselves.
>
> —A STUDENT

The groups in this paragraph are arranged in a climactic order, but complexity or familiarity may also serve to organize a classification. This paragraph also illustrates several principles of classification. First, the subject being classified is plural (parents), in contrast to the singular subject of division. Second, the classes or groups are alike in at least one basic way: all hire sitters for their children. And third, the classes do not overlap, as would parents who work and parents who don't because both groups include some uncaring and some caring parents.

How is it like, or different from, other things?

Asking about similarities and differences leads to **comparison and contrast.** The two may be used separately or together to develop an idea or to relate two or more things. In the following paragraph the author contrasts two styles of basketball play to support his point about consistency in sentence 1.

> Consistency is also always potentially dull, even when 1
> the consistency demonstrated happens to be excellence. John 2
> Havlicek, the former basketball star of the Boston Celtics, al-
> most never made a mistake on the court. He used the back- 3
> board with astounding precision, and stood exactly where he
> was supposed to on every fast break. Yet Havlicek was a far 4
> less satisfying player to watch than Philadelphia's Julius Erv-

ing, who continually surprises spectators and defenses with moves no one (including himself) could possibly anticipate. One might argue that Erving is consistently amazing, but the 5 reason he so grasps a crowd's imagination, the reason thousands of people roar whenever Erving simply lays a hand on the ball, is that the man seems the epitome of the unpredictable, the thoroughly free and spontaneous soul.
—ROGER ROSENBLATT, "Consistency as a Minor Virtue"

This paragraph illustrates one of two common ways of organizing a comparison and contrast: **subject-by-subject,** with the two subjects discussed separately, first one and then the other. The next paragraph illustrates the other common organization: **point-by-point,** with the two subjects discussed side by side and matched feature for feature.

This emphasis on the unfairness of language to women is 1
misplaced. We should be erasing all bias from language, and 2
that means bias against men as well. If a female pilot should 3
not be stigmatized as an "aviatrix," then a male pilot should
not be stigmatized as a "fly-boy." If it is unfair to label women 4
as "witches," then it is equally unfair to label men as "cads."
If a woman should not be called a "dog," then a man should 5
not be called a "nerd" or a "wimp." If it demeans the homeless 6
woman to call her "baglady," then it also demeans the homeless man to call him a "bum." —A STUDENT

The most effective comparisons show similarities between subjects usually perceived as different, such as the words used for women and men in the preceding paragraph. Contrasts, however, are most effective when they show differences between subjects usually perceived as similar, such as the two basketball players in Rosenblatt's paragraph.

Is it comparable to something that is in a different class but more familiar?

Whereas we draw comparisons and contrasts between elements in the same general class (basketball players, words), we link elements in different classes with a special kind of comparison called **analogy.** Most often in analogy we illuminate or explain an unfamiliar, complex, abstract class of things with a familiar and concrete class of things. In the following paragraph the author develops an analogy between writing style (abstract) and a distance runner (concrete).

The good style is the lean style. Like a good distance run- 1,2
ner, it hasn't an ounce of excess fat anywhere on it. And like 3
the good distance runner, it moves without excess motion. Its 4

IMITATING PARAGRAPHS

Choose a successful paragraph (student or professional) with a clear pattern, and discuss it in class. Then ask students to write paragraphs imitating the pattern but not the content of the model paragraph.

arms don't flail out in all directions; they swing easily at the sides in a beautiful economy of effort. A good style has the same grace and beauty in its motion as a good athlete because there's nothing wasted. Everything is there for a purpose.

–LAURENCE PERRINE, "Fifteen Ways to Write Five Hundred Words"

In the next paragraph the author draws an analogy between the weather and human combat.

In an age all too familiar with war the yearly cycle of the weather is well imagined in terms of combat. It is a war in which a stronghold or citadel sometimes beats off assault after assault. More often the battle-line shifts quickly back and forth across thousands of miles—a war of sudden raids and swift counterattacks, of stern pitched battles, of deep forays and confused struggles high in the air. In the Northern Hemisphere the opponents are the Arctic and the Tropics, North against South. Uncertain ally to the South—now bringing, now withdrawing aid—the sun shifts among the signs of the zodiac. And the chief battle-line is known as the Polar Front.

–GEORGE R. STEWART, *Storm*

What are its causes or its effects?

When you analyze why something happened or what is likely to happen, then you are determining causes and effects. **Cause-and-effect analysis** is especially useful in writing about social, economic, or political events or problems, as the next paragraphs illustrate. In the first, the author looks at the causes of Japanese collectivism, which he elsewhere contrasts with American individualism.

The *shinkansen* or "bullet train" speeds across the rural areas of Japan giving a quick view of cluster after cluster of farmhouses surrounded by rice paddies. This particular pattern did not develop purely by chance, but as a consequence of the technology peculiar to the growing of rice, the staple of the Japanese diet. The growing of rice requires the construction and maintenance of an irrigation system, something that takes many hands to build. More importantly, the planting and the harvesting of rice can only be done efficiently with the cooperation of twenty or more people. The "bottom line" is that a single family working alone cannot produce enough rice to survive, but a dozen families working together can produce a surplus. Thus the Japanese have had to develop the capacity to work together in harmony, no matter what the forces of disagreement or social disintegration, in order to survive.

–WILLIAM OUCHI, *Theory Z: How American Business Can Meet the Japanese Challenge*

COMBINING FOR EMPHASIS

Put together a group of sentences or bits of information about a topic, perhaps drawing the material from an essay in a reader or a magazine article. Ask students, working individually or in groups, to combine the material into a paragraph that has a distinct point of view. You might, for example, provide information about a recent controversial incident and ask for a paragraph emphasizing one perspective toward the incident or one perspective on its causes and effects.

¶ dev
3c

In sentences 1, 2, and 6 Ouchi specifies an effect: the Japanese live close together and work in harmony. The middle sentences explain the conditions that caused this effect: the Japanese depend heavily on rice, and growing rice demands collective effort.

Cause-and-effect paragraphs tend to focus either on causes, as Ouchi's does, or on effects, as the next paragraph does.

> There is something uneasy in the Los Angeles air this af-
> ternoon, some unnatural stillness, some tension. What it
> means is that tonight a Santa Ana will begin to blow, a hot
> wind from the northeast whining down through the Cajon
> and San Gorgonio Passes, blowing up sandstorms out along
> Route 66, drying the hills and the nerves to the flash point.
> For a few days now we will see smoke back in the canyons,
> and hear sirens in the night. I have neither heard nor read
> that a Santa Ana is due, but I know it, and almost everyone I
> have seen today knows it too. We know it because we feel it.
> The baby frets. The maid sulks. I rekindle a waning argument
> with the telephone company, then cut my losses and lie down,
> given over to whatever it is in the air. To live with the Santa
> Ana is to accept, consciously or unconsciously, a deeply mech-
> anistic view of human behavior.
> —JOAN DIDION, "Los Angeles Notebook"

Didion's second sentence specifies a cause: the Santa Ana wind. All the sentences in the paragraph describe the effects of the wind.

How does it work?

When you explain how something works, you explain the steps in a **process.** Paragraphs developed by analyzing a process are usually organized chronologically or spatially, as the steps in the process occur. Some process analyses tell the reader how to do something. For example:

> Car owners waste money when they pay a mechanic to
> change the engine oil. The job is not difficult, even for some-
> one who knows little about cars. All one needs is a wrench to
> remove the drain plug, a large, flat pan to collect the draining
> oil, plastic bottles to dispose of the used oil, and fresh oil.
> First, warm up the car's engine so that the oil will flow more
> easily. When the engine is warm, shut it off and remove its oil-
> filler cap (the owner's manual shows where this cap is). Then
> locate the drain plug under the engine (again consulting the
> owner's manual for its location) and place the flat pan under
> the plug. Remove the plug with the wrench, letting the oil
> flow into the pan. When the oil stops flowing, replace the plug
> and, at the engine's filler hole, add the amount and kind of
> fresh oil specified by the owner's manual. Pour the used oil

into the plastic bottles and take it to a waste-oil collector, which any garage mechanic can recommend. —A STUDENT

Other process analyses explain how a process is done or how it works in nature. The following paragraph, for example, explains how an island of mangrove trees begins "from scratch."

> Nor can a tree live without soil. A hurricane-born mangrove island may bring its own soil to the sea. But other mangrove trees make their own soil—and their own islands—from scratch. These are the ones which interest me. The seeds germinate in the fruit on the tree. The germinated embryo can drop anywhere—say, onto a dab of floating muck. The heavy root end sinks; a leafy plumule unfurls. The tiny seedling, afloat, is on its way. Soon aerial roots shooting out in all directions trap debris. The sapling's networks twine, the interstices narrow, and water calms in the lee. Bacteria thrive on organic broth; amphipods swarm. These creatures grow and die at the tree's wet feet. The soil thickens, accumulating rainwater, leaf rot, seashells, and guano; the island spreads.
>
> —ANNIE DILLARD, "Sojourner"

Combining patterns of development

Whatever pattern you choose as the basis for developing a paragraph, other patterns may also prove helpful. We have seen combined patterns often throughout this section: Tuchman uses contrast to define *quality* (pp. 104–05); Rosenblatt uses examples to contrast consistency and inconsistency (pp. 106–07); Perrine uses analogy to define a good writing style (pp. 107–08).

As we will see in 3e, the paragraphs within an essay inevitably will be developed with a variety of patterns, even when one controlling pattern develops and structures the entire essay.

3 **Checking length**

The average paragraph contains between 100 and 150 words, or between four and eight sentences. These numbers are averages, of course. The actual length of a paragraph depends on its topic, the role it plays in developing the thesis of the essay, and its position in the essay. Nevertheless, very short paragraphs are often inadequately developed; they may leave readers with a sense of incompleteness. And very long paragraphs often contain irrelevant details or develop two or more topics; readers may have difficulty sorting out or remembering ideas.

When you are revising your essay, reread the paragraphs that

DEVELOPING PARAGRAPHS

Take underdeveloped paragraphs on subjects likely to be familiar to students and ask them to develop the paragraphs fully by drawing on their own knowledge. Student paragraphs often provide good material for this exercise.

seem very long or very short, checking them especially for unity and adequate development. If the paragraph wanders, cut everything from it that does not support your main idea (such as sentences that you might begin with *By the way*). If it is underdeveloped, supply the specific details, examples, or reasons needed, or try one of the methods of development we have discussed here.

¶ dev 3c

EXERCISE 12

Great Exercise

The following paragraphs are not well developed. Analyze them, looking especially for general statements that lack support or leave questions in your mind. Then rewrite one into a well-developed paragraph, supplying your own concrete details or examples.

1. One big difference between successful and unsuccessful 1
teachers is the quality of communication. A successful teacher 2
is sensitive to students' needs and excited by the course subject. In contrast, an unsuccessful teacher seems uninterested 3
in students and bored by the subject.

2. Gestures are one of our most important means of com- 1
munication. We use them instead of speech. We use them to 2,3
supplement the words we speak. And we use them to com- 4
municate some feelings or meanings that words cannot adequately express.

3. Children who have been disciplined too much are often 1
easy to spot. Their behavior toward adults may reflect the 2
harsh treatment they have received from adults. And their be- 3
havior toward other children may be uncontrolled.

EXERCISE 13

Good

Identify the pattern or patterns of development in each of the following paragraphs. Where does the author supply specific information to achieve development?

1. A century of association has inevitably acculturated both 1
Hispanos and Anglo-Americans to some extent, but there still
persist a number of culture traits that neither group has relinquished altogether. Nothing is more disquieting to an Anglo- 2
American who believes that time is money than the time perspective of Hispanos. They usually refer to this attitude as the 3
"*mañana* [tomorrow] psychology." Actually, it is more of a 4
"today psychology," because Hispanos cultivate the present
to the exclusion of the future; because the latter has not arrived yet, it is not a reality. They are reluctant to relinquish 5
the present, so they hold onto it until it becomes the past. To 6
an Hispano, nine is nine until it is ten, so when he arrives at
nine-thirty, he jubilantly exclaims: "*¡Justo!*" [right on time].

ANSWERS: EXERCISE 12

1. Sentence 1 requires some expansion to explain *quality of communication*. Each of the next two sentences needs to be supported with specific examples of the two qualities named.

2. Sentences 2, 3, and 4 should each be followed by at least two specific examples of gestures to make the writer's meaning concrete.

3. Sentences 2 and 3 require specific support, perhaps both citations of studies that have demonstrated the effects mentioned and examples of children's behavior.

ANSWERS: EXERCISE 13

1. The paragraph is developed by comparison and contrast of Hispanos' and Anglo-Americans' attitudes toward time. Specific details appear primarily in sentences 6–10.

2. The paragraph is developed by illustration of the ways in which immigrants are "changing the American landscape." Sentences 2–5 each contain one or two specific examples.

3. The paragraph is developed by division of a dying person's attitude into five stages. Specific details appear in sentences 2–6, each sentence a description of a separate stage.

4. The paragraph is developed by a definition of *mooches*. Specific details appear particularly in sentences 3 and 5.

This may be why the clock is slowed down to a walk in Spanish while in English it runs. In the United States, our future-oriented civilization plans our lives so far in advance that the present loses its meaning. January magazine issues are out in December; 1973 cars have been out since October; cemetery plots and even funeral arrangements are bought on the installment plan. To a person engrossed in living today the very idea of planning his funeral sounds like the tolling of the bells.

—ARTHUR L. CAMPA, "Anglo vs. Chicano: Why?"

2.   They [newly arrived ethnic groups] are changing the American landscape, proliferating into unexpected niches, each following an irresistible ethnic call. Korean greengrocers have sprouted all over New York City, nestling bins of knobby and unexplained roots next to red Delicious apples, while Greeks have all but taken over the coffee shops, conquering the quick lunch business under their ubiquitous symbol: the drink container with a picture of a discus thrower. In New Orleans, Vietnamese immigrants have converted their housing-project lawns into vegetable gardens, irrigating them with the same long-handled canvas buckets they once dipped into the Mekong. The amplified call of the muezzin echoes through the south end of Dearborn, Michigan, five times a day, calling the faithful to prayer at their mosque. Just as Americans have finally digested the basics of soccer, cricket has emerged as the avant-garde immigrant sport, played by exuberant Samoans on the fields of Carson, California, and earnest Jamaicans and Trinidadians in Brooklyn's Prospect Park.

—"The New Immigrants," *Newsweek*

3.   A dying person may pass through five separate attitude stages, according to the psychiatrist Elisabeth Kübler-Ross. In the first stage, denial, the patient ignores symptoms of illness and refuses to accept diagnosis and sometimes even treatment. Then, in a stage of anger, the patient feels outraged at the injustice of dying. A stage of bargaining may follow, when the patient tries to make an exchange with the hospital staff or his or her family or God for a little more time. Then the patient may enter a period of depression that comes when he or she realizes that everything is soon to be finished, that life is almost over. And finally, the dying person may feel acceptance of death, a quiet resignation to the power of death.

—A STUDENT

4.   In American society there exist people classified by encyclopedia salesmen as "mooches." Mooches can be generally defined as people who like to buy the product; they see the encyclopedia salesman as the bearer of a rare and desirable gift. Mooches are people whose incomes and occupational levels exceed their educational attainments; persons whose income is in the middle-middle range but whose education doesn't ex-

ceed high school, or may not even attain that level. Without ⁴
education, mooches cannot have professional status, although ·
they might make as much money as a professional; consequently, mooches try to assume professionalism by accruing
what they think are indications of professional status. A con- ⁵
spicuously displayed set of encyclopedias tells the mooch's
friends that he can afford to consume conspicuously, that he
values a highly normative product over creature comforts,
and that he provides for the long-range benefit of his protec-
torate. The mooch associates all these characteristics with ⁶
professional persons. For him, then, encyclopedias function as ⁷
easily interpreted professional-status indicators.

—Lynn M. Buller, "The Encyclopedia Game"

EXERCISE 14

Write a well-developed paragraph on one of the following ideas
or an idea of your own. Or take an underdeveloped paragraph
from something you have written and revise it. Be sure your paragraph is unified and coherent as well as adequately developed
with specific information.

1. how billboards blight (or decorate) the landscape
2. why you like (or don't like) poetry
3. a place where you feel comfortable (or uncomfortable)
4. an unusual person you know
5. an instance of unusual kindness or cruelty

ANSWERS: EXERCISE 14
Individual response.

EXERCISE 15

Identify an appropriate pattern or patterns for developing a paragraph on each of the following topics. (Choose from narration,
description, illustration or support, definition, division or classification, comparison and contrast, analogy, cause-and-effect
analysis, and process analysis.)

1. the influences of a person's biorhythms or astrological sign
   on his or her behavior
2. a typical situation comedy on television
3. tuning an engine
4. rock music and country music
5. why read newspapers
6. what loyalty is
7. the picture of aliens shown by a recent science-fiction movie
8. dancing as pure motion, like a kite in the wind
9. an especially vivid moment in your life
10. the kinds of fans at a baseball game (or a game in some other
    sport)

POSSIBLE ANSWERS: EXERCISE 15
1. cause-and-effect analysis
2. illustration
3. process analysis
4. comparison and contrast
5. support with reasons
6. definition
7. illustration or definition
8. analogy
9. narration or description
10. classification

¶ dev
3c

ANSWERS: EXERCISE 16

Individual response.

ANSWERS: EXERCISE 17

Individual response.

EXERCISE 16

Write a paragraph about a topic from Exercise 15, using the development pattern you chose in that exercise. Or if you prefer, choose a topic of your own and develop it with one of the patterns discussed in the text. Be sure the paragraph is also unified and coherent.

EXERCISE 17

Write nine unified, coherent, and well-developed paragraphs, each one developed with a different pattern. Draw on the topics provided here or in Exercise 15. Or choose your own topics.

1. *Narration*
   an experience of public speaking
   a disappointment
   leaving home
   waking up

2. *Description (objective or subjective)*
   your room
   a crowded or deserted place
   a food
   an intimidating person

3. *Illustration or support*
   why study
   having a headache
   the best sports event
   usefulness (or uselessness) of a self-help book

4. *Definition*
   humor
   an adult
   fear
   authority

5. *Division and classification*
   the segments of a television news show
   factions in a campus controversy
   styles of playing poker
   parts of a barn

6. *Comparison and contrast*
   driving a friend's car and driving your own car
   AM and FM radio announcers
   high school and college football
   movies on TV and in a theater

7. *Analogy*
   paying taxes and giving blood
   the U.S. Constitution and a building's foundation
   graduating from high school and being released from prison

8. *Cause-and-effect analysis*
   connection between tension and anger
   causes of failing a course
   connection between credit cards and debt
   causes of a serious accident

9. *Process analysis*
   preparing for a job interview
   making a cabinet
   protecting your home from burglars
   making a jump shot

3d Writing special kinds of paragraphs

Several kinds of paragraphs do not always follow our guidelines for unity, coherence, development, and length because they serve special functions. These are the essay introduction, the essay conclusion, the transitional or emphatic paragraph, and the paragraph of spoken dialogue.

1 Opening an essay

Most essays open with a paragraph that draws readers from their world into the writer's world. An opening paragraph should focus readers' attention on the topic and arouse their curiosity about what the writer has to say. It should be concise. It should specify what the writer will discuss and what his or her attitude is. It should be sincere. And it should be interesting without misrepresenting the content of the essay that follows.

The safest kind of introduction opens with a statement of the essay's general subject, clarifies or limits the subject in one or more sentences, and then, in the thesis sentence, asserts the point of the essay (see 1g). This is the pattern in the following paragraph, which introduces an essay on the history of American bathing habits.

> We Americans are a clean people. We bathe or shower regularly and spend billions of dollars each year on soaps and deodorants to wash away or disguise our dirt and odor. Yet cleanliness is a relatively recent habit with us. From the time of the Puritans until the turn of the twentieth century, bathing in the United States was rare and sometimes even illegal.
>
> —A STUDENT

The writer's first two sentences offer her subject and elaborate on it, leading us to focus on something within our experience. Then, by introducing a less familiar but related idea, the third sentence forms a bridge from common experience to the writer's specific

---

SOME STRATEGIES FOR OPENING PARAGRAPHS

1. State the subject.
2. Use a quotation.
3. Relate an incident.
4. Create an image.
5. Ask a question.
6. State an opinion.
7. Make a historical comparison or contrast.

HIGHLIGHTS

This section addresses introductory and concluding paragraphs, the occasionally useful transitional and short emphatic paragraphs, and the conventions of paragraphing in dialogue. The emphasis you give to introductory and concluding paragraphs may vary with the experience of your students. For some, writing a straightforward introductory paragraph that simply sets the stage for the essay and presents a thesis statement will be an accomplishment. Others will benefit from experimenting with some of the variations illustrated. Most, however, will appreciate the list of "don'ts" for introductory paragraphs.

Because concluding paragraphs often present a special problem, you may wish to highlight the common inept endings that trap students and then suggest satisfactory alternatives.

¶ 3d

¶
3d

purpose. The fourth sentence, the thesis, states that purpose explicitly. Here is another example of this form of introductory paragraph.

> Can your home or office computer make you sterile? Can [1,2] it strike you blind or dumb? The answer is: probably not. [3] Nevertheless, reports of side effects relating to computer use [4] should be examined, especially in the area of birth defects, eye complaints, and postural difficulties. Although little conclu- [5] sive evidence exists to establish a causal link between computer use and problems of this sort, the circumstantial evidence can be disturbing.
>
> —THOMAS HARTMANN, "How Dangerous
> Is Your Computer?"

Several other types of introductions can be equally effective, though they are sometimes harder to invent and control. One kind begins with a quotation that leads into the thesis sentence.

> "It is difficult to speak adequately or justly of London," [1] wrote Henry James in 1881. "It is not a pleasant place; it is [2] not agreeable, or cheerful, or easy, or exempt from reproach. It is only magnificent." Were he alive today, James, a connois- [3,4] seur of cities, might easily say the same thing about New York or Paris or Tokyo, for the great city is one of the paradoxes of history. In countless different ways, it has almost always been [5] an unpleasant, disagreeable, cheerless, uneasy and reproachful place; in the end, it can only be described as magnificent.
>
> —*Time*

Another kind of introduction opens by relating an incident or creating an image that sets the stage for the thesis.

> Canada is pink. I knew that from the map I owned when [1,2] I was six. On it, New York was green and brown, which was [3] true as far as I could see, so there was no reason to distrust the map maker's portrayal of Canada. When my parents took me [4] across the border and we entered the immigration booth, I looked excitedly for the pink earth. Slowly it dawned on me: [5] this foreign, "different" place was not so different. I discov- [6] ered that the world in my head and the world at my feet were not the same.
> —ROBERT ORNSTEIN, *Human Nature*

An introduction may also start with a question, as in the earlier paragraph by Thomas Hartmann, or with an opinion, preferably a startling one that will grab the reader's attention.

> Caesar was right. Thin people need watching. I've been [1,2,3] watching them for most of my adult life, and I don't like what I see. When these narrow fellows spring at me, I quiver to my [4] toes. Thin people come in all personalities, most of them men- [5]

MAGAZINE MODELS

Magazines like *Time*, *Glamour*, *Outdoor Life*, and *Self* contain a variety of informative articles. The authors of these articles and students writing expository essays face a similar problem—how to get readers interested enough to keep reading. Have students collect effective openings and bring them to class for discussion. Students can also comb editorials and magazine articles for openings of argumentative essays.

acing. You've got your "together" thin person, your mechani- 6
cal thin person, your condescending thin person, your tsk-tsk
thin person. All of them are dangerous.   7
              —Suzanne Britt Jordan, "That Lean and Hungry Look"

A historical comparison or contrast may make an effective
introduction when some background to the essay topic is useful.

> Throughout the first half of this century, the American 1
> Medical Association, the largest and most powerful medical
> organization in the world, battled relentlessly to rid the coun-
> try of quack potions and cure-alls; and it is the AMA that is
> generally credited with being the single most powerful force
> behind the enactment of the early pure food and drug laws.
> Today, however, medicine's guardian seems to have done a 2
> complete about-face and become one of the pharmaceutical
> industry's staunchest allies—often at the public's peril and
> expense.   —Mac Jeffery, "Does Rx Spell Rip-off?"

An effective introductory paragraph need not be long, as the
following opener shows.

> I've often wondered what goes into a hot dog. Now I 1,2
> know and I wish I didn't.
>   —William Zinsser, *The Lunacy Boom*

When writing and revising an introductory paragraph, avoid
the following approaches that are likely to bore readers or make
them question your sincerity or control.

OPENING PARAGRAPHS TO AVOID

1. Don't simply mark time with vague generalities or repetition
   and then rely entirely on your thesis sentence to get moving.
   You may have needed a warm-up paragraph to start drafting,
   but your readers can do without it.
2. Don't start with "The purpose of this essay is . . . ," "In this
   essay I will . . . ," or any similar flat announcement of your
   intention or topic.
3. Don't refer to the title of the essay in the first sentence—for
   example, "This is my favorite activity" or "This is an interesting problem."
4. Don't start with "According to Webster . . ." or a similar
   phrase leading to a dictionary definition. A definition can be
   an effective springboard to an essay, but this kind of lead-in
   has become dull with overuse.
5. Don't apologize for your opinion or for inadequate knowledge
   of your subject with "I'm not sure if I'm right, but I think
   . . . ," "I don't know much about this, but . . . ," or similar
   lines.

LEARNING STRATEGIES
To help students learn effective strategies
for writing opening paragraphs, give the
class outlines of well-known essays and ask
students to construct opening paragraphs
based on the information provided. Compare students' opening paragraphs with
those of the essays. This exercise will expose
students to the numerous possibilities for
creating good opening paragraphs and will
promote discussion of the relative merits of
different techniques for a specific subject,
essay, or audience.

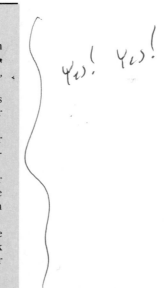

3d ¶

COMPARING CLOSINGS

Using the same essays gathered for the preceding exercise, ask students to read all but the conclusions. Then have them underline the thesis statement and the main ideas of each paragraph. Finally, have students write their own conclusions. This exercise will help students to recognize the structure, effectiveness, and importance of concluding paragraphs and will provide diverse examples of how key information may be arranged for variety and emphasis.

IMITATING OPENINGS AND CLOSINGS

When experienced writers have trouble beginning or ending essays, they usually turn to strategies that have been successful on other occasions. To help student writers develop similar resources, distribute opening and closing paragraphs that demonstrate particularly effective strategies and ask students to write their own paragraphs using the same strategies but containing different content.

2   Closing an essay

Most essays end with a closing statement or conclusion, a signal to readers that the writer has not simply stopped writing but has actually finished. The conclusion completes the essay, bringing it to a climax while assuring readers that they have understood the writer's intention. Usually set off in its own paragraph, the conclusion may consist of a single sentence or a group of sentences. It may summarize the evidence presented in the essay, restate the thesis with a fresh emphasis, suggest a course of action, ask a question, strike a note of hope or despair, introduce a startling fact, quote an authority, or tell an anecdote.

The following paragraph concludes the essay on bathing habits whose introduction we saw on page 115. The writer both summarizes her essay and echoes her introduction by proposing a link between the habits of history and the habits of today.

> Thus changed attitudes and advances in plumbing finally   1
> freed us to bathe whenever we want. Perhaps partly to make   2
> up for our ancestors' bad habits, we have transformed that
> freedom into a national obsession.   –A STUDENT

Maxine Hong Kingston uses a different technique—a vivid image—to conclude an essay on her aunt, a suicide by drowning.

> My aunt haunts me—her ghost drawn to me because   1
> now, after fifty years of neglect, I alone devote pages of paper
> to her, though not origamied into houses and clothes. I do not
> think she always means me well. I am telling on her, and she   2,3
> was a spite suicide, drowning herself in the drinking water.
> The Chinese are always very frightened of the drowned one,   4
> whose weeping ghost, wet hair hanging and skin bloated,
> waits silently by the water to pull down a substitute.
>   –Maxine Hong Kingston, "No Name Woman"

In the paragraph on the next page, the author concludes an essay on environmental protection with a statement of opinion and, in the last sentence, a call for action.

SOME STRATEGIES FOR CLOSING PARAGRAPHS

1. Summarize the paper.
2. Echo the introduction.
3. Create an image.
4. Use a quotation.

5. Give a symbolic or powerful fact or other detail.
6. Recommend a course of action.

Until we get the answers, I think we had better keep on [1] building power plants and growing food with the help of fertilizers and such insect-controlling chemicals as we now have. The risks are well known, thanks to the environmentalists. If [2,3] they had not created a widespread public awareness of the ecological crisis, we wouldn't stand a chance. But such aware- [4] ness by itself is not enough. Flaming manifestos and prophe- [5] cies of doom are no longer much help, and a search for scapegoats can only make matters worse. The time for sensations [6] and manifestos is about over. Now we need rigorous analysis, [7] united effort and very hard work.

—Peter F. Drucker, "How Best to Protect the Environment"

These three paragraphs illustrate ways of avoiding several pitfalls of conclusions.

CLOSING PARAGRAPHS TO AVOID

1. Don't simply restate your introduction—statement of subject, thesis sentence, and all. Presumably the paragraphs in the body of your essay have contributed something to the opening statements, and it's that something you want to capture in your conclusion.
2. Don't start off in a new direction, with a subject different from or broader than the one your essay has been about.
3. Don't conclude more than you reasonably can from the evidence you have presented. If your essay is about your frustrating experience trying to clear a parking ticket, you cannot reasonably conclude that *all* local police forces are too tied up in red tape to be of service to the people.
4. Don't apologize for your essay or otherwise cast doubt on it. Don't say, "Even though I'm no expert," or "This may not be convincing, but I believe it's true," or anything similar. Rather, to win your readers' confidence, display confidence.

---

3   **Using short transitional or emphatic paragraphs**

A short paragraph of a sentence or two may direct readers' attention to a turn in an essay or emphasize an idea that has been or will be developed. A transitional paragraph, because it is longer than a word or phrase and set off by itself, moves a discussion from one point to another more slowly or more completely than does a single transitional expression (3b-6) or even a transitional sentence attached to a paragraph (3a-2).

PAIRS OF IDEAS

Students may hone their skills with transitional paragraphs by being given pairs of seemingly unrelated ideas and being asked to link them. For example, using the topic of capital punishment, have students create a transitional paragraph linking the discussion of legal implications to the discussion of moral implications.

These, then, are the causes of the current expansion in hospital facilities. But how does this expansion affect the medical costs of the government, private insurers, and individuals?

The conclusion would seem to be obvious. To be sure, however, we must look at a few other facts.

So the debates were noisy and emotion-packed. But what did they accomplish? Historians agree on at least three direct results.

Use transitional paragraphs rarely—only to shift readers' attention when your essay makes a significant turn. A paragraph like the one below betrays a writer who is stalling; it does not redirect the flow but stops it altogether.

Now that we have examined these facts, we can look at some others that are equally important to an examination of this issue.

A short, emphatic paragraph gives unusual stress to an important idea, in effect asking the reader to pause and consider before moving on.

In short, all those who might have taken responsibility ducked it, and catastrophe was inevitable.

4   Writing dialogue

When recording a conversation between two or more people, start a new paragraph for each person's speech. The paragraphing establishes for the reader the point at which one speaker stops talking and another begins.

> The dark shape was indistinguishable. But once I'd flooded him with light, there he stood, blinking.
> "Well," he said eventually, "you're a sight for sore eyes. Should I stand here or are you going to let me in?"
> "Come in," I said. And in he came.
> —Louise Erdrich, *The Beet Queen*

Though dialogue appears most often in fictional writing (the source of the example above), it may occasionally freshen or enliven narrative or expository essays. (For guidance in using quotation marks and other punctuation in dialogue, see 24c.)

ANSWERS: EXERCISE 18

The introduction to the first draft rushes from a quick summary of Sommer's idea to the writer's thesis without showing readers how the topic relates to their experiences or

EXERCISE 18

Analyze the introductory and concluding paragraphs in the first and final drafts of the student essay in Chapter 2, pages 53–56 and 68–70. What is wrong with the first-draft paragraphs? Why are the final-draft paragraphs better? Could they be improved still further?

3e Linking paragraphs in the essay

Paragraphs do not stand alone but contribute to a larger piece of writing. Each unified, coherent, and well-developed paragraph adds something to a unified, coherent, and well-developed essay (see Chapter 1).

In a two- to four-page essay each paragraph between the introductory and concluding ones will develop and support a part of the essay's central idea, its thesis. The devices for achieving paragraph coherence—organization, transitional expressions, and the like—will also link paragraphs in a coherent whole. And the patterns for developing paragraphs—definition, division, and so on—will suit the needs of individual paragraphs in the larger context of the essay. Thus the paragraph patterns may or may not reflect the overall pattern of the whole essay, and they may vary from one paragraph to the next.

The following essay illustrates the way effective paragraphs can contribute to an effective essay.

> A hyperactive committee member can contribute to efficiency. A hyperactive salesperson can contribute to profits. But when a child is hyperactive, people—even parents—may wish he had never been born. To understand hyperactivity in children, we can visualize a collage of the thoughts, feelings, and attitudes of those who must cope with the problem: doctors, parents, even the child himself. 1
>
> The first part of our collage is the doctors. In their terminology the word *hyperactivity* is short for H-LD, a hyperkinesis–learning disability syndrome. They apply the word to children who are "abnormally or excessively busy." But doctors do not fully understand the problem and thus differ over how to treat it. For example, some recommend special diet; others, behavior-modifying drugs; and still others, who do not consider hyperactivity to be a medical problem, a psychiatrist for the entire family. The result is a merry-go-round of tests, confusion, and frustration for the parents and the child. 2
>
> As the parent of a hyperactive child, I can say what the word *hyperactivity* means to the parents who form the second part of the collage. It means a worry that is deep and enduring. It means a despair that is a companion on dark and sleepless nights. It means a fear that is heart twisting and constant, for the hyperactive child is most destructive toward himself. It means a mixture of frustration, guilt, and anger. And 3

why they should care about what the writer has to say. In contrast, the introduction to the final draft pulls readers in gradually: it opens with two sentences that recall an experience likely to be shared by most readers; it relates Sommer's idea to this experience and explains the idea more fully; and it introduces the analogy between buildings and people (formerly in the second paragraph) as a bridge to the thesis sentence.

The conclusion of the first draft is not ineffective, but the first of its two paragraphs seems to embark on a new subtopic (the condition of Detroit in the 1970s) rather than begin to close the essay. In the final draft the two paragraphs are combined in a tighter conclusion, with less background and a new last sentence that uses <u>rebirth</u> to echo <u>Renaissance</u> and <u>new life</u> and also repeats <u>insensitive</u> to recall the thesis sentence.

finally, since there are times when that anger goes out of control and the child is in danger from the parent, it means self-loathing.

The weight of hyperactivity, however, rests not on the 4 doctors or the parents but on the child. For him is reserved the final and darkest part of our collage because he is most affected. From early childhood he is dragged from doctor to doctor, is attached to strange and frightening machines, and is tested or discussed by physicians, parents, neighbors, teachers, peers. His playmates dislike him because of his temper and his unwillingness to follow rules; and even his pets fear and mistrust him, for he treats them erratically, often hurting them without meaning to. As time goes on, he sees his parents more and more often in tears and anger, and he knows that he is the cause. Though he is highly intelligent, he does poorly when he enters school because of his short attention span. He is fond of sports and games but never joins the other children on the playground because he has an uncontrollable temper and poor coordination. By the time he reaches age seven or eight, he is obsessed with one thought: "Mama," my son asks me repeatedly, "why do I have to be hyperactive?"

At last the collage is completed, and it is dark and som- 5 ber. *Hyperactivity*, as applied to children, is a word with uncertain, unattractive, and bitter associations. But the picture does have a bright spot, for inside every hyperactive child is a loving, trustful, calm person waiting to be recognized.

—A STUDENT

The overall pattern of development in this essay is division or analysis: the writer examines the human elements involved in hyperactivity. In addition, the writer creates an analogy, comparing those involved to the pieces in a collage. The essay's basic organization is climactic or general to specific, proceeding from the general notions of the seemingly distant doctors to the more specific and poignant experiences of a single child. Within this general scheme, however, each paragraph follows the course required by its topic and the writer's purpose. For instance, having shown in paragraph 2 that doctors do not agree on what hyperactivity is, the writer develops paragraph 3 by defining the word as she sees it. And she develops paragraph 4 by analyzing the effects of hyperactivity on the one most harmed by it, the child himself. This paragraph also follows a chronological organization in tracing the child's experiences.

Despite the varied organizational schemes and patterns of development in her paragraphs, the writer guides us smoothly and steadily from one paragraph to the next. She recalls the promise of the thesis sentence, a three-part collage, in the topic sentence of every succeeding paragraph. She links paragraphs with transitional words to remind us where we are in the essay: *first* (paragraph 2), *second* (3), *however* and *final* (4), *at last* (5). The entire first sentence of paragraph 4 is a transition from the earlier paragraphs. The writer repeats the key words of the essay, *collage* and *hyperactive* or *hyperactivity*, in the first or second sentence of every paragraph. At the end of paragraph 2, on doctors, she looks ahead to the next two paragraphs, on parents and the child. In the conclusion she echoes the distinction, first made in the introduction, between the useful hyperactivity of adults and the destructive hyperactivity of children. The combination of these techniques produces a tightly woven analysis that readers can easily understand.

EXERCISE 19

Analyze the ways in which paragraphs combine in the three student essays in Chapter 2, pages 68, 72, and 74. With what techniques, if any, does each writer link paragraphs to the thesis sentence and to each other? Where, if at all, does the writer seem to stray from the thesis or fail to show how paragraphs relate to it? How would you revise the essays to solve any problems they exhibit?

EXERCISE 20

Analyze the following paragraphs for unity, coherence, and development. For each paragraph, identify the central idea (even if it is not stated explicitly), the organizational scheme, the devices used to achieve coherence, and the pattern or patterns of development.

1. If it is the very essence of life you seek, visit Japan. The wine is served piping hot in the tiniest thimble bowls, and it is better than gulping beakers of cold sauterne. Some of the finest Japanese sculptures are no larger than a walnut and can be worn as the tassel to one's belt. In the Japanese dance, one tightly controlled gesture stands for an entire routine, and in the theater the merest corner of handkerchief pressed to the eye symbolizes unbearable grief.
    —James Michener, "Why I Like Japan"

2. To feel used is to have a sense of something of ours being taken away. But it is more than that. To feel used is to feel that our services have been separated from ourselves. It is a sense of the violation of our central worth, as though we ourselves are important to the other individual only because we are a vehicle for supplying the stuff that he desires. It may be most graphic and evident when what he desires is a material or physical thing—our money or our possession—but we are

(margin numbers for paragraph 1: 1,2 3 4)
(margin numbers for paragraph 2: 1 2,3 4 5)

ANSWERS: EXERCISE 19

1. Essay on page 68 ("Towering Insensitivity"): After a basic description of the Renaissance Center (paragraph 2), the writer links each of the next three paragraphs with opening transitional expressions that also clarify the spatial organization: <u>From close up</u>; <u>Seen from a greater distance</u>; <u>From afar</u>. Each paragraph is also linked to the thesis sentence by frequent repetition and restatement of the key idea of insensitivity: for example, <u>stands apart</u> (2); <u>remind . . . of their insignificance</u>, <u>barrier</u> (3); <u>fortress-like</u>, <u>exclusive</u>, <u>armor</u> (4); <u>insensitive</u>, <u>stands apart</u>, <u>no part of</u> (5); <u>did not care</u>, <u>insensitive</u>, <u>shut out</u> (6). (Further analysis of this essay appears in Chapter 2 of the handbook and in the answer to the previous exercise.)

2. Essay on page 72 ("Working in the Barnyard"): The paragraphs in this narrative essay relate clearly to the thesis and proceed smoothly from one incident to the next. Transitions are provided primarily by time markers such as <u>Last May</u> (second paragraph), <u>as soon as I arrived</u> (third paragraph), <u>after about a week</u> (fourth paragraph), <u>over the next seven weeks</u> (fifth paragraph), <u>Two months after I had started work</u> (sixth paragraph), <u>a month before school began</u> (concluding paragraph). (Further analysis of this essay appears in the answer to Chapter 2, Exercise 9.)

3. Essay on page 73 ("The Obsolete Hero"): The paragraphs of this essay most obviously are linked by frequent repetition of <u>cowboy(s)</u> and by the transitional expressions beginning paragraphs 3–5: <u>As the railroads moved westward</u>; <u>As civilization spread across the West</u>; <u>Today</u>. In addition, the main paragraphs (3–4) are linked by a roughly similar arrangement of points of comparison (trail drives, transportation, food, skills) and by frequent echoes of paragraph 3 in paragraph 4 (e.g., <u>Trail drives dwindled</u>; <u>instead of busting wild broncos</u>; <u>When the cowboy needs to search the bush</u>; <u>skills that used to be essential</u>). (Further analysis of this essay appears in the answer to Chapter 2, Exercise 9.)

ANSWERS: EXERCISE 20

1. The central idea is in sentence 1. The examples are organized climactically. Coherence is achieved primarily by repetition and restatement (<u>Japan</u>, <u>Japanese</u>; <u>tiniest</u>, <u>no larger than a walnut</u>, <u>tightly controlled</u>, <u>merest corner</u>). The paragraph is developed by illustration.

2. The central idea is in sentence 2. The paragraph is organized from general to specific. Coherence is achieved primarily by repetition and restatement (<u>To feel used</u>, <u>feel</u>, <u>sense</u>); by parallelism (<u>To feel used is to have . . . To feel used is to feel</u>; <u>But it is more . . . It is a sense . . . It may be most graphic</u>); and by pronouns (<u>it</u>; <u>ours</u>, <u>ourselves</u>, etc.; <u>he</u>). The paragraph is developed by definition.

3. The central idea is in sentence 2. The organization is chronological. Coherence is achieved by transitional expressions (<u>First</u>, <u>Second</u>, <u>Finally</u>); by the pronoun <u>they</u>; and by parallelism (<u>they should shop around . . . they should consult guides . . . they should refuse to accept . . . demand to see . . . decline to sign or accept</u>). The paragraph is developed by process analysis.

4. The central idea is in sentence 1. The organization is general to specific. Coherence is achieved primarily by repetition and restatement (e.g., <u>small versus large animals</u>, <u>small animals</u>, <u>large animals</u>, <u>large mammals</u>, <u>tiny shrews</u>, <u>blue whales</u>; <u>life</u>, <u>lives</u>); by parallelism (<u>Tiny shrews move frenetically . . . blue whales glide majestically</u>); and by the transitional expression <u>Most importantly</u>. The paragraph is developed by comparison and contrast.

5. The central idea is in sentence 2. The paragraph is organized from general to specific. Coherence is achieved primarily by repetition and restatement (<u>agriculture's</u>, <u>farm(s)</u>; <u>farm boys</u>; <u>technologists</u>, <u>invention</u>, <u>technical</u>, <u>mechanical</u>, <u>invented</u>; <u>Ford</u>, <u>mechanic</u>); by pronouns (<u>its</u>; <u>he</u>, <u>his</u>); and by transitional expressions (<u>another</u>, <u>Strictly speaking</u>, <u>Years later</u>). The paragraph is developed by cause-and-effect analysis and illustration.

equally offended when what is taken or used is our intelligence, our creativity, our companionship, or our love.

—WILLARD GAYLIN, "Feeling Used"

3. As more products and services become available to consumers, their quality and effectiveness seem to decline. To avoid unnecessary frustration and expense, consumers should be well informed before buying products and services. First, they should shop around, hunting among dealers for the best quality, price, and service available. Second, they should consult guides, such as *Consumer Reports*, that are published by nonprofit product-testing services. Finally, they should refuse to accept oral promises, demand to see relevant contracts and warranties, and decline to sign or accept any document they do not fully understand.

—A STUDENT

4. We may extend this conclusion for hearts to a general statement about the pace of life in small versus large animals. Small animals tick through life far more rapidly than large animals—their hearts work more quickly, they breathe more frequently, their pulse beats much faster. Most importantly, metabolic rate, the so-called fire of life, increases only three-fourths as fast as body weight in mammals. To keep themselves going, large mammals do not need to generate as much heat per unit of body weight as small animals. Tiny shrews move frenetically, eating nearly all their waking lives to keep their metabolic fire burning at the maximal rate among mammals; blue whales glide majestically, their hearts beating the slowest rhythm among active, warm-blooded creatures.

—STEPHEN JAY GOULD, *The Panda's Thumb*

5. In the nineteenth century one of American agriculture's bumper crops was extraordinary technologists. The revolution that made possible America's great cities was begun on farms. Elias Howe, Eli Whitney, Thomas Alva Edison, Alexander Graham Bell, George Westinghouse, Orville and Wilbur Wright, the American geniuses of invention, manufacturing, transportation, were farm boys all. And not altogether surprisingly. Whatever its limitations as a teacher of culture or sociability, the farm was a superior forcing house of technical ingenuity and mechanical skill. Henry Ford, another American farm boy, born on a farm outside Dearborn, Michigan, in 1863, was the most famous mechanic the world has known. Strictly speaking, Henry Ford invented nothing, but he tinkered with nearly everything. Years later, recalling his early days on his father's farm, Ford said: "My toys were all tools—they still are."

—JOSEPH EPSTEIN, *Ambition*

CHAPTER 4

Critical Thinking and Writing

Critical thinking—the ability to read (or listen) objectively, to analyze, and finally to argue a position—is a fundamental activity of academic life. In most contexts, thinking critically involves both reading *and* writing. For example, to determine the validity of an argument, you must first understand—objectively and accurately—the main points of that argument; and a good way to reach that understanding is to write a summary. Or as a critical reader you will identify and challenge questionable logic used in an argument, and as a writer of arguments you will use this same knowledge to avoid faulty reasoning. Being an accomplished critical reader *and* writer are flip sides of the same coin. When you learn to do one well, you need only apply what you've learned to do the other equally well.

Critical thinking and writing are associated with certain interrelated skills that are discussed in this chapter: summarizing a passage; reasoning effectively; evaluating an argument; and writing an argument.

4a Summarizing

A great deal of the writing you do in college is based on reading that you use in some way—perhaps as evidence for your assertions, as background information, or as the subject of your evaluation. To use reading, you need to understand the author's main points and be prepared, if the occasion requires, to restate these points objectively. The most efficient way to reach and demonstrate this understanding is to write a **summary:** a distillation of the author's text to its main points, in your own words.

HIGHLIGHTS

The special features of this chapter include (1) the treatment of both reading and writing as acts of critical thinking and (2) considerable attention to the construction of arguments as well as to analysis of their logic. In place of an artificial separation of these subjects, as is common among many other texts, *The Little, Brown Handbook* offers a unified view of the various activities involved in critical thinking.

The opening section of the chapter describes detailed and useful procedures for writing summaries, an activity that calls for both analytical reading and thoughtful composition. Since the aim of summarizing is to come to an understanding of the main points in a line of reasoning or argument, the habits of critical reading it encourages can provide a basis for effective reasoning and argumentative writing.

The patterns of reasoning that readers observe as they analyze a text critically and that writers employ to present their outlooks effectively and convincingly are the subject of the second section: inductive reasoning and deductive reasoning, as well as the faults that can undermine them.

The remaining sections look at the constructing of arguments, paying attention to both the writer's intention and the concerns of the audience for whom the argument is being prepared. The discussion includes a sample student essay, examines various kinds of assertions and their use or misuse, and concludes with advice about the kinds and reliability of supporting evidence.

4a

EXERCISE 1

Read and reread the passage below, and follow the instructions after it.

In Europe the clock very early became a *public* machine. 1 Churches expected communicants to assemble regularly and repeatedly for prayers, and flourishing cities brought people together to share a life of commerce and entertainment. When clocks took their places in church steeples and town belfries, they entered on a public stage. There they proclaimed themselves to rich and poor, awakening the interest even of those who had no personal reason to mark the hours. Machines that began as public instruments gradually became some of the most widely diffused private instruments. But instruments that began their lives in private might never become diffused into the wants and needs of the whole community. The first advertisement for the clock was the clock itself, performing for new publics all over Europe.

No self-respecting European town would be without its 2 public clock, which tolled all citizens together to defend, to celebrate, or to mourn. A community that could focus its resources in a dazzling public clock was that much more a community. The bell tolled for all and each, as the poet John Donne noted in 1623, and the tolling of the community's bells was a reminder that "I am involved in mankind."

Many communities, even before they had organized sew- 3 age disposal or a water supply, offered the town clock as a public service. In due course each citizen wanted his own private clocks—first for his household, then for his person. When more people had their private timepieces, more other people needed timepieces to fulfill their neighbors' expectations at worship, at work, and at play.

All the while, the clock was being secularized—another 4 way of saying it was being publicized. The first European clocks, as we have seen, alerted cloistered monks for their regular prayers, but when the clock moved into the church steeple and then into the town belfry, it moved out to a secular world. This larger public soon required the clock for the whole schedule of daily life. In Europe the artificial hour, the machine-made hour, took the calculations of time out of the calendar-universe, out from the penumbra of astrology, into the bright everyday light. When steam power, electric power, and artificial illumination kept factories going around the clock, when night was assimilated into day, the artificial hour, the clock-marked hour became the constant regimen for everyone. The story of the rise of the clock in the West, then, is the story of new modes and widening arenas of publicity.   —DANIEL J. BOORSTIN, *The Discoverers*

1. From the lists below, choose the one sentence for each paragraph that best summarizes the paragraph. Explain why the two remaining sentences are inappropriate summaries. Recall that a good summary is concise, complete, and objective.

Paragraph 1

a. Found in the churches and town squares of Europe, clocks were at first public machines that announced events of communal interest; but once displayed, they gradually gained value as private machines.

b. The invention of the clock, once introduced to the public, inevitably corrupted townspeople, who all too easily allowed a machine to dominate their lives.

c. Clocks were first used in churches to call people to prayer and were later moved to public settings in order to announce events of community interest, such as markets and entertainment. Once on public display, clocks became instruments desired by private individuals. Had their first use been private, one suspects that their *public* use would never have grown widespread.

Paragraph 2

a. It was a mark of civic pride for European towns to have a grand, publicly displayed clock that could summon citizens for communal needs—such as defense, celebration, or mourning—and remind all who heard the hourly tolling that individuals exist in a community, and that each person (as John Donne wrote) is "involved in mankind."

b. European townspeople placed great stock in impressing one another and visitors with the grandness of their public clocks.

c. European townspeople were proud of their public clocks, for clocks summoned individuals to a common cause and reminded them that they were interdependent.

Paragraph 3

a. Some early communities foolishly built public clocks before securing adequate water or arranging for the disposal of sewage, an attitude which explains perfectly the lamentable hygiene of those times.

b. The highly valued town clock after a time became an instrument desired by private citizens, whose increasing reliance on the "hourly" organization of the day created an ever greater demand for timepieces.

c. After a time, townspeople required private clocks.

Paragraph 4

a. The clock, both public and private, was perfectly suited

ANSWERS: EXERCISE 1

1. An effective summary is brief, complete, and objective. The sentences that do not adequately summarize Boorstin's paragraphs fail this test for the reasons mentioned:

Paragraph 1

The correct answer is a. Sentence b is biased: notice the introduced word <u>corrupted</u>; no sense of this word appears in the original. Sentence c though accurate, is too long. It is closer to a paraphrase than to a summary.

Paragraph 2

The correct answer is c. Sentence a is too long. As a summary, sentence b is incomplete because communal clocks are not mentioned.

Paragraph 3

The correct answer is b. Sentence a is biased. Notice that the word <u>foolishly</u> is introduced into the summary. The sentence also has a reference (<u>lamentable hygiene of those times</u>) not found in the original passage. Sentence c is incomplete.

Paragraph 4

The correct answer is c. Sentence a is incomplete, for it has no mention of the clock evolving from the cloister, through intermediate stages, to the factory. Sentence b is biased: notice that <u>unscrupulous</u> factory owners are introduced.

2. Here is a one-sentence summary, grouped with a slightly edited version of the paragraph summaries:

The introduction of clocks into early European history altered religious, private, and industrial relations. Found in the churches and town squares of Europe, clocks were at first public machines that announced events of communal interest. European townspeople were proud of these instruments, which summoned individuals to a common cause and reminded them of their interdependence.

4a

After a time, the highly valued town clock became an instrument desired by private citizens, whose increasing reliance on "hourly" organization of the day created ever greater demand for timepieces. Uses of the clock grew secular—moving from the church, originally, to the town belfry, to the home, and finally to the factory, when the "machine-made hour" (as opposed to the natural cycles of the sun, moon, and stars) came to organize everyday life.

to the advancements of the modern age and soon came to organize everyday life.

b. The advent of steam power and electric power, along with electric light, enabled unscrupulous factory owners to force day laborers into extending their "hours," or clock-time at the job, into the night.

c. Uses of the clock grew increasingly secular—moving from the church, originally, to the town belfry, to the home, and finally to the factory, at which point the "machine-made hour" (as opposed to the natural cycles of sun, moon, and stars) came to organize everyday life.

2. Now write your own one-sentence summary of the entire passage on clocks. Following this sentence, place the four sentences you have chosen as appropriate summaries of the separate paragraphs. Rewrite and rearrange the sentences as needed to achieve clarity, to eliminate repetition, and to ensure a smooth final draft.

EXERCISE 2

Read the passage below carefully, and follow the instructions after it to plan and write your own summary.

The whole art world of the Indian was completely and irrevocably upset by the appearance of the white man. This strange new person came in several waves, each exerting a different influence. Initially, the explorer brought little and took little; he perhaps levied the least toll. 1

But hard on his heels came the trader, eager to introduce new things in exchange for local resources. Moreover, what he had to give—cloth, metal, decorative materials—made the greatest single change in Indian art. With metal knives, carving could be done more efficiently; with new cloth, new garment designs were possible; and with the decorative materials such as dyestuffs and glass beads, a whole new world of applied ornament was opened. 2

Many new decorative materials were used in old ways— this is especially true of beads, which were applied more or less as the older porcupine quills had been. Careful examination of beadwork and quillwork will reveal the debt the one owes the other in style, technique, and execution. 3

Next came the missionary, whose whole purpose in life was to influence. By and large, this had a less happy effect on Indian art; there was no sensitivity to or interest in native aesthetic abilities, and little tolerance for a differing mode of life. The demand for conformity tended to bring about a loss of freedom of expression in many arts, and Indian religious art in particular suffered at the hand of the incoming nonbelievers. 4

ANSWERS: EXERCISE 2

1. Each <u>wave</u> of white men had its effect on Indian art:

The explorer had least effect. (Paragraph 1)

The trader introduced cloth, which expanded the possibiliy of garment design; metal, which made possible more efficient carving; and <u>decorative materials</u>, such as beads, which could be used as ornaments. (Paragraph 2)

The missionary's <u>demand for conformity</u> influenced Indian religious art by deny-

Mission schools, notably the French convents in Canada, established new design styles, as the young girls were taught to copy European models of the period. This occurred at a time when garment decoration was elaborately florid, which happened to fit in nicely with the curvilinear art so popular with the aboriginal artist. From this set of circumstances evolved an art form still in use today in the Eastern Woodlands region. 5

The settler's arrival was of more concern, since it brought a more lasting influence. The household possessions which these newcomers brought with them included many readily usable items which the Indian was quick to adopt. These articles affected art sizes, shapes, forms, and, to some extent, techniques. One example will suffice—the wealthy settler who brought along a few prized Oriental rugs then in vogue started a chain reaction he little suspected. These patterns seem to have made their way into Sioux beadwork, and became popular as "Indian design" when they were taken East with the Buffalo Bill shows. Eventually they turned up in Navajo weaving, after traders gave these patterns out to the weavers, convinced that the beadwork design would make rugs salable in the East. 6

—FREDERICK J. DOCKSTADER, *Indian Art in America*

1. What effects did the various "waves" of white men have on Indian art? State the effects of each wave in a sentence.
2. Follow the first of the two recommended techniques for writing a summary (see p. 126). Restate concisely, completely, and objectively the content of these six paragraphs. Your summary should be roughly one hundred words.
3. Compare your summary with that of a classmate. In principle, two summaries of the same passage should include the same information. Is this the case? If not, why?

EXERCISE 3

Choose a ten- to twelve-page article, essay, or chapter from a book, and write a summary by following the second technique given on page 126. Work on a passage that at least one other student is also summarizing, and compare your results.

ing native expression and encouraging European expression. (Paragraphs 4 and 5)

The settlers brought household possessions that Indians quickly adapted to their art—one example being the patterning in oriental rugs that was copied by Sioux artisans into their beadwork. (Paragraph 6)

2. A summary of the six paragraphs by Dockstader:

According to Frederick Dockstader, the various "waves" of white settlement "irrevocably upset" the world of Indian art. Explorers, who briefly passed through Indian territory, had least effect. Traders more profoundly affected Indian art, introducing such items as cloth, which expanded possibilities in garment design; metal, which made possible more efficient carving; and "decorative materials," such as beads, which could be used as ornaments. Missionaries demanded conformity of the Indians and influenced religious art by denying native expression and encouraging European expression. Finally, settlers brought with them household possessions that Indians quickly adapted to their art, one example being the patterning in oriental rugs that Sioux craftsmen copied in their beadwork.

3. Individual response.

ANSWERS: EXERCISE 3

Individual response.

RESOURCES AND IDEAS

Barbara Deane, "Putting the Inferential Process to Work in the Classroom," *College Composition and Communication* 27 (1976): 50–52. Deane describes activities to help students develop their ability to make accurate inferences.

4b **Effective reasoning**

In order to write an accurate summary of Dockstader's passage on Indian art, one needs to make an inference. Recall this sentence by Dockstader:

log
4b

> By and large, this [the missionaries' purpose of influencing] had a less happy effect on Indian art; there was no sensitivity to or interest in native aesthetic abilities, and little tolerance for a differing mode of life.

Dockstader's views on the value of Indian art are not stated directly here; rather, they are *implied* and must be *inferred* by the reader. What are the author's views? If Indian art was art that missionaries showed "no sensitivity" toward and if the art displayed "aesthetic abilities" that the missionaries did not appreciate, then —and here is the inference—Indian art in itself was valuable and worth preserving in its native form. An **inference** is a conclusion based on available evidence. Though the conclusion is not stated directly, the reader feels justified in attributing it to the author. The logical method that allows such an attribution is induction; its opposite is deduction. These methods figure not only in our reading and our formal writing but also in our everyday activities, as the following example demonstrates.

You want to buy a reliable used car. In thinking of what kind of car to buy, you follow specific steps of reasoning. (1) You consider your friends' experiences with used cars: one has had to spend a lot of money to repair her used Volkswagen; another has complained that his used Ford handles badly; and three others have raved about their used Toyotas. (2) You recall an article in *Consumer Reports* rating Toyota high among used cars. (3) You conclude that Toyota is the most reliable used car. So far your reasoning is **inductive.** You have made a series of specific observations about the reliability of different used cars. And you have induced, or inferred, from those observations the generalization that Toyota is the most reliable used car. The **generalization** is based on the assumption that what is applicable in one set of circumstances (your friends' experiences, *Consumer Reports'* tests) is or will be applicable as well in a similar set of circumstances (your own experiences). Having thus reasoned inductively, you then proceed with **deductive** reasoning, from the generalization to specific circumstances. You start with a generalization you believe to be true (Toyota is the most reliable used car) and apply it to particular circumstances (you want to buy a reliable used car) in order to reach a conclusion (you want to buy a used Toyota).

As this example demonstrates, induction and deduction are fundamental to our thought. They derive from our experience of the world as coherent (with one event related to another) and not fragmented. We activate these reasoning processes effortlessly and habitually in the daily business of living. We employ them more consciously in organizing essays and paragraphs from specific to general (inductively) and from general to specific (deductively). (See 1h-1 and 3b-1.) And we can use induction and deduc-

RESOURCES AND IDEAS

Charles W. Kneupper, "Teaching Argument: An Introduction to the Toulmin Model," *College Composition and Communication* 29 (1978): 237–41. Kneupper provides a brief review of Stephen Toulmin's simplified, practical logic, a system based primarily on three elements: data, claim, and warrant.

Gerald Levin, "On Freshman Composition and Logical Thinking," *College Composition and Communication* 28 (1977): 359–64. Levin suggests using essays on controversial topics as a basis for class discussion of the features and patterns of argument.

**QUESTIONS TO ASK ABOUT YOUR OWN
AND OTHERS' REASONING**

1. Has the writer (meaning you, if you are the writer) reasoned inductively or deductively, and to what effect? (See 4b-1 and 4b-2.)
2. Has the writer faced the questions implied by his or her assertions? (See 4b-3.)
3. Has the writer avoided faulty reasoning? (See 4b-4.)

---

tion methodically in reasoning about complex ideas—whether in what we read or in what we write. As a *reader,* you will need to determine the effectiveness of the author's reasoning. As a *writer,* you will want to present your own views as reasonably and thus convincingly as possible.

1 Inductive reasoning

Induction is the dominant method of reasoning in two situations: generalizing from observations and attributing a cause to a set of observed circumstances.

We saw an example of generalizing from observations in the identification of a reliable used car. In another case you might observe that few students attend showings of the school film society, which presents only serious foreign films; that your college friends seem to prefer science-fiction, adventure, and horror movies; and that a magazine article says these three kinds of entertainment films are most popular with people under twenty-five. From these observations you infer that most college students prefer entertainment movies. The more students you talk to and the more you read about the subject, the more certain you can be that your generalization is true.

Attributing a cause to circumstances is essentially the same process as generalizing from observations. You and your friends, and presumably most students, prefer science-fiction, adventure, and horror movies, which entertain you and offer relief from studying. The president of the student film society, however, programs only weighty foreign films, and few students attend. From these observations you conclude that the president is unaware of students' needs and preferences. True, with a little imagination you could also conclude that the president knows students' preferences but is determined to ignore them because she is a snob. You could even conclude that she is ignoring them because she wants to learn foreign languages. But the conclusion you do draw is the simplest because it adheres to the available evidence: the president does not demonstrate awareness of students' preferences. And the simplest explanation of cause, based exclusively on the evidence, is usually more reasonable than the more elaborate one for which supporting facts must be invented.

The more evidence a writer has, the more likely it is that his or her generalizations are valid, but absolute certainty is not possible. Instead, the goal is reasonableness: sound conclusions based on sound evidence.

EXERCISE 4

Study the following facts and then evaluate each of the numbered conclusions below them. Which of the generalizations are reasonable given the evidence, and which are not? Why?

> Between the 1970 and 1980 national censuses, the population of the United States increased 11.4 percent, to 226,504,825.
>
> The percentage increase from 1950 to 1960 was 18.5 percent; from 1960 to 1970, 13.3 percent.
>
> The population of the South and West regions increased 21.4 percent between 1970 and 1980.
>
> The population of the Northeast and North Central regions increased just over 2 percent between 1970 and 1980.
>
> More than 52 percent of the nation's people now live in the South and the West.

1. During the 1970s the population of the United States continued to grow at the same rapid pace set during the 1950s.
2. During the 1970s increasing numbers of Americans made their homes in the Sun Belt states of the South and West regions rather than in the states of the Northeast and North Central regions.
3. Many Americans prefer the pleasant climate of the South and West regions to the harsh climate of the Northeast and North Central regions.

2   Deductive reasoning

You reason deductively when you use some assertions to arrive at others. As when you determined that you should buy a used Toyota, in deduction you apply generalizations or conclusions that are accepted as true to slightly different but similar situations or issues. For example, if you know that all male members of your psychology class are on the football squad, and Albert is in the psy-

---

ANSWERS: EXERCISE 4

The unreasonable generalizations from the given evidence are statements 1 (contradicted by the facts) and 3 (the reasons for the population shift are not given in the facts).

RESOURCES AND IDEAS

John T. Gage, "Teaching the Enthymeme: Invention and Arrangement," *Rhetoric Review* 2 (1983): 38–50. Gage argues that students can gain awareness and control over the context, logic, and structure of their arguments by stating their reasoning in enthymemic fashion, as a sentence containing an assertion and a because clause.

chology class, then you conclude that Albert must be on the football squad. This group of three statements constitutes a **syllogism,** two premises stating facts or judgments that together lead to a conclusion.

1. *Premise:* English papers containing sentence fragments receive poor grades.
2. *Premise:* Your English paper contains sentence fragments.
3. *Conclusion:* Your English paper will receive a poor grade.

The first premise states a generalization that was already arrived at by induction. The second premise states a specific case of the generalization. The conclusion derives logically from the two premises.

Though it is rarely laid out as neatly as in the preceding syllogism, deductive reasoning underlies many arguments you read or write. The force of such arguments depends on the reliability of the premises and the care with which they are applied in drawing new conclusions. Two common sources of difficulty with deduction are unstated premises and overstated premises.

Many deductive arguments depend on **unstated premises**— that is, the basic premise is not explicitly stated but is understood. For instance:

> Ms. Chang has worked with drug addicts for fifteen years, so she should know a great deal about their problems. [Unstated premise: Anyone who has worked fifteen years with drug addicts knows about their problems.]

> As student government president, Jordan will have to deal with conflicting demands from all sides. [Unstated premise: A student government president must deal with conflicting demands.]

Problems arise when the unstated premise is wrong or unfounded, as in the following sentences.

> Since Jane Lightbow is a senator, she must receive money illegally from lobbyists. [Unstated premise: All senators receive money illegally from lobbyists.]

> Now that Sally Matlock's mother is in jail, Sally will become a behavior problem. [Unstated premise: All children whose mothers are jailed become behavior problems.]

As these sentences show, you must be alert to the logic of deductive reasoning when you read or write. Examine basic premises, especially when they are implied.

The second common problem in deduction, **overstated premises,** results from the difficulty in making a generalization that will apply to all instances, since ordinarily we must base any generalization on only a few instances. When such generalizations are premises in a deductive argument, they must contain or imply limiting words such as *some, many,* and *often* rather than absolute words such as *all, no one, never,* or *always.* Compare the difference in reasonableness in the following pairs of sentences.

OVERSTATED	Parents are *always* too busy to help their children solve problems.
MODIFIED	Parents are *often* too busy to help their children solve problems.
OVERSTATED	Movie theater ushers *are* a thing of the past; one *never* sees them in cinema complexes.
MODIFIED	Movie theater ushers *may be* a thing of the past; one *rarely* sees them in cinema complexes.

Even when a premise sounds reasonable, it still must be supportable. For instance, modifying the unstated assumption about Senator Lightbow might result in this sentence:

Since Jane Lightbow is a senator, she might receive money illegally from lobbyists. [Unstated premise: *Some* senators receive money illegally from lobbyists.]

But it does not necessarily follow that Senator Lightbow is one of the "some." The sentence, though logical, is not truly reasonable unless evidence demonstrates that Senator Lightbow should be linked with illegal activities.

ANSWERS: EXERCISE 5

1. Lung cancer can cause death.
2. Therefore, biology is a good course.
3. Children who receive no individual attention learn slowly.
4. Warren is a discus thrower.
5. The school will close if enrollments decline.

EXERCISE 5

Supply the element needed to complete each of the following syllogisms.

1. a. Cigarette smokers risk lung cancer.
   b.
   c. Therefore, cigarette smokers risk death.
2. a. The challenging courses are the good ones.
   b. Biology is a challenging course.
   c.
3. a.
   b. That child receives no individual attention.
   c. Therefore, that child learns slowly.
4. a. Discus throwers develop large pectoral muscles.
   b.
   c. Therefore, Warren has large pectoral muscles.
5. a.
   b. Enrollments will certainly decline.
   c. Therefore, the school will close.

EXERCISE 6

At least one of the following assertions is reasonable, but the others either generalize from inadequate evidence or depend on faulty or overstated assumptions. Circle the number preceding any sentence that seems reasonable, and explain what is wrong with each of the others.

1. Since capital punishment prevents murder, it should be the mandatory sentence for all murderers.
2. The mayor opposed pollution controls when he was president of a manufacturing company, so he may not support new controls or vigorously enforce existing ones.
3. The only way to be successful in the United States is to make money, because Americans measure success by income.
4. Keeping the library open until midnight has caused the increase in late-night crime on the campus.
5. Government demands so much honesty that we should not leave it to lawyers and professional politicians.

ANSWERS: EXERCISE 6

1. The assertion depends on the unproved assumption that capital punishment prevents murder.
2. A reasonable assertion.
3. The assertion depends on the overstated assumption that all Americans measure success by income and thus that there is only one way to be successful.
4. The assertion depends on the unproved assumption that the library's late hours have had something to do with the increase in crime.
5. The assertion is based on the faulty assumption that lawyers and politicians are mostly dishonest.

log
4b

3 Facing the question

Reasoning is likely to go awry if the writer does not directly face the questions implied by his or her statements. In an argument, for instance, the thesis usually centers on an issue or question: Should the risk of meltdown in a nuclear plant be lowered further? Could a program of mandatory government service help solve the nation's problems? Should the country adopt national health insurance? An effective argument faces the central issue squarely. It answers the question by stating relevant opinions about it and supporting those opinions with facts. But facing the question can be difficult. It is often easier to oversimplify complex issues or to argue superficially about them than it is to grapple with all the evidence. Sometimes, too, a favored opinion dies hard, though the evidence fails to support it. These circumstances can cause two common faults: begging the question (also called circular reasoning) and ignoring the question through inappropriate emotional appeals.

Begging the question

A writer **begs the question** by treating an opinion that is open to question as if it were already proved or disproved. (In essence, the writer begs readers to accept his or her ideas from the start.) For example, a writer begs the question when arguing that the expenses of the school library should be reduced by cutting subscriptions to useless periodicals. Without supplying the necessary evidence, the writer asserts that at least some of the library's periodicals are useless and then uses that unproved assertion to support the proposal.

The following sentence begs the question in a slightly different way.

> Teenagers should be prevented from having abortions, for they would not become pregnant in the first place if they weren't allowed to terminate their "mistakes."

The writer assumes—and asks us to agree—that the option of having an abortion leads teenagers to unwanted pregnancies; therefore, removing the option of abortion will remove the problem of pregnancy. But how can we agree when we still have no proof for the fundamental assertion? The writer has merely substituted one debatable assumption for another.

Ignoring the question

Appeals to readers' emotions are common in effective arguments, as we will see in 4c-2. But such appeals must be relevant and must supplement rather than substitute for facts, examples, and other evidence. If they do not, they obscure or **ignore the question.**

Writers sometimes ignore the question with **appeals to readers' fear, pity, or sense of decency.**

> By electing Susan Clark to the city council, you will prevent the city's economic collapse. [Trades on people's fears. Can Clark single-handedly prevent economic collapse?]

> She should not have to pay taxes because she is an aged widow with no friends or relatives. [Appeals to people's pity. Should age and loneliness, rather than income, determine a person's tax obligation?]

> Dr. Bowen is an honest man because he attends church regularly and participates in community activities. [Appeals to people's sense of decent behavior. Are churchgoers and community participants necessarily honest?]

Sometimes writers ignore the question by appealing to readers' sense of what other people believe or do. One approach is **snob appeal,** inviting readers to accept an assertion in order to be identified with others they admire.

> As any literate person knows, James Joyce is the best twentieth-century novelist. [But what qualities of Joyce's writing make him a superior novelist?]

Paul Newman's support for the governor proves that the governor is doing a good job. [What has the governor actually accomplished?]

A similar tactic invites readers to accept an assertion because everybody else does. This is the **bandwagon approach.**

> As everyone knows, marijuana use leads to heroin addiction. [What is the evidence?]
>
> No one in this town would consider voting for him. [What is the basis for judging him?]

Yet another diversion involves **flattery** of readers, in a way inviting them to join in a conspiracy.

> Since you are thoughtful and perceptive, you know how corrupt the insurance commissioners are. [What is the evidence of corruption?]
>
> We all understand campus problems well enough to see the disadvantages of such a backward policy. [What are the disadvantages of the policy?]

All these assertions resort to appeals having nothing to do with the issues they raise. A careless reader might be momentarily swayed by such appeals, but a careful reader is more likely to be put off by the writer's evasion.

One final kind of inappropriate emotional appeal addresses *not* the pros and cons of the issue itself but the real or imagined negative qualities of the people who hold the opposing view. This kind of argument is called **ad hominem,** Latin for "to the man."

> We need not listen to her arguments against national health insurance because she is wealthy enough to afford private insurance. [Her wealth does not necessarily discredit her views on health insurance.]
>
> One of the scientists has been treated for emotional problems, so his pessimism about nuclear war merits no attention. [Do the scientist's previous emotional problems invalidate his current views?]

You'll recognize most of these tricks for ignoring the question from advertising and political campaigns. Are your children's teeth cavity-free? Is your kitchen floor as spotless as your neighbor's? Are you the only person who does not eat a certain brand of cereal? Is that candidate as incompetent as his opponent says? You should be wary of these pitches in what you read and hear, for they betray carelessness at best, dishonesty at worst. And you should avoid these tactics in your own writing. Readers are unlikely to be persuaded by them, and their presence in your work could cause readers to mistrust everything else you say.

log
4b

ANSWERS: EXERCISE 7

1. The question is whether many women are bored with their lives. This statement begs the question by assuming the unproved truths that they are bored and that their boredom is caused by tedious jobs.

2. The question is whether Steven McRae is an effective spokesman. The statement ignores the question by presenting an irrelevant observation about his attitude toward himself, an *ad hominem* argument.

3. The question is whether teenagers should be allowed to use birth control. This statement begs the question by asserting that teenagers should not be allowed to use birth control because they are teenagers.

4. The question is what dangers there might be in giving nuclear capability to emerging nations, obviously a complex issue. The statement ignores the complexity of the question by appealing to fear.

5. The question is whether our souls are immortal. The statement begs the question by asserting immortality.

ANSWERS: EXERCISE 8

Individual response.

RESOURCES AND IDEAS

Angela A. Rapkin, "The Uses of Logic in the College Freshman English Curriculum," *Activities to Promote Critical Thinking*, ed. Jeff Golub (Urbana: NCTE, 1986), 130–35. Rapkin suggests emphasizing logic in all the papers in a course and describes in detail the use of ads in a final argumentation unit, a strategy that expands awareness of the logical fallacies students have been developing throughout the course.

EXERCISE 7

Identify the question implied by each of the following assertions, and evaluate the writer's effectiveness in facing the question.

1. Many women are bored with their lives because their jobs are tedious.
2. Steven McRae spends too much time making himself look good to be an effective spokesman for the student body.
3. Teenagers are too young to be allowed to use birth control.
4. Giving nuclear capability to emerging nations is dangerous because they will probably use it to wage war.
5. Our souls are immortal because they are not made of matter and thus are indestructible.

EXERCISE 8

Leaf through a magazine or watch television for half an hour, looking for advertisements that attempt to sell a product not on the basis of its worth but by snob appeal, flattery, or other inappropriate appeals to emotions. Be prepared to discuss the advertiser's techniques.

4 **Spotting faulty reasoning**

Some kinds of faulty inductive and deductive reasoning—errors called **fallacies**—are common in all sorts of writing. Like begging or ignoring the question, these fallacies weaken what you read and what you write.

Hasty generalization

A **hasty generalization** is based on too little evidence or on evidence that is unrepresentative (see 4e). For example:

Because it trains one for work, business is the only major worth pursuing. [Other majors train one for work, and other students may have different goals.]

When attendance is down and the team is losing, the basketball coach should be fired. [The sentence does not allow for other influences on the team's performance.]

A variation of the hasty generalization involves the use of absolute words such as *all*, *always*, *never*, and *no one* when your evidence cannot support such terms and what you really mean is *some*, *sometimes*, *rarely*, and *few* (see the overstated and modified assertions on p. 136).

Another common hasty generalization is the **stereotype,** a conventional and oversimplified characterization of a group of people. The ideas that the French are good lovers, the British reserved, and the Italians emotional are stereotypes. When you apply such a characterization to an individual Frenchman or Briton or Italian, you extend a prejudice, an opinion based on insufficient or unexamined evidence (see p. 153). Here are several other stereotypes: *People who live in cities are unfriendly. Californians are fad-crazy. Women are emotional. Men are less expressive than women.* (See also 31a-8 on sexist and other biased language.)

Oversimplification

A frequent fallacy in writing is **oversimplification** of the relation between causes and their effects. The fallacy (sometimes called the **reductive fallacy**) often involves linking two events as if one caused the other directly, whereas the causes may be more complex or the relation may not exist at all. For example:

> Poverty causes crime. [If so, then why do people who are not poor commit crimes? And why aren't all poor people criminals?]

> The better a school's athletic facilities are, the worse its academic programs are. [The sentence assumes a direct cause-and-effect link between athletics and scholarship.]

Post hoc fallacy

Related to oversimplification of cause and effect is the fallacy of assuming that because *A* preceded *B*, then *A* must have caused *B*. This fallacy is called in Latin *post hoc, ergo propter hoc,* meaning "after this, therefore because of this," or the ***post hoc* fallacy** for short.

> In the two months since he took office, Mayor Holcomb has allowed crime in the city to increase 2 percent. [The increase in crime is no doubt attributable to conditions existing before Holcomb took office.]

> The town council erred in permitting the adult bookstore to open, for shortly afterward two women were assaulted. [It cannot be assumed without evidence that the women's assailants visited or were influenced by the bookstore.]

Either/or fallacy

In the **either/or fallacy** (also called **false dilemma**) you assume that a complicated question has only two answers, one good and one bad, both bad, or both good.

City policemen are either brutal or corrupt.

Either we institute national health insurance or thousands of people will become sick or die.

Like the illustrations for the previous fallacies, these sentences oversimplify complex issues and relations to make the writer's perspective seem convincing. But no careful reader would be fooled. Many city policemen are neither brutal nor corrupt. And allowing people to sicken or die is not necessarily the only alternative to national health insurance.

Non sequitur

A **non sequitur** occurs when no logical relation exists between two or more connected ideas. In Latin *non sequitur* means "it does not follow." In the following sentences the second thought does not follow from the first.

If high school English were easier, fewer students would have trouble with the college English requirement. [Presumably, if high school English were easier, students would have *more* trouble.]

Kathleen Newsome has my vote for mayor because she has the best-run campaign organization. [Shouldn't one's vote be based on the candidate's qualities, not the campaign organization's?]

False analogy

An **analogy** is a comparison between two essentially unlike things for the purpose of definition or illustration. (See also 1d-6 and 3c-2.) In arguing by analogy, a writer draws a likeness between things on the basis of a single shared feature and then extends the likeness to other features. But analogy can only illustrate a point, never prove it. It can trick one into assuming that because things are similar in one respect, they *must* be alike in other respects. Here is an example of this fallacy, which is called **false analogy.**

The nonhuman primates such as chimpanzees and gorillas care for their young, clean and groom each other, and defend themselves and sometimes the group from attack. Why, then, must the human primates go so much further—Medicare, child care, welfare, Social Security, and so on—to protect the weak? [Taken to its logical extreme, this analogy would lead us to ask why we speak to each other when gorillas do not.]

EXERCISE 9

The following sentences exemplify the fallacies discussed in the text. Determine what is wrong with each sentence, and then revise it to make it more logical.

1. A successful marriage demands a maturity that no one under twenty-five possesses.
2. Students' persistent complaints about the grading system prove that it is unfair.
3. The United States got involved in World War II because the Japanese bombed Pearl Harbor.
4. People watch television because they are too lazy to talk or read or because they want mindless escape from their lives.
5. Working people are slaves to their corporate masters: they have no freedom to do what they want, and they can be traded to other companies.
6. The stories about welfare chiselers show that the welfare system supports only shirkers and cheats.
7. Mountain climbing is more dangerous than people think: my cousin has fainted three times since he climbed Pikes Peak.
8. Racial tension is bound to occur when people with different backgrounds are forced to live side by side.
9. If the United States does not supply military assistance to Central and South American countries, we will eventually be subjected to Communism.
10. She admits to being an atheist, so how can she be a good philosophy teacher?

EXERCISE 10

Evaluate the following brief essay for its effectiveness in persuading you (or any reader) to accept the writer's argument. Look especially for sound or unsound inductive or deductive reasoning, begged or ignored questions, overstated assumptions, and fallacies.

Let's Hear It for Asphalt

The truly disadvantaged students on this campus are the commuters. We pay our money and work hard for our degrees, yet we can never find places to park our cars. Commuters are regularly treated as second-class citizens compared with resident students. But nowhere is the discrepancy more noticeable than in the parking situation.

The fact is that there aren't enough parking spaces for half the cars on campus. Students are lucky to make their classes at all after driving around for hours looking for a place to stop their car. If parking were easier, students would get better grades, and the school administrators would probably have the higher enrollments they're so desperate for.

ANSWERS: EXERCISE 9

1. Hasty generalization. *No one* is absolute, and *under twenty-five* suggests stereotyping.
   A revision: A successful marriage demands a degree of maturity.
2. Hasty generalization.
   A revision: Students' persistent complaints about the unfairness of the grading system should be investigated.
3. Oversimplification.
   A revision: The United States got involved in World War II for many complex reasons. The bombing of Pearl Harbor was a triggering incident.
4. Either/or fallacy.
   A revision: People watch television for many reasons, but some watch because they are too lazy to talk or read or because they want mindless escape from their lives.
5. False analogy.
   A revision: Some working people see themselves as slaves to their corporate masters.
6. Hasty generalization.
   A revision: Stories about welfare chiselers show that some people on welfare do shirk and cheat.
7. *Post hoc* fallacy.
   A revision: We wonder whether my cousin's recent three fainting spells have anything to do with his climbing Pikes Peak.
8. Oversimplification.
   A revision: Racial tension may occur when people with different backgrounds live side by side.
9. Either/or fallacy.
   A revision: Failing to supply military assistance to Central and South American countries may encourage the spread of Communism.
10. Non sequitur.
    A revision: She admits to being an atheist, so how can she be a good Sunday school teacher?

4c

This essay is not persuasive. Exaggeration is common: *truly disadvantaged students; never; most maddening.* Instead of offering evidence—facts about numbers of cars and numbers of parking spaces—the writer begs or ignores the crucial questions of the argument or commits faults in reasoning. Examples:

> Commuters are regularly treated as second-class citizens. [Begs the question. Evidence?]

> If parking were easier, students would get better grades, and the school administrators would have the higher enrollments they're so desperate for. [Two non sequiturs.]

> The money probably goes toward a new faculty office building or dormitory. [Oversimplification. Evidence?]

> Why should the rich folks in charge of things care what happens to a few struggling students . . . ? [*Ad hominem* argument and appeal to pity.]

> The commuting students are like Jews wandering in the wilderness. . . . [False analogy.]

RESOURCES AND IDEAS

Katharyn Crabbe, "Debate/Write: An Approach to Writing Arguments," *College Composition and Communication* 27 (1976): 291–93. Crabbe suggests pairing students for discussion/debate about issues to move from personal to persuasive writing.

The most maddening thing is that we have to pay good money for parking tickets on top of tuition and everything else. The money probably goes toward a new faculty office building or dormitory or one of the other building projects that eat up what little parking space there is. Meanwhile, we commuters are pushed farther and farther away from the center of campus. But then why should the rich folks in charge of things care what happens to a few struggling students, some with families to support, who seek to better themselves?

The commuting students are like the Jews wandering in the wilderness. We need homelands for our cars and freedom from persecution by campus cops.

 4c ## Understanding the construction of arguments

Reading and writing arguments, a large part of what you do in college, can test all your critical skills. As a reader of arguments, you seek to understand, to determine validity, and to respond. You expect to have your views challenged, and you evaluate the validity of that challenge. As a writer of arguments, you work to offer a compelling, sound logic and ample evidence in hopes of changing the reader's views or behavior. The previous sections on writing summaries and reasoning effectively can help you to do these things well. This section and the next two address argumentation more specifically.

Whether you are reading an argument or trying to construct one, the knowledge involved is much the same. Use the checklist on the next page to help you evaluate any argument, including your own.

1 ### The general and the specific

In conversation with friends who trust your judgment, you might gain their acceptance of a general statement, such as *That movie is boring*, without supplying any supporting evidence. In a narrative essay you might gain readers' acceptance of the significance of an event by providing plentiful concrete details, without stating the significance outright. In argumentation, however, you cannot expect readers to accept your opinions unless you state them and provide the evidence to back them up. Nor should you, as a reader, accept the views of anyone who does not make a plain case and offer specific supporting evidence for it. An argumentative essay must present both general statements, or **assertions,**

CHECKLIST FOR READING OR WRITING AN ARGUMENT

1. What appeals does the writer (meaning you, if you are the writer) make to the reader? Emotional? Rational? A combination of the two? Are the appeals appropriate? (See 4c-2.)
2. Has the writer anticipated and responded to reasonable objections? (See 4c-3.)
3. What combination of fact, opinion, and belief constitutes the writer's assertions? Has the author defined the key terms of the assertions? (See 4d-1 and 4d-2.)
4. Has the writer supported the assertions with varying and appropriate kinds of evidence (i.e., facts, examples, expert opinions)? Is the evidence accurate, relevant, representative, and adequate? (See 4e-1 and 4e-2.)
5. Has the writer reasoned inductively or deductively? Is the reasoning effective? (See 4b-1 and 4b-2.) Has the writer faced the question? (See 4b-3.) Has the writer avoided faulty reasoning? (See 4b-4.)

4c

LISTING PRIORITIES AND VALUES

1. Ask groups of students first to list the five (or ten) issues they consider most worth arguing about and then to record their different opinions about the top two or three.
2. Ask students to prepare lists as in 1, above, but to restrict the list to a specific area, such as sports, the economy, or drugs. In so doing, you will create a situation in which students will need to go beyond obvious issues and opinions to complete their lists.

and the evidence to support those assertions. Neither is effective without the other. (We will discuss the kinds of assertions and evidence in detail in 4d and 4e.)

Most effective arguments state the central assertion of the essay in a thesis sentence (see 1g) so that readers understand the writer's purpose and know what they are supposed to agree with. The body of the essay then demonstrates the validity of the thesis by breaking it down into other assertions. Each assertion may be the topic sentence of a paragraph (see 3a), with the remainder of the paragraph consisting of the evidence for the assertion—the facts, examples, and so on that make the assertion true.

CUT AND PASTE

Ask groups of students to identify an issue, collect newspaper or magazine articles on it, and bring the articles to class (in photocopied form, if possible). Then ask them to identify what the articles say on the different sides of the issue and to cut out the assertions and paste them in columns (or simply write them out) according to the particular perspective on the argument they represent.

2 Appeals to reason and emotion

In Chapter 1 we discussed the way details and tone can gain readers' interest and support in any kind of writing (see 1f). Argumentation presents a special challenge to the writer because the aim is to affect, often to change, the way readers think and feel about a subject. Readers approached for this reason are also challenged to remain open to new ideas and evidence and yet not submit to sheer manipulation of their thoughts and feelings.

In forming convictions about arguable issues—capital punishment, gun control, defense spending, the best location for a new

RESOURCES AND IDEAS

Victoria Aarons, "Ethical Issues: A Rhetorical Methodology," *The Writing Instructor* 4 (1985): 83–88. Aarons suggests that using ethical issues for class discussion and writing engages students' interest and encourages critical thinking.

4c

town dump—we generally interpret the factual evidence through the filter of our values, beliefs, tastes, desires, and feelings. Mayor Jones may object to placing the new town dump in a particular wooded area because the facts suggest that the site is not large enough and that prevailing winds will blow odors back through the town. But Mayor Jones may also have fond memories of playing in the wooded area as a child, feelings that color his interpretation of the facts and strengthen his conviction that the dump should be placed elsewhere. His conviction is partly rational, because it is based on evidence, and partly emotional, because it is also based on feelings.

Most effective arguments combine **rational appeals** to readers' capacities for reasoning logically from evidence to a conclusion with **emotional appeals** to readers' beliefs and feelings. The following three passages, all expressing the same view on the same subject, illustrate how either a primarily rational or a primarily emotional appeal may be weaker than an approach that uses both.

RATIONAL APPEAL

In its report the commission expresses too strong a concern for the public image of nuclear power. The commission regards the Howe nuclear plant as now "safe," with the risk of meltdown "an acceptably low 3 in 10,000 per year." Yet it maintains that the general public may not accept the experts' judgments of safety. To "strengthen public faith in nuclear power," the commission calls for additional safety precautions to achieve a "slight" further reduction in risk, to 1 in 10,000. The report does not address the high cost of these additional precautions or how the financially unstable plant is to pay for them.

EMOTIONAL APPEAL

The commission is clearly more intent on improving the public image of nuclear power than on making this much-needed source of energy available for public use. In recommending additional and totally unnecessary safety precautions at the Howe nuclear plant, the commission shows blind unconcern that a minor improvement in public image might be gained at the expense of the plant's being shut down for good.

RATIONAL AND EMOTIONAL APPEALS

In its report the commission reveals itself to be more intent on improving the public image of nuclear power than on making this much-needed source of energy available for public use. The commission regards the Howe nuclear plant as now "safe," with the risk of meltdown "an acceptably low 3 in 10,000 per year." Yet it worries that the general public may not accept the experts' judgments of safety. To "strengthen public faith in nuclear power," the commission calls for additional safety precautions to achieve a "slight" further reduction in risk, to 1 in 10,000. The

COLLECTING APPEALS

Ask students to read, on their own, a relatively long and complex argumentative essay from a reader or a magazine of political or social opinion. In class, assign students to groups and ask each group (1) to identify purely logical appeals, purely emotional appeals, and mixed appeals in the essay and (2) to describe, if they can, the effect of each appeal on average readers (like the members of the group).

report does not acknowledge that these unnecessary precautions would be prohibitively expensive, especially for a plant that is already financially unstable. Apparently the commission is unconcerned that a minor improvement in public image might be gained at the expense of the plant's being shut down for good.

Notice the differences in these three passages. The first one emphasizes the evidence that supports the claim of the first sentence: the current risk, the desired risk, and the omissions from the report. The writer appeals to readers' reason by making an arguable assertion and then providing the facts to back it up; but he fails to address readers' feelings on the issue. The second passage emphasizes the writer's interpretation of the facts: merely to improve the public image of nuclear power, the commission requires unnecessary safety precautions that will jeopardize the availability of nuclear power. The writer appeals to readers' emotions—to their desire for more plentiful energy supplies, their receptiveness to nuclear energy, and even their distaste for public relations ploys—but he fails to provide supporting evidence. The third passage combines both kinds of appeal. Thus it gives readers both a rational and an emotional basis for accepting the writer's view that the commission is willing to sacrifice nuclear power out of concern for public relations alone, not for actual safety.

As the third passage illustrates, an appeal to emotion is a way to establish common ground between the writer and the reader. Writers use emotional appeals to demonstrate that they share with readers beliefs and desires that can and should influence the interpretation of the facts. For such an appeal to be successful, however, it must be appropriate for the audience and the argument. An appeal is inappropriate for the *audience* when it misjudges readers' actual feelings. The writer of the third passage assumed that his readers would want nuclear power to supplement other energy supplies. If, instead, his readers feared nuclear power, finding even a minimal risk too high, then he would fail to convince them that the commission's concerns were misplaced.

An appeal is inappropriate for the *argument* when it raises emotional issues that are irrelevant to the assertions and the evidence. For example, the writer of the third passage might have tried to bolster his case by stating that one member of the commission was once an executive with the regional natural-gas company. But the statement would be inappropriate on at least two counts: it would attack a member of the commission rather than the report of the entire commission; and the attack would be based on the unproved assumption that the member's past employment invalidated his current judgment. As a writer, you want to avoid inappropriate appeals. As a reader, you are justified in challenging a writer who makes inappropriate appeals.

4c

RESOURCES AND IDEAS

Stephen Hahn, "Counter-Statement: Using Written Dialogue to Develop Critical Thinking and Writing," *College Composition and Communication* 38 (1987): 97–100. Hahn asks students to create short dialogues focusing on an issue, beginning with a counter-statement such as "That's not music. That's junk." and then moving to response and further responses. In so doing, students can come to an understanding of the context of debate surrounding an issue.

RESOURCES AND IDEAS

Barbara E. Winder, "The Delineation of Values in Persuasive Writing," *College Composition and Communication* 29 (1978): 55–58. Winder asks writers to spell out both sides of an argument to make them sensitive to their own values and those of their readers.

See pages 137–39 for further examples of inappropriate appeals.

3 Anticipation of objections

By definition, an arguable issue has more than one side: however well supported a case is and however strongly the writer believes in it, others can marshal their own evidence to support a different view or even several different views. Some of these others are likely to be in any reading audience. But even readers who have no preconceptions about a subject will suspect that the one side presented in an argument is but *one* side. When a writer ignores the opposition or pretends that none exists, readers are justified in finding the resulting argument less sound than the writer claims and even in considering the argument dishonest.

As a reader, then, you may decide whether to agree or disagree with a writer partly on the basis of how he or she handles possible objections. As a writer, you need to acknowledge opposing views forthrightly, grant any validity they may have, and demonstrate why, despite their validity, the opposing views are less compelling than your own. The student who wrote the following paragraph took this approach.

> The athletic director argues against reducing university support for athletic programs on the grounds that they make money that goes toward academic programs. It is true that here at Springfield the surpluses from the football and basketball programs have gone into the general university fund, and some of that money may have made it into academic departments (the fund's accounting methods make it impossible to say for sure). But the athletic director misses the point. The problem is not that the athletic programs cost more than they take in but that they demand too much to begin with. For an institution that hopes to become first-rate academically, too many facilities, too much money, too much energy, and too many people are tied up in the effort to produce championship sports teams.

The writer first acknowledges the possible truth of the athletic director's defense of his programs. Then he shows that the director fails to address the central issue, the cost of the programs.

4 A sample argument

The following student essay illustrates the principles discussed so far in this section. As you read the essay, look especially for general assertions and supporting evidence and for rational and emotional appeals.

A Year for America

Among the many problems in the United States today, two are particularly troubling. One is the tendency of people to see those with different moral, religious, social, economic, and political views as "the enemy"—absolutely wrong, even somewhat less than human. The other is the tendency to see government not as the resolver of such differences—the place where compromises are hammered out—but as the chief problem itself, either too intrusive or not responsive enough, depending on one's point of view. The loss of respect and sympathy for the "other guy" and the loss of faith in government are depriving us of a sense of community —of belonging to, sharing in, and contributing to our great nation. One step toward restoring this sense of community could be achieved by requiring a year of government service from each citizen.

Introduction: identification of problems

Thesis: a proposal for a solution

A program of mandatory government service might be set up as follows. On finishing high school or reaching age eighteen, all young adults would be expected to spend one year working for the government (local, state, or federal). The service might be with the military, but it could also be with social-service agencies, hospitals, schools, national parks, data-processing centers, road-maintenance departments, or any other government group. Program participants would be paid the minimum wage and would work full-time throughout the year. There would be no deferments or exemptions from service, except possibly for severe economic hardship or mental or physical disability.

Explanation of the proposal

This program could substantially reduce the present polarization in our society. In keeping with the United States' melting-pot heritage, the program would be a great equalizer: male and female, rich and poor, black and white, urban and rural—all would serve together. Participants would be exposed to others whose backgrounds, experiences, and values were previously unknown or misunderstood. They would become more aware and tolerant of diversity, more sympathetic toward "different" people, more respectful of different views.

Support for the proposal: first advantage

In addition to learning about each other, the participants would also learn firsthand about their government. They would see for themselves the huge variety of services that we as a nation expect our government to deliver, from keeping roads free of litter to providing health care to the elderly. In many jobs they would come face to face with the people who benefit from government services—the middle-class home owner, the school-age child, the disabled veteran, the impoverished mother of five. In short, participants would see the many ways in which their government serves them and others. And that experience could

Support for the proposal: second advantage

turn their fear and mistrust of government into healthy appreciation and respect.

The participants would gain personally as well. The year of service would expose them to a broad range of career options, both in and out of government. They would gain some of the experience and information necessary to discover their talents and interests and to make realistic and appropriate decisions about further education and eventual career paths. They would also acquire marketable skills that would give them a boost in whatever work they chose. On a less practical level, participants would begin to see themselves as belonging and contributing to the larger community of which they were a part. Such awareness would reduce the sense of isolation and frustration that often disturbs young adults.

Support for the proposal: third advantage

The proposal for a mandatory year of government service is bound to meet at least two objections. First, the young adults who would be affected might not want to give up a year of their lives. However, since everyone else in their age group would be making the same sacrifice, they would not be at any disadvantage. And with public education, the young adults could be made to take pride in their sacrifice and service. The second major objection would be cost: with budget deficits already endangering our economy, how can we possibly afford such a program? Granted, the program would cost money in its initial stages, as the administrative machinery was set in motion and the low-level government employees being displaced by participants were retrained for jobs outside government. Eventually, however, the program could save money because the participants, receiving minimum wage, would cost less to do the same work now performed by relatively highly paid government employees. Furthermore, the government labor force would grow temporarily when participants began serving but before existing employees had been retrained and moved out. With a larger labor force, government could do many things it now cannot do because of inadequate labor, such as clean up city streets, give individual attention to disadvantaged children, and help the elderly with daily living. The money would be well spent.

Responses to probable objections

Despite its personal and monetary costs, a program of mandatory government service would be enormously beneficial to the United States. Its citizens, instead of viewing each other as enemies, would learn to work together creatively, despite their differences, to resolve problems. And instead of seeing their government as something *other* than themselves, a faceless giant either too intrusive or too unresponsive to be worth its cost, they would see it as something *of, by,* and *for* themselves and all other Americans.

Conclusion: summary of how the plan would solve the problems identified in the introduction

EXERCISE 11

Analyze the construction and effectiveness of the preceding essay by answering the following questions.

1. Where does the writer make general assertions related to her thesis sentence, and where does she provide examples or other evidence to support the assertions?
2. Where does the writer appeal primarily to reason, and where does she appeal primarily to emotion? What specific beliefs, values, and desires of readers does the writer appeal to?
3. What objections to her plan does the writer anticipate? What reasons does she give for dispensing with them?
4. How effective do you find this argument? To what extent do you agree with the writer about the problems identified in her introduction? To what extent does she convince you that her plan is desirable and workable and would solve those problems? Does she fail to anticipate any major objections to her plan?
5. Write a formal evaluation of "A Year for America." First summarize the writer's views. Then respond to those views by answering the questions posed in item 4, above.

EXERCISE 12

Identify each sentence below either as a general assertion in need of support or as possible evidence for some general assertion.

1. Drugs and alcohol are particularly dangerous for someone with a family history of substance abuse.
2. The IRS estimates that perhaps half of all taxpayers do not report all their income.
3. The city jail is so overcrowded that cells intended for two inmates now house three or four.
4. The university's policy of open admissions has benefited economically and educationally disadvantaged students.
5. Whatever her motivation, Ms. Horne has succeeded in refocusing employees' attention and energy on achieving corporate goals.

EXERCISE 13

Identify each sentence below either as a rational appeal or as an emotional appeal,

1. Only complacency, indifference, or selfishness could allow us to ignore these people's hunger.
2. As the data collected by the researchers demonstrate, a mandatory sentence for illegal possession of handguns can lead to reduction in handgun purchases.
3. The broadcasters themselves accept that children's television is a fair target for regulation.

ANSWERS: EXERCISE 11

4c

1. General assertions related to thesis sentence: the first sentence of paragraph 2, the first and last sentences of paragraphs 3 and 4, the last two sentences of paragraph 5, the first sentence of paragraph 6, and the conclusion. Supporting examples and other evidence: paragraph 2, sentences 2–5; paragraph 3, sentences 2–3; paragraph 4, sentences 2–3; paragraph 5, sentences 2–5; paragraph 6, sentences 3–4 and 6–9.

2. Examples of appeals to reason: the explanation of the proposal (paragraph 2); the examples and reasons given as evidence (paragraphs 3–6); the response to probable objections (paragraph 6). Examples of appeals to emotion: *our great nation* (paragraph 1); *melting-pot heritage* (paragraph 3); *sacrifice and service* (paragraph 6); *see [the government] as something of, by, and for themselves and all other Americans* (paragraph 7). Throughout the essay, the writer appeals to readers' feelings of distance from and impatience with government and their wish for community, sense of fairness, pride in their nation, and willingness to make sacrifices for others. In paragraph 5, she appeals specifically to readers' career anxieties.

3. Objections anticipated (paragraph 6): personal sacrifice and monetary cost. However, personal sacrifice would be required of all young adults, not just some, and it could become a source of pride. And cost would be offset by initially improved services and eventual savings.

4. Answers will vary.

5. Individual response.

ANSWERS: EXERCISE 12

1. General assertion.
2. Possible evidence.
3. Possible evidence.
4. General assertion.
5. General assertion.

ANSWERS: EXERCISE 13

1. Emotional appeal.
2. Rational appeal.
3. Rational appeal.

4. Emotional appeal.
5. Rational appeal.

4. Anyone who cherishes life in all its diversity could not help being appalled by the mistreatment of laboratory animals.
5. Many experts in constitutional law have warned that the rule violates the right to free speech.

4d Testing assertions

As we saw in the preceding section, assertions are fundamental to an argument. Though an assertion must generally be well supported for readers to accept it fully, the likelihood of acceptance can be improved or diminished by the nature of the assertion and its degree of concreteness or abstraction.

1 Fact, opinion, belief, and prejudice

Most statements we hear, read, or make in speaking and writing are assertions of fact, opinion, belief, or prejudice. In argumentation the usefulness and acceptability of an assertion depends partly on which of these categories it falls into.

A **fact** is verifiable—that is, one can determine whether it is true. It may involve numbers or dates: *The football field is 100 yards long. World War II ended in 1945.* Or the numbers may be implied: *The earth is closer to the sun than Saturn is. The cost of medical care is rising.* Or the fact may involve no numbers at all: *The city council adjourned without taking a vote. The President vetoed the bill.* The truth of the fact is beyond argument if one can assume that measuring devices or records or memories are correct. Facts provide crucial support for the assertions of an argument. But because they are inarguable, they do not make worthwhile assertions by themselves.

An **opinion** is a judgment *based* on facts, an honest attempt to draw a reasonable conclusion from evidence. For example, you know that millions of people go without proper medical care because they can't afford it, and so you form the judgment that the country should institute national health insurance even though it would cost billions of dollars. This opinion expresses a viewpoint. It is arguable because the same facts might lead another reasonable person to a different opinion (for instance, that the country simply can't afford costly national health insurance, even if people must go without proper medical care). And the opinion is potentially changeable: with more evidence you might conclude that the problem of inadequate medical care could be solved by other means less costly than national health insurance.

ANALYZING ISSUES

Have students, in groups, discuss a campus issue like residential policies, parking arrangements, or library or computer services, trying to identify the assertions and supporting evidence on each side of the argument. List the assertions and evidence on the board so that students can distinguish fact from opinion and identify terms that need defining. If students know enough about issues of public policy (such as gun control, capital punishment, or nuclear disarmament), these topics, too, can be used for discussion.

The thesis of an argument is always an opinion, and other, more specific opinions generally form the backbone of the argument supporting the thesis. By themselves, however, opinions do not make arguments. A writer must always let readers know what the evidence is and how it has led to each opinion, and readers must always satisfy themselves that the writer has fulfilled this responsibility. (See 4e on evidence.)

An opinion is not the same as a **belief,** a conviction based on cultural or personal faith, morality, or values. Statements such as *Capital punishment is legalized murder* and *The primary goal of government should be to provide equality of opportunity for all* are often called opinions because they express viewpoints. Unlike opinions, however, such beliefs are not based on facts and other evidence. They cannot be disproved by facts or even contested on the basis of facts. Thus they should not serve as the thesis of an argument because they, like facts, are inarguable. However, as we saw in the earlier discussion of emotional appeals, statements of belief can be effective in argumentation if readers share the writer's feelings. For instance, a writer might support an argument that the country should institute national health insurance not only with facts demonstrating the need but also with the assertion that a nation cannot be strong while millions of its citizens suffer needlessly from poor health. If you as reader agree with this assertion, you will probably be more open to other parts of the writer's argument.

One kind of assertion that has no place in argumentation is **prejudice,** an opinion based on insufficient or unexamined evidence: *Women are bad drivers. Fat people are jolly. Teenagers are irresponsible.* Unlike a belief, a prejudice is testable: it can be contested and disproved on the basis of facts. Very often, however, we form prejudices or accept them from others—parents, friends, the communications media—without questioning their meaning or testing their truth. At best, they are thoughtless oversimplifications: *some* women are bad drivers, but so are *some* men. At worst, assertions of prejudice reflect a narrow-minded view of the world. Writers who display prejudice are not likely to win the confidence and agreement of readers. Readers who accept prejudice are not thinking critically. (See also 31a-8 on avoiding sexist and other biased language.)

2   Defined terms

In any argument, but especially in arguments about abstract ideas, clear and consistent definition of terms is essential. In the following assertion the writer is not clear about what she means by *justice.*

4d

Over the past few decades justice has deteriorated so badly that it almost does not exist anymore.

We can't tell what the writer is asserting because we don't know what *justice*, the crucial term of the sentence, means to her. The word is abstract; it does not refer to anything specific or concrete and in fact has varied meanings. (The seven definitions in *The American Heritage Dictionary* include "the principle of moral rightness" and "the administration and procedure of law.") When the writer specifies her meaning, her assertion is much clearer.

If by *justice* we mean treating people fairly, punishing those who commit crimes, and protecting the victims of those crimes, then justice has deteriorated badly over the past few decades.

Of course, we need to see how this writer supports her assertion before we can accept it, but at least we now understand her definition of *justice*.

Highly abstract words such as *justice, equality, success,* and *maturity* may require an entire paragraph of definition if they are central to an argument. See Chapter 3, pages 104–05, for more on definition and a paragraph defining the abstract word *quality*.

ANSWERS: EXERCISE 14

The paragraph is reprinted below, with *F* for fact, *O* for opinion, *B* for belief, and *P* for prejudice.

(F) Cigarette advertising has already been banned from television and radio, and *(O)* the time has come to ban it from newspapers, magazines, and billboards as well. *(F)* Numerous research studies have linked smoking with disease and death, and *(B)* it is simply wrong to advertise a health- and life-threatening activity. Nonetheless, *(F)* the major tobacco companies continue to spend more than $1.5 billion a year advertising their products. In sharp contrast, *(F)* the federal government and health organizations such as the American Lung Association spend perhaps $20 *million* a year on programs and advertisements designed to educate the public about the dangers of smoking. Clearly, *(O)* these efforts cannot begin to counterbalance the onslaught of the tobacco companies' messages that smoking gives a person romance, beauty, fun, and happiness. And even if there were more balance in what the public is told about smoking, *(P)* people who smoke are so mindless that they would ignore the warnings and heed only the sales pitches.

EXERCISE 14

Identify the assertions of fact, opinion, belief, and prejudice in the following paragraph.

Cigarette advertising has already been banned from television and radio, and the time has come to ban it from newspapers, magazines, and billboards as well. Numerous research studies have linked smoking with disease and death, and it is simply wrong to advertise a health- and life-threatening activity. Nonetheless, the major tobacco companies continue to spend more than $1.5 billion a year advertising their products. In sharp contrast, the federal government and health organizations such as the American Lung Association spend perhaps $20 *million* a year on programs and advertisements designed to educate the public about the dangers of smoking. Clearly, these efforts cannot begin to counterbalance the onslaught of the tobacco companies' messages that smoking gives a person romance, beauty, fun, and happiness. And even if there were more balance in what the public is told about smoking, people who smoke are so mindless that they would ignore the warnings and heed only the sales pitches.

EXERCISE 15

The following paragraph fails to define important words clearly enough for us to pin down the meaning intended. Identify the undefined terms and revise the paragraph as you see fit to eliminate the problems.

> The best solution to current problems is one we don't hear of very often: self-sufficiency. If we were more self-sufficient, we would not have to rely so much on scarce resources to satisfy basic needs. Sure, some of us play at gardening, sewing, and other skills, but very few of us try to free ourselves of the grocery store's vegetables or the department store's clothes. If we were more self-sufficient, we would be more secure because independence ultimately creates a bond between individuals.

4e Weighing evidence

As we saw in Chapters 1 and 3, evidence is crucial in any kind of writing to make readers understand meaning and to engage their interest. In argumentation, however, evidence must do even more: it must demonstrate to readers the validity of the writer's opinions. A clear and reasonable assertion will open readers' minds to evidence. But if the evidence is then inadequate or questionable, readers should and probably will reject the assertion, and the writer's cause will be at least partly and perhaps wholly lost. In the following sections we will look at the kinds of evidence used in argumentation and then at the criteria for evaluating such evidence.

1 Kinds of evidence

Writers draw on several kinds of evidence to support their assertions. One discussed already is **facts,** statements whose truth is subject to verification (see p. 152).

> Poland is slightly smaller than New Mexico.
> Insanity is grounds for divorce in a majority of the states.

Facts employing numbers are **statistics.**

> Of those polled, 62 percent stated a preference for a flat tax.
> In 1981 there were 2,049,000 men and women in the U.S. armed forces.
> The average American household consists of 2.73 persons.

Another kind of evidence is **examples,** specific instances of the point being made, including historical precedents. The following passage uses a personal anecdote as partial support for the assertion in the first sentence.

4e

ANSWERS: EXERCISE 15

The meaning of *current problems* is vague and shifting. At first, the writer seems to mean the high cost of living caused by scarcities. But in the last sentence a new problem appears: insecurity. *Self-sufficiency* is similarly vague, defined only by the examples of freeing ourselves from grocery and department stores. A possible revision:

> The best solution to one current problem—helplessness in the face of rising prices—is one you don't hear very often: self-sufficiency. If we were more self-sufficient, we would not have to rely so much on scarce resources to satisfy basic needs. Instead, we could draw on our innate or easily learned capacities to provide for ourselves. With an inexpensive sewing machine, some fabric, some skill, and time, a person can be at least partly independent of clothing stores. With a good-sized garden, some tools and supplies, and work, a family can grow a year's supply of vegetables and be completely independent of the grocery store's produce section. Any degree of self-sufficiency provides not only the economic reward of avoiding high prices but also the psychological reward of no longer feeling helpless.

EVIDENCE IN EDITORIALS

Distribute copies of newspaper editorials, and ask students, in groups, to examine the evidence the editorials contain in order to (1) identify facts, statistics, examples, and expert opinions and (2) evaluate the evidence for accuracy, relevance, representativeness, adequacy, and reliability. Then ask the groups to compare the results of their analysis and evaluation.

4e

Besides broadening students' knowledge, required courses can also introduce students to possible careers that they otherwise would have known nothing about. Somewhat reluctantly, I enrolled in a psychology course to satisfy the social science requirement. But what I learned in the course has led me to consider becoming a clinical psychologist instead of an engineer.

A third kind of evidence is **expert opinions,** the judgments formed by authorities on the basis of their own examination of the facts. In the following passage the writer cites the opinion of an expert to support the assertion in the first sentence.

Despite the fact that affirmative action places some individuals at a disadvantage, it remains necessary to right the wrongs inflicted historically on whole groups of people. Howard Glickstein, a past director of the U.S. Commission on Civil Rights, maintains that "it simply is not possible to achieve equality and fairness" unless the previous grounds for discrimination (such as sex, race, and national origin) are now used as the grounds for admission to schools and jobs.

As this passage illustrates, a citation of expert opinion is generally accompanied by a reference to the expert's credentials. (See also 36f-2, p. 583.)

| 2 | **The reliability of evidence** |

To support assertions and convince readers, evidence must be reliable—that is, it must be accurate, relevant, representative, and adequate.

Accurate evidence is drawn from trustworthy sources, quoted exactly, and presented with the original meaning unchanged. In researching an essay in favor of gun control, for instance, you might consult statistics provided by the anticontrol National Rifle Association as well as those provided by procontrol groups to ensure that your evidence is sound from both perspectives. In quoting a source, be careful to preserve the author's true meaning, not just a few words that happen to support your argument. For instance, you would distort the writer's meaning if you quoted only the first sentence in the following passage as evidence of the positive effect of television.

Television can be an effective force for education and understanding, for appreciation of people and their troubles and accomplishments. But it assumes that role so rarely that we have only fleeting glimpses of the possibilities. We know better the dull-witted, narrow-minded fare that monopolizes the set from one year to the next.

RESOURCES AND IDEAS

Richard A. Katula and Richard W. Roth, "A Stock Issues Approach to Writing Arguments," *College Composition and Communication* 31 (1980): 183–96. The authors present a logical and practical system for inventing and structuring arguments based on the conflicts that arise in trying to convince an audience of a particular solution to a problem.

Not just opinions but also facts and examples may be misinterpreted or distorted. Suppose you were reading an argument for extending a three-year-old law allowing the police to stop vehicles randomly as a means of apprehending drunk drivers. If the author cited statistics showing that the number of drunk-driving accidents dropped in the first two years of the law, but failed to note that the numbers rose back to the previous level in the third year, then the evidence would be distorted and thus inaccurate. You or any reader would be justified in questioning the entire argument, no matter how accurate the rest seemed.

Relevant evidence comes from sources with authority on a topic and relates directly to the point the writer is making. Unless your uncle is a recognized expert on the Central Intelligence Agency, or unless you can establish his authority, his opinion of whether the CIA meddles illegally in other countries' affairs is not relevant to your paper on the subject. If your aunt is a member of the town council, however, her views may very well be relevant evidence in an essay on how a new shopping mall will hurt the town merchants.

Representative evidence reflects the full range of the sample from which it is said to be drawn. For instance, in an essay arguing that dormitories should stay open during school holidays, a writer might cite the opinions of the school's 5000 students. But that writer would mislead you and other readers if, on the basis of a poll among her roommates and dormitory neighbors, she reported as evidence that "the majority of students favor leaving the dormitories open." A few dormitory residents could not be said to represent the entire student body, particularly the nonresident students. To be representative, the poll would have to take in many more students in proportions that reflect the numbers of resident and nonresident students on campus.

Adequate evidence is plentiful and specific enough to support a writer's assertions. To convince readers of an opinion, a writer must tell them what information it is based on. If you are writing an essay about animal abuse, you cannot hope to win over your readers solely with statements like *Too many animals are deliberately injured or killed by humans every year.* You need to supply facts instead of the vague *too many.* How many animals are injured? How many die? You need to specify the conditions under which animals are injured or killed. And you need to demonstrate that the actions are deliberate, perhaps with examples of animal abuse. Adequate, well-selected evidence is crucial to an effective argument.

As a writer, you are responsible for the accuracy, relevance, representativeness, and adequacy of your evidence. As a reader, you should be alert to these qualities (or their absence) and sensi-

RESOURCES AND IDEAS

Kathleen McCormick, "Teaching Critical Thinking and Writing," *The Writing Instructor* 2 (1983): 137–44. McCormick suggests having students develop critical and analytical skills by critiquing flawed essays, and she describes several units in a course employing this strategy.

ANSWERS: EXERCISE 16

1. The assertion to be supported is that a college education is *too costly* or *a good value.* For either, details of the cost of an education would have to be weighed

4e

against examples of the gains from an education.

2. The assertion is based on the definition of a "good model" for the group selected. If the *Cosby Show*, for example, fills in the blank as a model for parents, evidence might include the senior Cosbys' good humor, affection, and fair discipline.

3. The development must first establish the characteristics that define *good*. Then examples of behavior that exhibits those qualities would support the assertion.

4. The question is whether Americans waste energy. Perhaps compare the number of cars (on campus, for example, or in a shopping-center parking lot) to the number of bicycles or pedestrians. Mention lights that burn for twenty-four hours and other examples of apparent waste.

5. The assertion requires a precise definition of *better driver* and, as evidence, examples of how the content of a driver-education course helps one drive better or statistics on the records of drivers who have and have not taken driver education.

ANSWERS: EXERCISE 17

1. First, the evidence is inadequate and unrepresentative; the passage contains only one example of *our rivers and streams*, and only a few details of its pollution. Second, the prohibition of swimming is not explained; the river's current, hidden rocks, or water snakes could be at fault as well. Third, the minister is an irrelevant authority.

2. This paragraph does give evidence—examples—of crime, though the examples are not representative enough to establish that crime is *out of control*. Some hard facts are needed, such as statistics on crime in the past month. The three examples can then become illustrations to make the facts immediate.

tive to how the quality and quantity of evidence affects your responses.

EXERCISE 16

Supply at least two pieces of evidence—examples from your own experience or facts or expert opinions from other sources—to support each of the following general assertions.

1. A college education is too costly (or is a good value for the money).

2. _____ is a television program (or movie or book) that should be a model for all entertainment aimed at adolescents (or children or parents).

3. _____ is a good teacher (or employer, doctor, or politician).

4. Americans are energy spendthrifts.

5. Driver education makes one a better driver.

EXERCISE 17

Locate the statements of evidence in the following passages, and evaluate each one against the four criteria of accuracy, relevance, representativeness, and adequacy.

1. Our rivers and streams are becoming choked by pollution. For example, swimming is now prohibited along stretches of the Mississippi River. My minister says there are portions of the river where fish can't survive. Are we a nation that does not care enough about its resources to conserve them?

2. Crime is out of control in this city. Three months ago my parents' house was burglarized. The thieves stole their food processor and their vibrating bed as well as their television and stereo. Then a month ago my roommate had her pocket picked on the subway. And last week I saw a confused old man trying to describe to the police how muggers had stolen his wallet and his groceries as he walked home from the corner market.

PART II

Grammatical Sentences

CHAPTER 5

Understanding Sentence Grammar

Grammar describes how language works. Many people who write well would have difficulty explaining in grammatical terms how their sentences work. But when something goes wrong in a sentence, a knowledge of grammar helps in recognizing the problem and provides a language for discussing it.

Grammar can help us understand sentences even if we don't know the meaning of all the words in the sentence.

> The rumfrum biggled the pooba.

We don't know what that sentence means. But we can infer that something called a *rumfrum* did something to a *pooba*. He (or she, or it) *biggled* it, whatever that means. We know this because we understand the basic grammar and word order of simple English sentences. We understand that this sentence seems like *The boy kicked the ball* or *The student passed the test*. As in those sentences, a single word following *the* names something; words with *-ed* endings usually denote action of some sort, especially when they fall in patterns like *the rumfrum biggled;* and the word groups beginning with *the* and *that*, coming after words like *biggled*, usually name something that receives the action indicated.

In the sense that we understand *The rumfrum biggled the pooba*, we can understand more complex sentences such as the following:

> The stintless rumfrums biggled the jittish poobas who were kerpesting the gloots.

We don't know what *stintless* and *jittish* mean, but we do know that they describe *rumfrums* and *poobas*, respectively, and that the *poobas were kerpesting* (doing something to) *the gloots*, probably more than one *gloot*. We understand these relations among the words because we recognize structures that recur in everyday talking and writing. Each statement is a **sentence,** the basic unit of writing.

5a   Understanding the basic sentence

The basic grammar of sentences consists of the kinds of words that compose them, the functions of those words, the patterns on which sentences are built, and the ways those patterns can be expanded and elaborated. Understanding basic grammar can help you create clear sentences that effectively relate your ideas.

1   Identifying subjects and predicates

Most sentences make statements. First they name something; then they make an assertion about or describe an action involving that something. These two sentence parts are the **subject** and the **predicate.**

SUBJECT	PREDICATE
Amanda	took the money to the bank.
Leroy	rode his bicycle down the middle of the street.
All the members of my family	were churchgoers from their earliest years.

2   Identifying the basic words: nouns and verbs

If we study the following five simple sentences, we find that they consist almost entirely of two quite different kinds of words.

SUBJECT	PREDICATE
The earth	trembled.
The earthquake	destroyed the city.
The result	was chaos.
The government	sent the city aid.
The citizens	considered the earthquake a disaster.

In these sentences the words *earth, earthquake, government,* and *citizens* name things; in contrast, the words *trembled, destroyed,* and *sent* express actions. These two groups of words work

mar can contribute to their writing. As may be obvious, this chapter of the handbook was prepared in the belief that a clear understanding of the essential structure of English sentences and of the uses of syntactic groups and compound structures can help many students not only to punctuate correctly but also to gain greater control of subordination and emphasis within their sentences. This process will take place only if students get a chance to put knowledge into action through exercises that ask them to manipulate and create sentences. In this regard, the sentence-combining exercises in the chapter can be coordinated with those in other chapters of the text to create a program of sentence combining designed to complement instruction in essay and paragraph writing.

gr
5a

RESOURCES AND IDEAS

Does grammar instruction help? The effectiveness of grammar instruction in improving writing and in helping students achieve correctness in their prose is still a hotly debated issue. Martha Kolln, in "Closing the Books on Alchemy," *College Composition and Communication* 32 (1981): 139–51, defends instruction in formal grammar. The opposite position is articulated by Patrick Hartwell in "Grammar, Grammars, and the Teaching of Grammar," *College English* 47 (February 1985): 105–27 (reprinted in *A Sourcebook for Basic Writing Teachers*, ed. Theresa Enos [New York: Random, 1987], 348-72).

Perhaps the most useful treatment of the issue, however, is Sarah D'Eloia's "The Uses—and Limits—of Grammar," *Journal of Basic Writing* 3 (1977): 1–48 (reprinted in *A Sourcebook for Basic Writing Teachers*, ed. Theresa Enos [New York: Random, 1987], 373–416). D'Eloia argues that grammar instruction can help alert students to errors and suggests ways to integrate instruction in writing and grammar. These methods include dictation, paraphrase and conversion, imitation, follow-ups to writing assignments, and exercises that ask students to "discover" a rule from examples of it in operation. The article also provides a detailed syllabus for teaching the verb phrase.

in different ways. We can have one *citizen* or many *citizens*, but we cannot have one or more *destroyeds*. If we drop the *-ed* from *destroyed*, we change the time of the action. But we cannot add *-ed* to *citizen* and have *citizened*. The word *citizen* just doesn't work that way.

Grammar reflects these differences by identifying **parts of speech** or **word classes.** Except for the words *the* and *a*, which simply point to and help identify the words after them, our five sentences consist of two parts of speech: **nouns,** words that name; and **verbs,** words that express an action or an occurrence or a state of being. These are the basic words in English; without them we cannot form even the simplest sentences. The nouns and verbs in our sample sentences appear below.

NOUNS	VERBS
earth	trembled
earthquake	destroyed
result	was
government	sent
citizens	considered
city	
chaos	
aid	
disaster	

We can identify nouns and verbs both by their meanings and by their forms.

Nouns

MEANING

Nouns name. They may name a person (*Lily Tomlin, Johnny Carson, astronaut*), a thing (*chair, book, spaceship*), a quality (*pain, mystery, simplicity*), a place (*city, Washington, ocean, Red Sea*), or an idea (*reality, peace, success*). Whatever exists or can be thought to exist has a name. Its name is a noun.

FORM

Almost all nouns that name countable things add an *-s* to distinguish between the singular, meaning "one," and the plural, meaning "more than one": *earthquake, earthquakes; city, cities; citizen, citizens.* A few nouns form irregular plurals: *man, men; child, children; goose, geese.* Nouns also form a possessive by adding *-'s: citizen, citizen's; city, city's; father, father's.* This possessive form shows ownership (*Sheila's books*) and source (*Auden's poems*) as well as some other relationships.

Some nouns in our sample sentences—*chaos* and *earth*—do

THE PARTS OF SPEECH

(For more information, consult the sections or pages in parentheses.)

Nouns name persons, places, things, ideas, or qualities: *Roosevelt, girl, Schuylkill River, coastline, Koran, table, strife, happiness.* (See opposite page and Guide to Nouns, p. 201.)

Pronouns usually substitute for nouns and function as nouns: *I, you, he, she, it, we, they, myself, this, that, who, which, everyone.* (See p. 165 and Guide to Pronouns, p. 202.)

Verbs express actions, occurrences, or states of being: *run, bunt, inflate, become, be.* (See next page and Guide to Verbs and Verbals, p. 203.)

Adjectives describe or modify nouns or pronouns: *gentle, small, helpful.* (See p. 171 and Guide to Modifiers, p. 205.)

Adverbs describe or modify verbs, adjectives, other adverbs, or whole groups of words: *gently, helpfully, almost, really, someday.* (See p. 171 and Guide to Modifiers, p. 205.)

Prepositions relate nouns or pronouns to other words in a sentence: *about, at, down, for, of, with.* (See 5c-1.)

Conjunctions link words, phrases, and clauses. **Coordinating conjunctions** and **correlative conjunctions** link words, phrases, or clauses of equal importance: *and, but, or, nor; both . . . and, not only . . . but also, either . . . or.* (See 5d-1.) **Subordinating conjunctions** introduce subordinate clauses and link them to main clauses: *although, because, if, whenever.* (See 5c-4.)

Interjections express feeling or command attention, either alone or in a sentence: *hey, oh, darn, wow.* (See 20e, 21c-4.)

gr
5a

RESOURCES AND IDEAS

Related to the controversy over the effectiveness of instruction in formal grammar (see above) is the argument over the influence of nonstandard dialects on writing. In his article "Grammar, Grammars, and the Teaching of Grammar," *College English* 47 (February 1985): 105–27 (reprinted in *A Sourcebook for Basic Writing Teachers*, ed. Theresa Enos [New York: Random, 1987], 348–72), Patrick Hartwell argues that writers struggling to master print literacy display similar patterns of error regardless of dialect.

In contrast, Mary Epes argues that nonstandard dialects have a marked influence on writing and that "direct instruction in the grammar of standard written English is essential for nonstandard dialect speakers" ("Tracing Errors to the Sources: A Study of the Encoding Processes of Adult Basic Writers," *Journal of Basic Writing* 41 [1985]: 4–33).

Though the issue is clearly far from resolved, the perspective offered by Marcia Farr and Harvey Daniels is promising. They look at standard and nonstandard dialects in the context of linguistic research and provide suggestions for shaping writing instruction as a whole (including instruction in formal grammar) in ways that are likely to benefit speakers of nonstandard dialects (*Language Diversity and Writing Instruction* [New York: ERIC Clearinghouse on Urban Education, 1986]).

not usually form plurals. These words belong to a subgroup called **mass nouns.** They name something that is not usually countable, such as *sugar, silver,* and *gravel;* or they name qualities, such as *courage, fortitude,* and *anger.* Other important groups of nouns not illustrated in our sentences are **proper nouns** such as *Ann, Cairo,* and *Ohio River,* which name specific people, places, and things; and **collective nouns** such as *army, family,* and *herd,* which name groups.

NOUNS WITH *THE*, *A*, AND *AN*

Nouns are often preceded by *the* or *a* (*an* before a vowel sound: *an apple*). These words are usually called **articles,** but they may be described as **noun markers** since they always indicate that a noun will soon follow.

Verbs

MEANING

Verbs express an action (*bring, change, grow*), an occurrence (*become, happen*), or a state of being (*be, seem*).

FORM

Almost all verbs change form to indicate a difference between present and past time. To show past time, most verbs add *-d* or *-ed* to the form listed in the dictionary: *They play today. They played yesterday.* Some verbs indicate past time irregularly: *eat, ate; begin, began.* (See 7a.)

All verbs except *be* and *have* add *-s* or *-es* to their dictionary forms when their subjects are singular nouns or singular pronouns such as *he, she*, and *it: The bear escapes. It escapes. The woman begins. She begins.* When their subjects are plural nouns or pronouns, verbs retain their dictionary forms: *The bears escape. The women begin. The -s* forms of *be* and *have* are *is* and *has;* and *are* is the form of *be* with plural subjects. (See Chapter 7, pp. 217–19, for a fuller discussion of verb forms.)

HELPING VERBS

The dictionary form of all verbs can combine with the words *do, does, did, can, could, may, might, will, would, shall, should*, and *must: could run, may escape, must help.* These words are called **helping verbs** or **auxiliary verbs.** They and a few others combine with special forms of verbs to make verb phrases such as *will be running, might have escaped*, and *could have been helped.* (See Chapter 7, pp. 218 and 224.)

A note on form and function

In different sentences an English word may serve different functions, take correspondingly different forms, and belong to different word classes. For example, *aid* functions as a noun in the sentence *The government sent the city aid.* But in *The government aids the city*, the word *aid* functions as a verb, taking the characteristic *-s* ending of a verb with a singular subject, *government.* In *The light burns*, the word *light* functions as a noun; but in *The lanterns light the path*, the word *light* functions as a verb. Because words can function in different ways, we must always determine how a particular word works in a sentence before we can identify what part of speech it is. The *function* of a word in a sentence always determines its part of speech in that sentence.

DICTATION

Read to your class the words in the list below (or in a similar one) and then go through the list again, giving students a minute or two to write sentences using the words in as many different roles (parts of speech) as they can. The word *good*, for example, can be an adjective or a noun.

well	post
set	bill
that	needle
while	bit
turn	

---

gr
5a

Pronouns

Before looking at the five basic sentence patterns in English, we need to look at a third group of words, the pronouns.

Susanne enlisted in the Air Force. *She* leaves for her training in two weeks. Susanne is one of the people *who* took advanced physics in high school.

Most **pronouns** substitute for nouns and function in sentences as nouns do. In the sentences above, the pronoun *she* substitutes for *Susanne*, and the pronoun *who* substitutes for *people*.

Pronouns fall into several subclasses depending on their form or function. **Personal pronouns** refer to a specific individual or to individuals. They are *I, you, he, she, it, we,* and *they*. **Indefinite pronouns,** such as *everybody* and *some*, do not substitute for any specific nouns, though they function as nouns (*Everybody likes Tim*). **Demonstrative pronouns,** including *this, that,* and *such*, identify or point to nouns (*This is the gun she used*). The **relative pronouns** *who, which,* and *that* relate groups of words to nouns or other pronouns (*Jim spoke to the boys who broke the window*). Intensive and reflexive pronouns have different functions but the same form: a personal pronoun plus *-self* (*himself, yourself*). **Intensive pronouns** emphasize a noun or other pronoun (*She herself asked the question*). **Reflexive pronouns** indicate that the sentence subject also receives the action of the verb (*You might hurt yourself*). Finally, **interrogative pronouns,** including *who, which,* and *what*, introduce questions (*Who will come to the concert?*).

The personal pronouns *I, he, she, we,* and *they* and the relative pronoun *who* change form depending on their function in the sentence. (For a discussion of these form changes, see Chapter 6.)

EXERCISE 1

Identify the subject and the predicate of each sentence below. Then use each sentence as a model to create a sentence of your own.

Example:
An important scientist spoke at commencement.
        SUBJECT   PREDICATE
An important scientist | spoke at commencement.
The hungry family ate at the diner.

1. The leaves fell.
2. October ends soon.
3. The orchard owners made apple cider.
4. They examined each apple carefully before using it.
5. Over a hundred people will buy cider at the roadside stand.

gr
5a

ANSWERS: EXERCISE 1

        SUBJECT | PREDICATE
1. The leaves | fell.
   Sample imitation: The kite soared.

      SUBJECT | PREDICATE
2. October | ends soon.
   Sample imitation: My class begins soon.

                SUBJECT | PREDICATE
3. The orchard owners made | apple cider.
   Sample imitation: The couple grew summer squash.

SUBJECT | PREDICATE
4. They | examined each apple carefully before using it.
   Sample imitation: They dried each glass gingerly after washing it.

                SUBJECT | PREDICATE
5. Over a hundred people will | buy cider at the roadside stand.
   Sample imitation: Few pool owners will swim at the public beach.

ANSWERS: EXERCISE 2

1. The trees died.
   N   V
2. They caught a disease.
   P   V   N
3. The disease was a fungus.
      N   V   N
4. It ruined a grove that we treasured.
   P   V   N   P   P   V
5. Our great-grandfather planted the
   P   N   V
   grove in the last century.
   N   N

SAMPLE ANSWERS: EXERCISE 3

1. Noun and verb.
   Blow out the candles and make a
   wish. [Noun.] The child wished for a
   new bicycle. [Verb.]
2. Noun and verb.
   Many people purchase ties as Father's
   Day presents. [Noun.] Tie the rope
   into a square knot. [Verb.]
3. Noun and verb.
   The swing hung from a large oak tree.
   [Noun.] Ted picked up his niece and
   swung her around and around. [Verb.]
4. Noun and verb.
   The mail does not come on national
   holidays. [Noun.] Mail the package to
   her home address. [Verb.]
5. Verb.
   He spends his free time doing volunteer work.
6. Noun and verb.
   The label bore a poison warning.
   [Noun.] The companies must label
   their products. [Verb.]
7. Noun.
   The door flew open by itself.
8. Noun.
   My younger sister was good company.
9. Noun and verb.
   The whistle released us from work.
   [Noun.] We whistle all the way home.
   [Verb.]
10. Noun and verb.
    The glue stuck to my hands. [Noun.]
    We glue our models together. [Verb.]

EXERCISE 2

In the following sentences identify all words functioning as nouns with *N*, all words functioning as verbs with *V*, and all pronouns with *P*.

Example:
We took the tour through the museum.

We took the tour through the museum.
 P   V   N   N

1. The trees died.
2. They caught a disease.
3. The disease was a fungus.
4. It ruined a grove that was treasured.
5. Our great-grandfather planted the grove in the last century.

EXERCISE 3

Identify each of the following words as a noun, as a verb, or as both. Then create sentences of your own, using each word in each possible function.

Example:
fly
Noun and verb.
The *fly* sat on the meat loaf. [Noun.] The planes *fly* low. [Verb.]

1. wish	5. spend	8. company
2. tie	6. label	9. whistle
3. swing	7. door	10. glue
4. mail		

3   **Forming sentence patterns with nouns and verbs**

The five sample sentences introduced earlier reappear below with an *N* over each noun and a *V* over each verb.

1. The earth trembled.
       N   V
2. The earthquake destroyed the city.
       N   V   N
3. The result was chaos.
       N   V   N
4. The government sent the city aid.
       N   V   N   N
5. The citizens considered the earthquake a disaster.
       N   V   N   N

gr
5a

THE FIVE BASIC SENTENCE PATTERNS

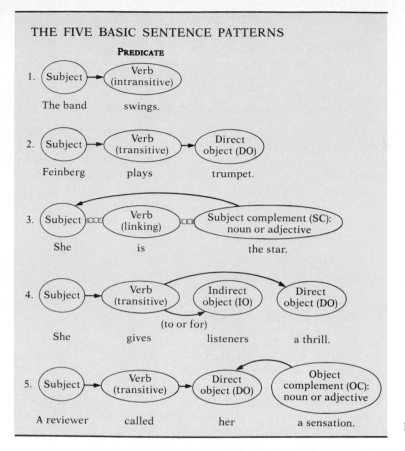

These five sentences typify the five basic patterns on which we build all our sentences, even the most complex. The subjects of the sentences are similar, consisting only of a noun and an article or marker. But each predicate is different because the relation between the verb and the remaining words is different. The five patterns are diagrammed above. The following discussion examines each pattern in turn.

Pattern 1: The earth trembled.

In the simplest pattern the predicate consists only of the verb. Verbs in this pattern do not require following words to complete their meaning and thus are called **intransitive** (from Latin words meaning "not passing over").

RESOURCES AND IDEAS

Andrea Lunsford, "Cognitive Development and the Basic Writer," *College English* 41 (1979): 38–46 (reprinted in *A Sourcebook for Basic Writing Teachers*, ed. Theresa Enos [New York: Random, 1986], 449–59). Lunsford presents exercises and assignments adapted to the cognitive level of basic writers and designed to help students identify sentence parts and functions and to help them write sentences using a number of basic patterns.

Marilyn Sternglass, "Composition Teacher as Reading Teacher," *College Composition and Communication* 27 (1976): 378–82. Sternglass suggests analytical reading as a way to help students understand the varieties of basic sentence structure.

SUBJECT	PREDICATE
	Intransitive verb
The earth	trembled.
Mosquitoes	buzz.
We	have been swimming.

Pattern 2: The earthquake destroyed the city.

In sentence 2 the predicate consists of a verb followed by a noun. The noun completes the meaning of the verb by identifying who or what receives the action of the verb. This noun is a **direct object** (DO). Verbs that require direct objects to complete their meaning are called **transitive** ("passing over").

SUBJECT	PREDICATE	
	Transitive verb	*Direct object*
The earthquake	destroyed	the city.
The man	stubbed	his toe.
The people	wanted	peace.

Pattern 3: The result was chaos.

In sentence 3 the predicate also consists of a verb followed by a single noun. But here the verb *was* serves merely to introduce a word that renames or describes the subject. We could write the sentence *The result = chaos*. The noun following the verb in this kind of sentence is a **subject complement** (SC), or a **predicate noun**. Verbs in this pattern are called **linking verbs** because they link their subjects to the description that follows.

SUBJECT	PREDICATE	
	Linking verb	*Subject complement*
The result	was	chaos.
Jenn	is	an engineer.
The man	became	an accountant.

Subject complements in this sentence pattern may also be adjectives, words such as *tall* and *hopeful* (see 5b-1). Adjectives serving as complements are often called **predicate adjectives.**

SUBJECT	PREDICATE	
	Linking verb	*Subject complement*
The result	was	chaotic.
The house	seemed	expensive.

gr
5a

Pattern 4: The government sent the city aid.

In sentence 4 the predicate consists of a verb followed by two nouns. The second noun is a direct object, identifying what was sent. But the first noun, *city*, is different. This noun is an **indirect object** (IO), identifying to or for whom or what the action of the verb is performed. The direct object and indirect object refer to different things, people, or places.

SUBJECT	PREDICATE		
	Transitive verb	*Indirect object*	*Direct object*
The government	sent	the city	aid.
Neighbors	gave	the dog	a bone.
The boys	asked	their teacher	a question.
George	tossed	me	an apple.

Pattern 5: The citizens considered the earthquake a disaster.

In sentence 5 the predicate again consists of a verb followed by two nouns. But in this pattern the first noun is a direct object and the second noun renames or describes it. Here the second noun is an **object complement** (OC).

SUBJECT	PREDICATE		
	Transitive verb	*Direct object*	*Object complement*
The citizens	considered	the earthquake	a disaster.
The manager	made	him	an assistant.
The class	elected	Joan O'Day	president.
We	declared	her	the winner.

Notice that the relation between a direct object and an object complement is the same as that between a subject and a subject complement in pattern 3. Just as the subject complement renames or describes a subject, so an object complement renames or describes a direct object. And just as we can use either nouns or adjectives in pattern 3, so we can use either nouns or adjectives as object complements in this last pattern.

SUBJECT	PREDICATE		
	Transitive verb	*Direct object*	*Object complement*
The citizens	considered	the earthquake	disastrous.
The results	proved	Sweeney	wrong.
Success	makes	some people	nervous.

The five sentence patterns above are the basic frameworks for most written English sentences. However long or complicated a sentence is, one or more of these basic patterns forms its foundation. A question may change the order of the subject and verb (*Is she a doctor?*), a command may omit the subject entirely (*Be quiet!*), and the order of the parts may be different in some statements (see 5e), but the same basic sentence parts will be present or clearly understood.

gr
5a

ANSWERS: EXERCISE 4

1. <u>Find</u> is transitive.
   Many people find the <u>movie offensive</u>.
   (DO) (OC)
2. <u>Stalled</u> is intransitive.
   No objects or complements.
3. <u>Lost</u> is transitive.
   I lost my dry-cleaning <u>ticket</u>.
   (DO)
4. <u>Is</u> is linking.
   The building is <u>unusual</u>.
   (SC)
5. <u>Calls</u> is transitive.
   Marie calls her <u>boyfriend</u> a <u>genius</u>.
   (DO) (OC)
6. <u>Was</u> is linking.
   The dentist's bill was five hundred <u>dollars</u>.
   (SC)
7. <u>Read</u> is transitive.
   I read my <u>brother</u> *Charlotte's Web*.
   (IO) (DO)
8. <u>Bought</u> is transitive.
   Then I bought <u>him</u> his own <u>copy</u>.
   (IO) (DO)
9. <u>Was</u> is linking.
   The counterfeiter was a <u>child</u>.
   (SC)
10. <u>Showed</u> is transitive.
    The magician showed the <u>audience</u> his <u>tricks</u>.
    (IO) (DO)

SAMPLE ANSWERS: EXERCISE 5

1. The audience laughed at the comedian.
2. The town elected Flynn mayor.
3. Pip stole the pie.
4. Josie caught the ball.
5. My uncle brought me a cake.
6. Marilou seems unhappy.
7. One candidate called the other a crook.
8. We became reckless.
9. We bought ourselves a television set.
10. No one studied.

EXERCISE 4

In the following sentences, identify each verb as intransitive, transitive, or linking. Then identify each direct object (DO), indirect object (IO), subject complement (SC), and object complement (OC).

Example:
Children give their parents both headaches and pleasures.
Give is a transitive verb.

Children give their *parents* both headaches and *pleasures*.
(IO) (DO) (DO)

1. Many people find the movie offensive.
2. The car stalled.
3. I lost my dry-cleaning ticket.
4. The building is unusual.
5. Marie calls her boyfriend a genius.
6. The dentist's bill was five hundred dollars.
7. I read my brother *Charlotte's Web*.
8. Then I bought him his own copy.
9. The counterfeiter was a child.
10. The magician showed the audience his tricks.

EXERCISE 5

Create sentences by using each of the following verbs in the pattern indicated. You may want to change the form of the verb.

Example: give (S–V–IO–DO)
Sam gave his brother a birthday card.

1. laugh (S–V)
2. elect (S–V–DO–OC)
3. steal (S–V–DO)
4. catch (S–V–DO)
5. bring (S–V–IO–DO)
6. seem (S–V–SC)
7. call (S–V–DO–OC)
8. become (S–V–SC)
9. buy (S–V–IO–DO)
10. study (S–V)

5b Expanding the basic sentence with single words

We have been studying simple sentences and their basic structures. But most of the sentences we read, write, or speak are more complex and also more informative and interesting. Most sentences contain one or more of the following: (1) modifying words; (2) word groups, called phrases and clauses; and (3) combinations of two or more words or word groups of the same kind. These sentence expanders are the subjects of this and the next two sections.

1 Using adjectives and adverbs

The simplest expansion of sentences occurs when we add modifying words to describe or limit the nouns and verbs. Modifying words add details.

Recently, the earth trembled.
The earthquake *nearly* destroyed the *old* city.
The *federal government soon* sent the city aid.

The added words do not all act the same way. *Old* and *federal* modify nouns, but *recently, nearly,* and *soon* do not. We don't speak of a *recently earthquake* or a *soon government*. Nor do we say *old sent*. We are dealing with two different parts of speech. **Adjectives** (such as *old, federal, heartless, friendly*) describe or modify nouns and pronouns. **Adverbs** (such as *recently, nearly, soon, never, always*) describe the action of verbs and also modify adjectives, other adverbs, and whole groups of words.

We cannot always identify adjectives and adverbs by their form. Although an *-ly* ending often signals an adverb, many adverbs—*never* and *always*, for example—have a different form. Moreover some adjectives end in *-ly:* in *likely candidate* and *lovely breeze, likely* and *lovely* clearly modify nouns and are thus adjectives. Therefore, to determine whether a word is an adjective or an adverb, we must identify the word or words it modifies.

Adjectives modify only nouns and pronouns. Adverbs may modify verbs, but they may also modify adjectives and other adverbs: *extremely unhappy* (adverb-adjective); *bitterly cold* (adverb-adjective); *very quickly* (adverb-adverb). Adverbs may also modify whole sentences or groups of words within a sentence. In *Unfortunately, we have no money*, for example, *unfortunately* modifies the whole sentence that follows it. In *She ran almost to the end of the street*, the adverb *almost* modifies *to the end of the street*.

RESOURCES AND IDEAS

Anne J. Herrington, "Grammar Recharted: Sentence Analysis for Writing," in *Writing Exercises from "Exercise Exchange,"* vol. 2 (Urbana: NCTE, 1984), 276–87. Herrington suggests using a five-column chart to analyze sentence patterns and help make students aware of syntax. The five columns in the chart—Preceding Subject, Subject, Between Subject and Verb, and Following Verb—allow the system to account for both relatively simple sentences and those to which considerable information has been added. The columns can be layered as well to account for compound sentences.

gr
5b

gr
5b

ANSWERS: EXERCISE 6

        ADJ   ADJ
1. The <u>icy</u> rain created <u>glassy</u> patches on the roads.
Sample imitation: The blue bird turned graceful circles in the air.

   ADV   ADJ
2. <u>Happily</u>, children played in the <u>slip-pery</u> streets.
Sample imitation: Quietly, we peeked into the silent cathedral.

    ADV   ADJ   ADV
3. <u>Fortunately</u>, <u>no</u> cars ventured <u>out</u>.
Sample imitation: Impatiently, the old man gazed ahead.

ADJ   ADV
4. <u>Wise</u> parents stayed <u>indoors</u> where
            ADJ   ADJ
they could be <u>warm</u> and <u>dry</u>.
Sample imitation: Smart children go outdoors when they feel noisy and rambunctious.

            ADV   ADJ
5. The dogs slept <u>soundly</u> near the <u>warm</u> radiators.
Sample imitation: The babies lay quietly in their small cribs.

SAMPLE ANSWERS: EXERCISE 7

1. skillfully
The weaver was <u>skillful</u> at his craft. The waiter <u>skillfully</u> balanced the three trays.
2. wise
The minister spoke <u>wisely</u> to the congregation. The <u>wise</u> child knows his or her own parent.
3. newly
The <u>new</u> book smelled of wood. The <u>newly</u> planted petunias wilted in the sun.
4. brightly
The <u>bright</u> colors were unflattering. The sun glinted <u>brightly</u> off the tin roof.
5. fortunate
<u>Fortunately,</u> I passed the test. We are <u>fortunate</u> to be living in these times.

Adverbs usually indicate where, when, how, or to what extent, as in the following sentences.

Send all the mail *here*. [*Here* is *where* the mail is to be sent.]

Fred will arrive *tomorrow*. [*Tomorrow* is *when* Fred will arrive.]

Jeremy answered *angrily*. [*Angrily* is *how* Jeremy answered.]

We are *completely* satisfied. [*Completely* indicates *to what extent* we are satisfied.]

Adjectives and adverbs appear in three forms distinguished by degree. The **positive degree** is the basic form, the one listed in the dictionary: *good, green, angry; badly, quickly, angrily.* The **comparative** form indicates a greater degree of the quality named by the word: *better, greener, angrier; worse, more quickly, more angrily.* The **superlative** form indicates the greatest degree of the quality named: *best, greenest, angriest; worst, most quickly, most angrily.* (For further discussion of the forms and uses of comparatives and superlatives, see 9e.)

EXERCISE 6

Identify the adjectives and adverbs in the following sentences. Then use each sentence as a model for creating a sentence of your own.

Example:

The *red* barn sat uncomfortably among *modern* buildings.

     ADJ   ADV   ADJ
The *red* barn sat *uncomfortably* among *modern* buildings.

The little girl complained loudly to her busy mother.

1. The icy rain created glassy patches on the roads.
2. Happily, children played in the slippery streets.
3. Fortunately, no cars ventured out.
4. Wise parents stayed indoors where they could be warm and dry.
5. The dogs slept soundly near the warm radiators.

EXERCISE 7

Change each of the following adjectives into an adverb, and change each adverb into an adjective. Then write one sentence using the adjective and another using the adverb.

Example:

sorrowful: *sorrowfully*.

Her expression was *sorrowful*.

David watched *sorrowfully* as the firefighters removed the charred remains of his furniture.

1. skillful	5. fortunately	8. painfully
2. wisely	6. bluntly	9. stupid
3. new	7. happy	10. sturdy
4. bright		

2 Using other words as modifiers

We have already observed that a particular word may function sometimes as a noun, sometimes as a verb. Similarly, nouns and special forms of verbs may sometimes serve as modifiers of other nouns. In combinations such as *office buildings, Thanksgiving prayer,* and *shock hazard,* the first noun modifies the second. In combinations such as *singing birds, corrected papers,* and *broken finger,* the first word is a verb form modifying the following noun. (These modifying verb forms are discussed in more detail in 5c-2.) Again, the part of speech to which we assign a word always depends on its function in a sentence.

EXERCISE 8

Use each of the following verb forms to modify a noun in a sentence of your own.

Example:

smoking
Only a *smoking cigar* remained.

1. scrambled	5. painted	8. ripened
2. twitching	6. written	9. known
3. rambling	7. charging	10. driven
4. typed		

EXERCISE 9

To practice expanding the basic sentence patterns with single-word modifiers, combine each group of sentences below into one sentence. You will have to delete and rearrange words.

Example:

The speaker told us the facts. The speaker told us calmly. The facts were terrifying.

The speaker *calmly* told us the *terrifying* facts.

1. A painting hung on a wall. The painting was religious. The wall was wooden.
2. The clock ticked. The clock was big. It was a wall clock. It ticked noisily.
3. The parents comforted their children. The parents were departing. The children were nervous.

6. blunt
   She **bluntly** stated her opinion. The knife is too **blunt** to cut the cardboard.
7. happily
   Two **happy** people left the church. The child skipped **happily** along the street.
8. painful
   She spoke **painfully**. It was a **painful** decision.
9. stupidly
   It was **stupid** of me to oversleep. He **stupidly** forgot to make an extra copy.
10. sturdily
    The **sturdy** table was fifty years old. The little boy faced the dog **sturdily**.

gr
5b

SAMPLE ANSWERS: EXERCISE 8

1. Jack woke up craving **scrambled eggs**.
2. The **twitching limb** relaxed when the sedative took effect.
3. The treasurer's **rambling speech** covered more topics than I can remember.
4. The **typed manuscript** contained many errors.
5. **Painted birds** decorate the window.
6. He wanted to know the origins of the **written word**.
7. The man escaped the **charging animal**.
8. We picked the **ripened fruit**.
9. All the **known facts** contradict his theory.
10. **Driven people** may have hypertension.

POSSIBLE ANSWERS: EXERCISE 9

1. A religious painting hung on a wooden wall.
2. The big wall clock ticked noisily.
3. The departing parents comforted their nervous children.
4. The abandoned house sheltered homeless people.
5. Growing children leave behind many broken toys.
6. The wrecked car is a silver Chevrolet.

7. We recently bought our father a carving knife.
8. The brass doors open inward.
9. The deep oceans contain peculiar fish.
10. The hiccupping boy drank the water quickly.

gr
5c

RESOURCES AND IDEAS

Dealing with Error

David Bartholomae, "The Study of Error," *College Composition and Communication* 31 (1980): 253–69. Bartholomae suggests that asking basic writers to read their papers aloud helps identify sources of error and can contribute to improvement in writing.

Mina P. Shaughnessey, *Errors and Expectations: A Guide for the Teacher of Basic Writing* (New York: Oxford UP, 1977). This valuable book focuses on basic writing but is also an important work for teachers of writing at all levels. It provides a detailed analysis of the causes of student errors as well as useful strategies for dealing with writing problems.

Patricia Laurence, "Error's Endless Train: Why Students Don't Perceive Errors," *Journal of Basic Writing* 1 (1975): 23–42. The author discusses why students do not perceive errors and presents exercises to help make students aware of inflections and easily confused words.

Carroll Viera, "Helping Students to Help Themselves: An Approach to Grammar," *College Composition and Communication* 37 (1986): 94–96. Viera suggests having students analyze their own grammatical problems, do research in their handbooks, and present minilessons in small groups.

RESOURCES AND IDEAS

Sentence Combining: Background and Suggestions

Much has been written about sentence combining over the past two decades. The twenty-three essays in *Sentence Combining:*

4. The house sheltered people. The people were homeless. The house was abandoned.
5. Children leave toys. The children are growing. They leave the toys behind. The toys are many. The toys are broken.
6. The car is a Chevrolet. The car is wrecked. The car is silver.
7. We bought our father a knife. We bought the knife recently. It is for carving.
8. The doors open. The doors are brass. They open inward.
9. The oceans are deep. The oceans contain fish. The fish are peculiar.
10. The boy drank the water. The boy was hiccupping. He drank the water quickly.

5c Expanding the basic sentence with word groups

We have seen that nouns and verbs are the basic words of our language. Naming and asserting, they are all we need to build the basic sentence patterns. Adjectives and adverbs are the simplest modifiers, permitting us to qualify or limit nouns and verbs. But most sentences we read or write contain whole word groups that *serve* as nouns and modifiers. Such word groups enable us to combine several bits of information into one sentence and to make the relations among them clear.

Consider the following sentence:

When the ice cracked, the skaters, fearing an accident, sought safety at the lake's edge.

The skeleton of this sentence—the basic subject and predicate—is *The skaters sought safety.* The sentence pattern is subject (*skaters*), verb (*sought*), and direct object (*safety*). But attached to this skeleton are three other groups of words that add related information. Each word group could itself be stated as a basic sentence pattern: *The ice cracked. The skaters feared an accident. The lake's edge was safe.* In the sample sentence, however, each of these statements is reduced to something less than a sentence and then is inserted into the basic pattern *The skaters sought safety.* The reduced constructions are phrases and clauses.

A **phrase,** such as *at the lake's edge* and *fearing an accident,* is a group of related words that lacks either a subject or a predicate or both. A **clause,** in contrast, contains both a subject and a predicate. Both *The skaters sought safety* and *When the ice cracked* are clauses, though only the first can stand alone as a sentence. We will examine the various kinds of phrases and clauses in the following sections.

1 **Using prepositional phrases**

Prepositions are connecting words. Unlike nouns, verbs, and modifiers, which may change form according to their meaning and use in a sentence, prepositions never change form. We use many prepositions with great frequency.

COMMON PREPOSITIONS

about	beneath	in spite of	round
above	beside	instead of	since
according to	between	into	through
across	beyond	like	throughout
after	by	near	till
against	concerning	next to	to
along	despite	of	toward
along with	down	off	under
among	during	on	underneath
around	except	onto	unlike
as	except for	out	until
aside from	excepting	out of	up
at	for	outside	upon
because of	from	over	with
before	in	past	within
behind	in addition to	regarding	without
below	inside		

A preposition always connects a noun, a pronoun, or a word group functioning as a noun to another word in the sentence: *Robins nest in trees.* The noun, pronoun, or word group so connected (*trees*) is the **object of the preposition.** The preposition plus its object and any modifiers is a **prepositional phrase.**

PREPOSITION	OBJECT
of	spaghetti
on	the surface
with	great satisfaction
upon	entering the room
from	where you are standing

Prepositions normally come before their objects. But sometimes the preposition comes after its object, particularly in speech.

What do you want to see him *about?*
They know the *town* we are *from.*

Prepositional phrases usually function as adjectives (modifying nouns) or as adverbs (modifying verbs, adjectives, or other

A Rhetorical Perspective, ed. Donald A. Daiker, Andrew Kerek, and Max Morenberg (Carbondale: Southern Illinois UP, 1985), provide excellent perspectives on the strengths and weaknesses of sentence combining as a way of improving the quality of writing and of developing an understanding of language and style.

The following articles are also useful resources:

Donald Daiker, Andrew Kerek, and Max Morenberg, "Sentence-Combining and Syntactic Maturity in Freshman English," *College Composition and Communication* 29 (1978): 36–41. The authors discuss the results of an experiment demonstrating the effectiveness of sentence combining over fifteen weeks of intensive instruction.

William Strong, "Sentence Combining: Back to the Basics and Beyond," *English Journal* 65 (1976): 56, 60–64. Strong explains different kinds of exercises and suggests ways to use them in class.

M. Beverly Swan, "Sentence Combining in College Composition: Interim Measures and Patterns," *Research in the Teaching of English* 13 (1979): 217–24. Swan reports that the amount of instruction students receive in sentence combining is less important than the amount of time they are given to absorb the instruction. She suggests that instruction should take place over a relatively long period, perhaps a fifteen-week semester.

gr
5c

RESOURCES AND IDEAS

Many of the exercises in this chapter can be used as the basis for a sequence of sentence-combining activities. The appropriate exercises are 9, 11, 13, 14, 16, 17, 18, and 22.

Exercises in other chapters that can be part of a sentence-combining sequence are listed in the discussion "A Sequence for Sentence Combining" in the essay "The Handbook in Composition Courses" at the beginning of this *Annotated Instructor's Edition.*

gr
5c

adverbs). As modifiers, they add details that make sentences clearer and more interesting for readers.

PREPOSITIONAL PHRASES AS ADJECTIVES

Terry is the boy *in the pink shirt.* [Phrase describes *boy.*]

Life *on a raft in the Mississippi* was an opportunity *for adventure.* [*On a raft* describes *life; in the Mississippi* describes *raft;* and *for adventure* describes *opportunity.*]

PREPOSITIONAL PHRASES AS ADVERBS

She had driven steadily *for four hours from Baltimore.* [Both phrases describe *driven.*]

Our Great Dane, Joshua, buries his bones *behind the garage.* [Phrase describes *buries.*]

Occasionally, prepositional phrases also function as nouns, though rarely in writing.

PREPOSITIONAL PHRASE AS NOUN

Across the river is too far to go for ice cream. [Phrase functions as sentence subject.]

Punctuating prepositional phrases

Since a prepositional phrase lacks a subject and a predicate, it should not be punctuated as a complete sentence. If it is, the result is a **sentence fragment:**

FRAGMENT   Toward the sun.

The phrase must be attached to another group of words containing both a subject and a predicate:

REVISED   The plane turned *toward the sun.*

See Chapter 10 for a full discussion of how to recognize and revise sentence fragments.

A prepositional phrase that introduces a sentence is set off with punctuation, usually a comma, unless it is short (see 21b).

According to the newspaper and other sources, the governor has reluctantly decided to veto the bill.

In 1865 the Civil War finally ended.

A prepositional phrase that interrupts or concludes a sentence is *not* set off with punctuation when it restricts the meaning of the word or words it modifies (see 21c).

Nothing *about him* surprises me.
We saw her riding *in Sandy's car.*

When an interrupting or concluding prepositional phrase does *not* restrict meaning, but merely adds information to the sentence, then it *is* set off with punctuation, usually a comma or commas (see 21c).

> The governor, *according to the newspaper and other sources,* has reluctantly decided to veto the bill.

> The governor has reluctantly decided to veto the bill, *according to the newspaper and other sources.*

As all the preceding examples illustrate, a preposition and its object are not separated by a comma (see 21j-1).

EXERCISE 10

Identify the prepositional phrases in the following passage. Indicate whether each phrase functions as an adjective or as an adverb, and name the word that the phrase modifies.

> *Example:*
> After an hour I finally arrived at the home of my professor.
>
> **ADV PHRASE**   **ADV PHRASE**   **ADJ PHRASE**
> *After an hour* I finally arrived *at the home of my professor.*
> [*After an hour* and *at the home* modify *arrived; of my professor* modifies *home.*]

The woman in blue socks ran from the policeman on horseback. She darted down Bates Street and then into the bus depot. At the depot the policeman dismounted from his horse and searched for the woman. The entrance to the depot and the interior were filled with travelers, however, and in the crowd he lost sight of the woman. She, meanwhile, had boarded a bus on the other side of the depot and was riding across town.

EXERCISE 11

To practice writing sentences with prepositional phrases, combine each pair of sentences below into one sentence that includes one or two prepositional phrases. You will have to add, delete, and rearrange words. Some items have more than one possible answer.

> *Example:*
> I will start working. The new job will pay the minimum wage.
> I will start working *at a new job for the minimum wage.*

1. A doctor first discovered the cure. New York was where the doctor lived.

ANSWERS: EXERCISE 10

POSSIBLE ANSWERS: EXERCISE 11

1. A doctor from New York first discovered the cure.
2. A young couple with two small children bought the house for little money.
3. The lawyer accepted the case without hesitation.
4. The band members held a party for one hundred people.
5. We are required to write the exam in pencil on white paper.

gr
5c

gr
5c

6. The interview continued for two hours.
7. Jan received a glass paperweight from an unknown admirer.
8. They took a long walk along the stream and across the bridge.
9. The wagging tail of a dog toppled the lamp.
10. Everyone except Vicky and Carlos attended the lecture.

2. A young couple bought the house. The couple had two small children. The house cost little money.
3. The lawyer accepted the case. She had no hesitation.
4. The band members held a party. They invited one hundred people.
5. We are required to write the exam. We must use pencil and white paper.
6. The interview continued. Two hours was the time it took.
7. Jan received a glass paperweight. An unknown admirer gave it.
8. They took a long walk. They followed the stream and crossed the bridge.
9. The wagging tail toppled the lamp. The tail belonged to the dog.
10. Everyone attended the lecture. Only Vicky and Carlos did not go.

2   Using verbals and verbal phrases

Verbals are special verb forms like *smoking* or *hidden* or *to win* that can function as nouns (*smoking is dangerous*) or as modifiers (*the hidden money, the urge to win*). Verbals *cannot* stand alone as the complete verb in the predicate of a sentence. For example, *The man smoking* and *The money hidden* are not sentences but sentence fragments (see 10a). Any verbal must combine with a helping verb to serve as the predicate of a sentence: *The man was smoking. The money is hidden.*

Because verbals cannot serve alone as sentence predicates, they are sometimes called **nonfinite verbs** (in essence, they are "unfinished"). **Finite verbs,** in contrast, can make an assertion or express a state of being without a helping verb (they are "finished"). Either of two tests can distinguish finite and nonfinite verbs.

TESTS FOR FINITE AND NONFINITE VERBS (VERBALS)

TEST 1: Does the word require a change in form when a third-person subject changes from singular to plural?

> **Yes.** Finite verb: *It sings. They sing.*
> **No.** Nonfinite verb (verbal): *bird singing, birds singing*

TEST 2: Does the word require a change in form to show the difference in present, past, and future?

> **Yes.** Finite verb: *It sings. It sang. It will sing.*
> **No.** Nonfinite verb (verbal): *The bird singing is/was/will be a robin.*

There are three kinds of verbals: participles, gerunds, and infinitives.

Participles

All verbs have two participle forms, a present and a past. The **present participle** consists of the dictionary form of the verb plus the ending *-ing: beginning, completing, hiding.* The **past participle** of most verbs consists of the dictionary form plus *-d* or *-ed: believed, completed.* Some common verbs have an irregular past participle: *begun, hidden.* (See 7a.)

Both present and past participles function as adjectives to modify nouns and pronouns.

> The *freezing* rain made the roads dangerous. [Modifies *rain*.]
> The *exhausted* miners were rescued. [Modifies *miners*.]
> Oliver found his *typing* job *boring*. [Both participles modify *job*.]
> *Disgusted*, he quit that night. [Modifies *he*.]

Gerunds

Gerund is the name given to the *-ing* form of the verb when it serves as a noun.

> Unfortunately, *studying* always bored Michael. [Sentence subject.]
> His sister Annie hated *swimming*. [Object of *hated*.]
> Both Michael and Annie preferred *loafing* to *working*. [*Loafing* is the object of *preferred; working* is the object of *to*.]
> Their principal occupation was *loafing*. [Subject complement.]

Present participles and gerunds can be distinguished *only* by their function in a sentence. If the *-ing* form functions as an adjective (*a teaching degree*), it is a present participle. If the *-ing* form functions as a noun (*Teaching is difficult*), it is a gerund.

Infinitives

The **infinitive** is the *to* form of the verb, the dictionary form preceded by the infinitive marker *to: to begin, to hide, to run.* Infinitives may function as nouns, adjectives, or adverbs.

> He plans *to go*. [The infinitive functions as a noun, the object of *plans*.]
> He is the man *to elect*. [The infinitive functions as an adjective, modifying *man*.]
> Some physics problems are difficult *to solve*. [The infinitive functions as an adverb, modifying *difficult*.]

---

gr
5c

USING READINGS

Students can analyze passages from an essay in a reader (or some other source), looking for verbal phrases, passive sentences, compound and complex sentences, or any other features that you feel contribute to the effect of the essay and should be part of the students' prose style.

REDO THE READINGS

Using the passages from the activity above (or other passages), ask students to transform each occurrence of a structure—verbal phrases or compound sentences, etc.—into alternate structures of their choice without changing the meaning of the passage. Then ask students to comment on how the changes affect the passage, if at all. This activity is particularly well suited for collaborative work.

Verbal phrases

Participles, gerunds, and infinitives—like other forms of verbs—may take subjects, objects, or complements, and they may be modified by adverbs. The verbal and all the words immediately related to it make up a **verbal phrase.** With verbal phrases, we can create concise sentences packed with information.

PARTICIPIAL PHRASES

Like participles, **participial phrases** always serve as adjectives, modifying nouns or pronouns.

Chewing his pencil steadily, Dick stared into the air. [Modifies *Dick.*]

He was frustrated by the paper *lying before him.* [Modifies *paper.*]

Defeated by the same blank paper earlier in the day, Dick knew he must somehow write something. [Modifies *Dick.*]

GERUND PHRASES

Gerund phrases, like gerunds, always serve as nouns.

Eating an entire lemon pie for lunch was easy for Wesley. [Sentence subject.]

His mother was annoyed at *his eating the whole pie.* [Object of preposition *at. His* is the subject of the gerund; see 6h.]

But she had hidden a second pie because she anticipated *his doing it.* [Object of *anticipated.*]

INFINITIVE PHRASES

Infinitive phrases may serve as nouns, adjectives, or adverbs.

To lie repeatedly is *to deny reality.* [Both phrases function as nouns, the first as the sentence subject and the second as a subject complement.]

We wanted *him to go.* [The phrase functions as a noun, the object of *wanted. Him* is the subject of the infinitive; see 6f.]

Jimmy's is the best place *to eat pancakes.* [The phrase functions as an adjective, modifying *place.*]

Frank jogged *to keep himself fit.* [The phrase functions as an adverb, modifying *jogged.*]

Jack was too young *to understand the story.* [The phrase functions as an adverb, modifying *young.*]

NOTE: When an infinitive or infinitive phrase serves as a noun after verbs such as *hear, let, help, make, see,* and *watch,* the infinitive marker *to* is omitted: *We all heard her (to) tell the story.*

gr
5c

Punctuating verbals and verbal phrases

Like prepositional phrases, verbal phrases punctuated as complete sentences are sentence fragments. A complete sentence must contain a subject and a finite verb (p. 178).

FRAGMENT	*Treating* the patients kindly.
REVISED	*She treats* the patients kindly.

See Chapter 10 on sentence fragments.

A verbal or verbal phrase serving as a modifier is almost always set off with a comma when it introduces a sentence (see 21b).

To pay her tuition, she worked at two jobs.
Breathing evenly, the cat lay asleep on the rug.

A modifying verbal or verbal phrase that interrupts or concludes a sentence is *not* set off with punctuation when it restricts the meaning of the word or words it modifies (see 21c).

The boy *selling hotdogs* is my brother.
She worked at two jobs *to pay her tuition.*

When an interrupting or concluding verbal modifier does *not* restrict meaning, but merely adds information to the sentence, it *is* set off with punctuation, usually a comma or commas (see 21c).

The cat, *breathing evenly,* lay asleep on the rug.
The cat lay asleep on the rug, *breathing evenly.*

EXERCISE 12

The following sentences contain participles, gerunds, and infinitives as well as participial, gerund, and infinitive phrases. First identify each verbal or verbal phrase. Then indicate whether it is used as an adjective, an adverb, or a noun.

Example:
Laughing, the talk-show host prodded her guest to talk.

  ADJ   **ADV**
Laughing, the talk-show host prodded her guest *to talk.*

1. Shunned by the community, Hester Prynne went into exile.
2. She is self-confident enough to laugh at her own faults.
3. Sliding and slipping, they moved across the ice to greet their friends.
4. Eating at a nice restaurant is a relaxing way to end a hectic week.
5. To fly was one of humankind's recurring dreams.
6. Because of the dwindling water supply, the remaining vacationers decided to leave for another campground.
7. The periodic firing of the rifle kept the hungry wolves at bay.

ANSWERS: EXERCISE 12

             ADJ
1. Shunned by the community,   Hester Prynne went into exile.
2. She   is   self-confident   enough
            ADV
to laugh at her own faults.
     ADJ   **ADJ**
3. Sliding and slipping, they moved
               ADV
across the ice to greet their friends.
  N
4. Eating at a nice restaurant   is   a
   ADJ   **ADJ**
relaxing way to end a hectic week.
  N
5. To fly   was   one   of   humankind's
    ADJ
recurring dreams.

gr
5c

6. Because of the dwindling [ADJ] water supply, the remaining [ADJ] vacationers decided to leave for another campground. [N]

7. The periodic firing of the rifle [N]   kept
the hungry wolves at bay.

8. The train moved too fast for
us to enjoy the countryside. [N]

9. Three misbehaving [ADJ] children ruined our
attempt   to stage a play in the el- [ADJ]
ementary school.

10. After missing rehearsal three times in [N]
a row, I received a call from the conductor.

POSSIBLE ANSWERS: EXERCISE 13

1. The sound grew louder, swelling as
the airplanes approached.
2. By importing flowers from all over the
world, florists manage to sell tulips in
December.
3. The highway leading into town is
lined with fast-food restaurants.
4. The ancient Greeks gave their children cheese to reward good behavior.
5. The islands of Japan form a thousand-
mile-long archipelago lying mostly in
the temperate zone.
6. Falling far behind the other runners,
Lee knew she had lost the race.
7. The letter, opened by mistake, was
lying on the table.
8. Shopping in supermarkets with their
parents is an early experience that almost all children share.
9. I must get a job to support myself.
10. Cleaning the cellar, they discovered a
box of old money.

8. The train moved too fast for us to enjoy the countryside.
9. Three misbehaving children ruined our attempt to stage a
play in the elementary school.
10. After missing rehearsal three times in a row, I received a call
from the conductor.

EXERCISE 13

To practice writing sentences with verbals and verbal phrases,
combine each pair of sentences below into one sentence. You will
have to add, delete, change, and rearrange words. Each item has
more than one possible answer.

Example:

My father took pleasure in mean pranks. For instance, he hid
my neighbors' cat.

My father took pleasure in mean pranks such as *hiding the
neighbors' cat.*

1. The sound grew louder. It swelled as the airplanes approached.
2. Florists import flowers from all over the world. In this way
they manage to sell tulips in December.
3. The highway leads into the town. It is lined with fast-food
restaurants.
4. The ancient Greeks gave their children cheese. The cheese
rewarded good behavior.
5. The islands of Japan form a thousand-mile-long archipelago. The archipelago lies mostly in the temperate zone.
6. Lee knew she had lost the race. She was falling far behind
the other runners.
7. The letter had been opened by mistake. It was lying on the
table.
8. Children shop in supermarkets with their parents. This is an
early experience that almost all children share.
9. I must get a job. I must support myself.
10. They discovered a box of old money. They were cleaning the
cellar.

3   **Using absolute phrases**

Absolute phrases consist of a noun or pronoun and a participle, plus any modifiers.

The parade passed by slowly, *the bands blaring, the crowds
shouting.*

The old tree stood alone, *its trunk stripped and rotting.*

Their work nearly finished, the men rested.

These phrases are called *absolute* (from a Latin word meaning "free") because they have no specific grammatical connection to any word in the rest of the sentence. Instead, they modify the entire rest of the sentence, adding information or clarifying meaning.

Notice that absolute phrases, unlike participial phrases, always contain a subject. Compare the following.

> The large man *standing before me* turned to speak. [Participial phrase modifying *man*, the sentence subject.]

> *A large man having moved in front of me*, I could see nothing. [Absolute phrase having its own subject, *A large man*, and modifying the rest of the sentence.]

We often omit the participle from an absolute phrase when it is some form of *be* such as *being* or *having been*.

> Sammy watched intently, *his mouth (being) wide open*.

Punctuating absolute phrases

Absolute phrases are always set off from the rest of the sentence with punctuation, usually a comma or commas (see 21d).

> *Its finish waxed and buffed*, the car looked almost new.
> The car, *its finish waxed and buffed*, looked almost new.
> The car looked almost new, *its finish waxed and buffed*.

EXERCISE 14

To practice writing sentences with absolute phrases, combine each pair of sentences below into one sentence that contains an absolute phrase. You will have to add, delete, change, and rearrange words.

> *Example:*
> The flower's petals wilted. It looked pathetic.
> *Its petals wilted*, the flower looked pathetic.

1. Her face turned pale. She stared at the woman ahead of her.
2. The steelworkers called a strike. The factory was closed down.
3. We were forced to cancel the annual picnic. The funds had run out.
4. The thief stood before the safe. His fingers twitched eagerly.
5. The swimmer rose again to the surface. His arms thrashed.

RESOURCES AND IDEAS

Martha Solomon, "Teaching the Nominative Absolute," *College Composition and Communication* 26 (1975): 356–61. Solomon offers advice on analyzing and teaching the absolute.

gr
5c

POSSIBLE ANSWERS: EXERCISE 14

1. Her face turning pale, she stared at the woman ahead of her.
2. The steelworkers having called a strike, the factory was closed down.
3. We were forced to cancel the annual picnic, the funds having run out.
4. The thief stood before the safe, his fingers twitching eagerly.
5. The swimmer rose again to the surface, his arms thrashing.

4 Using subordinate clauses

As we noted earlier, a **clause** is any group of words that contains both a subject and a predicate. There are two kinds of clauses, and the distinction between them is important. A **main** or **independent clause** can stand alone as a sentence: *The sky darkened.* A **subordinate** or **dependent clause** is just like a main clause *except* that it begins with a subordinating word: *when the sky darkened. When* and other subordinating words such as *because, if, who,* or *that* express particular relationships between the clauses they introduce and the main clauses to which they are attached. Clauses that have been subordinated can *never* stand alone as sentences (see the discussion of punctuation on p. 186). The following examples show the differences between the two kinds of clauses.

Two main clauses

The chair is expensive. We cannot buy it.

First clause subordinated

Because the chair is expensive, we cannot buy it.

Two main clauses

I met a man. He was selling boa constrictors.

Second clause subordinated

I met a man *who was selling boa constrictors.*

We use two kinds of subordinating words to connect subordinate clauses with main clauses. The first kind is **subordinating conjunctions** or **subordinators.** They always come at the beginning of subordinate clauses. Like prepositions, subordinating conjunctions are few and never change form in any way.

COMMON SUBORDINATING CONJUNCTIONS

after	because	in order that	than	when
although	before	now that	that	whenever
as	even if	once	though	where
as if	even though	rather than	till	whereas
as long as	if	since	unless	wherever
as though	if only	so that	until	while

The second kind of connecting word is the **relative pronoun.** It also introduces a subordinate clause and links it with an independent clause.

RELATIVE PRONOUNS

which	what	who (whose, whom)
that	whatever	whoever (whomever)

Like subordinating conjunctions, relative pronouns link one clause with another. But unlike subordinating conjunctions, relative pronouns also usually act as subjects or objects in their own clauses, and two of them (*who* and *whoever*) change form accordingly (see 6g).

Subordinate clauses function as adjectives, adverbs, and nouns and are described as adjective, adverb, or noun clauses according to their use in a particular sentence. Only by determining its function in a sentence can we identify a particular clause.

ADJECTIVE CLAUSES

Adjective clauses modify nouns and pronouns, providing necessary or helpful information about them. They usually begin with the relative pronouns listed above, although a few adjective clauses begin with *when* or *where* (standing for *in which, on which,* or *at which*). The relative pronoun is the subject or object of the clause it begins. The clause ordinarily falls immediately after the noun or pronoun it modifies.

> My family still lives in the house *that my grandfather built.* [Modifies *house.*]
>
> Dale is the girl *who always gets there early.* [Modifies *girl.*]
>
> My yellow Volkswagen, *which I bought seven years ago,* has traveled 78,000 miles. [Modifies *Volkswagen.*]
>
> There comes a time *when each of us must work.* [Modifies *time.*]

ADVERB CLAUSES

Like adverbs, adverb clauses modify verbs, adjectives, other adverbs, and whole groups of words. They usually tell how, why, when, where, under what conditions, or with what result. They always begin with subordinating conjunctions.

> Calvin liked to go *where there was action.* [Modifies *go.*]
>
> Elaine is friendlier *when she's talking on the telephone.* [Modifies *friendlier.*]
>
> *Because he did not study,* Donald failed. [Modifies *failed.*]
>
> She came as quickly *as she could.* [Modifies *quickly.*]

An adverb clause can often be separated from the word it modifies. In both sentences below, the adverb clause modifies *ended.*

> The game ended *before he had a chance to play.*
> *Before he had a chance to play,* the game ended.

NOUN CLAUSES

Noun clauses function as subjects, objects, and complements in sentences. They begin either with relative pronouns or with the words *when, where, whether, why,* and *how.* Unlike adjective and adverb clauses, noun clauses *replace* a word (a noun) within a main clause; therefore, they can be difficult to identify.

> *The lecture* pleased the audience. [*The lecture* is the sentence subject.]
>
> *What the lecturer said* pleased the audience. [The noun clause replaces *The lecture* as the sentence subject.]

Here are some typical noun clauses.

> Everyone knows *what a panther is.* [Object of *knows.*]
>
> *Whoever calls the station first* will win a case of bean soup. [Subject of sentence.]
>
> They thought about *whether they could afford the trip.* [Object of preposition *about.*]

ELLIPTICAL CLAUSE

A subordinate clause that is grammatically incomplete but clear in meaning is an **elliptical clause** (*ellipsis* means "omission"). The meaning of the clause is clear because the missing element can be supplied from the context. Most often the elements omitted are the relative pronouns *that, which,* and *whom* from adjective clauses or the predicate from the second part of a comparison.

> Thailand is among the countries (*that* or *which*) he visited.
> Ellen dances better *than Martha* (*dances*).

Here are other typical elliptical clauses.

> *When* (*she was*) *only a child,* Julia saw a great gray owl.
>
> *Though* (*they are*) *rare south of Canada,* great gray owls sometimes appear in Massachusetts.

Punctuating subordinate clauses

Subordinate clauses punctuated as complete sentences are sentence fragments. Though a subordinate clause contains a subject and a predicate and thus resembles a complete sentence, it also contains a subordinating word that makes its meaning dependent on a main clause.

FRAGMENT	Because the door was ajar.
REVISED	The door was ajar.
REVISED	I overheard *because the door was ajar.*

See Chapter 10 on sentence fragments.

A subordinate clause serving as an adverb is almost always set off with a comma when it introduces a sentence (see 21b).

> *Although the project was almost completed,* it lost its funding.

RESOURCES AND IDEAS

Richard B. Larsen, "Sentence Patterning," *College Composition and Communication* 37 (1986): 103–04. Larsen describes a sequence in which students are introduced to a variety of sentence patterns and then asked to use the patterns in their writing, including paragraph-length compositions.

gr
5c

A modifying subordinate clause that interrupts or concludes a main clause is *not* set off with punctuation when it restricts the meaning of the word or words it modifies (see 21c).

The woman *who spoke* is a doctor.
The project lost its funding *because it was not completed on time.*

When an interrupting or concluding subordinate clause does *not* restrict meaning, but merely adds information to the sentence, it *is* set off with punctuation, usually a comma or commas (see 21c).

The woman, *who is a doctor,* cares for her invalid father.
The project lost its funding, *although it was almost completed.*

EXERCISE 15

Identify the subordinate clauses in the following sentences. Then indicate whether each is used as an adjective, an adverb, or a noun. If the clause is a noun, indicate its function in the sentence.

Example:

The article explained how one could build an underground house.

The article explained *how one could build an underground house.* [Object of *explained.*]

1. They were not interested in what the tour guide said.
2. The auctioneer opened the bidding once everyone was seated.
3. Whenever the economy is uncertain, people tend to become anxious.
4. Whoever wants to graduate must pass all the required courses.
5. I knew the ending would be unhappy when the main character started falling apart.
6. That Stefanie has not gone to college is a disappointment to her parents.
7. Ever since she was a small child, they have saved money for her education.
8. Stefanie decided, though, that she wanted to work a year or two before college.
9. Until she makes up her mind, Stefanie's education money is collecting interest.
10. Her parents are the kind who let their children think for themselves.

EXERCISE 16

To practice writing sentences with subordinate clauses, combine each pair of main clauses below into one sentence. Use either subordinating conjunctions or relative pronouns as appropriate,

gr
5c

ANSWERS: EXERCISE 15

1. They were not interested in
   N (object of preposition)
   what the tour guide said.
2. The auctioneer opened the bidding
   ADV
   once everyone was seated.
   ADV
3. Whenever the economy is uncertain, people tend to become anxious.
   N (subject)
4. Whoever wants to graduate must pass all the required courses.
5. I knew the ending would be unhappy
   ADV
   when the main character started falling apart.
   N (subject)
6. That Stefanie has not gone to college is a disappointment to her parents.
   ADV
7. Ever since she was a small child, they have saved money for her education.
8. Stefanie decided, though, that she
   N (direct object)
   wanted to work a year or two before college.
   ADV
9. Until she makes up her mind, Stefanie's education money is collecting interest.
10. Her parents are the kind who let
    ADJ
    their children think for themselves.

POSSIBLE ANSWERS: EXERCISE 16

1. The phone lines went dead after a fire destroyed much of the central office.
2. Taxpayers should understand that the IRS does not make exceptions.
3. The critic reviewed the Frank Capra movie that was playing at the revival theater.

gr
5c

4. He is an accountant who rarely makes mistakes.
5. We came to the gate where we had first seen the deer tracks.
6. Someone who is fickle cannot be relied on.
7. When the town government canceled the new playground, small children demonstrated in the streets.
8. Those dogs have a master who gives them equal discipline and praise.
9. Although the basketball team has had a losing season, the team still shows promise.
10. He did not bother to undress for bed because he was too tired.

CREATE YOUR OWN

Divide the class into groups. Ask each group to create its own set of sentence-combining exercises following the pattern of the exercises in the handbook. Then ask the groups to trade exercises, work on them, and return them to the authors with both positive comments and criticisms.

referring to the lists on page 184 if necessary. You will have to add, delete, and rearrange words. Each item has more than one possible answer.

Example:
She did not have her tire irons with her. She could not change her bicycle tire.

Because she did not have her tire irons with her, she could not change her bicycle tire.

1. The phone lines went dead. Earlier a fire destroyed much of the central office.
2. Taxpayers should understand something. The IRS does not make exceptions.
3. The critic reviewed the Frank Capra movie. It was playing at the revival theater.
4. He is an accountant. He rarely makes mistakes.
5. We came to the gate. We had first seen the deer tracks there.
6. Someone is fickle. This person cannot be relied on.
7. The town government canceled the new playground. Then small children demonstrated in the streets.
8. Those dogs have a master. He gives them equal discipline and praise.
9. The basketball team has had a losing season. The team still shows promise.
10. He did not bother to undress for bed. He was too tired.

5 Using appositives

An **appositive** is a word or word group that renames the word or word group before it. (The word *appositive* derives from a Latin word that means "placed near to" or "applied to.") The most common appositives are nouns that rename other nouns.

Her sister *Jean* attends law school. [Noun as appositive.]

Bizen ware, *a dark stoneware*, has been produced in Japan since the fourteenth century. [Noun phrase as appositive.]

His first love, *racing stock cars*, was his last love. [Gerund phrase as appositive.]

All appositives can replace the words they refer to: *A dark stoneware has been produced in Japan. Racing stock cars was his last love.*

Appositives are often introduced by words and phrases such as *or, that is, such as, for example,* and *in other words.*

Kangaroos, opossums, and wombats are all marsupials, *that is, mammals that carry their young in external abdominal pouches.*

Jujitsu, *or judo,* is based on the principle that an opponent's strength may be used to defeat him or her.

Although most appositives are nouns that rename other nouns, they may also be and rename other parts of speech.

All papers should be proofread carefully, that is, *checked for spelling, punctuation, and mechanics.* [The appositive defines the verb *proofread.*]

Noun appositives can always be stated as clauses with some form of the verb *be.*

Bizen ware, *(which is) a dark stoneware,* has been produced in Japan since the fourteenth century.

Thus appositives are economical alternatives to adjective clauses containing a form of *be.*

Punctuating appositives

Appositives punctuated as complete sentences are sentence fragments (see Chapter 10). Correcting such fragments generally involves connecting the appositive to the main clause containing the word referred to.

FRAGMENT	An exceedingly tall man with narrow shoulders.
REVISED	I stood next to a basketball player, *an exceedingly tall man with narrow shoulders.*

An appositive is *not* set off with punctuation when it restricts the meaning of the word it refers to (see 21c).

The verb *howl* comes from the Old English verb *houlen.*

When an appositive does *not* restrict the meaning of the word it refers to, it *is* set off with punctuation, usually a comma or commas (see 21c).

An aged elm, the tree was struck by lightning.
The tree, *an aged elm,* was struck by lightning.
Lightning struck the tree, *an aged elm.*

A nonrestrictive appositive is sometimes set off with a dash or dashes, especially when it contains commas (see 25b-2).

Three people—*Will, Carolyn, and Tom*—objected to the new procedure.

A concluding appositive is sometimes set off with a colon (see 25a-1).

Two principles guide the judge's decisions: *justice and fairness.*

POSSIBLE ANSWERS: EXERCISE 17

1. The poet, an egocentric boor, is rarely invited to read.
2. The part of Nathan Detroit, a gambler, is played by Frank Sinatra.
3. The tapestry depicted a unicorn, the fabled horse-like animal with one horn.
4. Cactus growing, a hobby with no immediate rewards, attracts patient people.
5. The most popular professional sports—football, baseball, basketball, and hockey—pay their players well.
6. Edgar Allan Poe, a writer of fantastic, scary stories, was also a poet and a journalist.
7. The house, a five-room adobe structure, was bought by a neighborhood group.
8. English adopted many words for animals—such as *moose, opossum,* and *raccoon*—from the Algonquin Indians.
9. Jerry's aim, to avoid all productive labor, will surely change when his parents stop supporting him.
10. Their Beatles memorabilia—records, photographs, posters, and T-shirts—occupied a room in their basement.

EXERCISE 17

To practice writing sentences with appositives, combine each pair of sentences into one sentence that contains an appositive. You will have to delete and rearrange words. Some items have more than one possible answer.

Example:

The largest land animal is the elephant. The elephant is also one of the most intelligent animals.

The largest land animal, *the elephant*, is also one of the most intelligent animals.

1. The poet is an egocentric boor. He is rarely invited to read.
2. The part of Nathan Detroit is played by Frank Sinatra. Detroit is a gambler.
3. The tapestry depicted a unicorn. That is the fabled horselike animal with one horn.
4. Cactus growing attracts patient people. It is a hobby with no immediate rewards.
5. The most popular professional sports pay their players well. They are football, baseball, basketball, and hockey.
6. Edgar Allan Poe was a writer of fantastic, scary stories. He was also a poet and a journalist.
7. The house was a five-room adobe structure. It was bought by a neighborhood group.
8. English adopted many words for animals from the Algonquin Indians. These are words such as *moose, opossum,* and *raccoon*.
9. Jerry's aim in life is to avoid all productive labor. His aim will surely change when his parents stop supporting him.
10. Their Beatles memorabilia occupied a room in their basement. The memorabilia consisted of records, photographs, posters, and T-shirts.

5d Compounding words, phrases, and clauses

We have seen how to modify the nouns and verbs of the basic sentence patterns and how to use word groups in place of single nouns and modifiers. Here we examine how to combine words and word groups that are closely related and parallel in importance.

Bonnie spent the afternoon in the park. Her father spent the afternoon in the park.

Bonnie and her father spent the afternoon in the park.

Curt was tired. He was sick. He was depressed.

Curt was *tired, sick, and depressed.*

Brenda went to the drugstore. She bought some vitamins. She returned as soon as possible.

Brenda *went to the drugstore, bought some vitamins, and returned as soon as possible.*

In the first pair of examples the two different subjects, *Bonnie* and *her father,* become a **compound subject,** thus avoiding repetition of the same predicate in two sentences. In the second pair of examples the three adjective complements become a **compound complement** (*tired, sick, and depressed*) that describes the common subject *Curt* after the common linking verb *was.* And in the last pair of examples the three different predicates become a **compound predicate** (*went . . . , bought . . . , and returned . . .*) with the common subject *Brenda.* In every example *and* joins the parts.

1 **Using coordinating conjunctions and correlative conjunctions**

The word *and* is a **coordinating conjunction.** Like prepositions and subordinating conjunctions, coordinating conjunctions are few and do not change form.

COORDINATING CONJUNCTIONS			
and	nor	for	yet
but	or	so	

The coordinating conjunctions *and, but, nor,* and *or* always connect words or word groups of the same kind—that is, two or more nouns, verbs, adjectives, adverbs, phrases, subordinate clauses, or main clauses.

Stewart *or* Linda will have to go.
The chair was unfashionable *but* charming.
Alison worked every day *and* partied every evening.
He studied day and night, *but* he could not pass the course.

The conjunctions *for* and *so* cannot connect words, phrases, or subordinate clauses, but they can connect main clauses. *For* may also function as a preposition (*a present for the girls*). When it functions as a conjunction, it indicates cause. *So* indicates result.

Amy stayed home, *for* she had work to do.
Jasper was tired, *so* he went to bed early.

RESOURCES AND IDEAS

Donna Gorrell, "Controlled Composition for Basic Writers," *College Composition and Communication* 32 (1981): 308–16. Gorrell suggests having students manipulate and alter previously written material to develop basic skills.

The word *yet* often functions as an adverb (*She has not left yet*), but it can also function as a coordinating conjunction. Like *but*, it indicates contrast.

> He tended the goldfish carefully, *yet* it died.

Some conjunctions pair up with other words to form **correlative conjunctions**.

COMMON CORRELATIVE CONJUNCTIONS

both . . . and	neither . . . nor
not only . . . but also	whether . . . or
not . . . but	as . . . as
either . . . or	

> *Both* Bonnie *and* her father went to the park.
> The basketball is *either* on the shelf *or* in the closet.
> The class stood *neither* when he arrived *nor* when he left.
> We consume energy *not only* when awake *but also* when asleep.

Punctuating compounded words, phrases, and clauses

Unless they form a series of three or more, words, phrases, and subordinate clauses that are connected by a coordinating conjunction are *not* separated by commas (see 21j-2).

> The *boys and girls* segregated themselves.
> The cat jumped *off the roof and into the tree.*
> The robbery occurred *after I left but before Jim arrived.*

When two *main* clauses are joined into one sentence with a coordinating conjunction, a comma precedes the conjunction (see 21a).

> The test was difficult, *but* I think I did well.

When two main clauses are joined *without* a coordinating conjunction, they must be separated with a semicolon to avoid the error called a **comma splice** (see 11a).

> The joke was not funny; it was insulting.

The semicolon sometimes separates two main clauses joined by a coordinating conjunction when the clauses are long or contain commas (see 22c). The semicolon *always* separates two main clauses related by a conjunctive adverb (see the next section).

In a series of three or more items, commas separate the items, with *and* usually preceding the last item (see 21f-1).

The curtains were mostly white with splotches of pink, yellow, *and* brown.

Semicolons sometimes separate the items in a series if they are long or contain commas (see 22d).

The comma also separates coordinate adjectives (those which modify a noun or pronoun equally) when the adjectives are not joined by a coordinating conjunction (see 21f-2).

Wet, slick roads made driving dangerous.

The comma does *not* separate adjectives when the one nearer the noun is more closely related to it in meaning (see 21f-2).

She gave the teacher a *large red* apple.

2 Using conjunctive adverbs

One other kind of connecting word, called a **conjunctive adverb,** relates only main clauses, not words, phrases, or subordinate clauses.

COMMON CONJUNCTIVE ADVERBS			
accordingly	furthermore	moreover	similarly
also	hence	namely	still
anyway	however	nevertheless	then
besides	incidentally	next	thereafter
certainly	indeed	nonetheless	therefore
consequently	instead	now	thus
finally	likewise	otherwise	undoubtedly
further	meanwhile		

Unlike coordinating and subordinating conjunctions, conjunctive adverbs do not bind the two clauses into a grammatical unit. Rather, as adverbs, they describe the relation of the *ideas* in two clauses. Compare the following examples:

The game was exciting; *consequently,* we stayed to the end.
The game was exciting, *and* we stayed to the end.
Because the game was exciting, we stayed to the end.

In the first sentence the conjunctive adverb *consequently* describes how the second independent statement relates to the first, but it does not form the two statements into a grammatical unit. In the second sentence the coordinating conjunction *and* does join the two main clauses into a unit. In the third sentence the subordinating conjunction *because* reduces the first clause from a main clause to an adverb modifier.

A simple test can distinguish a conjunctive adverb from a coordinating or subordinating conjunction. Because a conjunctive adverb is an adverb, it can be moved from where it appears to elsewhere in the clause.

> The game was long and boring; *however,* we stayed to the end.
> The game was long and boring; we stayed, *however,* to the end.
> The game was long and boring; we stayed to the end, *however.*

In contrast, coordinating and subordinating conjunctions cannot be moved. For example, we would not write *we stayed to the end but* or *the game although was long and boring.*

These differences among conjunctive adverbs, coordinating conjunctions, and subordinating conjunctions are important because they determine very different punctuation between clauses. (See the discussion of punctuation below.)

NOTE: Just as some words may serve as nouns, verbs, or modifiers depending on their function in a sentence (see pp. 164 and 173), so some connecting words may have more than one use. *After, before, until,* and some other words may be either prepositions or subordinating conjunctions. Some prepositions, such as *behind, in,* and *outside,* can serve also as adverbs, as in *He trailed behind.* Most relative pronouns are used also as interrogative pronouns to ask questions: *What time is it? Who left?* And some conjunctive adverbs, particularly *however,* may also serve simply as adverbs in sentences such as *However much it costs, we must have it.* Again, the part of speech of a word depends on its function in a sentence.

Punctuating sentences containing conjunctive adverbs

Because the two main clauses related by a conjunctive adverb remain independent units, they must be separated by a semicolon (see 22b). If they are separated by a comma, the result is a **comma splice.**

COMMA SPLICE	We hoped for sunshine, *instead,* we got rain.
REVISED	We hoped for sunshine; *instead,* we got rain.

See Chapter 11 for a full discussion of comma splices.

A conjunctive adverb is almost always set off from its clause with a comma or commas.

No one was injured; *however,* the car was totaled.
No one was injured; the car, *however,* was totaled.
No one was injured; the car was totaled, *however.*

The comma or commas are optional with some one-syllable conjunctive adverbs (especially *hence, now, then,* and *thus*) and are not used with a few others when they appear inside or at the ends of clauses.

Interest rates rose; *thus* real estate prices declined.

All the performances were sold out; the play *therefore* made a profit.

We hoped for sunshine; we got rain *instead.*

EXERCISE 18

To practice compounding words, phrases, and clauses, combine each pair of sentences below into one sentence that is as short as possible without altering meaning. Use an appropriate connecting word of the type specified in parentheses, referring to the lists on pages 191–93 if necessary. You will have to add, delete, and rearrange words, and you may have to change or add punctuation.

> *Example:*
>
> The encyclopedia had some information. It was not detailed enough. (*Conjunctive adverb.*)
>
> The encyclopedia had some information; *however,* it was not detailed enough.

1. Frank Lloyd Wright was an influential architect. He is considered the leading American architect of the twentieth century. (*Conjunctive adverb.*)
2. Wright is best known for his houses from the early twentieth century. He did not stop building then. (*Coordinating conjunction.*)
3. Wright did not have an architecture degree. He did not have an engineering degree. (*Correlative conjunction.*)
4. Physics is a difficult subject. It is an enjoyable subject. (*Coordinating conjunction.*)
5. The cheerleaders missed the bus. The back-up center also missed the bus. (*Coordinating conjunction.*)
6. Politicians cannot be shy people. They must be outgoing. (*Conjunctive adverb.*)
7. The newspaper publishes interesting feature articles. It publishes feeble editorials. (*Coordinating conjunction.*)

POSSIBLE ANSWERS: EXERCISE 18

1. Frank Lloyd Wright was an influential architect: <u>indeed</u>, he is considered the leading American architect of the twentieth century.
2. Wright is best known for his houses from the early twentieth century, <u>but</u> he did not stop building then.
3. Wright did not have <u>either</u> an architecture <u>or</u> an engineering degree.
4. Physics is a difficult <u>but</u> enjoyable subject.
5. The cheerleaders <u>and</u> the back-up center missed the bus.
6. Politicians cannot be shy people; <u>indeed</u>, they must be outgoing.
7. The newspaper publishes interesting feature articles <u>but</u> feeble editorials.
8. <u>Both</u> my mother <u>and</u> my mother-in-law attended Thomas Jefferson High School.
9. The news stories from Uganda were censored; <u>furthermore</u>, they were out of date because the censor had held on to them for so long.
10. The crocuses were in bloom, <u>but</u> there were no other signs of spring.

8. My mother attended Thomas Jefferson High School. My mother-in-law also attended Thomas Jefferson High School. (*Correlative conjunction.*)
9. The news stories from Uganda were censored. They were out of date because the censor had held on to them for so long. (*Conjunctive adverb.*)
10. The crocuses were blooming. There were no other signs of spring. (*Coordinating conjunction.*)

5e **Changing the usual order of the sentence**

So far, all the examples of basic sentence grammar have been similar: the subject of the sentence comes first, naming the performer of the predicate's action, and the predicate comes second. This arrangement of subject and predicate describes most sentences that occur in writing, but we need to look briefly at four other kinds of sentences that alter this basic pattern.

1 Forming questions

We form questions in one of several ways. We may invert the normal subject-verb arrangement of statements:

The dog is barking. Is the dog barking?

We may use a question word such as *how, what, who, when, where, which,* or *why:*

What dog is barking?

Or we may use some combination of the two methods:

Why is the dog barking?

In each case a question mark signals that the sentence is a question.

2 Forming commands

We construct commands even more simply than we construct questions: we merely delete the subject of the sentence, *you.*

Open the window.	Eat your spinach.
Go to the store.	Leave me alone.

3 Writing passive sentences

In any sentence that uses a transitive verb—that is, in any sentence where the verb takes an object—we can move the object to the position of the subject and put the subject in the predicate. The result is a **passive sentence,** using the **passive voice** of the verb rather than the **active voice.** (See also Chapter 7, pp. 235–37.)

Greg *wrote* the paper. [Active voice.]

The paper *was written* by Greg. [Passive voice.]

A passive sentence is so called because its subject does not perform or initiate the action indicated by the verb. Rather, the subject *receives* the action. In passive sentences the verb is always a phrase consisting of some form of the verb *be* and the past participle of the main verb (*paper was written, exams are finished*). The prepositional phrase specifying the subject of the active verb (the actor) may be omitted entirely if the actor is unknown or unimportant: *The house was flooded.*

(See 7h and 18d concerning overuse of the passive voice.)

4 Writing sentences with postponed subjects

The subject follows the predicate in two sentence patterns that are not questions, commands, or passive sentences. In one pattern the normal word order is reversed for emphasis: *Then came the dawn. Up walked Henry.* This pattern occurs most often when the normal order is subject–intransitive verb–adverb. Then the adverb moves to the front of the sentence while subject and predicate reverse order.

A second kind of sentence with a postponed subject begins with either *it* or *there*, as in the following:

     V   S
There will be eighteen people attending the meeting.

  V   S
It was surprising that Marinetti was nominated.

The words *there* and *it* in such sentences are **expletives.** Their only function is to postpone the sentence subject. Expletive sentences are common, but they can be unemphatic because they add words and delay the sentence subject. Usually, the normal subject-predicate order is more effective: *Eighteen people will attend the meeting. Marinetti's nomination was surprising.* (See also 18e and 31c-3.)

gr
5f

SAMPLE ANSWERS: EXERCISE 19

1. <u>Will</u> the <u>water</u> <u>boil</u>?
   <u>Boil</u> the <u>water</u>, please.
2. <u>Did</u> the <u>music</u> <u>stop</u>?
   <u>Stop</u> the <u>music</u>.
3. <u>Have</u> you <u>set</u> the <u>table</u>?
   <u>Set</u> the <u>table</u>.
4. <u>Have</u> you <u>rolled</u> the <u>dice</u> yet?
   <u>Roll</u> the <u>dice</u>.
5. <u>Who</u> <u>can use</u> the <u>telephone</u>?
   <u>Use</u> the <u>telephone</u>.

ANSWERS: EXERCISE 20

1. <u>Francis Scott Key wrote</u> "The Star-Spangled Banner."
2. The <u>chef added</u> the tarragon to the stew.
3. The <u>quarterback threw</u> the football for more than forty yards.
4. <u>Whether microwave ovens are dangerous is</u> uncertain.
5. An <u>audience</u> of nearly ten thousand <u>attended</u> the outdoor concert.

EXERCISE 19

Form a question and a command from the following noun and verb pairs.

> *Example:*
> split, wood
> *Did* you *split* all this *wood?*
> *Split* the *wood* for our fire.

1. water, boil
2. music, stop
3. table, set
4. roll, dice
5. telephone, use

EXERCISE 20

Rewrite each passive sentence below as active, and rewrite each expletive construction to restore normal subject-predicate order. (For additional exercises with the passive voice and with expletives, see pp. 237, 348, and 481.)

1. "The Star-Spangled Banner" was written by Francis Scott Key.
2. The tarragon was added to the stew by the chef.
3. The football was thrown by the quarterback for more than forty yards.
4. It is uncertain whether microwave ovens are dangerous.
5. There was an audience of nearly ten thousand at the outdoor concert.

5f Classifying sentences

We describe and classify sentences in two different ways: by function (statement, question, command, exclamation, and so forth) or by structure. Four basic sentence structures are possible: simple, compound, complex, and compound-complex.

1 Writing simple sentences

Simple sentences consist of a single main clause. The clause may contain phrases, and the subject, the verb, and its objects may be compound; but the sentence is simple as long as it contains only one complete main clause and no subordinate clause.

Last July was unusually hot.

In fact, both July and August were vicious months.

The summer made farmers leave the area for good or reduced them to bare existence. [Two predicates but only one subject.]

2 Writing compound sentences

A **compound sentence** consists of two or more main clauses. The clauses may be joined by a coordinating conjunction and a comma, by a semicolon alone, or by a conjunctive adverb and a semicolon.

Last July was hot, but August was even hotter.

The hot sun scorched the land to powder; the lack of rain made the soil untillable.

The government later provided assistance; consequently, the remaining farmers gradually improved their lot.

3 Writing complex sentences

A sentence is **complex** if it contains one main clause and one or more subordinate clauses.

Rain finally came, although many had left the area by then. [Main clause, then subordinate clause.]

When the rain came, people rejoiced. [Subordinate clause, then main clause.]

Those who remained were able to start anew because the government came to their aid. [Main clause containing subordinate clause, then another subordinate clause.]

Notice that length does not determine whether a sentence is complex or simple; both kinds can be short or long.

4 Writing compound-complex sentences

A **compound-complex sentence** has the characteristics of both the compound sentence (two or more main clauses) and the complex sentence (at least one subordinate clause).

Even though government aid finally came, many people had already been reduced to poverty, and others had been forced to leave the area. [Subordinate clause, then main clause, then another main clause.]

Some of the farmers who had left the area moved back gradually

gr
5f

DECODING THE SENTENCE

Divide the class into small groups, and have each group write a set of nonsense sentences that conform to English syntax and punctuation. Students should be sure to include nonsense prepositional phrases, verbals, appositives, absolutes, and subordinate and coordinate structures. Warn students to punctuate the sentences carefully. Students can use the nonsense sentences at the beginning of Chapter 5 as models.

Once the sentences are written, have groups exchange sentences or write them on the board and try to identify the part of speech for each nonsense word. If the creators of the sentences have made any errors in punctuation, the puzzle-solvers should be prepared to correct them. This exercise should help students see how grammar and punctuation work together to define a word's role in a sentence and to create different kinds of sentences.

to their original homes, but several years passed before the land became as fertile as before. [Main clause containing subordinate clause, then another main clause, then another subordinate clause.]

EXERCISE 21

Mark the main clauses and subordinate clauses in the following sentences. Identify each sentence as simple, compound, complex, or compound-complex.

Example:

The police began patrolling more often when crime in the neighborhood increased.

Complex: ⌒————— MAIN —————⌒ The police began patrolling more often ⌒————— SUBORDINATE —————⌒ when crime in the neighborhood increased.

1. Joseph Pulitzer endowed the Pulitzer Prizes.
2. Pulitzer, incidentally, was the publisher of the New York newspaper *The World*.
3. Although the first prizes were for journalism and letters only, Pulitzers are now awarded in music and other areas.
4. The police strike lasted a week, but no robberies occurred in that time.
5. Even though some say football has supplanted baseball as the national pastime, millions of people watch baseball every year, and they don't seem ready to stop.

EXERCISE 22

Combine each of the following groups of simple sentences to produce the kind of sentence specified in parentheses. You will have to add, delete, change, and rearrange words.

Example:

The traffic passed her house. It never stopped. (*Complex*.)
The traffic that passed her house never stopped.

1. Dinner was tasty. It did not fill us up. (*Compound*.)
2. The storm was predicted to be fierce. It passed by quickly. (*Complex*.)
3. The musical notes died away. Then a strange object filled the sky. (*Complex*.)
4. The wolves were afraid. They feared the fire. (*Simple*.)
5. We wanted the rumors to stop. We hoped for that. They did not. (*Compound-complex*.)

ANSWERS: EXERCISE 21

1. Simple: ⌒——— MAIN ——— Joseph Pulitzer endowed the Pulitzer Prizes.
2. Simple: ⌒ Pulitzer, incidentally, was the ——— MAIN ——— publisher of the New York newspaper *The World*.
3. Complex: ⌒—SUBORDINATE——— Although the first prizes were for journalism and letters only, ⌒——— MAIN ——— Pulitzers are now awarded in music and other areas.
4. Compound: ⌒——— MAIN ——— The police strike lasted a week, ⌒——— MAIN ——— but no robberies occurred in that time.
5. Compound-complex: ⌒ Even though some ——— SUBORDINATE ——— say football has supplanted baseball as the national pastime, ⌒——— MAIN ——— millions of people watch baseball every year, and ⌒ they ——— MAIN ——— don't seem ready to stop.

POSSIBLE ANSWERS: EXERCISE 22

1. Dinner was tasty, but it did not fill us up.
2. Although the storm was predicted to be fierce, it passed by quickly.
3. When the musical notes died away, a strange object filled the sky.
4. The wolves were afraid of the fire.
5. We hoped that the rumors would stop, but they did not.

gr 5f

GUIDE TO NOUNS

Summary and index of information in this book (consult sections or pages in parentheses).

Description of nouns

Nouns as sentence subjects (5a-1, 5a-2)

Nouns as direct and indirect objects (5a-3), object complements (5a-3), objects of prepositions (5c-1), appositives (5c-5), modifiers (9g)

Classes of nouns: proper, common, collective, count, mass, concrete, abstract (5a-2; pp. 740–41)

Forms of nouns: subjective and objective case (p. 207), possessive case (23a), and plural (34b-6)

Other structures serving as nouns: gerunds and gerund phrases (5c-2), infinitives and infinitive phrases (5c-2), subordinate clauses (5c-4)

Conventions regarding nouns

FORMS OF NOUNS

Possessive forms: *boy's* vs. *boys'*; *Park's* vs. *Parks's* vs. *Parkses'* (23a)

Possessives before gerunds: *Nguyen's writing is clear.* (6h)

Plurals of nouns and compound nouns: *dish, dishes; child, children; mother-in-law, mothers-in-law* (34b-6)

NOUNS AND OTHER SENTENCE PARTS

Agreement of subjects and verbs: *The <u>towel was</u> wet. The <u>towels were</u> wet.* (8a)

Agreement of antecedents and pronouns: *The <u>children</u> surrounded <u>their</u> father.* (8b)

Grammatical fit between subjects and predicates (avoiding mixed grammar): *In the supervision of others is the best preparation for a management career.→The <u>supervision</u> of others <u>is</u> the best preparation for a management career.* (15a)

Fit in meaning of subjects and predicates (avoiding faulty predication): *The use of the airwaves is the ideal medium for campaigning.→The <u>airwaves are</u> the ideal medium for campaigning.* (15b)

CLARITY AND EFFECTIVENESS

Nouns as modifiers (avoiding overuse): *adult education grants workshop → workshop on grants for adult education* (9g)

Consistency in subjects and the voice of verbs: *Tony woke suddenly, but his eyes were kept shut.→Tony woke suddenly, but <u>he kept</u> his eyes shut.* (13c)

gr

GUIDE TO PRONOUNS

Summary and index of information in this book (consult sections or pages in parentheses).

Description of pronouns

Pronouns as substitutes for nouns (5a-2, 8b)

Pronouns as subjects, objects, complements, appositives, modifiers (pp. 207–09)

Case forms of pronouns: subjective, objective, possessive (pp. 207–09)

Person, number, and gender of personal pronouns (8b)

Classes of pronouns: personal, relative, interrogative, demonstrative, reflexive, intensive, reciprocal, indefinite (5a-2)

Conventions regarding pronouns

FORMS OF PRONOUNS

Subjective case for subjects and subject complements: *You and I can talk. It was she.* (6a)

Objective case for objects: *Ken gave me a dog. He gave her to me.* (6b)

We or *us* with nouns: *We drivers like highways. Many of us drivers like highways.* (6c)

Case in appositives: *Two drivers, she and Nell, won the award. The state rewarded two drivers, her and Nell.* (6d)

Case after *than* or *as*: *Nell likes Buddy more than (she likes) him. Nell likes Buddy more than he (likes Buddy).* (6e)

Objective case for subjects and objects of infinitives: *We invited him to meet her.* (6f)

Who vs. *whom*: *Who can predict whom he will ask?* (6g)

Possessives before gerunds: *his working* (6h)

Possessive forms of personal pronouns: *hers* (not *her's*); *theirs* (not *their's*) (23b)

Possessive pronouns vs. contractions: *its* vs. *it's; your* vs. *you're; their* vs. *they're* (23c)

PRONOUNS AND OTHER SENTENCE PARTS

Agreement of pronoun subjects and verbs: *Neither he nor they are late. Everybody is finished.* (8a)

Agreement of pronouns and antecedents: *Everybody finished his/ her/his or her paper. Lisa or Maria left her notebook.* (8b)

Reference of pronouns to antecedents (avoiding unclear or remote reference): *The first act of the play seemed weak, but then it improved.→The first act of the play started weakly but then improved.* Or: *Though the first act was weak, the play then improved.* (12a–12f)

GUIDE TO VERBS AND VERBALS

Summary and index of information in this book (consult sections or pages in parentheses).

Description of verbs and verbals

Verb as sentence predicate (5a-1, 5a-2, 5a-3)
Transitive, intransitive, and linking verbs (5a-3)
Forms of verbs: infinitive, past tense, past participle, present participle, -*s* form (pp. 217–19)
Regular vs. irregular verbs (7a)
Finite vs. nonfinite verbs (5c-2)
Helping (auxiliary) verbs (pp. 218, 224)
Tense of verbs: present, past, future, etc. (pp. 225–27)
Mood of verbs: indicative, imperative, subjunctive (pp. 233–34)
Voice of verbs: active and passive (pp. 235–36)
Verbals and verbal phrases: participles, gerunds, infinitives (5c-2)

Conventions regarding verbs and verbals

FORMS AND TENSES OF VERBS

Principal parts of common irregular verbs: e.g., *begin, began, begun; run, ran, run* (7a)
Sit vs. *set* and *lie* vs. *lay* (7b)
Needed -*s* and -*ed* endings: *He asks/asked too much.* (7c)
Needed helping verbs: *He is asking too much.* (7d)
Present tense (*runs*) and perfect tenses (*has/had/will have run*) (7e)
Sequence of tenses: e.g., *We would like to have gone* vs. *We would have liked to go.* (7f)
Subjunctive mood: *I wish I were there.* (7g)

VERBS AND OTHER SENTENCE PARTS

Agreement of verbs and subjects: *The guests are here. Nobody is missing.* (8a)
Unseparated verb phrases and infinitives: *They had before long agreed to voluntarily surrender.→Before long they had agreed to surrender voluntarily.* (14e)
Grammatical fit between subjects and predicates (avoiding mixed grammar): *By saving is how they could buy a car.→By saving, they could buy a car.* (15a)
Fit in meaning of subjects and predicates (avoiding faulty predication): *The reason is because they were frugal.→The reason is that they were frugal.* (15b)

(continued)

gr

GUIDE TO VERBS AND VERBALS (*continued*)

PROBLEMS WITH VERBALS

Verbs required in complete sentences (avoiding sentence fragments with verbals): *Rain falling silently.→Rain fell silently.* (10a, 10c)

Clear and logical modifiers (avoiding dangling modifiers): *Flying home, her thoughts remained behind.→As she flew home, her thoughts remained behind.* (14f)

PUNCTUATION WITH VERBALS

Commas after introductory verbal modifiers: *Struggling for air, the climbers reached the summit.* (21b)

Commas to set off nonrestrictive verbal modifiers: *The climbers, struggling for air, reached the summit.* (21c)

CLARITY AND EFFECTIVENESS

Active rather than passive voice: *Hands were raised by the students.→The students raised their hands.* (7h)

Consistency in voice: *Before you tighten the bolts, the car should be lowered to the ground.→Before you tighten the bolts, you should lower the car to the ground.* (13c)

Consistency in tense: *The hero escapes, but he was captured. →The hero escapes, but he is captured.* (13b)

Consistency in mood: *Unscrew the bolts, and then you remove the wheel.→Unscrew the bolts, and then remove the wheel.* (13b)

Strong rather than weak verbs (avoiding wordiness): *The book is a depiction of family strife.→The book depicts family strife.* (31c-3)

GUIDE TO MODIFIERS

Summary and index of information in this book (consult the sections or pages in parentheses).

Description of modifiers

Functions of adjectives: modifying nouns and pronouns (p. 252)

Functions of adverbs: modifying verbs, adjectives, other adverbs, phrases, and clauses (p. 252)

Forms of adjectives and adverbs: positive, comparative, superlative (9e)

Irregular adjectives and adverbs (9e-2)

Classes of adjectives: descriptive, limiting, proper, attributive, predicate (p. 731)

Classes of adverbs: modifiers of verbs, adjectives, and other adverbs (p. 732); sentence modifiers (21b); conjunctive adverbs (5d-2)

Other structures serving as modifiers: nouns (9g); prepositional phrases (5c-1); participles and participial phrases (5c-2); infinitives and infinitive phrases (5c-2); subordinate clauses (5c-4)

Conventions regarding modifiers

DISTINCTIONS BETWEEN ADJECTIVES AND ADVERBS

Adverbs (not adjectives) to modify verbs, adjectives, adverbs: *Susan writes well* (not *good*). (9a)

Adjectives after linking verbs, adverbs to modify other verbs: *I feel bad. She sings badly.* (9b)

Adjectives to modify objects, adverbs to modify verbs: *We believed him honest. We treated him honestly.* (9c)

FORMS OF ADJECTIVES AND ADVERBS

Short vs. *-ly* forms of adverbs: *slow* vs. *slowly* (9d)

Comparatives and superlatives: *steady, steadier/more steady, steadiest/most steady* (9e-1); *good/well, better, best* (9e-2); *most steadiest→most steady* (9e-3); *the bigger of two* and *the biggest of three* (9e-4); *most unique→unique* (9e-5)

MODIFIERS AND OTHER SENTENCE PARTS

Clear placement of modifiers: *We waited for the rain to stop in a doorway.→We waited in a doorway for the rain to stop.* (14a–14e)

Clear and logical modifiers (avoiding dangling modifiers): *Watching the rain, our hands and feet froze.→As we watched the rain, our hands and feet froze.* (14f)

(continued)

gr

205

GUIDE TO MODIFIERS (*continued*)

PUNCTUATION AND MECHANICS WITH MODIFIERS

Commas after most introductory modifiers: *Happily, we have friends.* (21b)

Commas to set off nonrestrictive modifiers: *Ellen, who is our best friend, checks in every day.* (21c)

Commas to set off absolute phrases: *Her workday finished, she calls us.* (21d)

Commas for coordinate adjectives: *She is a steady, reliable friend.* (21f-2)

Commas with conjunctive adverbs: *Traffic was bad; we left, however, before it could get worse.* (5d-2, 22b)

Semicolons between clauses related by conjunctive adverbs: *We did not leave right away; instead, we waited for Ellen.* (11b, 22b)

Capital letters for proper adjectives: *Indian tea; Buddhist chant* (26d)

Figure vs. words for numbers: *327* vs. *twenty-three* (29a)

Hyphens in compound adjectives and numbers: *well-spoken words* vs. *words well spoken* (34d-1); *thirty-two minutes* (34d-2)

CLARITY AND EFFECTIVENESS

Clear negation (avoiding double negatives): *They don't want no interruptions.→They don't want any interruptions.* Or: *They want no interruptions.* (9f)

Nouns as modifiers (avoiding overuse): *business managers spreadsheet analysis seminar→seminar in spreadsheet analysis for business managers* (9g)

Complete and logical comparisons: *The value of friendship is greater than money.→The value of friendship is greater than the value of* (or *that of*) *money.* (15d)

CHAPTER 6

Case of Nouns and Pronouns

HIGHLIGHTS

The forms that nouns and pronouns take according to their role in a sentence are relatively few in English when compared with some other languages. Nonetheless, most students are likely to find compound subjects and objects or questions of *who* and *whom* occasionally troublesome. Others may need to review pronoun forms more extensively to gain control over this part of their writing.

This chapter opens with a review of the functions a pronoun can perform, functions that determine the form, or case, of the pronoun. In addition to the familiar list of forms of the personal pronouns, the chapter provides sentences illustrating the wide variety of uses for pronouns. Following this are brief discussions of the proper case for pronouns in contexts that usually cause difficulty for student writers, including compound subjects and objects, appositives, comparisons using *than* or *as*, possessive case with gerunds, and the different uses of *who* and *whom*.

The exercises ask students to select the appropriate forms of pronouns in the troublesome contexts treated in the discussion, to correct any case errors in a paragraph, and to combine sentences so as to use *who* or *whom* in relative clauses.

Case is the form of a noun or pronoun that shows the reader how it functions in a sentence—that is, whether it functions as a subject, as an object, or in some other way. The pronouns *I, we, he, she, they,* and *who* have separate forms for three cases: subjective, possessive, and objective. Most other pronouns and all nouns have only two case forms, subjective and possessive, with the subjective form serving all functions except that of the possessive. The case forms are summarized in the chart on the next page. Since only *I, we, he, she, they,* and *who* change form for each case, we will focus on these pronouns in this chapter.

The **subjective form** is used when a pronoun is the subject of a sentence, the subject of a clause, the complement of a subject, or an appositive identifying a subject. (See 5a and 5c.)

SUBJECT OF SENTENCE

She and *I* skied three days last week.
They tried to save the house.

SUBJECT OF SUBORDINATE CLAUSE

Give the money to the kids *who* cleaned up the house.
He is the man *who* I thought would win.

SUBJECT OF UNDERSTOOD VERB

Sarah has more money than *he* (has).
I am not as smart as *she* (is).

SUBJECT COMPLEMENT

The editors of the paper were *he* and *I*.
They assumed it was *I*.

APPOSITIVE IDENTIFYING SUBJECT

Only two members, Susan and *I*, went to the jazz festival.

THE CHART

Students may be tempted to skip over this chart of the case forms of nouns and pronouns. Get them to pay attention by asking them to fill out the whole chart in class—without looking at the text. The act of remembering the forms or figuring them out will be more valuable than listening to an explanation. Students who have trouble completing the chart probably need to spend time reviewing the chapter.

CASE FORMS OF NOUNS AND PRONOUNS

	SUBJECTIVE	**POSSESSIVE**	**OBJECTIVE**
NOUNS	boy	boy's	boy
	Jessie	Jessie's	Jessie
PERSONAL PRONOUNS			
Singular			
1st person	**I**	**my, mine**	**me**
2nd person	you	your, yours	you
3rd person	**he**	**his**	**him**
	she	**her, hers**	**her**
	it	its	it
Plural			
1st person	**we**	**our, ours**	**us**
2nd person	you	your, yours	you
3rd person	**they**	**their, theirs**	**them**
RELATIVE AND INTERROGATIVE PRONOUNS			
	who	**whose**	**whom**
	whoever	—	**whomever**
	which, that, what	—	which, that, what
INDEFINITE PRONOUNS			
	everybody	everybody's	everybody

The **objective form** is used when a pronoun is the direct or indirect object of a verb or verbal, the object of a preposition, the subject of an infinitive, or an appositive identifying an object. (See 5a and 5c.)

OBJECT OF VERB

Lisa likes both Tom and *him.*
The woman *whom* they elected was experienced.
The exam gave *him* a headache.

OBJECT OF PREPOSITION

Most of *us* hated to get up.
I didn't know *whom* they laughed at.

OBJECT OF VERBAL

Electing *her* was easy. [Object of gerund.]

BACK TO NOUNS

Distribute copies of a paragraph taken from a magazine article, an essay in a reader, or a student paper. Ask students to rewrite it, substituting the appropriate noun for each pronoun. This exercise will help students to understand the role of pronouns and see the relationship between the case of a pronoun and the function of the noun it stands for.

Having elected *her*, the committee adjourned. [Object of past participle.]

Mary ran to help *him*. [Object of infinitive.]

SUBJECT OF INFINITIVE

We invited *them* to eat with us.

They asked *me* to speak.

APPOSITIVE IDENTIFYING OBJECT

The judge fined both defendants, Joe and *her*.

The **possessive form** of a pronoun is used before nouns and gerunds.

BEFORE A NOUN

His sisters needed *our* bicycles.

BEFORE A GERUND

Their flying to Nashville was my suggestion.

In addition, the possessive forms *mine, ours, yours, his, hers,* and *theirs* (and only those forms) may be used without a following noun, in the position of a noun.

IN NOUN POSITIONS

Hers is the racket on the table.

The blue car is *mine* (*ours, yours, his, theirs*).

(For the possessive forms of nouns, see 23a.)

6a **Use the subjective case for all parts of compound subjects and for subject complements.**

In compound subjects use the same pronoun form you would use if the pronoun stood alone as a subject.

SUBJECTS

Joan and *I* left, but *Bill* and *he* stayed.

After *she* and *I* left, the fight started.

If you are in doubt about the correct form, try each part of the subject in a separate sentence: *Joan left. I left.* Therefore, *Joan and I left.*

A pronoun following the forms of the verb *be* (*am, is, are, was, were*) is a subject complement (see 5a-3). Since it renames the subject, the pronoun is in the subjective case.

SUBJECT COMPLEMENTS

The ones who paid the bill were *you* and *I*.
It was *she* whom the governor finally appointed.

Sentences like these may sound stilted because expressions such as *It's me* and *It was her* are common in speech. In writing, unless you seek special emphasis, use the more natural order: *You and I were the ones who paid the bill. The governor finally appointed her.*

6b Use the objective case for all parts of compound objects.

In compound objects use the same pronoun form you would use if the pronoun stood alone as an object.

OBJECTS OF VERBS

We wanted to invite *Larry* and *her*. [Direct object.]
The coach gave *her* and *me* a lecture. [Indirect object.]

OBJECTS OF PREPOSITIONS

Marty gave presents to *Gloria* and *me*.
The gift was divided between *him* and *me*.

If you are in doubt about the correct form, try each part of the object in a separate sentence: *We wanted to invite Larry. We wanted to invite her.* Therefore, *We wanted to invite Larry and her.*

ANSWERS: EXERCISE 1

1. I
2. she, I, we
3. her, me
4. she, I, we
5. us, we
6. her, me
7. her, me
8. she, I
9. I, we
10. her, me

EXERCISE 1

From the pairs in parentheses, select the appropriate subjective or objective pronoun(s) for each of the following sentences.

Example:

"Between you and (*I, me*)," the salesman said, "this deal is a steal."

"Between you and *me*," the salesman said, "this deal is a steal."

1. Jody and (*I, me*) had been hunting for jobs.
2. The best employees at our old company were (*she, her*) and (*I, me*), so (*we, us*) expected to find jobs quickly.
3. One company did offer jobs to both (*she, her*) and (*I, me*).
4. After (*she, her*) and (*I, me*) had discussed the offers with several people, however, (*we, us*) both decided to decline.
5. The jobs did not seem appropriate for (*we, us*) if (*we, us*) wanted to become management trainees.

6. That left (*she, her*) with only one offer and (*I, me*) with none.
7. Between (*she, her*) and (*I, me*) the job search had lasted two months, and still it had barely begun.
8. Slowly, (*she, her*) and (*I, me*) stopped sharing leads.
9. It was obvious that Jody and (*I, me*) could not be as friendly as (*we, us*) had been.
10. Sadly, money seemed to mean more to (*she, her*) and (*I, me*) than our friendship.

6c **Use the appropriate case when the plural pronouns *we* and *us* occur with a noun.**

The case of the first-person plural pronoun used with a noun depends on the use of the nouns.

Freezing weather is welcomed by *us* skaters. [*Skaters* is the object of the preposition *by.*]

We skaters welcome freezing weather. [*Skaters* is the subject of the sentence.]

6d **In appositives the case of a pronoun depends on the function of the word it describes or identifies.**

The class elected two representatives, Debbie and *me*. [*Representatives* is the object of the verb *elected*, so the words in the appositive, *Debbie and me*, take the objective case.]

Two representatives, Debbie and *I*, were elected. [*Representatives* is the subject of this sentence, so the words in the appositive, *Debbie and I*, take the subjective case.]

If you are in doubt about case in an appositive, try the sentence without the word the appositive identifies: *The class elected Debbie and me; Debbie and I were elected.*

EXERCISE 2

From the pairs in parentheses, select the appropriate subjective or objective pronoun for each of the following sentences.

Example:

Convincing (*we, us*) veterans to vote yes on this issue will be difficult.

Convincing *us* veterans to vote yes on this issue will be difficult.

US THE PEOPLE

If students try out pronoun forms in sentences, they can often "hear" the contrast between correct and incorrect forms by relying on their implicit understanding of the language or by using familiar phrases as touchstones:

Us the people.
Us are the world.
Are you going with *we?*
Take *we* to the movies.

This approach will not work, of course, with students for whom standard English is a second language or a second dialect.

ANSWERS: EXERCISE 2

1. us
2. we
3. him
4. us
5. we, I

1. Obtaining enough protein is important to (*we, us*) vegetarians.
2. Instead of obtaining protein from meat, (*we, us*) vegetarians get our protein from other sources.
3. Jeff claims to know only two vegetarians, Helena and (*he, him*), who avoid all animal products, including milk.
4. Some of (*we, us*) vegetarians eat fish, which is a good source of protein.
5. (*We, Us*) vegetarians in my family, my parents and (*I, me*), drink milk and eat fish.

 6e **The case of a pronoun after *than* or *as* in a comparison depends on the meaning.**

When we use *than* and *as* in comparisons, we often do not complete the clauses they introduce: *Joe likes spaghetti more than (he likes) ravioli.* Without the words in parentheses, this sentence is clear because it can have only one sensible meaning. But in *Annie liked Ben more than Joe*, we cannot tell whether *Annie liked Ben more than (she liked) Joe* or *Annie liked Ben more than Joe (liked him).*

When such sentences end with a pronoun, the case of the pronoun indicates what words have been omitted. When the pronoun is subjective, it must serve as the subject of the omitted verb.

Annie liked Ben more than *he* (liked Ben).

When the pronoun is objective, it must serve as the object of the omitted verb.

Annie liked Ben more than (she liked) *him*.

Be careful to choose the pronoun form that fits your meaning.

6f **Use the objective case for pronouns that are subjects or objects of infinitives.**

SUBJECT OF INFINITIVE

We wanted Gail and *her* to win the bowling tournament. [*Gail and her* is the compound subject of the infinitive *to win*.]

OBJECT OF INFINITIVE

They expect to meet *him*. [*Him* is the object of the infinitive *to meet*.]

6g The form of the pronoun *who* depends on its function in its clause.

1 At the beginning of questions use *who* if the question is about a subject, *whom* if it is about an object.

To determine the form of *who* at the beginning of a question, construct an answer to the question, using a personal pronoun in the answer. The case of the pronoun in the answer will indicate the required case of *who* in the question.

(*Who, Whom*) left the freezer door open? *She* left it open. Therefore, *Who* left the freezer door open?

(*Who, Whom*) does one ask? One asks *him.* Therefore, *Whom* does one ask?

(*Who, Whom*) is the pizza for? It is for *them.* Therefore, *Whom* is the pizza for?

In speech the subjective case *who* is commonly used whenever it is the first word of a question, regardless of whether it is a subject or an object. But writing requires a distinction between the forms.

SPOKEN   *Who* should we blame?

WRITTEN   *Whom* should we blame? [Object of verb *blame.*]

2 In subordinate clauses use *who* and *whoever* for all subjects, *whom* and *whomever* for all objects.

The case of a pronoun in a subordinate clause depends on its function in the clause, regardless of whether the clause itself functions as a subject, an object, or a modifier. (See 5c-4.)

Give the clothes to *whoever* needs them. [*Whoever* is the subject of *needs.* The entire clause *whoever needs them* is the object of the preposition *to.*]

I don't know *whom* the mayor appointed. [*Whom* is the object of *appointed: the mayor appointed whom.* The whole clause *whom the mayor appointed* is the object of the verb *know.*]

Whom he appointed is not my concern. [Again, *whom* is the object of *appointed.* This time the clause is the subject of the sentence.]

Larry is the man *whom* most people prefer. [*Whom* is the object of *prefer: people prefer whom.* The clause *whom most people prefer* modifies the noun *man.*]

ca

6g

If you have trouble determining which form to choose, rewrite the subordinate clause as a separate sentence, substituting a personal pronoun for the *who* form. The form of the personal pronoun will be the same as the required form of *who*. For instance:

I remember (*who, whom*) was sitting on the sofa. *He* was sitting on the sofa. Therefore, I remember *who* was sitting on the sofa.

The manager hired the woman (*who, whom*) his boss recommended. His boss recommended *her*. Therefore, the manager hired the woman *whom* his boss recommended.

NOTE: Don't let expressions such as *I think* and *she says* confuse you when they come between the subject *who* and its verb.

He is the man *who* I think *was* on duty yesterday. [*Who* is the subject of *was*, not the object of *think*.]

I asked the mechanic *who* Barbara said *was* her friend. [*Who* is the subject of *was*, not the object of *said*.]

To choose between *who* and *whom* in such constructions, delete the interrupting phrase: *I asked the mechanic who was her friend.*

ANSWERS: EXERCISE 3

1. whom	6. whom
2. who	7. who
3. whoever	8. whomever
4. Who	9. who
5. Whom	10. whom

EXERCISE 3

From the pairs in parentheses, select the appropriate form of the pronoun in each of the following sentences.

Example:

My mother asked me (*who, whom*) I was going out with.
My mother asked me *whom* I was going out with.

1. The school administrators suspended Jurgen, (*who, whom*) they suspected of setting the fire.
2. Jurgen had been complaining to other custodians, (*who, whom*) reported him.
3. He constantly complained of unfair treatment from (*whoever, whomever*) happened to be passing in the halls, including pupils.
4. "(*Who, Whom*) here has heard Mr. Jurgen's complaints?" the police asked.
5. "(*Who, Whom*) did he complain most about?"
6. His coworkers agreed that Jurgen seemed less upset with the staff or students, most of (*who, whom*) he did not even know, than with the building itself.
7. "He took out his aggressions on the building," claimed one coworker (*who, whom*) often witnessed Jurgen's behavior.
8. "He cursed and kicked the walls and (*whoever, whomever*) he saw nearby."
9. The coworker thought that Jurgen might have imagined

people (*who, whom*) instructed him to behave the way he did.

10. "He's someone (*who, whom*) other people can't get next to," said the coworker.

EXERCISE 4

Combine each pair of sentences below into one sentence that contains a clause beginning with *who* or *whom*. Be sure to use the appropriate case form. You will have to add, delete, and rearrange words. Each item may have more than one possible answer.

Example:

David is the candidate. We think David deserves to win.
David is the candidate *who* we think deserves to win.

1. Some children have undetected hearing problems. These children may do poorly in school.
2. They may not hear important instructions and information from teachers. Teachers may speak softly.
3. Classmates may not be audible. The teacher calls on those classmates.
4. Some hearing-impaired children may work harder to overcome their handicap. These children get a lot of encouragement at home.
5. Some hearing-impaired children may take refuge in fantasy friends. They can rely on these friends not to criticize or laugh.

POSSIBLE ANSWERS: EXERCISE 4

1. Some children who have undetected hearing problems may do poorly in school.
2. They may not hear important instructions and information from teachers who speak softly.
3. Classmates whom the teacher calls on may not be audible.
4. Some hearing-impaired children who get a lot of encouragement at home may work harder to overcome their handicap.
5. Some hearing-impaired children may take refuge in fantasy friends whom they can rely on not to criticize or laugh.

6h **Ordinarily, use the possessive form of a pronoun or noun immediately before a gerund.**

A **gerund** is the *-ing* form of the verb (*running, sleeping*) used as a noun (see 5c-2). Like nouns, gerunds are commonly preceded by possessive nouns and pronouns: *her marriage* (noun), *her marrying* (gerund), *our vote* (noun), *our voting* (gerund).

He disapproved of *their* exercising. [Compare *their exercise.*]
Jo's failing in history surprised us. [Compare *Jo's failure.*]

Notice the difference between the gerund and the present participle. Both have the same *-ing* form. But whereas the gerund serves as a subject or object, the participle serves as an adjective.

We often met *John* coming home late. [*Coming home late* is a participial phrase modifying *John.*]

John's coming home late worried us. [*Coming home late* is a gerund phrase serving as the subject of *worried.*]

CREATE A STORY

On the board, write a sentence or two that introduces as many people's names as possible. For example, you might write,

Bob went to a party last night, and there he saw his first-grade teacher, Mrs. West; his neighbor George; his old girlfriend Sarah; and her children Susan and Jason. In the middle of the party, Bob's dog Bowser came racing into the living room.

Divide the class into small groups and ask each group to write a one-paragraph story that grows out of the sentences on the board. (In the example above, students would probably describe what happened after the dog's entrance.) In writing their story, students should try to use as many pronouns as possible without introducing any ambiguity into the tale.

Groups should then read their stories aloud or write them on the board so that other students can try to understand the stories and verify that all the pronoun cases are accurate.

The case of a noun or pronoun before the *-ing* form of a verb can subtly influence the meaning of a sentence.

> We noticed *Ann* driving. [The emphasis is on *Ann*, who happened to be driving when she was noticed. *Driving* is a participle.]
>
> We noticed *Ann's* driving. [The emphasis is on Ann's activity— her driving. *Driving* is a gerund.]

Note that a gerund usually is not preceded by the possessive when the possessive would create an awkward construction.

AWKWARD	We heard a rumor about everybody's on the team wanting to quit.
LESS AWKWARD	We heard a rumor about everybody on the team wanting to quit.
BETTER	We heard a rumor that everybody on the team wants to quit.

ANSWERS: EXERCISE 5

Mike and I arrived at the campground just after sunset. The manager, <u>who</u> we thought looked like a movie star, was naturally reluctant to let <u>us</u> ruffians in, but eventually she showed us to a tiny campsite. When we unpacked the tent, Mike and <u>I</u> discovered that we were missing two tent pegs. Searching in the dark, Mike managed to find some sturdy sticks to use as pegs, and between <u>him</u> and <u>me</u> we managed to set up the tent. But Mike was apparently more tired than <u>I</u>, because he didn't drive his pegs deeply enough into the ground. Several hours later, when <u>he</u> and <u>I</u> had finally dozed off, the tent collapsed on top of us. <u>Our</u> yelling at each other woke the people in the next campsite, who were even less amused than <u>we</u> by our plight. We piled everything into the car as fast as possible and took off down the road for a motel.

EXERCISE 5

Correct all inappropriate case forms in the following paragraph, and explain the function of each case form.

Mike and I arrived at the campground just after sunset. The manager, whom we thought looked like a movie star, was naturally reluctant to let we ruffians in, but eventually she showed us to a tiny campsite. When we unpacked the tent, Mike and me discovered that we were missing two tent pegs. Searching in the dark, Mike managed to find some sturdy sticks to use as pegs, and between he and I we managed to set up the tent. But Mike was apparently more tired than me, because he didn't drive his pegs deeply enough into the ground. Several hours later, when him and me had finally dozed off, the tent collapsed on top of us. Us yelling at each other woke the people in the next campsite, who were even less amused than us by our plight. We piled everything into the car as fast as possible and took off down the road for a motel.

CHAPTER 7

Verb Forms, Tense, Mood, and Voice

VERB FORMS

All verbs except *be* have five basic forms. The first three forms—infinitive, past tense, and past participle—are the verb's **principal parts.** The **infinitive** (sometimes called the **plain form**) is the dictionary form of the verb. It is the form we use when the verb's action occurs in the present and the subject is a plural noun or the pronoun *I, we, you,* or *they.*

> We *live* in the city.
> Examinations *frighten* me.
> They *go* downtown.

The **past-tense form** indicates that the verb's action occurred in the past. It is usually formed by adding *-d* or *-ed* to the infinitive, although for some irregular verbs it is formed in other ways (see 7a).

> We *lived* in the city.
> Examinations *frightened* me.
> They *went* downtown. [Irregular verb.]

VERB FORMS

INFINITIVE: close, run

PAST TENSE: closed, ran

PAST PARTICIPLE: closed, run

PRESENT PARTICIPLE: closing, running

-*s* FORM: closes, runs

HIGHLIGHTS

Verbs can cause trouble for writers regardless of their level of skill. For some inexperienced writers, choosing the correct tense or form of a verb is a challenge. Verb endings and the forms of irregular verbs (inflections) can be quite confusing, especially if the writer's spoken dialect employs differing forms of a verb. Even experienced writers may occasionally stumble over the forms of *lie* and *lay* or worry about maintaining a correct sequence of tenses in a complicated writing task, such as a summary of a secondary source in a research paper.

For all these needs (and many others as well) this chapter can be useful, though it cannot provide the kind of sustained support and practice some students may require. (Students who need additional work may benefit from tutoring in a writing center or from the supplemental exercises available in *The Little, Brown Workbook.*)

Students looking for help with verb *forms* will benefit from the chapter's thorough explanations, list of the principal parts of frequently used irregular verbs, discussion of the troublesome pairs *sit/set* and *lie/lay,* and treatment of two problems often associated with dialect interference: omitted *-s* and *-ed* endings and omitted helping verbs.

Students looking for help with verb *tense* can make use of the chapter's discussion of the major tenses and of appropriate sequences of tenses. Tense sequence becomes increasingly important as students begin to write ambitious narratives and expository or argumentative essays.

The closing sections of the chapter deal with mood and voice, reviewing uses of the subjunctive and placing special emphasis on appropriate and inappropriate uses of the passive voice.

RESOURCES AND IDEAS

Speakers of black English vernacular may tend to use the verb forms of this dialect in their writing rather than those of standard written English, particularly by dropping -s and -ed endings. Becoming aware of the verb system of standard written English and the differences between it and the verb system of black English vernacular is an important step for students seeking control over their writing. But as Marcia Farr and Harvey Daniels point out in *Language Diversity and Writing Instruction* (New York: ERIC Clearing House on Urban Education and Urbana: NCTE, 1986), awareness of and practice in identifying and using the verb forms are useful only if they take place in a context that includes a wide range of reading and writing experiences; substantial practice in writing; collaborative activities; sentence combining or similar activities; and flexible, sensitive feedback from the instructor. Farr and Daniels also offer a detailed discussion of dialects and language variations, along with concrete suggestions for teaching.

The **past participle** is the verb form we use with *have, has,* or *had* (*have climbed, had opened*); with a form of *be* in the passive voice (*was created;* see 7h); and by itself to modify nouns and pronouns (*sliced bread*). Except for some irregular verbs (see 7a), the past participle is the same as the past-tense form.

We have *lived* in the city.
Examinations have *frightened* me.
They had *gone* downtown. [Irregular verb.]

In addition to the three principal parts, all verbs have two other forms, a present participle and an -s form. We form the **present participle** by adding -ing to the verb's infinitive, as in *acting, eating, living, studying.* The present participle can modify nouns and pronouns (*boiling water, the girl driving*); and, as a gerund, the same form functions as a noun (*Running exhausts me*). In addition, the present participle may combine with forms of the verb *be* (*am, is, are, was,* and *were*) to indicate continuing action: *is buying, was finishing, were swimming.*

The **-s form** of the verb is the one ending in -s or -es (*begs, lives, is, has*). We use it when the verb's action occurs in the present and the subject is third-person singular—that is, a singular noun (*dog, Harry*), a singular indefinite pronoun (*everybody, someone*), or the personal pronoun *he, she,* or *it.*

The dog *begs.*　　　　Everybody *is* asleep.
Harry *lives* in town.　　She *has* a car.

The verb *be* has eight forms rather than the five forms of most other verbs. In addition to its infinitive *be,* its present participle *being,* and its past participle *been, be* has three distinct forms in the present tense and two in the past tense.

	I	*he, she, it*	*we, you, they*
PRESENT TENSE	am	is	are
PAST TENSE	was	was	were

Helping verbs, also called **auxiliary verbs,** combine with a verb's infinitive, present participle, or past participle to indicate time and other kinds of meaning, as in *can run, was sleeping, had been eaten.* These combinations are **verb phrases** (see also 7d). Since the infinitive, present participle, or past participle in any verb phrase always carries the principal meaning, it is sometimes called the **main verb.**

Some helping verbs—*shall* and *will; have, has,* and *had; do, does,* and *did;* and the forms of *be* (*am, is, are, was, were, been,* and *being*)—combine with main verbs to indicate time and voice (see pp. 225 and 235).

I *will go.*	The doors *were opened.*
She *had run.*	The child *was awakened.*
Sylvia *did* not *want* grapes.	They *have been seen.*

Helping verbs such as *can, could, may, might, must, ought, shall, should, will,* and *would* combine with main verbs to indicate necessity, obligation, permission, possibility, and other conditions.

She *can write.*	You *must go.*
I *should study.*	I *might come.*

The two kinds of helping verbs sometimes work together to create complex verb phrases.

You *might have told* me.
I *may be sleeping.*
You *ought to have eaten.*

vb
7a

7a Use the correct form of regular and irregular verbs.

As indicated above, most verbs are **regular;** that is, they form their past tense and past participle by adding *-d* or *-ed* to the infinitive.

INFINITIVE	PAST TENSE	PAST PARTICIPLE
live	lived	lived
act	acted	acted

Since the past tense and past participle are created simply by adding to the infinitive and since the two are identical, the forms of regular verbs do not often cause problems in speech and writing (but see 7c).

Some verbs, however, do not follow the pattern of regular verbs. About two hundred English verbs are **irregular;** that is, they form their past tense and past participle in some irregular way. We have to learn the parts of the verbs by memorizing them, just as we learn new words.

Most irregular verbs form the past tense and the past participle by changing an internal vowel.

INFINITIVE	PAST TENSE	PAST PARTICIPLE
begin	began	begun
come	came	come

Some irregular verbs change an internal vowel and add an *-n* in the past participle.

MEMORY AID—REGULAR VERBS

The individual forms of irregular verbs require memorization. For regular verbs, however, the word *INFEDS* can help students identify past tense and past participle: *INFEDS* = infinitive + *-ed* or *-es.*

INFINITIVE	PAST TENSE	PAST PARTICIPLE
break	broke	broken
draw	drew	drawn

Some irregular verbs have the same form in both the past tense and the past participle or in all three forms.

INFINITIVE	PAST TENSE	PAST PARTICIPLE
sleep	slept	slept
let	let	let

Check a dictionary if you have any doubt about a verb's principal parts. The form listed there is the infinitive. If no other forms are listed, the verb is regular; that is, both the past tense and the past participle add -d or -ed to the infinitive (*agree, agreed; sympathize, sympathized; talk, talked*). If the verb is irregular, the dictionary will list the infinitive, the past tense, and the past participle in that order (*speak, spoke, spoken; go, went, gone*). If the dictionary gives only two forms (as in *hear, heard* or *think, thought*), then the past tense and the past participle are the same.

The following list includes the most common irregular verbs. (When a principal part has two possible forms, as in *dove* and *dived*, both are included.) Look over this list to find verbs whose parts you are unsure of. Then spend some time memorizing the parts and trying them in sentences.

PRINCIPAL PARTS OF COMMON IRREGULAR VERBS

INFINITIVE	PAST TENSE	PAST PARTICIPLE
arise	arose	arisen
become	became	become
begin	began	begun
bid	bid	bid
bite	bit	bitten, bit
blow	blew	blown
break	broke	broken
bring	brought	brought
burst	burst	burst
buy	bought	bought
catch	caught	caught
choose	chose	chosen
come	came	come
cut	cut	cut
dive	dived, dove	dived
do	did	done
draw	drew	drawn
dream	dreamed, dreamt	dreamed, dreamt
drink	drank	drunk
drive	drove	driven

INFINITIVE	PAST TENSE	PAST PARTICIPLE
eat	ate	eaten
fall	fell	fallen
find	found	found
flee	fled	fled
fly	flew	flown
forget	forgot	forgotten, forgot
freeze	froze	frozen
get	got	got, gotten
give	gave	given
go	went	gone
grow	grew	grown
hang (suspend)	hung	hung
hang (execute)	hanged	hanged
hear	heard	heard
hide	hid	hidden
hold	held	held
keep	kept	kept
know	knew	known
lay	laid	laid
lead	led	led
leave	left	left
let	let	let
lie	lay	lain
lose	lost	lost
pay	paid	paid
prove	proved	proved, proven
ride	rode	ridden
ring	rang	rung
rise	rose	risen
run	ran	run
say	said	said
see	saw	seen
set	set	set
shake	shook	shaken
sing	sang, sung	sung
sink	sank, sunk	sunk
sit	sat	sat
slide	slid	slid
speak	spoke	spoken
spring	sprang, sprung	sprung
stand	stood	stood
steal	stole	stolen
swim	swam	swum
take	took	taken
tear	tore	torn
throw	threw	thrown
wear	wore	worn
write	wrote	written

vb
7a

ONE-FORM PARAGRAPHS

Using groups of three to five verbs, have students create paragraphs using only one form of the verbs. Then have students rewrite the paragraphs using a different verb form. This exercise will reinforce consistent use of form and may make students more aware of the element of time in verb usage. Following are student-written examples that use the past-participle form of the verbs *break, bring, burst, buy,* and *catch*.

Because his bubble had burst and she had broken his heart, he had caught the next train home and had brought his mother some flowers. —Jennifer Haas

We had brought the dishes out to the table to set it. When we looked we realized that we had broken some of them. We had burst out laughing, but it wasn't too funny when we realized that my mother had caught us. —Nicole Hanna

He had broken the vase that she had brought. She had burst into tears. If only he had caught it. —Jim Rosen

vb
7b

ANSWERS: EXERCISE 1

1. The world population has <u>grown</u> by two-thirds of a billion people in less than a decade. (Past participle.)
2. Recently it <u>broke</u> the 5 billion mark. (Past tense.)
3. Experts have <u>drawn</u> pictures of a crowded future. (Past participle.)
4. They predict that the world population may have <u>slid</u> up to as much as 16 billion by 2100. (Past participle.)
5. Though the food supply <u>rose</u> in the last decade, the share to each person <u>fell</u>. (Both past tense.)
6. At the same time the water supply, which had actually <u>become</u> healthier over the previous century, <u>sank</u> in size and quality. (Past participle and past tense.)
7. The number of animal species on earth <u>shrank</u> by 20 percent. (Past tense.)
8. Changes in land use <u>ran</u> nomads and subsistence farmers off the land. (Past tense.)
9. Yet all has not been <u>lost</u>. (Past participle.)
10. Recently human beings have <u>begun</u> to heed these and other problems and to explore how technology can be <u>driven</u> to help the earth and all its populations. (Both past participles.)

EXERCISE 1

For each irregular verb in parentheses, supply either the past tense or past participle, as appropriate, and identify the form you used.

> *Example:*
> Though we had (*hide*) the cash box, it was (*steal*).
> Though we had *hidden* the cash box, it was *stolen*. [Two past participles.]

1. The world population has (*grow*) by two-thirds of a billion people in less than a decade.
2. Recently it (*break*) the 5 billion mark.
3. Experts have (*draw*) pictures of a crowded future.
4. They predict that the world population may have (*slide*) up to as much as 16 billion by the year 2100.
5. Though the food supply (*rise*) in the last decade, the share to each person (*fall*).
6. At the same time the water supply, which had actually (*become*) healthier over the previous century, (*sink*) in size and quality.
7. The number of animal species on earth (*shrink*) by 20 percent.
8. Changes in land use (*run*) nomads and subsistence farmers off the land.
9. Yet all has not been (*lose*).
10. Recently human beings have (*begin*) to heed these and other problems and to explore how technology can be (*drive*) to help the earth and all its populations.

7b ### Distinguish between *sit* and *set* and between *lie* and *lay*.

The principal parts of *sit* and *set* and of *lie* and *lay* are easy to confuse. Here are the forms of the four verbs.

INFINITIVE	PAST TENSE	PAST PARTICIPLE
sit	sat	sat
set	set	set
lie	lay	lain
lay	laid	laid

Sit and *lie*, as in *Sit down* and *Lie down*, mean "be seated" and "recline," respectively. They are both **intransitive verbs:** they cannot take objects. *Set* and *lay*, as in *Set the eggs down carefully* and *Lay the floor boards there*, mean "put" or "place." They are **transitive verbs** and usually take objects. (See 5a-3.)

Angela *lies* down every afternoon. [No object.]
Carter *laid* the plans on the table. [*Plans* is the object of *laid*.]
The dog *sits* by the back door. [No object.]
Mr. Flood *set* the jug down roughly. [*Jug* is the object of *set*.]

EXERCISE 2

Choose the correct verb from the pair given in parentheses and then supply the past tense or past participle, as appropriate.

Example:

After I washed all the windows, I (*lie, lay*) down the squeegee and then I myself (*lie, lay*) down for a nap.

After I washed all the windows, I *laid* down the squeegee and then I myself *lay* down for a nap.

1. Last Christmas, Jay (*lie, lay*) in bed all day with a fever.
2. When he awoke, Millard (*sit, set*) up in his chair, picked up the fallen book, and (*sit, set*) it on the table.
3. The spider (*sit, set*) in its web and (*lie, lay*) in wait for its prey.
4. After she had (*sit, set*) the table, she (*lie, lay*) a cloth over it.
5. Joan's wallet had (*lie, lay*) in the street for two days.

ANSWERS: EXERCISE 2

1. Last Christmas, Jay <u>lay</u> in bed all day with a fever.
2. When he awoke, Millard <u>sat</u> up in his chair, picked up the fallen book, and <u>set</u> it on the table.
3. The spider <u>sat</u> in its web and <u>lay</u> in wait for its prey.
4. After she had <u>set</u> the table, she <u>laid</u> a cloth over it.
5. Joan's wallet had <u>lain</u> in the street for two days.

7c **Use the *-s* and *-ed* forms of the verb when they are required.**

Some English dialects use the infinitive of the verb instead of the *-s* form that is required by standard English whenever the subject is third-person singular and the verb's action occurs in the present.

The roof *leak* (*leaks*). Nobody *have* (*has*) a car.
Harry *live* (*lives*) in town. She *be* (*is*) happy.
He *don't* (*doesn't*) care.

In sentences like these, standard English requires the forms in parentheses.

Some dialects also omit the *-ed* or *-d* ending from the past tense or past participle of regular verbs when the ending is not clearly pronounced.

We *bag* (*bagged*) groceries. I bought a *use* (*used*) book.
He was *suppose* (*supposed*) Sue has *ask* (*asked*) for help.
   to call.

In standard English, however, the *-ed* and *-d* ending is required for regular verbs whenever (1) the verb's action occurred in the past (*we bagged*); (2) the past participle functions as a modifier (*used books*); and (3) the past participle combines with a form of *be* or *have* (*were supposed, has asked*).

ANSWERS: EXERCISE 3

A teacher sometimes <u>asks</u> too much of a student. In high school I was once <u>punished</u> for being sick. I had <u>missed</u> some school, and I <u>realized</u> that I would fail a test unless I had a chance to make up the class work. I <u>discussed</u> the problem with the teacher, but he said I was <u>supposed</u> to make up the work while I was sick. At that I <u>walked</u> out of the class. I <u>received</u> a failing grade then, but it did not change my atttitudes. Today I still balk when a teacher <u>makes</u> unreasonable demands or <u>expects</u> too much.

EXERCISE 3

Supply the correct form of each verb in parentheses. Be careful to include *-s* and *-ed* (or *-d*) endings where they are needed for standard English.

A teacher sometimes (*ask*) too much of a student. In high school I was once (*punish*) for being sick. I had (*miss*) some school, and I (*realize*) that I would fail a test unless I had a chance to make up the class work. I (*discuss*) the problem with the teacher, but he said I was (*suppose*) to make up the work while I was sick. At that I (*walk*) out of the class. I (*receive*) a failing grade then, but it did not change my attitude. Today I still balk when a teacher (*make*) unreasonable demands or (*expect*) miracles.

7d Use helping verbs when they are required.

Helping verbs combine with the infinitives, present participles, and past participles of verbs to indicate time and other kinds of meaning (see p. 218). In some English dialects the helping verb is omitted:

The owl (*is*) *hooting*.	Sara (*has*) *been* at home.
I (*have*) *taken* French.	That (*would*) *be* awful.

However, standard English requires the helping verbs in these sentences and in others like them.

Often, the omission of a helping verb creates an incomplete sentence, or **sentence fragment,** because a present participle (*hooting*) or an irregular past participle (*taken, been*) cannot stand alone as the only verb in a sentence (see Chapter 10).

FRAGMENTS	Few people *smoking*. The toy *broken*.
REVISED	Few people *were smoking*. The toy *was broken*.

Smoking and *broken* are **nonfinite,** or "unfinished," verbs: they can modify other words, but they cannot serve as sentence predicates. Only a **finite,** or "finished," verb can serve as a sentence predicate, and to be made finite a nonfinite verb must be combined with a helping verb. (See p. 178 for additional discussion of finite and nonfinite verbs.)

EXERCISE 4

Add helping verbs in the following sentences where they are needed for standard English.

1. The floors squeak loudly, and we been meaning to repair them.
2. The essay written by a woman who earned a degree in biology and worked as a laboratory technician.
3. They expected that the play be canceled because of poor attendance.
4. Joey complaining that his course load leaves him no time for running, and he talking about dropping physics.
5. Most of the harsh words spoken at the meeting been left out of the minutes.

ANSWERS: EXERCISE 4

1. The floors squeak loudly, and we <u>have</u> been meaning to repair them.
2. The essay <u>was</u> written by a woman who earned a degree in biology and worked as a laboratory technician.
3. They expected that the play <u>would</u> be canceled because of poor attendance.
4. Joey <u>was</u> complaining that his course load leaves him no time for running, and he <u>was</u> talking about dropping physics.
5. Most of the harsh words spoken at the meeting <u>have</u> been left out of the minutes.

t
7

TENSE

Tense is the attribute of a verb that shows the time of the verb's action in relation to the time at which the writer writes or the speaker speaks. The table on the next two pages shows all the tense forms for a regular and an irregular verb in the active voice. (See pp. 235–37 on voice.)

The **simple tenses** indicate that an action or state of being is present, past, or future relative to the speaker or writer. The present tense uses the verb's infinitive (*work, write*), or, for third-person singular subjects, its *-s* form (*he works, she writes*). The past tense uses the verb's past-tense form (*worked, wrote*). The future tense uses the helping verb *will* or *shall* and the verb's infinitive.

The **perfect tenses** indicate that an action was or will be completed before another time or action. (The term *perfect* derives from the Latin *perfectus*, meaning "completed.") The perfect tenses consist of the verb's past participle (*worked, written*) preceded by a form of the helping verb *have*.

All verbs also have a set of **progressive forms,** sometimes called the **progressive tense,** which indicate continuing (therefore progressive) action. The progressive uses the *-ing* form of the verb plus a form of *be* (*is working, were writing*). Regular and irregular verbs do not differ.

We use the helping verb *do* (*does*) or its past tense *did*, together with the infinitive of the verb, in asking questions, making negative statements, and showing emphasis.

Does he *write* every day? [Question.]
He *did* not *write* every day. [Negation.]
He *does write* every day. [Emphasis.]

t
7

TENSES OF A REGULAR AND AN IRREGULAR VERB (ACTIVE VOICE)

	SINGULAR	PLURAL
SIMPLE TENSES		
Present		
1st person	I work/write	we work/write
2nd person	you work/write	you work/write
3rd person	he/she/it works/writes	they work/write
Past		
1st person	I worked/wrote	we worked/wrote
2nd person	you worked/wrote	you worked/wrote
3rd person	he/she/it worked/wrote	they worked/wrote
Future		
1st person	I will work/write	we will work/write
2nd person	you will work/write	you will work/write
3rd person	he/she/it will work/write	they will work/write
PERFECT TENSES		
Present perfect		
1st person	I have worked/written	we have worked/written
2nd person	you have worked/ written	you have worked/ written
3rd person	he/she/ it has worked/ written	they have worked/ written
Past perfect		
1st person	I had worked/written	we had worked/written
2nd person	you had worked/ written	you had worked/ written
3rd person	he/she/it had worked/ written	they had worked/ written
Future perfect		
1st person	I will have worked/ written	we will have worked/ written
2nd person	you will have worked/ written	you will have worked/ written
3rd person	he/she/it will have worked/written	they will have worked/ written
PROGRESSIVE TENSES		
Present progressive		
1st person	I am working/writing	we are working/writing
2nd person	you are working/writing	you are working/writing
3rd person	he/she/it is working/ writing	they are working/ writing

PROGRESSIVE TENSES *(continued)*

Past progressive

1st person	I was working/writing	we were working/writing
2nd person	you were working/writing	you were working/writing
3rd person	he/she/it was working/writing	they were working/writing

Future progressive

1st person	I will be working/writing	we will be working/writing
2nd person	you will be working/writing	you will be working/writing
3rd person	he/she/it will be working/writing	they will be working/writing

Present perfect progressive

1st person	I have been working/writing	we have been working/writing
2nd person	you have been working/writing	you have been working/writing
3rd person	he/she/it has been working/writing	they have been working/writing

Past perfect progressive

1st person	I had been working/writing	we had been working/writing
2nd person	you had been working/writing	you had been working/writing
3rd person	he/she/it had been working/writing	they had been working/writing

Future perfect progressive

1st person	I will have been working/writing	we will have been working/writing
2nd person	you will have been working/writing	you will have been working/writing
3rd person	he/she/it will have been working/writing	they will have been working/writing

7e **Use the appropriate tense to express your meaning.**

For native speakers of English, the selection of an appropriate verb tense usually presents few problems. Most errors in tense are actually errors in verb form like those discussed in the preceding sections—misusing the principal parts of irregular verbs, omitting -*d* or -*ed* endings, and omitting helping verbs. Still, errors in tense do sometimes occur, so it is a good idea to edit your work carefully to ensure that the tenses of verbs accurately express your meaning.

Any problems in verb tense are most likely to occur with some special uses of the present tense and with the perfect tenses.

1 **Observe the special uses of the present tense.**

The present tense generally indicates action occurring at the time of speaking, as in *She understands what you mean* or *From here I see the river and the docks.* It is also used in several special situations.

TO INDICATE HABITUAL OR RECURRING ACTION

Abby *goes* to New York every Friday.
The store *opens* at ten o'clock.

TO STATE A GENERAL TRUTH

The mills of the gods *grind* slowly.
The earth *is* round.

TO DISCUSS THE CONTENT OF LITERATURE, FILM, AND SO ON (SEE ALSO pp. 652–53)

Huckleberry Finn *has* adventures we all envy.
In that article the author *examines* several causes of crime.

TO INDICATE FUTURE TIME

Our friends *arrive* the day after tomorrow.
Ted *leaves* in the next half-hour.

(Notice that in sentences like the last two, time is really indicated by *the day after tomorrow* and *in the next half-hour.*)

2 **Observe the uses of the perfect tenses.**

The perfect tenses generally indicate an action completed before another specific time or action. The present perfect tense also indicates action begun in the past and continued into the present.

PRESENT PERFECT

Hannah *has fed* the dog, so we can go. [The action is completed at the time of the statement.]

Hannah *has* always *fed* the dog. [The action began in the past but continues now.]

t

7e

MEMORY AID

To help students remember special uses of the present tense, you might suggest that they use the acronym *FACT* as a memory aid:

*F*uture time
*A*ction recurring
*C*ontent of literature
*T*ruth, general

PAST PERFECT

Hannah *had fed* the dog by the time we were ready. [The action was completed before another past action.]

FUTURE PERFECT

Hannah *will have fed* the dog a thousand times by the end of the month. [The action was begun in the past and will be completed by a specified time in the future.]

She *will have fed* the dog at least another seven hundred meals by this time next year. [The action begins now or in the future and will be completed by a specified time in the future.]

t seq

7f

7f Use the appropriate sequence of verb tenses.

The term **sequence of tenses** refers to the relation between the verb in a main clause and the verbs or verbals in subordinate clauses or verbal phrases (see 5c). The tenses need not be identical as long as they reflect changes in actual or relative time. For example, in the sentence *He had left before I arrived* the past tense *arrived* is in normal sequence with the past perfect *had left*. The principal conventions governing tense sequence are discussed below. (For a discussion of tense shifts—changes *not* required by meaning—see 13b.)

PICTURES AND EVENTS—VERB TENSE AND SEQUENCE

Show students a picture containing a scene that suggests some preceding events as well as some that might follow. Ask students to write a brief narrative describing the sequence of events and making use of proper verb forms and the correct sequence of tenses.

1 Generally, the verb in a subordinate clause may be in any tense required by meaning.

As long as the tense of the verb in the main clause is neither past nor past perfect (see 7f-2 below), the tense in the subordinate clause need only reflect your meaning. In the following sentences all the verb forms follow a clear and natural sequence, though the tenses in main and subordinate clauses are different.

Mike *knows* that Susan *visited* New Orleans. [Mike's present knowledge is about something that happened in the past, Susan's visit.]

Mike *has known* all along that Susan *will visit* New Orleans. [Mike's knowledge began in the past and continues; Susan's going to New Orleans lies in the future.]

Susan *will explain* to Mike why she *changed* her plans. [The explanation lies in the future, but the change of plans occurred at some time in the past.]

Note that any change of tense between a main and a subordinate clause must be logical. The sentence *My family always keeps pets because we liked them* does not seem logical because *liked* indicates that the liking is past and thus is not a reason to keep pets in the present.

t seq

7f

CREATING A STORY

Write on the board a sentence containing one or more characters and an action. Here are some examples:

> As he rounded the corner, John heard a loud noise, somewhere between a crash and a bang.

> As he came into the classroom, Jim noticed that Carolyn was already there reviewing her notes.

Ask students to form groups, and then require the groups to write paragraph-length (seven to eight sentences) stories. The stories should begin with the sentence you have provided, and individual members of the group should add sentences to the narrative one by one until it is complete. The final story should maintain a correct sequence of tenses, contain proper verb forms, and use a variety of action verbs.

2 **The verb in a subordinate clause must be past or past perfect if the verb in the main clause is past or past perfect.**

The past or past perfect tense in a main clause refers to an action already completed (*smiled, had smiled*). Since the meaning of a subordinate clause depends on that of the main clause, the verb in the subordinate clause must also be completed and thus past or past perfect.

> We *talked* for a long time after we *returned* home. [Since the talking took place in the past, the return home must also have occurred in the past. The past perfect *had returned* would also indicate that the return occurred at a time before the past talking. But the present *return* or the future *will return* would make no sense in the sentence.]

> My friend *had left* before I *arrived*. [The past perfect *had left* indicates that the friend's leaving occurred earlier than the past arrival.]

EXCEPTION: When a subordinate clause expresses a general truth such as *The earth is round*, use the present tense even though the verb of the main clause is in the past or past perfect tense.

> I never *realized* that many marriages *are* genuinely happy.

3 **Observe the appropriate tense sequence with infinitives.**

The tense of an infinitive is determined by the tense of the verb in the predicate. The **present infinitive** is the verb's plain form preceded by *to* (see 5c-2). It indicates action *at the same time* as or *later* than that of the verb.

> I *went to see* a World Series game last year. [The going and the seeing occurred at the same time in the past.]

> I *want to see* a World Series game this year. [The wanting is present; the seeing is still in the future.]

> I *would have liked to see* (not *to have seen*) the other World Series games last year. [The present infinitive indicates the same past time as *would have liked*.]

The verb's **perfect infinitive** consists of *to have* followed by the past participle, as in *to have talked, to have won*. It indicates action *earlier* than that of the verb.

> Sarah *would like* (not *would have liked*) *to have heard* Sylvia Plath read her poetry. [The liking occurs in the present; the hearing would have occurred in the past.]

> The election *was thought to have been rigged*. [The rigging of the election occurred before the thinking about it.]

t seq

7f

4 **Observe the appropriate tense sequence with participles.**

Like the tense of an infinitive, the tense of a participle is determined by the tense of the verb in the predicate. The present participle shows action occurring *at the same time* as that of the verb.

> *Driving* across the United States, he *was astonished* by the vast spaces. [The driving and the astonishment occurred in the same past time.]

The past participle and the present perfect participle show action occurring *earlier* than that of the verb.

> *Exhausted* by overwork, Sheila *remained* at home for two weeks. [The exhaustion occurred before Sheila remained home.]

> *Having lived* all his life in the country, he *is frightened* by cities. [Life in the country preceded the fear of cities.]

EXERCISE 5

Revise the following sentences so that the sequence of verb tenses is appropriate. If a sentence is already correct as given, circle the number preceding it. Some items have more than one possible answer.

Example:
Hedy had hoped to have been elected.
Hedy had hoped *to be elected*.

1. In a history of hospitals in the United States, Charles E. Rosenberg describes how changes in medicine and in American society have fostered increasing dependence on hospitals.
2. Until well into the nineteenth century, hospitals were mainly places to house the desperately sick who have been poor and alone.
3. The sick in hospitals usually received little professional care and usually improved, if at all, simply because time has elapsed.

ANSWERS: EXERCISE 5

1. Sentence correct.
2. Until well into the nineteenth century, hospitals were mainly places to house the desperately sick who <u>were</u> poor and alone.
3. The sick in hospitals usually received little professional care and usually improved, if at all, simply because time <u>elapsed</u>.
4. As doctors learned more about infectious disease, they also decided that the hospital was the best place <u>to train</u> young doctors and <u>to conduct</u> medical research.
5. <u>Having tended</u> the wounded in the Crimean War, the British nurse Florence Nightingale then campaigned for hospital improvements and training of nurses.

6. Surgeons increasingly believed that <u>to perform</u> their work properly required a hospital setting.
7. Sentence correct.
8. Before World War I had begun, the number of hospitals in the U.S. <u>had reached</u> more than 4400.
9. Sentence correct.
10. Now many Americans <u>would like</u> <u>to reconsider</u> whether it is healthy to rely so heavily on hospitals.

4. As doctors learned more about infectious disease, they also decided that the hospital was the best place to have trained young doctors and to have conducted medical research.
5. Tending the wounded in the Crimean War, the British nurse Florence Nightingale then campaigned for hospital improvements and training of nurses.
6. Surgeons increasingly believed that to have performed their work properly required a hospital setting.
7. In addition, doctors of all kinds saw hospitals as places to improve their knowledge and to gain new patients.
8. Before World War I had begun, the number of hospitals in the U.S. reaches more than 4400.
9. Having learned to depend heavily on hospitals, Americans soon found that the services were very expensive.
10. Now many Americans would have liked to have reconsidered whether it is healthy to rely so heavily on hospitals.

ANSWERS: EXERCISE 6

1. Diaries that Adolf Hitler <u>was supposed</u> to have written <u>had surfaced</u> in Germany.
2. Many people <u>believed</u> that the diaries <u>were</u> authentic because a well-known historian <u>had declared</u> them so.
3. The historian's evaluation <u>was questioned</u>, however, by other authorities who <u>called</u> the diaries forgeries.
4. They <u>claimed</u>, among other things, that the paper <u>was</u> not old enough to have been used by Hitler.
5. Eventually, the doubters <u>won</u> the debate because they <u>had</u> the best evidence.

EXERCISE 6

The tenses in each of the following sentences are in correct sequence. Change the tense of one verb as instructed in parentheses. Then change the tense of infinitives, participles, and other verbs as necessary to restore correct sequence. Some items have more than one possible answer.

Example:
He will call when he reaches his destination. (*Change <u>will call</u> to <u>called</u>.*)
He called when he *reached* (or *had reached*) his destination.

1. Diaries that Adolf Hitler is supposed to have written have surfaced in Germany. (*Change <u>have surfaced</u> to <u>had surfaced</u>.*)
2. Many people believe that the diaries are authentic because a well-known historian has declared them so. (*Change <u>believe</u> to <u>believed</u>.*)
3. However, the historian's evaluation has been questioned by other authorities, who call the diaries forgeries. (*Change <u>has been questioned</u> to <u>was questioned</u>.*)
4. They claim, among other things, that the paper is not old enough to have been used by Hitler. (*Change <u>claim</u> to <u>claimed</u>.*)
5. Eventually, the doubters will win the debate because they have the best evidence. (*Change <u>will win</u> to <u>won</u>.*)

MOOD

Mood in grammar is a verb form that indicates the writer's or speaker's attitude toward what he or she is saying. The **indicative mood** states a fact or opinion or asks a question.

They *need* our help. [Opinion.]
Marie *works* only on Saturday. [Fact.]
Why *does* she *work* on Saturday? [Question.]

The **imperative mood** expresses a command or gives a direction. It omits the subject of the sentence, *you.*

Work hard. [Command.]
Turn right at the light. [Direction.]

The **subjunctive mood** expresses a requirement, a suggestion, or a desire, or it states a condition that is contrary to fact (that is, imaginary or hypothetical).

Her father urged that she *work* only on Saturdays. [Suggestion.]

Rules require that applications *be* in writing. [Requirement.]

I wish that I *swam* better. [Desire.]

He could have the job if he *were* harder working. [Present condition contrary to fact.]

The movie would have been more interesting if the lead actor *had been* tougher. [Past condition contrary to fact.]

With all subjects the subjunctive uses only the infinitive of the verb for suggestions and requirements (*work, be*). For desires and present conditions contrary to fact, the subjunctive uses the past tense of the verb (*swam*) or, for *be,* the past-tense form *were.* For past conditions contrary to fact, the subjunctive uses the past perfect (*had known, had been*). With conditions contrary to fact, notice that the verb in the main clause also expresses the imaginary or hypothetical with the helping verb *could* (*could have*) or *would* (*would have been*).

(For a discussion of keeping mood consistent within and among sentences, see 13b.)

vb
7g

7g Use the subjunctive verb forms appropriately.

Although in the past English used distinctive subjunctive verb forms in many contexts, such forms appear now only in two kinds of constructions and in a few idiomatic expressions.

1 Use the subjunctive in contrary-to-fact clauses beginning with *if* or expressing desire.

If I *were* you, I would see a doctor.
If you *saw* a doctor, the rash would disappear.
I wish Jeannie *were* my doctor.

DISCUSSION STORY

Put a lead sentence (as in *Creating a Story*—above) on the board, and ask the class as a whole to decide on the events that follow it. Summarize the events briefly; then ask groups of students to write out the story as in the preceding activity, making it as vivid as they can. This entire exercise will provide both oral and written practice with verb tense and sequence.

Note: The indicative form *was* (*I wish Jeannie was my doctor*) is common in speech and in some informal writing, but the subjunctive *were* is usual in formal English.

Not all clauses beginning *if* express conditions contrary to fact. In the sentence *If Joe is out of town, he hasn't heard the news*, the verb *is* is correct because the clause refers to a condition presumed to exist.

2 **Don't use *would* or *could* in the *if* clause of a conditional statement.**

As discussed above, the helping verb *would* or *could* appears in the main clause of a sentence expressing a condition contrary to fact. The helping verb does *not* appear in the subordinate clause beginning *if*.

Not	I would have called if I *would have* known.
But	I would have called if I *had* known.

3 **Use the subjunctive in *that* clauses following verbs that demand, request, or recommend.**

Verbs such as *ask, insist, urge, require, recommend,* and *suggest* often precede subordinate clauses beginning with *that* and containing the substance of the request or suggestion. The verb in such *that* clauses should be in the subjunctive mood.

The psychologist urged that the patient *be released.*
The law required that he *report* weekly.
Julie's mother insisted that she *stay* home.
Instructors commonly ask that papers *be finished* on time.

Note: These constructions have widely used alternative forms that do not require the subjunctive, such as *The law required him to report weekly* or *Julie's mother insisted on her staying home.*

4 **Use the subjunctive in some set phrases and idioms.**

Several English expressions commonly use the subjunctive. For example:

Come rain or *come* shine.
Be that as it may.
The people *be* damned.

EXERCISE 7

Revise the following sentences with appropriate subjunctive verb forms.

> *Example:*
> I would help the old man if there was a way I could reach him.
> I would help the old man if there *were* a way I could reach him.

1. The audience would have walked out if the performance would have been any worse.
2. The letter requests that we are patient.
3. If I was a rich man, I would still clip coupons from the paper.
4. The syllabus requires that each student writes three papers and takes two essay tests.
5. I wish the lighting in the office was better because my eyes are strained.

ANSWERS: EXERCISE 7

1. The audience would have walked out if the performance <u>had</u> been any worse.
2. The letter requests that we <u>be</u> patient.
3. If I <u>were</u> a rich man, I would still clip coupons from the paper.
4. The syllabus requires that each student <u>write</u> three papers and <u>take</u> two essay tests.
5. I wish the lighting in the office <u>were</u> better because my eyes are strained.

vb

7

VOICE

Verbs that take objects (transitive verbs) can show whether their subjects are acting or are acted upon. In the **active voice** the subject names the actor.

> *David wrote* the paper.
> *Bookies coordinate* illegal bets.

In the **passive voice** the subject names the object or receiver of the action. The actor may be named in a prepositional phrase or omitted.

> *The paper was written* by David.
> *Illegal bets are coordinated* by bookies.
> *Illegal bets are coordinated.* [Actor omitted.]

The passive voice of a verb always consists of the appropriate form of the helping verb *be* plus the past participle of the main verb. Other helping verbs may also be present.

> Senators *are elected* for six-year terms.
> Jerry *has been given* complete freedom.

To change a sentence from active to passive voice, we convert the direct object or the indirect object of the verb into the subject of the verb.

> **ACTIVE**   We *gave* Jerry complete freedom.

PASSIVE SENTENCES—COUNT THE WORDS

Write on the board a number of sentences in the active voice, the sentences ranging from simple to relatively complex. Ask students to change the sentences into the passive voice and then to count the number of words in each version. Finally, ask students to read some of the passive sentences aloud and comment on their effectiveness. This exercise will allow you to check students' understanding of the passive voice and at the same time demonstrate its wordiness.

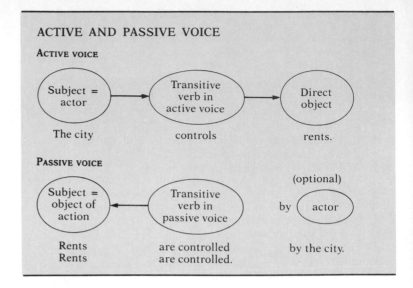

ACTIVE AND PASSIVE VOICE

ACTIVE VOICE

Subject = actor → Transitive verb in active voice → Direct object

The city   controls   rents.

PASSIVE VOICE

Subject = object of action ← Transitive verb in passive voice   (optional) by (actor)

Rents   are controlled   by the city.
Rents   are controlled.

PASSIVE	Jerry *was given* complete freedom. [Indirect object becomes subject.]
PASSIVE	Complete freedom *was given* (to) Jerry. [Direct object becomes subject.]

To change a sentence from passive to active voice, we convert the verb's subject into a direct or an indirect object and substitute a new subject for the previous one.

PASSIVE	Sally *was bitten* by Jamie's dog.
ACTIVE	Jamie's dog *bit* Sally.
PASSIVE	The statement *was read* at a press conference.
ACTIVE	The company's representative *read* the statement at a press conference.

7h Generally, prefer the active voice. Use the passive voice when the actor is unknown or unimportant.

Because the passive omits or de-emphasizes the actor (the performer of the verb's action), it can deprive writing of vigor and is often vague or confusing. The active voice is usually stronger, clearer, and more forthright.

WEAK PASSIVE The exam was thought by us to be unfair because we were tested on material that was not covered in the course.

STRONG ACTIVE We thought the exam unfair because it tested us on material the course did not cover.

The passive voice is useful in two situations: when the actor is unknown and when the actor is unimportant or less important than the object of the action.

Ray Appleton *was murdered* after he returned home. [The murderer is presumably unknown, and in any event Ray Appleton's death is the point of the sentence.]

In the first experiment acid *was added* to the solution. [The person who added the acid, perhaps the writer, is less important than the fact that acid was added. Passive sentences are common in scientific writing.]

Except in such situations, however, you should prefer the active voice in your writing. (See 18d and 31c-3 for additional cautions against the passive voice.)

EXERCISE 8

To practice using the two voices of the verb, convert the following sentences from active to passive or from passive to active. (In converting from passive to active, you may have to add a subject for the new sentence.) Which version of each sentence seems more effective, and why? (For additional exercises with the passive voice, see pp. 198, 348, and 481.)

Example:
The aspiring actor was discovered in a nightclub.
A *talent scout discovered* the aspiring actor in a nightclub.
1. When the Eiffel Tower was built in 1889, it was thought by the French to be ugly.
2. At that time many people still resisted industrial technology.
3. The tower's naked steel construction epitomized this technology.
4. Beautiful ornament was expected to grace fine buildings.
5. Further, the tower could not even be called a building because it had no solid walls.

EXERCISE 9

Circle all the verbs and verbals in the following paragraph and correct their form, tense, or mood if necessary.

PASSIVE SENTENCES—FINDING PASSAGES

Have students, working in groups, locate passive sentences in an essay from a reader or a similar source. Ask them to decide if the passive voice provides emphasis appropriate for the essay or if the active voice would be better. Tell them to be ready to defend their choice of the passive or to offer a revision of the sentence in the active voice.

POSSIBLE ANSWERS: EXERCISE 8

1. When <u>engineers</u> <u>built</u> the Eiffel Tower in 1889, the <u>French</u> <u>thought</u> it was ugly.
2. At that time industrial <u>technology</u> <u>was</u> still resisted <u>by</u> many people.
3. The <u>technology</u> <u>was</u> <u>epitomized</u> by the tower's naked steel construction.
4. <u>People</u> <u>expected</u> beautiful ornament to grace fine buildings.
5. Further, <u>people</u> <u>could</u> <u>not</u> even <u>call</u> the tower a building because it had no solid walls.

ANSWERS: EXERCISE 9

For centuries the <u>natives</u> of Melanesia, a group of islands (lying) northeast of Australia (have practiced) an unusual religion. It (began) in the eighteenth century when European explorers first (visited) the islands. The natives (were fascinated) by the rich goods or "cargo" (possessed) by the explorers. They (saw) the wealth as treasures of the gods, and cargo cults eventually (arose) among them. Over the centuries some Melanesians (turned) to Christianity in the belief that the white man's religion (would bring) them the white man's treasures. During World War II, American soldiers, (having arrived) by boat and airplane (to occupy) some of the islands, (introduced) new and even more wonderful cargo. Even today some leaders of the cargo cults (insist) that the airplane (be worshipped) as a vehicle of the Melanesians' future salvation.

vb

7

For centuries the natives of Melanesia, a group of islands laying northeast of Australia, have practice an unusual religion. It began in the eighteenth century when European explorers first have visited the islands. The natives were fascinated by the rich goods or "cargo" possessed by the explorers. They saw the wealth as treasures of the gods, and cargo cults eventually had arised among them. Over the centuries some Melanesians turned to Christianity in the belief that the white man's religion will bring them the white man's treasures. During World War II, American soldiers, having arrived by boat and airplane to have occupied some of the islands, introduced new and even more wonderful cargo. Even today some leaders of the cargo cults insist that the airplane is worship as a vehicle of the Melanesians' future salvation.

CHAPTER 8

Agreement

Agreement is the correspondence in form between subjects and verbs and between pronouns and their **antecedents,** the nouns or other pronouns they refer to. Agreement helps readers understand the relations between elements in a sentence. The aspects of agreement are explained on the next page.

Subjects and verbs agree in number and in person.

Sarah often *speaks* up in class. [Both subject and verb are in the third-person singular form.]

Even though *we understand,* *we* still *dislike* it. [Both subjects and verbs are in the first-person plural form.]

Pronouns and their antecedents agree in person, number, and gender.

Claude resented their ignoring *him*. [Both the pronoun *him* and its antecedent *Claude* are masculine and third-person singular.]

The *dogs* stand still while *they* are judged. [The pronoun *they* and its antecedent *dogs* are both third-person plural.]

8a Make subjects and verbs agree in number.

Most subject-verb agreement problems arise when endings are omitted from subjects or verbs, when the subject is not clearly singular or plural, or when words come between subject and verb and blur their relationship. The following conventions cover these and other situations that affect subject-verb agreement.

ASPECTS OF AGREEMENT

PERSON

1st person, the speaker(s): *I, we*
2nd person, the person(s) spoken to: *you*
3rd person, the person(s) or thing(s) spoken about: *he, she, it, they;* nouns; indefinite and relative pronouns

NUMBER

Singular, one: *I, you, he, she, it;* nouns naming one; indefinite and relative pronouns referring to plural nouns and pronouns
Plural, more than one: *we, you, they;* nouns naming more than one; indefinite and relative pronouns referring to plural nouns and pronouns

GENDER

Masculine: *he;* nouns naming males; indefinite and relative pronouns referring to males
Feminine: *she;* nouns naming females; indefinite and relative pronouns referring to females
Neuter: *it;* nouns naming places, things, qualities, and ideas; indefinite and relative pronouns referring to same

---

 Use the verb ending *-s* or *-es* with all third-person singular subjects. Use the noun ending *-s* or *-es* to make most nouns plural.

Adding *-s* or *-es* to a noun usually makes the noun *plural*, whereas adding *-s* or *-es* to a present-tense verb makes the verb *singular*. Thus if the subject noun is plural, it will end in *-s* or *-es* and the verb will not. If the subject is singular, it will not end in *-s* and the verb will.

SINGULAR	**PLURAL**
The boy eat*s*.	The boy*s* eat.
The bird soar*s*.	The bird*s* soar.

The only exceptions to these rules involve the nouns that form irregular plurals, such as *child/children; woman/women.* The irregular plural still requires a plural verb: *The children play.*

Writers often omit *-s* and *-es* endings from nouns or verbs because they are not pronounced clearly in speech (as in *asks* and *lists*) or because they are not used regularly in some English dialects. However, the endings are required in standard English.

NONSTANDARD	Julie *resist* any kind of change.
STANDARD	Julie *resists* any kind of change.
NONSTANDARD	Their *action* demand a response.
STANDARD	Their *actions* demand a response.

Remember that the verb *be* is irregular. In the present tense we use *is* with *he, she, it*, and singular nouns (*tree is*) and *are* with all plurals (*trees are*). In the past tense we use *was* with *he, she, it*, and singular nouns (*tree was*) and *were* with all plurals (*trees were*). (See Chapter 7, pp. 218 and 223, for more on these verb forms.)

NOTE: In a verb phrase (verb plus helping verb), the helping verb sometimes reflects the number of the subject and sometimes does not: *The car does run; The cars do run; The car/cars will run.* The verb itself (*run*) does not change in any way.

2 **Subject and verb should agree even when other words come between them.**

When the subject and verb are interrupted by other words, particularly nouns, then agreement errors may result from connecting the verb to the nearest noun instead of the actual subject.

A catalog of courses and requirements often *baffles* (not *baffle*) students. [The verb must agree with the subject, *catalog*, not the nearer word *requirements*.]

The profits earned by the cosmetic industry *are* (not *is*) high. [The subject is *profits*, not *industry*.]

NOTE: Phrases beginning with *as well as, together with, along with, in addition to*, and similar expressions do not change the number of the subject.

The governor, as well as his advisers, *has* (not *have*) agreed to attend the protest rally.

If you really mean *and* in such a sentence, you can avoid awkwardness by using it. Then the subject is compound, and the verb should be plural: *The governor and his advisers have agreed to attend.*

3 **Subjects joined by *and* usually take plural verbs.**

Two or more subjects joined by *and* usually take a plural verb, whether one or all of the subjects are singular.

agr
8a

WIDELY SEPARATED SUBJECTS AND VERBS

Ask students (working individually or in groups and using the handbook as a guide) to identify the sentence strategies that often result in widely separated subjects and verbs. Then ask them to write in their own words a description of these strategies (i.e., the grammatical rules governing them). Finally, ask students to write sentences using the strategies and containing proper subject-verb agreement. (This exercise can also be used with compound subjects, collective nouns, inverted word order, or other strategies that frequently lead to agreement problems.)

DICKENS

Sometimes the sample sentences we offer to students by way of illustrating a point of grammar or style seem a bit artificial or a bit too simple. Nineteenth-century novels, particularly those by Dickens, offer sentences with considerable variety and flair in structure that can be used either as models themselves or as patterns for sentences with a more contemporary content and cast. Here, as a starter, is a sentence from *Dombey and Sons:*

> Florence, with her hand upon the Captain's arm, so sorrowful and timid, and the Captain with his rough face and burly figure, so quietly protective of her, stood in the rosy light of the bright evening sky, without saying a word. (plural subject/plural verb)

Frost and Roethke *are* her favorite poets.
The dog, the monkey, the children, and the tent *were* in the car.

EXCEPTIONS: When the parts of the subject form a single idea or refer to a single person or thing, then they take a singular verb.

Avocado and bean sprouts *is* my favorite sandwich.
The winner and new champion *was* in the shower.

When a compound subject is preceded by the adjective *each* or *every*, then the verb is usually singular.

At customs, every box, bag, and parcel *is* inspected.
Each man, woman, and child *has* a right to be heard.

But when a compound subject is *followed* by *each*, the verb is plural.

The man and the woman each *have* different problems.

4 **When parts of a subject are joined by *or* or *nor*, the verb agrees with the nearer part.**

When all parts of a subject joined by *or* or *nor* are singular, the verb is singular; when all parts are plural, the verb is plural.

Neither the teacher nor the student *knows* the answer.
The rabbits or the woodchucks *have eaten* my lettuce.

Problems with subjects joined by *or* or *nor* occur most often when one part of the subject is singular and the other plural. In that case the verb should agree with the subject part closer to it. To avoid awkwardness in such sentences, place the plural part closer to the verb.

AWKWARD   Neither the players nor the coach *was* on time.
IMPROVED   Neither the coach nor the players *were* on time.

The same problem arises when the subject consists of nouns and pronouns of different person requiring different verb forms: *neither Jim nor I, either he or you.* In this case, too, the verb agrees with the part of the subject nearer to it.

Neither Jim nor I *am* late.
Either she or you *are* late.

Since observing this convention often results in awkwardness, avoid the problem altogether by rewording the sentence.

AWKWARD   Either she or you *are* late.
IMPROVED   Either she *is* late, or you *are*.

5   **Generally, use singular verbs with indefinite pronouns.**

An **indefinite pronoun** is one that does not refer to a specific person or thing.

COMMON INDEFINITE PRONOUNS			
all	each	neither	one
any	either	nobody	some
anybody	everybody	none	somebody
anyone	everyone	no one	someone
anything	everything	nothing	something

Most indefinite pronouns are singular in meaning (they refer to a single unspecified person or thing), and they take singular verbs.

> Something *smells*.   Neither *is* right.

A few indefinite pronouns like *all, any, none,* and *some* may be either singular or plural in meaning. The verbs you use with these pronouns depend on the meaning of the nouns or pronouns they refer to.

> All of the money *is* reserved for emergencies. [*All* refers to the singular noun *money,* so the verb is singular.]
>
> When the men finally arrive, all *go* straight to work. [*All* refers to the plural noun *men,* so the verb is plural.]

6   **Collective nouns take singular or plural verbs depending on meaning.**

A **collective noun** has singular form but names a group of individuals or things—for example, *army, audience, committee, crowd, family, group, team.* When used as a subject, a collective noun may take a singular or plural verb, depending on the context. When considering the group as one unit, use a singular verb.

> The group *agrees* that action is necessary.
> Any band *sounds* good in that concert hall.

But when considering the group's members as individuals who act separately, use the plural form of the verb.

> The old group *have* gone their separate ways.
> The band *do* not agree on where to play.

NOTE: Even when the plural verb form is properly used, as in

ARE EVERYONE READY?

Though many students will not, at first, hear anything wrong with sentences like "Everyone ought to pay attention to their own business" (a pattern that has wide acceptance in speech), almost all will find sentences like these unacceptable: "Are everyone ready for lunch?" "Do everybody have enough money to buy tickets for the rides?" Anyone who finds the latter sentences acceptable is probably having trouble recognizing the singular and plural forms of verbs. Sample sentences can, therefore, help you identify the real source of a student's problems with agreement.

these examples, it often sounds awkward. For this reason you may prefer to rephrase such sentences with plural subjects, as in *The members of the old group have gone their separate ways.*

The collective noun *number* may be singular or plural. Preceded by *a*, it is plural; preceded by *the*, it is singular.

> A number of my friends *have* decided to live off campus.
> *The* number of people in debt *is* very large.

7 **The verb agrees with the subject even when the normal word order is inverted.**

Inverted subject-verb order occurs in questions.

> *Is* voting a right or a privilege? [*Voting* is the subject; *is* is the verb. Compare *Voting is a right or a privilege.*]
>
> *Are* Madigan and Harris married? [*Madigan and Harris* is the compound subject; *are* is the verb. Compare *Madigan and Harris are married.*]

Inverted subject-verb order also occurs in expletive constructions beginning with *there* or *it* and a form of *be* (see 5e-4).

> There *are* too many students in that class. [*Students* is the subject; *are* is the verb. Compare *Too many students are in that class.*]
>
> After many years there *is* finally peace in that country. [*Peace* is the subject; *is* is the verb. Compare *Peace is in that country.*]

In expletive constructions, *there is* may be used before a compound subject when the first element in the subject is singular.

> There *is* much work to do and little time to do it.

Word order may sometimes be inverted for emphasis. The verb still agrees with its subject.

> From the mountains *comes* an eerie, shimmering light.

8 **A linking verb agrees with its subject, not the subject complement.**

When a linking verb is followed by a subject complement, make the verb agree with its subject, the first element, not with the noun or pronoun serving as a subject complement (see 5a-3).

> Henry's sole support *is* his mother and father. [The subject is *support.*]
>
> Henry's mother and father *are* his sole support. [The subject is *mother and father.*]

9 **When used as subjects, *who, which,* and *that* take verbs that agree with their antecedents.**

The relative pronouns *who, which,* and *that* do not have different singular and plural forms. When one of these pronouns serves as a subject, its verb should agree with the noun or other pronoun that the relative pronoun refers to (its antecedent).

> Mayor Garber ought to listen to the people who *work* for her. [*Who* refers to the plural *people,* so the verb is plural.]

> Jane is the person who usually *solves* our problems. [*Who* refers to the singular *person,* so the verb is singular.]

Agreement problems often occur with relative pronouns when the sentence includes *one of the* or *the only one of the* before the pronoun.

> Roberts is one of the teachers who *give* difficult tests. [*Who* refers to the plural *teachers.* Several teachers give difficult tests; Roberts is one of them.]

> Roberts is the only one of the teachers who *has* paid attention to me. [*Who* refers to *one.* Among the teachers only one, Roberts, has paid attention.]

10 **Nouns with plural form but singular meaning take singular verbs.**

Some nouns with plural form (that is, ending in *-s*) are usually regarded as singular in meaning. They include *athletics, economics, mathematics, measles, news, politics, physics,* and *statistics.*

> After so long a wait, the news *has* to be good.
> Statistics *is* required of psychology majors.

Measurements and figures ending in *-s* may also be singular when the quantity they refer to is a unit.

> Three years *is* a long time to wait.
> Three-fourths of her library *consists* of reference books.

These words and amounts are plural in meaning when they describe individual items rather than whole groups or whole bodies of activity or knowledge.

> The statistics *prove* him wrong. [*Statistics* refers to facts, individual items.]

> Two-fifths of the cars on the road *are* unsafe. [The cars are unsafe separately.]

A LITTLE INTERVENTION

Agreement problems with *who, which,* and *that* are often the result of a phrase separating the subject from the relative clause. Give students a few examples of such phrases:

> is one of those people who

> is the only one of the workers that

> are often believed to be creatures that

> are generally considered to be people who

> is representative of those executives who

Then ask them to write sample sentences of their own employing these or similar phrases and avoiding problems of agreement.

agr
8a

11 **Titles and words named as words take singular verbs.**

When your sentence subject is the title of a corporation or a work (such as a book or a movie) or a word you are defining or describing, the verb should be singular even if the title or the word is plural.

Hakada Associates *is* a new firm.
Dream Days remains one of her favorite books.
Folks is a down-home word for *people.*

ANSWERS: EXERCISE 1

1. Weinstein & Associates <u>is</u> a consulting firm that <u>tries</u> to make businesspeople laugh.
2. Statistics from recent research <u>suggest</u> that humor relieves stress.
3. Reduced stress in businesses in turn <u>reduces</u> illness and absenteeism.
4. Reduced stress can also reduce friction within an employee group, which then <u>works</u> together more productively.
5. In special conferences held by one consultant, each of the participants <u>practices</u> making the others laugh.
6. "<u>Aren't</u> there enough laughs within you to spread the wealth?" the consultant asks his students.
7. Sentence correct.
8. Such self-deprecating comments in public <u>are</u> uncommon among business managers, the consultant says.
9. Each of the managers in a typical firm <u>takes</u> the work much too seriously.
10. The humorous boss often feels like the only one of the managers who <u>has</u> other things in mind besides profits.
11. One consultant to many companies <u>suggests</u> cultivating office humor with practical jokes such as a rubber fish in the water cooler.
12. When employees or their manager regularly <u>posts</u> cartoons on the bulletin board, office spirit usually picks up.
13. Sentence correct.

EXERCISE 1

Revise the verbs in the following sentences as needed to make subjects and verbs agree in number. If the sentence is already correct as given, circle the number preceding it.

Example:

Each of the job applicants type sixty words per minute.
Each of the job applicants *types* sixty words per minute.

1. Weinstein & Associates are a consulting firm that try to make businesspeople laugh.
2. Statistics from recent research suggests that humor relieves stress.
3. Reduced stress in businesses in turn reduce illness and absenteeism.
4. Reduced stress can also reduce friction within an employee group, which then work together more productively.
5. In special conferences held by one consultant, each of the participants practice making the others laugh.
6. "Isn't there enough laughs within you to spread the wealth?" the consultant asks his students.
7. The consultant quotes Casey Stengel's rule that the best way to keep your management job is to separate the underlings who hate you from the ones who have not decided how they feel.
8. Such self-deprecating comments in public is uncommon among business managers, the consultant says.
9. Each of the managers in a typical firm take the work much too seriously.
10. The humorous boss often feels like the only one of the managers who have other things in mind besides profits.
11. One consultant to many companies suggest cultivating office humor with practical jokes such as a rubber fish in the water cooler.
12. When employees or their manager regularly post cartoons on the bulletin board, office spirit usually picks up.
13. When someone who has seemed too easily distracted is en-

trusted with updating the cartoons, his or her concentration often improves.
14. In the face of levity, the former sourpuss becomes one of those who hides bad temper.
15. Every one of the consultants caution, however, that humor has no place in life-affecting corporate situations such as employee layoffs.

14. In the face of levity, the former sourpuss becomes one of those who <u>hide</u> bad temper.
15. Every one of the consultants <u>cautions</u>, however, that humor has no place in life-affecting corporate situations such as employee layoffs.

8b	**Make pronouns and their antecedents agree in person and number.**

The **antecedent** of a pronoun is the noun or other pronoun it refers to. The antecedent usually comes before the pronoun that refers to it, but it may follow the pronoun.

Every *dog* in that kennel has received *its* shots. [*Dog* is the antecedent of *its*.]

Having received *their* tax bills, the *home owners* worried about payment. [*Home owners,* the subject of the main clause, is the antecedent of *their* in the introductory phrase.]

As these examples show, a pronoun agrees with its antecedent in gender (masculine, feminine, neuter), person (first, second, third), and number (singular, plural). (See p. 240 for an explanation of these terms.) Since pronouns derive their meaning from their antecedents, pronoun-antecedent agreement is essential for the reader to understand what you are saying.

1   **Antecedents joined by *and* usually take plural pronouns.**

Two or more antecedents joined by *and* usually take a plural pronoun, whether one or all of the antecedents are singular.

My adviser and I can't coordinate *our* schedules.
Their argument resolved, George and Jennifer made up.

EXCEPTIONS: When the compound antecedent refers to a single idea, person, or thing, then the pronoun is singular.

The athlete and scholar forgot both *his* javelin and *his* books.

When the compound antecedent follows *each* or *every,* the pronoun is singular.

Every girl and woman took *her* seat.

USING MAGAZINES OR A READER

Using essays from a reader or magazine articles, have students work in groups to find sentence structures often associated with agreement problems. Ask the groups to decide how important these structures are for expository prose and to write out what they consider to be the rules governing agreement within these structures.

2 **When parts of an antecedent are joined by *or* or *nor*, the pronoun agrees with the nearer part.**

When the parts of an antecedent are connected by *or* or *nor*, the pronoun should agree with the part closer to it.

Steve or John should have raised *his* hand.

Either consumers or car manufacturers will have *their* way.

Neither the student nor the elderly people will retrieve *their* deposits from that landlord.

When one subject is plural and the other singular, as in the last example, the sentence will be awkward unless you put the plural subject second.

> **AWKWARD**   Either the dogs or the cat will have to be returned to the shop *it* came from.

> **REVISED**   Either the cat or the dogs will have to be returned to the shop *they* came from.

3 **Generally, use a singular pronoun when the antecedent is an indefinite pronoun.**

Indefinite pronouns such as *anybody* and *something* refer to persons or things in general rather than to a specific person or thing. (See p. 243 for a list.) Most indefinite pronouns are singular in meaning. When these indefinite pronouns serve as antecedents to other pronouns, the other pronouns are singular.

Everyone on the team had *her* own locker.
Each of the boys likes *his* teacher.

Using a singular pronoun to refer to an indefinite pronoun may result in an awkward sentence when the indefinite pronoun clearly means "many" or "all."

> **AWKWARD**   After everyone left, I shut the door behind *him*.

In speech we commonly avoid such awkwardness with a plural pronoun: *After everyone left, I shut the door behind them*. In writing, however, you should rewrite the sentence.

> **REWRITTEN**   After *all the guests* left, I shut the door behind *them*.

The generic *he*

The meaning of an indefinite pronoun often includes both masculine and feminine genders, not one or the other. The same is

RESOURCES AND IDEAS

Martha Kolln, "Everyone's Right to Their Own Language," *College Composition and Communication* 37 (February 1986): 100–102. The frequency with which students treat indefinite pronouns as plural suggests that the widely accepted rules of usage discussed in this section may in some ways conflict with practice. Kolln takes a radical stance, arguing that "dicta that designate all indefinite pronouns as singular have no basis either in actual usage or in the rules of logic" (102).

true of other indefinite words such as *child, adult, individual,* and *person.* In such cases we traditionally use *he* (or *him* or *his*) to refer to the antecedent. But many people see the so-called **generic *he*** (or generalized *he*) as excluding females. Thus many writers now avoid using *he* in these situations by rewriting their sentences.

ORIGINAL	Everyone had *his* book in class.
BROADER	Everyone had *his or her* book in class. [Overused, this option can be wordy or awkward.]
PLURAL	*All the students* had *their* books in class. [This option can be used frequently without creating awkwardness.]

In speech we often solve the problem of the generic *he* by combining a plural pronoun with an indefinite pronoun, as in *Everyone brought their books to class.* But many readers view this construction as wrong, so it should be avoided in writing.

For more on avoiding bias in writing, see 31a-8.

4 **Collective noun antecedents take singular or plural pronouns depending on meaning.**

Collective nouns such as *army, committee, family, group,* and *team* have singular form but may be referred to by singular or plural pronouns, depending on the meaning intended. When you are referring to the group as a unit—all its members acting together—then the pronoun is singular.

The committee voted to disband *itself.*
The team attended a banquet in *its* honor.

When you are referring to the individual members of the group, the pronoun is plural.

The audience arose quietly from *their* seats.
The old group have gone *their* separate ways.

The last example demonstrates the importance of being consistent in verb use as well as pronoun choice when assigning a singular or plural meaning to a collective noun (see also 8a-6).

INCONSISTENT	The old group *has* gone *their* separate ways.
CONSISTENT	The old group *have* gone *their* separate ways.

EXERCISE 2

Revise the following sentences so that pronouns and their antecedents agree in person and number. Some items have more than

ANSWERS: EXERCISE 2

1. Almost any child will quickly astound observers with <u>his</u> or <u>her</u> capabilities. OR: <u>Most</u> <u>children</u> will quickly astound observers with their capabilities.

agr
8b

2. Sentence correct.
3. Of course, the family has a tremendous influence on the development of a child in <u>its</u> midst.
4. Each of the members of the immediate family exerts <u>his</u> <u>or</u> <u>her</u> own unique pull on the child.
5. Other relatives, teachers, and friends can also affect the <u>children's</u> view of the world and themselves. (Avoiding the generic <u>he</u>, the only alternative to a plural antecedent is the awkward: <u>the world and himself or herself</u>.)
6. Genetics and physiology also strongly influence the development of children, but <u>they</u> may never be fully understood.
7. The psychology community often cannot agree in <u>their</u> views of whether nurture or nature is more important in a child's development.
8. Another debated issue is whether the <u>children's</u> emotional development or their intellectual development is more central. OR: . . . whether the child's <u>emotional or intellectual development</u> is more central. OR: . . . whether the child's emotional development or <u>his or her</u> intellectual development is more central.
9. Just about everyone has <u>his</u> <u>or</u> <u>her</u> strong opinion on these issues, often backed up by evidence.
10. Sentence correct.

ANSWERS: EXERCISE 3

1. Recently, <u>some</u> <u>psychologists</u> <u>have</u> published <u>their</u> ideas about the entire process of child development.
2. <u>These</u> <u>theories</u> <u>mesh</u> social and intellectual development and illuminate the connection between them.
3. Stanley Greenspan, a child psychiatrist, proposes that <u>the</u> <u>child</u> <u>proceeds</u> through stages in <u>his or her</u> first ten years. (<u>His</u> would also be correct, but some would consider it sexist.)
4. <u>The</u> <u>stages</u> <u>integrate</u> emotions and cognition, and <u>they</u> <u>prepare</u> the way for following stages.

one possible answer. Try to avoid the generic *he* (see p. 248), and if you change the subject of a sentence be sure to change verbs as necessary for agreement. If the sentence is already correct as given, circle the number preceding it.

Example:
Each of the Boudreaus' children brought their laundry home at Thanksgiving.

Each of the Boudreaus' children brought *his or her* laundry home at Thanksgiving. *Or: All* of the Boudreaus' children brought *their* laundry home at Thanksgiving.

1. Almost any child will quickly astound observers with their capabilities.
2. Despite their extensive research and experience, neither child psychologists nor parents have yet figured out how children work.
3. Of course, the family has a tremendous influence on the development of a child in their midst.
4. Each of the members of the immediate family exerts their own unique pull on the child.
5. Other relatives, teachers, and friends can also affect the child's view of the world and themselves.
6. Genetics and physiology also strongly influence the development of children, but it may never be fully understood.
7. The psychology community often cannot agree in its views of whether nurture or nature is more important in a child's development.
8. Another debated issue is whether the child's emotional development or their intellectual development is more central.
9. Just about everyone has their strong opinion on these issues, often backed up by evidence.
10. Neither the popular press nor scholarly journals devote much of their space to the wholeness of the child.

EXERCISE 3

In the following sentences subjects agree with verbs, and pronouns agree with antecedents. Make the change specified in parentheses after each sentence, and then revise the sentence as necessary to maintain agreement. Try to avoid the generic *he* (see p. 248). Some items have more than one possible answer.

Example:
The student attends weekly conferences with her teacher. (*Change <u>The student</u> to <u>Students</u>.*)

Students *attend* weekly conferences with *their* teacher.

1. Recently, one psychologist has published his ideas about the entire process of child development. (*Change <u>one psychologist</u> to <u>some psychologists</u>.*)

agr
8b

2. This theory meshes social and intellectual development and illuminates the connection between them. (*Change This theory to These theories.*)
3. Stanley Greenspan, a child psychiatrist, proposes that children proceed through stages in their first ten years. (*Change children to the child.*)
4. Each stage integrates emotions and cognition, and it prepares the way for following stages. (*Change Each stage to The stages.*)
5. In the first stage, for example, the child learns some self-regulation as a means of protecting himself from overstimulation. (*Change the child to children.*)
6. But self-regulation also helps the child organize his immediate experience, so it serves a cognitive purpose for him as well. (*Change the child to children.*)
7. At a much later stage, around age nine, children identify strongly with adults of the same sex and imitate their roles and behaviors. (*Change children to the child.*)
8. Children also become preoccupied with their peers at this stage and begin to seek stable relationships. (*Change Children to The child.*)
9. Yet the child's interaction with peers is often guided by strict rules, indicating that it has a cognitive function. (*Change interaction to interactions.*)
10. The child is organizing experience that is abstract and complex, not just immediate and concrete as in infancy. (*Change experience to experiences.*)

EXERCISE 4

Revise the sentences in the following paragraph to correct errors in agreement between subjects and verbs or between pronouns and their antecedents.

Everyone has their favorite view of professional athletes. A common view is that the athletes are like well-paid children who have no real work to do, have no responsibilities, and simply enjoy the game and the good money. But this view of professional athletes fail to consider the grueling training the athletes have to go through to become professionals. Either training or competing lead each athlete to take risks that can result in their serious injury. The athletes have tremendous responsibility to the team they play on, which need to function as a unit at all times to win their games. Most athletes are finished as active team players by the age of forty, when he is too stiff and banged-up to go on. Rather than just listening to any of the people who criticizes professional athletes, everyone interested in sports need to defend the athletes. They take stiff physical punishment so neither the sports fanatic nor the casual observer are deprived of their pleasure.

5. In the first stage, for example, <u>children</u> <u>learn</u> some self-regulation as a means of protecting <u>themselves</u> from overstimulation.
6. But self-regulation also helps children organize <u>their</u> immediate experience, so it serves a cognitive purpose for <u>them</u> as well.
7. At a much later stage, around age nine, <u>the</u> <u>child</u> <u>identifies</u> strongly with adults of the same sex and <u>imitates</u> their roles and behaviors.
8. <u>The</u> <u>child</u> also <u>becomes</u> preoccupied with <u>his</u> or <u>her</u> peers at this stage and <u>begins</u> to seek stable relationships.
9. Yet the child's <u>interactions</u> with peers <u>are</u> often guided by strict rules, indicating that <u>they</u> <u>have</u> a cognitive function.
10. The child is organizing <u>experiences</u> that <u>are</u> abstract and complex, not just immediate and concrete as in infancy.

ANSWERS: EXERCISE 4

Everyone has *his* (or *his or her*) favorite view of professional athletes. A common view is that the athletes are like well-paid children who have no real work to do, have no responsibilities, and simply enjoy the game and the good money. But this view of professional athletes *fails* to consider the grueling training the athletes have to go through to become professionals. Either training or competing *leads* each athlete to take risks that can result in *his* (or *his or her*) serious injury. The athletes have tremendous responsibility to the team they play on, which *needs* to function as a unit at all times to win *its* games. Most athletes are finished as active team players by the age of forty, when *they are* too stiff and banged-up to go on. Rather than just listening to any of the people who *criticize* professional athletes, everyone interested in sports *needs* to defend the athletes. They take stiff physical punishment so neither the sports fanatic nor the casual observer *is* deprived of *his* (or *his or her*) pleasure.

Many readers view misuse of adjectives and adverbs as a sign of ignorance or carelessness. You should alert students to the potential effect of errors, of course, and remind them that this text offers helpful advice.

Yet fear of failure can disrupt the writing process and cause students to drop effective phrases and sentences from an essay because they are uncertain about the correct form of a word. This chapter therefore takes a positive approach, showing students the correct way to use adjectives and adverbs rather than emphasizing the "don'ts." It also offers easily remembered advice to guide writers over trouble spots. The exercises in the chapter ask students not only to recognize errors but also to revise sentences to make sure adjectives and adverbs are used appropriately.

CHAPTER 9

Adjectives and Adverbs

Adjectives and adverbs are modifiers that describe, restrict, or otherwise qualify the words to which they relate.

FUNCTIONS OF ADJECTIVES AND ADVERBS

Adjectives modify nouns: *serious* student
pronouns: *ordinary* one
Adverbs modify verbs: *warmly* greet
adjectives: *only* three people
adverbs: *quite* seriously
phrases: *nearly* to the edge of the cliff
clauses: *just* when we were ready to leave
sentences: *Fortunately*, she is now employed.

Many of the most common adjectives are familiar one-syllable words such as *good, bad, strange, true, false, large, right,* and *wrong.* Many others are formed by adding endings such as *-al, -able, -ful, -less, -ish, -ive,* and *-y* to nouns or verbs: *optional, fashionable, beautiful, fruitless, selfish, expressive, dreamy.*

Most adverbs are formed by adding *-ly* to adjectives: *badly, strangely, falsely. largely, beautifully, selfishly.* But note that we cannot depend on *-ly* to identify adverbs, since some adjectives also end in *-ly* (*fatherly, lonely, silly*) and since some common adverbs do not end in *-ly* (*always, forever, here, not, now, often, quite, then, there*). Thus the only sure way to distinguish between adjectives and adverbs is to determine how an individual word functions in its sentence. If a word modifies a noun or pronoun, it is an adjective; if it modifies a verb, an adjective, another adverb, or an entire word group, it is an adverb.

| **9a** | **Don't use adjectives to modify verbs, adverbs, or other adjectives.** |

Adjectives modify only nouns and pronouns. Using adjectives instead of adverbs to modify verbs, adverbs, or other adjectives is nonstandard.

| NONSTANDARD | They took each other *serious*. |
| STANDARD | They took each other *seriously*. |

| NONSTANDARD | Jenny read the book *easy*. |
| STANDARD | Jenny read the book *easily*. |

The adjectives *good* and *bad* often appear where standard English requires the adverbs *well* and *badly*.

| NONSTANDARD | Playing *good* is the goal of practicing baseball. |
| STANDARD | Playing *well* is the goal of practicing baseball. |

| NONSTANDARD | The band played *bad* last night. |
| STANDARD | The band played *badly* last night. |

Although in informal speech the adjective forms *real* and *sure* are often used in place of the adverb forms *really* and *surely*, formal speech and writing require the *-ly* adverb form.

| INFORMAL | After a few lessons Dan drove *real* well. |
| FORMAL | After a few lessons Dan drove *really* well. |

| INFORMAL | I *sure* was shocked by his confession. |
| FORMAL | I *surely* was shocked by his confession. |

| **9b** | **Use an adjective after a linking verb to modify the subject. Use an adverb to modify a verb.** |

A **linking verb** is one that links, or connects, a subject and its complement: *They are golfers* (noun complement); *He is lucky* (adjective complement). (See also 5a-3.) The verbs most often used as linking verbs are forms of *be* and verbs associated with our five senses (*look, sound, smell, feel, taste*), as well as a few others (*appear, seem, become, grow, turn, prove, remain*). But some of these verbs may or may not be linking, depending on their meaning in the sentence. When the word after the verb modifies the subject, the verb is linking and the word should be an adjective. When the word modifies the verb, however, it should be an adverb.

Hallie felt *bad* after she lost the race. [Adjective *bad*, meaning "ill" or "unhappy," modifies *Hallie*.]

She had lost the race *badly*. [Adverb *badly* modifies *had lost*.]

The evidence proved *conclusive*. [Adjective *conclusive* modifies *evidence*.]

The evidence proved *conclusively* that the defendant was guilty. [Adverb *conclusively* modifies *proved*.]

9c After a direct object, use an adjective to modify the object and an adverb to modify the verb.

If the direct object of a verb is followed by a word that modifies the verb, that word must be an adverb: *She repeated the words angrily*. If, in contrast, the direct object is followed by a word that modifies the object itself (an object complement), that word must be an adjective: *Campus politics made Martin angry*. (See also 5a-3.) You can test whether a modifier should be an adjective or an adverb by trying to separate it from the direct object. If you can separate it, it should be an adverb: *She angrily repeated the words*. If you cannot separate it, it is probably an adjective.

The instructor considered the student's work *thorough*. [The adjective can be moved in front of *work* (*student's thorough work*), but it cannot be separated from *work*.]

The instructor considered the student's work *thoroughly*. [The adverb can be separated from *work*. Compare *The instructor thoroughly considered the student's work*.]

9d When an adverb has a short form and an *-ly* form, distinguish carefully between the forms.

Some adverbs have two forms, one with an *-ly* ending and one without. These include the following:

cheap, cheaply	loud, loudly	sharp, sharply
high, highly	near, nearly	slow, slowly
late, lately	quick, quickly	wrong, wrongly

With some of these pairs the choice of form is a matter of idiom, for the two forms have developed entirely separate meanings.

He went *late*.	Winter is drawing *near*.
Lately he has been eating more.	Winter is *nearly* here.

In other pairs the long and short forms have the same meaning.

However, the short forms generally occur in informal speech and writing. The *-ly* forms are preferable in formal writing.

INFORMAL	Drive *slow.*
FORMAL	The funeral procession moved *slowly* through town.
INFORMAL	Jones wants to get rich *quick.*
FORMAL	Harrison became rich *quickly* when she invested in the stock market.

EXERCISE 1

Identify the adjectives and adverbs in the following sentences, and determine what part of speech each one modifies. Then compose a sentence of your own that parallels each sentence.

Example:

The angry man shouted loudly and moved inside.

The *angry* man shouted *loudly* and moved *inside.*

The *hungry* child cried *plaintively* and fussed *about.*

1. The weary tourists slowly filed into the large gray bus.
2. During the rapid descent through the thick clouds, passengers muttered tensely among themselves.
3. Everyone in the class answered the hardest question wrong.
4. He was such an exciting person that everyone felt bad when he left.
5. As the Ferris wheel slowly turned, raising him higher in the air, he became increasingly ill.

EXERCISE 2

Revise the following sentences to make adjectives modify nouns and pronouns and to make adverbs modify verbs, adjectives, and other adverbs. If any sentence is already correct as given, circle the number preceding it.

Example:

The announcer warned that traffic was moving very slow.
The announcer warned that traffic was moving very *slowly.*

1. I was real surprised when Martin and Emily bought a Thunderbird.
2. If you take your lessons more serious, you will improve faster.
3. That perfume smelled similarly to my mother's.
4. Thinking about the accident, Jerry felt bad.
5. After playing poor for six games, the hockey team finally had a game that went good.

9d *ad*

ANSWERS: EXERCISE 1

1. The <u>weary</u> tourists <u>slowly</u> filed into the <u>large gray</u> bus.
   Sample imitation: The trembling contestant hesitantly climbed onto the high wooden platform.
2. During the <u>rapid</u> descent through the <u>thick</u> clouds, passengers muttered <u>tensely</u> among themselves.
   Sample imitation: During the much-needed renovation of the South Wing, cars must park illegally on the side streets.
3. Everyone in the class answered the <u>hardest</u> question <u>wrong</u>.
   Sample imitation: Somebody in the crowd yelled a rude remark loudly.
4. He was <u>such</u> an <u>exciting</u> person that everyone felt <u>bad</u> when he left.
   Sample imitation: Susan is such an energetic woman that anyone seems lazy in comparison.
5. As the <u>Ferris</u> wheel <u>slowly</u> turned, raising him <u>higher</u> in the air, he became <u>increasingly</u> ill.
   Sample imitation: When the gray dog loudly barked, baring his teeth menacingly, I felt strangely unafraid.

ANSWERS: EXERCISE 2

1. I was <u>really</u> surprised when Martin and Emily bought a Thunderbird.
2. If you take your lessons more <u>seriously</u>, you will improve faster.
3. That perfume smelled <u>similar</u> to my mother's.
4. Sentence correct.
5. After playing <u>poorly</u> for six games, the hockey team finally had a game that went <u>well</u>.

Use the comparative and superlative forms of adjectives and adverbs appropriately.

Adjectives and adverbs can show different degrees of quality or amount with the endings *-er* and *-est* or with the words *more* and *most* (to compare upward) or *less* and *least* (to compare downward). Most modifiers have three forms. The **positive form** is the dictionary form and simply describes without comparing.

> a *big* book
> spoke *forcefully*

The **comparative form** compares the thing modified with one other thing.

> a *bigger* book
> spoke *more* (or *less*) *forcefully*

The **superlative form** compares the thing modified with two or more other things.

> the *biggest* book
> spoke *most* (or *least*) *forcefully*

 When word length or sound requires, use *more* and *most* instead of the endings *-er* and *-est*.

For downward comparisons, all adjectives and adverbs use *less* for the comparative (*less open*) and *least* for the superlative (*least successfully*). For upward comparisons, most one-syllable adjectives and adverbs and many two-syllable adjectives take the endings *-er* and *-est: red, redder, reddest; lucky, luckier, luckiest; fast, faster, fastest.*

Many two-syllable adjectives can either add *-er* and *-est* or use the words *more* and *most: steady, steadier* or *more steady, steadiest* or *most steady.* The use of *more* or *most* tends to draw the comparison out and so places more emphasis on it.

Using *more* and *most* is the only way to form the comparative and superlative for adjectives of three or more syllables and for most adverbs of two or more syllables (including nearly all ending in *-ly*): *beautiful, more beautiful, most beautiful; often, more often, most often; sadly, more sadly, most sadly.*

If you are in doubt about how to form a comparative or superlative, consult a dictionary. If the degrees can be formed with the endings *-er* and *-est,* the dictionary will give those forms. Otherwise, use *more* and *most.*

2 **Use the correct form of irregular adjectives and adverbs.**

The irregular modifiers change the spelling of their positive form to show comparative and superlative degrees.

DEGREES OF IRREGULAR ADJECTIVES AND ADVERBS

POSITIVE	COMPARATIVE	SUPERLATIVE
Adjectives		
good	better	best
bad	worse	worst
little	little, less	littlest, least
many ⎫		
some ⎬	more	most
much ⎭		
Adverbs		
well	better	best
badly	worse	worst

3 **Don't use double comparatives or double superlatives.**

A doubled comparative or superlative combines the *-er* or *-est* ending with the word *more, most, less,* or *least*. It is redundant and should be avoided.

He was the *wisest* (not *most wisest*) man I ever knew.
My sister gets privileges because she's *older* (not *more older*).

4 **In general, use the comparative form for comparing two things and the superlative form for comparing three or more things.**

She was the *taller* of the two girls. [Comparative.]
Of all those books, *The Yearling* is the *best*. [Superlative.]

In conversation the superlative form is often used even though only two things are being compared: *When two people argue, the angriest one is usually wrong.* But the distinction between the forms should be observed in writing.

HOMEMADE QUIZZES

Ask students to follow the pattern of the sample sentences and exercises in the chapter and make up sentences containing common errors in the use of adjectives and adverbs. The uses of *well* and *good, bad* and *badly* are good starters. Collect the papers and distribute them as quizzes during the next class. Correct them in small groups.

ANSWERS: EXERCISE 3

The sentences are sample answers.

1. badly, worse, worst
   The favored horse performed <u>badly</u> in the race. He performed <u>worse</u> than all but one other horse. The horse that performed <u>worst</u> broke stride and left the race.
2. great, greater, greatest
   A <u>great</u> tremor shook the earth. The tremor was <u>greater</u> than the earlier one. The <u>greatest</u> tremor was still to come.
3. lively, livelier, liveliest
   The children were <u>lively</u> yesterday. They are <u>livelier</u> today. The <u>liveliest</u> child sets the pattern for the others.
4. steady, steadier, steadiest
   The stool was not <u>steady</u>. It's <u>steadier</u> now that I've planed one leg. But it's still not the <u>steadiest</u> stool in the house.
5. some, more, most
   <u>Some</u> apples are in the basket.
   <u>More</u> apples are in the cooler.
   <u>Most</u> apples are red or green.
6. often, more often, most often
   We do not see our grandparents <u>often</u>. We would like to see them <u>more often</u>. <u>Most often</u>, we see our cousins.
7. good, better, best
   The fruit tasted <u>good</u>. The cheese tasted <u>better</u>. The chocolate pie tasted <u>best</u>.
8. well, better, best
   Julie did <u>well</u> on the test. Jack did <u>better</u> than Julie. Ellen did <u>best</u> of all.
9. elegant, more elegant, most elegant
   The Princess of Wales is an <u>elegant</u> woman. She is <u>more elegant</u> than the Queen. Of all the members of the Royal Family, she is the <u>most elegant</u>.
10. understanding, more understanding, most understanding
    Professor Najarian was <u>understanding</u> about my late paper. She was <u>more understanding</u> than I had expected. She must be the <u>most understanding</u> professor in the department.

5 **In general, don't use comparative or superlative forms for modifiers that cannot logically be compared.**

Adjectives and adverbs that cannot logically be compared include *perfect*, *unique*, *dead*, *impossible*, and *infinite*. These words are absolute; that is, they are not capable of greater or lesser degrees because their positive form describes their only state. Although they can be preceded by adverbs like *nearly* or *almost* that mean "approaching," they cannot logically be modified by *more*, *most*, *less*, or *least* (as in *most perfect*). This distinction is sometimes ignored in speech, but it should always be made in writing.

NOT	He was the *most unique* teacher we had.
BUT	He was a *unique* teacher.

EXERCISE 3

Write the comparative and superlative forms of each adjective or adverb below. Then use all three forms in sentences of your own.

Example:

heavy: heavier (comparative), heaviest (superlative)

The barbells were too *heavy* for me. The magician's trunk was *heavier* than I expected. Joe Clark was the *heaviest* person on the team.

1. badly
2. great
3. lively
4. steady
5. some
6. often
7. good
8. well
9. elegant
10. understanding

EXERCISE 4

Revise the following sentences so that the comparative and superlative forms of adjectives and adverbs are appropriate for formal usage.

Example:

Attending classes full-time and working at two jobs was the most impossible thing I ever did.

Attending classes full-time and working at two jobs was *impossible* (or *the hardest thing I ever did*).

1. Brad is the smallest of the two boys.
2. That is the most saddest story I have ever heard.
3. Of the two major problems with nuclear power plants—waste disposal and radiation leakage—radiation leakage is the most terrifying.
4. If I study hard, I should be able to do more better on the next economics test.

5. Working last summer as an assistant to my representative was one of the more unique experiences I have ever had.

9f   Avoid double negatives.

A **double negative** is a construction in which two negative words such as *no, none, neither, barely, hardly,* or *scarcely* cancel each other out. For instance, in *Jenny did not feel nothing,* the negatives *not* and *nothing* in essence produce a positive: the sentence asserts that Jenny felt other than nothing, or something. For the opposite meaning, one of the negatives must be eliminated or changed to a positive: *She felt nothing* or *She did not feel anything.*

FAULTY	We could *not hardly* hear the speaker. *None* of her ideas *never* made it to the back of the room.
REVISED	We could *hardly* hear the speaker. *None* of her ideas made it to the back of the room.
REVISED	We could *not* hear the speaker. Her ideas *never* made it to the back of the room.

9g   Avoid overuse of nouns as modifiers.

We often use one noun to modify another. For example:

father figure	slave trade	child care
flood control	truth serum	security guard

Carefully conceived, such phrases can be both clear and concise: *security guard* seems preferable to *guard responsible for security.* But overuse of noun modifiers can lead to flat, even senseless, writing. To avoid awkwardness or confusion, observe two principles. First, prefer possessives or adjectives as modifiers.

NOT	Glenn took the state medical *board* exams to become a *dentist* technician.
BUT	Glenn took the state medical *board's* exams to become a *dental* technician.

Second, use only short nouns as modifiers and use them only in two- or three-word sequences.

CONFUSING	Minimex maintains a *plant employee relations improvement program.*
REVISED	Minimex maintains a *program* for *improving relations* among *plant employees.*

ANSWERS: EXERCISE 4

1. Brad is the <u>smaller</u> of the two boys.
2. That is the <u>saddest</u> story I have ever heard.
3. Of the two major problems with nuclear power plants—waste disposal and radiation leakage—radiation leakage is the <u>more</u> terrifying.
4. If I study hard, I should be able to do <u>better</u> on the next economics test.
5. Working last summer as an assistant to my congressman was <u>a unique</u> experience.

ad
9g

CORRECTING ERRORS

Take an acceptable passage from a student paper, an essay in a reader, or a magazine article and rewrite it to introduce errors in the use of adjectives and adverbs. Distribute the passage to students and ask them to correct it. Then distribute the original version and ask students to comment on any differences between their corrections and the original version.

ANSWERS: EXERCISE 5

1. She batted <u>really</u> well this session, but she didn't field <u>well</u> enough to make the all-county team.
2. It was the <u>most</u> <u>nearly</u> <u>perfect</u> apartment we saw.
3. All three candidates claimed to be the <u>most</u> responsive.
4. Todd felt <u>strange</u> the next day, and he was sure his exam would go <u>badly</u>.
5. The cat stalked its prey <u>carefully</u> and <u>quietly</u>.
6. That argument sounds too illogical to take <u>seriously</u>.
7. The <u>university</u> <u>administration's</u> <u>policy</u> <u>on</u> <u>student</u> <u>absenteeism</u> was controversial.
8. Jerry could barely remember his older brother.
9. Sentence is correct.
10. One can buy a tape player <u>cheaply</u>, but the cheap players rarely work <u>well</u> or last long.

EXERCISE 5

Revise the following sentences so that they conform to formal usage of adjectives and adverbs as described in this chapter. If a sentence is already correct as given, circle the number preceding it.

Example:

Of the three books in the trilogy, the third is the better.
Of the three books in the trilogy, the third is the *best*.

1. She batted real well this season, but she didn't field good enough to make the all-county team.
2. It was the most totally perfect apartment we saw.
3. All three candidates claimed to be the more responsive.
4. Todd felt strangely the next day, and he was sure his exam would go bad.
5. The cat stalked its prey careful and quiet.
6. That argument sounds too illogical to take serious.
7. The university administration student absenteeism policy was controversial.
8. Jerry could not barely remember his older brother.
9. He remained firm, refusing to give in even though we asked him nicely.
10. One can buy a tape player cheap, but the cheap players rarely work good or last long.

PART III

Clear
Sentences

HIGHLIGHTS

This chapter opens with a positive approach, showing students how to test sentences for completeness, revise any fragments, and punctuate revised fragments. Following the opening section are discussions of particular structures that are often mispunctuated as complete sentences: subordinate clauses; verbal and prepositional phrases; and other word groups such as appositives, parts of compound predicates, and nouns plus modifiers. The chapter concludes with a discussion of the acceptable uses of incomplete sentences.

CHAPTER 10

Sentence Fragments

A **sentence fragment** is part of a sentence that is set off as if it were a whole sentence by an initial capital letter and a final period or other end punctuation. Unlike a complete sentence, a sentence fragment lacks a subject or a verb or both, or it is a subordinate clause not attached to a complete sentence.

FRAGMENT	The sign leaning against the wall. [The word group lacks a verb.]
FRAGMENT	Feeling sick. [The word group lacks both a subject and a verb.]
FRAGMENT	When it is time. [The word group is a subordinate clause.]

Although writers occasionally use fragments deliberately and effectively (see 10e), readers perceive most fragments as serious er-

---

COMPLETE SENTENCES VERSUS SENTENCE FRAGMENTS

A complete sentence

1. contains a subject and a verb (*Candy is* sweet);
2. *and* is not a subordinate clause (beginning with a subordinating conjunction such as *because* and *whereas* or a relative pronoun such as *who* and *that*).

A sentence fragment

1. lacks a verb (*The horse running away*);
2. *or* lacks a subject (*And ran away*);
3. *or* is a subordinate clause not attached to a complete sentence (*Because it was confused*).

---

rors because they are distracting or confusing. (Before proceeding with this chapter, you may find it helpful to review 5a and 5c on sentences and clauses.)

10a | **Test your sentences for completeness, and revise any fragments.**

The following three tests will help you determine whether a word group punctuated as a sentence is actually a complete sentence. If the word group does not pass *all three* tests, it is a fragment and needs to be revised.

RESOURCES AND IDEAS

Muriel Harris, "Mending the Fragmented Free Modifier," *College Composition and Communication* 32 (1981): 175–82. Harris presents strategies for identifying kinds of fragments and correcting them.

frag
10a

Test 1: Find a verb.

Look for a verb in the group of words. If you do not have one, the word group is a fragment.

> FRAGMENT   Four years of study and then graduation. [The group contains no verb. Compare a complete sentence: *Four years of study precede gradua-tion.*]

To function as the verb in a complete sentence, any verb form you find must be a **finite verb,** one that is capable of making an assertion without the aid of a helping verb. (See also 5c-2.) A finite verb changes form at least once to show the difference in present, past, and future time. Verbals such as *working* and *to work* do not change and thus are not finite verbs.

	FINITE VERBS	**VERBALS IN FRAGMENTS**
PRESENT	The riveters *work.*	The riveters *working.*
PAST	The riveters *worked.*	The riveters *working.*
FUTURE	The riveters *will work.*	The riveters *working.*

A finite verb in the present tense also changes form when the subject changes from singular to plural. A verbal does not.

	FINITE VERBS	**VERBALS IN FRAGMENTS**
SINGULAR	The riveter *works.*	The riveter *working.*
PLURAL	The riveters *work.*	The riveters *working.*

Fragments like those above require a change in the verbal or the addition of a helping verb to become complete sentences.

> FRAGMENT   The statue standing by the door [Compare a complete sentence: *The statue is* (or *was* or *will be*) *standing by the door.*]

FRAGMENT	The skies having darkened. [Compare a complete sentence: *The skies have* (or *had* or *will have*) *darkened.*]

Test 2: Find a subject.

If you find a finite verb, look for its subject by asking who or what performs the action or makes the assertion of the verb. The subject will usually come before the verb. If there is no subject, the word group is a fragment unless it is a command.

FRAGMENT	And closed the door quietly. [The word group lacks a subject and is not a command. Compare complete sentences: *And he closed the door quietly. And close the door quietly.*]

Test 3: Look for a subordinating word.

If you find a finite verb and its subject, look for a subordinating conjunction (*although, because, when,* and so on) or a relative pronoun (*who, whoever, which, that*). These words almost always signal subordinate clauses, which do not express complete, independent thoughts and must be attached to main clauses. (See 5c-4.)

FRAGMENT	As the plane lifted from the runway. [The word group contains a finite verb, *lifted*, and a subject, *plane*. But the subordinating conjunction *as* reduces the word group to a subordinate clause, so the thought is incomplete. Compare a complete sentence: *The plane lifted from the runway.*]
FRAGMENT	The plane that he had missed. [The word group contains two possible subjects, *plane* and *he*, and a finite verb, *had missed*. But the verb is in a subordinate clause beginning with *that*, so the thought about the plane is incomplete. Compare a complete sentence: *The plane that he had missed took off.*]

If the word group begins with *how, who, whom, whose, which, where, when, what,* or *why*—words that may introduce either subordinate clauses or questions—the group is a fragment unless it is attached to a complete main clause or asks a question.

FRAGMENT	When she goes to the office. [The word group contains a finite verb, *goes*, and a subject, *she*. But it begins with *when* and does not ask a question. Compare complete sentences: *She goes to the office. When does she go to the office?*]

frag
10a

NEWSCASTERS

The breathless style of radio and television newscasters often includes fragments. Ask students to write down examples from the evening news. Newpapers, especially tabloids, can be a good source, too.

Revising sentence fragments

Almost all sentence fragments can be corrected in one of two ways, the choice depending on the importance of the information in the fragment. First, the fragment can be made into a complete sentence. This method gives the information in the fragment the same importance as that in other complete sentences.

FRAGMENT	The baboon waited for his challenger. *Poised for combat.*
REVISED	The baboon waited for his challenger. *He was* poised for combat.
FRAGMENT	He stared at the woman. *Who had once been his wife.*
REVISED	He stared at the woman. *She* had once been his wife.

Once the fragment is corrected, it can be punctuated as a separate sentence (as in the preceding examples), or it can be separated from another main clause with a semicolon (see 22a).

FRAGMENT	She hesitated briefly. *Then blurted out her idea.*
REVISED	She hesitated briefly; then *she* blurted out her idea.

The second method of correcting a fragment is to combine it with a main clause. This method subordinates the information in the fragment to the information in the main clause.

FRAGMENT	The baboon waited for his challenger. *Poised for combat.*
REVISED	The baboon, poised for combat, waited for his challenger.

In this example, commas separate the inserted phrase from the rest of the sentence because the phrase does not restrict the meaning of any word in the main clause but simply adds information (see 21c). When a phrase or subordinate clause *does* restrict the meaning of a word in the main clause, a comma or commas do not separate the two elements.

FRAGMENT	He stared at the woman. *Who had once been his wife.*
REVISED	He stared at the woman who had once been his wife.

Sometimes a fragment may be combined with the main clause using a colon or a dash (see 25a and 25b, respectively).

FRAGMENT	His sculptures use four materials. *Wood, iron, plastic, and paper.*
REVISED	His sculptures use four materials: wood, iron, plastic, and paper.
FRAGMENT	*A shortage of money, the illness of her father, a fear of failure.* These were her reasons for dropping out of school.
REVISED	A shortage of money, the illness of her father, a fear of failure—these were her reasons for dropping out of school.

frag
10b

ANSWERS: EXERCISE 1

The sentences are sample answers.

1. Lacks a subject and a verb.
   Complete: An <u>article</u> about vandalism against works of art <u>was</u> interesting.
   Combined: In an interesting article about vandalism against works of art, <u>the author says the vandals' motives vary widely</u>.
2. Lacks a verb.
   Complete: The motives of the vandals <u>vary</u> widely.
   Combined: The motives of the vandals varying widely, researchers can make few generalizations.
3. Complete sentence.
4. Lacks a subject and a verb.
   Complete: But <u>the</u> <u>vandal</u> <u>is</u> not necessarily <u>angry</u> at the artist or the owner.
   Combined: <u>Whoever harms artwork is usually angry</u>, but not necessarily at the artist or the owner.
5. Lacks a verb for the subject <u>man</u>.
   Complete: For instance, <u>a man hammered at</u> Michelangelo's *Pietà*.
   Combined: For instance, a man who hammered at Michelangelo's *Pietà* was angry at the Roman Catholic Church.
6. Lacks a subject.
   Complete: <u>He</u> knocked off the Virgin Mary's nose.
   Combined: A man hammered at Mi-

EXERCISE 1

Apply the tests for completeness to each of the following word groups. If a word group is a complete sentence, circle the number preceding it. If it is a sentence fragment, revise it in two ways: by making it a complete sentence, and by combining it with a main clause written from the information given in other items.

> *Example:*
> And could not find his money.
>
> The word group has a verb (*could . . . find*) but no subject.
>
> Revised into a complete sentence: And *he* could not find his money.
>
> Combined with a new main clause: *He was lost* and could not find his money.

1. In an interesting article about vandalism against works of art.
2. The motives of the vandals varying widely.
3. Those who harm artwork are usually angry.
4. But not necessarily at the artist or the owner.
5. For instance, a man who hammered at Michelangelo's *Pietà*.
6. And knocked off the Virgin Mary's nose.
7. Because he was angry at the Roman Catholic Church.
8. Which knew nothing of his grievance.
9. Although many damaged works can be repaired.
10. Usually even the most skillful repairs are forever visible.

10b **Don't set off a subordinate clause as a sentence.**

Subordinate clauses contain both subjects and verbs, but they always begin with a subordinating conjunction (*although, because, if,* and so on) or a relative pronoun (*who, which, that*). (See

5c-4.) Subordinate clauses cannot stand alone as complete sentences.

To correct a subordinate clause set off as a sentence, combine it with the main clause or remove or change the subordinating word to create a main clause.

FRAGMENT	Many pine trees bear large cones. *Which appear in August.* [The fragment is a subordinate clause modifying *cones.*]
REVISED	Many pine trees bear large cones, which appear in August. [The subordinate clause is combined with the main clause.]
REVISED	Many pine trees bear large cones. They appear in August. [Substituting *They* for *Which* makes the fragment into a complete sentence.]
FRAGMENT	The decision seems fair. *Because it considers all parties.*
REVISED	The decision seems fair because it considers all parties.
REVISED	The decision seems fair. It considers all parties.

EXERCISE 2

Correct any sentence fragment below either by combining it with a main clause or by making it a main clause. If an item contains no sentence fragment, circle the number preceding it.

Example:

Jujitsu can be an excellent form of self-protection. Because it enables one to overcome an opponent without the use of weapons.

Jujitsu can be an excellent form of self-protection because it enables one to overcome an opponent without the use of weapons.

1. In the nineteenth century chemists began synthesizing perfume oils. Which previously could be made only from natural sources.
2. After Medieval Crusaders returned from the East. European perfumers began using animal oils as well as plant oils in their mixtures.
3. The most popular animal oil for perfume today is musk. Although some people dislike its heavy, sweet odor.
4. Musk oil goes a long way. Because of its pungency very little is needed to make a strong perfume.
5. Synthetic musk oil would help conserve a certain species of deer. Whose gland is the source of musk.

chelangelo's *Pietà* and knocked off the Virgin Mary's nose.
7. Begins with subordinating conjunction.
Complete: He was angry at the Roman Catholic Church.
Combined: A man hammered at Michelangelo's *Pietà* because he was angry at the Roman Catholic Church.
8. Begins with which but is not a question.
Complete: The Church knew nothing of his grievance.
Combined: He was angry at the Roman Catholic Church, which knew nothing of his grievance.
9. Begins with subordinating conjunction.
Complete: Many damaged works can be repaired.
Combined: Although many damaged works can be repaired, even the most skillful repairs are forever visible.
10. Complete sentence.

frag
10b

POSSIBLE ANSWERS: EXERCISE 2

1. In the nineteenth century chemists began synthesizing perfume oils, which previously could be made only from natural sources.
2. After Medieval Crusaders returned from the East, European perfumers began using animal oils as well as plant oils in their mixtures.
3. The most popular animal oil for perfume today is musk, although some people dislike its heavy, sweet odor.
4. No sentence fragment.
5. Synthetic musk oil would preserve a certain species of deer whose gland is the source of musk.

10c Don't set off a verbal phrase or a prepositional phrase as a sentence.

A **verbal phrase** consists of an infinitive (*to choose*), a past participle (*chosen*), or a present participle or gerund (*choosing*) together with any objects and modifiers it may have (see 5c-2). Verbal phrases cannot serve as the verbs in complete sentences. Fragments consisting of verbal phrases are most easily corrected by combining them with the main clauses they are related to. Verbal phrases can be converted into main clauses only by rewriting.

FRAGMENT	He backed closer and closer to the end of the diving board. *At last falling into the water.*
REVISED	He backed closer and closer to the end of the diving board, at last falling into the water. [The phrase is combined with the main clause.]
REVISED	He backed closer and closer to the end of the diving board. At last *he fell* into the water. [The phrase is made into a complete sentence by changing *falling* to the verb *fell* and by adding the subject *he*.]

A **prepositional phrase** consists of a preposition (such as *in*, *on*, *to*, and *with*) together with its object and modifier (see 5c-1). A prepositional phrase cannot stand alone as a complete sentence. It may be combined with a main clause or rewritten as a main clause.

FRAGMENT	More than anything else, I wanted to get away from the heat. *To someplace cooler.*
REVISED	More than anything else, I wanted to get away from the heat to someplace cooler. [The phrase is combined with the main clause.]
REVISED	More than anything else, I wanted to get away from the heat. *I longed for* someplace cooler. [With a new subject and verb, *I longed for*, the phrase becomes a complete sentence.]

CREATING PROBLEMS

If students have been assigned Chapter 11, "Comma Splices and Fused Sentences," along with this chapter, ask them to write sample sentences containing fused sentences, comma splices, and fragments. Then have them exchange papers and check to see if the errors have been executed properly. This exercise will help students recognize fused sentences, comma splices, and fragments. (It's much harder to create intentional errors, particularly sentence fragments than most students will think.)

POSSIBLE ANSWERS: EXERCISE 3

1. Deliberately scenting the <u>air is</u> a behavior that originated in prehistory.
2. Some sources say that the custom arose as an attempt to cover up the smell of burning fles<u>h d</u>uring sacrifices to the gods.
3. The sacred use of perfume survive<u>s in</u> the incense burned during religious services.

EXERCISE 3

Correct any sentence fragment below either by combining it with a main clause or by rewriting it as a main clause. If an item contains no sentence fragment, circle the number preceding it.

Example:
A hobby can contribute to a fulfilling life. Engaging one in activities outside work.
A hobby can contribute to a fulfilling life, engaging one in activities outside work.

1. Deliberately scenting the air. It is a behavior that originated in prehistory.
2. Some sources say that the custom arose as an attempt to cover up the smell of burning flesh. During sacrifices to the gods.
3. The sacred use of perfume survives. In the incense burned during religious services.
4. Perfumes became religious offerings in their own right. Being expensive to make, they were highly prized.
5. The earliest historical documents from the Middle East record the use of fragrances. Not only in religious ceremonies but on the body.
6. The Egyptians, Greeks, and Romans used fragrance extravagantly. Applying different scents to hair, arms, feet, and clothing.
7. To smell like several open perfume bottles. This was apparently desirable in earlier centuries.
8. The interest in perfume fell with Rome. For hundreds of years the Catholic Church forbade personal use of fragrance.
9. The Crusaders returned to Europe between the eleventh and fourteenth centuries. Bearing exotic scents from the Near and Far East.
10. Spreading rapidly throughout the continent. Perfume once again adorned human bodies.

4. No sentence fragment.
5. The earliest historical documents from the Middle East record the use of fragrances, _not_ only in religious ceremonies but on the body.
6. The Egyptians, Greeks, and Romans used fragrance extravagant<u>ly,</u> applying different scents to hair, arms, feet, and clothing.
7. To smell like several open perfume <u>bottles was</u> apparently desirable in earlier centuries. OR: To smell like several open perfume <u>bottles—this</u> was apparently desirable in earlier centuries.
8. No sentence fragment.
9. The Crusaders returned to Europe between the eleventh and fourteenth centuries<u> bearing</u> exotic scents from the Near and Far East.
10. Spreading rapidly throughout the continent,<u> perfume</u> once again adorned human bodies.

frag
10d

10d

 Don't set off any other word group as a sentence if it lacks a subject or a verb or both.

Besides subordinate clauses and verbal and prepositional phrases, several other word groups are often mistakenly punctuated as complete sentences—especially nouns plus their modifiers, appositives, and parts of compound predicates.

We often follow a noun with a phrase or subordinate clause that modifies the noun. No matter how long the noun and its modifier are, they cannot stand alone as a sentence.

FRAGMENTS	*People waving flags and cheering. Lined the streets for the parade.*
REVISED	People waving flags and cheering lined the streets for the parade. [The two fragments are combined into one sentence.]
FRAGMENT	*Veterans who fought in Vietnam.* They are finally being honored.
REVISED	Veterans who fought in Vietnam are finally being honored. [The fragment replaces *They* as the modified subject of the main clause.]

ADVERTISING

Advertisements and public announcements frequently contain fragments, fused sentences, and comma splices. In fact, some people speculate that this incidence may be one source of problems in student writing. Ask students to read Chapters 10 and 11 carefully. Then collect examples from magazine ads, junk mail, signs, and similar sources, and ask students to spot and correct the errors. Here are two examples, the first from an advertisement, the second from a hotel restaurant's menu.

Introducing the Satellite
News Channel.
The first all-live, all-news TV channel.
News with no fillers. No reruns. No nonsense. No fat.
  SNC is live-action news, delivered fresh every 18 minutes. Powered by the worldwide resources of ABC Television and Group W. Broadcasting. With the depth of 24 award-winning regional news teams.
  Available 24-hours a day. Seven days a week.

Picnic Lunch Available
Please give your order 1 hour in advance. Before 10:00 A.M. Good Morning we hope you will have a pleasant day.

This activity is particularly effective in groups because some students may wish to argue that the fragments they find are used appropriately, while others will insist on a strict interpretation of the rules they find in the handbook. The ensuing discussion is likely to be worthwhile, particularly if it touches on the importance of rhetorical context and convention in determining punctuation rules.

Appositives are nouns, or nouns and their modifiers, which rename or describe other nouns (see 5c-5). They cannot stand alone as sentences.

FRAGMENT	When I was a child, my favorite adult was an old uncle. *A retired sea captain who always told me long stories of wild adventures in faraway places.*
REVISED	When I was a child, my favorite adult was an old uncle, a retired sea captain who always told me long stories of wild adventures in faraway places. [The appositive is combined with the main clause.]

Compound predicates are predicates made up of two or more verbs and their objects, if any. A verb or its object cannot stand alone as a sentence.

FRAGMENT	Pat worked all day. *And danced at night.*
REVISED	Pat worked all day and danced at night. [The fragment, part of the compound predicate *worked . . . and danced*, is combined with the main clause.]
FRAGMENT	If his friends were in trouble, Henry always offered them much advice. *But no real help.*
REVISED	If his friends were in trouble, Henry always offered them much advice but no real help. [The fragment, part of the compound object of *offered*, is combined with the main clause.]

NOTE: Beginning a sentence with a coordinating conjunction such as *and* and *but* can lead to a sentence fragment. Check every sentence you begin with a coordinating conjunction to be sure it is complete.

POSSIBLE ANSWERS: EXERCISE 4

1. Human beings who perfume themselves are not much different from other animals.
2. Animals as varied as insects and dogs release pheromones, chemicals that signal other animals.
3. No sentence fragment.
4. Human beings have a diminished sense of smell and do not consciously detect most of their own species' pheromones.
5. The human substitute for pheromones

EXERCISE 4

Correct any sentence fragment below either by combining it with a main clause or by rewriting it as a main clause. If an item contains no sentence fragment, circle the number preceding it.

Example:

Lynn graduated from college in 1983. But did not begin working until 1985.

Lynn graduated from college in 1983 but did not begin working until 1985.

Lynn graduated from college in 1983. But *she* did not begin working until 1985.

1. Human beings who perfume themselves. They are not much different from other animals.
2. Animals as varied as insects and dogs release *pheromones*. Chemicals that signal other animals.
3. The chemicals sometimes repel other animals. But more often they perform a sexual function by attracting a member of the opposite sex.
4. Human beings have a diminished sense of smell. And do not consciously detect most of their own species' pheromones.
5. The human substitute for pheromones may be perfumes. Especially musk and other fragrances derived from animal oils.

may be perfumes, especially musk and other fragrances derived from animal oils.

10e   Be aware of the acceptable uses of incomplete sentences.

A few word groups lacking the usual subject-predicate combination are incomplete sentences, but they are not fragments because they conform to the expectations of most readers. They include exclamations (*Oh no!*); questions and answers (*Where next? To Kansas.*); and commands (*Move along. Shut the window.*). Exclamations and questions and answers occur most often in speech or in writing that records speech; commands occur in speech and in written directions. Another kind of incomplete sentence, which occurs in special situations, is the transitional phrase (*So much for the causes, now for the results. One final point.*).

Professional writers sometimes use incomplete sentences that *are* sentence fragments when they want to achieve a special effect. Such fragments appear more in informal than in formal writing. Unless you are experienced and thoroughly secure in your own writing, you should avoid all fragments and concentrate on writing clear, well-formed sentences.

RESOURCES AND IDEAS

Charles R. Kline, Jr., and W. Dean Memering, "Formal Fragments: The English Minor Sentence," *Research in the Teaching of English* 11 (1977): 97–110. The authors identify the kinds of fragments (minor sentences) often used and considered acceptable in formal writing.

POSSIBLE ANSWERS: EXERCISE 5

1. The President came to town. Secret Service men were everywhere.
2. They concealed themselves in the woods. The woods surrounded the outdoor theater where the President was to speak.
3. They stopped pedestrians to question them. They even frisked them.
4. They were suspicious-looking in dark glasses and sober suits. They stood erect on street corners.

EXERCISE 5

Break each of the following sentences at the vertical line, and then add, delete, or change words and punctuation as necessary to produce two *complete* sentences.

Example:

Classes may not resume after vacation | because the school has run out of money.

Classes may not resume after vacation. The school has run out of money.

5. Their presence gave a sinister cast to the event. It was supposed to be a celebration.

1. When the President came to town, | Secret Service agents were everywhere.
2. They concealed themselves in the woods | surrounding the outdoor theater where the President was to speak.
3. They stopped pedestrians to question them | and even to frisk them.
4. Suspicious-looking in dark glasses and sober suits, | they stood erect on street corners.
5. Their presence gave a sinister cast to the event, | which was supposed to be a celebration.

ANSWERS: EXERCISE 6

Possible Revision

Hiring Steele as manager of the baseball team was a stupid move_or a very clever maneuver, depending on whether one is thinking like a fan or like the team's owner. Fans claim it was stupid because Steele is hard to get along with and unfair. They say he is also a poor manager, failing to make the best use of the team's talents_and creating friction among the players. But the team's owner may have had a good reason for hiring such a manager. Some people think the owner hired Steele only temporarily_in order to make the team less attractive to unfriendly buyers_who have been threatening a hostile takeover of the team. Hiring Steele could have been intended to prevent the takeover_and in the long run save the team, not ruin it.

EXERCISE 6

Revise the following paragraph to eliminate sentence fragments by combining them with main clauses or rewriting them as main clauses.

Hiring Steele as the manager of the baseball team was a stupid move. Or a very clever maneuver. Depending on whether one is thinking like a fan or like the team's owner. Fans claim it was stupid. Because Steele is hard to get along with and unfair. They say he is also a poor manager. Failing to make the best use of the team's talents. And creating friction among the players. But the team's owner may have had a good reason for hiring such a manager. Some people think the owner hired Steele only temporarily. In order to make the team less attractive to unfriendly buyers. Who have been threatening a hostile takeover of the team. Hiring Steele could have been intended to prevent the takeover. And in the long run save the team. Not ruin it.

frag
10

CHAPTER 11

Comma Splices and Fused Sentences

HIGHLIGHTS

This chapter begins with a summary of the accepted methods for punctuating consecutive main clauses and follows with advice for recognizing and correcting comma splices and fused sentences. Correction of comma splices and fused sentences may involve strategies that students should employ more frequently in their sentences, particularly subordination and use of the semicolon. To encourage variety in sentence structure along with the avoidance of error, exercises for the chapter ask students to combine sentences following different strategies as well as to recognize and revise comma splices and fused sentences.

When two or more main clauses appear consecutively, readers expect them to be clearly separated from each other in one of four ways:

1. With a period:

   The ship was huge. Its mast stood thirty feet high.

2. With a semicolon:

   The ship was huge; its mast stood thirty feet high.

3. With a comma preceding a coordinating conjunction that joins the clauses and specifies the relation between them:

   The ship was huge, *and* its mast stood thirty feet high.

4. Occasionally with a colon when the second clause explains the first (see 25a):

   The ship was huge: its mast stood thirty feet high.

Two problems commonly occur in punctuating consecutive main clauses. One is the **comma splice,** in which the clauses are joined (or spliced) *only* with a comma instead of a comma and coordinating conjunction or instead of a period, semicolon, or colon.

COMMA SPLICE

The ship was huge, its mast stood thirty feet high.

The other problem is the **fused sentence** (also called a **run-on sentence**), in which no punctuation or coordinating conjunction appears between the clauses.

FUSED SENTENCE

The ship was huge its mast stood thirty feet high.

RESOURCES AND IDEAS

Teachers and tutors who have little trouble punctuating sentences themselves may find it difficult to understand why some students have such difficulty with punctuation. In *The Practical Tutor* (New York: Oxford UP, 1987, 177–201), Emily Meyer and Louise Z. Smith offer detailed explanations of the causes of error and advice for diagnosing the roots of a student's punctuation difficulties. The teaching strategies they suggest include reading aloud, reading unpunctuated passages, asking probing questions (examples provided), and using simple diagrams.

CS

11a

SITUATIONS THAT MAY PRODUCE COMMA SPLICES AND FUSED SENTENCES

1. Balanced negative and positive clauses:

SPLICE	Mary is not a nurse, she is a doctor.
REVISED	Mary is not a nurse; she is a doctor.

2. Amplification or illustration in the second clause:

FUSED	She did well in college she had a 3.9 average.
REVISED	She did well in college; she had a 3.9 average.

3. Conjunctive adverb in the second clause (see 11b):

SPLICE	She had intended to become a biologist, *however*, she switched to premed.
REVISED	She had intended to become a biologist; *however*, she switched to premed.

4. Same subject in both clauses:

FUSED	*Mary* is an internist *she* practices in Topeka.
REVISED	*Mary* is an internist. *She* practices in Topeka.

5. An attempt to link related ideas or smooth choppy sentences:

SPLICE	She is very committed to her work, she devotes almost all her time to patient care.
REVISED	*Because* she is very committed to her work, she devotes almost all her time to patient care.

Like sentence fragments (see Chapter 10), comma splices and fused sentences are serious errors because they generally force the reader to reread for sense.

COMMA SPLICES

 Separate two main clauses with a comma *only* when they are joined by a coordinating conjunction.

A comma cannot separate main clauses unless they are linked by a coordinating conjunction (*and, but, or, nor, for, so, yet*). Readers expect the same sentence to continue after a comma.

When they find themselves reading a second sentence before they realize they have finished the first, they may have to reread to understand the writer's meaning.

COMMA SPLICE   Rain had fallen steadily for sixteen hours, many basements were flooded.

COMMA SPLICE   Cars would not start, many people were late to work.

EXCEPTION: Experienced writers sometimes use commas between very brief main clauses that are grammatically parallel.

He's not a person, he's a monster.

However, many readers view such punctuation as incorrect. Unless you are certain that your readers will not object to the comma in a sentence like this one, separate the clauses with periods or semicolons, as described below.

You have four main options for correcting a comma splice. The option you choose depends on the relation you want to establish between the clauses.

cs
11a

REVISING COMMA SPLICES

1. Make the clauses into separate sentences.
2. Insert an appropriate coordinating conjunction after the comma between clauses.
3. Insert a semicolon between clauses.
4. Subordinate one clause to the other.

Making separate sentences

Revising a comma splice by making separate sentences from the main clauses will always be correct.

Rain had fallen steadily for sixteen hours. Many basements were flooded.

The period is not only correct but preferable if the ideas expressed in the two main clauses are only loosely related.

COMMA SPLICE   Chemistry has contributed much to our understanding of foods, many foods such as wheat and beans can be produced in the laboratory.

REVISED   Chemistry has contributed much to our understanding of foods. Many foods such as wheat and beans can be produced in the laboratory.

RESOURCES AND IDEAS

Betty Bamberg, "Periods Are Basic: A Strategy for Eliminating Comma Faults and Run-On Sentences," in *Teaching the Basics—Really!* ed. Ouida Clapp (Urbana: NCTE, 1977), 97–99. Bamberg suggests using oral reading to identify and correct problems.

Inserting a coordinating conjunction

When the ideas in the main clauses are closely related and equally important, you may choose to correct a comma splice by inserting the appropriate coordinating conjunction immediately after the comma to join the clauses.

Cars would not start, *and* many people were late to work.

COMMA SPLICE	He had intended to work all weekend, his friends arrived Friday and stayed until Sunday.
REVISED	He had intended to work all weekend, *but* his friends arrived Friday and stayed until Sunday.

Notice that the relation indicated by a coordinating conjunction can be complementary (*and*), contradictory (*but, yet*), causal (*for, so*), or alternate (*or, nor*).

Many people were late to work, *for* cars would not start.

People were late to work, *or* they stayed home to pump out flooded basements.

Using a semicolon

If the relation between the ideas expressed in the main clauses is very close and obvious without a conjunction, you can separate the clauses with a semicolon. (See also 11b.)

Rain had fallen steadily for sixteen hours; many basements were flooded.

COMMA SPLICE	Rhoda and Nate were more than close friends, they were inseparable.
REVISED	Rhoda and Nate were more than close friends; they were inseparable.

Subordinating one clause

When the idea in one clause is more important than that in the other, you can express the less important idea in a phrase or a subordinate clause. (See p. 184 for a list of subordinating conjunctions.)

After rain had fallen steadily for sixteen hours, many basements were flooded. [The addition of the subordinating conjunction *After* reduces the first sentence to a subordinate clause indicating time.]

After sixteen hours of steady rain, many basements were flooded. [The clause is reduced to a prepositional phrase.]

Subordination is often more effective than forming separate sentences because it defines the relation between ideas more precisely.

COMMA SPLICE	The examination was finally over, Becky felt free to enjoy herself once more.
REVISED	The examination was finally over. Becky felt free to enjoy herself once more. [Both ideas receive equal weight.]
IMPROVED	*When* the examination was finally over, Becky felt free to enjoy herself once more. [Emphasis on the second idea.]
COMMA SPLICE	The house was for sale, the price was reasonable.
REVISED	The house was for sale. The price was reasonable.
IMPROVED	The house was for sale at a reasonable price.

^{CS}

11b

11b Use a period or semicolon to separate main clauses related by conjunctive adverbs.

Conjunctive adverbs are modifiers such as *consequently, however, nevertheless, then,* and *therefore* (see p. 193 for a more complete list). Conjunctive adverbs frequently relate main clauses, and then the clauses must be separated by a period (forming two separate sentences) or by a semicolon (see 22b). The adverb is also generally set off by a comma or commas.

COMMA SPLICE	Most Americans refuse to give up unhealthful habits, consequently our medical costs are higher than those of many other countries.
REVISED	Most Americans refuse to give up unhealthful habits. Consequently, our medical costs are higher than those of many other countries.
REVISED	Most Americans refuse to give up unhealthful habits; consequently, our medical costs are higher than those of many other countries.

Unlike coordinating and subordinating conjunctions, conjunctive adverbs do not join two clauses into a grammatical unit but merely describe the way the clauses relate in meaning. Also unlike conjunctions, which must be placed between the word groups they join (coordinating) or at the beginning of the word group they introduce (subordinating), conjunctive adverbs may usually be moved from one place to another in the clause (see 5d-2). No mat-

CREATING PROBLEMS

If students have been assigned Chapter 10, "Sentence Fragments," along with this chapter, ask them to write sample sentences containing comma splices, fused sentences, and fragments. Then have them exchange papers and check to see if the errors have been executed properly. This exercise will help students recognize comma splices, fused sentences, and fragments. (It's much harder to create intentional errors, particularly fused sentences and sentence fragments, than most students will think.)

ter where in the clause a conjunctive adverb appears, however, the clause must be separated from another main clause by a period or a semicolon.

COMMA SPLICE

The increased time devoted to watching television is not the only cause of the decline in reading ability, it is one of the important causes.

COMMA AND COORDINATING CONJUNCTION

The increased time devoted to watching television is not the only cause of the decline in reading ability, *but* it is one of the important causes.

SUBORDINATING CONJUNCTION

Although the increased time devoted to watching television is not the only cause of the decline in reading ability, it is one of the important causes.

PERIOD AND CONJUNCTIVE ADVERB

The increased time devoted to watching television is not the only cause of the decline in reading ability. *However,* it is one of the important causes.

SEMICOLON AND CONJUNCTIVE ADVERB

The increased time devoted to watching television is not the only cause of the decline in reading ability; *however,* it is one of the important causes.

The increased time devoted to watching television is not the only cause of the decline in reading ability; it is, *however,* one of the important causes.

The increased time devoted to watching television is not the only cause of the decline in reading ability; it is one of the important causes, *however.*

CS

11b

IN CONTEXT

Identifying sentence problems in the context of an essay can be more challenging and rewarding than working with single-sentence examples. The content and flow of an essay can draw attention away from punctuation and sentence structure, making it hard to identify errors but also providing an experience similar to that of proofreading. To supplement the paragraph exercise at the end of this chapter (or at the end of Chapter 10), revise part of a professional essay to introduce errors (or find an error-filled student essay), and then distribute the essay to the class, asking students to locate and revise the errors.

POSSIBLE ANSWERS: EXERCISE 1

1. Money has a long history. It goes back at least as far as the earliest records. Money has a long history that goes back at least as far as the earliest records.
2. Many of the earliest records concern financial transactions; indeed, early history must often be inferred from commercial activity.
   Many of the earliest records concern financial transactions. Indeed, early history must often be inferred from commercial activity.
3. No comma splice.

EXERCISE 1

Correct each comma splice below in *two* of the following ways: make separate sentences of the main clauses; insert an appropriate coordinating conjunction after the comma; substitute a semicolon for the incorrect comma; or subordinate one clause to another. If an item contains no comma splice, circle the number preceding it.

Example:

Carolyn still had a headache, she could not get the childproof cap off the aspirin bottle.

> Carolyn still had a headache because she could not get the child-proof cap off the aspirin bottle. [Subordination.]
>
> Carolyn still had a headache, for she could not get the child-proof cap off the aspirin bottle. [Coordinating conjunction.]

1. Money has a long history, it goes back at least as far as the earliest records.
2. Many of the earliest records concern financial transactions, indeed, early history must often be inferred from commercial activity.
3. Every known society has had a system of money, though the objects serving as money have varied widely.
4. Sometimes the objects have had real value, in modern times, however, their value has been more abstract.
5. Cattle, fermented beverages, and rare shells have served as money, each one had actual value for the society.
6. As money, however, these objects acquired additional value because they represented other goods.
7. Today money may be made of worthless paper, it may even consist of a bit of data in a computer's memory.
8. We think of money as valuable, only our common faith in it makes it valuable.
9. That faith is sometimes fragile, consequently, currencies themselves are fragile.
10. Economic crises often shake the belief in money, such weakened faith helped cause the Great Depression of the 1930s.

FUSED SENTENCES

 11c **Don't combine two main clauses without using an appropriate connector or punctuation mark between them.**

When two main clauses are joined without a word to connect them or a punctuation mark to separate them, the result is a **fused sentence**, sometimes called a **run-on sentence.** Fused sentences can rarely be understood on first reading, and they are never acceptable in standard written English.

> **Fused**   Many people would be lost without television they would not know how to amuse themselves.
>
> **Fused**   Our foreign policy is not well defined it confuses many countries.

Fused sentences may be corrected in the same ways as comma splices (see 11a).

4. Sometimes the objects have had real value. In modern times, however, their value has been more abstract.
   Sometimes the objects have had real value; in modern times, however, their value has been more abstract.
5. Cattle, fermented beverages, and rare shells have served as money, and each one had actual value for the society.
   Cattle, fermented beverages, and rare shells have served as money. Each one had actual value for the society.
6. No comma splice.
7. Today money may be made of worthless paper; it may even consist of a bit of data in a computer's memory.
   Today money may be made of worthless paper. It may even consist of a bit of data in a computer's memory.
8. Although we think of money as valuable, only our common faith in it makes it valuable.
   We think of money as valuable, but only our common faith in it makes it valuable.
9. That faith is sometimes fragile; consequently, currencies themselves are valuable.
   That faith is sometimes fragile. Consequently, currencies themselves are valuable.
10. Economic crises often shake the belief in money. Such weakened faith helped cause the Great Depression of the 1930s.
    Economic crises often shake the belief in money; such weakened faith helped cause the Great Depression of the 1930s.

fs
11c

NEWSCASTERS
The breathless style of radio and television newscasters often includes groups of words that sound like fused sentences. Ask students to write down examples from the evening news. Newspapers, especially tabloids, can be a good source, too. (This activity also works well for sentence fragments.)

REVISING FUSED SENTENCES
1. Make the clauses into separate sentences.
2. Insert a comma and an appropriate coordinating conjunction between clauses.
3. Insert a semicolon between clauses.
4. Subordinate one clause to the other.

POSSIBLE ANSWERS: EXERCISE 2

1. Throughout history money and religion were closely linked <u>because</u> there was little distinction between government and religion.

   Throughout history money and religion were closely linked; <u>for</u> there was little distinction between government and religion.

2. The head of state and the religious leader were often the same person<u>. All</u> power rested in one ruler.

   The head of state and the religious leader were often the same person<u>; all</u> power rested in one ruler.

3. These powerful leaders decided what objects would serve as money<u>, and</u> their backing encouraged public faith in the money.

   These powerful leaders decided what objects would serve as money<u>. Their</u> backing encouraged public faith in the money.

4. <u>When</u> coins were minted of precious metals, the religious overtones of money were then strengthened.

   Coins were minted of precious metals<u>.</u> The religious overtones of money were then strengthened.

5. People already believed the precious metals to be divine<u>, so</u> their use in money intensified its allure.

   People already believed the precious metals to be divine<u>;</u> their use in money intensified its allure.

POSSIBLE ANSWERS: EXERCISE 3

1. The exact origin of paper money is unknown <u>because</u> <u>it</u> has not survived as coins, shells, and other durable objects have.

2. Scholars disagree over where paper

SEPARATE SENTENCES

Our foreign policy is not well defined. It confuses many countries. [The two main clauses are made into separate sentences.]

COMMA AND COORDINATING CONJUNCTION

Our foreign policy is not well defined, *and* it confuses many countries. [The two main clauses are separated by a comma and a coordinating conjunction.]

SEMICOLON

Our foreign policy is not well defined; it confuses many countries. [The two main clauses are separated by a semicolon.]

SUBORDINATING CONJUNCTION

Because our foreign policy is not well defined, it confuses many countries. [*Because* subordinates the first clause to the second.]

EXERCISE 2

Revise each of the fused sentences below in *two* of the four ways shown above.

Example:

Tim was shy he usually refused invitations.
Tim was shy, *so* he usually refused invitations.
Tim was shy; he usually refused invitations.

1. Throughout history money and religion were closely linked there was little distinction between government and religion.
2. The head of state and the religious leader were often the same person all power rested in one ruler.
3. These powerful leaders decided what objects would serve as money their backing encouraged public faith in the money.
4. Coins were minted of precious metals the religious overtones of money were then strengthened.
5. People already believed the precious metals to be divine their use in money intensified its allure.

EXERCISE 3

Combine each pair of sentences below into one sentence without creating comma splices or fused sentences. Combine sentences by supplying a comma and coordinating conjunction, supplying a semicolon, or subordinating one clause to the other. You will have to add, delete, or change words as well as punctuation.

Example:

The sun sank lower in the sky. The colors gradually faded.

As the sun sank lower in the sky, the colors gradually faded. [The first clause is subordinated to the second.]

1. The exact origin of paper money is unknown. It has not survived as coins, shells, and other durable objects have.
2. Scholars disagree over where paper money originated. Many scholars believe it was first used in Europe, however.
3. Perhaps goldsmiths were also bankers. Thus they held the gold of their wealthy customers.
4. The goldsmiths probably gave customers receipts for their gold. These receipts were then used in trade.
5. The goldsmiths were something like modern-day bankers. Their receipts were something like modern-day money.
6. The goldsmiths became even more like modern-day bankers. They began issuing receipts for more gold than they actually held in their vaults.
7. Today's bankers owe more to their customers than they actually have in reserve. They keep enough assets on hand to meet reasonable withdrawals.
8. In economic crises bank customers sometimes fear the loss of their money. Consequently, they demand their deposits.
9. Depositors' demands may exceed a bank's reserves. The bank may collapse.
10. The government now regulates banks to protect depositors. Bank failures are less frequent than they once were.

EXERCISE 4

Identify and revise the comma splices and fused sentences in the following paragraph.

A good way to meet new people during the summer is to take evening courses, many colleges, high schools, and adult-education centers offer them. They attract different kinds of people who share common interests. Last summer in my woodworking class I met a woman who was also interested in colonial chairs we have been touring antique shows ever since. This summer in my singing class I met several people who enjoy country music as much as I do, we have gone to numerous concerts together, we are planning a trip to Nashville. If I had not attended evening classes, I would not have met these new friends, they have enriched my life.

cs, fs
11c

money originated; many scholars believe it was first used in Europe, however.
3. Perhaps goldsmiths were also bankers; thus they held the gold of their wealthy customers.
4. The goldsmiths probably gave customers receipts for their gold; and these receipts were then used in trade.
5. The goldsmiths were something like modern-day bankers; their receipts were something like modern-day money.
6. The goldsmiths became even more like modern-day bankers when they began issuing receipts for more gold than they actually held in their vaults.
7. Today's bankers owe more to their customers than they actually have in reserve, but they keep enough assets on hand to meet reasonable withdrawals.
8. In economic crises bank customers sometimes fear the loss of their money; consequently, they demand their deposits.
9. If depositors' demands exceed a bank's reserves, the bank may collapse.
10. The government now regulates banks to protect depositors, so bank failures are less frequent than they once were.

ANSWERS: EXERCISE 4

Possible Revision

A good way to meet new people during the summer is to take evening courses. Many colleges, high schools, and adult-education centers offer them. They attract different kinds of people who share common interests. Last summer in my woodworking class I met a woman who was also interested in colonial chairs. We have been touring antique shows ever since. This summer in my singing class I met several people who enjoy country music as much as I do. We have gone to numerous concerts together, and we are planning a trip to Nashville. If I had not attended evening classes, I would not have met these new friends. They have enriched my life.

HIGHLIGHTS

Writers at all levels—advanced or struggling—will be likely to consult this chapter often, for problems with pronoun reference can arise in short, uncomplicated sentences as well as in papers that are ambitious in style and content. The discussion covers a number of particularly troublesome problems: unclear or ambiguous antecedents; broad reference with *this, that, which,* and *it;* indefinite use of *it* and *they;* and inappropriate use of *who, which,* and *that.* In each case, the discussion stresses the need for precision in reference as a way of ensuring that readers can follow the meaning of a passage. The examples and exercises mostly show reference problems within sentences as a way of keeping the discussion as simple and accessible as possible; however, the text points out that reference problems are just as likely to occur between sentences, and the paragraph exercise at the end of the chapter stresses this fact. Because strings of pronouns are an important device for creating coherence over long stretches of discourse, reference problems between or among sentences can cause considerable misunderstanding.

CHAPTER 12

Pronoun Reference

A **pronoun** such as *it* or *they* derives its meaning from its **antecedent,** the noun it substitutes for. Therefore, a pronoun must refer clearly and unmistakably to its antecedent in order for the sentence containing the pronoun to be clear. A sentence such as *Jim told Mark he was not invited* is not clear because the reader does not know whether *he* refers to Jim or to Mark.

Whether a pronoun and its antecedent appear in the same sentence or in adjacent sentences, you should be certain their relation is clear. One way to achieve clarity is to ensure that pronoun and antecedent agree in person and number (see 8b). The other way is to ensure that the pronoun refers unambiguously to a single, close, specific antecedent.

12a Make a pronoun refer clearly to one antecedent.

A pronoun may, of course, refer to two or more nouns in a compound antecedent, as in *Jenkins and Wilson pooled their resources and became partners.* But when either of two nouns can be a pronoun's antecedent, the reference will not be clear.

CONFUSING	The men removed all the furniture from the room and cleaned *it.* [Does *it* refer to the room or to the furniture?]
CLEAR	The men removed all the furniture from the room and cleaned *the room* (or *the furniture*).
CLEAR	After removing all the furniture from it, the men cleaned the room.
CLEAR	The men cleaned all the furniture after removing it from the room.

282

PRINCIPAL CAUSES OF UNCLEAR PRONOUN REFERENCE

1. More than one possible antecedent (12a):

   CONFUSING   To keep birds from eating seeds, soak *them* in blue food coloring.

   CLEAR   To keep birds from eating seeds, soak *the seeds* in blue food coloring.

2. Antecedent too far away (12b):

   CONFUSING   Employees should consult with their supervisor *who* require personal time.

   CLEAR   Employees *who* require personal time should consult with their supervisor.

3. Antecedent only implied (12c):

   CONFUSING   Many children begin reading on their own by watching television, but *this* should be discounted in government policy.

   CLEAR   Many children begin reading on their own by watching television, but *such self-instruction* should be discounted in government policy.

See also 12d, 12e, and 12f.

**ref
12a**

Clarifying pronoun reference may require simply replacing the pronoun with the appropriate noun, as in the first revision above. But to avoid repetition, you may want to restructure the sentence so that the pronoun can refer to only one possible antecedent, as in the second and third revisions.

Sentences that report what someone said, using verbs like *said* or *told*, often require direct rather than indirect quotation.

   CONFUSING   Oliver told Bill that he was mistaken.

   CLEAR   Oliver told Bill, "I am mistaken."

   CLEAR   Oliver told Bill, "You are mistaken."

NOTE: Avoid the awkward device of using a pronoun followed by the appropriate noun in parentheses.

   WEAK   Mary should help Joan, but *she (Joan)* should help herself first.

   IMPROVED   Mary should help Joan, but *Joan* should help herself first.

RETRIEVING SENTENCES

Reverse the process of sentence combining by asking students to reconstruct (or retrieve) the shorter (kernel) sentences that lie behind a long sentence containing a reference error. You may wish to use sentences from the text as a basis for the exercise. This activity will help students spot ambiguity or vague reference in the long sentence. After they have found the shorter sentences, ask students to recombine, this time avoiding the reference problem.

Original sentence: After the van hit John's car, its engine stopped running and its radiator started leaking.

Kernels: The van hit John's car. The van's engine stopped running. The van's radiator started leaking.

Recombined sentence: After the van hit John's car, the van's engine stopped running and its radiator started leaking.

ref
12b

12b	**Place a pronoun close enough to its antecedent to ensure clarity.**

When the relative pronoun *who*, *which*, or *that* introduces a clause that modifies a noun, the pronoun generally should fall immediately after its antecedent to prevent confusion. (See also 14b.)

CONFUSING   Jody found a dress in the attic *that* her aunt had worn. [Her aunt had worn the attic?]

CLEAR   In the attic Jody found a *dress that* her aunt had worn.

Even when only one word could possibly serve as the antecedent of a pronoun, the relationship between the two may still be unclear if they are widely separated.

CONFUSING   Denver, where my grandmother grew up, was once the scene of a mad gold rush with fortune seekers, plush opera houses, makeshift hotels, noisy saloons, and dirt streets. When I was a child, *she* often retold the stories she had heard of those days. [*She* can sensibly refer only to *grandmother*, but the pronoun is too far from its antecedent to be clear.]

CLEAR   Denver, where my grandmother grew up, was once the scene of a mad gold rush with fortune seekers, plush opera houses, makeshift hotels, noisy saloons, and dirt streets. When I was a child, *my grandmother* often retold the stories she had heard of those days. [The noun is repeated for clarity.]

The confusing separation of pronoun and antecedent is most likely to occur in long sentences and, as illustrated by the preceding example, in adjacent sentences within a paragraph.

POSSIBLE ANSWERS: EXERCISE 1

1. When Mrs. Krieger was away, she telephoned her daughter often.
   Or: When her daughter was away, Mrs. Krieger telephoned her often.
2. The picture on the cover of the novel was disturbing; one expects the novel to be more gruesome than it is.
3. Two brothers had built the town's oldest barn, which over the years had served as a cow barn, a blacksmith

EXERCISE 1

Rewrite the following sentences to eliminate unclear pronoun reference. If you use a pronoun in your revision, be sure that it refers to only one antecedent and that it falls close enough to its antecedent to ensure clarity.

Example:
Saul found an old gun in the rotting shed that was just as his grandfather had left it.

In the rotting shed Saul found an old gun that was just as his grandfather had left it.

1. Mrs. Krieger telephoned her daughter often when she was away.
2. The picture on the cover of the novel is disturbing; one expects it to be more gruesome than it is.
3. Two brothers had built the town's oldest barn, which over the years had served as a cow barn, a blacksmith shop, and a studio for artisans. However, no one could remember their names.
4. Lee played a piece on the piano that dated from the seventeenth century.
5. Since Colson was operating the rented backhoe that ran over Mrs. Gibb's fence, he is responsible for the damage it suffered.
6. If your pet cheetah will not eat raw meat, cook it.
7. My father and his sister have not spoken for thirty years because she left the family when my grandfather was ill and never called or wrote. But now he is thinking of resuming communication.
8. There is a difference between the heroes of today and the heroes of yesterday: they have flaws in their characters.
9. Jan held the sandwich in one hand and the telephone in the other, eating it while she talked.
10. Tom told his brother that he was in trouble with their grandparents.

shop, and a studio for artisans. However, no one could remember <u>the brothers'</u> names.
4. Lee played <u>a piano piece</u> that dated from the seventeenth century.
5. Since Colson was operating the rented backhoe that ran over Mrs. Gibb's fence, he is responsible for the damage <u>the backhoe</u> (or <u>the fence</u>) suffered.
6. If your pet cheetah will not eat raw meat, cook <u>the meat</u>.
7. My father and his sister have not spoken for thirty years because she left the family when my grandfather was ill and never called or wrote. But now <u>my father</u> is thinking of resuming communication.
8. There is a difference between the heroes of today and the heroes of yesterday: <u>today's heroes</u> have flaws in their characters.
9. Jan held the sandwich in one hand and the telephone in the other, eating <u>the sandwich</u> while she talked.
10. Tom told his brother, "<u>I am</u> (or <u>You are</u>) in trouble with our grandparents."

ref

12c

12c Make a pronoun refer to a specific antecedent rather than to an implied one.

As a rule, the meaning of a pronoun will be clearest when it refers to a specific noun or other pronoun. When the antecedent is not specifically stated but is implied by the context, the reference can only be inferred by the reader.

1 Use *this, that, which,* and *it* cautiously in referring to whole statements.

The most common kind of implied reference occurs when the pronoun *this, that, which,* or *it* refers to a whole idea or situation described in the preceding clause, sentence, or even paragraph. Such reference, often called **broad reference,** is acceptable only when the pronoun refers clearly to the entire preceding clause. In the following sentence, *which* could not possibly refer to anything but the whole preceding clause.

> I can be kind and civil to people, *which* is more than you can.
> —GEORGE BERNARD SHAW

RESOURCES AND IDEAS

Leonard Moskovit, "When Is Broad Reference Clear?" *College Composition and Communication* 34 (1983): 454–469. The question of the acceptability of broad reference is a complicated one, as Moskovit points out, and anyone interested in looking at how broad reference operates in sophisticated prose will enjoy his essay.

But if a pronoun might possibly confuse a reader, you should re-cast the sentence to avoid using the pronoun or to provide an appropriate noun.

ref
12c

CONFUSING	I knew nothing about economics, *which* my instructor had not learned. [*Which* could refer to *economics* or to the whole preceding clause.]
CLEAR	I knew nothing about economics, *a fact* my instructor had not learned.
CLEAR	I knew nothing about economics *because* my instructor knew nothing about it.
CONFUSING	The faculty members reached agreement on a change in the requirements, but *it* took time. [Does *it* refer to reaching agreement or to the change?]
CLEAR	The faculty members agreed on a change in the requirements, but *arriving at agreement* took time.
CLEAR	The faculty members reached agreement on a change in the requirements, but *the change* took time to implement.
CONFUSING	The British knew little of the American countryside and had no experience with the colonists' guerrilla tactics. *This* gave the colonists an advantage. [Does *This* refer to the whole preceding sentence, to the ignorance alone, or to the inexperience alone?]
CLEAR	The British knew little of the American countryside and had no experience with the colonists' guerrilla tactics. *Their ignorance and inexperience* gave the colonists an advantage.

2 **Don't use a pronoun to refer to a noun implied by a modifier.**

Adjectives, nouns used as modifiers, and the possessives of nouns or pronouns make unsatisfactory antecedents. Although they may imply a noun that could serve as an antecedent, they do not supply the specific antecedent needed for clarity.

WEAK	In the President's speech *he* outlined plans for tax reform.
REVISED	In *his* speech *the President* outlined plans for tax reform.

WEAK	Liz drove a red car; *it* was her favorite color.
REVISED	Liz drove a red car because *red* was her favorite color.
REVISED	Liz drove a car *that was red,* her favorite color.

3 | **Don't use a pronoun to refer to a noun implied by some other noun or phrase.**

WEAK	Jim talked at length about entrepreneurship, although he had never been *one.*
REVISED	Jim talked at length about entrepreneurship, although he had never been *an entrepreneur.*
WEAK	Jake was bitten by a rattlesnake, but *it* was not serious.
REVISED	Jake was bitten by a rattlesnake, but *the bite* was not serious.

4 | **Don't use part of a title as an antecedent in the opening sentence of a paper.**

The title of a paper is entirely separate from the paper itself, so a pronoun cannot be used to refer to the title. If you open a paper with a reference to the title, repeat whatever part of the title is necessary for clarity.

TITLE	How to Row a Boat
NOT	*This* is not as easy as it looks.
BUT	*Rowing a boat* is not as easy as it looks.

12d | **Avoid the indefinite use of *it* and *they.* Use *you* only to mean "you, the reader."**

In conversation we commonly use expressions such as *It says in the paper* or *In Texas they say.* But such indefinite use of *it* and *they* is inappropriate in writing. The constructions are not only unclear but wordy.

| WEAK | In Chapter 4 of this book *it* describes the early flights of the Wright brothers. |
| REVISED | In Chapter 4 of this book *the author* describes the early flights of the Wright brothers. |

ref
12d

WEAK	In the average television drama *they* present a false picture of life.
REVISED	The average television *drama* presents a false picture of life.

Using *you* with indefinite reference to people in general is also well established in conversation: *You can tell that my father was a military man.* The indefinite *you* frequently occurs in informal writing, too. And in all but very formal writing, *you* is acceptable when the meaning is clearly "you, the reader," as in *You can learn the standard uses of pronouns.* But the context must be appropriate for such a meaning. Consider this example:

INAPPROPRIATE	In the fourteenth century *you* had to struggle simply to survive. [Clearly, the meaning cannot be "you, the reader."]
REVISED	In the fourteenth century *one* (or *a person* or *people*) had to struggle simply to survive.

12e   **Avoid using the pronoun *it* more than one way in a sentence.**

We use *it* idiomatically in expressions such as *It is raining.* We use *it* to postpone the subject in sentences such as *It is true that more jobs are available to women today.* And, of course, we use *it* as a personal pronoun in sentences such as *Joan wanted the book, but she couldn't find it.* All these uses are standard, but two of them in the same sentence can confuse the reader.

CONFUSING	When *it* is rainy, shelter your bicycle and wipe *it* often. [The first *it* is idiomatic; the second refers to *bicycle*.]
REVISED	*In rainy weather*, shelter your bicycle and wipe *it* often.

12f   **Be sure the relative pronouns *who, which,* and *that* are appropriate for their antecedents.**

The relative pronouns *who, which,* and *that* commonly refer to persons, animals, or things. *Who* refers most often to persons but may also refer to animals that have names.

Travis is the boy *who* leads the other boys into trouble.
Their dog Wanda, *who* is growing lame, has difficulty running.

IT, WHICH, AND THEY

Distribute copies of a student paper that uses *it, which, they,* and other pronouns in sentences without supplying clear antecedents in preceding sentences. Ask students to work in groups to correct the reference problems. Ask them also to construct an explanation of how a string of pronouns can be used properly to bring coherence to writing.

CORRECTING A NARRATIVE

Find or write a brief narrative containing several events and more than one character. Introduce enough reference problems so that readers have difficulty unraveling the events. If you wish, include dialogue in the narrative in such a way that the reference

ref 12f

Which refers to animals and things.

> The Orinoco River, *which* is 1600 miles long, flows through Venezuela into the Atlantic Ocean.

That refers to animals and things and occasionally to persons when they are collective or anonymous.

> The jade tree *that* my grandmother gave me suddenly died.
> Infants *that* walk need constant tending.

(See also 21c-1 for the use of *which* and *that* in nonrestrictive and restrictive clauses.)

The possessive *whose* generally refers to people but may refer to animals and things to avoid awkward and wordy *of which* constructions.

> The book *whose* binding broke had been my father's. [Compare *The book of which the binding broke had been my father's.*]

problems make it hard to identify the speakers. (Using "He said" as a tag when there are two men in the narrative is one possibility.) Ask students to work in groups to untangle the problems in the narrative and to rewrite it, removing vague and ambiguous references.

ref

12f

EXERCISE 2

Many of the pronouns in the following sentences do not refer to specific, appropriate antecedents. Revise the sentences as necessary to make them clear.

> *Example:*
> In Grand Teton National Park they have moose, elk, and trumpeter swans.
> *Moose, elk, and trumpeter swans live* in Grand Teton National Park.

1. Sandra Day O'Connor has been a Supreme Court Justice since 1981, when she was appointed to it by Ronald Reagan.
2. Ever since I read a book on the Buddhists' beliefs, I've been thinking of becoming one.
3. In impressionist paintings they used color to imitate reflected light.
4. Six or seven bearskin rugs decorated the rooms of the house, and Sam claimed to have killed them.
5. In Japan they are very loyal to the companies they work for.
6. Thompson is a painter that works primarily in oils.
7. In my weight-training class, the instructors advise you to leave two or three days between workouts.
8. The play was supposed to open the first week in March, but because of casting problems this did not happen.
9. We receive warnings to beware of nuclear fallout, pesticides, smog, and even our food, but I try not to think about it.
10. In F. Scott Fitzgerald's novels he wrote about the Jazz Age.
11. Macbeth is a complicated and ambiguous hero, and that makes it a good play.

POSSIBLE ANSWERS: EXERCISE 2

1. Sandra Day O'Connor has been a Supreme Court Justice since 1981, when she was appointed to <u>the Court</u> by Ronald Reagan.
2. Ever since I read a book on the Buddhists' beliefs, I've been thinking of becoming <u>a Buddhist</u>.
3. <u>Impressionist painters</u> used color to imitate reflected light.
4. Six or seven bearskin rugs decorated the rooms of the house, and Sam claimed to have killed <u>the bears</u>.
5. <u>The Japanese are very loyal</u> to the companies they work for.
6. Thompson is a painter <u>who</u> works primarily in oils.
7. In my weight-training class, the instructors advise <u>us</u> to leave two or three days between workouts.
8. The play was supposed to open the first week in March, but because of casting problems <u>it did not</u>.
9. We receive warnings to beware of nuclear fallout, pesticides, smog, and even our food, but I try not to think about <u>these dangers</u>.
10. In <u>his</u> novels <u>F. Scott Fitzgerald</u> wrote about the Jazz Age.

11. <u>Because the title character</u> is a complicated and ambiguous hero, *Macbeth* is a good play.

12. <u>Urban redevelopment projects</u> are attempts to make neighborhoods safe and attractive.

13. <u>The nineteenth century didn't offer</u> many options in motorized transportation.

14. It rained for a week, but <u>we may be able to</u> save the crop.

15. We argue constantly, and <u>it bothers me that</u> he never looks straight at me.

ANSWERS: EXERCISE 3

Sample Revision

In Charlotte Brontë's *Jane Eyre,* Jane is a shy young woman <u>who</u> takes a job as governess. Her employer is a rude, brooding man named Rochester. He lives in a mysterious mansion on the English moors, <u>and both the mansion and the moors</u> contribute an eerie quality to Jane's experience. Eerier still are the fires, strange noises, and other unexplained happenings in the house; but Rochester refuses to discuss <u>them</u>. Eventually, <u>Jane and Rochester</u> fall in love. On the day they are to be married, however, Jane learns that <u>Rochester</u> has a wife hidden in the house. <u>The wife</u> is hopelessly insane and violent and must be guarded at all times, <u>circumstances that explain Rochester's</u> strange behavior. Heartbroken, Jane leaves the moors, and many years pass before <u>she and Rochester</u> are reunited.

12. In urban redevelopment projects they try to make neighborhoods safe and attractive.

13. In the nineteenth century you didn't have many options in motorized transportation.

14. It rained for a week, but it is possible that we can save the crop.

15. We argue constantly and he never looks straight at me, which bothers me.

EXERCISE 3

Revise the following paragraph so that each pronoun refers clearly to a single specific and appropriate antecedent.

In Charlotte Brontë's *Jane Eyre* she is a shy young woman that takes a job as governess. Her employer is a rude, brooding man named Rochester. He lives in a mysterious mansion on the English moors, which contributes an eerie quality to Jane's experience. Eerier still are the fires, strange noises, and other unexplained happenings in the house; but Rochester refuses to discuss this. Eventually, they fall in love. On the day they are to be married, however, she learns that he has a wife hidden in the house. She is hopelessly insane and violent and must be guarded at all times, which explains his strange behavior. Heartbroken, Jane leaves the moors, and many years pass before they are reunited.

CHAPTER 13

Shifts

HIGHLIGHTS

Shifts in person and number, in tense and mood, in subject and voice, or between direct and indirect quotation can be irritating to readers and occasionally make it hard to follow the meaning of a passage. Often, however, students are not fully aware of the shifts or their effect on a reader. This chapter describes in detail and illustrates the various shifts so that students can learn to identify the problems in their own writing. The exercises ask students to revise sentences and a longer passage, much as they will need to in revising their own work.

A sentence or a group of related sentences should be consistent: grammatical elements such as tense, mood, voice, person, and number should remain the same unless grammar or meaning requires a shift. Unnecessary shifts in these elements confuse readers and distort meaning.

13a | **Keep a sentence or related sentences consistent in person and number.**

Person in grammar refers to the distinction among the person talking (first person), the person spoken to (second person), and the person, object, or concept being talked about (third person). **Number** refers to the distinction between one (singular) and more than one (plural). Both nouns and personal pronouns change form to show differences in number, but only personal pronouns have distinctive forms for the three persons.

Shifts in person

The most common faulty shifts in person are shifts from second to third and from third to second person. They occur because we can refer to people in general, including our readers, either in the third person (*a person, one; people, they*) or in the second person (*you*).

People should not drive when *they* have been drinking.
One should not drive when *he or she* has been drinking.
You should not drive when *you* have been drinking.

291

Although any one of these possibilities is acceptable in an appropriate context, a mixture of them is inconsistent.

INCONSISTENT	If a *person* works hard, *you* can accomplish a great deal.
REVISED	If *you* work hard, *you* can accomplish a great deal.
REVISED	If a *person* works hard, *he or she* can accomplish a great deal.
BETTER	If *people* work hard, *they* can accomplish a great deal.

Shifts in number

Inconsistency in number occurs most often between a pronoun and its antecedent (see 8b).

INCONSISTENT	If a *student* does not understand a problem, *they* should consult the instructor.
REVISED	If a *student* does not understand a problem, *he or she* should consult the instructor.
BETTER	If *students* do not understand a problem, *they* should consult the instructor.

Inconsistency in number can also occur between other words (usually nouns) that relate to each other in meaning.

| INCONSISTENT | All the *boys* have a good *reputation*. |
| REVISED | All the *boys* have good *reputations*. |

The consistency in the revised sentence is called **logical agreement** because the number of the nouns is logically consistent.

ANSWERS: EXERCISE 1

1. When a student is waiting to hear from college admissions committees, <u>he or she begins</u> to notice what time the mail carrier arrives. *Or:* When <u>students are</u> waiting to hear from college admissions committees, <u>they</u> begin to notice what time the mail carrier arrives.
2. If tourists cannot find the Arts Center, <u>they</u> should ask for directions.
3. When taxpayers do not file their <u>returns</u> on time, they may be penalized.
4. If a student misses too many classes, <u>he or she</u> may fail a course. *Or:* If <u>students miss</u> too many classes, <u>they</u> may fail a

EXERCISE 1

Revise the following sentences to make them consistent in person and number.

Example:
A plumber will fix burst pipes, but they won't repair waterlogged appliances.

Plumbers will fix burst pipes, but they won't repair waterlogged appliances.

1. When a student is waiting to hear from college admissions committees, you begin to notice what time the mail carrier arrives.
2. If tourists cannot find the Arts Center, one should ask for directions.

3. When taxpayers do not file their return on time, they may be penalized.
4. If a student misses too many classes, you may fail a course.
5. One should not judge other people's actions unless they know the circumstances.

course. *Or:* If <u>you miss</u> too many classes, you may fail a course.
5. One should not judge other people's actions unless <u>one knows</u> the circumstances.

 Keep a sentence or related sentences consistent in tense and mood.

Shifts in tense

Certain changes in tense within a sentence or from one sentence to another may be required to indicate changes in actual or relative time (see 7f). For example:

Ramon *will graduate* from college twenty-three years after his father *arrived* in the United States. [Ramon's graduation is still in the future, but his father arrived in the past.]

But changes that are not required by meaning distract readers. Unnecessary shifts from past to present or from present to past in passages narrating a series of events are particularly confusing.

INCONSISTENT	Immediately after Booth *shot* Lincoln, Major Rathbone *threw* himself upon the assassin. But Booth *pulls* a knife and *plunges* it into the major's arm. [Tense shifts from past to present.]
REVISED	Immediately after Booth *shot* Lincoln, Major Rathbone *threw* himself upon the assassin. But Booth *pulled* a knife and *plunged* it into the major's arm.

The present tense is used to describe what another author has written, including the action in literature or a film (see also 38b-3).

INCONSISTENT	The main character in the novel *suffers* psychologically because he *has* a clubfoot, but he eventually *triumphed* over his handicap.
REVISED	The main character in the novel *suffers* psychologically because he *has* a clubfoot, but he eventually *triumphs* over his handicap.

Shifts in mood

Shifts in the mood of verbs occur most frequently in directions when the writer moves between the imperative mood (*Unplug the appliance*) and the indicative mood (*You should unplug the appliance*). (See 7g.) Directions are usually clearer and more concise in the imperative, as long as its use is consistent.

> **INCONSISTENT**   *Cook* the mixture slowly, and *you should stir* it until the sugar is dissolved. [Mood shifts from imperative to indicative.]
>
> **REVISED**   *Cook* the mixture slowly, and *stir* it until the sugar is dissolved. [Consistently imperative.]

ANSWERS: EXERCISE 2

1. Misunderstandings sometimes <u>occur</u> when people of one culture do not understand the rules of appropriate behavior in another culture.
2. Soon after he joined the union, Lester <u>appeared</u> at a rally and <u>made</u> a speech.
3. First sand down any paint that is peeling; then <u>paint</u> the bare wood with primer.
4. Rachel was walking down the street, and suddenly she stopped as a shot <u>rang</u> out.
5. To buy a tape deck, find out what features you need and <u>decide</u> what you want to pay.

CLASS READING

Use the passage below, or find or write another that contains several kinds of shifts. Distribute copies to the class and read through the passage with students, asking them to identify the problems. This exercise will help make students aware of the different kinds of shifts as they appear in the context of an essay.

As soon as the avalanche was over, Jim pulls himself out of the snowbank and yells, "Where's everybody?" and were we still alive. As each of us in turn started digging out, you could see the damage the huge wall of snow had caused. The snow had destroyed the lodge and cars were swept away. . . .

EXERCISE 2

Revise the following sentences to make them consistent in tense and mood.

> *Example:*
>
> Lynn ran to first, rounded the base, and keeps running until she slides into second.
>
> Lynn ran to first, rounded the base, and *kept* running until she *slid* into second.

1. Misunderstandings sometimes occurred when people of one culture do not understand the rules of appropriate behavior in another culture.
2. Soon after he joined the union, Lester appears at a rally and makes a speech.
3. First sand down any paint that is peeling; then you should paint the bare wood with primer.
4. Rachel was walking down the street, and suddenly she stopped as a shot rings out.
5. To buy a tape deck, find out what features you need and you should decide what you want to pay.

13c   **Keep a sentence or related sentences consistent in subject and voice.**

When a verb is in the active voice, the subject names the actor: *Linda passed the peas.* When a verb is in the passive voice, the subject names the receiver of the action; the actor may not be mentioned or may be mentioned in a prepositional phrase: *The peas were passed* (*by Linda*). (See pp. 235–36.)

A shift in voice may sometimes help focus the reader's attention on a single subject, as in *The candidate campaigned vigorously and was nominated on the first ballot.* However, most shifts in subject and voice not only are unnecessary but also may create confusion or error.

INCONSISTENT	In the morning the *children rode* their bicycles; in the afternoon *their skateboards were given* a good workout. [The shift in subject from *children* to *skateboards* is confusing. Without a named actor the second clause implies that people other than the children used the skateboards.]
REVISED	In the morning the *children rode* their bicycles; in the afternoon *they gave* their skateboards a good workout.
INCONSISTENT	As *we looked* out over the ocean, *ships could be seen* in the distance. [Since the main clause does not name an actor, the reader cannot be sure who is looking.]
REVISED	As *we looked* out over the ocean, *we could see* ships in the distance.

shift

13d

EXERCISE 3

Make the following sentences consistent in subject and voice.

Example:

At the reunion they ate hot dogs and volleyball was played.
At the reunion they ate hot dogs and *played volleyball.*

1. Some arrowheads were dug up, and the researchers found some pottery that was almost undamaged.
2. They started the game after some practice drills were run.
3. The tornado ripped off the roof, and it was deposited in a nearby lot.
4. The debate was begun by the senator when he introduced the new bill.
5. If you learn how to take good notes in class, much extra work will be avoided.

ANSWERS: EXERCISE 3

1. <u>The researchers dug up</u> some arrowheads, and they found some pottery that was almost undamaged.
2. They started the game after <u>they ran</u> some practice drills.
3. The tornado ripped off the roof and <u>deposited it</u> in a nearby lot.
4. <u>The senator began</u> the debate when he introduced the new bill.
5. If you learn how to take good notes in class, you <u>will avoid</u> much extra work.

ANSWERS: EXERCISE 4

1. Muhammad Ali bragged that he was the greatest and <u>that he not only knocked them out but picked the round.</u> *Or:* Muhammad Ali bragged, "I am the greatest. Not only do I knock 'em out, I pick the round."
2. Coach Butler said that our timing was terrible and <u>that he would rather cancel the season than watch us play.</u> *Or:* Coach Butler said, "Your timing is terrible. I would rather cancel the season than watch you play."
3. The report concluded <u>that drought is a serious threat</u> and that we must begin conserving water now. *Or:* The report

13d Don't shift unnecessarily between indirect and direct quotation.

Direct quotation reports, in quotation marks, the exact words of a speaker: *He said, "I am going."* **Indirect quotation** reports what was said but not necessarily in the speaker's exact words: *He said that he was going.*

INCONSISTENT	Sue asked whether we had repaired the car and "Is anything else likely to happen?"

concluded, "Drought is a serious threat. <u>We must begin conserving water now.</u>"

4. The author claims that adults pass through emotional stages and <u>that no stage can be avoided</u>. *Or:* The author claims, "<u>Adults pass through emotional stages, and</u> no stage can be avoided."

5. My grandfather says <u>that gardening keeps him alive</u> and that, in any event, the exercise helps ease his arthritis. *Or:* My grandfather says, "Gardening helps keep me alive, <u>and, in any event, the exercise helps ease my arthritis.</u>"

ANSWERS: EXERCISE 5

Sample revision:

Driving in snow need not be dangerous if you practice a few simple rules. First, <u>avoid</u> fast starts, which prevent the wheels from gaining traction and may result in the car's getting stuck. Second, drive more slowly than usual, and <u>pay</u> attention to the feel of the car: if the steering <u>seems</u> unusually loose or the wheels <u>do</u> not seem to be grabbing the road, slow down. Third, avoid fast stops, which lead to skids. <u>Be alert</u> for other cars and intersections that may necessitate <u>applying the brakes</u> suddenly. If you need to slow down, <u>reduce the car's momentum</u> by downshifting as well as by applying the brakes. When braking, don't press the pedal to the floor but <u>pump it</u> in short bursts. If you feel the car skidding, <u>release the brakes</u> and <u>turn the wheel</u> into the direction of the skid, and then <u>pump the brakes</u> again. Repeating these motions <u>will stop the skid</u> and <u>reduce the speed</u> of the car.

CHECK YOUR OWN

If shifts are a problem in the essays your class submits, go over the chapter in detail in class, and then ask students to go through their papers and circle each shift they find. This activity can be done on the day papers are to be handed in or with a set of graded papers on which you have not marked the shifts. The activity is also a good small-group exercise; students are often good at spotting shifts in someone else's writing.

REVISED	Sue asked, "Have you repaired the car? Is anything else likely to happen?"
REVISED	Sue asked whether we had repaired the car and whether anything else was likely to happen.

EXERCISE 4

Revise each of the following sentences twice, once to make the form of quotation consistently indirect and once to make it consistently direct.

Example:

Tom asked whether the host had arrived and "Are the cameras ready?"

Tom asked whether the host had arrived and *whether the cameras were ready.*

Tom asked, *"Has the host arrived? Are the cameras ready?"*

1. Muhammad Ali bragged that he was the greatest and "Not only do I knock 'em out, I pick the round."
2. Coach Butler said that our timing was terrible and "I would rather cancel the season than watch you play."
3. The report concluded, "Drought is a serious threat" and that we must begin conserving water now.
4. The author claims that adults pass through emotional stages and "No stage can be avoided."
5. My grandfather says, "Gardening keeps me alive" and that, in any event, the exercise helps ease his arthritis.

EXERCISE 5

Revise the following paragraph to eliminate unnecessary shifts in person, number, tense, mood, and voice.

Driving in snow need not be dangerous if you practice a few rules. First, one should avoid fast starts, which prevent the wheels from gaining traction and may result in the car's getting stuck. Second, drive more slowly than usual, and you should pay attention to the feel of the car: if the steering seemed unusually loose or the wheels did not seem to be grabbing the road, slow down. Third, avoid fast stops, which lead to skids. One should be alert for other cars and intersections that may necessitate that the brakes be applied suddenly. If you need to slow down, the car's momentum can be reduced by downshifting as well as by applying the brakes. When braking, don't press the pedal to the floor, but it should be pumped in short bursts. If you feel the car skidding, the brakes should be released and the wheel should be turned into the direction of the skid, and then the brakes should be pumped again. If one repeated these motions, the skid would be stopped and the speed of the car would be reduced.

CHAPTER 14

Misplaced and Dangling Modifiers

HIGHLIGHTS

Misplaced and dangling modifiers often interest students because the faulty constructions can be amusing. To tie together all the different problems discussed in the chapter, however, you may want to point out that they all illustrate the importance of position and arrangement in sentences. Split constructions (14d and 14e) conveniently emphasize the need to keep the parts of related syntactic groups clearly unified. Yet both standard speech and formal writing provide frequent examples of freely placed limiting modifiers and of split infinitives. Part of our difficulty in teaching composition is in giving students effective advice about when freedom is constructive and when it is confusing. As in all such matters, the advice of the handbook is largely conservative; you may therefore want to modify it somewhat.

In reading a sentence in English, we depend principally on the arrangement of the words to tell us how they are related. In writing, we usually follow unconsciously the arrangements readers expect. But we may create confusion if we fail to connect modifiers to the words they modify.

MISPLACED MODIFIERS

We say that a modifier is **misplaced** if it appears to modify the wrong part of the sentence or if we cannot be certain what part of the sentence the writer intended it to modify. Misplaced modifiers may be awkward, unintentionally amusing, or genuinely confusing.

14a Place modifiers where they will clearly modify the words intended.

Readers tend to link a modifying word, phrase, or clause to the nearest word it could modify: *I saw a man in a green hat*. Thus the writer must place the phrase so that it clearly modifies the intended word and not some other.

CONFUSING	She served hamburgers to the men *on paper plates*. [Surely the hamburgers, not the men, were on paper plates.]
CLEAR	She served the men hamburgers *on paper plates*.

297

CONFUSING	He was unhappy that he failed to break the record *by a narrow margin*. [The sentence implies that he wanted to break the record only by a narrow margin.]
CLEAR	He was unhappy that he failed *by a narrow margin* to break the record.
CONFUSING	According to police records, many dogs are killed by automobiles and trucks *roaming unleashed*. [The phrase appears to modify *automobiles*.]
CLEAR	According to police records, many dogs *roaming unleashed* are killed by automobiles and trucks.
CONFUSING	The mayor was able to cut the ribbon and then the band played *when someone found scissors*. [The clause appears to modify *the band played*.]
CLEAR	*When someone found scissors*, the mayor was able to cut the ribbon and then the band played.

mm
14a

ANSWERS: EXERCISE 1

1. The senator returned to Capitol Hill <u>on Monday</u> after a long illness.
2. <u>In my hospital bed</u> I watched a film clip of the accident.
3. <u>At a summer retreat</u> the artist painted a canvas that imitated Monet's style.
4. The consulate received the letter with exotic stamps <u>from a messenger</u>.
5. Trisha delivered a party platter <u>wrapped in cellophane</u>.
6. The electric typewriter <u>in the library</u> needs repair.
7. Marie opened the book <u>by Charles Dickens</u> given to her last Christmas.
8. The bell <u>that you hear chiming</u> is an heirloom.
9. <u>With flashing eyes</u> she stared at the people standing nearby.
10. <u>From Niagara Falls</u>, Buffalo gains a huge supply of hydroelectric power that will never be exhausted.

EXERCISE 1

Revise the following sentences so that prepositional phrases and subordinate clauses clearly modify the words they are intended to modify.

Example:
I came to enjoy flying over time.
Over time I came to enjoy flying.

1. The senator returned to Capitol Hill after a long illness on Monday.
2. I watched a film clip of the accident in my hospital bed.
3. The artist painted a canvas at a summer retreat that imitated Monet's style.
4. The consulate received the letter from a messenger with exotic stamps.
5. Trisha delivered a party platter to the host wrapped in cellophane.
6. The electric typewriter needs repair in the library.
7. Marie opened the book given to her last Christmas by Charles Dickens.
8. The bell is an heirloom that you hear chiming.
9. She stared at the people standing nearby with flashing eyes.
10. Buffalo gains a huge supply of hydroelectric power from Niagara Falls that will never be exhausted.

14b Place limiting modifiers carefully.

Limiting modifiers include *almost, even, exactly, hardly, just, merely, nearly, only, scarcely,* and *simply.* They modify the expressions that immediately follow them. Compare the uses of *just* in the following sentences:

The instructor *just nodded* to me as he came in.
The instructor nodded *just to me* as he came in.
The instructor nodded to me *just as he came in.*

In speech several of these modifiers frequently occur before the verb, regardless of the words they are intended to modify. In writing, however, these modifiers should fall immediately before the word or word group they modify to avoid any ambiguity.

UNCLEAR	They *only* saw each other during meals. [They had eyes only for each other, or they met only during meals?]
CLEAR	They saw *only* each other during meals.
CLEAR	They saw each other *only* during meals.

NOTE: *Only* is acceptable immediately before the verb when it modifies a whole statement.

He *only* wanted his guest to have fun.

EXERCISE 2

Use each of the following limiting modifiers in two versions of the same sentence.

Example:
only
He is the *only* one I like.
He is the one *only* I like.

1. almost
2. even
3. hardly
4. simply
5. nearly

14c Avoid squinting modifiers.

A **squinting modifier** is one that may refer to either a preceding or a following word, leaving the reader uncertain about what it is intended to modify. A modifier can modify only *one* grammatical element in a sentence. It cannot serve two elements at once.

SAMPLE ANSWERS: EXERCISE 2

1. <u>Almost</u> everybody hates him.
   Everybody <u>almost</u> hates him.
2. <u>Even</u> now I remember the details of the event.
   Now I remember <u>even</u> the details of the event.
3. We <u>hardly</u> heard him call our names.
   We heard him <u>hardly</u> call our names.
4. Write <u>simply</u>.
   <u>Simply</u> write.
5. I <u>nearly</u> missed the performance that was booed off the stage.
   I missed the performance that was <u>nearly</u> booed off the stage.

mm
14c

MOVING *ONLY*

Ask students to create sentences whose meaning changes as a modifier like *only* moves from place to place:

Only students were asked to bring gym shorts and running shoes.

Students were *only* asked to bring gym shorts and running shoes.

Students were asked *only* to bring gym shorts and running shoes.

Students were asked to bring *only* gym shorts and running shoes.

ANSWERS: EXERCISE 3

1. People who <u>frequently</u> sunbathe can damage their skin.
   People who sunbathe can <u>frequently</u> damage their skin.
2. The contestant who <u>completely</u> answered the first question lost his concentration during the second round.
   The contestant who answered the first question lost his concentration <u>completely</u> during the second round.
3. The baseball team that <u>most of the time</u> wins championships has excellent pitching.
   The baseball team that wins championships has excellent pitching <u>most of the time</u>.
4. <u>When the game was over</u>, I told my son I would play with him.
   I told my son I would play with him <u>when the game was over</u>.
5. People who <u>occasionally</u> see psychologists will feel better.
   People who see psychologists will <u>occasionally</u> feel better.

SQUINTING	Snipers who fired on the soldiers *often* escaped capture.
CLEAR	Snipers who *often* fired on the soldiers escaped capture.
CLEAR	Snipers who fired on the soldiers escaped capture *often*.

When an adverb modifies an entire main clause, as in the last example, it can usually be moved to the beginning of the sentence: *Often, snipers who fired on the soldiers escaped capture.*

EXERCISE 3

Revise each of the following sentences twice so that the squinting modifier applies clearly first to one element and then to the other.

Example:

The work that he hoped would satisfy him completely frustrated him.

The work that he hoped would *completely* satisfy him frustrated him.

The work that he hoped would satisfy him frustrated him *completely*.

1. People who sunbathe frequently can damage their skin.
2. The contestant who answered the first question completely lost his concentration during the second round.
3. The baseball team that wins championships most of the time has excellent pitching.
4. I told my son when the game was over I would play with him.
5. People who see psychologists occasionally will feel better.

14d **Avoid separating a subject from its verb or a verb from its object or complement.**

When we read a sentence, we expect the subject, verb, and object or complement to be close to each other. If adjective phrases or clauses separate them, the meaning is usually clear.

The wreckers who were demolishing the old house discovered a large box of coins. [The subject, *wreckers*, and the verb, *discovered*, are separated by the adjective clause beginning *who*.]

However, if an adverb phrase or clause interrupts the movement from subject to verb to object or complement, the resulting sentence is likely to be awkward and confusing.

AWKWARD	The *wreckers,* soon after they began demolishing the old house, *discovered* a large box of coins. [The clause beginning *soon after* interrupts the movement from subject to verb.]
REVISED	Soon after they began demolishing the old house, the *wreckers discovered* a large box of coins.
AWKWARD	Three of the wreckers *lifted,* with great effort, *the heavy box.* [The phrase beginning *with* interrupts the movement from verb to object.]
REVISED	Three of the wreckers *lifted the heavy box* with great effort.

14e Avoid separating the parts of a verb phrase or the parts of an infinitive.

A verb phrase consists of a helping verb plus a main verb, as in *will call, was going, had been writing.* Such phrases constitute close grammatical units. We regularly insert single-word adverbs in them without causing awkwardness: *Joshua <u>had</u> almost <u>completed</u> his assignment.* But when longer word groups interrupt verb phrases, the result is almost always awkward.

AWKWARD	Many students *had,* by spending most of their time on the assignment, *completed* it.
REVISED	By spending most of their time on the assignment, many students *had completed* it.
REVISED	Many students *had completed* the assignment by spending most of their time on it.

Infinitives consist of the marker *to* plus the plain form of a verb: *to produce, to enjoy.* The two parts of the infinitive are widely regarded as a grammatical unit that should not be split.

AWKWARD	The weather service expected temperatures *to not rise.*
REVISED	The weather service expected temperatures not *to rise.*

Note, however, that a split infinitive may sometimes be natural and preferable, though it may still bother some readers.

Several U.S. industries expect *to* more than *triple* their use of robots within the next decade.

We could recast the sentence entirely: *Several U.S. industries expect*

mm
14e

THE MEDIA

Radio and television newscasts are rich sources of dangling and misplaced modifiers, perhaps because reporters have little time to pay attention to the structure of their sentences. Have students listen to newscasts and record errors; doing so will help them to understand the perspective of a reader who comes across similar errors in an essay. Newspaper headlines and public announcements are also rich sources; from time to time, magazine articles and paperback books appear with collections of particularly humorous errors. But students will be able to find many on their own by looking at the newspaper for headlines like "Young Man, 17, Slain by Road."

HOME-GROWN STAR REPORTERS

Ask students to form groups in order to write their own newscasts filled with the kinds of errors they might spot through the activity above. The newscasts (and the errors) should be plausible in style and content, though the content will probably have to be the product of students' imaginations. Having heard many newscasts, however, students will probably have little trouble parodying them in form and matter.

*to increase their use of robots by over 200 percent within the next dec-
ade.* But the split construction seems acceptable for economy.

ANSWERS: EXERCISE 4

1. <u>After two weeks</u>, the mail carrier returned the undelivered letter.
2. <u>Although he was later accused of dereliction of duty</u>, the lieutenant had
given the correct orders.
3. The girls loved to sun <u>daily</u> beside the
pool.
4. Ballet will be one of the country's most
popular arts <u>if the present interest continues to grow</u>.
5. The beavers abandoned their dam
<u>when the new housing construction be-
gan</u>.

RESOURCES AND IDEAS

Elaine Chaika, "Grammars and Teaching," *College English* 39 (1978): 770–83.
Chaika offers fresh explanations from a
linguistic perspective for a number of
standard errors, including dangling
modifiers.

William H. Pixton, "The Dangling Ger-
und: A Working Definition," *College Composition and Communication* 24 (1973):
193–99. Pixton reviews discussions of
dangling modifiers and, using a variety
of sample sentences, formulates a definition of the dangling gerund.

EXERCISE 4

Revise the following sentences to connect separated parts
(subject-predicate, verb-object-complement, verb phrase, infinitive).

Example:

Most children have by the time they are seven lost a tooth.
By the time they are seven, most children have lost a tooth.

1. The mail carrier returned, after two weeks, the undelivered
letter.
2. The lieutenant had given, although he was later accused of
dereliction of duty, the correct orders.
3. The girls loved to daily sun beside the pool.
4. Ballet will, if the present interest continues to grow, be one
of the country's most popular arts.
5. The beavers, when the new housing construction began,
abandoned their dam.

DANGLING MODIFIERS

14f **Avoid dangling modifiers.**

A **dangling modifier** does not sensibly modify anything in its
sentence.

DANGLING	*Passing the building*, the vandalism was clearly visible. [The modifying phrase seems to describe *vandalism*. The writer has not said who was passing the building or who saw the vandalism.]
DANGLING	*Shortly after leaving home*, the accident occurred. [The modifying phrase seems to describe *accident*. The writer has not said who left home or who was in the accident.]

Dangling modifiers occur most often when certain kinds of
modifying word groups precede the main clause of the sentence.
These word groups include participial phrases (*passing the building*); infinitive phrases (*to see*); prepositional phrases in which the
object of the preposition is a gerund (*after leaving home*); and elliptical clauses in which the subject and perhaps the verb are understood (*while at work*). (See 5c.) These phrases and clauses are

IDENTIFYING AND REVISING DANGLING MODIFIERS

1. If the modifier lacks a subject of its own (e.g., *running away*), identify what it describes.
2. Verify that what the modifier describes is in fact the subject of the main clause. If it is not, the modifier is probably dangling.
3. Revise a dangling modifier (*a*) by recasting it with a subject of its own or (*b*) by changing the subject of the main clause.

	MODIFIER **DESCRIBES DIGGERS**	**SUBJECT IS** **WATER**
DANGLING	Having sweltered in the sun, the water tasted wonderful to the diggers.	
REVISION A	*After the diggers had* sweltered in the sun, the water tasted wonderful.	
REVISION B	Having sweltered in the sun, *the diggers thought* the water tasted wonderful.	

dm
14f

about something, but their subjects are not expressed. Thus readers take them to modify the following noun, the subject of the main clause. If they do not sensibly define or describe the following noun, they are dangling modifiers.

DANGLING	*Being very tired,* Morton's alarm failed to disturb his sleep. [Participial phrase.]
DANGLING	*To get up on time,* a great effort was needed. [Infinitive phrase.]
DANGLING	*On rising,* coffee was essential to waken Morton. [Prepositional phrase.]
DANGLING	*Until completely awake,* work was impossible. [Elliptical clause.]

These sentences are illogical: alarm clocks don't get tired, effort doesn't get up, coffee doesn't rise, and work doesn't awaken. Note that a modifier may be dangling even when the sentence elsewhere contains a word the modifier might seem to describe, such as *Morton's* and *Morton* in the first and third examples. In addition, a dangling modifier may fall at the end of a sentence:

DANGLING	Work came easily *when finally awake.*

We correct dangling modifiers by recasting the sentences in which they appear. We can change the subject of the main clause to a word the modifier properly defines or describes. Or we can recast the dangling modifier as a complete clause. The following examples illustrate these revisions.

DANGLING	*Being crowded in the car*, the trip was uncomfortable.
REVISED	Being crowded in the car, *we* were uncomfortable. [New subject.]
REVISED	*Because we were* crowded in the car, the trip was uncomfortable. [Rewritten modifier.]
DANGLING	*After unlocking the door*, the cat refused to go out.
REVISED	After *I had unlocked* the door, the cat refused to go out. [Rewritten modifier.]
DANGLING	*To take sharp action pictures*, the shutter speed should be fast.
REVISED	To take sharp action pictures, *a photographer* should use a fast shutter speed. [New subject.]
REVISED	*If a photographer wants* to take sharp action pictures, the shutter speed should be fast. [Rewritten modifier.]
DANGLING	The stitches were removed from Larry's wound *while still in the hospital*.
REVISED	*Larry* had the stitches removed while still in the hospital. [New subject.]
REVISED	The stitches were removed from Larry's wound while *he was* still in the hospital. [Rewritten modifier.]

dm
14f

SENTENCE COMBINING

Exercise 6 below requires students to combine pairs of sentences whose content and structure make them likely causes of misplaced or dangling modifiers. Extend this activity by having students create their own sentences that would be easy to miscombine. Choose the best pairs, copy them, and have the class do them for an exercise. This activity leads to considerable discussion and some imaginative and amusing results when the students work in groups.

POSSIBLE ANSWERS: EXERCISE 5

1. The room looked less dingy <u>when I turned the lights down</u>.
2. To file a formal complaint, <u>you must submit</u> a statement.
3. Having prepared thoroughly, <u>I found the exam easy</u>.
4. Though <u>she was</u> usually energetic, emotional problems had sapped her strength.
5. <u>While I was</u> staring at the ceiling, the idea became clear.
6. <u>Because his house was</u> sagging and <u>needed</u> a new coat of paint, Mr. Preston called the house painter.
7. <u>I let</u> Monday <u>pass</u> me by without <u>my</u> accomplishing anything.
8. To obtain disability income, <u>an employee must have a doctor certify that the employee cannot work</u>.

EXERCISE 5

Revise the following sentences to eliminate any dangling modifiers. Each item has more than one possible answer.

Example:

Driving north, the vegetation became increasingly sparse.

Driving north, *we noticed* that the vegetation became increasingly sparse.

As we drove north, the vegetation became increasingly sparse.

1. By turning the lights down, the room looked less dingy.
2. To file a formal complaint, a statement must be submitted.
3. Having prepared thoroughly, the exam was easy for me.
4. Though usually energetic, emotional problems had sapped her strength.
5. Staring at the ceiling, the idea became clear.
6. Sagging and needing a new coat of paint, Mr. Preston called the house painter.
7. Monday passed me by without accomplishing anything.
8. To obtain disability income, a doctor must certify that an employee cannot work.

9. When only a ninth grader, my grandmother tried to teach me double-entry bookkeeping.
10. After weighing the alternatives, his decision became clear.

EXERCISE 6

Combine each pair of sentences below into a single sentence by rewriting one as a modifier. Make sure the modifier applies clearly to the appropriate word. You will have to add, delete, and rearrange words, and you may find that more than one answer is possible in each case.

Example:

Bob demanded a hearing from the faculty. Bob wanted to appeal the decision.

Wanting to appeal the decision, Bob demanded a hearing from the faculty.

1. We were taking our seats. The announcer read the line-up.
2. I was rushing to the interview. My shoelace broke.
3. The children crowded into the buses. The children were from the fifth grade.
4. She was trying to cheer Jason up. Her Halloween mask terrified Jason instead.
5. They were holding hands. A man crept up behind them.
6. She rested her bandaged foot on the stool. She was wearing a yellow satin robe.
7. My uncle said he had never received good advice. He was fifty years old then.
8. Several people saw the ranch hand. The people had been shopping in town.
9. We reached the end of the road. A vast emptiness surrounded us.
10. Sylvie received a letter announcing she had won. The letter came the day after she returned from vacation.

EXERCISE 7

Revise the following paragraph to eliminate any misplaced or dangling modifiers.

Town legend has it that Mr. Potter was as an infant left on the doorstep of a church in a basket. After a few days he was placed in the care of experienced foster parents along with two other orphans who provided love and strong guidance. Eventually adopted by his foster parents, Mr. Potter's life was seemingly happy and uneventful through law school. His bizarre behavior only started after his law practice began to completely fail.

---

9. When **I was** only a ninth grader, my grandmother tried to teach me double-entry bookkeeping.
10. After **he weighed** the alternatives, his decision became clear.

dm
14f

POSSIBLE ANSWERS: EXERCISE 6

1. As we were taking our seats, the announcer read the line-up.
2. As I was rushing to the interview, my shoelace broke.
3. The children from the fifth grade crowded into the buses.
4. While trying to cheer Jason up, she terrified him instead with her Halloween mask.
5. They were holding hands when a man crept up behind them.
6. Wearing a yellow satin robe, she rested her bandaged foot on the stool.
7. At fifty years old, my uncle said he had never received good advice.
8. Several people who had been shopping in town saw the ranch hand.
9. When we reached the end of the road, a vast emptiness surrounded us.
10. The day after she returned from vacation, Sylvie received a letter announcing she had won.

ANSWERS: EXERCISE 7

Sample revision

Town legend has it that <u>as an infant</u> Mr. Potter was left <u>in a basket</u> on the doorstep of a church. After a few days he, <u>along with two other orphans</u>, was placed in the care of experienced foster parents who provided love and strong guidance. Eventually adopted by his foster parents, <u>Mr. Potter led a seemingly happy and uneventful life</u> through law school. His bizarre behavior started <u>only</u> after his law practice began <u>to fail completely</u>.

CHAPTER 15

Mixed and Incomplete Sentences

MIXED SENTENCES

A **mixed sentence** contains two or more parts that are incompatible—that is, the parts do not fit together. The misfit may be in grammar or in meaning.

MIXED GRAMMAR	After watching television for twelve hours was the reason his head hurt.
MIXED MEANING	The work involved in directing the use of resources is the definition of management.

15a Be sure that the parts of your sentences, particularly subjects and predicates, fit together grammatically.

Many mixed sentences occur when we start a sentence with one grammatical plan or construction in mind but end it with a different one. Such sentences often result from a confusion between two ways of making a statement.

MIXED	In all her efforts to please others got her into trouble.

In this mixed sentence the writer starts with a modifying prepositional phrase and then tries to make that phrase work as the subject of *got*. But prepositional phrases can very seldom function as sentence subjects. The sentence needs a new subject for *got*.

REVISED	In all her efforts to please others, *she* got into trouble. [The necessary subject *she* is added to the main clause.]

306

REVISED   *All her efforts* to please others got her into trouble. [The preposition *In* is dropped, leaving the subject *All her efforts*.]

Each group of sentences below illustrates a similar confusion between two sentence plans and gives ideas for revising the subject and sometimes the predicate so that they fit grammatically.

MIXED   Although he was seen with a convicted thief does not make him a thief. [The writer has used an adverb clause, beginning *Although*, as the subject of *does*. An adverb clause cannot serve as a subject.]

REVISED   *That* he was seen with a convicted thief does not make him a thief. [*That* changes the clause into a noun clause, a grammatical subject.]

REVISED   Although he was seen with a convicted thief, *he is* not necessarily a thief. [A new subject and verb are supplied for the main clause.]

MIXED   Among those who pass the entrance examinations, they do not all get admitted to the program. [The modifying phrase beginning *Among* demands a subject that gives an amount, such as *all or many*, not the general *they*.]

REVISED   Among those who pass the entrance examinations, *not all* get admitted to the program.

REVISED   Among those who pass the entrance examinations, *many* do not get admitted to the program.

REVISED   *Not all those* who pass the entrance examinations get admitted to the program.

15b Be sure that the subjects and predicates of your sentences fit together in meaning.

The mixed sentences examined above are confusing because their parts do not fit together grammatically. Another kind of mixed sentence fails because its subject and predicate do not fit together in meaning: the subject is said to be or do something it cannot logically be or do. Such a mixture is sometimes called **faulty predication.**

The most common form of faulty predication occurs when the linking verb *be* connects a subject and its complement. Since such a sentence forms a kind of equation, the subject and complement must be items that can be sensibly equated. If they are not, the sentence goes awry.

ACTIVITIES AND ASSIGNMENTS

Because the mixed and incomplete sentences in student writing have complicated causes and because the problems in one student's essay are likely to differ widely from those in another student's paper, most instructors choose simply to discuss the chapter and use some of the exercises rather than elaborate with classroom activities and assignments. In working with individual students, however, most instructors are able to devise activities that suit individual needs. Instructors who wish to alert students to the problem of incomplete compound constructions, incomplete comparisons, and omission of needed words can draw from a student paper or write a passage containing these problems and then ask students to work with the passage, perhaps in small groups, proofreading it and correcting the errors.

mixed
15b

RESOURCES AND IDEAS

Valerie Krishna, "The Syntax of Error," *Journal of Basic Writing* 1 (1975): 43–49. The author views problems like mixed constructions and shifts as the result of a weak sentence core, and she encourages teachers to pay attention to this underlying problem in helping students avoid such errors.

> **FAULTY** A *compromise* between the city and the town would be the ideal *place* to live.

In this sentence the subject *compromise* is equated with the complement *place*. Thus the sentence says that *a compromise is a place*, clearly not a sensible statement. Sometimes such mixed sentences seem to result from the writer's effort to compress too many ideas into a single word or phrase. The sentence above can be revised to state the writer's meaning more exactly.

> **REVISED** A *community* that offered the best qualities of both city and town would be the ideal *place* to live.

A special kind of faulty predication occurs when a clause beginning *when* or *where* follows a form of *be* in a definition, as in *Suffrage is where you have the right to vote*. Though the construction is common in speech, written definitions require nouns or noun clauses on both sides of *be: Suffrage is the right to vote*.

> **FAULTY** An *examination* is *when you are tested* on what you know.
>
> **REVISED** An *examination* is *a test* of what you know.
>
> **REVISED** *In an examination you are tested* on what you know.

A similar kind of faulty predication occurs when a *because* clause follows the subject-verb pattern *The reason is*, as in *The reason is because I don't want to*. This construction is common in speech, but it is redundant since the conjunction *because* means *for the reason that*. The construction should not appear in writing.

> **FAULTY** The *reason* we were late *is because* we had an accident.
>
> **REVISED** The *reason* we were late is *that* we had an accident.
>
> **REVISED** We were late *because* we had an accident.

Faulty predications are not confined to sentences with *be*. In the following sentences the italicized subjects and verbs highlight the misfit between them.

> **FAULTY** The *use* of emission controls *was created* to reduce air pollution. [The controls, not their use, were created.]
>
> **REVISED** Emission *controls were created* to reduce air pollution.

FAULTY	The *area* of financial mismanagement *poses* a threat to small businesses. [Mismanagement, not the area, poses the threat.]
REVISED	Financial *mismanagement poses* a threat to small businesses.

In some mixed sentences the combination of faults is so confusing that the writer has little choice but to start over.

MIXED	My long-range goal is through law school and government work I hope to deal with those problems I deal with more effectively.
POSSIBLE REVISION	My long-range goal is to go to law school and then work in government so that I can deal more effectively with problems I face.

mixed
15b

EXERCISE 1

Revise the following sentences so that their parts fit together both in grammar and in meaning. Each item has more than one possible answer.

Example:

When they found out how expensive pianos are is why they were discouraged.

They were discouraged *because* they found out how expensive pianos are.

When they found out how expensive pianos are, *they* were discouraged.

1. The different accents of students is in where they grew up.
2. Because he believes news programs are misleading is why he does not watch them.
3. By simply increasing the amount of money we spend will not solve the problem of crime.
4. An antique is when an object is one hundred or more years old.
5. Among the polished stones, they were all beyond my price range.
6. Schizophrenia is when a person withdraws from reality and behaves in abnormal ways.
7. Any government that can support an expedition to Mars, they should be able to solve their country's social problems too.
8. Needlepoint is where you work with yarn on a mesh canvas.
9. Through the help of his staff is how the mayor got reelected.
10. The reason many people don't accept the theory of evolution is because it goes contrary to their religious beliefs.

POSSIBLE ANSWERS: EXERCISE 1

1. Students have different accents because they grew up in different regions.
2. He does not watch news programs, because he believes they are misleading.
3. Simply increasing the amount of money we spend will not solve the problem of crime.
4. An antique is an object that is one hundred or more years old.
5. The polished stones were all beyond my price range.
6. Schizophrenia is a psychological disorder causing a person to withdraw from reality and behave in abnormal ways.
7. Any government that can support an expedition to Mars should be able to solve its country's social problems too.
8. Needlepoint is the craft of working with yarn on a mesh canvas.
9. The help of his staff got the mayor reelected.
10. Many people don't accept the theory of evolution because it contradicts their religious beliefs.

INCOMPLETE SENTENCES

The most serious kind of incomplete sentence is the fragment (see Chapter 10). But sentences are also incomplete when the writer omits one or more words needed to make a phrase or clause clear or accurate.

15c	Be sure that omissions from compound constructions are consistent with grammar or idiom.

In both speech and writing we commonly use **elliptical constructions,** constructions that omit words not necessary for meaning (see 5c-4). In the following sentences the words in parentheses can be omitted without confusing or distracting the reader. Notice that they all involve compound constructions.

My car has been driven 80,000 miles; his (has been driven) only 20,000 (miles).

Some people heat by oil, some (heat) by gas and some (heat) by electricity.

She had great hopes for her sons and (for) their children.

Such omissions are possible only when the words omitted are common to all the parts of a compound construction. When the parts differ in grammar or idiom, all words must be included in all parts.

My car *has been driven* 80,000 miles; their cars *have been driven* only 20,000 miles.

I *am* firm; you *are* stubborn; he *is* pigheaded.

The students *were* invited and *were* happy to go. [Each *were* has a different grammatical function: the first is a helping verb in the passive verb phrase *were invited;* the second is a linking verb with the complement *happy.*]

She had faith *in* and hopes *for* the future. [Idiom requires different prepositions with *faith* and *hopes,* so both must be included.]

Notice that in the sentence *My brother and friend moved to Dallas,* the omission of *my* before *friend* indicates that *brother* and *friend* are the same person. If two different persons are meant, the modifier or article must be repeated: *My brother and my friend moved to Dallas.*

(See 31b-3 for a list of English idioms and 17a for a discussion of grammatical parallelism.)

15d   Be sure that all comparisons are complete and logical.

Comparisons make statements about the relation between two or more things, as in *Dogs are more intelligent than cats* or *Bones was the most intelligent dog we ever had.* To be complete and logical, a comparison must state the relation fully enough to ensure clarity; it must compare only items that can sensibly be compared; and it must include all and only the items being compared.

1   State a comparison fully enough to ensure clarity.

In a comparison such as *John likes bowling better than (he likes) tennis*, we can omit *he likes* because only one meaning is possible. But sentences such as *John likes bowling better than Jane* may mean either "better than he likes Jane" or "better than Jane likes bowling." Therefore, we must be careful to state such sentences fully enough to prevent any misreading.

UNCLEAR	They worry more about money than their child.
CLEAR	They worry more about money than their child *does*.
CLEAR	They worry more about money than *about* their child.

2   Be sure that the items being compared are in fact comparable.

A comparison is logical only if it compares items that can sensibly be compared. We can compare one food with another or one car with another, but we cannot sensibly compare food with cars. We are likely to make illogical comparisons unintentionally.

ILLOGICAL	The cost of a typewriter is greater than a calculator. [The writer compares the cost of something with a calculator.]
REVISED	The cost of a typewriter is greater than *the cost of* (or *that of*) a calculator.

3   In comparing items in the same class, use *other* or *any other*. In comparing items in different classes, use *any*.

When we compare a person or thing with all others in the same group, we form two units: (1) the individual person or thing and (2) all *other* persons or things in the group. The two units need to be distinguished.

Joshua [the individual] was more stubborn than *any other* child in the family [all the others in the group].

ILLOGICAL Los Angeles is larger than *any* city in California. [Since Los Angeles is itself a city in California, the sentence seems to say that Los Angeles is larger than itself.]

LOGICAL Los Angeles is larger than *any other* city in California. [Adding *other* excludes Los Angeles from the group of the state's other cities.]

When a person or thing is compared with the members of a *different* group, the two units are logically separate.

Some American cars [one group] are cheaper than *any* foreign car [a different group].

ILLOGICAL Los Angeles is larger than *any other* city in Canada. [The cities in Canada constitute a group to which Los Angeles does not belong.]

LOGICAL Los Angeles is larger than *any* city in Canada. [Omitting the word *other* makes a separate group of the Canadian cities.]

4 **Avoid comparisons that do not state what is being compared.**

Brand X gets clothes *whiter*. [Whiter than what?]
Brand Y is so much *better*. [Better than what?]

15e **Be careful not to omit articles, prepositions, or other needed words.**

In haste or carelessness writers sometimes omit small words such as articles and prepositions that are needed for clarity.

INCOMPLETE Regular payroll deductions are a type painless savings. You hardly notice missing amounts, and after period of years the contributions can add a large total.

REVISED Regular payroll deductions are a type *of* painless savings. You hardly notice *the* missing amounts, and after *a* period of years the contributions can add *up to* a large total.

In both speech and writing we often omit *that* when it introduces a noun clause following a verb: *We knew* (*that*) *he was coming.* But such an omission can sometimes be confusing.

INCOMPLETE	She observed many people who had been invited were missing. [At first reading, *many people* appears to be the object of *observed* rather than the subject of the entire subordinate clause.]
REVISED	She observed *that* many people who had been invited were missing.

Attentive proofreading is the only insurance against the kind of omissions described in this section. (See 2d.) *Proofread all your papers carefully.*

inc

15e

EXERCISE 2

Revise the following sentences so that they are complete, logical, and clear. Some items have more than one possible answer.

Example:

Our house is closer to the courthouse than the subway stop.

Our house is closer to the courthouse than *it is to* the subway stop.

Our house is closer to the courthouse than the subway stop *is.*

1. I get along with my parents better than my sister.
2. Councilor Dougherty not only believes but works for tax reform.
3. Wally believed people who came to him with their problems were using him.
4. His tip was larger than any customer I ever waited on.
5. With an altitude of 6288 feet, New Hampshire's Mount Washington is higher than any mountain in New England.
6. The largest bookstore the United States stocks two three copies most books in print.
7. The dog is only a puppy; the cats both ten years old.
8. My chemistry text is more interesting to me than any other social science text.
9. Inventors usually have an interest and talent for solving practical problems.
10. The legal question raised by the prosecution was relevant and considered by the judge.

EXERCISE 3

Revise the following paragraph to eliminate mixed or incomplete constructions.

ANSWERS: EXERCISE 2

1. I get along with my parents better than my sister <u>does</u>. *Or:* I get along with my parents better than <u>with</u> my sister.
2. Councilor Dougherty not only believes <u>in</u> but works for tax reform.
3. Wally believed <u>that</u> people who came to him with their problems were using him.
4. His tip was larger than <u>that of</u> any <u>other</u> customer I ever waited on.
5. With an altitude of 6288 feet, New Hampshire's Mount Washington is higher than any <u>other</u> mountain in New England.
6. The largest bookstore <u>in</u> the United States stocks two <u>or</u> three copies <u>of</u> most books in print.
7. My dog is only a puppy; the cats <u>are</u> both ten years old.
8. My chemistry text is more interesting to me than <u>any</u> social science text.
9. Inventors usually have an interest <u>in</u> and <u>a</u> talent for solving practical problems.
10. The legal question raised by the prosecution was relevant and <u>was</u> considered by the judge.

ANSWERS: EXERCISE 3

Possible revision

The Hancock Tower in Boston is <u>a</u> thin mirror-glass slab that rises almost 800 feet. When it was being constructed in the early 1970s<u>, its</u> windows began cracking, and some fell crashing to the ground. In order to minimize risk<u>s, the</u> architects and owners replaced over a third <u>of</u> the huge windows with plywood until the problem could be found and solved. With its plywood sheath, the building was homelier than any <u>other</u> skyscraper, the butt of many jokes. Eventually, however, it was discovered <u>that the</u> windows <u>cracked because the</u> joint between the double panes of glass was too <u>rigid.</u> <u>Thicker</u> single-pane windows <u>were</u> installed, and the silly plywood building crystallized into <u>a</u> reflective jewel.

The Hancock Tower in Boston is thin mirror-glass slab that rises almost 800 feet. When it was being constructed in the early 1970s was when its windows began cracking, and some fell crashing to the ground. In order to minimize risks is why the architects and owners replaced over a third the huge windows with plywood until the problem could be found and solved. With its plywood sheath, the building was homelier than any skyscraper, the butt of many jokes. Eventually, however, it was discovered that the reason the windows cracked was because joint between the double panes of glass was too rigid. The solution of thicker single-pane windows was installed, and the silly plywood building crystallized into reflective jewel.

HIGHLIGHTS

The discussion in this chapter emphasizes how writers can use coordination and subordination to relate ideas and distinguish central ideas from less important material. The opening section illustrates how coordination relates facts and ideas and then goes on to address the problems of excessive and faulty coordination. The second section follows a parallel pattern in discussing subordination, focusing on subordinate clauses. But since effective writing depends on a writer's ability to work with the whole range of subordinate structures, the uses of single words; appositives; and prepositional, verbal, and absolute phrases are also illustrated. The final section cautions briefly against the often unclear and misused connectors *like*, *while*, and *as*.

Included in this chapter are subsections on punctuating coordinated elements (16a), designed to help students not only punctuate correctly but also see punctuation as an instrument and extension of effective sentence structure. The exercises in this chapter ask students to revise sentences and longer passages and to combine sentences in ways that implement the sentence strategies introduced in the chapter.

CHAPTER 16

Using Coordination and Subordination

To communicate effectively, you often need to combine several statements into a single sentence, fitting thoughts together according to their relative importance. You can **coordinate** the facts and ideas you wish to emphasize equally, such as the thoughts about insurance in the sentence *Car insurance is costly, but medical insurance is almost a luxury.* You can **subordinate** statements of lesser importance to those you wish to emphasize. In the sentence *Because accidents and theft are frequent, car insurance is expensive*, the clause beginning *Because* is grammatically subordinate to the main clause. The information you decide to subordinate may be important to the total meaning of the sentence, providing necessary explanation or support, but readers will almost always see it as less important than that presented in the main clause.

The box on the facing page and the following sections provide guidelines for using coordination and subordination effectively in constructing sentences.

16a Coordinating to relate equal ideas

Two or more simple sentences in a row will seem roughly equal in importance but distinct, even if they are related in content. Thus readers will have to detect on their own the specific relations among the sentences. By linking sentences and ideas with coordinating conjunctions or conjunctive adverbs, a writer can help readers see the relations more easily. Compare the following passages.

We should not rely so heavily on coal, oil, and uranium. We have a substantial energy resource in the moving waters of our rivers.

316

PRINCIPAL WAYS TO COORDINATE AND SUBORDINATE INFORMATION IN SENTENCES

Use **coordination** to relate ideas of equal importance (16a).

1. Link main clauses with a comma and a coordinating conjunction: *and, but, or, nor, for, so, yet* (5d-1).

   Independence Hall in Philadelphia is now restored, *but* fifty years ago it was in bad shape.

2. Relate main clauses with a semicolon alone or a semicolon and a conjunctive adverb: *however, indeed, thus,* etc. (5d-2).

   The building and others nearby still stood; *however,* they suffered from decay and vandalism.

3. Within clauses, link words and phrases with a coordinating conjunction: *and, but, or, nor* (5d-1).

   The people *and* officials of Philadelphia were indifferent to Independence Hall *or* took it for granted.

Use **subordination** to de-emphasize ideas (16b).

1. Use a subordinate clause beginning with a subordinating conjunction: *although, because, if, whereas,* etc. (5c-4).

   Although some citizens had tried to rescue the building, they had not gained substantial public support.

2. Use a subordinate clause beginning with a relative pronoun: *who, whoever, which, that* (5c-4).

   The first strong step was taken by the federal government, *which made the building a national monument in the 1950s.*

3. Use a prepositional, verbal, or absolute phrase (5c-1 to 5c-3).

   Like most national monuments, Independence Hall is protected by the National Park Service. [Prepositional phrase.]

   The service, *protecting many popular tourist sites,* is a highly visible government agency. [Verbal phrase.]

   Visitors can always learn something at national parks, *the rangers being helpful and informative.* [Absolute phrase.]

4. Use an appositive (5c-5).

   The National Park Service, *a branch of the Department of Interior,* also runs Yosemite and other wilderness parks.

5. Use a modifying word.

   At the *red brick* Independence Hall, park rangers give *guided* tours and protect the *irreplaceable* building from vandalism.

RESOURCES AND IDEAS

Evelyn B. Melamed and Harvey Minkoff, "Transitions: A Key to Mature Reading and Writing," *Teaching the Basics—Really!* ed. Ouida Clapp (Urbana: NCTE, 1977), 17–21. The authors describe exercises to help students make logical links between sentences and parts of sentences with transitions.

coord
16a

RESOURCES AND IDEAS
You may wish to remind students that section 5d of the handbook contains a detailed discussion of coordinating conjunctions. If students make a simple list of the conjunctions, they may find themselves becoming more aware of the words and their functions as they read and write:

and	or
but	for
nor	so
yet	

coord
16a

Smaller streams add to the total volume of water. The resource renews itself. Coal and oil are irreplaceable. Uranium is also irreplaceable. The cost of water does not increase much over time. The costs of coal, oil, and uranium rise dramatically.

We should not rely so heavily on coal, oil, and uranium, for we have a substantial energy resource in the moving waters of our rivers and streams. Coal, oil, and uranium are irreplaceable and thus subject to dramatic cost increases; water, however, is self-renewing and more stable in cost.

The information in both passages is essentially the same, but the second is shorter and considerably easier to read and understand. Whereas the first passage strings ideas together in short, simple sentences without relating them to each other, the second passage builds connections among coordinate ideas: the availability of water in rivers and streams (first sentence); the relation between renewal and cost (second sentence); and the contrast between water and the other resources (both sentences).

Punctuating coordinated words, phrases, and clauses

Most coordinated words, phrases, and subordinate clauses are not punctuated with commas (see 21j-2). The exceptions are items in a series and coordinate adjectives.

We rely heavily on *coal, oil, and uranium.* [A series; see 21f-1.]

Dusty, dog-eared books littered his rooms. [Coordinate adjectives; see 21f-2.]

In a sentence consisting of two main clauses, punctuation depends on whether a coordinating conjunction, a conjunctive adverb, or no connecting word links the clauses.

Oil is irreplaceable, *but* water is self-renewing. [See 21a.]

Oil is irreplaceable; *however*, water is self-renewing. [See 22b.]

Oil is irreplaceable; water is self-renewing. [See 22a.]

1 Avoiding faulty coordination

Faulty coordination occurs when no logical connection seems to exist between two coordinated statements or when the connection expressed by the coordinating conjunction contradicts common sense.

FAULTY	Forecasters had predicted a mild winter, and temperatures were lower than normal.
REVISED	Forecasters had predicted a mild winter, *but* temperatures were lower than normal.

Sometimes faulty coordination occurs because the writer omits necessary information, as in the following example.

FAULTY	Julie is a hairdresser, and she has developed a skin allergy.
REVISED	As a hairdresser, Julie *must use products containing strong chemicals; consequently,* she has developed a skin allergy.
REVISED	*Because* her work as a hairdresser *requires that she use products containing strong chemicals,* Julie has developed a skin allergy.

Often, as the second revision shows, the intended relation between clauses can be clarified by subordinating one of the ideas if it modifies or explains the other one. Here is another example.

FAULTY	John Stuart Mill was a utilitarian, and he believed that actions should be judged by their usefulness or by the happiness they cause.
REVISED	John Stuart Mill, *a utilitarian,* believed that actions should be judged by their usefulness or by the happiness they cause.

2 Avoiding excessive coordination

A stringy compound sentence—a sequence of main clauses linked with coordinating conjunctions—creates the same effect as a series of simple sentences: it obscures the relative importance of ideas and details.

EXCESSIVE COORDINATION	We were near the end of the trip, and the storm kept getting worse, and the snow and ice covered the windshield, and I could hardly see the road ahead, and I knew I should stop, but I kept on driving, and once I barely missed a truck.

This sentence contains two main assertions: *the storm kept getting worse* and *I kept on driving.* All the rest is detail elaborating on these simple statements. The information in the sentence needs to be recombined using subordination so that the reader can easily distinguish between main assertions and the details that support them.

REVISED	As we neared the end of the trip, *the storm kept getting worse,* covering the windshield with snow and ice until I could barely see the road ahead. Even though I knew I should stop, *I kept on driving,* once barely missing a truck.

RESOURCES AND IDEAS

You may wish to remind students that section 5d of the handbook contains a detailed discussion of conjunctive adverbs. You can help create awareness of conjunctive adverbs by asking students to make a list of the words. As they read and write later, students may pay greater attention to the conjunctive adverbs and their functions:

also	further
next	then
certainly	likewise
similarly	undoubtedly
however	anyway
therefore	now
meanwhile	finally
namely	still
besides	indeed
otherwise	thus

coord
16a

Be careful not to overuse *so* as a connector.

<table>
<tr><td>**EXCESSIVE COORDINATION**</td><td>Jim had an examination that day, so he came home late, so he missed seeing the fire, so he was not able to describe it to us.</td></tr>
</table>

As with other varieties of excessive coordination, the best way to revise such sentences is to separate the main statement from dependent details.

<table>
<tr><td>**REVISED**</td><td>*Jim was not able to describe the fire to us* because he had an examination that day and arrived home too late to see the fire.</td></tr>
</table>

Excessive coordination is not always as obvious as it is in the two preceding examples. The following passage contains only two compound sentences, but they still connect facts so loosely that the reader is left to distinguish their importance.

<table>
<tr><td>**EXCESSIVE COORDINATION**</td><td>A man came out of the liquor store. He wore a pair of frayed corduroy pants, and he wore a brown sweater. He started toward a blue car, and the police arrested him.</td></tr>
</table>

In revising this passage, a writer might use subordination to show which ideas are important and which less important. The essential fact that the police arrested the man could become the main clause and all other details part of a single subordinate *when* clause.

<table>
<tr><td>**REVISED**</td><td>When a man wearing frayed corduroy pants and a brown sweater came out of the liquor store and started toward a blue car, *the police arrested him.*</td></tr>
</table>

coord
16a

ANSWERS: EXERCISE 1

Possible Revisions

1. Many chronic misspellers do not have the time <u>or</u> motivation to master spelling rules. They rely on dictionaries to catch misspellings,<u> but</u> most dictionaries list words under their correct spellings. One kind of dictionary is designed for chronic misspellers. It lists each word under its common *mis*spellings <u>and</u> then provides the correct spelling <u>and</u> definition.

2. Henry Hudson was an English explorer<u>, but</u> he captained ships for the Dutch East India Company. On a voyage in 1610 he passed Greenland <u>and</u> sailed into a great bay in today's northern Canada. He thought

Good!

EXERCISE 1

<u>Combine sentences in the following passages to coordinate related ideas in the way that seems most effective to you. You will have to supply coordinating conjunctions or conjunctive adverbs and the appropriate punctuation.</u>

1. Many chronic misspellers do not have the time to master spelling rules. They may not have the motivation. They rely on dictionaries to catch misspellings. Most dictionaries list words under their correct spellings. One kind of dictionary is designed for chronic misspellers. It lists each word under its common *mis*spellings. It then provides the correct spelling. It also provides the definition.

2. Henry Hudson was an English explorer. He captained ships for the Dutch East India Company. On a voyage in 1610 he

passed by Greenland. He sailed into a great bay in today's northern Canada. He thought he and his sailors could winter there. The cold was terrible. Food ran out. The sailors mutinied. The sailors cast Hudson adrift in a small boat. Eight others were also in the boat. Hudson and his companions perished.

Good!

EXERCISE 2

Revise the following sentences to eliminate faulty or excessive coordination. Relate ideas effectively by adding or subordinating information or by forming more than one sentence. Each item has more than one possible answer.

Example:

My dog barks, and I have to move out of my apartment.

Because my dog's barking *disturbs my neighbors*, I have to move out of my apartment.

1. The candidate was an Independent, and she disagreed with both the Republican and the Democrat.
2. He is almost always cheerful, and he has few friends.
3. The dean was furious, and she let the police know it, but they refused to listen, and they began patrolling the campus anyway.
4. The dogs escaped from the pen because the keeper forgot to secure the latch, and the dogs wanted freedom, and they got it by running away, and it took the rest of the day to find them.
5. The weather in March is cold and rainy, but sometimes it is warm and sunny, and the inconsistency makes it impossible to plan outdoor activities, yet everyone wants to be outdoors after the long winter.
6. The gun sounded, and I froze, but an instant later I was running with a smooth, pumping motion, and I knew I would win the race.
7. The citizens of Vermont are determined to preserve their environment, and they have some of the nation's toughest antipollution laws.
8. Two days last month were legal holidays, and the school held classes as usual.
9. Registering for classes the first time is confusing, and you have to find your way around, and you have to deal with strangers.
10. Air traffic in and out of major cities increases yearly, and the congestion is becoming dangerous, but the current regulations are inadequate, and they cannot control even the present traffic.

he and his sailors could winter there, but the cold was terrible and food ran out. The sailors mutinied and cast Hudson and eight others adrift in a small boat. Hudson and his companions perished.

POSSIBLE ANSWERS: EXERCISE 2

1. The candidate, an Independent, disagreed with both the Republican and the Democrat.
2. Even though he is almost always cheerful, he has few friends.
3. Although the dean let the police know she was furious, they refused to listen and began patrolling the campus anyway.
4. Wanting freedom, the dogs escaped from the pen when the keeper forgot to secure the latch. They ran away, and it took the rest of the day to find them.
5. Although the weather in March is cold and rainy, sometimes it is warm and sunny. Everyone wants to be outdoors after the long winter, but the inconsistency in weather makes it impossible to plan outdoor activities.
6. I froze when the gun sounded, but an instant later I was running with a smooth, pumping motion. I knew I would win the race.
7. Because they are determined to preserve their environment, the citizens of Vermont have some of the nation's toughest antipollution laws.
8. Although two days last month were legal holidays, the school held classes as usual.
9. Registering for classes the first time is confusing because you have to find your way around and deal with strangers.
10. Although air traffic in and out of major cities increases yearly so that congestion is becoming dangerous, the current regulations are inadequate to control even the present traffic.

coord

16a

16b Subordinating to distinguish main ideas

Like paragraphs, many sentences consist of a main idea amplified and supported by details. Usually, the main idea appears in the main clause, and the details appear in subordinate structures such as phrases or subordinate clauses. This arrangement helps readers distinguish principal ideas from supporting information. In the following sentence the writer does not provide such assistance.

> In recent years computer prices have dropped, and production costs have dropped more slowly, and computer manufacturers have had to contend with shrinking profits.

The writer gives three facts: computer prices have decreased, production costs have decreased, and profits have shrunk. By loosely coordinating these three facts, the writer suggests some relation among them. But *in recent years* and *more slowly* provide the only explicit relations. We do not know which fact the writer considers most important or how the others qualify or support it. Look at the improvement in these revisions.

> *Because* production costs have dropped more slowly than computer prices in recent years, computer manufacturers have had to contend with shrinking profits.

> In recent years computer manufacturers have had to contend with shrinking profits *on account of* a slower drop in production costs than in computer prices.

> *Faced with* a slower drop in production costs than in computer prices, computer manufacturers have had to contend with shrinking profits in recent years.

In these revisions the words *because, on account of,* and *faced with* indicate specific cause-and-effect relations among the three facts. Each sentence makes clear that computer manufacturers' profits decline when prices fall more quickly than production costs, but the emphasis varies from one version to another.

No rules can specify what information in a sentence you should make primary and what you should subordinate; the decision will depend on your meaning. But, in general, you should consider using subordinate structures for details of time, cause, condition, concession, purpose, and identification (size, location, and the like). Consider the use of subordinate clauses in the following pairs of examples. (Some appropriate subordinating conjunctions and relative pronouns are listed in parentheses.)

TIME (*after, before, since, until, when, while*)

> The mine explosion killed six workers. The owners adopted safety measures.

(margin) sub
16b

After the mine explosion killed six workers, the owners adopted safety measures.

CAUSE (*because, since*)

Jones has been without work for six months. He is having trouble paying his bills.

Because Jones has been without work for six months, he is having trouble paying his bills.

CONDITION (*if, provided, since, unless*)

Mike attends no lectures and studies infrequently. He has little chance of passing his biology examination.

Since Mike attends no lectures and studies infrequently, he has little chance of passing his biology examination.

CONCESSION (*although, as if, even though, though*)

The horse looked gentle. It proved high-spirited and hard to manage.

Although the horse looked gentle, it proved high-spirited and hard to manage.

PURPOSE (*in order that, so that, that*)

Congress passed new immigration laws. Many Vietnamese refugees could enter the United States.

Congress passed new immigration laws *so that* many Vietnamese refugees could enter the United States.

IDENTIFICATION (*that, when, where, which, who*)

The old factory now manufactures automobile transmissions. It stands on the south side of town and covers three acres.

The old factory, *which* stands on the south side of town and covers three acres, now manufactures automobile transmissions.

Using subordinate clauses to distinguish main ideas from supporting information is an important strategy for creating effective sentences. But you can use other grammatical constructions as well to indicate the subordinate role of certain statements or information. A verbal or prepositional phrase, an appositive, an absolute phrase, or even a single-word modifier will often be the appropriate choice. In general, a subordinate clause places greatest emphasis on the subordinate information; verbal phrases, appositives, and absolute phrases give less weight; prepositional phrases still less; and single words the least. The following sets of examples illustrate the differences among subordinate constructions.

Old barns are common in New England. They are often painted red. [Separate sentences.]

Old barns, *which are often painted red*, are common in New England. [Subordinate clause.]

IDENTIFYING

Have students, working in groups, identify the connectors (subordinating and coordinating conjunctions) in several essays: an essay from a reader, a news item in a newspaper, or a student essay. If the uses of subordination and coordination and the kinds of connectors differ in each kind of essay, ask students to try to account for the differences.

sub
16b

Old barns, *often painted red*, are common in New England. [Verbal phrase.]

Old *red* barns are common in New England. [Single word.]

The horse looked gentle. It proved high-spirited and hard to manage. [Separate sentences.]

Although the horse looked gentle, it proved high-spirited and hard to manage. [Subordinate clause.]

Despite its gentle appearance, the horse proved high-spirited and hard to manage. [Prepositional phrase.]

The horse, *a gentle-looking animal*, proved high-spirited and hard to manage. [Appositive.]

The *gentle-looking* horse proved high-spirited and hard to manage. [Single word.]

Punctuating subordinate constructions

A modifying word, phrase, or clause that introduces a sentence is usually set off from the rest of the sentence with a comma (see 21b).

Fortunately, I got the job.
In a little over six months, the company will open a new plant.
Buffeted by the wind, the boat drifted out to sea.
When the crisis passed, everyone was relieved.

A modifier that interrupts or concludes a main clause is *not* set off with punctuation when it restricts the meaning of a word or words in the clause (see 21c).

Her article *about a bank failure* won a prize.

The article *that won the prize* appeared in the local newspaper.

She wrote the article *because the bank failure affected many residents of the town.*

When an interrupting or concluding modifier does *not* restrict meaning, but simply adds information to the sentence, it *is* set off with punctuation, usually a comma or commas (see 21c).

The bank, *over forty years old,* never reopened.

The bank managers, *who were cleared of any wrongdoing,* all found new jobs.

The customers of the bank never recovered all their money, *although most of them tried to do so.*

Like a modifier, an appositive is set off with punctuation (usually a comma or commas) only when it does *not* restrict the meaning of the word it refers to (see 21c-2).

GETTING A NEW LOOK AT YOUR WRITING

Give students a fresh look at their own writing by asking them to revise a portion of a graded essay following specific directions, such as, "Add subordination" or "Use more imaginative subordinating words."

REDUCING

To help students practice subordination, create several groups, and give each group a different passage. Ask the groups to first reduce sentences to clauses and then, if possible, to phrases and words. After they have reduced the modifiers in these stages, ask the students in each group to reach consensus on the version they find most effective. At the end of the activity, the groups can explain to the rest of the class the changes they made. Or the groups can exchange passages and repeat the process, comparing their work at the end with the work of the prior group.

The movie, *a science-fiction adventure,* was a huge success.
The movie *Star Wars* was directed by George Lucas.

A dash or dashes may also be used to set off a nonrestrictive appositive, particularly when it contains commas (see 25b-2). A concluding appositive is sometimes set off with a colon (see 25a-1).

1 Avoiding faulty subordination

Faulty subordination occurs when a writer uses a subordinate clause or other subordinate structure for what seems clearly to be the most important idea in the sentence. Often, faulty subordination merely reverses the dependent relation the reader expects.

FAULTY	Ms. Angelo was in her first year of teaching, although she was a better instructor than others with many years of experience. [The sentence suggests that Ms. Angelo's inexperience is the main idea, whereas the writer almost certainly intended to stress her skill *despite* her inexperience.]
REVISED	Although Ms. Angelo was in her first year of teaching, *she was a better instructor than others with many years of experience.*
FAULTY	Marty's final interview that was to determine his admission to law school began at two o'clock. [Common sense says that the important fact is the interview's purpose, not its time.]
REVISED	*Marty's final interview,* which began at two o'clock, *was to determine his admission to law school.*

sub
16b

2 Avoiding excessive subordination

Excessive subordination sometimes occurs when a writer tries to cram too much loosely related information into one long sentence.

OVERLOADED	The boats that were moored at the dock when the hurricane, which was one of the worst in three decades, struck were ripped from their moorings, because the owners had not been adequately prepared, since the weather service had predicted the storm would blow out to sea, which they do at this time of year.

AVOIDING EXCESSIVE SUBORDINATION

Choose paragraphs from student essays that demonstrate overuse or faulty use of subordination, and distribute them to the class. Have students rewrite the paragraphs and then compare their versions to determine which are the most clear and effective revisions. This exercise may be used for small-group or individual work.

POSSIBLE ANSWERS: EXERCISE 3

1. Harrods in London is the largest department store in the world, consisting of over 250 departments.
   With over 250 departments, Harrods in London is the largest department store in the world.
2. When the man saw a ship approaching, he fell to his knees.
   Seeing a ship approaching, the man fell to his knees.
3. Although Route 93 is the most direct route to school, it is under construction.
   Route 93, the most direct route to school, is under construction.
4. Dedicated to social reform, Frances Perkins was the first female cabinet member in the U.S.
   Frances Perkins, the first female cabinet member in the U.S., was dedicated to social reform.
5. James Joyce, who has been praised as the greatest writer since Milton and condemned as a writer of "latrine literature," is one of the century's most controversial writers.
   Praised as the greatest writer since Milton and condemned as the writer of "latrine literature," James Joyce is one of the century's most controversial writers.
6. The Amish live peaceful but austere lives, most of them refusing to use modern technology.
   Living peaceful but austere lives, most of the Amish refuse to use modern technology.
7. Hernando de Soto, the legendary European discoverer of the Mississippi River, supposedly died on the river's banks.
   Hernando de Soto, who is the legendary European discoverer of the Mississippi River, supposedly died on the river's banks.
8. Because computerized newspaper operations speed up and simplify copy preparation, they are favored by editors and reporters.

sub
16b

Since such sentences usually have more than one idea that deserves a main clause, they are best revised by sorting their details into more than one sentence.

REVISED   Struck by one of the worst hurricanes in three decades, *the boats at the dock were ripped from their moorings. The owners were unprepared* because the weather service had said that hurricanes at this time of year blow out to sea.

A common form of excessive subordination occurs with a string of adjective clauses beginning *which*, *who*, or *that*, as in the following:

STRING OF ADJECTIVE CLAUSES   Every Christmas we all try to go to my grandfather's house, which is near Louisville, which is an attractive city where my parents now live.

To revise such sentences, consider recasting some of the subordinate clauses as other kinds of modifying structures. In the following revision, for example, the clause *which is near Louisville* has been reduced to a simple modifier, and the clause *which is an attractive city* has been changed to an appositive.

REVISED   Every Christmas we all try to go to my grandfather's house *near Louisville, an attractive city* where my parents now live.

EXERCISE 3

Combine each of the following pairs of sentences twice, each time using one of the subordinate structures in parentheses to make a single sentence. You will have to add, delete, change, and rearrange words.

Example:
During the late eighteenth century, workers carried beverages in brightly colored bottles. The bottles had cork stoppers. (*Clause beginning that. Phrase beginning with.*)
During the late eighteenth century, workers carried beverages in brightly colored bottles *that had cork stoppers*.
During the late eighteenth century, workers carried beverages in brightly colored bottles *with cork stoppers*.

1. Harrods in London is the largest department store in the world. It consists of over 250 departments. (*Phrase beginning consisting. Phrase beginning with.*)
2. The man saw a ship approaching. He fell to his knees. (*Clause beginning when. Phrase beginning seeing.*)
3. Route 93 is the most direct route to school. It is under construction. (*Clause beginning although. Appositive beginning the most.*)

4. Frances Perkins was the first female cabinet member in the U.S. She was dedicated to social reform. (*Phrase beginning dedicated. Appositive beginning the first.*)
5. James Joyce is one of the century's most controversial writers. He has been praised as the greatest writer since Milton and condemned as a writer of "latrine literature." (*Clause beginning who. Phrase beginning praised.*)
6. The Amish live peaceful but austere lives. Most of them refuse to use modern technology. (*Absolute phrase beginning most. Phrase beginning living.*)
7. Hernando de Soto is the legendary European discoverer of the Mississippi River. He supposedly died on the river's banks. (*Clause beginning who. Appositive beginning the legendary.*)
8. Computerized newspaper operations speed up and simplify copy preparation. They are favored by editors and reporters. (*Clause beginning because. Phrase beginning favored.*)
9. Andrew Bradford began the American magazine industry. He first published *American Magazine* in 1741. (*Clause beginning who. Clause beginning when.*)
10. In World War I, German forces set out to capture Verdun. Verdun was a fortress in northeastern France. (*Clause beginning which. Appositive beginning a fortress.*)

EXERCISE 4

Rewrite the following paragraph in the way you think most effective to subordinate the less important ideas to the more important ones. Use subordinate clauses and other subordinate constructions as appropriate.

Many students today are no longer majoring in the liberal arts. I mean by "liberal arts" such subjects as history, English, and the social sciences. Students think a liberal arts degree will not help them get jobs. They are wrong. They may not get practical, job-related experience from the liberal arts, but they will get a broad education, and it will never again be available to them. Many employers look for more than a technical, professional education. They think such an education can make an employee's views too narrow. The employers want open-minded employees. They want employees to think about problems from many angles. The liberal arts curriculum instills such flexibility. The flexibility is vital to the health of our society.

EXERCISE 5

Revise the following sentences to eliminate faulty or excessive subordination by reversing main and subordinate ideas, by coordinating ideas, or by making separate sentences. Some items have more than one possible answer.

Favored by editors and reporters, computerized newspaper operations speed up and simplify copy preparation.

9. Andrew Bradford, who first published *American Magazine* in 1741, began the American magazine industry.

   When Andrew Bradford first published *American Magazine* in 1741, he began the American magazine industry.

10. In World War I, German forces set out to capture Verdun, which was a fortress in northeastern France.

    In World War I, German forces set out to capture Verdun, a fortress in northeastern France.

sub
16b

ANSWERS: EXERCISE 4

Possible Revision

Many students today are no longer majoring in the liberal arts—that is, in such subjects as history, English, and the social sciences. Although students think a liberal arts degree will not help them get jobs, they are wrong. They may not get practical, job-related experience from the liberal arts, but they will get a broad education that will never again be available to them. Many employers look for more than a technical, professional education because they think such an education can make an employee's views too narrow. Instead, they want open-minded employees who can think about problems from many angles. This sort of flexibility—vital to the health of our society—is just what the liberal arts curriculum instills.

POSSIBLE ANSWERS: EXERCISE 5

1. Because of government funding, standby and discounted tickets are available for every performance at the National Theatre in London.

2. Although he had experienced two near air disasters, he continued to fly.
3. My boss's new car, parked in front of the store, rolled into my bike.
4. Because reasonable people no longer think that there's anything wrong with women who want to become career officers, a woman who wants a career in the armed forces is better off now.
5. Though invited on short notice when our planned guest speaker canceled, the Sierra Club speaker nonetheless gave an informative talk about our need to preserve wilderness areas from extinction.

Example:
Terrified to return home, he had driven his mother's car into a corn field.
Having driven his mother's car into a corn field, he was terrified to return home.

1. The National Theatre in London is government funded, which means that stand-by and discounted tickets are available for every performance.
2. He had experienced two near air disasters, although he continued to fly.
3. The car that my boss parked in front of the store, which rolled into my bike, was the car that he had just bought.
4. A woman who wants a career in the armed forces is better off now than she used to be because reasonable people no longer think that there's anything wrong with women who want to become career officers, which used to be a problem.
5. The speaker from the Sierra Club, whom we had invited on short notice when our planned speaker canceled, nonetheless gave an informative talk about the need to preserve our wilderness areas, which he said were in danger of extinction.

16c Choosing clear connectors

Most connecting words signal specific and unambiguous relations; for instance, the coordinating conjunction *but* clearly indicates contrast, and the subordinating conjunction *because* clearly indicates cause. A few connectors, however, require careful use, either because they are ambiguous in many contexts and may therefore confuse the reader or because they are often misused in current English.

REWRITING

Give students a passage from a student or professional essay, and ask them to rewrite it following a specified strategy: adding subordination, using different subordinators, or adding coordination. This exercise can be extended by having students rewrite the passage to change its emphasis.

1 Avoiding ambiguous connectors: *as* and *while*

The subordinating conjunction *as* can indicate several kinds of adverbial relations, including comparison and time.

COMPARISON   He was working *as* rapidly as he could.

TIME   The instructor finally arrived *as* the class was leaving.

As is sometimes used to indicate cause, but in that sense it is often ambiguous and should be avoided.

AMBIGUOUS   *As* I was in town, I visited some old friends. [Time or cause intended?]

| CLEAR | *When* I was in town, I visited some old friends. [Time]. |
| CLEAR | *Because* I was in town, I visited some old friends. [Cause.] |

The subordinating conjunction *while* can indicate either time or concession. Unless the context makes the meaning of *while* unmistakably clear, choose a more exact connector.

AMBIGUOUS	*While* we were working nearby, we did not hear the burglars enter. [Time or concession?]
CLEAR	*When* we were working nearby, we did not hear the burglars enter. [Time.]
CLEAR	*Although* we were working nearby, we did not hear the burglars enter. [Concession.]

2 Avoiding misused connectors: *as*, *like*, and *while*

The use of *as* as a substitute for *whether* or *that* is nonstandard—that is, it violates the conventions of spoken and written standard English.

| NONSTANDARD | He was not sure *as* he could come. |
| REVISED | He was not sure *whether* (or *that*) he could come. |

Although the preposition *like* is often used as a conjunction in informal speech and in advertising (*Dirt-Away works like a soap should*), writing and formal speech generally require the conjunction *as*, *as if*, or *as though*.

| INFORMAL SPEECH | It seemed *like* the examination would never end. |
| WRITING | It seemed *as if* (*as though*) the examination would never end. |

The subordinating conjunction *while* is sometimes carelessly used in the sense of *and* or *but*, creating false subordination.

| FAULTY | My sister wants to study medicine *while* I want to study law. |
| REVISED | My sister wants to study medicine, *and* I want to study law. |

EXERCISE 6

Substitute a clear or correct connector in the following sentences where *as*, *while*, and *like* are ambiguous or misused.

ANSWERS: EXERCISE 6

1. The poet looked <u>as if</u> he had never read in public before.

2. Many writers use <u>he</u> to denote both males and females, <u>but</u> others avoid the usage.
3. <u>Because</u> I was going home for Thanksgiving, my mother cooked a squash pie for me.
4. Some banks now charge for each transaction, <u>as if</u> the monthly charge weren't enough of a burden for customers.
5. <u>Because</u> teachers and legislators worry about the literacy of high school students, the situation may improve.

ANSWERS: EXERCISE 7

Possible Revision

Sir Walter Raleigh personified the Elizabethan Age, <u>the</u> period during which Elizabeth I ruled England, <u>in</u> the last half of the sixteenth century. Raleigh was a <u>courtier, a poet, an explorer, and an entrepreneur.</u> Supposedly, he gained Queen Elizabeth's favor by throwing his cloak beneath her feet at the right moment, <u>just as she was</u> about to step over a puddle. <u>Although</u> there is no evidence for this <u>story, it</u> illustrates Raleigh's dramatic and dynamic personality. His energy drew others to <u>him, and</u> he was one of Elizabeth's favorites. She supported <u>him and</u> dispensed favors to him. However, he lost his queen's good <u>will when without</u> her permission he <u>seduced and eventually married</u> one of her maids of honor. <u>After Elizabeth died,</u> her successor, <u>James I,</u> imprisoned Raleigh in the Tower of London <u>on false charges of treason.</u> Raleigh was released after thirteen <u>years but</u> arrested again two years later on the old treason charges. At the age of sixty-six he was beheaded.

Example:
He looked to me like he had slept in his clothes.
He looked to me *as if* he had slept in his clothes.

1. The poet looked like he had never read in public before.
2. Many writers use *he* to denote both males and females, while others avoid the usage.
3. As I was going home for Thanksgiving, my mother cooked a squash pie for me.
4. Some banks now charge for each transaction, like the monthly charge weren't enough of a burden for customers.
5. As teachers and legislators worry about the literacy of high school students, the situation may improve.

EXERCISE 7

The following paragraph consists entirely of simple sentences. Use coordination and subordination to combine sentences in the way you think most effective to emphasize main ideas.

Sir Walter Raleigh personified the Elizabethan Age. That was the period of Elizabeth I's rule of England. The period occurred in the last half of the sixteenth century. Raleigh was a courtier and poet. He was also an explorer and entrepreneur. Supposedly, he gained Queen Elizabeth's favor. He did this by throwing his cloak beneath her feet at the right moment. She was just about to step over a puddle. There is no evidence for this story. It does illustrate Raleigh's dramatic and dynamic personality. His energy drew others to him. He was one of Elizabeth's favorites. She supported him. She also dispensed favors to him. However, he lost his queen's good will. Without her permission he seduced one of her maids of honor. He eventually married the maid of honor. Elizabeth died. Then her successor imprisoned Raleigh in the Tower of London. Her successor was James I. Raleigh was charged falsely with treason. He was released after thirteen years. He was arrested again two years later on the old treason charges. At the age of sixty-six he was beheaded.

sub
16c

CHAPTER 17

Using Parallelism

HIGHLIGHTS

This discussion of parallelism is divided into two sections, and it moves from correctness to effective style. The opening section addresses the obligatory use of parallelism in coordinate constructions—those linked by coordinating conjunctions and correlative conjunctions; those in comparisons and contrasts; and those in lists, outlines, and the like. The second section examines how parallelism can be used within and among sentences to increase coherence, emphasize meaning, and heighten the effect. For some students you may wish to emphasize the items in the opening section. But students who have no trouble maintaining obligatory parallelism can often profit by working more creatively with parallelism to tighten and clarify their writing. Exercise 3, a sentence-combining exercise, is designed to give students a chance to explore the options for expression that parallelism provides. The exercise is likely to be most effective when students are given a chance to (1) discuss with one another the impact of various combinations or (2) work collaboratively in exploring various sentence-combining options.

Parallelism is a similarity of grammatical form between two or more coordinated elements.

The air is dirtied by ‖ factories ‖ belching ‖ smoke
 and ‖ cars ‖ spewing ‖ exhaust.

Parallel structure reinforces and highlights a close relation or a contrast between compound sentence elements, whether they be words, phrases, or entire clauses.

The principle underlying parallelism is that form should reflect meaning: since the parts of compound constructions have the same function and importance, they should have the same grammatical form. (See the box on p. 332.) For the writer, parallelism is both a way to emphasize related ideas and a grammatical requirement to be observed in constructing sentences. In the following sections we will look at both roles of parallelism.

17a Using parallelism for coordinate elements

Parallel structure is necessary wherever coordination exists: wherever elements are connected by coordinating conjunctions or by correlative conjunctions, wherever elements are compared or contrasted, and wherever items are arranged in a list or outline. The elements should match each other in structure, though they need not match word for word, as the previous sentence of this paragraph illustrates. In the following sentence the coordinate prepositional phrases are parallel even though the second phrase contains more words.

We passed *through the town* and *into the vast, unpopulated desert.*

PATTERNS OF PARALLELISM

PARALLEL WORDS

In 1988 a Greek cyclist, backed up by ‖ engineers,
‖ physiologists,
and ‖ athletes,
broke the world's record for human flight
with neither ‖ a boost
nor ‖ a motor.

PARALLEL PHRASES

‖ Pedalling ‖ a superlight plane
and ‖ sipping ‖ a special nutritious drink,
the pilot made an over-water journey of
‖ more than ‖ seventy-four miles
and ‖ fewer than ‖ four hours.

To conserve energy, the pilot
both ‖ kept ‖ to the straightest possible course
and ‖ stayed ‖ near the surface of the water.

PARALLEL SUBORDINATE CLAUSES

The plane was escorted by several boats
‖ whose equipment ‖ tracked ‖ the wind
and ‖ whose passengers ‖ monitored ‖ the pilot's health.

PARALLEL MAIN CLAUSES

‖ The plane ‖ alighted just thirty feet offshore,
and ‖ the pilot ‖ swam to a welcoming crowd.

//
17a

1 Using parallelism for elements linked by coordinating conjunctions

The coordinating conjunctions *and, but, or, nor,* and *yet* always signal a need for parallelism, as the following sentences show.

> Miracle Grill will cook your food *in the kitchen* or *on the patio.*
>
> Political candidates *often explain what they intend to do* but *rarely explain how they are going to do it.*
>
> In Melanie's home, children had to account for *where they had been* and *what they had been doing.*

Sentence elements linked by coordinating conjunctions should be parallel in structure; otherwise, their coordination will be weakened and the reader distracted.

FAULTY	Three reasons why steel companies keep losing money are that their plants are inefficient, high labor costs, and foreign competition is increasing.
REVISED	Three reasons why steel companies keep losing money are inefficient plants, high labor costs, and increasing foreign competition.

All the words required by idiom or grammar must be stated in compound constructions (see also 15c).

FAULTY	The boy demonstrated an interest and a talent for writing.
REVISED	The boy demonstrated an interest *in* and a talent for writing. [Idiom dictates different prepositions with *interest* and *talent*.]
FAULTY	The thieves were careless and apprehended.
REVISED	The thieves were careless and *were* apprehended. [Each *were* serves a different grammatical function—the first as a linking verb, the second as a helping verb.]

Often, the same word must be repeated to avoid confusion.

CONFUSING	Thoreau stood up for his principles by not paying his taxes and spending a night in jail. [Did he spend a night in jail or not?]
REVISED	Thoreau stood up for his principles by not paying his taxes and by spending a night in jail.

Be sure that clauses beginning *and who* or *and which* are coordinated only with preceding *who* and *which* clauses.

FAULTY	Marie is a young woman of great ability and who wants to be a lawyer.
REVISED	Marie is a young woman *who has* great ability and who wants to be a lawyer.
REVISED	Marie is a young woman of great ability *who wants* to be a lawyer.

SAMPLE ESSAYS

Ask students to look for parallelism in essays from a reader or a similar source. If the students are working in groups, ask them not only to reach consensus on which elements are parallel but also to decide what functions the parallelism performs.

//

17a

2 Using parallelism for elements linked by correlative conjunctions

Correlative conjunctions are pairs of connectors such as *both . . . and, not only . . . but also,* and *either . . . or* (see 5d-1). They stress equality and balance and thus emphasize the relation between elements, even long phrases and clauses. The elements should be parallel to confirm their relation.

17a

ADDING PARALLELISM

Take a loose-jointed student essay or a professional essay and distribute it to students (working individually or in groups), asking them to make the sentences denser by adding parallelism wherever possible. Ask them also to decide when the parallelism adds to the essay and when it detracts.

It is not *a tax bill* but *a tax relief bill*, providing relief not *for the needy* but *for the greedy*.　—FRANKLIN DELANO ROOSEVELT

At the end of the novel, Huck Finn both *rejects society's values by turning down money and a home* and *affirms his own values by setting out for "the territory."*

Most errors in parallelism with correlative conjunctions occur when the element after the second connector does not match the element after the first connector.

| NONPARALLEL | He told the boys either to brush the horse or feed the chickens. |
| REVISED | He told the boys either to brush the horse or *to* feed the chickens. |

| NONPARALLEL | We were warned that we must either pay our rent or we must vacate the apartment. |
| REVISED | We were warned that we must either pay our rent or *vacate* the apartment. |

3　Using parallelism for elements being compared or contrasted

Elements being compared or contrasted should ordinarily be cast in the same grammatical form.

It is better *to live rich* than *to die rich*.　—SAMUEL JOHNSON

WEAK	Jody wanted a job rather than to apply for welfare.
REVISED	Jody wanted a job rather than *welfare payments*.
REVISED	Jody wanted *to find a job* rather than to apply for welfare.

4　Using parallelism for items in lists or outlines

The elements of a list or outline that divides a larger subject are coordinate and should be parallel in structure. (See also 1h-2 on outlining.)

FAULTY	IMPROVED
The Renaissance in England was marked by	The Renaissance in England was marked by
1. an extension of trade routes	1. the extension of trade routes
2. merchant class became more powerful	2. the increasing power of the merchant class

3. the death of feudalism
4. upsurging of the arts
5. the sciences were
   encouraged
6. religious quarrels began

3. the death of feudalism
4. the upsurge of the arts
5. the encouragement of the
   sciences
6. the rise of religious quarrels

EXERCISE 1

Identify the parallel elements in the following sentences. How
does parallelism contribute to the effectiveness of each sentence?

1. While not as pointless as *The Three Musketeers* or as lengthy
   as *Harrigan 'n' Hart* or as becalmed as *Quilters*, this show
   does lead the pack in such key areas as incoherence (total),
   vulgarity (boundless), and decibel level (stratospheric, with
   piercing electronic feedback). —FRANK RICH
2. This apparent amnesia, which Freud labelled infantile or
   childhood amnesia, applies only to our memories about the
   self, not to our memory for words learned or objects and
   people recognized. —PATRICK HUYGHE
3. They [pioneer women] rolled out dough on the wagon seats,
   cooked with fires made out of buffalo chips, tended the sick,
   and marked the graves of their children, husbands and each
   other. —ELLEN GOODMAN
4. The mornings are the pleasantest times in the apartment,
   exhaustion having set in, the sated mosquitoes at rest on
   ceiling and walls, sleeping it off, the room a swirl of tortured
   bedclothes and abandoned garments, the vines in their full
   leafiness filtering the hard light of day, the air conditioner
   silent at last, like the mosquitoes. —E. B. WHITE
5. Aging paints every action gray, lies heavy on every movement, imprisons every thought. —SHARON CURTIN

EXERCISE 2

Revise the following sentences to make coordinate, compared, or
listed elements parallel in structure. Add or delete words or rephrase as necessary to increase the effectiveness of each sentence.

   Example:
   After emptying her bag, searching the apartment, and having called the library, Jennifer realized she had lost the
   book.
   After emptying her bag, searching the apartment, and *calling* the library, Jennifer realized she had lost the book.

1. The reviews of the play were uniformly positive: unstinting

ANSWERS: EXERCISE 1

1. The two sets of parallel constructions
   (*pointless . . . lengthy . . . becalmed* and
   *incoherence . . . , vulgarity . . . , decibel
   level*) condemn the reviewed show by
   repeated association with other inept
   shows and then separate it into its own
   realm of ineptness. After such a tight
   sentence structure, the final break in
   parallelism (*stratospheric, with piercing electronic feedback*) gives a sense of
   the writer's exasperation and pain.
2. The parallel phrases (*applies only to our
   memories about . . . not to our memory
   for*) clarify what the definition includes
   and excludes.
3. The parallel verbs (*rolled out . . . cooked
   . . . tended . . . marked*) stress the number and variety of the women's responsibilities.
4. Supporting *pleasantest* is a wealth of
   detail expressed in five parallel absolute phrases: *exhaustion . . . in; the
   sated mosquitoes . . . off; the room . . .
   garments; the vines . . . day;* and *the air
   conditioner . . . mosquitoes.* The phrases
   convey no action, emphasizing the
   stillness of the scene.
5. The limiting effects of aging are emphasized by the increasingly narrow
   parallel verbs—*pants, lies, imprisons*—and the parallel objects—*every
   action, every movement,* and *every
   thought.*

**//
17a**

POSSIBLE ANSWERS: EXERCISE 2

1. The reviews of the play were uniformly positive: unstinting praise for
   the actors; <u>acclaim for</u> the director's
   interpretation; and <u>applause for</u> the
   playwright's technique.
2. Her tennis coach taught her how to
   serve and <u>how to rush</u> the net and <u>win</u>
   the point.
3. The unprepared student wished for either a blizzard or <u>a</u> blackout on the
   examination day.

4. Working last summer as a waitress, I learned <u>how to choose and serve wine</u> and <u>how to make</u> small talk while wrestling the cork from the bottle.
5. My favorite winter activities are skiing, reading, and <u>drinking</u> herbal tea by the fire.
6. To receive an A in that class, one must have both a perfect attendance record and <u>a perfect</u> academic record.
7. In moving from Vermont to California, I was bothered less by the distance <u>than by</u> the climate change and <u>especially</u> the warm, snowless Christmases.
8. After a week on a construction job, Leon felt not so much exhausted as <u>invigorated</u> by the physical labor.
9. To lose weight, cut down on the amount you eat, eat fewer calories in the food you do consume, and <u>exercise</u> regularly.
10. Her generosity, <u>sympathy</u>, and <u>ability</u> to motivate employees make her an excellent supervisor.

praise for the actors; the director's interpretation was acclaimed; and the reviews applauded the playwright's technique.
2. Her tennis coach taught her how to serve and rushing the net and winning the point.
3. The unprepared student wishes for either a blizzard or to have a blackout on the examination day.
4. Working last summer as a waitress, I learned about choosing wine, how to serve wine, and making small talk while wrestling the cork from the bottle.
5. My favorite winter activities are skiing, reading, and to drink herbal tea by the fire.
6. To receive an A in that class, one must have both a perfect attendance record and academic record.
7. In moving from Vermont to California, I was bothered less by the distance than to experience the climate change and especially that Christmases are warm and snowless.
8. After a week on a construction job, Leon felt not so much exhausted as that he was invigorated by the physical labor.
9. To lose weight, cut down on what you eat, eat fewer calories in the food you do consume, and you should exercise regularly.
10. Her generosity, sympathetic nature, and the fact that she is able to motivate employees make her an excellent supervisor.

17b
//

RESOURCES AND IDEAS

Phyllis Brooks, "Mimesis: Grammar and the Echoing Voice," *College English* 35 (1973): 161–68. Brooks suggests the writing of paragraphs that imitate the style of a writer but use different content. She indicates that the practice helps students learn to use a variety of structures, including parenthetical expressions, appositives and modifiers, and parallelism plus reference.

Robert L. Walker, "The Common Writer: A Case for Parallel Structure," *College Composition and Communication* 21 (1970): 373–79. Walker believes that students should be encouraged to use a variety of sentence structures and parallelism, which he considers important features of mature sentences.

17b Using parallelism to increase coherence

Parallelism not only ensures similarity of form for coordinated structures but also enhances coherence by clearly relating paired or opposed units. Consider this sentence:

NONPARALLEL During the early weeks of the semester, the course reviews fundamentals, but little emphasis is placed on new material or more advanced concepts.

Here "the course" is doing two things—or doing one thing and not doing the other—and these are opposites. But the nonparallel construction of the sentence (*the course reviews . . . little emphasis is placed*) does not help the reader see the connection quickly.

REVISED During the early weeks of the semester, the course reviews fundamentals but *places little emphasis* on new material or more advanced concepts.

Effective parallelism will enable you to combine in a single, well-ordered sentence related ideas that you might have expressed in two or three separate sentences. Compare the following three sentences with the original single sentence written by H. L. Mencken.

> Slang originates in the effort of ingenious individuals to make language more pungent and picturesque. They increase the store of terse and striking words or widen the boundaries of metaphor. Thus a vocabulary for new shades and differences in meaning is provided by slang.

> Slang originates in the effort of ingenious individuals to make the language more pungent and picturesque—to increase the store of terse and striking words, to widen the boundaries of metaphor, and to provide a vocabulary for new shades and differences in meaning.
> —H. L. MENCKEN

Parallel structure works as well to emphasize the connections among related sentences in a paragraph (see 3b-2).

> Style is an extraordinary thing. It is one of the subtlest secrets of all art. . . . *In painting, it is* composition, colour-sense, and brushwork. *In sculpture, it is* the treatment of depths and surfaces and the choice of stones and metals. *In music, it is* surely the melodic line, the tone-colour, and the shape of the phrase. . . . *In prose and poetry, it is* the choice of words, their placing, and the rhythms and melodies of sentence and paragraph.
> —GILBERT HIGHET

Here, Highet clarifies and emphasizes his assertion that style is common to all forms of art by casting four successive sentences in the same structure (*In . . . , it is . . .*).

17b

EXERCISE 3

Combine each group of sentences below into one concise sentence in which parallel elements appear in parallel structures. You will have to add, delete, change, and rearrange words. Each item has more than one possible answer.

Example:
Christin sorted the books neatly into piles. She was efficient about it, too.
Christin sorted the books neatly *and efficiently* into piles.

1. The professor spoke rapidly. Moreover, his voice was almost inaudible.
2. The cyclists finally arrived at their destination. They arrived after riding uphill most of the day. They had also endured a hailstorm.

PATTERNS FOR PARALLELISM

Working on their own, students might find it difficult to write many sentences containing correlative conjunctions, lists, and coordinate structures that require parallelism, but if you ask them to do this in groups, they can probably generate quite a few. As part of the assignment, ask students to vary the sentences as much as they can in content and in use of parallelism. Then ask the groups to judge each other's work for originality, clarity, and effectiveness.

POSSIBLE ANSWERS: EXERCISE 3

1. The professor spoke rapidly <u>and</u> almost <u>inaudibly.</u>
2. The cyclists finally arrived at their destination after riding uphill most of the day <u>and</u> enduring a hailstorm.
3. I go to jazz class on Wednesday evenings <u>and</u> sometimes on Friday afternoons.
4. Finding an apartment requires <u>spending</u> time and energy, <u>paying</u> close attention to newspaper advertisements, <u>and learning</u> the city's neighborhoods.
5. After making several costly mistakes, he stopped to consider the jobs available to him <u>and</u> his goals for a job.

6. To make a good stew, marinate the meat<u>, add</u> plenty of vegetables<u>, include</u> wine for flavor<u>, and</u> simmer the whole thing for at least two hours.
7. Carlone had three desires<u>: f</u>irst, money<u>;</u> second, <u>fame; and</u> third<u>,</u> happiness.
8. The sun looks small at its zenith <u>but</u> large <u>at</u> the horizon.
9. Most people who saw the movie were unimpressed with or frankly <u>critical of</u> the acting.
10. We returned from camping very tired, dirty<u>, and</u> covered <u>with</u> mosquito bites.

ANSWERS: EXERCISE 4

Possible Revision

The great white shark has an undeserved bad reputation. Many people consider the great white not only swift and powerful <u>but also a</u> cunning and cruel predator on humans. However, scientists claim that the great white attacks humans not by choice <u>but by</u> chance. To a shark, our behavior in the water is similar to that of porpoises, seals, and sea lions—the shark's favorite foods. These sea mammals are both agile enough <u>and fast</u> enough to evade the shark. Thus the shark must attack <u>swiftly</u> and noiselessly to surprise the prey and <u>give</u> it little chance to escape. Humans become the shark's victims not because the shark has any preference <u>for</u> or hatred of humans but because humans can neither outswim <u>nor outmaneuver</u> the shark. If the fish were truly a cruel human-eater, it would prolong the terror of its attacks, perhaps by circling or bumping into its intended victims before <u>attacking them</u>.

3. I go to jazz class on Wednesday evenings. Sometimes I attend on Friday afternoons.
4. Finding an apartment requires expenditures of time and energy. It requires paying close attention to newspaper advertisements. It also requires that one learn the city's neighborhoods.
5. After making several costly mistakes, he stopped to consider the jobs available to him. He thought about his goals for a job.
6. To make a good stew, marinate the meat. There should be plenty of vegetables added. Wine should be included for flavor. Simmer the whole thing for at least two hours.
7. Carlone had three desires. First, he wanted money. Second, he wanted to be famous. The third desire was for happiness.
8. The sun looks small at its zenith. But it looks large when it reaches the horizon.
9. Most people who saw the movie were unimpressed with the acting. Or they frankly criticized the acting.
10. We returned from camping very tired. We were dirty. Mosquito bites covered us.

EXERCISE 4

Revise the following paragraph to create parallelism wherever it is required for grammar or for coherence.

The great white shark has an undeserved bad reputation. Many people consider the great white not only swift and powerful but also to be a cunning and cruel predator on humans. However, scientists claim that the great white attacks humans not by choice but as a result of chance. To a shark, our behavior in the water is similar to that of porpoises, seals, and sea lions—the shark's favorite foods. These sea mammals are both agile enough and can move fast enough to evade the shark. Thus the shark must attack with swiftness and noiselessly to surprise the prey and giving it little chance to escape. Humans become the shark's victims not because the shark has any preference or hatred of humans but because humans can neither outswim nor can they outmaneuver the shark. If the fish were truly a cruel human-eater, it would prolong the terror of its attacks, perhaps by circling or bumping into its intended victims before they were attacked.

CHAPTER 18

Emphasizing Main Ideas

Effective writing uses coordination, subordination, and parallelism to help readers understand the relationship of ideas and details. It also emphasizes important information by making it readily apparent to readers.

18a Arranging ideas effectively

In arranging ideas within sentences for emphasis, you should keep two principles in mind. First, the beginnings and endings of sentences are the most emphatic positions, and endings are generally more emphatic than beginnings. Second, a parallel series of words, phrases, or clauses will be most emphatic if the elements appear in order of increasing importance.

WAYS TO EMPHASIZE IDEAS

1. Put important ideas in the beginnings or endings of sentences (18a-1).
2. Arrange series items in order of increasing importance (18a-2).
3. Use an occasional balanced sentence (18a-2).
4. Use judicious repetition of key words and phrases (18b).
5. Set off important ideas with punctuation (18c).
6. Use the active voice (18d).
7. Write concisely (18e).

HIGHLIGHTS

This chapter looks at two ways to achieve emphasis within sentences: by the distribution of information and by the choice of strategies to create a specific effect. Special features of the chapter are its treatment of cumulative and periodic sentences and discussion that stresses the rhetorical effect of each sentence pattern. The sentence-combining exercises that accompany the discussion are designed to help students feel comfortable using these patterns in their writing. The opening discussion also looks at the importance of sentence beginnings and endings and at the effective arrangement of items in a series. Most students benefit from some work with these basic ways of controlling emphasis as well as from discussion of using the active voice (18d) and of being concise (18e). Students who have problems with sentence structure, however, may have more difficulty with the effective uses of repetition (18b) and separation (18c) for emphasis.

emph
18a

RESOURCES AND IDEAS

An understanding of the roles of topics and comments and of the possible relationships of old and new information can be very useful for writers seeking greater clarity and more effective emphasis in their writing. To supplement the discussion in this section of the handbook you may wish to turn to two excellent texts:

William J. Vande Koppel, *Clear and Coherent Prose* (Glenview: Scott, 1989).

Joseph M. Williams, *Style: Ten Lessons in Clarity and Grace*, 2nd ed. (Glenview: Scott, 1984).

RESOURCES AND IDEAS

Francis Christensen, "A Generative Rhetoric of the Sentence," in *Notes Toward a New Rhetoric: Nine Essays for Teachers*, ed. Francis Christensen and Bonniejean Christensen, 2nd ed. (New York: Harper, 1978), 23–44. Christensen demonstrates how to analyze the levels of generality in sentences and discusses and illustrates the structure of the cumulative sentence.

1 Using sentence beginnings and endings

Readers automatically seek a writer's principal meaning in the basic sentence—that is, in the subject that names a topic and the predicate that comments on the topic (see 5a). Thus you can help ensure that readers understand your intended meaning by controlling the relation of the basic sentence to any other words, phrases, or clauses that modify all or parts of it.

Just as in speech we stress the beginning and the ending of a sentence, so in reading we expect the beginning and the ending to contain important information. Thus the most effective way to call attention to information is to place it first or last in the sentence, reserving the middle for incidentals.

UNEMPHATIC	Education remains the most important single means of economic advancement, in spite of its shortcomings.
REVISED	In spite of its shortcomings, education remains the most important single means of economic advancement.
REVISED	Education remains, in spite of its shortcomings, the most important single means of economic advancement.

The topic (*education*), the comment (*remains . . . advancement*), and the modifier (*in spite . . . shortcomings*) are worded the same in all three sentences. But the first sentence focuses our attention on education's shortcomings, even though the writer clearly wished to emphasize its importance. The first revision stresses the qualifying phrase a bit by placing it at the beginning but emphasizes education's importance by reserving it for the end. The second revision de-emphasizes the qualification by placing it in the middle.

Many sentences begin with the subject and predicate plus their modifiers and then add more modifiers. Such sentences are called **cumulative** (because they accumulate information as they proceed) or **loose** (because they are not tightly structured).

CUMULATIVE	Jim staggered through the doorway, his pants torn, his shirt ripped open, his face scraped.
CUMULATIVE	Most of the Great American Desert is made up of bare rock, rugged cliffs, mesas, canyons, mountains, separated from one another by broad flat basins covered with sun-baked mud and alkali, supporting a sparse and measured growth of sagebrush or creosote or saltbush, depending on location and elevation.
	—EDWARD ABBEY

As these examples illustrate, a cumulative sentence completes its main statement (topic and comment) and then explains, amplifies, or illustrates it. By thus accumulating information, the sentence parallels the way we naturally think.

The opposite kind of sentence, called **periodic,** saves the main clause until just before the end (the period) of the sentence. Everything before the main clause points toward it.

> PERIODIC   His pants torn, his shirt ripped open, his face scraped, Jim staggered through the doorway.
>
> PERIODIC   In the Mason jars stacked up dusty and fly-specked on the side shelves, in the broken-webbed snowshoes hung there, the heap of rusty hinged traps waiting this long to be oiled and set to catch something in the night, was the visible imprint of the past we were rooted in.   —JOAN CHASE

A variation of the periodic sentence names the subject at the beginning, follows it with a modifier, and then fills in the predicate.

> Thirty-eight-year-old Dick Hayne, who works in jeans and loafers and likes to let a question cure in the air for a while before answering it, bears all the markings of what his generation used to call a laid-back kind of guy.   —GEORGE RUSH

Whether the subject comes first or is delayed along with the predicate, the periodic sentence creates suspense for the reader by reserving the important information of the main clause for the end. But it requires careful planning so that the reader can remember all the information leading up to the main clause. Most writers save periodic sentences for when their purpose demands climactic emphasis.

2 **Arranging parallel elements effectively**

Series

Parallelism requires that you express coordinate ideas in similar grammatical structures (see Chapter 17). In addition, you should arrange the coordinate ideas in order of importance. A series of grammatically parallel elements can be weak if you arrange the elements randomly.

> UNEMPHATIC   The storm ripped the roofs off several buildings, killed ten people, and knocked down many trees in town.

MEMORY AID

Thinking About Cumulative and Periodic Sentences

The following examples may help students remember how to formulate and how to distinguish between cumulative and periodic sentences:

1. Cumulative Sentences
   A cumulative sentence is created much like a portrait, detail by detail. The diver (for example) paused at the end of the board, gazing down at the smooth, greenish-blue water meters below, his arms stretched out in front, his legs trembling slightly with anticipation and tension, drops of water falling from his fingertips into the swirling wind filled with murmurs from the crowd below and behind his solitary figure.

2. Periodic Sentences
   In a form that parallels the dramatic movement of a tragedy, the meaning of a periodic sentence is built from words and phrases preceding the main clause. In Shakespeare's play *Othello*, step by step, with slowly gathering force and filled with increasing tension and foreboding, the opening scenes create a situation that makes the tragic events inevitable.

emph
18a

In this sentence the most serious damage (*killed ten people*) is buried in the middle. The revised sentence below presents the items in order of increasing importance.

> EMPHATIC   The storm knocked down many trees in town, ripped the roofs off several buildings, and killed ten people.

You may want to use an unexpected item at the end of a series for humor or for another special effect.

> Early to bed and early to rise makes a man healthy, wealthy, and dead.   —JAMES THURBER

But be careful not to use such a series unintentionally. The following series seems thoughtlessly random rather than intentionally humorous.

> UNEMPHATIC   The painting has subdued tone, great feeling, and a length of about three feet.
>
> EMPHATIC   The painting, about three feet long, has subdued tone and great feeling.

Balanced sentences

When the clauses of a compound or complex sentence are parallel, the sentence is **balanced.**

> The fickleness of the women I love is equalled only by the infernal constancy of the women who love me.
> —GEORGE BERNARD SHAW

In a pure balanced sentence two main clauses are exactly parallel: they match item for item.

> The love of liberty is the love of others; the love of power is the love of ourselves.   —WILLIAM HAZLITT

But the term is commonly applied to sentences that are only approximately parallel or that have only some parallel parts.

> If thought corrupts language, language can also corrupt thought.
> —GEORGE ORWELL

> The secret of learning to act lies not in the study of methods but in the close observation of those who have already learned.

Balanced sentences are heavily emphatic but require thoughtful planning. When used carefully, they can be an especially effective way to alert readers to a strong contrast between two ideas.

---

emph
18a

MORE COMBINING

Give students a list of information about a topic, and ask them to combine the information to emphasize certain features or to achieve a particular rhetorical purpose. They can do the combining in groups or meet together to discuss the results.

ANSWERS: EXERCISE 1

1. The main clause is *One . . . Mouse*. The sentence is cumulative. Rewritten as a periodic sentence:
An idiot optimist, each week marching forth in Technicolor against a battalion

EXERCISE 1

Underline the main clause in each sentence below, and identify the sentence as cumulative or periodic. Then rewrite each cumulative sentence as a periodic one and each periodic sentence as a cumulative one.

1. One of the most disastrous cultural influences ever to hit America was Walt Disney's Mickey Mouse, that idiot optimist who each week marched forth in Technicolor against a battalion of cats, invariably humiliating them with one clever trick after another. —JAMES A. MICHENER
2. At length, in the beginning of May, with the help of my acquaintances, rather to improve so good an occasion for neighborliness than from any necessity, I set up the frame of my house. —HENRY DAVID THOREAU
3. Thirty years later, when the country was aroused by a rash of political assassinations—the Kennedys, King, Malcolm X—Congress passed the Gun Control Act of 1968. —JERVIS ANDERSON
4. Matthew's children worked two years to get him out of jail—writing letters, seeing lawyers, attending meetings—because they knew him to be honest and believed him to be innocent.
5. Aspiring writers can learn much from waiting on tables, eavesdropping on conversations to sharpen their ear for dialogue and to pick up promising story material.

EXERCISE 2

Combine each group of sentences below into a single cumulative sentence and then into a single periodic sentence. You will have to add, delete, change, and rearrange words. Each item has more than two possible answers. Does the cumulative or the periodic sentence seem more effective to you?

Example:
The woman refused any treatment. She felt that her life was completed. She wished to die.
Cumulative: The woman refused any treatment, feeling that her life was completed and wishing to die.
Periodic: Feeling that her life was completed and wishing to die, the woman refused any treatment.

1. The lead singer aroused the audience. He was spinning around the stage. He was dancing with the microphone stand.
2. Many writers now use computerized word processors. The machines make both revising and editing easier and faster.
3. The swan took flight. Its wings beat against the water. Its neck stretched forward.

of cats, invariably humiliating them with one clever trick after another, Walt Disney's Mickey Mouse was one of the most disastrous influences ever to *hit America*.

2. The main clause is *I . . . house*. The sentence is periodic. Rewritten as a cumulative sentence:
I set up the frame of my house at length, in the beginning of May, with the help of some of my acquaintances, rather to improve so good an occasion for neighborliness than from any necessity.

3. The main clause is *Congress . . . 1968*. The sentence is periodic. Rewritten as a cumulative sentence:
Congress passed the Gun Control Act of 1968 thirty years later, when the country was aroused by a rash of political assassinations—the Kennedys, King, Malcolm X.

4. The main clause is *Matthew's . . . jail*. The sentence is cumulative. Rewritten as a periodic sentence:
Writing letters, seeing lawyers, and attending meetings—because they knew their father to be honest and believed him to be innocent—Matthew's children worked two years to get him out of jail.

5. The main clause is *Aspiring . . . tables*. The sentence is cumulative. Rewritten as a periodic sentence:
Eavesdropping on conversations to sharpen their ear for dialogue and to pick up promising story materials, aspiring writers can learn much from waiting on tables.

POSSIBLE ANSWERS: EXERCISE 2

1. *Cumulative*: The lead singer aroused the audience, spinning around the stage and dancing with the microphone stand.
Periodic: Spinning around the stage and dancing with the microphone stand, the lead singer aroused the audience.

emph
18a

2. *Cumulative*: Many writers now use computerized word processors because the machines make both revising and editing faster and easier.
   Periodic: Because computerized word processors make both revising and editing faster and easier, many writers now use the machines.
3. *Cumulative*: The swan took flight, its wings beating against the water, its neck stretching forward.
   Periodic: Its wings beating against the water, its neck stretching forward, the swan took flight.
4. *Cumulative*: The abandoned car was a neighborhood eyesore, its windows smashed, its body rusted and dented.
   Periodic: Its windows smashed, its body rusted and dented, the abandoned car was a neighborhood eyesore.
5. *Cumulative*: Carl hid his shame, walking with his back straight, holding his head high, and staring straight ahead.
   Periodic: Walking with his back straight, holding his head high, and staring straight ahead, Carl hid his shame.

ANSWERS: EXERCISE 3

1. Remembering summers at my grandmother's makes me happy, but <u>remembering</u> later summers at camp makes me angry.
2. Good scientists seek the truth regardless of personal success, whereas bad scientists <u>seek</u> success <u>regardless of</u> truth.
3. The car had several problems: the left rear window would not open, the upholstery was torn, and the engine was missing.
4. The explosion at the chemical factory started a fire in a building, blew up half a city block, and killed six workers.
5. In the 1950s Americans wanted to keep up with the Joneses; in the 1980s <u>Americans want to keep</u> up with change.

4. The abandoned car was a neighborhood eyesore. Its windows were smashed. Its body was rusted and dented.
5. Carl walked with his back straight. He held his head high. He stared straight ahead. He hid his shame.

EXERCISE 3

Revise the following sentences so that elements in a series or balanced elements are arranged to give maximum emphasis to main ideas.

Example:

The campers were stranded without matches, without food or water, and without a tent.

The campers were stranded without matches, without a tent, and without food or water.

1. Remembering summers at my grandmother's makes me happy, but I get angry when I remember later summers that I spent at camp.
2. Good scientists seek the truth regardless of personal success, whereas for bad scientists personal success is more important than the truth.
3. The car had several problems: the upholstery was torn, the engine was missing, and the left rear window would not open.
4. The explosion at the chemical factory blew up half a city block, killed six workers, and started a fire in a building.
5. In the 1950s Americans wanted to keep up with the Joneses; keeping up with change is what America wants in the 1980s.

18b Repeating ideas

Although careless repetition results in weak and wordy sentences, judicious repetition of key words and phrases can be an effective means of emphasis. Such repetition often combines with parallelism. It may occur in a series of sentences within a paragraph (see 3b-3). Or it may occur in a series of words, phrases, or clauses within a sentence, as in the following examples.

We have the tools, all the tools—we are suffocating in tools—but we cannot find the actual wood to work or even the actual hand to work it.   —ARCHIBALD MACLEISH

Government comes from below, not above; government comes from men, not from kings or lords or military masters; government looks to the source of all power in the consent of men.   —HENRY STEELE COMMAGER

emph
18b

18c Separating ideas

When you save important information for the end of a sentence, you can emphasize it even more by setting it off from the rest of the sentence. The second example below illustrates how putting an important idea in a separate sentence can highlight it.

> Boys are wild animals, rich in the treasures of sense, but the New England boy had a wider range of emotions than boys of more equable climates, for he felt his nature crudely, as it was meant.

> Boys are wild animals, rich in the treasures of sense, but the New England boy had a wider range of emotions than boys of more equable climates. He felt his nature crudely, as it was meant.
> —HENRY ADAMS

You can vary the degree of emphasis by varying the extent to which you separate one idea from the others. A semicolon provides more separation than a comma, and a period provides still more separation. Compare the following sentences.

> Most of the reading which is praised for itself is neither literary nor intellectual, but narcotic.

> Most of the reading which is praised for itself is neither literary nor intellectual; it is narcotic.

> Most of the reading which is praised for itself is neither literary nor intellectual. It is narcotic. —DONALD HALL

Sometimes a dash or a pair of dashes will isolate and thus emphasize a part of a statement (see also 25b).

> His schemes were always elaborate, ingenious, and exciting— and wholly impractical.

> Athletics—that is, winning athletics—have become a profitable university operation.

REWRITE

Take a passage from a student essay or a professional essay and ask students to rewrite it, using different sentence patterns that give different emphasis to the content of the sentences. Split the class into groups and have them compare their versions with the original, trying to identify a new version that is in some ways clearer than the original and that contains more appropriate emphasis on the main ideas. Since students may well have decided to emphasize different ideas from those emphasized by the original writer, their analysis of the versions may involve matters of content as well as style.

emph
18c

EXERCISE 4

Emphasize the main idea in each sentence or group of sentences below by following the instructions in parentheses: either combine sentences so that parallelism and repetition stress the main idea, or place the main idea in a separate sentence. Each item has more than one possible answer.

Example:

I try to listen to other people's opinions. When my mind is closed, I find that other opinions open it. And they can change my mind when it is wrong. (*Parallelism and repetition.*)

POSSIBLE ANSWERS: EXERCISE 4

1. Without funding, the center will close: <u>without funding, the counseling program will end.</u>
2. Roger worked harder than usual to win the chemistry prize that his father had won before him. <u>He could not let his father down.</u>

3. One of the few worthwhile habits is daily reading: <u>reading</u> for information, <u>reading</u> for entertainment, <u>reading</u> for a broader view of the world.

4. My parents fear <u>change in</u> morals, <u>change in</u> their neighborhood, and <u>change in</u> their own children.

5. By the time the rescuers reached the crash site, the wind had nearly covered the small plane with snow. <u>No one had survived</u>.

I try to listen to other people's opinions, for they can open my mind when it is closed and they can change my mind when it is wrong.

1. Without funding, the center will close. The counseling program will end if funding stops. (*Parallelism and repetition.*)

2. Roger worked harder than usual to win the chemistry prize that his father had won before him, for he could not let his father down. (*Separation.*)

3. One of the few worthwhile habits is daily reading. One can read for information. One can read for entertainment. Reading can give one a broader view of the world. (*Parallelism and repetition.*)

4. My parents fear change. They fear change in morals. They are afraid their neighborhood will change. They are afraid of change in their own children. (*Parallelism and repetition.*)

5. By the time the rescuers reached the crash site, the wind had nearly covered the small plane with snow and no one had survived. (*Separation.*)

emph
18d

18d Preferring the active voice

In the active voice of the verb, the subject acts (*I peeled the onions*). In the passive voice, the subject is acted upon and the actor is either relegated to a phrase (*The onions were peeled by me*) or omitted entirely (*The onions were peeled*). (See Chapter 7, p. 235.) The passive voice is thus indirect because it obscures or removes the actor. The active voice is more direct, vigorous, and emphatic. Further, all sentences turn on their verbs, which give sentences their motion, pushing them along. And active verbs push harder than passive ones.

PASSIVE	For energy conservation it is urged that all lights be turned off when not being used. [Who is urging? Who is to turn the lights off?]
ACTIVE	To save energy, students should turn off all lights they are not using.
PASSIVE	The new outpatient clinic was opened by the hospital administration so that the costs of non-emergency medical care would be reduced.
ACTIVE	The hospital administration opened the new outpatient clinic to reduce the costs of non-emergency medical care.

Sometimes the actor is unknown or unimportant, and much technical writing deliberately omits the actor in order give impersonal emphasis to what is being acted upon. In these cases the passive voice can be useful.

> Wellington was called the "Iron Duke."
> Thousands of people are killed annually in highway accidents.
> The mixture was then stirred.

Except in these situations, however, rely on the active voice. It is economical and creates movement. (See also 31c-3.)

18e Being concise

Conciseness—brevity of expression—aids emphasis no matter what the sentence structure. Unnecessary words detract from necessary words. They clutter sentences and obscure ideas.

One common structure that may contribute to wordiness is the expletive construction, which inverts the normal subject-verb order by beginning a sentence with *there* or *it* and a form of the verb *be* (see 5e-4).

WEAK	*There are* likely to be thousands of people attending the rally against nuclear arms.
EMPHATIC	*Thousands of people are* likely to attend the rally against nuclear arms.

Some frequently used qualifying phrases such as *in my opinion*, *more or less*, and *for the most part* are also unnecessarily wordy. They can always be reworded more concisely and can often be omitted entirely.

WEAK	*In my opinion*, the competition for grades distracts many students from their goal of obtaining a good education.
EMPHATIC	*I think* the competition for grades distracts many students from their main goal of obtaining a good education.
MORE EMPHATIC	The competition for grades distracts many students from their goal of obtaining a good education.

(See 31c for a longer discussion of concise writing.)

EXERCISE 5

Revise the following sentences to make them more emphatic by converting passive voice to active voice, by eliminating expletive

---

CLEAR THE CONFUSION

Choose a particularly confusing or unemphatic passage from a student essay, give it to student groups, and ask them to decide what devices covered in the chapter could be used to improve the passage. Ask them to make the changes as a group, and have a representative of each group write the revised passage on the board so that the class as a whole can compare the various revisions.

emph
18e

emph
18e

POSSIBLE ANSWERS: EXERCISE 5

1. The major weakness of the <u>restaurant is</u> that the service is surly.
2. The contestant <u>sat</u> behind a screen so that <u>the judges could not see her</u> while <u>she performed</u>.
3. After all these years <u>something still calls</u> me back to the town where I lived as a child.
4. <u>The police ordered</u> the protesters to clear the sidewalk when the motorcade was approaching.
5. <u>He must have had</u> some reason <u>for acting</u> as he did, whether conscious or unconscious.

ANSWERS: EXERCISE 6

Possible Revision

<u>Preparing pasta requires</u> common sense and imagination rather <u>than complicated</u> recipes. The key to <u>success is</u> fresh ingredients for the sauce and perfectly cooked pasta. The sauce <u>may contain</u> just about any fresh fish, meat, cheese, herb, or vegetable. <u>The pasta itself may</u> be dried or fresh, although <u>many experienced cooks find fresh pasta</u> more delicate and flavorful. Dried pasta is fine with zesty sauces; <u>fresh pasta is best with light oil and cream sauces</u>. Dried pasta <u>takes longer to cook than fresh pasta does</u>. <u>The cook should follow</u> the package directions <u>and test</u> the pasta before the cooking time is up. <u>According to the Italians, who ought to know</u>, the pasta is done when the texture is neither tough nor mushy but <u>al dente</u>, or "firm to the bite."

constructions, or by condensing or eliminating wordy phrases. (For additional exercises with the passive voice, see pp. 197, 237, and 481.)

Example:

The problem in this particular situation is that we owe more money than we can afford under present circumstances.

The *problem is* that we owe more money than we can afford.

1. As far as I am concerned, the major weakness of the restaurant in question is that the service is surly, in a manner of speaking.
2. The contestant was seated behind a screen so that she could not be seen by the judges while her performance was heard.
3. After all these years there is still something calling me back to the town where I lived as a child.
4. The protesters were ordered by the police to clear the sidewalk when the motorcade was approaching.
5. There must have been some reason, whether conscious or unconscious, why he acted as he did.

EXERCISE 6

Drawing on the advice in this chapter, rewrite the following paragraph to emphasize main ideas and to de-emphasize less important information.

In preparing pasta, there is a requirement for common sense and imagination rather than for complicated recipes. The key to success in this area is fresh ingredients for the sauce and perfectly cooked pasta. The sauce may be made with just about any fresh fish, meat, cheese, herb, or vegetable. As for the pasta itself, it may be dried or fresh, although fresh pasta is usually more delicate and flavorful, as many experienced cooks have found. Dried pasta is fine with zesty sauces; with light oil and cream sauces fresh pasta is best used. There is a difference in the cooking time for dried and fresh pasta, with dried pasta taking longer. It is important that the package directions be followed by the cook and that the pasta be tested before the cooking time is up. The pasta is done when the texture is neither tough nor mushy but *al dente*, or "firm to the bite," according to the Italians, who ought to know.

CHAPTER 19

Achieving Variety

HIGHLIGHTS

This chapter asks students to think of sentences not as single units but as a sequence of ideas working together. Coordination, subordination, parallelism, and emphasis—topics covered in the preceding chapters—all come into play in the examples in this chapter. You will probably want to direct attention to the introduction to this chapter and to the first two sections, covering strategies for varying the length and structure of sentences and for varying sentence beginnings. You may have to decide, though, how much time to devote to the last two sections, which cover the occasional uses of inverted sentence order and of minor sentence types such as questions and commands.

In a paragraph or an essay, sentences do not stand one by one. Rather, each stands in relation to those before and after it. To make sentences work together effectively, the writer must vary their length, structure, and word order to reflect the importance and complexity of ideas. Although experienced writers generally find that variety takes care of itself as they commit ideas to paper, inexperienced writers often have difficulty achieving variety without guidance and practice.

A series of similar sentences will prove monotonous and ineffective, as this passage illustrates:

> Ulysses S. Grant and Robert E. Lee met on April 9, 1865. Their meeting place was the parlor of a modest house at Appomattox Court House, Virginia. They met to work out the terms for the surrender of Lee's Army of Northern Virginia. One great chapter of American life ended with their meeting, and another began. Grant and Lee were bringing the Civil War to its virtual finish. Other armies still had to surrender, and the fugitive Confederate government would struggle desperately and vainly. It would try to find some way to go on living with its chief support gone. Grant and Lee had signed the papers, however, and it was all over in effect.

Individually, these eight sentences are perfectly clear and adequately detailed. But together they do not make pleasant reading, and their relative importance is obscure. Their lengths are roughly the same, they are about equally detailed, and they all consist of one or two main clauses beginning with the subject. At the end of the passage we have a sense of names, dates, and events but no sure sense of how they relate.

RESOURCES AND IDEAS

Jane R. Walpole, "The Vigorous Pursuit of Grace and Style," *The Writing Instructor* 1 (1982): 163–69. Walpole describes six ways students can manipulate a good but not great passage (improving their own prose in the process), along with an example to show how the procedure works.

19

> **WAYS TO ACHIEVE VARIETY AMONG SENTENCES**
>
> 1. Vary the length and structure of sentences so that important ideas stand out (19a).
> 2. Vary the beginnings of sentences with modifiers, transitional words and expressions, and occasional expletive constructions (19b).
> 3. Occasionally, invert the normal order of subject, predicate, and object or complement (19c).
> 4. Use an occasional command, question, or exclamation (19d).

Now compare the preceding passage with the actual passage written by Bruce Catton.

> When Ulysses S. Grant and Robert E. Lee met in the parlor of a modest house at Appomattox Court House, Virginia, on April 9, 1865, to work out the terms for the surrender of Lee's Army of Northern Virginia, a great chapter in American life came to a close, and a great new chapter began.
> These men were bringing the Civil War to its virtual finish. To be sure, other armies had yet to surrender, and for a few days the fugitive Confederate government would struggle desperately and vainly, trying to find some way to go on living now that its chief support was gone. But in effect it was all over when Grant and Lee signed the papers.   —BRUCE CATTON, "Grant and Lee"

The information in these two passages is almost identical. The differences lie chiefly in the sentence variety of the second and the sharp focus on the end of war which that variety underscores. Catton's four sentences range from eleven to fifty-five words, and only one of the sentences begins with its subject. The first sentence brings together in one long *when* clause all the details of place, time, and cause contained in the first three sentences of the first passage. The sentence is periodic (see 18a-1), and the suspense it creates forces us to focus on the significance of the meeting described in the two main clauses at the end. The very brief second sentence, contrasting sharply with the one before it, quickly recapitulates the reason for the meeting. The third sentence, a long, cumulative one (see 18a-1), reflects the lingering obstacles to peace. And the fourth sentence, another short one, tersely indicates the futility of future struggle. Together, the four sentences clearly, even dramatically, convey that the meeting ended the war and marked a turning point in American history.

The rest of this chapter suggests how you can vary your sentences for the kind of interest and clarity achieved by Catton.

19a Varying sentence length and structure

The sentences of a stylistically effective essay will differ most obviously in their length. Further, some sentences will consist only of one main clause with modifiers, others of two main clauses; some will be cumulative, and a few perhaps will be periodic. (See 18a-1.) This variation in length and structure marks mature writing, making it both readable and clear.

Neither short sentences nor long sentences are intrinsically better. But in most contemporary writing, sentences tend to vary from about ten words on the short side to about forty words on the long, with an average of between fifteen and twenty-five words, depending on the writer's purpose and style. Your sentences generally should not be all at one extreme or the other, for if they are, your readers may have difficulty focusing on main ideas and seeing the relations among them. If most of your sentences contain thirty-five words or more, you probably need to break some up into shorter, simpler sentences. If most of your sentences contain fewer than ten or fifteen words, you probably need to add details to them or combine them through coordination and subordination. Examine your writing particularly for a common problem: strings of main clauses, subjects first, in either simple or compound sentences.

1 Avoiding strings of brief and simple sentences

A series of brief and simple sentences is both monotonous and hard to understand because it forces the reader to sort out relations among ideas. If you find that you depend on brief, simple sentences, work to increase variety by combining some of them into longer units that emphasize and link new and important ideas while de-emphasizing old or incidental information. (See 16a, 16b, and 18a.)

The following example shows how a string of simple sentences can be revised into an effective piece of writing.

WEAK

The moon is now drifting away from the earth. It moves away at the rate of about one inch a year. Our days on earth are getting longer. They grow a thousandth of a second longer every century. A month might become forty-seven of our present days long. We might eventually lose the moon altogether. Such great planetary movement rightly concerns astronomers. It need not worry us. The movement will take 50 million years.

REVISED

The moon is now drifting away from the earth, moving at the rate of about one inch a year. And at the rate of a thousandth of a second or so every century, our days on earth are getting longer. Someday, a month will be forty-seven of our present days long, if we don't eventually lose the moon altogether. Such great planetary movement rightly concerns astronomers, but it need not concern us. It will take 50 million years.

In the first passage the choppy movement of the nine successive simple sentences leaves the reader with nine independent facts and a lame conclusion. The revision retains all the facts of the original but compresses them into five sentences that are structured to emphasize main ideas—the moon's movement (sentence 1), our lengthening days (2), and the enormous span of time involved (5)—and to show relations among ideas.

2   Avoiding excessive compounding

Because compound sentences are usually just simple sentences linked with conjunctions, a series of them will be as weak as a series of brief simple sentences, especially if the clauses of the compound sentences are all about the same length.

WEAK

The hotel beach faces the south, and the main street runs along the north side of the hotel. The main street is heavily traveled and often noisy, but the beach is always quiet and sunny. It was Sunday afternoon, and we were on the hotel beach. We lay stretched out on the sand, and the sun poured down on us.

REVISED

The main street, heavily traveled and often noisy, runs along the north side of the hotel. But on the south side the hotel beach is always quiet and sunny. On Sunday we lay there stretched out on the sand, letting the sun pour down on us.

The first passage creates a seesaw effect. The revision, with some main clauses changed into modifiers and repositioned, is both clearer and more emphatic. (See 16a-2 for additional discussion of how to avoid excessive coordination within sentences.)

EXERCISE 1

Rewrite the following paragraphs to increase variety so that important ideas receive greater emphasis than supporting information does. You will have to change some main clauses into modifiers and then combine and reposition the modifiers and the remaining main clauses.

1. Charlotte Perkins Gilman was a leading intellectual in the women's movement during the first decades of this century. She wrote *Women and Economics*. This book challenged Victorian assumptions about differences between the sexes. It explored the economic roots of women's oppression. Gilman wrote little about gaining the vote for women. Many feminists were then preoccupied with this issue. Historians have since focused their analyses on this issue. As a result, Gilman's contribution to today's women's movement has often been overlooked.

2. Nathaniel Hawthorne was one of America's first great writers, and he was descended from a judge. The judge had presided at some of the Salem witch trials, and he had condemned some men and women to death. Hawthorne could never forget this piece of family history, and he always felt guilty about it. He never wrote about his ancestor directly, but he did write about the darkness of the human heart. He wrote *The Scarlet Letter* and *The House of the Seven Gables*, and in those books he demonstrated his favorite theme of a secret sin.

19b Varying sentence beginnings

Most English sentences begin with their subjects.

The defendant's lawyer relentlessly cross-examined the stubborn witness for two successive days.

However, an unbroken sequence of sentences beginning with the subject quickly becomes monotonous, as shown by the altered passage on Grant and Lee at the start of this chapter (p. 349). Your final arrangement of sentence elements should always depend on two concerns: the relation of a sentence to those preceding and following it and the emphasis required by your meaning. When you do choose to vary the subject-first pattern, you have several options.

Adverb modifiers can often be placed at a variety of spots in a sentence. Consider the different emphases created by moving the adverbs in the basic sentence above.

For two successive days, the defendant's lawyer *relentlessly* cross-examined the stubborn witness.

Relentlessly, the defendant's lawyer cross-examined the stubborn witness *for two successive days*.

Relentlessly, for two successive days, the defendant's lawyer cross-examined the stubborn witness.

ANSWERS: EXERCISE 1
Possible Revisions

1. Charlotte Perkins Gilman was a leading intellectual in the women's movement during the first decades of this century. Her book *Women and Economics* challenged Victorian assumptions about the differences between the sexes and explored the economic root of women's oppression. Gilman wrote little about gaining the vote for women, the issue that then preoccupied feminists and that historians have since focused their analyses on. As a result, Gilman's contribution to today's women's movement has often been overlooked.

2. Nathaniel Hawthorne was one of America's first great writers. He was descended from a judge who had presided at some of the Salem witch trials and had condemned some men and women to death. Hawthorne could never forget about this piece of family history, and he always felt guilty about it. Though he never wrote about his ancestor directly, he did write about the darkness of the human heart. In *The Scarlet Letter* and *The House of the Seven Gables*, he demonstrated his favorite theme: a secret sin.

var 19b

RESOURCES AND IDEAS
William J. Vande Kopple, *Clear and Coherent Prose: A Functional Approach* (Glenview: Scott, 1989). Vande Kopple offers detailed advice about creating clear and emphatic sentences, including helpful suggestions for sentence beginnings.

Notice that the last sentence, with both modifiers at the beginning, is periodic and thus highly emphatic (see 18a-1).

Beginning a sentence with a participial phrase also postpones the subject and sometimes creates a periodic sentence.

> The lawyer thoroughly cross-examined the witness and then called the defendant herself to testify.
>
> *Having thoroughly cross-examined the witness*, the lawyer called the defendant herself to testify.

When the relation between two successive sentences demands, you may begin the second with a coordinating conjunction or with a transitional expression such as *first, for instance, however, in addition, moreover, or therefore*. (See 3b-6 for a list of transitional expressions.)

> The witness expected to be dismissed after his first long day of cross-examination. He was not; the defendant's lawyer called him again the second day.
>
> The witness expected to be dismissed after his first long day of cross-examination. *But* he was not; the defendant's lawyer called him again the second day.
>
> The price of clothes has risen astronomically in recent years. The cotton shirt that once cost $6.00 and now costs $25.00 is an example.
>
> The price of clothes has risen astronomically in recent years. *For example*, a cotton shirt that once cost $6.00 now costs $25.00.

Occasionally, an expletive construction—*it* or *there* plus a form of *be*—may be useful to delay and thus emphasize the subject of the sentence.

> His judgment seems questionable, not his desire.
> *It is* his judgment that seems questionable, not his desire.

However, expletive constructions are more likely to flatten writing by adding extra words. You should use them rarely, only when you can justify doing so. (See also 18e.)

var
19b

Good

ANSWERS: EXERCISE 2

1. The loan application was denied by the bank. <u>Consequently</u>, the business had to close its doors.
2. <u>If the school builds</u> a new athletic complex, it will tear down the old field house.

EXERCISE 2

Revise each pair of sentences below, following the instructions in parentheses to make a single sentence that begins with an adverb modifier or a participial phrase, or to make one of the two sentences begin with an appropriate coordinating conjunction or transitional expression.

Example:
The *Seabird* took first place. It moved quickly in the wind.
(*One sentence with participial phrase beginning <u>moving</u>.*)

> *Moving quickly in the wind*, the *Seabird* took first place.

1. The loan application was denied by the bank. The business had to close its doors. (*Two sentences with transitional expression*.)
2. The school may build a new athletic complex. It will tear down the old field house. (*One sentence with adverb modifier beginning* if.)
3. Voting rights for women seemed a possibility in the 1860s. Women were not actually given the vote for nearly sixty years. (*Two sentences with coordinating conjunction*.)
4. Robert had orders to stay in bed. He returned to work immediately. (*One sentence with adverb modifier beginning* although.)
5. The rescuers were careful as they handled the ropes. They lowered the frightened climber from the ledge. (*One sentence with participial phrase beginning* carefully.)

EXERCISE 3 *Nice!*

Revise the following paragraph to vary sentence beginnings by using each of the following at least once: an adverb modifier, a participial phrase, a coordinating conjunction, and a transitional expression.

The instructor found himself in class alone. He waited patiently for his students to arrive. He went over his lecture notes. He read yesterday's newspaper. No one arrived. He noticed an article on the front page of the paper instructing readers to turn their clocks back one hour. He realized his mistake. He smiled.

---

3. Voting rights for women seemed a possibility in the 1860s. Yet women were not actually given the vote for nearly sixty years.
4. Although Robert had orders to stay in bed, he returned to work immediately.
5. Carefully handling the ropes, the rescuers lowered the frightened climber from the ledge.

ANSWERS: EXERCISE 3

Possible Revision

When the instructor found himself in the class alone, he waited patiently for his students to arrive. He went over his lecture notes. He read yesterday's paper. But no one arrived. Finally, he noticed an article on the front page of the paper instructing readers to turn their clocks back one hour. Realizing his mistake, he smiled.

var
19c

19c Inverting the normal word order

Inverted sentences such as *Up came the down* and *Mutton he didn't like* are infrequent in modern prose. Because the word order of subject, verb, and object or complement is so strongly fixed in English, an inverted sentence can be emphatic.

Harry had once been a dog lover. Then his neighbor's barking dogs twice raced through his garden. Now *all dogs*, especially barking dogs, *Harry detests*.

Inverting the normal order of subject, verb, and complement can be useful in two successive sentences when the second expands on the first.

Critics have not been kind to Presidents who have tried to apply the ways of private business to public affairs. Particularly *explicit was the curt verdict* of one critic of President Hoover: Mr. Hoover was never President of the United States; he was four years chairman of the board.   —Adapted from EMMET JOHN HUGHES, "The Presidency vs. Jimmy Carter"

Inverted sentences used without need are artificial. Avoid descriptive sentences such as *Up came Larry and down went Cindy's spirits.*

**var
19d**

19d Mixing types of sentences

Most written sentences make statements. Occasionally, however, questions, commands, or, more rarely, exclamations may enhance variety. Questions may set the direction of a paragraph, as in *What does a detective do?* or *How is the percentage of unemployed workers calculated?* More often, though, the questions used in exposition or argumentation do not require answers but simply emphasize ideas that readers can be expected to agree with. These **rhetorical questions** are illustrated in the following passage.

> Another word that has ceased to have meaning due to overuse is *attractive. Attractive* has become verbal chaff. Who, by some stretch of language and imagination, cannot be described as attractive? And just what is it that attractive individuals are attracting?   —DIANE WHITE

Imperative sentences occur frequently in an explanation of a process, particularly in directions, as this passage on freewriting illustrates.

> The idea is simply to write for ten minutes (later on, perhaps fifteen or twenty). Don't stop for anything. Go quickly without rushing. Never stop to look back, to cross something out, to wonder how to spell something, to wonder what word or thought to use, or to think about what you are doing.   —PETER ELBOW

Notice that the authors of these examples use questions and commands not merely to vary their sentences but to achieve some special purpose. Variety occurs because a particular sentence type is effective for the context, not because the writer set out to achieve variety for its own sake.

USING FORMS

Tell students to write a paragraph making use of the strategies suggested in this chapter. Leave the content of the paragraph up to them; they will discover how form can help suggest content.

SAMPLE ANSWERS: EXERCISE 4

1. How many cars are registered on this campus?
2. Try to find a parking space on this campus any weekday morning after nine o'clock.

EXERCISE 4

Imagine that you are writing an essay either on the parking problem at your school or on the problems of living in a dormitory. Practice varying sentences by composing a sentence or passage to serve each purpose listed below.

1. Write a question that could open the essay.
2. Write a command that could open the essay.
3. Write an exclamation that could open the essay.
4. For the body of the essay, write an appropriately varied paragraph of at least five sentences, including at least one short and one long sentence beginning with the subject; at least one sentence beginning with an adverb modifier; at least one sentence beginning with a coordinating conjunction or transitional expression; and one rhetorical question or command.

EXERCISE 5

Examine the following paragraph for sentence variety. By analyzing your own response to each sentence, try to explain why the author wrote each short or long sentence, each cumulative or periodic sentence, each sentence beginning with its subject or beginning some other way, and each question.

That night in my rented room, while letting the hot water run over my can of pork and beans in the sink, I opened [H. L. Mencken's] *A Book of Prefaces* and began to read. I was jarred and shocked by the style, the clear, clean, sweeping sentences. Why did he write like that? And how did one write like that? I pictured the man as a raging demon, slashing with his pen, consumed with hate, denouncing everything American, extolling everything European or German, laughing at the weaknesses of people, mocking God, authority. What was this? I stood up, trying to realize what reality lay behind the meaning of the words. Yes, this man was fighting, fighting with words. He was using words as a weapon, using them as one would use a club. Could words be weapons? Well, yes, for here they were. Then, maybe, perhaps, I could use them as a weapon? No. It frightened me. I read on and what amazed me was not what he said, but how on earth anybody had the courage to say it.

—Richard Wright, *Black Boy*

EXERCISE 6

The following paragraph consists entirely of simple sentences that begin with their subjects. As appropriate, use the techniques discussed in this chapter to vary sentences so that the paragraph is more readable and its important ideas stand out clearly. You will have to delete, add, change, and rearrange words.

The Italian volcano Vesuvius had been dormant for many years. It then exploded on August 24 in the year A.D. 79. The ash, pumice, and mud from the volcano buried two busy towns. Herculaneum is one. The more famous is Pompeii. The ruins of both towns lay undiscovered for many centuries. Herculaneum and

3. What an unexpected pleasure to find a parking space within two blocks of the library!
4. Can the frustration caused by the parking problem be healthy for the student? He drives round and round the campus, the minutes of lost study or class time ticking away. Tension builds. As he passes filled row upon filled row in one lot after another, the driver begins to tremble, sweat, and swear. And the anger and panic, instead of abating when finally the car is safely stowed, stays with the student throughout the day.

POSSIBLE ANSWER: EXERCISE 5

The shortest sentence is one word: *No*. The longest is sentence 5, *I pictured the man as. . . .* The opening periodic sentence sets the scene before coming to the point. The longest sentence gains its length and power from the six modifying verbal phrases that convey Wright's first impression of Mencken. Wright relies on questions interspersed with tentative answers to show his own incremental awakening on discovering Mencken. Repetition—*fighting, fighting; using . . . using; maybe, perhaps*—also show Wright wrestling with what he has found. The last question leads to the conclusion of the final three sentences, which gradually increase in length and complexity.

ANSWER: EXERCISE 6

Possible revision

After being dormant for many years, the Italian volcano Vesuvius exploded on August 24 in the year A.D. 79. The ash, pumice, and mud from the volcano buried two towns—Herculaneum and the more famous Pompeii—which lay undiscovered until 1709 and 1748, respectively. The excavation of Pompeii was the more systematic, the occasion for initiating modern methods

var
19

of conservation and restoration. <u>Whereas</u> Herculaneum was simply looted of its most valuable finds <u>and</u> then left to disintegrate, Pompeii appears much as it did during the eruption. A luxurious house opens onto a lush central garden. An election poster decorates a wall. <u>And</u> a dining table is set for breakfast.

Pompeii were discovered in 1709 and 1748, respectively. The excavation of Pompeii was the more systematic. It was the occasion for initiating modern methods of conservation and restoration. The methods replaced earlier practices. Herculaneum was simply looted of its most valuable finds. It was then left to disintegrate. Pompeii appears much as it did before the eruption. A luxurious house opens onto a lush central garden. An election poster decorates a wall. A dining table is set for breakfast.

var
19

PART V

Punctuation

HIGHLIGHTS

This chart provides sentence examples covering the main features of sentence punctuation, including the comma, the semicolon, the colon, dashes, and parentheses. It also provides a quick reference for such troublesome features as restrictive and nonrestrictive modifiers and items in a series. Students can locate on the chart a sentence like one they have just written to determine how to punctuate it, or they can look at the chart for a particular feature of punctuation whose name they have forgotten and therefore cannot locate in the handbook's index or table of contents.

Because the various punctuation strategies appear together in a short space in this list, students will be able to see the options available to them as they write. In addition, the cross references give students a chance to explore these options in depth. Instructors, too, should be able to find many uses for the chart, both in class and in working with individual students.

USING THE PUNCTUATION CHAPTERS

The use you make of the chapters in this unit of the text is likely to depend partly on your students and partly on whether you choose to use the chapters solely to teach punctuation or as part of a sentence-combining program. Many college students should need no formal instruction in punctuation, although they,

MAJOR INTERNAL SENTENCE PUNCTUATION
Commas, Semicolons, Colons, Dashes, and Parentheses

(For explanations, consult the sections in parentheses.)

Sentences with two main clauses

The bus stopped, *but* no one got off. (21a)
The bus stopped; no one got off. (22a)
The bus stopped; *however,* no one got off. (22b)
The mechanic replaced the battery, the distributor cap, and the starter; *but* still the car would not start. (22c)
His duty was clear: he had to report the theft. (25a-1)

Introductory elements

MODIFIERS (21b)

After the argument was over, we laughed at ourselves.
Racing over the plain, the gazelle escaped the lion.
To dance in the contest, he had to tape his knee.
Suddenly, the door flew open.
With 125 passengers aboard, the plane was half full.
In 1983 he won the Nobel Prize.

ABSOLUTE PHRASES (21d)

Its wing broken, the bird hopped around on the ground.

Interrupting and concluding elements

NONRESTRICTIVE MODIFIERS (21c-1)

Jim's car, *which barely runs,* has been impounded.
We consulted the dean, *who had promised to help us.*
The boy, *like his sister,* wants to be a pilot.
They moved across the desert, *shielding their eyes from the sun.*
The men do not speak to each other, *although they share a car.*

NONRESTRICTIVE APPOSITIVES

Bergen's daughter, *Candice,* became an actress. (21c-2)
The residents of three counties—*Suffolk, Springfield, and Morrison*—were urged to evacuate. (25b-2)
Our father demanded one promise: *that we not lie to him.* (25a-1)

RESTRICTIVE MODIFIERS (21j-3)

The car *that hit mine* was uninsured.
We consulted a teacher *who had promised to help us.*
The boy *in the black hat* is my cousin.
They were surprised to find the desert *teeming with life.*
The men do not speak to each other *because they are feuding.*

Restrictive appositives (21j-3)

Shaw's play *Saint Joan* was performed last year.
Their sons *Tony, William, and Steve* all chose military careers, leaving only Joe to run the family business.

Parenthetical expressions

We suspect, *however*, that he will not come. (21c-3)
Jan is respected by many people—*including me*. (25b-2)
George Balanchine (*1904–1983*) was a brilliant choreographer. (25c-1)

Absolute phrases (21d)

The bird, *its wing broken*, hopped about on the ground.
The bird hopped about on the ground, *its wing broken*.

Phrases expressing contrast (21e)

The humidity, *not just the heat*, gives me headaches.
My headaches are caused by the humidity, *not just the heat*.

Concluding summaries and explanations

The movie opened to bad notices: *the characters were judged shallow and unrealistic*. (25a-1)
We dined on gumbo, blackened fish, and jambalaya—*a Cajun feast*. (25b-3)

Items in a series

Three or more items

Chimpanzees, gorillas, orangutans, and gibbons are all apes. (21f-1)
The cities singled out for praise were *Birmingham, Alabama; Lincoln, Nebraska; Austin, Texas; and Madison, Wisconsin*. (22d)

Two or more adjectives before a noun or pronoun (21f-2)

Dingy, smelly clothes decorated their room.
The luncheon consisted of *one tiny watercress* sandwich.

Introductory series (25b-3)

Appropriateness, accuracy, and necessity—these criteria should govern your selection of words.

Concluding series

Every word should be *appropriate, accurate, and necessary*. (25a-3)
Every word should meet three criteria: *appropriateness, accuracy, and necessity*. (25a-1)
Pay attention to your words—*to their appropriateness, their accuracy, and their necessity*. (25b-3)

---

like all of us, will need to check on particular conventions as they write. Other students may require specific work with the principal uses of the comma, the semicolon, and the apostrophe, and some students may profit from a review of end punctuation.

Almost all students, however, find punctuation of restrictive and nonrestrictive elements a problem, and the extensive discussion in Chapter 21 should prove helpful. Two special features of this discussion are the practical tests for determining if an element is restrictive or nonrestrictive and the discussion of how the context of a sentence helps determine the role an element plays.

The sentence-combining exercises in Chapters 21 and 22 give students a chance to practice using the comma and the semicolon. These exercises also ask students to create sentences with the structures those marks of punctuation make possible, such as independent clauses joined with a semicolon, nonrestrictive clauses and phrases, and compound sentences. By asking students to complete these exercises, you can encourage variety in sentence structure and style.

If time allows, you might wish to point out to your class how punctuation marks often substitute for other grammatical and semantic signals used in speech.

P

HIGHLIGHTS

This chapter discusses the three marks of end punctuation: the period, the question mark, and the exclamation point. Although many college students will need no formal instruction in punctuation, some students will benefit from a review of end punctuation. Such a review might emphasize the important role punctuation plays in conveying meaning and in creating subtle shades of meaning—a role students often overlook.

CHAPTER 20

End Punctuation

THE PERIOD

 20a Use the period to end sentences that are statements, mild commands, or indirect questions.

STATEMENTS

These are exciting and trying times.

The airline went bankrupt.

The violins played quietly in the background.

MILD COMMANDS

Please do not smoke.

Think of the possibilities.

Turn to page 146.

If you are unsure whether to use an exclamation point or a period after a command, use a period. The exclamation point should be used only rarely (see 20f).

An **indirect question** reports what someone has asked but not in the original speaker's own words.

INDIRECT QUESTIONS

The judge asked why I had been driving with my lights off in the middle of the night.

Students sometimes wonder whether their teachers read the papers they write.

Abused children eventually stop asking why they are being punished.

20b Use periods with most abbreviations.

Ordinarily, use periods with abbreviations.

p.   B.A.   A.D.   Mr.
D.C.   Ph.D.   A.M., a.m.   Mrs.
M.D.   e.g.   P.M., p.m.   Ms.
Dr.   B.C.

When an abbreviation falls at the end of a sentence, use only one period: *Government, not industry, is the business of Washington, D.C.*

Periods are usually dropped from abbreviations for organizations, corporations, and government agencies when more than two words are abbreviated. For example:

IBM   USMC   NFL   AFL-CIO

Check a dictionary for the preferred form of such abbreviations, and see Chapter 28 on abbreviations.

Note that **acronyms**—pronounceable words, such as UNESCO, NATO, VISTA, and WHO, formed from the initial letters of the words in a name—never require periods (see 28b).

EXERCISE 1

Revise the following sentences so that periods are used correctly.

> *Example:*
> Several times I wrote to ask when my subscription ended?
> Several times I wrote to ask when my subscription ended.

1. The instructor asked when Plato wrote *The Republic?*
2. Give the date within one century
3. The exact date is not known, but it is thought to be around 370 BC..
4. Dr Arn will lecture on Plato at 7:30 PM.
5. The area of the lecture hall is only 1600 sq ft

ANSWERS: EXERCISE 1

1. The instructor asked when Plato wrote *The Republic*.
2. Give the date within one century.
3. The exact date is not known, but it is thought to be around 370 B.C.
4. Dr. Arn will lecture on Plato at 7:30 P.M.
5. The lecture hall is only 1600 sq. ft.

THE QUESTION MARK

20c Use the question mark after direct questions.

DIRECT QUESTIONS

Who will follow her?
What is the difference between these two people?
Will economists ever really understand the economy?

After indirect questions, use a period: *My mother asked why I came in so late.* (See 20a.)

Questions in a series are each followed by a question mark.

The officer asked how many times the suspect had been arrested. Three times? Four times? More than that?

The use of capital letters for questions in a series is optional (see 26a).

NOTE: Question marks are never combined with other question marks, exclamation points, periods, or commas.

FAULTY	I finally asked myself, "Why are you working at a job you hate?."
REVISED	I finally asked myself, "Why are you working at a job you hate?"

20d **Use a question mark within parentheses to indicate doubt about the correctness of a number or date.**

The Greek philosopher Socrates was born in 470 (?) B.C. and died in 399 B.C. from drinking poison after having been condemned to death.

NOTE: Don't use a question mark within parentheses to express sarcasm or irony. Express these attitudes through sentence structure and diction. (See Chapters 18 and 31.)

FAULTY	Her friendly (?) criticism did not escape notice.
REVISED	Her criticism, *too rough to be genuinely friendly,* did not escape notice.

ANSWERS: EXERCISE 2

1. In Homer's *Odyssey*, Ulysses took seven years to travel from Troy to Ithaca. Or was it eight years? Or more?
2. Ulysses must have wondered wether he would ever make it home.
3. "What man are you and whence?" asks Ulysses's wife, Penelope.
4. Why does Penelope ask, "Where is your city? Your parents?"
5. Penelope does not recognize Ulysses and asks who this stranger is.

EXERCISE 2

Revise the following sentences so that question marks (along with other punctuation marks) are used correctly.

Example:
"When will it end?," cried the man dressed in rags.
"When will it end?" cried the man dressed in rags.

1. In Homer's *Odyssey*, Ulysses took seven years to travel from Troy to Ithaca. Or was it eight years. Or more?
2. Ulysses must have wondered whether he would ever make it home?
3. "What man are you and whence?," asks Ulysses's wife, Penelope.

4. Why does Penelope ask, "Where is your city? Your parents?"?

5. Penelope does not recognize Ulysses and asks who this stranger is?

THE EXCLAMATION POINT

20e Use the exclamation point after emphatic statements and interjections, and after strong commands.

No! We must not lose this election!
When she saw her rain-soaked term paper, she gasped, "Oh, no!"
Come here immediately!
"Stop!" he yelled.

Follow mild interjections and commands with commas or periods, as appropriate.

No, the response was not terrific.
To prolong your car's life, change its oil regularly.

NOTE: Exclamation points are never combined with other exclamation points, question marks, periods, or commas.

| FAULTY | My father was most emphatic. "I will not give you any more money!," he roared. |
| REVISED | My father was most emphatic. "I will not give you any more money!" he roared. |

20f Avoid overusing exclamation points.

Don't express sarcasm, irony, or amazement with the exclamation point. Rely on sentence structure and diction to express these attitudes. (See Chapters 18 and 31.)

| FAULTY | After traveling 1.24 billion miles through space, *Voyager 2* missed its target by 41 miles (!). |
| REVISED | After traveling 1.24 billion miles through space, *Voyager 2* missed its target by *a mere* 41 miles. |

Relying on the exclamation point for emphasis is like crying wolf: the mark loses its power to impress the reader. Frequent exclamation points can also make writing sound overemotional. In the following passage, the writer could have conveyed her ideas more effectively by punctuating sentences with periods.

EXTRA HELP

The *Little, Brown Workbook* provides additional exercises for students who need more practice with the end marks of punctuation.

!
20f

Our city government is a mess! After just six months in office, the mayor has had to fire four city officials! In the same period the city councilors have done nothing but argue! And city services decline with each passing day!

ANSWERS: EXERCISE 3

1. As the firefighters moved their equipment into place, the police shouted, "Move back<u>!</u>"
2. A child's cries could be heard from above: "Help me<u>!</u> Help<u>!</u>"
3. When the child was rescued, the crowd called, "Hooray<u>!</u>"
4. The rescue was the most exciting event of the day<u>.</u>
5. Correct.

EXERCISE 3

Revise the following sentences so that exclamation points (along with other punctuation marks) are used correctly. If a sentence is punctuated correctly as given, circle the number preceding it.

Example:
"Well, now!," he said loudly.
"Well, now!" he said loudly.

1. As the firefighters moved their equipment into place, the police shouted, "Move back!."
2. A child's cries could be heard from above: "Help me. Help."
3. When the child was rescued, the crowd called "Hooray."
4. The rescue was the most exciting event of the day!
5. Let me tell you about it.

ANSWERS: EXERCISE 4

When visitors first arrive in Hawaii, they often encounter an unexpected language barrier<u>.</u> Standard English is the language of business and government, but many of the people speak Pidgin English<u>.</u> Instead of an excited "Aloha<u>!</u>" the visitors may be greeted with an excited Pidgin "Howzit<u>!</u>" or asked if they know "how fo' find one good hotel<u>.</u>" Many Hawaiians question whether Pidgin will hold children back because it prevents communication with the *haoles*, or Caucasians, who run businesses<u>.</u> Yet many others feel that Pidgin is a last defense of ethnic diversity on the islands<u>.</u> To those who want to make Standard English the official language of the state, these Hawaiians may respond, "Just 'cause I speak Pidgin no mean I dumb<u>.</u>" They may ask, "Why you no listen<u>?</u>" or, in Standard English, "Why don't you listen<u>?</u>"

! 20f

EXERCISE 4

Insert appropriate punctuation (periods, question marks, or exclamation points) where needed in the following paragraph.

When visitors first arrive in Hawaii, they often encounter an unexpected language barrier Standard English is the language of business and government, but many of the people speak Pidgin English Instead of an excited "Aloha" the visitors may be greeted with an excited Pidgin "Howzit" or asked if they know "how fo' find one good hotel" Many Hawaiians question whether Pidgin will hold children back because it prevents communication with the *haoles*, or Caucasians, who run businesses Yet many others feel that Pidgin is a last defense of ethnic diversity on the islands To those who want to make standard English the official language of the state, these Hawaiians may respond, "Just 'cause I speak Pidgin no mean I dumb" They may ask, "Why you no listen" or, in standard English, "Why don't you listen"

NOTE: See page 434 for a punctuation exercise combining periods with other marks of punctuation such as commas and semicolons.

CHAPTER 21

The Comma

HIGHLIGHTS

This chapter deals with one of the most frequently misused marks of punctuation—the comma. Although some of the trouble that students have with comma usage may stem from speech patterns (ill-timed pauses, for example) and may be corrected through attention to speech patterns and sentence rhythm, the remainder of the problems generally arise from unfamiliarity with the rules of punctuation. One way to overcome this trouble is to memorize the rules. The chapter, therefore, provides both the rules and examples of the rules in use in a format designed for easy notation and memorization.

The comma is the most frequently used—and misused—mark of internal punctuation. In general, commas function within sentences to separate elements (see the box on the next page). Commas also have several conventional uses, as in dates. Omitting needed commas or inserting needless ones can confuse the reader, as the following sentences show.

COMMA NEEDED	Though very tall Abraham Lincoln was not an overbearing man.
REVISED	Though very tall, Abraham Lincoln was not an overbearing man.
UNNEEDED COMMAS	The hectic pace of Beirut, broke suddenly into frightening chaos when the city became, the focus of civil war.
REVISED	The hectic pace of Beirut broke suddenly into frightening chaos when the city became the focus of civil war.

21a   Use a comma before a coordinating conjunction linking main clauses.

The coordinating conjunctions are

for	and	or
so	but	nor
yet		

Words or phrases joined by a coordinating conjunction are *not* separated by a comma: *Bill plays and sings Irish and English folk songs* (see 21j-2). However, main clauses joined by a coordinating con-

367

PRINCIPAL USES OF THE COMMA

1. To separate main clauses linked by a coordinating conjunction (21a).

The steering was stiff, *but* the car rode smoothly.

2. To set off most introductory elements (21b).

Fortunately, the ride would be comfortable.

3. To set off nonrestrictive elements (21c).

We dreaded the trip, *which would take sixteen hours.*

Our destination, *Oklahoma City,* was unfamiliar to us.

4. To separate items in a series (21f-1).

We would need *a new home, new schools, and new friends.*

5. To separate coordinate adjectives (21f-1).

A *bumpy, cramped* ride would have been unbearable.

Other uses of the comma:

> To set off absolute phrases (21d).
> To set off phrases expressing contrast (21e).
> To separate parts of dates, addresses, and long numbers (21g).
> To separate quotations and explanatory words (21h).
> To prevent misreading (21i).

See also 21j for when *not* to use the comma.

21a

junction *are* separated by a comma. Main clauses are those which have a subject and a predicate (but no subordinating word at the beginning) and make complete statements (see 5c).

> She was perfectly at home in what she knew, *and* what she knew has remained what all of us want to know.
> —EUDORA WELTY on Jane Austen

> He would have turned around again without a word, *but* I seized him. —FYODOR DOSTOYEVSKY

> Seventeen years ago this month I quit work, *or*, if you prefer, I retired from business. —F. SCOTT FITZGERALD

> They made their decision with some uneasiness, *for* they knew that in such places any failure to conform could cause trouble.
> —RICHARD HARRIS

> In putting on trousers a man always inserts the same old leg first. . . . All men do it, *yet* no man thought it out and adopted it of set purpose. —MARK TWAIN

> Near evening I was too jittery to attend to chores, *so* Bailey volunteered to do all before his bath. —MAYA ANGELOU

EXCEPTIONS: Some writers prefer to use a semicolon before *so* and *yet*.

> Many people say that the institution of marriage is in decline; *yet* recent evidence suggests that the institution is at least holding steady.

When the main clauses in a sentence are very long or grammatically complicated, or when they contain internal punctuation, a semicolon before the coordinating conjunction will clarify the division between clauses (see 22c).

> Life would be dull without its seamier side, its violence, filth, and hatred; *for* otherwise how could we appreciate the joys?
> —ELLEN STEPIK

When main clauses are very short and closely related in meaning, you may omit the comma between them as long as the resulting sentence is clear.

> She opened her mouth *but* no sound came out of it.
> —FLANNERY O'CONNOR

> My heart raced *and* I felt ill.

If you are in doubt about whether to use a comma in such sentences, use it. It will always be correct.

RESOURCES AND IDEAS

Though writing instructors often treat commas and other marks of punctuation as if they were primarily cues to grammatical structures, these marks also function legitimately as stylistic cues, as indicators of the writer's voice—or so argues Wallace Chafe in "What Good Is Punctuation?" (*The Quarterly of the National Writing Project and the Center for the Study of Writing* 10 [1988]: 8–11). Chafe supports his argument with examples from the work of Herman Melville and James Agee and concludes with some useful advice for teaching:

> Students, in addition to being sensitized to their inner voices, will benefit from knowing the range of punctuating options that are available, and from being shown, through examples, what is most appropriate to one style and another. They can learn from practice in writing advertising copy as well as the more academic kinds of exposition, and from experimenting with fiction that mimics the very different punctuation styles of, say, Melville and Agee. At the same time, developing writers need to know that there are certain specific rules for punctuating that violate the prosody of their inner voices and that simply have to be learned. These arbitrary rules are few in number and well defined, and to learn them need be no burden. . . . The bottom line is that punctuation contributes substantially to the effectiveness of a piece of writing, and that its successful use calls for an awareness of something that is, for this and other reasons, essential to good writing: a sensitivity to the sound of written language. (11)

RESOURCES AND IDEAS

Emily Meyer and Louise Z. Smith, *The Practical Tutor* (New York: Oxford, 1987), Chapter 9, "Punctuation." The authors offer detailed advice for the often frustrating task of helping students develop effective punctuation skills.

21a

ANSWERS: EXERCISE 1

1. Parents once automatically gave their children the father's surname, but some no longer do.
2. Instead, they bestow the mother's name, for they believe that the mother's importance should be recognized.
3. The child's surname may be just the mother's, or it may link the mother's and the father's with a hyphen.
4. Sometimes the first and third children will have the mother's surname, and the second child will have the father's.
5. Occasionally the mother and father combine parts of their names, and a new hybrid surname is born.

POSSIBLE ANSWERS: EXERCISE 2

1. Parents were once legally required to bestow the father's surname on their children, but these laws have been contested in court and found invalid.
2. Parents may now give their children any surname they choose, and the arguments for bestowing the mother's surname are often strong and convincing.
3. Critics sometimes question the effects of unusual surnames on children, or they wonder how confusing or fleeting the new surnames will be.
4. Children with surnames different from their parents' may suffer embarrassment or identity problems, for giving children their father's surname is still very much the norm.
5. Hyphenated names are awkward and difficult to pass on, so some observers think they will die out in the next generation or before.

21a

EXERCISE 1

Insert a comma before each coordinating conjunction that links main clauses in the following sentences.

Example:

I would have attended the concert and the reception but I had to baby-sit for my niece.

I would have attended the concert and the reception, but I had to baby-sit for my niece.

1. Parents once automatically gave their children the father's surname but some no longer do.
2. Instead, they bestow the mother's name for they believe that the mother's importance should be recognized.
3. The child's surname may be just the mother's or it may link the mother's and the father's with a hyphen.
4. Sometimes the first and third children will have the mother's surname and the second child will have the father's.
5. Occasionally the mother and father combine parts of their names and a new hybrid surname is born.

EXERCISE 2

Combine each group of sentences below into one sentence that contains only two main clauses connected by the coordinating conjunction in parentheses. Separate the main clauses with a comma. You will have to add, delete, and rearrange words.

Example:

The circus had come to town. The children wanted to see it. Their parents wanted to see it. (*and*)

The circus had come to town, *and* the children and their parents wanted to see it.

1. Parents were once legally required to bestow the father's surname on their children. These laws have been contested in court. They have been found invalid. (*but*)
2. Parents may now give their children any surname they choose. The arguments for bestowing the mother's surname are often strong. They are often convincing. (*and*)
3. Critics sometimes question the effects of unusual surnames on children. They wonder how confusing the new surnames will be. They wonder how fleeting the surnames will be. (*or*)
4. Children with surnames different from their parents' may suffer embarrassment. They may suffer identity problems. Giving children their father's surname is still very much the norm. (*for*)
5. Hyphenated names are awkward. They are also difficult to pass on. Some observers think they will die out in the next generation. Or they may die out before. (*so*)

21b Use a comma to set off most introductory elements.

An introductory element modifies a word or words in the main clause that follows. Such elements include subordinate clauses serving as adverbs (5c-4); participles, infinitives, and participial and infinitive phrases serving as adjectives and adverbs (5c-2); prepositional phrases (5c-1); and sentence modifiers such as *unfortunately, certainly,* and *of course.* These elements are usually set off from the rest of the sentence with a comma.

> *If Ernest Hemingway had written comic books,* they would have been just as good as his novels. [Subordinate clause.]
> —STAN LEE

> *Exhausted,* the runner collapsed at the finish line. [Participle.]

> *To win the most important race of her career,* she had nearly killed herself. [Infinitive phrase.]

> *From Columbus and Sir Walter Raleigh onward,* America has been traveling the road west. [Prepositional phrase.]
> —PETER DAVISON

> *Unfortunately,* the diamond was fake. [Sentence modifier.]

The comma may be omitted following short introductory prepositional and infinitive phrases and subordinate clauses if its omission does not create confusion. (If you are in doubt, however, the comma is always correct.)

CLEAR	*By the year 2000* the world population will be more than 6 billion. [Prepositional phrase.]
CLEAR	*To write clearly* one must think clearly. [Infinitive phrase.]
CLEAR	*When snow falls* the city collapses. [Subordinate clause.]
CONFUSING	At eighteen people are considered young adults.
REVISED	At eighteen, people are considered young adults.

NOTE: Take care to distinguish verbals used as modifiers from verbals used as subjects. The former almost always take a comma; the latter never do.

> *Jogging through the park,* I was unexpectedly caught in a downpour. [Participial phrase used as modifier.]
> *Jogging through the park* has become a popular form of recreation for city dwellers. [Gerund phrase used as subject.]

RESOURCES AND IDEAS

Joseph Collignon, "Why Leroy Can't Write," *College English* 39 (1978): 852–59. Collignon suggests using oral reading to help students punctuate correctly and to provide them with models for writing.

21b

To dance professionally, he trained for years. [Infinitive phrase used as modifier.]

To dance professionally is his one desire. [Infinitive phrase used as subject.]

In addition, do not use a comma to separate a verbal from the noun or pronoun it modifies when the verbal restricts the meaning of the noun or pronoun (see also 21c).

Shuttered houses lined the street. [*Shuttered* restricts *houses*.]

Shuttered, the houses were protected from the elements. [*Shuttered* does not restrict *houses*.]

21b

ANSWERS: EXERCISE 3

1. Veering sharply to the right, a large flock of birds neatly avoids a high wall.
2. Correct.
3. With the help of complex computer simulations, zoologists are learning more about this movement.
4. Because it is sudden and apparently well coordinated, the movement of flocks and schools has seemed to be directed by a leader.
5. Almost incredibly, the group could behave with more intelligence than any individual seemed to possess.
6. However, new studies have discovered that flocks and schools are leaderless.
7. Correct.
8. When each bird or fish senses a predator, it follows individual rules for fleeing.
9. To keep from colliding with its neighbors, each bird or fish uses other rules for dodging.
10. Multiplied over hundreds of individuals, these responses look as if they have been choreographed.

EXERCISE 3

Insert commas where needed after introductory elements in the following sentences. If a sentence is punctuated correctly as given, circle the number preceding it.

Example:

After the new library opened the old one became a student union.

After the new library opened, the old one became a student union.

1. Veering sharply to the right a large flock of birds neatly avoids a high wall.
2. Moving in a fluid mass is typical of flocks of birds and schools of fish.
3. With the help of complex computer simulations zoologists are learning more about this movement.
4. Because it is sudden and apparently well coordinated the movement of flocks and schools has seemed to be directed by a leader.
5. Almost incredibly the group could behave with more intelligence than any individual seemed to possess.
6. However new studies have discovered that flocks and schools are leaderless.
7. Evading danger turns out to be an individual response.
8. When each bird or fish senses a predator it follows individual rules for fleeing.
9. To keep from colliding with its neighbors each bird or fish uses other rules for dodging.
10. Multiplied over hundreds of individuals these responses look as if they have been choreographed.

EXERCISE 4

Combine each pair of sentences below into one sentence that begins with an introductory phrase or clause as specified in parentheses. Follow the introductory element with a comma. You will have to add, delete, change, and rearrange words.

Example:

The girl was humming to herself. She walked upstairs. (*Phrase beginning* <u>Humming</u>.)

Humming to herself, the girl walked up the stairs.

1. Scientists have made an effort to explain the mysteries of flocks and schools. They have proposed bizarre magnetic fields and telepathy. (*Phrase beginning* <u>In</u>.)
2. Scientists developed computer models. They have abandoned earlier explanations. (*Clause beginning* <u>Since</u>.)
3. The movement of a flock or school starts with each individual. It is rapidly and perhaps automatically coordinated among individuals. (*Phrase beginning* <u>Starting</u>.)
4. One zoologist observes that human beings seek coherent patterns. He suggests that investigators saw purpose in the movement of flocks and schools where none existed. (*Phrase beginning* <u>Observing</u>.)
5. One may want to study the movement of flocks or schools. Then one must abandon a search for purpose or design. (*Phrase beginning* <u>To</u>.)

21c Use a comma or commas to set off nonrestrictive elements.

Restrictive and nonrestrictive sentence elements contribute differently to meaning and require different punctuation. A **restrictive element** limits, or restricts, the meaning of the word or words it applies to. Thus it is essential to the meaning of the sentence and cannot be omitted without significantly changing that meaning. Restrictive elements are never set off with punctuation.

RESTRICTIVE ELEMENT

Employees *who work hard* will receive raises.

A **nonrestrictive element** gives added information about the word or words it applies to, but it does not limit the word or words. It can be omitted from the sentence without changing the essential meaning. Nonrestrictive elements are always set off with punctuation.

NONRESTRICTIVE ELEMENT

Molly Berman, *who lives next door,* got a raise.

The relation of restriction and punctuation is an inverse one: when

RESTRICTIVE AND NONRESTRICTIVE PAIRS

Give students a sentence containing a modifying element and ask them to write two brief groups of sentences, one providing a context that requires that the element in the original sentence be restrictive, another requiring a nonrestrictive element.

the element is *not* essential, the punctuation *is;* and when the element *is* essential, the punctuation is *not.*

Commas are most commonly used to set off nonrestrictive elements, although dashes or parentheses are sometimes used to emphasize or de-emphasize them (see 25b-2 and 25c-1, respectively, and especially the box on p. 426). Whatever punctuation mark you select, be sure to use a pair if the nonrestrictive element falls in the middle of a sentence—one *before* and another *after* the element.

A test can help you determine whether a sentence element is restrictive or nonrestrictive: does the fundamental meaning of the sentence change when the element is removed? It does in the restrictive example above, for *Employees will receive raises* does not provide the same information about employees as the original sentence did. The employees are no longer defined or limited to a specific group, the ones who work hard, but instead encompass all employees, whatever their work habits. Conversely, *Molly Berman got a raise* has essentially the same meaning as the original nonrestrictive example. No matter where Molly Berman lives, she still got the raise.

The presence or absence of commas around a sentence element can change the meaning of a single sentence, as the following examples illustrate.

> The band *playing old music* held the audience's attention.
> The band, *playing old music,* held the audience's attention.

In the first sentence the absence of commas restricts the subject to a particular band, the one playing old music, and thus implies that more than one band played more than one kind of music. In the second sentence, however, the commas setting off the phrase imply that only one band played, because the phrase does not restrict the subject to a particular band. Which punctuation is correct depends on the writer's intended meaning and on the context in which the sentence appears. For example:

RESTRICTIVE

Not all the bands were equally well received, however. The band *playing old music* held the audience's attention. The other groups created much less excitement.

NONRESTRICTIVE

A new band called Fats made its debut on Saturday night. The band, *playing old music,* held the audience's attention. If this performance is typical, the group has a bright future.

1 **Use a comma or commas to set off nonrestrictive clauses and phrases.**

Clauses and phrases serving as adjectives and adverbs may be either nonrestrictive or restrictive. Only nonrestrictive clauses and phrases are set off with punctuation, as the following examples illustrate.

NONRESTRICTIVE CLAUSES

Three-year-old Nancy, *whose blue eyes shone with mischief,* had to be rescued more than once from her adventures. [Compare *Three-year-old Nancy had to be rescued more than once from her adventures.* The look of the child's eyes does not restrict the meaning.]

The American farming system, *which is the envy of the world,* is the despair of the American farmer. [Compare *The American farming system is the despair of the American farmer.* The meaning of the subject is unchanged.] —CHARLES KURALT

Puerto Rico was a Spanish colony until 1898, *when it was ceded to the United States.* [Compare *Puerto Rico was a Spanish colony until 1898.* The meaning of the main clause remains the same without the deleted clause.]

NOTE: Most subordinate clauses serving as adverbs are restrictive because they describe conditions necessary to the main clause. They are set off by a comma only when they introduce sentences (see 21b) and when they are truly nonrestrictive, adding incidental information (as in the last example above) or expressing a contrast beginning *although, even though, though, whereas,* and the like.

NONRESTRICTIVE PHRASES

The Capitol Building, *at one end of Independence Mall,* is an imposing sight. [Compare *The Capitol Building is an imposing sight.* The building's name identifies it; its location does not supply further restriction.]

The library's most valuable book, *bought at auction in 1962,* is a thirteenth-century Bible. [Compare *The library's most valuable book is a thirteenth-century Bible.* Assuming that a more valuable book was not purchased in some other year, the details of the Bible's purchase do not restrict it further.]

He beat the other runners, *reaching the finish line in record time.* [Compare *He beat the other runners.* The meaning of the main clause remains the same.]

NOTE: When a participial phrase is separated from the noun or pronoun it modifies, as in the last example above, a comma is es-

RESOURCES AND IDEAS

Francis Christensen, "Restrictive and Nonrestrictive Modifiers Again," in *Notes Toward a New Rhetoric: Nine Essays for Teachers,* ed. Francis Christensen and Bonniejean Christensen, 2nd ed. (New York: Harper, 1978), 117–32. Christensen discusses and illustrates uses of the comma with a variety of modifying elements.

21c

WORD PUZZLES

Divide the class into small groups, and give them word puzzles like the following. Each of these puzzles can be solved only if the reader knows how restrictive and nonrestrictive phrases are punctuated.

1. You are a CIA agent whose job is to keep track of all the Russian spies in Melopolia. One day you receive this telegram from Washington: "All the Russian spies, formerly residing in the Russian embassy, have been sent home."

Is there anyone left for you to watch?

2. After a long and successful season the university basketball team played its cross-state rival for the conference championship. Pandemonium broke out when a long shot dropped in at the buzzer to give the university the victory. Parties were held all over campus.

When Professor Kean arrived at class the next morning, the students, who had celebrated long into the night, were fast asleep at their desks.

Can you tell what portion of the class was asleep?

3. A severe electrical storm swept through town just after noon. Lightning struck several buildings, including the computer center. Technicians repairing damage there found that the microcomputers which were not equipped with electrical surge protectors needed to have their circuit boards replaced.

Are any of the microcomputers still usable?

sential to clarify that the phrase does not modify the word closest to it. Without the comma, the reader automatically connects the phrase to *runners: He beat the other runners reaching the finish line in record time.*

RESTRICTIVE CLAUSES

Every question *that has a reasonable answer* is justifiable. [Compare *Every question is justifiable*, which clearly alters the writer's meaning.]　　　　　　　　　　　　　　　　　　–KONRAD LORENZ

He wore the look of one *who knows he is the victim of a terrible disease and understands his helplessness.* [Compare *He wore the look of one.* Without its modifying clause, *one* is meaningless.]
　　　　　　　　　　　　　　　　　　　　　　　　–STEPHEN CRANE

Books fall apart *when they are not well bound.* [Compare *Books fall apart*, which omits the limiting circumstances and thus implies that all books always fall apart. See the note on the preceding page about adverb clauses.]

RESTRICTIVE PHRASES

A student *seeking an easy course* should not enroll *in History 101.* [Compare *A student should not enroll*, which fails to limit the kind of student who should not enroll and does not specify the course to be avoided.]

The ongoing taboo *against women dating men shorter than themselves* is among the strictest of this society. [Compare *The ongoing taboo is among the strictest of this society*, which no longer specifies what taboo.]　　　　　　　　　　　　–RALPH KEYES

The sealed crates *containing the records of my past* were drawn from storage and opened. [Compare *The sealed crates were drawn from storage and opened.* The crates are no longer limited by their contents.]　　　　　　　　　　　　–JOHN GREGORY DUNNE

NOTE: Whereas both nonrestrictive and restrictive clauses may begin with *which*, only restrictive clauses begin with *that*. Some writers prefer *that* exclusively for restrictive clauses and *which* exclusively for nonrestrictive clauses. See the Glossary of Usage, page 729, for advice on the use of *that* and *which*.

2 **Use a comma or commas to set off nonrestrictive appositives.**

An **appositive** is a noun or noun substitute that renames and could substitute for another noun immediately preceding it. (See 5c-5.) Many appositives are nonrestrictive; thus they are set off, usually with commas. Take care *not* to set off restrictive appositives; like restrictive phrases and clauses, they limit or define the noun or nouns they refer to.

NONRESTRICTIVE APPOSITIVES

The Chapman lighthouse, *a three-legged thing erect on a mud-flat,* shone strongly. [Compare *The Chapman lighthouse shone strongly.*] —JOSEPH CONRAD

John Kennedy Toole's only novel, *A Confederacy of Dunces,* won the Pulitzer Prize. [Compare *John Kennedy Toole's only novel won the Pulitzer Prize.*]

RESTRICTIVE APPOSITIVES

Paul Scott's novel *The Jewel in the Crown* is about India under British rule. [Compare *Paul Scott's novel is about India under British rule,* which implies wrongly that Scott wrote only one novel.]

The philosopher *Alfred North Whitehead* once wrote that the history of philosophy was a series of footnotes to Plato. [Compare *The philosopher once wrote that the history of philosophy was a series of footnotes to Plato.*]

Our language has adopted the words *garage, panache,* and *fanfare* from French. [Compare *Our language has adopted the words from French.*]

 3 **Use a comma or commas to set off parenthetical expressions.**

Parenthetical expressions are explanatory, supplementary, or transitional words or phrases. (Transitional expressions include *however, indeed, consequently, as a result, of course, for example,* and *in fact;* see 3b-6 for a longer list.) Parenthetical expressions are usually set off by a comma or commas.

The Cubist painters, *for example,* were obviously inspired by the families of crystals. —JACOB BRONOWSKI

The only option, *besides locking him up,* was to release him to his parents' custody.

The film is one of Redford's best, *according to the judgment of the critics.*

Any writer, *I suppose,* feels that the world into which he was born is nothing less than a conspiracy against the cultivation of his talent. —JAMES BALDWIN

(Dashes and parentheses may also set off parenthetical elements. See 25b-2 and 25c-1, respectively, and see especially the box on p. 426.)

21c

4 Use a comma or commas to set off *yes* and *no*, tag questions, words of direct address, and mild interjections.

YES AND NO

Yes, the editorial did have a point.
No, that can never be.

TAG QUESTIONS

Jones should be allowed to vote, *should he not?*
They don't stop to consider others, *do they?*

DIRECT ADDRESS

Cody, please bring me the newspaper.
With all due respect, *sir,* I will not do that.

MILD INTERJECTIONS

Well, you will never know who did it.
Oh, they forgot all about the baby.

(You may want to use exclamations to set off forceful interjections. See 20e.)

21c

ANSWERS: EXERCISE 5

1. Italians insist that Marco Polo, the thirteenth-century explorer, did not import pasta from China.
2. Pasta, which consists of flour and water and often egg, existed in Italy long before Marco Polo left for his travels.
3. Correct.
4. Most Italians dispute this account, although their evidence is shaky.
5. Wherever it originated, the Italians are now the undisputed masters in making and cooking pasta.
6. Correct.
7. Most cooks must buy dried pasta, lacking the time to make their own.
8. Correct.
9. Pasta manufacturers choose hard durum wheat because it makes firmer cooked pasta than common wheat does.
10. Pasta made from common wheat tends to get soggy in boiling water.

EXERCISE 5

Insert commas in the following sentences to set off nonrestrictive elements, and delete any commas that incorrectly set off restrictive elements. If a sentence is correct as given, circle the number preceding it.

Example:

Elizabeth Blackwell who attended medical school in the 1840s was the first American woman to receive a medical degree.

Elizabeth Blackwell, who attended medical school in the 1840s, was the first American woman to receive a medical degree.

1. Italians insist that Marco Polo the thirteenth-century explorer did not import pasta from China.
2. Pasta which consists of flour and water and often egg existed in Italy long before Marco Polo left for his travels.
3. A historian who studied pasta places its origin in the Middle East in the fifth century.
4. Most Italians dispute this account although their evidence is shaky.
5. Wherever it originated, the Italians are now the undisputed masters, in making and cooking pasta.

6. Marcella Hazan, who has written several books on Italian cooking, insists that homemade and hand-rolled pasta is the best.
7. Most cooks must buy dried pasta lacking the time to make their own.
8. The finest pasta is made from semolina, a flour from hard durum wheat.
9. Pasta manufacturers choose hard durum wheat, because it makes firmer cooked pasta than common wheat does.
10. Pasta, made from common wheat, tends to get soggy in boiling water.

EXERCISE 6

Combine each pair of sentences below into one sentence that uses the element described in parentheses. Insert commas as appropriate. You will have to add, delete, change, and rearrange words. Some items have more than one possible answer.

Example:

Mr. Ward's oldest sister helped keep him alive. She was a nurse in the hospital. (*Nonrestrictive clause beginning who.*)

Mr. Ward's oldest sister, *who was a nurse in the hospital*, helped keep him alive.

1. Most sources say it was the Italians. The Italians introduced pasta as a main dish. (*Restrictive clause beginning who.*)
2. The Italians use the word to mean only tubular pasta. The word is *maccheroni*. (*Restrictive appositive.*)
3. American manufacturers use *macaroni* to mean all flour-and-water pasta. These manufacturers are unlike the Italians. (*Nonrestrictive phrase beginning unlike.*)
4. Americans also use *spaghetti* for all flour-and-water pasta. The meaning is "little strings" in Italian. (*Nonrestrictive phrase beginning meaning.*)
5. American colonists first imported pasta from the English. The English had discovered it as tourists in Italy. (*Nonrestrictive clause beginning who.*)
6. The English returned from their grand tours of Italy. They were called *macaronis* because of their fancy airs. (*Restrictive phrase beginning returning.*)
7. A hairstyle was also called *macaroni*. It had elaborate curls. (*Restrictive phrase beginning with.*)
8. The song "Yankee Doodle" refers to this hairdo. It reports that Yankee Doodle "stuck a feather in his cap and called it macaroni." (*Restrictive clause beginning when.*)
9. The song was actually intended to poke fun at unrefined

POSSIBLE ANSWERS: EXERCISE 6

1. Most sources say it was the Italians who introduced pasta as a main dish.
2. The Italians use the word *maccheroni* to mean only tubular pasta.
3. American manufacturers, unlike the Italians, use *macaroni* to mean all flour-and-water pasta.
4. Americans also use *spaghetti*, meaning "Little strings" in Italian, for all flour-and-water pasta.
5. American colonists first imported pasta from the English, who discovered it as tourists in Italy.
6. The English, returning from their grand tours of Italy, were called *macaronis* because of their fancy airs.
7. A hairstyle with elaborate curls was also called *macaroni*.
8. The song "Yankee Doodle" refers to this hairdo when it reports that Yankee Doodle "stuck a feather in his cap and called it macaroni."
9. The song, a creation of the English, was actually intended to poke fun at unrefined American colonists.
10. The colonists adopted the jolly tune, turning it to their advantage.

21c

American colonists. It was a creation of the English. (*Non-restrictive appositive.*)

10. The colonists adopted the jolly tune. They turned it to their advantage. (*Nonrestrictive phrase beginning* <u>turning</u>.)

| **21d** | **Use a comma or commas to set off absolute phrases.** |

An **absolute phrase** modifies a whole main clause rather than any word or word group in the clause; it is not connected to the rest of the sentence by a conjunction, preposition, or relative pronoun. (See 5c-3.) Absolute phrases usually consist of at least a participle and its subject (a noun or pronoun), as in the following:

Their work finished, the men quit for the day.

Absolute constructions can occur at almost any point in the sentence. Whatever their position, they are always set off by a comma or commas.

Their homework done, the children may watch whatever they want on television.

After reaching Eagle Rock, we pointed our canoes toward shore, *the rapids ahead being rough.*

His clothes, *the fabric tattered and the seams ripped open,* looked like Salvation Army rejects.

ANSWERS: EXERCISE 7

1. The election having ended, officials felt somewhat secure in their posts.
2. Prices having risen rapidly, the government debated a price freeze.
3. A price freeze was no one's perfect solution, the measure being always controversial.
4. Businesses, their profits otherwise made vulnerable, would demand a wage freeze as well.
5. They would threaten employee layoffs, their threats carrying some weight with the President.
6. A price freeze would be welcomed by labor, workers' incomes already suffering from inflation.

EXERCISE 7

Insert commas in the following sentences to set off absolute constructions.

Example:

The recording contract was canceled the band having broken up.

The recording contract was canceled, the band having broken up.

1. The election having ended officials felt somewhat secure in their posts.
2. Prices having risen rapidly the government debated a price freeze.
3. A price freeze was no one's perfect solution the measure being always controversial.
4. Businesses their profits otherwise made vulnerable would demand a wage freeze as well.

5. They would threaten employee layoffs their threats carrying some weight with the President.
6. A price freeze would be welcomed by labor workers' incomes already suffering from inflation.
7. Workers their real income having been eaten away by rising prices and taxes would resist any wage freeze.
8. The President would have to persuade businesses to accept a price freeze his methods depending on their recalcitrance.
9. No doubt the President his advisers having urged it would first try a patriotic appeal.
10. Arm-twisting having worked for previous Presidents this one might resort to it.

7. Workers, their real income having been eaten away by rising prices and taxes, would resist any wage freeze.
8. The President would have to persuade businesses to accept a price freeze, his methods depending on their recalcitrance.
9. No doubt the President, his advisers having urged it, would first try a patriotic appeal.
10. Arm-twisting having worked for previous Presidents, this one might resort to it.

21e Use a comma or commas to set off phrases expressing contrast.

The essay needs less wit, *more pith*.

His generosity, *not his good looks*, won him friends.

Style is the manner of a sentence, *not its matter*.   —DONALD HALL

It is not light that is needed, *but fire;* it is not the gentle shower, *but thunder*.   —FREDERICK DOUGLASS

NOTE: Writers often omit commas around contrasting phrases beginning *but*.

His life was long *but sadly empty*.   —HERMAN CRATSLEY

21e

EXERCISE 8

Insert commas in the following sentences to set off phrases that express contrast.

Example:
Susan not her sister was the one who attended college in Michigan.

Susan, not her sister, was the one who attended college in Michigan.

1. The expense of heating homes not just the cold makes the winter months difficult in northern states.
2. Many people must forego necessities not just luxuries to pay their heating bills.
3. People use their gas ovens more for heat less for cooking.
4. Using a gas oven for heat is extremely dangerous not safe as many people believe.
5. The gas fumes not the flames are the source of danger.

ANSWERS: EXERCISE 8

1. The expense of heating homes, not just the cold, makes the winter months difficult in northern states.
2. Many people must forego necessities, not just luxuries, to pay their heating bills.
3. People use their gas ovens more for heat, less for cooking.
4. Using a gas oven for heat is extremely dangerous, not safe as many people believe.
5. The gas fumes, not the flames, are the source of danger.

21f Use commas between items in a series and between coordinate adjectives.

1 Use commas between words, phrases, or clauses forming a series.

Place commas between all elements of a **series**—that is, three or more items of equal importance.

> The names *Belial, Beelzebub, and Lucifer* sound ominous.

> He felt cut off from them *by age, by understanding, by sensibility, by technology, and by his need to measure himself against the mirror of other men's appreciation.*   —RALPH ELLISON

> The ox was *solid black, stood five feet high at the shoulder, had a five-foot span of horns, and must have weighed 1,200 pounds on the hoof.*   —RICHARD B. LEE

Though some writers omit the comma before the coordinating conjunction in a series (*Breakfast consisted of coffee, eggs and kippers*), the final comma is never wrong and it always helps the reader see the last two items as separate. Use it consistently and your writing will be clearer, as the following example shows.

> CONFUSING   The job involves typing, answering the phone, filing and reading manuscripts.
>
> CLEAR   The job involves typing, answering the phone, filing, and reading manuscripts.

EXCEPTION: When items in a series are long and grammatically complicated, they may be separated by semicolons. When the items contain commas, they must be separated by semicolons. (See 22d.)

2 Use commas between coordinate adjectives not linked by conjunctions.

Coordinate adjectives are two or more adjectives that modify equally the same noun or pronoun. The individual adjectives are separated either by coordinating conjunctions or by commas.

> The *sleek* and *shiny* car was a credit to the neighborhood.

> The *dirty, rusty, dented* car was an eyesore.

> Nothing is more essential to *intelligent, profitable* reading than sensitivity to connotation.   —RICHARD ALTICK

Adjectives are not coordinate—and should *not* be separated by commas—when the one nearer the noun is more closely related to the noun in meaning.

The house overflowed with *ornate electric* fixtures. [*Ornate* modifies *electric fixtures*.]

The museum's most valuable object is a *sparkling diamond* necklace. [*Sparkling* modifies *diamond necklace*.]

Two tests will help you determine whether adjectives are coordinate: (1) Can the adjectives be rearranged without changing the meaning? (2) Can the word *and* be inserted between the adjectives without changing the meaning? If the answer to both these questions is *yes*, then the adjectives are coordinate. In the sentence *She was a faithful sincere friend*, the adjectives can be rearranged (*sincere faithful friend*), and they can be separated by *and* (*faithful and sincere friend*). Thus the adjectives are coordinate, and a comma belongs between them: *She was a faithful, sincere friend.* However, in the sentence *They are dedicated medical students*, the adjectives cannot be rearranged (*medical dedicated students*) or separated by *and* (*dedicated and medical students*). Thus the adjectives are not coordinate, and no comma belongs between them.

Notice that numbers are not coordinate with other adjectives.

FAULTY	Among the junk in the attic was *one, lovely* vase.
REVISED	Among the junk in the attic was *one lovely* vase.

Do not use a comma between the final coordinate adjective and the noun.

FAULTY	Spring evenings in the South are *warm, sensuous,* experiences.
REVISED	Spring evenings in the South are *warm, sensuous* experiences.

21f

EXERCISE 9

Insert commas in the following sentences to separate coordinate adjectives or elements in series. Circle the number preceding each sentence whose punctuation is already correct.

Example:

Although quiet by day, the club became a noisy smoky dive at night.

Although quiet by day, the club became a noisy, smoky dive at night.

1. Shoes with high heels originated to protect feet from the mud garbage and animal waste in the streets.
2. The first known high heels worn strictly for fashion appeared in the sixteenth century.

SAMPLE PAPERS

Take one of the sample papers from the chapter "Evaluating Student Essays" at the beginning of this annotated edition and revise it to introduce punctuation errors of the kind you have been emphasizing in class. Distribute copies of the altered paper, and ask students to correct it. You may also wish to use a student paper from one of your own classes.

ANSWERS: EXERCISE 9

1. Shoes with high heels originated to protect feet from the mud, garbage, and animal waste in the streets.
2. Correct.
3. The heels were worn by men and made of colorful silk brocades, soft suedes, or smooth leathers.
4. High-heeled shoes received a boost when the short, powerful King Louis XIV of France began wearing them.
5. Louis's influence was so strong that men and women of the court, priests

and cardinals, and even household servants donned high heels.
6. Eventually only wealthy, fashionable French women wore high heels.
7. Correct.
8. High-heeled shoes for women spread to other courts, most European and North American countries, and almost all social classes.
9. Now high heels are commonplace, though their heights and shapes undergo wide, often baffling swings.
10. Correct.

3. The heels were worn by men and made of colorful silk brocades soft suedes or smooth leathers.
4. High-heeled shoes received a boost when the short powerful King Louis XIV of France began wearing them.
5. Louis's influence was so strong that men and women of the court priests and cardinals and even household servants donned high heels.
6. Eventually only wealthy fashionable French women wore high heels.
7. In the seventeenth and eighteenth centuries, French culture represented the one true standard of elegance and refinement.
8. High-heeled shoes for women spread to other courts most European and North American countries and almost all social classes.
9. Now high heels are commonplace, though their heights and shapes undergo wide often baffling swings.
10. A Paris store recently showed a pair of purple satin pumps with tiny jeweled bows and four-inch stiletto heels.

21g Use commas according to convention in dates, addresses, place names, and long numbers.

The items in a date, address, or place name are conventionally separated with commas, as illustrated below. When they appear within sentences, dates, addresses, and place names punctuated with commas are also ended with commas.

DATES

July 4, 1776, was the day the Declaration of Independence was signed.

The bombing of Pearl Harbor on Sunday, December 7, 1941, prompted American entry into World War II.

Commas are not used between the parts of a date in inverted order: *Their anniversary on 15 December 1982 was their fiftieth.* Commas need not be used in dates consisting of a month or season and a year: *For the United States the war began in December 1941 and ended in August 1945.*

ADDRESSES AND PLACE NAMES

Use the address 5262 Laurie Lane, Memphis, Tennessee, for all correspondence.

Send inquires to Box 3862, Pasadena, California.

Columbus, Ohio, is the location of Ohio State University.

The population of Garden City, Long Island, New York, is 30,000.

Commas are not used between state names and zip codes in addresses: *Berkeley, California 94720, is the place of my birth.*

LONG NUMBERS

Use the comma to separate the figures in long numbers into groups of three, counting from the right. The comma with numbers of four digits is optional.

A kilometer is 3,281 feet (*or* 3281 feet).
Russia's 8,649,490 square miles make it the largest country in the world.

EXERCISE 10

Insert commas as needed in the following sentences.

Example:

The house cost $27000 fifteen years ago.
The house cost $27,000 fifteen years ago.

1. The festival will hold a benefit dinner and performance on March 10 1990 in Asheville.
2. The organizers hope to raise more than $100000 from donations and ticket sales.
3. Performers are expected from as far away as Milan Italy and Kyoto Japan.
4. All inquiries sent to Mozart Festival P.O. Box 725 Asheville North Carolina 28803 will receive a quick response.
5. The deadline for ordering tickets by mail is Saturday February 10 1990.

ANSWERS: EXERCISE 10

1. The festival will hold a benefit dinner and performance on March 10, 1990, in Asheville.
2. The organizers hope to raise more than $100,000 from donations and ticket sales.
3. Performers are expected from as far away as Milan, Italy, and Kyoto, Japan.
4. All inquiries sent to Mozart Festival, P.O. Box 725, Asheville, North Carolina 28803, will receive a quick response.
5. The deadline for ordering tickets by mail is Saturday, February 10, 1990.

21h

21h Use commas with quotations according to standard practice.

The words used to explain a quotation (*he said, she replied,* and so on) may come before, after, or in the middle of the quotation. They must always be separated from the quotation by punctuation, usually a comma or commas. (See pp. 414–15 for a summary of conventions regarding quotations.)

1 Ordinarily, use a comma to separate introductory and concluding explanatory words from quotations.

General Sherman summed up the attitude of all thoughtful soldiers when he said, "War is hell."

"Knowledge is power," wrote Francis Bacon.

EXCEPTIONS: Do not use a comma when explanatory words follow a quotation ending in an exclamation point or a question mark (see 20c and 20e).

> "Claude!" Mrs. Harrison called.
> "Why must I come home?" he asked.

Do not use commas with a quotation introduced by *that* or with a short quotation in a sentence that does more than merely introduce or explain the quotation.

> The warning that "cigarette smoking is dangerous to your health" has fallen on many deaf ears.

> People should always say "Excuse me" when they bump into fellow pedestrians.

Use a colon instead of a comma to separate explanatory words from a quotation when there is an emphatic break between them in meaning or in grammar or when the quotation is very formal or longer than a sentence. (See also 25a.) For instance:

> The Bill of Rights is unambiguous: "Congress shall make no law respecting an establishment of religion, or prohibiting the free exercise thereof."

RESOURCES AND IDEAS

Kenneth S. Benson, "Profitable Proofreading," in *Teaching the Basics—Really!* ed. Ouida Clapp (Urbana: NCTE, 1977), 80–81. Benson describes exercises in proofreading and in getting students to pay attention to correction symbols.

21h

2 Use a comma after the first part of a quotation interrupted by explanatory words. Follow the explanatory words with the punctuation required by the quotation.

QUOTATION

"When you got nothin', you got nothin' to lose."

EXPLANATORY WORDS

"When you got nothin'," Kris Kristofferson sings, "you got nothin' to lose." [The explanatory words interrupt the quotation at a comma and thus end with a comma.]

QUOTATION

"That part of my life was over; his words had sealed it shut."

EXPLANATORY WORDS

"That part of my life was over," she wrote; "his words had sealed it shut." [The explanatory words interrupt the quotation at a semicolon and thus end with a semicolon.]

QUOTATION

"This is the faith with which I return to the South. With this new faith we will be able to hew out of the mountain of despair a stone of hope."

EXPLANATORY WORDS

"This is the faith with which I return to the South," Martin Luther King, Jr., proclaimed. "With this new faith we will be able to hew out of the mountain of despair a stone of hope." [The explanatory words interrupt the quotation at the end of a sentence and thus end with a period.]

NOTE: Using a comma instead of a semicolon or a period in the last two examples would result in the error called a comma splice: two main clauses separated only by a comma, without a linking coordinating conjunction. (See 11a.)

3   **Place commas that follow quotations within quotation marks.**

"That's my seat," she said coldly.

"You gave it up," I replied evenly, "so you have no right to it."

EXERCISE 11

Insert commas or semicolons in the following sentences to correct punctuation with quotations. Circle the number preceding any sentence whose punctuation is already correct.

Example:
The shoplifter declared "I didn't steal anything."
The shoplifter declared, "I didn't steal anything."

1. The writer and writing teacher Peter Elbow suggests that an "open-ended writing process . . . can change you, not just your words."
2. "I think of the open-ended writing process as a voyage in two stages" Elbow says.
3. "The sea voyage is a process of divergence, branching, proliferation, and confusion" Elbow continues "the coming to land is a process of convergence, pruning, centralizing, and clarifying."
4. "Keep up one session of writing long enough to get loosened up and tired" advises Elbow "long enough in fact to make a bit of a voyage."
5. "In coming to new land" Elbow says "you develop a new conception of what you are writing about."

ANSWERS: EXERCISE 11

1. Correct.
2. "I think of the open-ended writing process as a voyage in two stages," Elbow says.
3. "The sea voyage is a process of divergence, branching, proliferation, and confusion," Elbow continues; "the coming to land is a process of convergence, pruning, centralizing, and clarifying."
4. "Keep up one session of writing long enough to get loosened up and tired," advises Elbow, "long enough in fact to make a bit of a voyage."
5. "In coming to new land," Elbow says, "you develop a new conception of what you are writing about."

21i

21i   **Use commas to prevent misreading.**

The comma tells the reader to pause slightly before moving on. In some sentences words may run together in unintended and confusing ways unless a comma separates them. Use a comma in such sentences even though no rule requires one.

CONFUSING	Soon after she left town for good. [A short introductory phrase does not require a comma, but clarity requires it in this sentence.]
REVISED	Soon after, she left town for good.
CONFUSING	The students who can usually give some money to the United Fund. [Without a comma the sentence seems incomplete.]
REVISED	The students who can, usually give some money to the United Fund.

ANSWERS: EXERCISE 12

1. Though happy, people still have moments of self-doubt.
2. In research, subjects have reported themselves to be generally happy people.
3. Yet those who have, described sufferings as well as joys.
4. Of fifty, eight subjects reported bouts of serious depression.
5. For half, the preceding year had included at least one personal crisis.

EXERCISE 12

Insert commas in the following sentences to prevent misreading.

Example:

To Laura Ann symbolized decadence.

To Laura, Ann symbolized decadence.

1. Though happy people still have moments of self-doubt.
2. In research subjects have reported themselves to be generally happy people.
3. Yet those who have described sufferings as well as joys.
4. Of fifty eight subjects reported bouts of serious depression.
5. For half the preceding year had included at least one personal crisis.

21j **Avoid misusing or overusing the comma.**

Although commas are useful and often necessary to signal pauses in sentences, they can make sentences choppy and even confusing if they are used more often than needed or in violation of rules 21a through 21h. Examine every sentence you write to be sure you have used commas appropriately.

1 **Don't use a comma to separate a subject from its verb, or a verb or a preposition from its object, unless the words between them require punctuation.**

FAULTY	The returning *soldiers, expected* a warmer welcome than they received. [Separation of subject and verb.]
REVISED	The returning *soldiers expected* a warmer welcome than they received.

FAULTY	After deciding that she could do one but not both, my sister *chose, to have children* rather than pursue a career. [Separation of verb and object.]
REVISED	After deciding that she could do one but not both, my sister *chose to have children* rather than pursue a career.
FAULTY	Amazingly, the refund arrived *after, only three weeks*. [Separation of preposition and object.]
REVISED	Amazingly, the refund arrived *after only three weeks*.

In the following sentence, commas are needed to set off the nonrestrictive clause that interrupts subject and verb (see 21c).

Americans, who are preoccupied with other sports, have not developed a strong interest in professional soccer.

2 Don't use a comma to separate words or phrases joined by coordinating conjunctions.

FAULTY	*The defense attorney, and the presiding judge* disagreed with the verdict. [Compound subject.]
REVISED	*The defense attorney and the presiding judge* disagreed with the verdict.
FAULTY	Television advertising is *expensive, and sometimes very effective*. [Compound complement.]
REVISED	Television advertising is *expensive and sometimes very effective*.
FAULTY	The sale of *handguns, and other weapons* is increasing alarmingly. [Compound object of a preposition.]
REVISED	The sale of *handguns and other weapons* is increasing alarmingly.
FAULTY	The boys *hiked up the mountain, and camped for the night* on the summit. [Compound predicate.]
REVISED	The boys *hiked up the mountain and camped for the night* on the summit.
FAULTY	Banks *could, and should* help older people manage their money. [Compound helping verb.]
REVISED	Banks *could and should* help older people manage their money.

CREATING SENTENCES

Choose a mark of punctuation you wish to emphasize in class—the comma, for this chapter—and ask students to write sentences using the punctuation strategy correctly. You may wish to use this activity as a quiz.

no ⌃
21j

(See 21a and 21f-1, respectively, for the appropriate use of commas with coordinating conjunctions when they link main clauses or elements in a series.)

3 **Don't use commas to set off restrictive elements.**

FAULTY   The land, *that both families claim as theirs*, is mostly swamp. [The clause beginning *that* restricts the meaning of the subject *land*.]

REVISED   The land *that both families claim as theirs* is mostly swamp.

FAULTY   Hawthorne's work, *The Scarlet Letter*, was the first major American novel. [The title of the novel is essential to distinguish the novel from the rest of Hawthorne's work.]

REVISED   Hawthorne's work *The Scarlet Letter* was the first major American novel.

FAULTY   Birds, *heading south*, signal the end, *of summer*. [*Heading south* limits *birds*, and *of summer* limits *end*.]

REVISED   Birds *heading south* signal the end *of* summer.

FAULTY   Buckle your seat belt, *whenever you travel by car*. [The clause specifies when to buckle up.]

REVISED   Buckle your seat belt *whenever you travel by car*.

(See 21c for further discussion of identifying and punctuating nonrestrictive and restrictive elements in sentences.)

no ʅ
21j

REPUNCTUATING

Take an essay from a reader or a similar source, remove the punctuation you wish to emphasize, make copies of the essay, and ask students to work in groups in order to reach consensus about how it should be punctuated. Tell them not to look at the handbook but to decide on their own the best way to serve the reader's needs through punctuation. When the students have finished, they can compare their work with the original and, using the handbook as a reference, decide which punctuation they think best serves the needs of the essay and the reader. If they decide to disagree with the advice given in the handbook, ask them to write out their own punctuation rules.

4 **Don't use a comma before the first or after the last item in a series unless a rule requires it.**

FAULTY   The *forsythia, daffodils, and tulips*, turned the garden into a rush of color. [The comma after *tulips* separates subject and verb.]

REVISED   The *forsythia, daffodils, and tulips* turned the garden into a rush of color.

FAULTY   Among other things, the Europeans brought to the New World, *horses, advanced technology, and new diseases*. [The comma after *World* separates verb and object.]

REVISED   Among other things, the Europeans brought to the New World *horses, advanced technology, and new diseases*.

In the following sentence the commas before and after the series are appropriate because the series is a nonrestrictive appositive (see 21c-2).

The three major television networks, *ABC, CBS, and NBC,* face fierce competition from the cable networks.

However, many writers prefer to use dashes rather than commas to set off series functioning as appositives (see 25b-2).
(See 21f-1 for further discussion of punctuating series.)

---

5 | **Don't use commas to set off an indirect quotation or a single word unless it is a nonrestrictive appositive.**

INDIRECT QUOTATION

FAULTY   The students asked, why they had to take a test the day before vacation.

REVISED   The students asked why they had to take a test the day before vacation.

QUOTED OR ITALICIZED WORD

FAULTY   James Joyce's story, "Araby," was assigned last year, too. [The story title is a restrictive appositive. The commas imply wrongly that Joyce wrote only one story.]

REVISED   James Joyce's story "Araby" was assigned last year, too.

FAULTY   The word, *open,* can be both a verb and an adjective. [*Open* is a restrictive appositive.]

REVISED   The word *open* can be both a verb and an adjective.

The following sentence requires commas because the quoted title is a nonrestrictive appositive.

Her only poem about death, "Mourning," was printed in *The New Yorker.*

(See 21c-2 for more on punctuating appositives.)

EXERCISE 13

Revise the following sentences to eliminate needless or misused commas. Circle the number preceding each sentence that is already punctuated correctly.

no ᐱ
21j

ANSWERS: EXERCISE 13

1. In Greek mythology Theseus is protected by the god␣Poseidon.
2. Theseus is an adventurer␣and a hero of the Athenians.

3. In one of his adventures Theseus sails_to Crete_to kill the Minotaur, which has been devouring young Athenians.
4. Correct.
5. Each year Minos captures fourteen young Athenians_and throws them to the Minotaur in revenge for the death of his son in Athens.
6. When Theseus arrives in Crete, Minos challenges him by_throwing a gold ring into the sea and ordering him to retrieve it.
7. Under the water Theseus meets a woman_who is Poseidon's wife and who hands him the ring to return to Minos.
8. Correct.
9. She warns_that the Minotaur's victims have been too exhausted from being lost in the maze to fight for their lives.
10. With a ball of string Theseus can leave a trail behind him_and find his way through_and out of the maze.
11. Theseus does_as Ariadne urges_and conserves the energy_needed to kill the Minotaur.
12. He also rescues some youths_whom the Minotaur has not yet killed.
13. Theseus, the youths, and Ariadne_all flee from Crete in Theseus's ship.
14. They travel to the island_of Naxos, where Theseus deserts Ariadne.
15. One version of the myth explains_that another god, Dionysus, orders Theseus away so that he can have Ariadne for himself.

no ↕
21j

ANSWERS: EXERCISE 14

Ellis Island, New York, has reopened for business, but now the customers are tourists, not immigrants. This spot, which lies in New York Harbor, was the first American soil seen_or touched by many of the nation's immigrants. Though other places also served as ports of entry for foreigners, none has the symbolic power of_Ellis Island. Between its opening in 1892 and its closing in 1954, over 20 million people, about two-

Example:

The portrait of the founder, that hung in the dining hall, was stolen by pranksters.

The portrait of the founder that hung in the dining hall was stolen by pranksters.

1. In Greek mythology Theseus is protected by the god, Poseidon.
2. Theseus is an adventurer, and a hero of the Athenians.
3. In one of his adventures Theseus sails, to Crete, to kill the Minotaur, which has been devouring young Athenians.
4. The Minotaur, half-bull and half-human, is kept by the king of Crete, Minos, in his maze-like palace.
5. Each year Minos captures fourteen young Athenians, and throws them to the Minotaur in revenge for the death of his son in Athens.
6. When Theseus arrives in Crete, Minos challenges him by, throwing a gold ring into the sea and ordering him to retrieve it.
7. Under the water Theseus meets a woman, who is Poseidon's wife and who hands him the ring to return to Minos.
8. Theseus later meets Minos's only daughter, Ariadne, and she gives him a ball of string so that he can find his way out of the maze.
9. She warns, that the Minotaur's victims have been too exhausted from being lost in the maze to fight for their lives.
10. With a ball of string Theseus can leave a trail behind him, and find his way through, and out of the maze.
11. Theseus does, as Ariadne urges, and conserves the energy, needed to kill the Minotaur.
12. He also rescues some youths, whom the Minotaur has not yet killed.
13. Theseus, the youths, and Ariadne, all flee from Crete in Theseus's ship.
14. They travel to the island, of Naxos, where Theseus deserts Ariadne.
15. One version of the myth explains, that another god, Dionysus, orders Theseus away so that he can have Ariadne for himself.

EXERCISE 14

Insert commas in the following paragraphs wherever they are needed, and eliminate any misused or needless commas.

Ellis Island New York has reopened for business but now the customers are tourists not immigrants. This spot which lies in New York Harbor was the first American soil seen, or touched by many of the nation's immigrants. Though other places also served as ports of entry for foreigners none has the symbolic power of, Ellis Island. Between its opening in 1892 and its closing in 1954, over 20 million people about two-thirds of all immigrants were detained there before taking up their new lives in the United States. Ellis Island processed over 2000 newcomers a day when immigration was at its peak between 1900 and 1920.

As the end of a long voyage and the introduction to the New World Ellis Island must have left something to be desired. The "huddled masses" as the Statue of Liberty calls them indeed were huddled. New arrivals were herded about kept standing in lines for hours or days yelled at and abused. Assigned numbers they submitted their bodies to the pokings and proddings of the silent nurses and doctors, who were charged with ferreting out the slightest sign of sickness, disability or insanity. That test having been passed the immigrants faced interrogation by an official through an interpreter. Those, with names deemed inconveniently long or difficult to pronounce, often found themselves permanently labeled with abbreviations, of their names, or with the names, of their hometowns. But of course millions survived the examination humiliation and confusion, to take the last short boat ride to New York City. For many of them and especially for their descendants Ellis Island eventually became not a nightmare but the place where life began.

NOTE: See page 434 for a punctuation exercise combining commas with other marks of punctuation such as semicolons and colons.

thirds of all immigrants, were detained there before taking up their new lives in the United States. Ellis Island processed over 2000 [or 2,000] newcomers a day when immigration was at its peak between 1900 and 1920.

As the end of a long voyage and the introduction to the New World, Ellis Island must have left something to be desired. The "huddled masses," as the Statue of Liberty calls them, indeed were huddled. New arrivals were herded about, kept standing in lines for hours or days, yelled at, and abused. Assigned numbers, they submitted their bodies to the pokings and proddings of the silent nurses and doctors_who were charged with ferreting out the slightest sign of sickness, disability, or insanity. That test having been passed, the immigrants faced interrogation by an official through an interpreter. Those_with names deemed inconveniently long or difficult to pronounce_often found themselves permanently labeled with abbreviations of their names_or with the names_of their hometowns. But, of course, millions survived the examination, humiliation, and confusion_to take the last short boat ride to New York City. For many of them, and especially for their descendants, Ellis Island eventually became not a nightmare, but the place where life began.

no ⌃
21j

GROUP PROOFREADING

On the day papers are due, ask students to form small groups and to proofread one another's papers, identifying errors by circling them, but not correcting them. Ask the authors to correct their own errors and to turn to the group or the teacher for general advice. If you find that some students come to rely too heavily on the group to find their errors, vary the activity somewhat.

HIGHLIGHTS

The semicolon is frequently ignored or misused in student writing, as is the comma.
This chapter is divided into four sections
that explain appropriate uses of the semicolon: to separate main clauses not joined
by a coordinating conjunction; to separate
main clauses joined by a conjunctive adverb; to separate main clauses if they are
very long and complex or if they contain
commas, even when they are joined by a coordinating conjunction; and to separate
items in a series if they are long or contain
commas. The final section explains the most
frequent misuses of the semicolon.

CHAPTER 22

The Semicolon

22a Use a semicolon to separate main clauses not joined by a coordinating conjunction.

Main clauses contain a subject and a predicate and do not begin with a subordinating word (see 5c). They may be linked by a coordinating conjunction such as *and* or *but* and then separated by a
comma (see 21a). But when no coordinating conjunction is present,
the clauses should be separated with a semicolon.

> I was not led to the university by conventional middle-class am-
> bitions; my grip on the middle class was more tenuous than that
> on the school system.
> —ROBIN FOX

The box opposite distinguishes among the principal uses of
three often-confused marks: semicolon, comma, and colon. In
choosing among the three marks that separate main clauses—the
semicolon, the comma with a coordinating conjunction, and the
period—you need to decide what effect you want to achieve. A
semicolon provides less separation between main clauses than a
period and more separation than a comma with a coordinating
conjunction. Generally, the semicolon is most appropriate when
the first clause creates some suspense—some expectation in the
reader that an equally important and complementary statement is
coming. The semicolon then provides a pause before the second
clause fulfills the expectation.

> Directing movies was only one of his ambitions; he also wanted
> to direct theatrical productions of Shakespeare's plays.

NOTE: If you do not link main clauses with a coordinating conjunction and you separate them only with a comma or with no
punctuation at all, you will produce a comma splice or a fused sentence. See Chapter 11.

DISTINGUISHING THE COMMA, THE SEMICOLON, AND THE COLON

The **comma** chiefly separates both equal and unequal sentence elements.

—It separates main clauses when they are linked by a coordinating conjunction (21a).

An airline once tried to boost sales by advertising the tense alertness of its crews, *but* nervous fliers did not want to hear about pilots' sweaty palms.

—It separates subordinate information that is part of or attached to a main clause, such as a nonrestrictive modifier or an introductory element (21b–21h).

Although the airline campaign failed, many advertising agencies, including some clever ones, copied its underlying message.

The **semicolon** chiefly separates equal and balanced sentence elements.

—It separates complementary main clauses that are *not* linked by a coordinating conjunction (22a).

The airline campaign had highlighted only half the story; the other half was buried in the copy.

—It separates complementary main clauses that are related by a conjunctive adverb (22b).

The campaign should not have stressed the seller's insecurity; *instead*, the campaign should have stressed the improved performance resulting from that insecurity.

The **colon** chiefly separates unequal sentence elements.

—It separates a main clause from a following explanation or summary, not necessarily a complete main clause (25a).

Many successful advertising campaigns have used this message: anxious seller as harder working and smarter than the competition.

;

22a

EXCEPTION: Writers sometimes use a comma instead of a semicolon between very short and closely parallel main clauses.

The poor live, the rich just exist.

But a semicolon is safer, and it is always correct.

ANSWERS: EXERCISE 1

1. More and more musicians are playing computerized instruments; more and more listeners are worrying about the future of acoustic instruments.
2. The computer is not the first new technology in music; the pipe organ and saxophone were also technological breakthroughs in their day.
3. Musicians have always experimented with new technology; audiences have always resisted the experiments.
4. Most computer musicians are not merely following the latest fad; they are discovering new sounds and new ways to manipulate sound.
5. Few musicians have abandoned acoustic instruments; most value acoustic sounds as much as electronic sounds.

POSSIBLE ANSWERS: EXERCISE 2

1. Electronic instruments are prevalent in jazz and rock music; they are less common in classical music.
2. Jazz and rock change rapidly; they nourish experimentation and improvisation.
3. Traditional classical music does not change; its notes and instrumentation were established by a composer writing decades or centuries ago.
4. Contemporary classical music not only can draw on tradition; it also can respond to innovations such as jazz rhythms and electronic sounds.
5. Much contemporary electronic music is more than just jazz, rock, or classical; it is a fusion of all three.

22a

EXERCISE 1

Insert semicolons or substitute them for commas to separate main clauses in the following sentences.

Example:

One man at the auction bid prudently another did not.
One man at the auction bid prudently; another did not.

1. More and more musicians are playing computerized instruments more and more listeners are worrying about the future of acoustic instruments.
2. The computer is not the first new technology in music the pipe organ and saxophone were also technological breakthroughs in their day.
3. Musicians have always experimented with new technology audiences have always resisted the experiments.
4. Most computer musicians are not merely following the latest fad they are discovering new sounds and new ways to manipulate sound.
5. Few musicians have abandoned acoustic instruments most value acoustic sounds as much as electronic sounds.

EXERCISE 2

Combine each set of three sentences below into one sentence containing only two main clauses, and insert a semicolon between the clauses. You will have to add, delete, change, and rearrange words. Most items have more than one possible answer.

Example:

The painter Andrew Wyeth is widely admired. He is not universally admired. Some critics view his work as sentimental.

The painter Andrew Wyeth is widely but not universally admired; some critics view his work as sentimental.

1. Electronic instruments are prevalent in jazz. They are also prevalent in rock music. They are less common in classical music.
2. Jazz and rock change rapidly. They nourish experimentation. They nourish improvisation.
3. Traditional classical music does not change. Its notes and instrumentation were established by a composer. The composer was writing decades or centuries ago.
4. Contemporary classical music not only can draw on tradition. It also can respond to innovations. These are innovations such as jazz rhythms and electronic sounds.
5. Much contemporary electronic music is more than just one type of music. It is more than just jazz, rock, or classical. It is a fusion of all three.

22b Use a semicolon to separate main clauses related by a conjunctive adverb.

Conjunctive adverbs include *consequently, hence, however, indeed, instead, nonetheless, otherwise, still, then, therefore,* and *thus.* (See p. 193 for more explanation and a fuller list.) When a conjunctive adverb relates two main clauses, the clauses should be separated by a semicolon.

The Labor Department lawyers will be here in a month; *therefore,* the grievance committee should meet as soon as possible.

For the first time in twenty years, the accident rate in St. Louis did not rise; *indeed,* it actually declined.

The position of the semicolon between main clauses never changes, but the conjunctive adverb may move around within a clause. The adverb is usually set off with a comma or commas.

Blue jeans have become fashionable all over the world; *however,* the American originators still wear more jeans than anyone else.

Blue jeans have become fashionable all over the world; the American originators, *however,* still wear more jeans than anyone else.

Blue jeans have become fashionable all over the world; the American originators still wear more jeans than anyone else, *however.*

Commas are optional with *thus, hence,* and some other one-syllable conjunctive adverbs; and commas are usually omitted when *therefore, instead,* and a few other adverbs fall inside or at the ends of clauses.

She skipped first grade; *thus* she is younger than her classmates.

She skipped first grade; she is *therefore* younger than her classmates.

I did not buy the book; I borrowed it *instead.*

NOTE: If you use a comma or no punctuation at all between main clauses connected by a conjunctive adverb, you will produce a comma splice or a fused sentence. See Chapter 11.

EXERCISE 3

Insert a semicolon in each sentence below to separate main clauses linked by a conjunctive adverb, and insert a comma or commas where needed to set off the adverb.

Example:
He knew that tickets for the concert would be scarce therefore he arrived at the box office hours before it opened.

ADDITIONAL PRACTICE

The Little, Brown Workbook offers additional practice in using the semicolon.

; 22b

ANSWERS: EXERCISE 3

1. Music is a form of communication like language; the basic elements, however, are not letters but notes.
2. Computers can process any information that can be represented numerically; consequently, they can process musical information.

3. A computer's ability to process music depends on what software it can run; furthermore, it must be connected to a system that converts electrical vibration into sound.
4. Computers and their sound systems can produce many different sounds; indeed, the number of possible sounds is infinite.
5. The powerful music computers are very expensive; they are therefore used only by professional musicians. *or*: . . . they are, therefore, used by professional musicians.

22b

POSSIBLE ANSWERS: EXERCISE 4

1. Most music computers are too expensive for the average consumer; however, digital keyboard instruments can be inexpensive and are widely available.
2. Inside the keyboard is a small computer that controls a sound synthesizer; consequently, the instrument can both process and produce music.
3. The person playing the keyboard presses keys or other controls; then the computer and synthesizer convert these signals into vibrations and sounds.
4. The inexpensive keyboards can perform only a few functions; still, to the novice computer musician the range of drum rhythms and simulated instruments is exciting.
5. Would-be musicians can orchestrate whole songs from just the melody lines; thus they need never again play *Chopsticks.*

He knew that tickets for the concert would be scarce; therefore, he arrived at the box office hours before it opened.

1. Music is a form of communication like language the basic elements however are not letters but notes.
2. Computers can process any information that can be represented numerically consequently they can process musical information.
3. A computer's ability to process music depends on what software it can run furthermore it must be connected to a system that converts electrical vibration into sound.
4. Computers and their sound systems can produce many different sounds indeed the number of possible sounds is infinite.
5. The powerful music computers are very expensive they are therefore used only by professional musicians.

EXERCISE 4

Combine each set of three sentences below into one sentence containing only two main clauses. Connect the clauses with the conjunctive adverb in parentheses, and separate them with a semicolon. (Be sure conjunctive adverbs are punctuated appropriately.) You will have to add, delete, change, and rearrange words. Each item has more than one possible answer.

Example:

The Albanians censor their news. We get little news from them. And what we get is unreliable. (*therefore*)

The Albanians censor their news; *therefore*, the little news we get from them is unreliable.

1. Most music computers are too expensive for the average consumer. Digital keyboard instruments can be inexpensive. They are widely available. (*however*)
2. Inside the keyboard is a small computer. The computer controls a sound synthesizer. The instrument can both process and produce music. (*consequently*)
3. The person playing the keyboard presses keys or manipulates other controls such as switches. The computer and synthesizer convert these signals. The signals are converted into vibrations and sounds. (*then*)
4. The inexpensive keyboards can perform only a few functions. To the novice computer musician, the range is exciting. The range includes drum rhythms and simulated instruments. (*still*)
5. Would-be musicians can orchestrate whole songs. They start from just the melody lines. They need never again play *Chopsticks.* (*thus*)

22c **Use a semicolon to separate main clauses if they are long and complex or if they contain commas, even when they are joined by a coordinating conjunction.**

You would normally use a comma with the coordinating conjunctions *and, but, or, nor,* and *for* between main clauses. But placing semicolons between clauses punctuated with commas or between long and grammatically complicated clauses makes a sentence easier to read.

> Lewis and Clark led the men of their party with consummate skill, inspiring and encouraging them, doctoring and caring for them; *and* they kept voluminous notes and journals.
> —PAGE SMITH

> By a conscious effort of the mind, we can stand aloof from actions and their consequences; *and* all things, good and bad, go by us like a torrent. —HENRY DAVID THOREAU

Many writers prefer to use a semicolon instead of a comma between main clauses joined by the coordinating conjunctions *so* and *yet,* even when the clauses are not complicated or internally punctuated.

> The day was rainy and blustery; *so* the food vendors kept their fruits and vegetables indoors.

> Three truckloads of supplies arrived at the construction site; *yet* we still did not have enough cement.

;
22c

EXERCISE 5

Substitute semicolons for commas in the following sentences to separate main clauses that are long or grammatically complicated or that are internally punctuated.

Example:

She enjoyed dancing to popular music, often joined a group for square dancing, and even danced the fox trot with her father and brothers, but she preferred ballet.

She enjoyed dancing to rock music, often joined a group for square dancing, and even danced the fox trot with her father and brothers; but she preferred ballet.

1. Legends of the towns of the Old West create a lively picture of constant saloon brawls, bank robberies, and gunfights, but the picture is distorted.
2. Many of the towns lacked saloons or banks, not to mention gun-toting strangers, and they were sparsely populated.
3. For towns such as Last Chance, with a population of sixty, the arrival of a stagecoach bearing supplies and mail was

ANSWERS: EXERCISE 5

1. Legends of the towns of the Old West create a lively picture of constant saloon brawls, bank robberies, and gunfights; but the picture is distorted.
2. Many of the towns lacked saloons or banks, not to mention gun-toting strangers; and they were sparsely populated.
3. For towns such as Last Chance, with a population of sixty, the arrival of a stagecoach bearing supplies and mail was the only excitement; and that event occurred only once a month.
4. In between stagecoach visits, the townspeople worked hard at their business, whether ranching, homemaking, shopkeeping, or preaching; but they rarely caroused.

5. Gambling, dancing, drinking, fighting, and other forms of fast living were not the style of the citizens of Last Chance and similar Old West towns; for eking out a living took most of their energy.

the only excitement, and that event occurred only once a month.
4. In between stagecoach visits, the townspeople worked hard at their business, whether ranching, homemaking, shopkeeping, or preaching, but they rarely caroused.
5. Gambling, dancing, drinking, fighting, and other forms of fast living were not the style of the citizens òf Last Chance and similar Old West towns, for eking out a living took most of their energy.

POSSIBLE ANSWERS: EXERCISE 6

1. The most respected citizens of Last Chance were not wealthy, well-educated, good looking, or fast with guns; but they worked hard.
2. The respected citizens were ranchers, a family of eight including the mother, the father, and six children; and every one of them worked the ranch full-time.
3. The ranchers were named Starch, which especially suited them, given their rectitude; and the townspeople sometimes joked about the name, despite their respect for the Starches.
4. Generally, however, the townspeople spoke only admiringly of the Starches, holding them aloft as models of industry, strength, and virtue; for they saw these values as essential if the West was to be tamed.
5. For their part the Starches left no record of their feelings about being set on a pedestal; so we cannot know whether they were proud of their special status or perhaps isolated, embarrassed, or even offended by it.

EXERCISE 6

Combine each set of sentences below into one sentence containing only two main clauses. Link the clauses with the coordinating conjunction in parentheses, and separate them with a semicolon. You will have to add, delete, change, and rearrange words. Each item has more than one possible answer.

Example:

The election will be close. Perhaps it will be a tie. The nominees have hardly campaigned. They do not seem worried. (*but*)

The election will be close, perhaps a tie; *but* the nominees have hardly campaigned and do not seem worried.

1. The most respected citizens of Last Chance were not wealthy. They were not well educated or good looking. They were not fast with guns. They worked hard. (*but*)
2. The respected citizens were ranchers. They were a family of eight including the mother, the father, and six children. Every one of them worked the ranch full-time. (*and*)
3. The ranchers were named Starch. The name especially suited them, given their rectitude. The townspeople sometimes joked about the name. They did so despite their respect for the Starches. (*and*)
4. Generally, however, the townspeople spoke only admiringly of the Starches. They held them aloft as models of industry, strength, and virtue. They saw these values as essential if the West was to be tamed. (*for*)
5. For their part the Starches left no record of their feelings. We do not know how they felt about being set on a pedestal. We cannot know whether they were proud of their special status. Or perhaps they felt isolated, embarrassed, or even offended by it. (*so*)

 Use semicolons to separate items in a series if they are long or contain commas.

You normally use commas to separate items in a series (see 21f-1). But use semicolons instead when the items are long or internally punctuated. The semicolons help the reader identify the items.

> The custody case involved Amy Dalton, the child; Ellen and Mark Dalton, the parents; and Ruth and Hal Blum, the grandparents.

> One may even reasonably advance the claim that the sort of communication that really counts, and is therefore embodied into permanent records, is primarily written; that "words fly away, but written messages endure," as the Latin saying put it two thousand years ago; and that there is no basic significance to at least fifty per cent of the oral interchange that goes on among all sorts of persons, high and low.   —MARIO PEI

EXERCISE 7

Substitute semicolons for commas in the following sentences to separate long or internally punctuated items in a series.

> *Example:*

> After graduation he debated whether to settle in San Francisco, which was temperate but far from his parents, New York City, which was exciting but expensive, or Atlanta, which was close to home but already familiar.

> After graduation he debated whether to settle in San Francisco, which was temperate but far from his parents; New York City, which was exciting but expensive; or Atlanta, which was close to home but already familiar.

1. The Indian subcontinent is separated from the rest of the world by clear barriers: the Bay of Bengal and the Arabian Sea to the east and west, respectively, the Indian Ocean to the south, and 1600 miles of mountain ranges to the north.

2. For thousands of years the subcontinent attracted immigrants, who fled poverty or oppression in their own lands, invaders, who aimed to conquer and rule the vast territory, and colonizers, who sought to enrich their own countries with India's labor and resources.

3. As a result, India is a nation of ethnic and linguistic diversity, with numerous religions, including Hinduism, Islam, and Christianity, with distinct castes as well as Aryan, Dravidian, and Mongoloid ethnic groups, and with sixteen languages, including the official Hindi and the "associate official" English.

4. Between the seventeenth and nineteenth centuries the British colonized most of India, taking control of government and the bureaucracy, running all significant mining, farming, industry, and trade, and assuming a social position above all Indians.

5. During British rule the Indians' own unresolved differences and their frustrations with the British erupted in violent in-

ANSWERS: EXERCISE 7

1. The Indian subcontinent is separated from the rest of the world by clear barriers: the Bay of Bengal and the Arabian Sea to the east and west, respectively; the Indian Ocean to the south; and 1600 miles of mountain ranges to the north.

2. For thousands of years the subcontinent attracted immigrants, who fled poverty or oppression in their own lands; invaders, who aimed to conquer and rule the vast territory; and colonizers, who sought to enrich their own countries with India's labor and resources.

3. As a result, India is a nation of ethnic and linguistic diversity, with numerous religions, including Hinduism, Islam, and Christianity; with distinct castes as well as Aryan, Dravidian, and Mongoloid ethnic groups; and with sixteen languages, including the official Hindi and the "associate official" English.

4. Between the seventeenth and nineteenth centuries the British colonized most of India, taking control of government and the bureaucracy; running all significant mining, farming, industry, and trade; and assuming a social position above all Indians.

5. During British rule the Indians' own unresolved differences and their frustrations with the British erupted in violent incidents such as the Sepoy

;
22d

Mutiny that began on February 26, 1857, and lasted two years; the Amritsar Massacre on April 13, 1919; and violence between Hindus and Moslems during World War II that resulted in the division of India into India and Pakistan.

POSSIBLE ANSWERS: EXERCISE 8

1. India's geography is varied, including the world's highest mountains, the Himalayas, in the North; some of the world's most fertile farmland farther south; still farther south, unpopulated deserts and tropical rain forests.
2. In the village of Cherrapunji the annual rainfall is 451 inches, one of the highest on earth; raindrops are sometimes as big as marbles; and the citizens wear straw armor to protect themselves from wind, rain, and flying debris.
3. Monsoon winds drive India's climate, bringing the hot, dry season between October and May; the cool, rainy season between June and September; and the short spells of moderate rain and temperature as the seasons change.
4. India's cultural life and economy are influenced by the monsoon, which may bring just the rain needed for a bountiful harvest; may deposit unusually long, hard rains that flood and ruin crops; or may withhold rain from drought- and famine-stricken lands.
5. In ancient Indian religions the moods of the monsoon were attributed to the moods of the gods: their pleasure with human beings brought the good monsoon of moderate rains; their anger at human trangressions brought scorching drought; their grief over still other transgressions brought crop-killing rains.

cidents such as the Sepoy Mutiny that began on February 26, 1857, and lasted two years, the Amritsar Massacre on April 13, 1919, and violence between Hindus and Moslems during World War II that resulted in the division of India into India and Pakistan.

EXERCISE 8

Combine each set of sentences below into one sentence that includes a series punctuated with semicolons. As appropriate, rewrite the items in the series into parallel constructions (see 17a). You will have to add, delete, change, and rearrange words. Each item has more than one possible answer.

Example:

He lived in a dream world. It was populated by chauffeurs who drove him about in expensive, fast cars. Servants fulfilled his every wish. Politicians sought his advice and money.

He lived in a dream world populated by chauffeurs who drove him about in expensive, fast cars; servants who fulfilled his every wish; and politicians who sought his advice and money.

1. India's geography is varied. It includes the world's highest mountains, the Himalayas, in the north. Some of the world's most fertile farmland is farther south. And still farther south are unpopulated deserts and tropical rain forests.
2. In the village of Cherrapunji the annual rainfall is 451 inches. It is one of the highest rainfalls on earth. Raindrops are sometimes as big as marbles. The citizens wear straw armor. They need to protect themselves from wind, rain, and flying debris.
3. Monsoon winds drive India's climate. The winds bring the hot, dry season between October and May. They bring the cool, rainy season between June and September. And they bring the short spells of moderate rain and temperature as the seasons change.
4. India's cultural life and economy are influenced by the monsoon. It may bring just the rain needed for a bountiful harvest. It may deposit unusually long, hard rains. These rains flood and ruin crops. Or it may withhold rain from drought- and famine-stricken lands.
5. In ancient Indian religions the moods of the monsoon were attributed to the moods of the gods. One mood was their pleasure with human beings. It brought the good monsoon of moderate rains. Another mood was their anger at human transgressions. It brought scorching drought. And another mood was their grief over still other transgressions. It brought crop-killing rains.

22e **Avoid misusing or overusing the semicolon.**

1 **Don't use a semicolon to separate a subordinate clause or a phrase from a main clause.**

The semicolon separates only equal sentence parts: main clauses and sometimes items in series. It does not separate unequal parts: subordinate clauses and main clauses, or phrases and main clauses.

FAULTY	According to African authorities; only about 35,000 Pygmies exist today.
REVISED	According to African authorities, only about 35,000 Pygmies exist today.
FAULTY	The world would be less interesting; if clothes were standardized.
REVISED	The world would be less interesting if clothes were standardized.

Many readers regard a phrase or subordinate clause set off with a semicolon as a sentence fragment. See Chapter 10.

2 **Don't use a semicolon to introduce a series.**

Colons and dashes, not semicolons, introduce explanations, series, and so forth. (See 25a and 25b.)

FAULTY	The teacher had heard all the students' reasons for doing poorly; psychological problems, family illness, too much work, too little time.
REVISED	The teacher had heard all the students' reasons for doing poorly: psychological problems, family illness, too much work, too little time.
REVISED	The teacher had heard all the students' reasons for doing poorly—psychological problems, family illness, too much work, too little time.

3 **Don't overuse the semicolon.**

Use the semicolon only occasionally. Too many semicolons, even when they are required by rule, often indicate repetitive sentence structure. Compare two versions of the same information.

; **22e**

MEMORY AID

Students may benefit from this brief list of ways *not* to use the semicolon:

Do not use a semicolon to separate a subordinate clause from a main clause.

Do not use a semicolon to introduce a series.

Do not overuse a semicolon.

SEMICOLON OVERUSED

The Make-a-Wish Foundation helps sick children; it grants the wishes of children who are terminally ill. The foundation learns of a child's wish; the information usually comes from parents, friends, or hospital staff; the wish may be for a special toy, perhaps, or a visit to Disneyland. The foundation grants some wishes with its own funds; for other wishes it appeals to those who have what the child desires.

REVISED

The Make-a-Wish Foundation grants the wishes of children who are terminally ill. From parents, friends, or hospital staff, the foundation learns of a child's wish for a special toy, perhaps, or a visit to Disneyland. It grants some wishes with its own funds; for other wishes it appeals to those who have what the child desires.

ANSWERS: EXERCISE 9

1. The main religion in India is Hinduism, a way of life as well as a theology and philosophy.
2. Unlike Christianity and Judaism, Hinduism is a polytheistic religion, with deities numbering in the hundreds.
3. Possible answer: Unlike many other religions, Hinduism allows its creeds and practices to vary widely from place to place and person to person. Whereas other religions have churches and principal prophets and holy books, Hinduism does not. And whereas other religions are centered on specially trained priests or other leaders, in Hinduism the individual is his or her own priest.
4. In Hindu belief there are four types of people: reflective, emotional, active, and experimental.
5. Each type of person has a different technique for realizing the true, immortal self, which has infinite existence, infinite knowledge, and infinite joy.

22e

EXERCISE 9

Revise the following sentences or groups of sentences to eliminate misused or overused semicolons, substituting other punctuation as appropriate.

Example:

The doctor gave all his patients the same advice; cut back on salt and fats, don't smoke and exercise regularly.

The doctor gave all his patients the same advice: cut back on salt and fats, don't smoke and exercise regularly.

1. The main religion in India is Hinduism; a way of life as well as a theology and philosophy.
2. Unlike Christianity and Judaism; Hinduism is a polytheistic religion; with deities numbering in the hundreds.
3. Hinduism is unlike many other religions; it allows its creeds and practices to vary widely from place to place and person to person. Other religions have churches; Hinduism does not. Other religions have principal prophets and holy books; Hinduism does not. Other religions are centered on specially trained priests or other leaders; in Hinduism the individual is his or her own priest.
4. In Hindu belief there are four types of people; reflective, emotional, active, and experimental.
5. Each type of person has a different technique for realizing the true, immortal self; which has infinite existence, infinite knowledge, and infinite joy.

EXERCISE 10

Insert semicolons in the following paragraph wherever they are needed. Eliminate any misused or needless semicolons, substituting other punctuation as appropriate.

The set, sounds, and actors in the movie captured the essence of horror films. The set was ideal; dark, deserted streets, trees dipping their branches over the sidewalks, mist hugging the ground and creeping up to meet the trees, looming shadows of unlighted, turreted houses. The sounds, too, were appropriate, especially terrifying was the hard, hollow sound of footsteps echoing throughout the film. But the best feature of the movie was its actors; all of them tall, pale, and thin to the point of emaciation. With one exception, they were dressed uniformly in gray and had gray hair. The exception was an actress who dressed only in black; as if to set off her pale yellow, nearly white, long hair; the only color in the film. The glinting black eyes of another actor stole almost every scene, indeed, they were the source of all the film's mischief.

NOTE: See page 434 for a punctuation exercise combining semicolons with other marks of punctuation such as commas and colons.

ANSWERS: EXERCISE 10

The set, sounds, and actors in the movie captured the essence of horror films. The set was ideal: dark, deserted streets; trees dipping their branches over the sidewalks; mist hugging the ground and creeping up to meet the trees; looming shadows of unlighted, turreted houses. The sounds, too, were appropriate; especially terrifying was the hard, hollow sound of footsteps echoing throughout the film. But the best feature of the movie was its actors, all of them tall, pale, and thin to the point of emaciation. With one exception, they were dressed uniformly in gray and had gray hair. The exception was an actress who dressed only in black, as if to set off her pale yellow, nearly white long hair, the only color in the film. The glinting black eyes of another actor stole almost every scene; indeed, they were the source of all the film's mischief.

;
22e

CHAPTER 23

The Apostrophe

Unlike other punctuation marks, which separate words, the apostrophe (') appears as *part* of a word to indicate possession, the omission of one or more letters, or (in a few cases) plural number.

RESOURCES AND IDEAS

Harvey S. Wiener, *The Writing Room: A Resource Book for Teachers of English* (New York: Oxford UP, 1981), 175–80. Wiener offers advice on explaining possession to students and describes several exercises designed to help them master the possessive forms of words.

23a Use the apostrophe to indicate the possessive case for nouns and indefinite pronouns.

The **possessive case** shows ownership or possession of one person or thing by another (see Chapter 6). Possession may be shown with an *of* phrase (*the hair of the dog*); or it may be shown with the addition of an apostrophe and, usually, an *-s* (*the dog's hair*). The possessive form functions as an adjective does to limit a noun. Keep in mind that the apostrophe or apostrophe plus *-s* is an addition: everything before this addition should spell the name of the owner or owners without dropped or added letters.

1 Add *-'s* to form the possessive case of singular or plural nouns or indefinite pronouns that do *not* end in *-s*.

The *cat's* eyes were pale blue.
Bill *Boughton's* skillful car tricks amaze his friends.
The *children's* parents were *everybody's* friends.

2 Add *-'s* to form the possessive case of singular words ending in *-s*.

Henry *James's* novels reward the patient reader.
Doris's term paper was read aloud in our English class.
The *business's* customers filed suit.

USES AND MISUSES OF THE APOSTROPHE

USES	**MISUSES**

USES

Possessives of nouns and indefinite pronouns (23a)

Chip's   weeks'
Park's   Parks'
everyone's

Contractions (23c)

won't   shouldn't
they're it's

Plurals of letters, numbers, and words named as words (23d)

C's   *6*'s   *if*'s

MISUSES

Possessives of personal pronouns (23b)

NOT it's   **BUT** its
      your's   yours

Third-person singulars of verbs (23b)

NOT swim's **BUT** swims
      go's   goes

Plurals of nouns (23b)

NOT book's **BUT** books
     Freed's   Freeds

EXCEPTION: We typically do not pronounce the possessive *-s* of a few singular nouns ending in an *s* or *z* sound, especially names with more than one *s* sound (*Moses*), names that sound like plurals (*Rivers*, *Bridges*), and other nouns when they are followed by a word beginning in *s*. In these cases, many writers add only the apostrophe to indicate possession.

> *Moses'* mother concealed him in the bulrushes.
> Joan *Rivers'* jokes offend many people.
> For *conscience'* sake she confessed her lie.

However, usage varies widely, and the final *-s* is not wrong with words like these (*Moses's, River's, conscience's*).

23a

---

3   **Add only an apostrophe to form the possessive case of plural words ending in -s.**

> The *teachers'* association called a strike.
> *Workers'* incomes have risen over the past decade, but not fast enough.
> She took two *years'* leave from school.
> The *Murphys'* car was stolen.

Note the difference in the possessives of singular and plural words ending in *-s*. The singular form usually takes *-'s*: *James's* (see above). The plural takes only the apostrophe: *Smiths'*.

4 Add -*'s* only to the last word to form the possessive case of compound words or word groups.

My *father-in-law's* birthday was yesterday.
The *council president's* address was a bore.
Go bang on *somebody else's* door.

5 When two or more words show individual possession, add -*'s* to them all. If they show joint possession, add -*'s* only to the last word.

INDIVIDUAL POSSESSION

Harry's and Gerry's dentists both use hypnotism. [Harry and Gerry have different dentists.]

JOINT POSSESSION

That living room is an example of *John and Martha's* bad taste. [John and Martha are jointly responsible for the living room.]

ANSWERS: EXERCISE 1

1. In the myths of the ancient Greeks, the <u>goddesses'</u> roles vary widely.
2. <u>Demeter's</u> responsibility is the fruitfulness of the earth.
3. <u>Athena's</u> role is to guard the city of Athens.
4. <u>Artemis's</u> function is to care for wild animals and small children.
5. <u>Athena and Artemis's</u> father, Zeus, is the king of the gods.
6. Even a single <u>goddess's</u> responsibilities are often varied.
7. Over several <u>centuries'</u> time, Athena changes from a mariner's goddess to the patron of crafts.
8. Athena is also concerned with fertility and with <u>children's</u> well-being, since <u>Athens's</u> strength depended on a large and healthy population.
9. Athena often changes into <u>birds'</u> forms.
10. In <u>Homer's</u> *Odyssey* she assumes a <u>sea eagle's</u> form.
11. In ancient Athens the myths of Athena were part of <u>everyone's</u> knowledge and life.
12. A cherished myth tells how Athena

23a

EXERCISE 1

Form the possessive case of each word or word group in parentheses.

Example:

The (*men*) blood pressures were higher than the (*women*).
The *men's* blood pressures were higher than the *women's*.

1. In the myths of the ancient Greeks, the (*goddesses*) roles vary widely.
2. (*Demeter*) responsibility is the fruitfulness of the earth.
3. (*Athena*) role is to guard the city of Athens.
4. (*Artemis*) function is to care for wild animals and small children.
5. (*Athena and Artemis*) father, Zeus, is the king of the gods.
6. Even a single (*goddess*) responsibilities are often varied.
7. Over several (*centuries*) time, Athena changes from a (*mariner*) goddess to the patron of crafts.
8. Athena is also concerned with fertility and with (*children*) well-being, since (*Athens*) strength depended on a large and healthy population.
9. Athena often changes into (*birds*) forms.
10. In (*Homer*) *Odyssey* she assumes a (*sea eagle*) form.
11. In ancient Athens the myths of Athena were part of (*everyone*) knowledge and life.
12. A cherished myth tells how Athena fights to retain possession of her (*people*) land when the god Poseidon wants it.
13. (*Athena and Poseidon*) skills are different, and each promises a special gift to the Athenians.

14. At the (*contest*) conclusion, Poseidon has given water and Athena has given an olive tree, for sustenance.
15. The other gods decide that the (*Athenians*) lives depend more on Athena than on Poseidon.

23b Don't use the apostrophe where it is not required.

Not all words ending in *-s* take an apostrophe. Three kinds of words are especially likely to attract unneeded apostrophes: plural nouns, third-person singular verbs, and the possessives of personal pronouns.

The plurals of nouns are generally formed by adding *-s* or *-es* (*boys, Smiths, families, Joneses*). Don't mistakenly add an apostrophe to form the plural.

FAULTY	The unleashed *dog's* began traveling in a pack.
REVISED	The unleashed *dogs* began traveling in a pack.
FAULTY	The *Jones'* and *Bass'* are feuding.
REVISED	The *Joneses* and *Basses* are feuding.

Present-tense verbs used with *he, she, it,* and other third-person singular subjects always end in *-s* and *never* take an apostrophe.

FAULTY	The subway break's down less often now.
REVISED	The subway breaks down less often now.

His, hers, its, ours, yours, theirs, and *whose* are possessive forms of the personal pronouns. They do not need apostrophes.

FAULTY	Credit for discovering the house is really *her's.*
REVISED	Credit for discovering the house is really *hers.*

The personal pronouns are often confused with contractions. See 23c below.

EXERCISE 2

Supply the appropriate form—possessive or plural—of each word given in parentheses. Some answers require apostrophes, and some do not.

Example:

A dozen Hawaiian (*shirt*), each with (*it*) own loud design, hung in the window.

A dozen Hawaiian *shirts,* each with *its* own loud design, hung in the window.

fights to retain possession of her people's land when the god Poseidon wants it.
13. Athena's and Poseidon's skills are different, and each promises a special gift to the Athenians.
14. At the contest's conclusion, Poseidon has given water and Athena has given an olive tree, for sustenance.
15. The other gods decide that the Athenians' lives depend more on Athena than on Poseidon.

23b

ANSWERS: EXERCISE 2

1. Demeter may be the oldest of the Greek gods, older than Zeus.
2. Many prehistoric cultures had earth goddesses like Demeter.
3. In myth she is the earth mother, which means that the responsibility for the fertility of both animals and plants is hers.
4. The goddess's power is so great that

world becomes desolate when she neglects <u>its</u> care.

5. Her <u>troubles</u> begin with the kidnapping of her daughter, Kore, by the god Hades.
6. <u>Hades's</u> domain is the underworld.
7. Both Demeter and Hades insist that Kore is rightfully <u>theirs</u>.
8. Eventually, like divorced <u>parents</u>, Demeter and Hades agree to share Kore.
9. Demeter restores the <u>earth's</u> fruitfulness.
10. The world owes a debt to Zeus, <u>whose</u> mediation encourages Demeter and Hades to compromise.

1. Demeter may be the oldest of the Greek (*god*), older than Zeus.
2. Many prehistoric (*culture*) had earth (*goddess*) like Demeter.
3. In myth she is the earth mother, which means that the responsibility for the fertility of both (*animal*) and (*plant*) is (*she*).
4. The (*goddess*) power is so great that the world becomes desolate when she neglects (*it*) care.
5. Her (*trouble*) begin with the kidnapping of her daughter, Kore, by the god Hades.
6. (*Hades*) domain is the underworld.
7. Both Demeter and Hades insist that Kore is rightfully (*they*).
8. Eventually, like divorced (*parent*), Demeter and Hades agree to share Kore.
9. Demeter restores the (*earth*) fruitfulness.
10. The world owes a debt to Zeus, (*who*) mediation encourages Demeter and Hades to compromise.

23c **Use an apostrophe to indicate the omission of one or more letters, numbers, or words in a standard contraction.**

it is	it's	does not	doesn't
they are	they're	were not	weren't
you are	you're	class of 1987	class of '87
who is	who's	of the clock	o'clock
cannot	can't	madam	ma'am

Contractions of verb phrases (*don't, weren't, isn't*) and of pronoun-verb pairs (*I'll, we're, she's*) are common in speech and in informal writing. They may also be used to relax style in more formal kinds of writing, as they are in this handbook. But be aware that many people disapprove of contractions in any kind of formal writing.

NOTE: Don't confuse the personal pronouns *its, their, your,* and *whose* with the contractions *it's, they're, you're,* and *who's.*

FAULTY *It's* messiness is not *you're* problem or *they're* problem. But *whose* going to clean up?

REVISED *Its* messiness is not *your* problem or *their* problem. But *who's* going to clean up?

EXERCISE 3

Form contractions from each set of words below. Use each contraction in a complete sentence.

Example:

we are

we*'re*

We're open to ideas.

1. she would
2. could not
3. they are
4. he is
5. do not
6. she will
7. hurricane of 1962
8. is not
9. we would
10. will not

EXERCISE 4

Revise the following sentences to correct mistakes in the use of contractions and personal pronouns. Circle the number preceding any sentence that is already correct.

Example:

The company gives it's employees their birthdays off.

The company gives *its* employees their birthdays off.

1. In Greek myth the goddess Demeter has a special fondness for Eleusis, near Athens, and it's people.
2. She finds rest among the people and is touched by their kindness.
3. Arriving in the disguise of an old woman, Demeter cares for a baby who's father is the king.
4. She tries to make the child immortal by laying it in fire to burn away its mortality.
5. Stopped by the baby's mother, the goddess announces, "You're eyes gaze on Demeter."
6. Demeter rewards the Eleusians with the secret for making they're land fruitful.
7. Demeter also presents the Eleusians with corn, and it's they who introduce the new food to the rest of the world.
8. The Eleusians begin a cult in honor of Demeter, whose worshipped in secret ceremonies.
9. At this point the ceremonies leave myth and enter history, for written texts record they're actual occurrence.
10. Yet its unknown what happened in the ceremonies, for no participant ever revealed their rituals.

23d Use an apostrophe plus *-s* to form the plurals of letters, numbers, and words named as words.

That sentence has too many *but*'s.

At the end of each chapter the author had written two *3*'s.

Remember to dot your *i*'s and cross your *t*'s, or your readers may not be able to distinguish them from *e*'s and *l*'s.

---

1. she'd
   <u>She'd</u> rather be dancing.
2. couldn't
   He <u>couldn't</u> see her in the crowd.
3. they're
   <u>They're</u> at the front door now.
4. he's
   <u>He's</u> my brother.
5. don't
   We <u>don't</u> like the beach.
6. she'll
   <u>She'll</u> speak her mind.
7. hurricane of '62
   The recent storm was nearly as bad as the <u>hurricane of '62.</u>
8. isn't
   <u>Isn't</u> that your cousin?
9. we'd
   <u>We'd</u> prefer you did not ask.
10. won't
    The door <u>won't</u> budge.

ANSWERS: EXERCISE 4

1. In Greek myth the goddess Demeter has a special fondness for Eleusis, near Athens, and <u>its</u> people.
2. Correct.
3. Arriving in the disguise of an old woman, Demeter cares for a baby <u>whose</u> father is the king.
4. Correct.
5. Stopped by the baby's mother, the goddess announces, "<u>Your</u> eyes gaze on Demeter."
6. Demeter rewards the Eleusians with the secret for making <u>their</u> land fruitful.
7. Correct.
8. The Eleusians begin a cult in honor of Demeter, <u>who's</u> worshipped in secret ceremonies.
9. At this point the ceremonies leave myth and enter history, for written texts record <u>their</u> actual occurrence.
10. Yet <u>it's</u> unknown what happened in the ceremonies, for no participant ever revealed their rituals.

23d

Notice that the letters, numbers, and words are italicized (underlined in typed or handwritten copy) but that the apostrophe and added *-s* are not. (See 27d on this use of italics or underlining.)

EXCEPTION: References to the years in a decade are not italicized and often omit the apostrophe. Thus either *1960's* or *1960s* is acceptable as long as usage is consistent.

EXERCISE 5

Form the plural of each letter, number, or word by using an apostrophe and *-s* and by underlining (italicizing) appropriately. Use the new plural in a complete sentence.

> *Example:* x
> Erase or white out typing mistakes. Do not use *x*'s.

1. 7
2. q
3. if
4. and
5. stop

EXERCISE 6

Correct any mistakes in the use of the apostrophe or any confusion between personal pronouns and contractions in the following paragraph.

> Landlocked Chad is among the worlds most troubled countries. The people's of Chad are poor: they're average per capita income equals $73 a year. No more than 15 percent of Chads population is literate, and every thousand people must share only two teacher's. The natural resources of the nation have never been plentiful, and now, as it's slowly being absorbed into the growing Sahara Desert, even water is scarce. Chads political conflicts go back beyond the turn of the century, when the French colonized the land by brutally subduing it's people. The rule of the French—who's inept government of the colony did nothing to ease tensions among racial, tribal, and religious group's—ended with independence in 1960. But since then the Chadians experience has been one of civil war and oppression, and now their threatened with invasions from they're neighbors.

NOTE: See page 434 for a punctuation exercise involving apostrophes along with other marks of punctuation.

SAMPLE ANSWERS: EXERCISE 5

1. 7's
   She drew 7's four times in a row.
2. q's
   She writes her q's with flourishes.
3. if's
   That's too many if's.
4. and's
   It's easy to use too many and's in writing.
5. stop's
   His job was to paint all the stop's in the parking lot.

ANSWERS: EXERCISE 6

Landlocked Chad is among the world's most troubled countries. The peoples of Chad are poor: their average per capita income equals $73 a year. No more than 15 percent of Chad's population is literate, and every thousand people must share only two teachers. The natural resources of the nation have never been plentiful, and now, as it's [correct] slowly being absorbed into the growing Sahara Desert, even water is scarce. Chad's political conflicts go back beyond the turn of the century, when the French colonized the land by brutally subduing its people. The rule of the French—whose inept government of the colony did nothing to ease tensions among racial, tribal, and religious groups—ended with independence in 1960. But since then the Chadians' experience has been one of civil war and oppression, and now they're threatened with invasions from their neighbors.

23d

CHAPTER 24

Quotation Marks

HIGHLIGHTS

The uses of quotation marks are the subject of this chapter. While many students are familiar with the basic rules of punctuation, review of the conventions governing quotation marks will be helpful, especially when the students are preparing papers that require the use of cited material.

The principal function of quotation marks—either double (" ") or single (' ')—is to enclose direct quotations from speech and from writing. The chart on the next two pages summarizes this and other uses. Always use quotation marks in pairs, one at the beginning of a quotation and one at the end.

24a Use double quotation marks to enclose direct quotations.

Direct quotations report what someone has said or written in the exact words of the original. Always enclose direct quotations in quotation marks.

"If a sentence does not illuminate your subject in some new and useful way," says Kurt Vonnegut, "scratch it out."

Indirect quotations report what has been said or written, but not in the exact words of the person being quoted. Indirect quotations are *not* enclosed in quotation marks.

Kurt Vonnegut advises writers to cross out any sentence that does not say something new and useful about their subject.

24b Use single quotation marks to enclose a quotation within a quotation.

When you quote a writer or speaker, use double quotation marks (see 24a). When the material you quote contains yet another

(*Text continues p. 416*)

HANDLING QUOTATIONS FROM SPEECH OR WRITING
(For explanations, consult the sections in parentheses.)

Direct and indirect quotation

DIRECT QUOTATION (24a)
According to Lewis Thomas, "We are, perhaps uniquely among the earth's creatures, the worrying animal. We worry away our lives."

QUOTATION WITHIN QUOTATION (24b)
Quoting a phrase by Lewis Thomas, the author adds, "We are 'the worrying animal.' "

INDIRECT QUOTATION (24a)
Lewis Thomas says that human beings are unique among animals in their worrying.

Quotation marks with other punctuation marks

COMMAS AND PERIODS (24g-1)
Human beings are "the worrying animal," says Thomas.
Thomas calls human beings "the worrying animal."

SEMICOLONS AND COLONS (24g-2)
Machiavelli said that "the majority of men live content"; in contrast, Thomas calls us "the worrying animal."

Thomas believes that we are "the worrying animal": we spend our lives afraid and restless.

QUESTION MARKS, EXCLAMATION POINTS, DASHES (24g-3)

When part of your own sentence

Who said that human beings are "the worrying animal"?
Imagine saying that we human beings "worry away our lives"!
Thomas's phrase—"the worrying animal"—seems too narrow.

When part of the original quotation

"Will you discuss this with me?" she asked.
"I demand that you discuss this with me!" she yelled.
"Please, won't you—" She paused.

Altering quotations

BRACKETS FOR ADDITIONS (25d)
"We [human beings] worry away our lives," says Thomas.

BRACKETS FOR ALTERED CAPITALIZATION (26a)
"[T]he worrying animal" is what Thomas calls us. He says that "[w]e worry away our lives."

ELLIPSIS MARKS FOR OMISSIONS (25e)
"We are . . . the worrying animal," says Thomas.

Our worrying places us "uniquely among the earth's creatures. . . . We worry away our lives."

Punctuating explanatory words

INTRODUCTORY EXPLANATORY WORDS (21h-1)
He says, "We worry away our lives."

An answer is in these words by Lewis Thomas: "We are, perhaps uniquely among the earth's creatures, the worrying animal."

Thomas says that "the worrying animal" is afraid and restless.

CONCLUDING EXPLANATORY WORDS (21h-1)
We are "the worrying animal," says Thomas.
"Who says?" she demanded.
"I do!" he shouted.

INTERRUPTING EXPLANATORY WORDS (21h-2)
"We are," says Thomas, "perhaps uniquely among the earth's creatures, the worrying animal."

"I do not like the idea," she said; "however, I agree with it."

We are "the worrying animal," says Thomas. "We worry away our lives."

See also:

SPECIAL KINDS OF QUOTED MATERIAL
Dialogue (3d-4, 24c)
Poetry (24c, 25f)
Prose passages of more than four lines (24c)

USING QUOTATIONS IN YOUR OWN TEXT
Quotations versus paraphrases and summaries (36c)
Avoiding plagiarism when quoting (36d)
Introducing quotations in your text (36f-2)
Citing sources for quotations (36i)

(*Continued from p. 413*)
quotation, distinguish the two by enclosing the second quotation in single quotation marks.

> "In formulating any philosophy," Woody Allen writes, "the first consideration must always be: What can we know? . . . Descartes hinted at the problem when he wrote, 'My mind can never know my body, although it has become quite friendly with my leg.' "

Notice that two different quotation marks appear at the end of the sentence—one single (to finish the interior quotation) and one double (to finish the main quotation).

ANSWERS: EXERCISE 1

1. "Why," the lecturer asked, "do we say 'Bless you!' or something else when people sneeze but not acknowledge coughs, hiccups, and other eruptions?"
2. Correct.
3. "Sneezes feel more uncontrollable than some other eruptions," she said.
4. "Unlike coughs and hiccups," she explained, "sneezes feel as if they come from inside the head."
5. She concluded, "People thus wish to recognize a sneeze, if only with a 'Gosh.' "

24c

EXERCISE 1

Insert single and double quotation marks as needed in the following sentences. Circle the number preceding any sentence that is already correct.

Example:

The purpose of this book, explains the preface, is to examine the meaning of the phrase Dance is poetry.

"The purpose of this book," explains the preface, "is to examine the meaning of the phrase 'Dance is poetry.' "

1. Why, the lecturer asked, do we say Bless you! or something else when people sneeze but not acknowledge coughs, hiccups, and other eruptions?
2. She said that sneezes have always been regarded differently.
3. Sneezes feel more uncontrollable than some other eruptions, she said.
4. Unlike coughs and hiccups, she explained, sneezes feel as if they come from inside the head.
5. She concluded, People thus wish to recognize a sneeze, if only with a Gosh.

24c Set off quotations of dialogue, poetry, and long prose passages according to standard practice.

Dialogue

When quoting conversations, begin a new paragraph for each speaker.

> "What shall I call you? Your name?" Andrews whispered rapidly, as with a high squeak the latch of the door rose.
> "Elizabeth," she said. "Elizabeth."
> —GRAHAM GREENE, *The Man Within*

NOTE: When you quote a single speaker for more than one paragraph, put quotation marks at the beginning of each paragraph but at the end of only the last paragraph. The absence of quotation marks at the end of each paragraph but the last tells readers that the speech is continuing.

Poetry

When you quote a single line from a poem, song, or verse play, place the line in the running text and enclose it in quotation marks.

Dylan Thomas remembered childhood as an idyllic time: "About the lilting house and happy as the grass was green."

Poetry quotations of two or three lines may be placed in the text or displayed separately. If you place such a quotation in the text, enclose it in quotation marks and separate the lines with a slash surrounded by space (see 25f).

Robert Frost's incisiveness shows in two lines from "Death of the Hired Man": "Home is the place where, when you have to go there, / They have to take you in."

Quotations of more than three lines of poetry should always be separated from the text with space and an indention. Do not add quotation marks.

Emily Dickinson rarely needed more than a few lines to express her complex thoughts:

> To wait an Hour—is long—
> If Love be just beyond—
> To wait Eternity—is short—
> If Love reward the end—

The *MLA Handbook*, the standard guide to manuscript format in English and some other disciplines, recommends the following spacings for displayed quotations: double-space above and below the quotation, indent it ten spaces from the left margin, and double-space the quoted lines. Unless your instructor specifies otherwise, follow these guidelines for your papers, whether typewritten or handwritten. (See Chapter 37, p. 610, for an example of a displayed quotation in a typed paper.)

NOTE: Be careful when quoting poetry to reproduce faithfully all line indentions, space between lines, spelling, capitalization, and punctuation, such as the capitals and dashes in the Dickinson poem above.

NOTE

If you are using this chapter as part of a review of citation, it may be helpful to mention the ellipsis mark (25e) at this point as a means of omitting unnecessary material within a quotation.

Long prose passages

Separate a prose quotation of more than four typed or handwritten lines from the body of your paper. Following the guidelines of the *MLA Handbook* (see above), double-space above and below the quotation, indent it ten spaces from the left margin, and double-space the quoted lines. Do not add quotation marks.

In his 1967 study of the lives of unemployed black men, Eliot Lebow observes that "unskilled" construction work requires more experience and skill than generally assumed.

> A healthy, sturdy, active man of good intelligence requires from two to four weeks to break in on a construction job. . . . It frequently happens that his foreman or the craftsman he services is not willing to wait that long for him to get into condition or to learn at a glance the difference in size between a rough 2 × 8 and a finished 2 × 10.

Do not use a paragraph indention when quoting a single complete paragraph or a part of a paragraph. Use paragraph indentions only when quoting two or more complete paragraphs.

SAMPLE ANSWERS: EXERCISE 2

1. "Do you have the tickets?" she asked, as they parked the car and started up the steps through the crowd.

"Of course," he said. "What do you think I am?" He stopped despite the crowd, patting his pockets. "Oh, no! My wallet!"

2. Do you know a poem that begins, "What is so rare as a day in June"?

3. The sonnet begins: "The world is too much with us; late and soon, / Getting and spending, we lay waste our powers."

The sonnet begins:

> The world is too much with us; late
> [and soon,
> Getting and spending, we lay waste
> [our powers.

4. Everyone should know by heart the first article of the Bill of Rights:

> Congress shall make no law respecting an establishment of religion, or prohibiting the free exercise thereof; or abridging the freedom of speech, or of the press; or the right of the people peaceably to assemble, and to petition the government for a redress of grievances.

EXERCISE 2

Practice using quotation marks in quoted dialogue, poetry, and long prose passages by completing each of the exercises below.

1. Write a short sketch of dialogue between two people.
2. Write a sentence that quotes a single line of poetry.
3. Write two sentences, each quoting the same two lines of poetry. In one, place the poetry lines in the text. In the other, separate the two lines from the text.
4. Write a sentence introducing a prose passage of more than four lines, and then set up the quotation appropriately.

24d Put quotation marks around titles according to standard practice.

Use quotation marks to enclose the titles of songs, short poems, articles in periodicals, short stories, essays, episodes of television and radio programs, and the subdivisions of books. Use italics (underlining) for all other titles, such as books, plays, periodicals, movies, television programs, and works of art. (See 27a.)

NOTE: Use single quotation marks for a quotation within a quoted title, as in the second article and second essay in the box opposite.

See 26b for guidelines on the use of capital letters in titles.

TITLES TO BE ENCLOSED IN QUOTATION MARKS

SONGS
"Lucy in the Sky with
   Diamonds"
"Mr. Bojangles"

SHORT POEMS
"Stopping by Woods on a
   Snowy Evening"
"Sunday Morning"

ARTICLES IN PERIODICALS
"Comedy and Tragedy
   Transposed"
"Does 'Scaring' Work?"

SHORT STORIES
"The Battler"
"The Gift of the Magi"

ESSAYS
"Politics and the English
   Language"
"Joey: A 'Mechanical Boy' "

**EPISODES OF TELEVISION AND
RADIO PROGRAMS**
"The Mexican Connection"
   (on *60 Minutes*)
"Cooking with Clams" (on
   Eating In)

SUBDIVISIONS OF BOOKS
"Voyage to the Houyhnhnms"
   (Part IV of *Gulliver's Travels*)
"The Mast Head" (Chapter 35
   of *Moby Dick*)

24e **Occasionally, quotation marks may be used to enclose defined words and words used in a special sense.**

By "charity," I mean the love of one's neighbor as oneself.
Pardon my pun, but I find that lawyer "appealing."

NOTE: In definitions, italics (or underlining) are more common than quotation marks (see 27d).

By *charity*, I mean the love of one's neighbor as oneself.

EXERCISE 3

Insert quotation marks as needed for titles and words in the following sentences. If quotation marks should be used instead of italics, insert them.

Example:
The students call her professor despite her youth.
The students call her "professor" despite her youth.

1. In Chapter 8, titled *How to Be Interesting*, the author explains the art of conversation.
2. The Beatles' Let It Be reminds him of his uncle.
3. Doom means simply judgment as well as unhappy destiny.

ANSWERS: EXERCISE 3

1. In Chapter 8, titled "How to Be Interesting," the author explains the art of conversation.
2. The Beatles' "Let It Be" reminds him of his uncle.
3. "Doom" [or *Doom*] means simply judgment as well as unhappy destiny.
4. The article that appeared in *Mental Health* was titled "Children of Divorce Ask, 'Why?' "
5. In my encyclopedia the discussion under "Modern Art" fills less than a column.

4. The article that appeared in *Mental Health* was titled *Children of Divorce Ask, "Why?"*
5. In my encyclopedia the discussion under Modern Art fills less than a column.

24f   Avoid using quotation marks where they are not required.

Don't use quotation marks in the titles of your papers unless they contain or are themselves direct quotations.

NOT	"The Death Wish in One Poem by Robert Frost"
BUT	The Death Wish in One Poem by Robert Frost
OR	The Death Wish in "Stopping by Woods on a Snowy Evening"

Don't use quotation marks to enclose common nicknames or technical terms that are not being defined.

NOT	Even as President, "Jimmy" Carter preferred to use his nickname.
BUT	Even as President, Jimmy Carter preferred to use his nickname.
NOT	"Mitosis" in a cell is fascinating to watch.
BUT	Mitosis in a cell is fascinating to watch.

Don't use quotation marks in an attempt to justify or apologize for slang and trite expressions that are inappropriate to your writing. If slang is appropriate, use it without quotation marks.

NOT	It "rained cats and dogs" for the whole week, so we made no "bread" working.
BUT	It rained hard for the whole week, so we made no money working.

(See 31a-1 and 31b-5 for more on slang and trite expressions.)

NOTE

Students should note that this rule applies even when closing quotation marks are both single and double. Example: "The author of the article pointed out that the rock group The Police coined the word 'synchronicity.'"

24g   Place other marks of punctuation inside or outside quotation marks according to standard practice.

1   Place commas and periods inside quotation marks.

"Your first check will come next month," the social worker said.
Without pausing he pointed and said, "That's the man."
Swift uses irony in his essay "A Modest Proposal."

(See 21h for the use of commas to separate quotations from words used to introduce or explain them.)

2 Place colons and semicolons outside quotation marks.

A few years ago the slogan in elementary education was "learning by playing"; now educators are concerned with teaching basic skills.

We all know what is meant by "inflation": more money buys less.

3 Place dashes, question marks, and exclamation points inside quotation marks only if they belong to the quotation.

When a dash, question mark, or exclamation point is part of the quotation, put it *inside* quotation marks.

"But must you—" Marcia hesitated, afraid of the answer.
Did you say, "Who is she?"
"Go away!" I yelled.

When a dash, question mark, or exclamation point applies only to the larger sentence, not to the quotation, place it *outside* quotation marks.

One of the most evocative lines in English poetry—"After many a summer dies the swan"—was written by Alfred, Lord Tennyson.
Who said, "Now cracks a noble heart"?
That woman called me "stupid"!

24g

EXERCISE 4

Revise the following sentences for the proper use of quotation marks. Insert quotation marks where they are needed, remove them where they are not needed, and be sure that other marks of punctuation are correctly placed inside or outside the quotation marks. Circle the number preceding any sentence that is already punctuated correctly.

Example:
The award-winning story was titled How to Say I'm Sorry to a Child.
The award-winning story was titled "How to Say 'I'm Sorry' to a Child."

1. The course reading included Virginia Woolf's essay The Anatomy of Fiction.

ANSWERS: EXERCISE 4

1. The course reading included Virginia Woolf's essay "The Anatomy of Fiction."
2. "No smoking on this bus!" the driver shouted.
3. The commercial says, "Lite Beer is a third less filling than your regular beer"; but how do they measure that?
4. Wearing calico and lace, she looked like a down-home girl.
5. How can we answer children who ask, "Will there be a nuclear war?"
6. In America the signs say, "Keep off the grass"; in England they say, "Please refrain from stepping on the lawn."

"Please refrain from stepping on the lawn."

7. In *King Richard II* Shakespeare calls England "This precious stone set in the silver sea."

8. The doctors gave my father an_electrocardiogram__but found nothing wrong.

9. Correct.

10. Must we regard the future with what Kierkegaard called "fear and trembling"?

2. No smoking on this bus! the driver shouted.

3. The commercial says, Lite Beer is a third less filling than your regular beer; but how do they measure that?

4. Wearing calico and lace, she looked like a "down-home girl."

5. How can we answer children who ask, Will there be a nuclear war?

6. In America the signs say, Keep off the grass; in England they say, Please refrain from stepping on the lawn.

7. In *King Richard II* Shakespeare calls England This precious stone set in the silver sea.

8. The doctors gave my father an "electrocardiogram" but found nothing wrong.

9. Our forests—in Longfellow's words, "The murmuring pines and the hemlocks"—are slowly succumbing to land development.

10. Must we regard the future with what Kierkegaard called fear and trembling?

ANSWERS: EXERCISE 5

In one class we talked about two lines from Shakespeare's "Sonnet 55":

Not marble, nor the gilded monuments
Of princes, shall outlive this powerful
rime.

"Why is this true?" the teacher asked. "Why does Shakespeare's 'powerful rime' indeed live longer than 'the gilded monuments / Of princes'? She then asked if the lines were protected only by Shakespeare's status as our greatest writer. "No," said one student. "It has more to do with the power of the language." Then another student added, "Even though paper is less durable than stone, ideas are more durable than monuments to dead princes." The whole discussion was an eye opener for those of us (including me) who had never given much credit to rhymes or the words that made them.

24g

EXERCISE 5

Insert quotation marks as needed in the following paragraph.

In one class we talked about two lines from Shakespeare's Sonnet 55:

Not marble, nor the gilded monuments
Of princes, shall outlive this powerful rime.

Why is this true? the teacher asked. Why does Shakespeare's powerful rime indeed live longer than the gilded monuments / Of princes? She then asked if the lines were protected only by Shakespeare's status as our greatest writer. No, said one student. It has more to do with the power of the language. Then another student added, Even though paper is less durable than stone, ideas are more durable than monuments to dead princes. The whole discussion was an eye opener for those of us (including me) who had never given much credit to rhymes or the words that made them.

NOTE: See page 434 for a punctuation exercise involving quotation marks along with other marks of punctuation.

Other Punctuation Marks

HIGHLIGHTS

Chapter 25 covers the marks of punctuation not treated in the preceding chapters (20–24): the colon, the dash, parentheses, brackets, the ellipsis mark, and the slash. In addition to exercises for these marks of punctuation, the chapter provides at the end an exercise that asks students to practice using all the punctuation marks covered in Chapters 20–25.

THE COLON

25a Use the colon to introduce and to separate.

1 Use a colon to introduce summaries, explanations, series, appositives ending sentences, long or formal quotations, and statements introduced by *the following* or *as follows*.

The colon is primarily a mark of introduction: it tells the reader that the preceding statement is about to be explained, amplified, or summarized; or it signals that a series or quotation follows. A colon is always preceded by a complete main clause, but it need not be followed by a main clause. Thus the colon differs from the semicolon, whose primary function is to separate main clauses expressing complementary and equally important ideas (see 22a, especially the box on p. 395). The colon is often interchangeable with the dash, though the dash is more informal and more abrupt (see 25b).

SUMMARY
They cannot pay their children's college costs because their money is tied up in their house and antique furniture: they are possession-rich and cash-poor.

EXPLANATION
It is a good thing to be old early: to have the fragility and sensitivity of the old, and a bit of wisdom, before the years of planning and building have run out.
—MARTIN GUMBERT

SUMMARY

25a Use the colon to introduce summaries, explanations, series, appositives ending sentences, long or formal quotations, and statements introduced by *the following* or *as follows*.

25b Use a dash or dashes to indicate sudden changes in tone or thought and to set off some sentence elements.

25c Use parentheses to enclose nonessential elements within sentences.

25d Use brackets only within quotations to separate your own comments from the words of the writer you quote.

25e Use the ellipsis mark to indicate omissions within quotations.

25f Use the slash between options and to separate lines of poetry that are run in to the text.

SERIES

It is impossible to dissociate language from science or science from language, because every natural science always involves three things: the sequence of phenomena on which the science is based; the abstract concepts which call these phenomena to mind; and the words in which the concepts are expressed.
—ANTOINE LAVOISIER

FINAL APPOSITIVE

Two chief elements make work interesting: first, the exercise of skill, and second, construction.   —BERTRAND RUSSELL

LONG OR FORMAL QUOTATION

He concluded with an ultimatum: "Either improve the mass transit system or anticipate further decay in your downtown area."

STATEMENT INTRODUCED BY *THE FOLLOWING* **OR** *AS FOLLOWS*

The relation between leisure and income is as follows: the quality of play depends on the quantity of pay.

NOTE: A complete sentence following a colon may begin with a small letter, as above, or with a capital letter.

2   Use a colon to separate titles and subtitles, the subdivisions of time, and the parts of biblical citations.

TITLES AND SUBTITLES

Charles Dickens: An Introduction to His Novels
Eros and Civilization: A Philosophical Inquiry into Freud

TIME	**BIBLICAL CITATIONS**
1:30	Isaiah 28:1–6
12:26	1 Corinthians 3:6–7

3   Avoid misusing the colon.

Use the colon only at the end of a main clause. Avoid using it between a verb and its object or between a preposition and its object.

NOT	Two entertaining movies directed by Stephen Speilberg are: *E.T.* and *Raiders of the Lost Ark.*
BUT	Two entertaining movies directed by Stephen Speilberg are *E.T.* and *Raiders of the Lost Ark.*
NOT	Shakespeare showed the qualities of a Renaissance thinker, such as: humanism and a deep

25a

interest in classical Greek and Roman literature.

BUT   Shakespeare showed the qualities of a Renaissance thinker, such as humanism and a deep
interest in classical Greek and Roman literature.

EXERCISE 1

Insert colons as needed in the following sentences, or delete colons that are misused.

Example:

Mix the ingredients as follows sift the flour and salt together, add the milk, and slowly beat in the egg yolk.

Mix the ingredients as follows: sift the flour and salt together, add the milk, and slowly beat in the egg yolk.

1. In the remote parts of many Third World countries, simple
signs mark human habitation a dirt path, a few huts, smoke
from a campfire.
2. In the built-up sections of industrialized countries, nature is
all but obliterated by signs of human life, such as: houses,
factories, skyscrapers, and highways.
3. The spectacle makes many question the words of Ecclesiastes 1:4 "One generation passeth away, and another generation cometh; but the earth abideth forever."
4. Yet many scientists see the future differently they hold that
human beings have all the technology necessary to clean up
the earth and restore the cycles of nature.
5. All that is needed is: a change in the attitudes of those who
use technology.

ANSWERS: EXERCISE 1

1. In the remote parts of many Third
World countries, simple signs mark human habitation: a dirt path, a few huts,
smoke from a campfire.
2. In the built-up sections of industrialized countries, nature is all but obliterated by signs of human life, such as
houses, factories, skyscrapers, and
highways.
3. The spectacle makes many question
the words of Ecclesiastes 1:4: "One
generation passeth away, and another
generation cometh; but the earth abideth forever."
4. Yet many scientists see the future differently: they hold that human beings
have all the technology necessary to
clean up the earth and restore the cycles of nature.
5. All that is needed is a change in the attitudes of those who use technology.

THE DASH

25b **Use a dash or dashes to indicate sudden changes
in tone or thought and to set off some sentence
elements.**

1 **Use a dash or dashes to indicate sudden shifts in tone,
new or unfinished thoughts, and hesitation in dialogue.**

SHIFT IN TONE

He tells us—does he really mean it?—that he will speak the
truth from now on.

UNFINISHED THOUGHT

If she found out—he did not want to think what she would do.

HESITATION IN DIALOGUE

"I was worried you might think I had stayed away because I was influenced by—" He stopped and lowered his eyes.

Astonished, Howe said, "Influenced by what?"

"Well, by—" Blackburn hesitated and for answer pointed to the table.   —LIONEL TRILLING

ALTERNATE EXAMPLES

Using a dash for definition:

Graphology—the study of handwriting—has recently gained attention as a valid tool for analyzing character and attitudes.

Using a dash for contrast:

The night was moonless, dark and brooding—the house was a joyful crash of color and light.

Dashes may be used to separate parenthetical expressions in dialogue or in quoted material:

"If you do not stop," he shouted, "I will have to"—his upper lip began to tremble—"leave."

25b

| 2 |

Use a dash or dashes to emphasize nonrestrictive elements.

Dashes may be used in place of commas (21c) or parentheses (25c-1) to set off and emphasize nonrestrictive elements such as modifiers, appositives, and parenthetical expressions. (See the box below.) Dashes are especially useful when these elements are internally punctuated. Be sure to use a pair of dashes when the element interrupts a main clause.

APPOSITIVE

The qualities Monet painted—sunlight, rich shadows, deep colors—abounded near the rivers and gardens he used as subjects.

DISTINGUISHING DASHES, COMMAS, AND PARENTHESES

Dashes, commas, and parentheses may all set off nonessential information such as nonrestrictive modifiers and parenthetical expressions.

Dashes give the information the greatest emphasis (25b-2):

Many students—including some employed by the college—disapprove of the new work rules.

Commas are less emphatic (21c):

Many students, including some employed by the college, disapprove of the new work rules.

Parentheses, the least emphatic, signal that the information is just worth a mention (25c-1):

Many students (including some employed by the college) disapprove of the new work rules.

MODIFIER

Though they are close together—separated by only a few blocks —the two neighborhoods could be in different countries.

PARENTHETICAL EXPRESSION

At any given time there exists an inventory of undiscovered embezzlement in—or more precisely not in—the country's businesses and banks. —JOHN KENNETH GALBRAITH

3 **Use a dash to set off introductory series and concluding series and explanations.**

INTRODUCTORY SERIES

Shortness of breath, skin discoloration or the sudden appearance of moles, persistent indigestion, the presence of small lumps— all these may signify cancer.

A dash sets off concluding series and explanations more informally and more abruptly than a colon does (see 25a-1).

CONCLUDING SERIES

We packed our camping gear—tent, sleeping bags, and stove.

CONCLUDING EXPLANATION

The country was the most beautiful he had seen—green, rolling hills dotted with stands of dark pine and etched with stone walls.

4 **Avoid misusing or overusing the dash.**

Don't use the dash when commas, semicolons, and periods are more appropriate. And don't use too many dashes. They can create a jumpy or breathy quality in writing.

NOT   In all his life—eighty-seven years—my great-grandfather never allowed his picture to be taken—not even once. He claimed the "black box"—the camera—would steal his soul.

BUT   In all his eighty-seven years my great-grandfather did not allow his picture to be taken even once. He claimed the "black box"—the camera—would steal his soul.

EXERCISE 2

Insert dashes as needed in the following sentences.

Example:

What would we do if someone like Adolf Hitler that monster appeared among us?

WRITING TIP

Dashes speed up a sentence; commas slow a sentence down.

—
25b

ANSWERS: EXERCISE 2

1. The movie-theater business is undergoing dramatic changes—changes that may affect what movies are made and shown.
2. The closing of independent theaters,

the control of theaters by fewer and fewer owners, and the increasing ownership of theaters by movie studios and distributors—these changes may reduce the availability of noncommercial films.

3. Yet at the same time the number of movie screens is increasing—primarily in multiscreen complexes—so that smaller films may find more outlets.

4. The number of active movie screens—that is, screens showing films or booked to do so—is higher now than at any time since World War II.

5. The biggest theater complexes seem to be something else as well—art galleries, amusement arcades, restaurants, spectacles.

What would we do if someone like Adolf Hitler—that monster—appeared among us?

1. The movie-theater business is undergoing dramatic changes changes that may affect what movies are made and shown.

2. The closing of independent theaters, the control of theaters by fewer and fewer owners, and the increasing ownership of theaters by movie studios and distributors these changes may reduce the availability of noncommercial films.

3. Yet at the same time the number of movie screens is increasing primarily in multiscreen complexes so that smaller films may find more outlets.

4. The number of active movie screens that is, screens showing films or booked to do so is higher now than at any time since World War II.

5. The biggest theater complexes seem to be something else as well art galleries, amusement arcades, restaurants, spectacles.

PARENTHESES

25c **Use parentheses to enclose nonessential elements within sentences.**

1 **Use parentheses to enclose parenthetical expressions.**

Parenthetical expressions include explanations, facts, digressions, and examples that may be helpful or interesting but are not essential to meaning. They are emphasized least when set off with a pair of parentheses instead of commas or dashes. (See the box on p. 426.)

He drove trucks (tractor-trailers, actually) to earn money for college tuition.

The population of Philadelphia (now about 1.7 million) has declined since 1950.

Unlike the creatures (some insects, for instance) that have been unchanged for five, ten, even fifty million years, man has changed over this time-scale out of all recognition.

—Jacob Bronowski

Note: Don't put a comma before a parenthetical expression enclosed in parentheses.

Not	The dungeon, (really the basement) haunted us.
But	The dungeon (really the basement) haunted us.

A comma or period falling after a parenthetical expression should be placed outside the closing parenthesis.

> We received numerous complaints (125 to be exact), but most harped on the same old theme (namely, high prices).

When it falls between other complete sentences, a complete sentence enclosed in parentheses has a capital letter and end punctuation.

> In general, coaches will tell you that scouts are just guys who can't coach. (But then, so are brain surgeons.) —ROY BLOUNT, JR.

2 Use parentheses to enclose letters and figures labeling items in lists within sentences.

> My father could not, for his own special reasons, even *like* me. He spent the first twenty-five years of my life acting out that painful fact. Then he arrived at two points in his own life: (1) his last years, and (2) the realization that he had made a tragic mistake.
> —RAY WEATHERLY

When lists are set off from the text, the numbers or letters labeling them are usually not enclosed in parentheses.

ALTERNATE EXAMPLE

When you are enclosing a complete sentence within another complete sentence, you need not start the sentence in parentheses with a capital letter nor end it with a punctuation mark. For example:

> I spent the weekend buried in books (this is my usual practice) and emerged on Monday in time to go to the library.

( )
25c

EXERCISE 3

Insert parentheses as needed in the following sentences.

> *Example:*
> Students can find good-quality, inexpensive furniture for example, desks, tables, chairs, sofas, even beds in junk stores.
> Students can find good-quality, inexpensive furniture (for example, desks, tables, chairs, sofas, even beds) in junk stores.

1. Many of those involved in the movie business agree that multiscreen complexes are good for two reasons: 1 they cut the costs of exhibitors; and 2 they offer more choices to audiences.
2. Those who produce and distribute films and not just the big studios argue that the multiscreen theaters give exhibitors too much power.
3. The major studios are buying movie theaters to gain control over important parts of the distribution process what gets shown and for how much money.
4. For twelve years 1938–1950 the federal government forced the studios to sell all their movie theaters.

ANSWERS: EXERCISE 3

1. Many of those involved in the movie business agree that multiscreen complexes are good for two reasons: (1) they cut the costs of exhibitors; and (2) they offer more choices to audiences.
2. Those who produce and distribute films (and not just the big studios) argue that the multiscreen theaters give exhibitors too much power.
3. The major studios are buying movie theaters to gain control over important parts of the distribution process (what gets shown and for how much money).
4. For twelve years (1938–1950) the federal government forced the studios to sell all their movie theaters.
5. But because they now have more competition (television and videocassette recorders), the studios are permitted to own theaters.

5. But because they now have more competition television and videocassette recorders, the studios are permitted to own theaters.

BRACKETS

25d Use brackets only within quotations to indicate your own comments or changes.

If you need to explain, clarify, or correct the words of the writer you quote, place your additions in a pair of brackets.

"That Texaco station [just outside Chicago] is one of the busiest in the nation," said a company spokesperson.

Also use brackets if you need to alter the capitalization of a quotation so that it will fit into your sentence. (See also 26a.)

"[O]ne of the busiest in the nation" is how a company spokesperson described the station.

You may also use a bracketed word or words to substitute for parts of the original quotation that would otherwise be unclear. In the sentence below, the bracketed word substitutes for *they* in the original.

"Despite considerable achievements in other areas, [humans] still cannot control the weather and probably will never be able to do so."

The word *sic* (Latin for "in this manner") in brackets indicates that an error in the quotation appeared in the original and was not made by you.

According to the newspaper report, "The car slammed thru [*sic*] the railing and into oncoming traffic."

But don't use *sic* to make fun of a writer or to note errors in a passage that is clearly nonstandard or illiterate.

ADDITIONAL POINT

Brackets may also be used to supply missing letters to complete names that are given partly in initials in a quotation.

THE ELLIPSIS MARK

25e Use the ellipsis mark to indicate omissions within quotations.

The **ellipsis mark** consists of three spaced periods (. . .). It is used most often to indicate an omission from a quotation, as illustrated in the following excerpts from this quotation about the Philippines:

ORIGINAL QUOTATION

"It was the Cuba of the future. It was going the way of Iran. It was another Nicaragua, another Cambodia, another Vietnam. But all these places, awesome in their histories, are so different from each other that one couldn't help thinking: this kind of talk was a shorthand for a confusion. All that was being said was that something was happening in the Philippines. Or more plausibly, a lot of different things were happening in the Philippines. And a lot of people were feeling obliged to speak out about it."
                                    —JAMES FENTON, "The Philippine Election"

OMISSION OF PART OF A SENTENCE

"But all of these places . . . are so different from each other that one couldn't help thinking: this kind of talk was a shorthand for a confusion."

"But . . . this kind of talk was a shorthand for a confusion."

OMISSION OF PARTS OF TWO SENTENCES

"All that was being said was that . . . a lot of different things were happening in the Philippines."

OMISSION OF ONE OR MORE SENTENCES

"It was the Cuba of the future. It was going the way of Iran. It was another Nicaragua, another Cambodia, another Vietnam. . . . All that was being said was that something was happening in the Philippines."

Notice that when the ellipsis mark follows a complete sentence, as in the example immediately above, four equally spaced periods result: the sentence period (closed up to the last word of the sentence) and the three periods of the ellipsis mark. Notice also that although Fenton's essay goes on after the quoted passage, an ellipsis mark is not used at the end of the quotation.

If you omit one or more lines of poetry or paragraphs of prose from a quotation, use a separate line of ellipsis marks across the full width of the quotation to show the omission.

NOTE: Pauses and unfinished statements in quoted speech may be indicated with an ellipsis mark instead of a dash (25b-1).

"I wish . . ." His voice trailed off.

EXERCISE 4

To practice using ellipsis marks to show omissions from quotations, follow each instruction below, using the following paragraph by Stewart Udall.

USING THE ELLIPSIS MARK—A SUMMARY

Use the ellipsis mark alone (. . .)

1. At the beginning or in the middle of a quoted sentence.
2. At the end of a quoted passage if the quotation is neither a grammatically complete sentence in itself nor a grammatically complete sentence in conjunction with the words preceding the quotation.

Use the ellipsis mark with a period (. . . .)

1. If the quoted material is either a grammatically complete sentence by itself or a grammatically complete sentence in conjunction with the words that precede the quotation.
2. To indicate the omission of material in a quotation when the omitted material comes between a grammatically complete sentence and another complete or incomplete sentence.

. . .
25e

ANSWERS: EXERCISE 4

1. "The most common trait of all primitive peoples is a reverence for the life-giving earth, and the native American shared this

elemental ethic: the land was alive to his loving touch, and he _ . . _ brother to all creatures."

2. "The most common trait of all primitive peoples is a reverence for the life-giving earth, and the native American shared this elemental ethic: the land was alive to his loving touch, and he, its son, was brother to all creatures. _ . . ._ During the long Indian tenure the land remained undefiled save for scars no deeper than the scratches of cornfield clearings or the farming canals of the Hohokams on the Arizona desert.

25f

/

The most common trait of all primitive peoples is a reverence for the life-giving earth, and the native American shared this elemental ethic: the land was alive to his loving touch, and he, its son, was brother to all creatures. His feelings were made visible in medicine bundles and dance rhythms for rain, and all of his religious rites and land attitudes savored the inseparable world of nature and God, the master of life. During the long Indian tenure the land remained undefiled save for scars no deeper than the scratches of cornfield clearings or the farming canals of the Hohokams on the Arizona desert.   —Stewart Udall

1. Quote the first sentence from the paragraph, but omit the words *its son* (and punctuation as necessary). Show the omission with an ellipsis mark.
2. Quote the paragraph, but omit the second sentence. Show the omission with an ellipsis mark.

THE SLASH

25f Use the slash between options and to separate lines of poetry that are run in to the text.

Option

I don't know why some teachers oppose pass/fail courses.

When used between options, the slash is not surrounded by extra space.

Note: The options *and/or* and *he/she* should be avoided. (See the Glossary of Usage, pp. 715 and 721.)

Poetry

More than fifty years after its introduction, people are still baffled by E. E. Cummings's unique form of expression, such as in the lines "next to of course god america i / love you land of the pilgrims' and so forth oh."

When used to separate lines of poetry, the slash is surrounded by space. (See 24c for more on quoting poetry.)

ANSWERS: EXERCISE 5

"Let all the learned say what they can, / 'Tis ready money makes the man." These two lines of poetry by the Englishman William Somerville (1645–1742) may apply to a current American economic problem. Non-American investors with plenty of "ready money" are pour-

EXERCISE 5

Insert colons, dashes, parentheses, brackets, ellipsis marks, or slashes as needed in the following paragraph. When different marks would be appropriate in the same place, be able to defend the choice you make.

"Let all the learned say what they can, 'Tis ready money makes the man." These two lines of poetry by the Englishman

William Somerville 1645–1742 may apply to a current American economic problem. Non-American investors with plenty of "ready money" are pouring some of it as much as $1.3 trillion in recent years into the United States. The investments of foreigners are varied stocks and bonds, savings deposits, service companies, factories, art works, even the campaigns of political candidates. Proponents of foreign investment argue that it revives industry, strengthens the economy, creates jobs more than 3 million, they say, and encourages free trade among nations. Opponents discuss the risks of heavy foreign investment it makes the American economy vulnerable to outsiders, sucks profits from the country, and gives foreigners an influence in governmental decision making. Proponents cite the jobs 3500 to be created by a new Japanese automobile factory in Kentucky. Opponents cite an attempt by the Russians the Russians! to buy California banks in order to spy on computer companies. On both sides, it seems, "the learned say 'Tis ready money makes the man or country." The question is, whose money?

NOTE: See the next page for a punctuation exercise combining colons, dashes, and parentheses with other marks of punctuation, such as commas and semicolons.

ing some of it—as much as $1.3 trillion in recent years—into the United States. The investments of foreigners are varied: stocks and bonds, savings deposits, service companies, factories, art works, even the campaigns of political candidates. Proponents of foreign investment argue that it revives industry, strengthens the economy, creates jobs (more than 3 million, they say), and encourages free trade among nations. Opponents discuss the risks of heavy foreign investment: it makes the American economy vulnerable to outsiders, sucks profits from the country, and gives foreigners an influence in governmental decision making. Proponents cite the jobs (3500) to be created by a new Japanese automobile factory in Kentucky. Opponents cite an attempt by the Russians [the Russians!] to buy California banks in order to spy on computer companies. On both sides, it seems "the learned say. . ./ 'Tis ready money makes the man [or country]." The question is, whose money?

/

25f

ANSWERS: EXERCISE ON CHAPTERS 20–25

Brewed coffee is the most widely consumed beverage in the world. The trade in coffee beans alone amounts to well over $6,000,000,000 a year, and the total volume of beans traded exceeds 4,250,000 tons a year. It's believed that the beverage was introduced into Arabia in the fifteenth century A.D., probably by Ethiopians. By the middle or late sixteenth century, the Arabs had introduced the beverage to the Europeans, who at first resisted it because of its strong flavor and effect as a mild stimulant. The French, Italians, and other Europeans incorporated coffee into their diets by the seventeenth century; the English, however, preferred tea, which they were then importing from India. Since America was colonized primarily by the English, Americans also preferred tea. Only after the Boston Tea Party (1773) did Americans begin drinking coffee in large quantities. Now, though, the U.S. is one of the top coffee-consuming countries, consumption having been spurred on by familiar advertising claims: "Good till the last drop," "Rich, hearty aroma," "Always rich, never bitter."

Produced from the fruit of an evergreen tree, coffee is grown primarily in Latin America, southern Asia, and Africa. Coffee trees require a hot climate, high humidity, rich soil with good drainage, and partial shade; consequently, they thrive on the east or west slopes of tropical volcanic mountains, where the soil is laced with potash and drains easily. The coffee beans—actually seeds—grow inside bright red berries. The berries are picked by hand, and the beans are extracted by machine, leaving a pulpy fruit residue that can be used for fertilizer. The beans are usually roasted in ovens, a chemical process that releases the beans' essential oil (caffeol), which gives coffee its distinctive aroma. Over a hundred different varieties of beans are produced in the world, each with a different flavor attributable to three factors: the species of plant (*Coffea arabia* and *Coffea robusta* are the most common) and the soil and climate where the variety was grown.

EXERCISE ON CHAPTERS 20–25
Periods, Commas, Semicolons, Apostrophes, Quotation Marks, Colons, Dashes, and Parentheses

The following paragraphs are unpunctuated except for end-of-sentence periods. Insert the appropriate punctuation marks where they are required. When different marks would be appropriate in the same place, be able to defend the choice you make.

Brewed coffee is the most widely consumed beverage in the world. The trade in coffee beans alone amounts to well over $6000000000 a year and the total volume of beans traded exceeds 4250000 tons a year. Its believed that the beverage was introduced into Arabia in the fifteenth century AD probably by Ethiopians. By the middle or late sixteenth century the Arabs had introduced the beverage to the Europeans who at first resisted it because of its strong flavor and effect as a mild stimulant. The French Italians and other Europeans incorporated coffee into their diets by the seventeenth century the English however preferred tea which they were then importing from India. Since America was colonized primarily by the English Americans also preferred tea. Only after the Boston Tea Party 1773 did Americans begin drinking coffee in large quantities. Now though the US is one of the top coffee-consuming countries consumption having been spurred on by familiar advertising claims Good till the last drop Rich hearty aroma Always rich never bitter.

Produced from the fruit of an evergreen tree coffee is grown primarily in Latin America southern Asia and Africa. Coffee trees require a hot climate high humidity rich soil with good drainage and partial shade consequently they thrive on the east or west slopes of tropical volcanic mountains where the soil is laced with potash and drains easily. The coffee beans actually seeds grow inside bright red berries. The berries are picked by hand and the beans are extracted by machine leaving a pulpy fruit residue that can be used for fertilizer. The beans are usually roasted in ovens a chemical process that releases the beans essential oil caffeol which gives coffee its distinctive aroma. Over a hundred different varieties of beans are produced in the world each with a different flavor attributable to three factors the species of plant *Coffea arabia* and *Coffea robusta* are the most common and the soil and climate where the variety was grown.

PART VI

Mechanics

Relatively few students will need to study or practice extensively the rules of capitalization covered in this chapter. A brief review, however, will be helpful for most students to clarify the rules for capitalization of titles, historical periods, specific places or institutions, people's titles, and similar matters.

CHAPTER 26

Capitals

Experienced writers generally agree on when to use capitals, but the conventions are constantly changing. Consult a recent dictionary if you have any doubt about whether a particular word should be capitalized.

RESOURCES AND IDEAS

Relatively little has been written about the teaching of capitalization, and most teachers probably assume that rules and drills are the only available instructional strategies. In *The Writing Room: A Resource Book for Teachers of English* (New York: Oxford UP, 1981, [172–74]), however, Harvey S. Wiener looks at the sources of capitalization problems for many basic writers—particularly problems of misunderstanding the rules governing sentence boundaries, of confusion over the capitalization of *I* and other personal pronouns, and of difficulty with the sometimes inexact categories of words that are to be treated as proper nouns. Wiener suggests looking for patterns of error in a student's writing, creating groups of words illustrating a particular rule, and asking a student to prepare sentences that demonstrate his or her grasp of a particular convention. These strategies can be used for more skilled writers as well.

26a Capitalize the first word of every sentence.

Every writer should own a good dictionary.
Will this rain ever stop?
Watch out!

When quoting other writers, you must reproduce the capital letters beginning their sentences or indicate that you have altered the source. Whenever possible, integrate the quotation into your own sentence so that its capitalization coincides with yours.

"Psychotherapists often overlook the benefits of self-deception," the author argues.

The author argues that "the benefits of self-deception" are not always recognized by psychotherapists.

If you need to alter the capitalization in the source, indicate the change with brackets (see 25d).

"[T]he benefits of self-deception" are not always recognized by psychotherapists, the author argues.

The author argues that "[p]sychotherapists often overlook the benefits of self-deception."

NOTE: Capitalization of questions in a series is optional. Both of the following examples are correct.

Is the population a hundred? Two hundred? More?
Is the population a hundred? two hundred? more?

Also optional is capitalization of the first word in a complete sentence after a colon (see 25a).

26b **Capitalize words in the titles of works according to standard practice.**

Capitalize all words in the title of a work *except* articles (*a, an, the*) and prepositions and conjunctions of fewer than five letters. Capitalize even these short words when they are the first or last word in a title or when they fall after a colon or semicolon.

The Sound and the Fury	*What Do I Live For?*
"Courtship Through the Ages"	"Once More to the Lake"
Merry England; Or, the History of a People	*Management: A New Approach*
	"Once Is Not Enough"

NOTE: Always capitalize the prefix or first word in a hyphenated word within a title. Capitalize the second word only if it is a noun or an adjective or is as important as the first word.

"Applying Stage Make-up"	*Through the Looking-Glass*
The Pre-Raphaelites	

26c **Always capitalize the pronoun *I* and the interjection *O*. Don't capitalize *oh* unless it begins a sentence.**

I love to stay up at night, but, oh, I hate to get up in the morning.
He who thinks himself wise, O heavens, is a great fool.
—VOLTAIRE

26d **Capitalize proper nouns, proper adjectives, and words used as essential parts of proper nouns.**

1 **Capitalize proper nouns and proper adjectives.**

Proper nouns name specific persons, places, and things: *Shakespeare, California, World War I*. **Proper adjectives** are formed from some proper nouns: *Shakespearean, Californian*. Capitalize all

cap
26d

EXTRA EXAMPLES

Capitalizing compound words:

un-American

post-Victorian

proper nouns and proper adjectives but not the articles (*a, an, the*) that precede them.

PROPER NOUNS AND ADJECTIVES TO BE CAPITALIZED

SPECIFIC PERSONS AND THINGS

Stephen King	the Leaning Tower of Pisa
Napoleon Bonaparte	Boulder Dam
Doris Lessing	the Empire State Building

SPECIFIC PLACES AND GEOGRAPHICAL REGIONS

New York City	the Mediterranean Sea
China	Lake Victoria
Europe	the Northeast
North America	the Rocky Mountains

DAYS OF THE WEEK, MONTHS, HOLIDAYS

Monday	Yom Kippur
May	Christmas
Thanksgiving	Columbus Day

HISTORICAL EVENTS, DOCUMENTS, PERIODS, MOVEMENTS

World War II	the Middle Ages
the Vietnam War	the Age of Reason
the Boston Tea Party	the Renaissance
the Treaty of Ghent	the Great Depression
the Constitution	the Romantic Movement

GOVERNMENT OFFICES OR DEPARTMENTS AND INSTITUTIONS

House of Representatives	Polk Municipal Court
Department of Defense	Warren County Hospital
Appropriations Committee	Northeast High School
Postal Service	York Board of Education

POLITICAL, SOCIAL, ATHLETIC, AND OTHER ORGANIZATIONS AND ASSOCIATIONS AND THEIR MEMBERS

Democratic Party, Democrats	Rotary Club, Rotarians
Communist Party, Communist	Eastern Star
Sierra Club	League of Women Voters
Girl Scouts of America, Scout	Boston Celtics
B'nai B'rith	Chicago Symphony Orchestra

RACES, NATIONALITIES, AND THEIR LANGUAGES

Native American	Germans
Afro-American, Negro	Swahili
Caucasian	Italian
But: blacks, whites	

RELIGIONS AND THEIR FOLLOWERS

Christianity, Christians   Judaism, Orthodox Jew
Protestantism, Protestants   Hinduism, Hindu
Catholicism, Catholics   Islam, Moslems *or* Muslims

RELIGIOUS TERMS FOR SACRED PERSONS AND THINGS

God   Buddha
Allah   the Bible (*but* biblical)
Christ   the Koran

NOTE: Capitalization of pronouns referring to God is optional in most contexts, but it is often used in religious texts and should be used where necessary to avoid confusion.

> **AMBIGUOUS**   Our minister spoke of God as though *he* loved every member of our congregation.
>
> **REVISED**   Our minister spoke of God as though *He* loved every member of our congregation.

2   **Capitalize common nouns used as essential parts of proper nouns.**

Common nouns name general classes of persons, places, or things, and they generally are not capitalized. However, capitalize the common nouns *street, avenue, park, river, ocean, lake, company, college, county,* and *memorial* when they are part of proper nouns naming specific places or institutions.

Main Street   Lake Superior
Central Park   Ford Motor Company
Mississippi River   Madison College
Pacific Ocean   George Washington Memorial Park

3   **Capitalize trade names.**

Trade names identify individual brands of certain products. When a trade name loses its association with a brand and comes to refer to a product in general, it is not capitalized. Refer to a dictionary for current usage when you are in doubt about a name.

Scotch tape   Xerox
Chevrolet   Bunsen burner
But: nylon, thermos

cap
26d

NOTE

You may wish to point out that when a generic term occurs with a proper name, the generic term is capitalized (the Congo River), but when the generic term occurs with two or more proper names, it is usually capitalized when it precedes the proper names but lowercased when it succeeds them (*L*akes Superior and Ontario; the Congo and Amazon *r*ivers).

NOTE

You may wish to tell students to capitalize kinship terms in direct address for preceding generations but not for terms of the same or succeeding generations. For example, *mother* and *grandma* are capitalized when used in direct address, but *brother* and *son* are not.

NOTE

You may wish to remind students not to capitalize *doctor*, *madame*, *sir*, or similar forms of address unless they occur directly before a name.

26e **Capitalize titles when they precede proper names but generally not when they follow proper names or are used alone.**

Professor Otto Osborne	Otto Osborne, a professor of English
Doctor Jane Covington	Jane Covington, a medical doctor
Senator Robert Dole	Robert Dole, senator from Kansas
the Reverend Ann Cole	Ann Cole, the minister

EXCEPTION: Many writers capitalize a title denoting very high rank even when it follows a proper name or is used alone.

Lyndon Johnson, past President of the United States
the Chief Justice of the United States

26f **Avoid unnecessary capitalization.**

In general, modern writers capitalize fewer words than earlier writers did. Capitalize only when a rule says you must.

1 **Don't capitalize common nouns used in place of proper nouns.**

UNNECESSARY   I am determined to take an Economics course before I graduate from College.

REVISED   I am determined to take an economics course before I graduate from college.

REVISED   I am determined to take Economics 101 before I graduate from Madison College.

2 **Don't capitalize compass directions unless they refer to specific geographical areas.**

The storm blew in from the northeast and then veered south along the coast. [Here *northeast* and *south* refer to general directions.]

Students from the South have trouble adjusting to the Northeast's bitter winters. [Here *South* and *Northeast* refer to specific regions.]

3 **Don't capitalize the names of seasons or the names of academic years or terms.**

spring	autumn	freshman year
fall	winter quarter	summer term

cap 26f

4   **Don't capitalize the names of relationships unless they form part of or substitute for proper names.**

my mother   the father of my friend
John's brother

But

I remember how Father scolded us.

Aunt Annie, Uncle Jake, and Uncle Irvin died within two months of each other.

EXERCISE

Capitalize words as necessary in the following sentence, or substitute small letters for unnecessary capitals. Consult a dictionary if you are in doubt. If the capitalization in a sentence is already correct, circle the number preceding the sentence.

Example:

The first book on my summer reading list is mark twain's *a connecticut yankee in king arthur's court.*

The first book on my summer reading list is Mark Twain's *A Connecticut Yankee in King Arthur's Court.*

1. The new State House is very imposing. it is made of reflective glass and steel.
2. My Grandmother told me stories about my Father and Uncle Bill.
3. Although Rashid is a moslem, he is very knowledgeable about the bible, especially the old testament.
4. Professor Kellogg recommended that *Sexist and non-sexist language* be a required text for all fall writing courses.
5. The photograph showed senator Ertel shaking hands with the Rabbi of the largest Synagogue in Florida.
6. The grand canyon is in arizona, not too far from phoenix.
7. Colson, the doctor, knew his medicine, but his manner made his patients nervous.
8. Our scavenger-hunt map directed us two blocks Southeast and two blocks Northeast to find an old sink.
9. The Suwannee river rises in the Okefenokee swamp and moves through Georgia and Florida to the gulf of Mexico.
10. The new Saunders theater is an acoustical triumph, but, Oh, it was expensive to build.

ANSWERS: EXERCISE

1. The new State House is very imposing. It is made of reflective glass and steel.
2. My grandmother told me stories about my father and Uncle Bill.
3. Although Rashid is a Moslem, he is very knowledgeable about the Bible, especially the Old Testament.
4. Professor Kellogg recommended that *Sexist and Non-Sexist Language* be a required text for all fall writing courses.
5. The photograph showed Senator Ertel shaking hands with the rabbi of the largest synagogue in Florida.
6. The Grand Canyon is in Arizona, not too far from Phoenix.
7. Correct.
8. Our scavenger-hunt map directed us two blocks southeast and two blocks northeast to find an old sink.
9. The Suwannee River rises in the Okefenokee Swamp and moves through Georgia and Florida to the Gulf of Mexico.
10. The new Saunders Theater is an acoustical triumph, but, oh, it was expensive to build.

cap
26f

Of all the chapters on mechanics, this chapter, on the uses of italics, most frequently needs to be reviewed, particularly by students writing essays or research papers that require incorporating material from outside the classroom. The chapter includes the rules for underlining titles; the names of various craft; foreign words and phrases that have not yet become part of the English language; and words, letters, numbers, and phrases named as words. It also gives the rules for underlining for emphasis.

CHAPTER 27

Italics

Type that slants upward to the right is known as *italic type.* We use italics to distinguish or emphasize certain words and phrases. In your handwritten or typed papers, <u>underline</u> to indicate material that would be italicized if set into type.

27a Underline titles according to standard practice.

Underline the titles of books, long poems, plays, periodicals, pamphlets, published speeches, long musical works, movies, television and radio programs, and works of visual art. (See the box on the facing page.) Use quotation marks for all other titles, such as songs, short poems, short stories, articles in periodicals, essays, and episodes of television and radio programs. (See 24d.)

NOTE: Be careful to underline marks of punctuation only if they are part of the title: *Did you read <u>Catch-22</u>?* (not *<u>Catch-22?</u>*). In titles of newspapers underline the name of the city only when it is part of the title.

NOTE

When an apostrophe or an apostrophe plus an *s* is added to a title, the addition is not underlined.

> Manchester *Guardian*
> *New York Times*

When giving the title of a periodical in your text, you do not need to capitalize or underline the article *the,* even if it is part of the title.

> She has the *New York Times* delivered to her in Alaska.

Omit the article entirely in bibliographic references (see Chapter 35, pp. 547–48).

TITLES TO BE UNDERLINED (ITALICIZED)

BOOKS

Catch-22
War and Peace
The Promise
The Bonfire of the Vanities

PLAYS

Equus
Hamlet
Summer and Smoke
The Phantom of the Opera

PAMPHLETS

The Truth About Alcoholism
*On the Vindication of the
    Rights of Women*

LONG MUSICAL WORKS

Tchaikovsky's *Swan Lake*
Bach's *St. Matthew Passion*
The Beatles' *Revolver*
But: Symphony in C

TELEVISION AND RADIO PROGRAMS

60 Minutes
The Shadow
L.A. Law

LONG POEMS

Beowulf
The Song of Roland
Paradise Lost
Song of Myself

PERIODICALS

Time
Philadelphia Inquirer
Yale Law Review
Mechanical Engineering

PUBLISHED SPEECHES

Lincoln's *Gettysburg Address*
Pericles's *Funeral Oration*

MOVIES

Gone with the Wind
Star Wars
Invasion of the Body Snatchers

WORKS OF VISUAL ART

Michelangelo's *David*
the *Mona Lisa*
Duchamp's *Standard Stoppages*

ital
27b

EXCEPTIONS: Legal documents, the Bible, and their parts are generally not italicized.

NOT	They registered their *deed.*
BUT	They registered their deed.
NOT	We studied the *Book of Revelation* in the *Bible.*
BUT	We studied the Book of Revelation in the Bible.

27b Underline the names of ships, aircraft, spacecraft, and trains.

Queen Elizabeth II
Spirit of St. Louis
Challenger

Apollo XI
Orient Express

27c Underline foreign words and phrases that are not part of the English language.

English tends to absorb foreign words and phrases that speakers and writers find useful. The French expression "bon voyage," for example, is now part of our language and need not be underlined. If a foreign word or phrase has not been absorbed into our language, it should be underlined. A dictionary will tell you whether or not the words you wish to use should be underlined.

The scientific name for the brown trout is *Salmo trutta*. [The scientific names for plants and animals are always underlined.]

What a life he led! He was a true *bon vivant*.

The Latin *De gustibus non est disputandum* translates roughly as "There's no accounting for taste."

NOTE

You may wish to remind students that when sounds (e.g., *ker-plunk, oof*) are represented in writing, they are usually underlined.

27d Underline words, letters, numbers, and phrases named as words.

Some people pronounce *th*, as in *thought*, with a faint *s* or *f* sound.

Carved into the middle of the column, twenty feet up, was a mysterious 7.

Try pronouncing *unique New York* ten times fast.

Italics may also be used instead of quotation marks in definitions (see 24e).

The word *syzygy* refers to a straight line formed by three celestial bodies, as in the alignment of earth, sun, and moon that produces an eclipse.

ADD THE MECHANICS

If you have assigned one or more of Chapters 26–30, this activity may be useful and interesting. Take an essay, either student or professional; remove capitals, italics, and the like; and ask students to work in groups reaching consensus on how to correct the mechanics in the "new" essay. Tell them not to look at the handbook but to decide on their own the best way to serve the readers' needs through mechanics. When the students have finished, they can compare their work with the original and, using the handbook as a reference, decide which choices in mechanics they think best serve the needs of the essay and the readers. If they decide to disagree with the advice given in the handbook, ask them to write out their own rules.

ital 27e Occasionally, underlining may be used for emphasis.

Compare these sentences:

I thought you had the key.   I *thought* you had the key.
I thought you had the key.   I thought *you* had the key.

In the absence of clues from context, the first sentence doesn't tell us where the emphasis should lie. The three following sentences, however, tell us exactly what word to emphasize, and the different emphases create different meanings. In this way italics (or underlining) can stress an important word or phrase, especially in re-porting how someone said something. But such emphasis should be used sparingly. Excessive underlining will make your writing sound immature or hysterical, as the following example illus-trates.

> The hunters had *no* food and *no* firewood. But they were *too* tired to do anything more than crawl into their *sopping* sleeping bags. Had it been ten degrees colder, *they might have frozen to death.*

If you find that you rely too much on underlining to achieve emphasis, consult Chapter 18 for other techniques to help you ac-cent your writing.

EXERCISE

Underline (italicize) words and phrases as needed in the follow-ing sentences, or circle any words or phrases that are italicized unnecessarily.

> *Example:*
> Of Hitchcock's movies, Psycho is the scariest.
> Of Hitchcock's movies, <u>Psycho</u> is the scariest.

1. The essay contains many puns and jeux de mots.
2. The author's stories have appeared in Redbook, Vogue, and Ms., among other magazines.
3. The director warned the writer that the screenplay for Opiela in Love had better be finished *tout de suite.*
4. The map was *so* out of date that it didn't even show the *town* Tammy lived in, let alone the *street* her *house* was on.
5. According to Publishers Weekly, Markosian's book is out of print.
6. San Francisco's major newspapers are the Chronicle and the Examiner.
7. Both the *Old Testament* and the *New Testament* of the *Bible* offer profound lessons in human nature.
8. No matter how many times I say it, the word euphemism comes out wrong.
9. Homo sapiens has evolved further than any other species.
10. Whether he's watching Masterpiece Theatre, Wide World of Sports, or the silliest situation comedy, Larry is happy in front of the television.

ANSWERS: EXERCISE

1. The essay contains many puns and <u>jeux de mots</u>.
2. The author's stories have appeared in <u>Redbook, Vogue</u>, and <u>Ms.</u>, among other magazines.
3. The director warned the writer that the screenplay for <u>Opiela in Love</u> had better be finished <u>tout de suite</u>.
4. The map was so out of date that it didn't even show the town Tammy lived in, let alone the street her house was on.
5. According to <u>Publishers Weekly</u>, Mar-kosian's book is out of print.
6. San Francisco's major newspapers are the <u>Chronicle</u> and the <u>Examiner</u>.
7. Both the Old Testament and the New Testament of the Bible offer profound lessons in human nature.
8. No matter how many times I say it, the word <u>euphemism</u> comes out wrong.
9. <u>Homo sapiens</u> has evolved further than any other species.
10. Whether he's watching <u>Masterpiece Theatre, Wide World of Sports</u>, or the silliest situation comedy, Larry is happy in front of the television.

ital
27e

HIGHLIGHTS

The discussion in this chapter covers the rules for using abbreviations in general writing. The first four sections cover the use of standard abbreviations for titles; the appropriate use of familiar abbreviations and acronyms; the abbreviations that accompany dates and numbers to show time and amount; and the use of common Latin abbreviations. The last two sections deal with the misuse of abbreviations.

CHAPTER 28

Abbreviations

All writers use certain standard abbreviations such as *Dr.* and *Ph.D.* because they are convenient and readily understood; and technical writers use a great many other abbreviations (see 28f). Nevertheless, only a few abbreviations are acceptable in general writing. For a list of abbreviations used in source citations, see Chapter 35, p. 560.

28a Use standard abbreviations for titles immediately before and after proper names.

BEFORE THE NAME	AFTER THE NAME
Dr. James Hsu	James Hsu, M.D.
Mr., Mrs., Ms., Hon.,	D.D.S., D.V.M., Ph.D.,
St., Rev., Msgr., Gen.	Ed.D., O.S.B., S.J., Sr., Jr.

(Note that the title *Ms.* is followed by a period, even though it is not actually an abbreviation: *Ms. Judith Boyer.*)

Use abbreviations such as *Rev., Hon., Prof., Rep., Sen., Dr.,* and *St.* (for *Saint*) only if they appear with a proper name. Spell them out in the absence of a proper name.

FAULTY	We learned to trust the *Dr.*
REVISED	We learned to trust the *doctor.*
REVISED	We learned to trust *Dr. Kaplan.*

The abbreviations for academic degrees—*Ph.D., M.A., B.A.,* and the like—may be used without a proper name.

My brother took seven years to get his *Ph.D.* It will probably take me just as long to earn my *B.A.*

28b Familiar abbreviations and acronyms for names of organizations, corporations, people, and some countries are acceptable in most writing.

An **acronym** is an abbreviation that spells a pronounceable word, such as WHO, UNESCO, and NATO. These abbreviations, written without periods, are acceptable in most writing as long as they are familiar. So are several familiar abbreviations of the names of organizations, corporations, people, and countries. When these abbreviate three or more words, they are usually written without periods.

ORGANIZATIONS	CIA, FBI, YMCA, AFL-CIO
CORPORATIONS	IBM, CBS, ITT
PEOPLE	JFK, LBJ, FDR
COUNTRIES	U.S.A. (or USA), U.S.S.R. (or USSR)

(See 20b for more information on when to use periods in abbreviations.)

NOTE: If a name or term (such as *operating room*) appears often in a piece of writing, then its abbreviation (*O.R.*) can cut down on extra words. Spell out the full term at its first appearance, indicate its abbreviation in parentheses, and use the abbreviation from then on. However, if the term occurs only a few times in a paper, the abbreviation will serve no useful purpose and may even confuse readers. In that case spell out the term each time it occurs.

28c Use *B.C., A.D., A.M., P.M., no.,* and *$* only with specific dates and numbers.

The abbreviation B.C. ("before Christ") always follows a date, whereas A.D. (*anno Domini,* Latin for "year of the Lord") precedes a date.

44 B.C.	8:05 P.M. (*or* p.m.)	no. 36 (*or* No. 36)
A.D. 1492	11.26 A.M. (*or* a.m.)	$7.41

FAULTY	Hospital routine is easier to follow in the A.M. than in the P.M.
REVISED	Hospital routine is easier to follow in the *morning* than in the *afternoon or evening.*

NOTE: The capitalized abbreviations above are often set in small capital letters in publications: B.C., A.D., A.M., P.M. In handwriting and typewriting, use B.C. and A.D. and either A.M./P.M. or

ADDITIONAL RULES

Civil and military titles are abbreviated only when used before a full name, not before the last name only.

Scholarly degrees are abbreviated when the degree follows a name. When a name is followed by an abbreviated title, no other title goes before the name.

ab
28c

SCHOLARLY ABBREVIATIONS

anon.	anonymous
b.	born
c	copyright
c. *or* ca.	about (with dates)
cf.	compare
col., cols.	column, columns
d.	died
ed.; eds.	editor, edited by; editors
e.g.	for example
esp.	especially
et al.	and others
i.e.	that is
ms., mss.	manuscript, manuscripts
n.b.	note carefully
n.d.	no date (of publication)
n.p.	no place (of publication), no publisher
p., pp.	page, pages
pref.	preface
rept.	report, reported by
sec., sect.; secs.	section; sections
v. *or* vs.	versus (legal)
vol., vols.	volume, volumes

**POSTAL ABBREVIATIONS
(U.S. AND CANADA)**

AB	Alberta
AL	Alabama
AK	Alaska
AR	Arkansas
AZ	Arizona
BC	British Columbia
CA	California
CO	Colorado
CT	Connecticut
DC	District of Columbia
DE	Delaware
FL	Florida
GA	Georgia
IA	Iowa
ID	Idaho
IL	Illinois
IN	Indiana
KS	Kansas
KY	Kentucky
LA	Louisiana
LB	Labrador
MA	Massachusetts
MB	Manitoba
MD	Maryland
ME	Maine
MI	Michigan
MN	Minnesota
MO	Missouri
MS	Mississippi
NB	New Brunswick
NC	North Carolina
ND	North Dakota
NE	Nebraska
NF	Newfoundland
NH	New Hampshire
NJ	New Jersey
NM	New Mexico
NS	Nova Scotia
NT	Northwest Territories
NV	Nevada
NY	New York
OH	Ohio
OK	Oklahoma
ON	Ontario
OR	Oregon
PA	Pennsylvania
PE	Prince Edward Island

a.m./p.m. The abbreviation for *number* may either be capitalized or not (No., no.).

28d Generally, reserve common Latin abbreviations such as *i.e., e.g.,* and *etc.* for use in source citations and comments in parentheses.

i.e.	that is (*id est*)
cf.	compare (*confer*)
e.g.	for example (*exempli gratia*)
et al.	and others (*et alii*)
etc.	and so forth (*et cetera*)
N.B.	note well (*nota bene*)

He said he would be gone a fortnight (i.e., two weeks).
Bloom et al., editors, *Anthology of Light Verse*
Trees, too, are susceptible to disease (e.g., Dutch elm disease).

(Note that these abbreviations are generally not italicized or underlined.) In formal writing use the appropriate English phrases instead of the Latin abbreviations.

FAULTY	The cabs of some modern farm machines—e.g., combines—look like airplane cockpits.
INFORMAL	The cabs of some modern farm machines (e.g., combines) look like airplane cockpits.
FORMAL	The cabs of some modern farm machines (for example, combines) look like airplane cockpits.
FORMAL	The cabs of some modern farm machines—for example, combines—look like airplane cockpits.

28e Don't use *Inc., Bros., Co.,* or *&* (for *and*) except when it is part of the official name of a business firm.

FAULTY	*The Santini bros.* operate a large moving firm in New York City.
REVISED	*The Santini brothers* operate a large moving firm in New York City.
REVISED	*Santini Bros.* is a large moving firm in New York City.
FAULTY	We read about the Hardy Boys & Nancy Drew.
REVISED	We read about the Hardy Boys *and* Nancy Drew.

28f In most writing don't abbreviate units of measurement; geographical names; names of days, months, and holidays; names of people; courses of instruction; and labels for divisions of written works.

Units of measurement, geographical names, specialized terms, and other words are often abbreviated in technical writing. In other academic writing and general writing, however, such words should be spelled out.

UNITS OF MEASUREMENT

The dog is thirty *inches* (not *in.*) high.
Dig a hole six *feet* (not *ft.*) deep.

EXCEPTIONS: Long phrases such as *miles per hour* (m.p.h.) or *cycles per second* (c.p.s.) are usually abbreviated, with or without periods: *The speed limit on that road was once 75 m.p.h.* (or *mph*).

GEOGRAPHICAL NAMES

The publisher is in *Massachusetts* (not *Mass.* or *MA*).
He came from Aukland, *New Zealand* (not *N.Z.*).
She lived on Morrissey *Boulevard* (not *Blvd.*).

EXCEPTIONS: The United States is often referred to as the U.S.A. (USA) or the U.S., and the Soviet Union as the U.S.S.R. (USSR). In writing of the U.S. capital, we use the abbreviation D.C. for District of Columbia when it follows the city's name: *Washington, D.C.*

NAMES OF DAYS, MONTHS, AND HOLIDAYS

The truce was signed on *Tuesday* (not *Tues.*), *January* (not *Jan.*) 16.
The *Christmas* (not *Xmas*) holidays were uneventful.

NAMES OF PEOPLE

James (not *Jas.*) Bennett ran for that seat.
Robert (not *Robt.*) Frost writes accessible poems.

COURSES OF INSTRUCTION

I'm majoring in *political science* (not *poli. sci.*).
Economics (not *Econ.*) is a tough course.

LABELS FOR DIVISIONS OF WRITTEN WORKS

The story begins on *page* (not *p.*)15 in *Volume* (not *Vol.*) 2.
Read *Chapter* (not *Ch.*) 6.

EXERCISE 1

Revise the following sentences as needed to correct faulty use of abbreviations. Circle the number preceding any sentence in which the abbreviations are already correct as written.

PQ	Quebec, Province du Quebec
PR	Puerto Rico
RI	Rhode Island
SC	South Carolina
SD	South Dakota
SK	Saskatchewan
TN	Tennessee
TX	Texas
UT	Utah
VA	Virginia
VT	Vermont
WA	Washington
WI	Wisconsin
WV	West Virginia
WY	Wyoming
YT	Yukon Territory

ab
28f

ANSWERS: EXERCISE 1

1. The kite was flying at about a hundred <u>feet</u> when the line snapped.
2. Old Louisville, a section of Louisville between Third and Fourth <u>Streets</u>, near Central <u>Park</u>, has some beautiful Victorian houses.
3. Jet lag—<u>that is</u>, disruption of sense of time, place, or well-being—often afflicts air travelers.
4. Upon his inauguration on <u>Friday, January</u> 20, 1961, John F. Kennedy became the first Roman Catholic President in American history.
5. Correct. It would also be correct to omit periods from the abbreviations: <u>USA</u> and <u>USSR</u>.
6. Mount Vesuvius erupted in <u>A.D.</u> 79 and buried Pompeii.
7. Correct.
8. The Lynch <u>brothers, William and Robert</u>, went bankrupt in the same year.
9. They asked the <u>reverend</u> to marry them on horseback.
10. There, in the middle of <u>Chapter 6</u>, between <u>pages</u> 128 <u>and</u> 129, was a leaf my mother had pressed as a child.

ANSWERS: EXERCISE 2

The advantages of a <u>graduate</u> degree are not lost on me. With a Ph.D. I might become a college <u>professor</u>, a job that would allow me to work only in the <u>afternoon</u>, so I wouldn't have to get up before 11:00 A.M., and only on <u>Tuesday, Wednesday,</u> and <u>Thursday</u>, my favorite days. Or I could get an M.D. and become a <u>doctor</u>. Though I might have to work long <u>hours</u>, I could earn plenty of <u>money</u> and, by serving on a professional association like the AMA, could have a lot of influence. I know about these advantages because my two older <u>brothers</u> are Prof. Giordano and Dr. Giordano. I also know how hard they had to work for their degrees, so I think I'll stick with <u>political science</u> courses and look for a nice, safe <u>government</u> job after I get my B.A.

Example:

One prof. spent five class hrs. reading from the textbook.

One *professor* spent five class *hours* reading from the textbook.

1. The kite was flying at about a hundred ft. when the line snapped.
2. Old Louisville, a section of Louisville between Third and Fourth Sts., near Central Pk., has some beautiful Victorian houses.
3. Jet lag—i.e., disruption of sense of time, place, or well-being—often afflicts air travelers.
4. Upon his inauguration on Fri., Jan. 20, 1961, JFK became the first Roman Catholic President in American history.
5. The relationship between the U.S.A. and the U.S.S.R. is one of the most analyzed subjects of the century.
6. Mount Vesuvius erupted in *anno Domini* 79 and buried Pompeii.
7. Mr. and Mrs. Harold Marsh, Jr., donated a new wing for the library.
8. The Lynch bros., Wm. & Robt., went bankrupt in the same year.
9. They asked the rev. to marry them on horseback.
10. There, in the middle of Ch. 6, between pp. 128 & 129, was a leaf my mother had pressed as a child.

EXERCISE 2

Spell out all inappropriate abbreviations in the following paragraph. If an abbreviation is appropriate in its context, leave it as is.

The advantages of a grad. degree are not lost on me. With a Ph.D. I might become a college prof., a job that would allow me to work only in the P.M., so I wouldn't have to get up before 11:00 A.M., and only on Tues., Wed., and Thurs., my favorite days. Or I could get an M.D. and become a dr. Though I might have to work long hrs., I could earn plenty of $ and, by serving on a professional association like the AMA, could have a lot of influence. I know about these advantages because my two older bros. are Prof. Giordano and Dr. Giordano. I also know how hard they had to work for their degrees, so I think I'll stick with poli. sci. courses and look for a nice, safe govt. job after I get my B.A.

ab
28f

CHAPTER 29

Numbers

HIGHLIGHTS

The representation of numbers in general writing is the subject of this chapter. The rules for when to use figures for numbers and when to write out numbers are few and easily memorized.

Experienced writers vary in their choice between writing numbers out and using figures. In scientific and technical writing, all numbers are usually written as figures. In business writing, all numbers over ten are usually written as figures. In general writing, numbers are more often spelled out. The following rules give conventions for general writing.

29a Use figures for numbers that require more than two words to spell out.

The leap year has *366* days.
The population of Minot, North Dakota, is about *32,500*.

Spell out numbers of one or two words. (See also 29b.)

That hotel can accommodate no more than *seventy-five* people.

The first writing we know of was done over *six thousand* years ago.

The collection included almost *twelve hundred* drawings and paintings.

A hyphenated number can be considered one word.

The ball game drew *forty-two thousand* people.

EXCEPTION: When you use several numbers together, they should be consistently spelled out or consistently expressed in figures.

| INCONSISTENT | Only *ninety-nine* students attended the first lecture, but the audience increased to *126* for the second lecture and *two hundred* for the third. |

REVISED   Only 99 students attended the first lecture, but the audience increased to *126* for the second lecture and *200* for the third.

29b Use figures instead of words according to standard practice.

Even when a number requires one or two words to spell out, we conventionally use figures for days and years; pages, chapters, volumes, acts, scenes, and lines; decimals, percentages, and fractions; addresses; scores and statistics; exact amounts of money; and the time of day.

DAYS AND YEARS

June 18, 1985   A.D. 12   456 B.C.

EXCEPTION: The day of a month may be expressed in words when it is not followed by a year (*June fifth; October first*).

PAGES, CHAPTERS, VOLUMES, ACTS, SCENES, LINES	DECIMALS, PERCENTAGES, AND FRACTIONS
Chapter 9, page 123	22.5
Isaiah 28:1 in the Bible	48% (or 48 percent)
Hamlet, Act 5 (*or* V), Scene 3 (*or* iii), lines 35–40	3½

ADDRESSES	SCORES AND STATISTICS
355 Clinton Avenue	21 to 7
419 Stonewall Street	a mean of 26
Washington, D.C. 20036	a ratio of 8 to 1

EXACT AMOUNTS OF MONEY	THE TIME OF DAY
$4.50	9:00
$3.5 million (*or* $3,500,000)	3:45
$2,763 (*or* $2763)	2:30

EXCEPTIONS: Round dollar or cent amounts of only a few words may be expressed in words: *seventeen dollars; fifteen hundred dollars; sixty cents.* When the word *o'clock* is used for the time of day, also express the number in words: *two o'clock* (not *2 o'clock*).

29c Always spell out numbers that begin sentences.

We are so accustomed to seeing a capital letter at the beginning of a sentence that a number there can make reading difficult.

ADDITIONAL EXAMPLES

ADDITIONAL EXAMPLES

Biblical reference

II Kings 3.6

Measurements

55 miles per hour

2 liters

1 tablespoon

9 × 12-inch paper *or* 9″ × 12″ paper

num
29c

Therefore, always spell out any number that begins a sentence. If the number requires more than two words, avoid further awkwardness by rewording the sentence so that the number falls later and can be expressed as a figure.

Awkward	*103* of the opening-night audience asked for a refund.
Awkward	*One hundred and three* of the opening-night audience asked for a refund.
Revised	Of the opening-night audience, *103* asked for a refund.

EXERCISE

Revise the following sentences to correct the use of numbers. Circle the number preceding any sentence in which numbers are already used appropriately.

Example:

Carol paid one hundred and forty-five dollars for a bridesmaid's dress she would never wear again.

Carol paid $145 for a bridesmaid's dress she would never wear again.

1. 1036 Colgate University students played Twister for three and one-half hours on May fifth, 1984, in the largest game on record.
2. I lost a trivia game because I forgot that sixteen hundred Pennsylvania Avenue is the White House.
3. Only 27 percent of the 350 consumers we polled preferred the new product to the old one.
4. The largest carousel in the United States is 100 feet tall and cost over a million and three-quarters dollars to build.
5. Covering four hundred and two acres, Angkor Wat in Cambodia is the largest religious building ever constructed.
6. A liter is equal to almost one and six-hundredths quarts.
7. Not until page ninety-nine, in the middle of Chapter five, does the author introduce the main character.
8. I was born on May fifteenth, six days after my dog.
9. Peter Minuit bought Manhattan Island from the Indians for twenty-four dollars.
10. Dominating the town's skyline was a sign that stood thirty feet off the ground and measured 112 feet by thirty-seven feet.

ANSWERS: EXERCISE

1. The number *1036* should be spelled out, but the sentence is best rewritten to avoid awkwardness: On May 5, 1984, in the largest Twister game on record, 1036 Colgate University students played for 3½ hours.
2. I lost a trivia game because I forgot that 1600 Pennsylvania Avenue is the White House.
3. Correct.
4. The largest carousel in the United States is 100 feet tall and cost over $1.75 million (or $1,750,000) to build.
5. Covering 402 acres, Angkor Wat in Cambodia is the largest religious building ever constructed.
6. A liter is equal to almost 1.06 quarts.
7. Not until page 99, in the middle of Chapter 5, does the author introduce the main character.
8. Numbers used appropriately, although May 15 is also correct.
9. Number used appropriately, although $24 is also correct.
10. Dominating the town's skyline was a sign that stood 30 feet off the ground and measured 112 feet by 37 feet.

num

29c

CHAPTER 30

Word Division

As much as possible, avoid dividing words. If you must divide a word between the end of one line and the beginning of the next, do so only between syllables. Put a hyphen at the end of the first line, never at the beginning of the second. Never divide the last word on a page, because in the act of turning the page the reader may forget the beginning of the word. If you are in doubt about how to break any word into syllables, consult a dictionary. Note, however, that not all syllable breaks are appropriate for word division. Use the following rules to decide when and how to divide words.

30a **Don't make a division that leaves a single letter at the end of a line or fewer than three letters at the beginning of a line.**

FAULTY   A newspaper or television editorial for or *a-gainst* a candidate can sway an election.

REVISED   A newspaper or television editorial for or *against* a candidate can sway an election.

FAULTY   Counseling is required for every child *abus-er.*

REVISED   Counseling is required for every child *abuser.*

30b **Don't divide one-syllable words.**

Since one-syllable words have no break in pronunciation, they should not be divided.

| FAULTY | The shiny, spinning space capsule *drop-ped* suddenly from the clouds. |
| REVISED | The shiny, spinning space capsule *dropped* suddenly from the clouds. |

30c Divide compound words only between the words that form them or at fixed hyphens.

Compound words are made up of two or more words (*drawback, homecoming*). Their component words may be separated by a hyphen (*well-paying, cross-reference*), in which case the hyphen is called **fixed.** Compound words should be divided only between their component words and at fixed hyphens.

FAULTY	If you want to have friends, be *good-na-tured.*
REVISED	If you want to have friends, be *good-natured.*
FAULTY	Sherlock Holmes exemplifies the *mas-termind.*
REVISED	Sherlock Holmes exemplifies the *master-mind.*

(See 34d for guidelines on when to use hyphens in spelling compound words.)

div
30d

30d Avoid confusing word divisions.

Some word divisions may momentarily confuse the reader because the first or second part by itself forms a pronounceable (or unpronounceable) unit that does not fit with the whole. For example: *poi-gnant, read-dress, in-dict.* Avoid word divisions like these.

CONFUSING	Her walking out of class was an act of *her-oism.*
CLEAR	Her walking out of class was an act of *hero-ism.*
CONFUSING	He claims that stealing never bothered his *con-science.*
CLEAR	He claims that stealing never bothered his *conscience.*

ANSWERS: EXERCISE

1. After my cousin graduated, she joined the <u>army</u> as an officer.
2. Correct.
3. The tarantella is a vivacious folk dance of southern <u>It-</u>
   <u>aly</u> (or Italy, without division).
4. He took bad advice from several <u>well-</u>
   <u>meaning</u> friends.
5. The product inspector detects any sur-faces that are not <u>smoothly</u> sanded.
6. Correct.
7. Each of the twenty-three apartments he looked at was <u>rented</u> before he could make a deposit on it.
8. Americans find any number of ways to keep from feeling <u>middle-aged</u> (or divide at fixed hyphen).
9. While the photographers snapped pic-tures, Dan <u>blushed</u> with embarrass-ment.
10. After the lecture Dotty felt she knew <u>enough</u> about the subject to pass the test.

EXERCISE

Revise the following sentences to repair any incorrect word divisions. Consult a dictionary if necessary. Circle the number preceding any sentence in which word division is already correct.

Example:

I thought Harry's joke was sidesplit-ting, but no one else even smiled.

I thought Harry's joke was *side-splitting*, but no one else even smiled.

1. After my cousin graduated, she joined the ar-my as an officer.
2. A travel agent booked a seat for me on a char-ter flight.
3. The tarantella is a vivacious folk dance of southern Ita-ly.
4. He took bad advice from several well-mean-ing friends.
5. The product inspector detects any surfaces that are not smo-othly sanded.
6. Last year I completely forgot to call my father on Fa-ther's day.
7. Each of the twenty-three apartments he looked at was rent-ed before he could make a deposit on it.
8. Americans find any number of ways to keep from feeling mid-dle-aged.
9. While the photographers snapped pictures, Dan blush-ed with embarrassment.
10. After the lecture Dotty felt she knew e-nough about the subject to pass the test.

div
30d

PART VII

Effective Words

Chapter 31 deals with appropriate usage, exactness, and the avoidance of wordiness. Of course, no instructional short cut can substitute for experience in choosing the appropriate word, in knowing when slang or a colloquialism is actually more effective than a standard word or expression, or in deciding when a technical term is useful or requires definition. But students are often interested in such matters, and some class time may usefully be spent considering how alternative choices affect students' own sentences or paragraphs, in addition to the sample sentences provided by the exercises. Similarly, denotation and connotation, abstract and concrete words, and general and specific words are topics that often generate lively discussion. Because the effect and even the meaning of words may depend as much on the reader's perspective as on the writer's intention, class discussion and collaborative work can be excellent approaches to understanding diction.

Avoiding wordiness, the subject addressed in the final section of this chapter, often causes problems for students, who are likely to mistake brevity for conciseness and to confuse simple lack of development with economy. Some practice with the ways of simplifying sentences and word groups can be useful, as can attention to the empty words and phrases and to the unnecessary repetition that are more obvious sources of flabbiness in writing.

CHAPTER 31

Controlling Diction

Diction is the choice and use of words. Controlling your diction will help you express yourself with precision and clarity, so that you affect your readers as you want. You should select words suited to your writing situation—that is, your purpose, your meaning, and your readers' backgrounds, interests, and expectations. And you should prune words that make your writing weak or inexact.

No firm rules dictate the proper words for every writing situation, but the following sections offer some guidelines for choosing words. The most useful advice, perhaps, is to suspect the first word that comes to mind and to be willing to search for a more appropriate or precise substitute.

31a Choosing the appropriate word

Words are appropriate when they suit your subject and the purpose of your writing, the role you are assuming, the attitude you want to project, and the readers you are writing for. We all use various kinds of language—various sets of words—depending on the context in which we are speaking or writing. Talking to friends, for example, you might say, *My sister decided to bag therapy because her shrink seemed even more strung out than she was.* Writing for a general audience, however, you would convey the same information quite differently, perhaps writing, *My sister decided to abandon therapy because her psychiatrist seemed even more disturbed than she was.* In each case the diction fits the occasion. When you talk or write to people you know well and share experiences with, you can relax into colloquial or slang expressions such as *bag, shrink,* and

---

APPROPRIATE AND INAPPROPRIATE DICTION

Appropriate in all writing situations:

Standard English (see below)

Appropriate in some writing situations:

Slang (31a-1)	Neologisms (31a-5)
Colloquial language (31a-2)	Technical language (31a-6)
Regional words and expressions (31a-3)	Euphemisms (31a-7)

Rarely or never appropriate in writing or speech:

Nonstandard language (31a-4)	Pretentious writing (31a-7)
Archaic and obsolete words (31a-5)	Biased language: sexist, racist, ethnocentric, etc. (31a-8)

---

strung out. Your friends expect such informality. But when you write for a general audience, you must be more formal, using words such as *abandon, psychiatrist,* and *disturbed.* These words are more widely understood, and they indicate your respect for your reader's seriousness and intelligence.

Most of your writing in college and after will be analyzing, explaining, and sometimes defending your understanding and interpretation of facts, events, and ideas. The words appropriate to such writing, like the conventions of grammar and usage described earlier in this handbook, are those of **standard** or **educated English**—that is, the English normally expected and used by educated readers and writers. The vocabulary of standard English is huge, allowing expression of an infinite range of ideas and feelings; but it does exclude words that only limited groups of people use, understand, or find inoffensive. Some of those more limited vocabularies should be avoided altogether; others should be used cautiously and in special situations, as when aiming for a special effect with an audience you know will appreciate it. Whenever you doubt a word's status, consult a dictionary (see 32b-2).

RESOURCES AND IDEAS

Mary Scott Simpson, "Teaching Writing: Beginning with the Word," *College English* 39 (1978): 934–39. The author describes class activities and readings designed to develop sensitivity to words and build vocabulary.

appr
31a

1   **Using slang only when appropriate**

All groups of people—from musicians and computer scientists to vegetarians and golfers—create **slang,** novel and colorful expressions that reflect the group's special experiences and set it off from others. Slang displays endless inventiveness. Some of it gives new meanings to old words. For example, several decades ago the word *cool* gained a meaning of "pleasing, excellent" (*The movie was cool*), and during the 1970s *into* came to describe personal commitment (*I'm really into plants*). More recently, the word *hacker* has been applied to computer buffs (*Enthusiastic hackers have produced innovative computer games*). Some slang comes from other languages: our word *chow* ("food" or "a meal") comes from the Chinese *chao*, meaning "to stir or fry"; and *schlep* ("to lug" or "a clumsy person") comes from the Yiddish *schleppen*, "to drag." Sometimes the slang of a particular ethnic group is widely adopted by the rest of the population. *Out to lunch, put on ice,* and *funky,* for example, are contributions of black slang.

Among those who understand it, slang may be vivid and forceful. It often occurs in dialogue, and an occasional slang expression can enliven an informal essay. Some slang, such as *dropout* (*she was a high school dropout*), has proved so useful that it has passed into the general vocabulary.

However, most slang is too flippant and imprecise for effective communication, and it is generally inappropriate for college or business writing. The writer who says that *many students start out pretty straight but then get weird* deprives her writing of seriousness while failing to specify what happens to the students. Avoiding imprecise slang and including specific, informative language would strengthen the sentence.

2 Using colloquial language only when appropriate

Colloquial language designates the words and expressions appropriate to everyday spoken language. Regardless of our backgrounds and how we live, we all try to *get along with* each other. We sometimes *get together with* our neighbors. We play with *kids*, *go crazy* about one thing, *crab* about something else, and in our worst moments try to *get back at* someone who has made us do the *dirty work*. These italicized words and expressions are not "wrong"; quite the contrary, more formal language might sound stilted and pompous in casual conversation and in some kinds of writing.

When you write informally, colloquial language may be appropriate to achieve the casual, relaxed effect of conversation. An occasional colloquial word dropped into otherwise more formal writing can also help you achieve a desired emphasis. And some formerly colloquial words (*rambunctious*, *trigger* as a verb) have gained acceptance in standard English. But colloquial language does not provide the exactness needed in more formal college, business, and professional writing. In such writing you should generally avoid any words and expressions labeled "informal" or "col-

HUCK FINN

You may wish to make the following examples the subject of class discussion. Students usually find them quite interesting.

In his explanatory note at the beginning of *The Adventures of Huckleberry Finn*, Mark Twain explains one of the difficulties with using nonstandard language:

In this book a number of dialects are used, to wit: the Missouri negro dialect; the extremist form of the backwoods Southwestern dialect; the ordinary "Pike County" dialect; and four modified varieties of this last. The shadings have not been done in a haphazard fashion, or by guesswork; but painstakingly, and with the trustworthy guidance and support of personal familiarity with these several forms of speech.

I make this explanation for the reason that without it many readers would suppose that all these characters were trying to talk alike and not succeeding.

—The Author

loquial" in your dictionary. Take special care to avoid **mixed diction,** a combination of standard and colloquial words.

MIXED DICTION	According to a Native American myth, the Great Creator *had a dog hanging around with him* when he created the earth.
CONSISTENT	According to a Native American myth, the Great Creator *was accompanied by a dog* when he created the earth.

3   Using regionalisms only when appropriate

Most national languages vary slightly from one geographical area to another. In American English, regional differences are most marked in pronunciation: a Texan overhearing a conversation between a New Yorker and a Georgian will not mistake either for a fellow Texan. But regional vocabularies differ somewhat, too. Southerners may say they *reckon,* meaning "think" or "suppose." People in Maine invite their Boston friends to come *down* rather than *up* (north) to visit. New Yorkers stand *on* (rather than *in*) line for a movie. Regional expressions are appropriate in writing addressed to local readers and may lend realism to regional description, but they should be avoided in writing intended for a general audience.

REGIONAL	The house where I spent my childhood was *down the road a piece* from a federal prison.
GENERAL	The house where I spent my childhood was *a short distance* from a federal prison.

4   Avoiding nonstandard language

Words and grammatical forms called **nonstandard** are used by many intelligent people who speak dialects other than standard English. In spoken and written standard English, however, these nonstandard forms are considered unacceptable. Examples include *nowheres;* such pronoun forms as *hisn, hern, hisself,* and *theirselves; them* as an adjective, as in *them dishes, them courses;* the expressions *this here* and *that there,* as in *that there elevator;* verb forms such as *knowed, throwed, hadn't ought,* and *could of;* and double negatives such as *didn't never* and *haven't no.* Dictionaries label such expressions "nonstandard" or "substandard." Avoid all nonstandard expressions in speaking and writing situations calling for standard English.

From the opening lines of *The Adventures of Huckleberry Finn:*

You don't know about me without you have read a book by the name of *The Adventures of Tom Sawyer;* but that ain't no matter. That book was made by Mr. Mark Twain, and he told the truth, mainly. There was things which he stretched; but mainly he told the truth. That is nothing. I never seen anybody but lied one time or another, without it was Aunt Polly, or the widow, or maybe Mary. Aunt Polly—Tom's Aunt Polly, she is—and Mary, and the widow Douglas is all told about in that book, which is mostly a true book, with some stretchers, as I said before.

appr
31a

5 Avoiding obsolete or archaic words and neologisms

Since our surroundings and our lives are constantly changing, some words pass out of use and others appear to fill new needs. **Obsolete** and **archaic** are dictionary labels for words or meanings of words that we never or rarely use but that appear in older documents and literature still read today. Obsolete words or meanings are no longer used at all—for example, *enwheel* ("to encircle") and *cote* ("to pass"). Archaic words or meanings occur now only in special contexts such as poetry—for example, *fast* ("near," as in *fast by the road*) and *belike* ("perhaps"). Both obsolete and archaic words are inappropriate in nonfiction writing for a general audience.

Neologisms are words created (or coined) so recently that they have not come into established use. An example is *prequel* (made up of *pre-*, meaning "before," and the ending of *sequel*), which is a movie or book that takes the story of an existing movie or book back in time. Some neologisms do become accepted as part of our general vocabulary. *Motel*, coined from *motor* and *hotel*, and *brunch*, meaning a combination of breakfast and lunch, are examples. But most neologisms pass quickly from the language. Unless such words serve a special purpose in your writing and are sure to be understood by your readers, you should avoid them.

6 Using technical words with care

All disciplines and professions rely on special words or give common words special meanings. Chemists speak of *esters* and *phosphatides*, geographers and mapmakers refer to *isobars* and *isotherms*, and literary critics write about *motifs* and *subtexts*. Printers use common words like *cut, foul,* and *slug* in special senses. Such technical language allows specialists to communicate precisely and economically with other specialists who share their vocabulary. But without explanation these words are meaningless to the nonspecialist. When you are writing for a general audience, avoid unnecessary technical terms. If your subject requires words the reader may not understand, be careful to define them. (See also 31c-4 for a discussion of jargon and overly technical and inflated language.)

7 Avoiding euphemisms and pretentious writing

A **euphemism** is a presumably inoffensive word that a writer or speaker substitutes for a word deemed potentially offensive or too blunt. Government officials use euphemism when they describe

appr
31a

an effort to cut waste in military spending as an *acquisitions-improvement program* or when they call nuclear war *nuclear engagement.* Because euphemisms conceal meaning instead of clarifying it, use them only when you know that blunt, truthful words would needlessly offend members of your audience.

People who write euphemistically also tend to decorate their prose with ornate phrases. Any writing that is more elaborate than its subject requires will sound pretentious, or excessively showy. Good writers choose their words for their exactness and economy. Pretentious writers choose them in the belief that fancy words will impress readers. They rarely will.

PRETENTIOUS   Many institutions of higher education recognize the need for youth at the threshold of maturity to confront the choice of life's endeavor and thus require students to select a field of concentration.

REVISED   Many colleges and universities force students to make decisions about their careers by requiring them to select a major.

When either of two words will say what you mean, prefer the small word to the big one, the common word to the uncommon one. If you want to say *It has begun to rain,* say so. Don't say *I perceive that moisture has commenced to precipitate earthward.*

8   Avoiding sexist and other biased language

Even when we do not mean it to, our language can reflect and perpetuate hurtful prejudices toward groups of people, especially racial, ethnic, religious, age, and sexual groups. (See 4d-1 for a discussion of the differences among prejudice, fact, opinion, and belief.) In any kind of speech or writing, a word such as *nigger, honky, mick, kike, fag, dike,* or *broad*—with or without additionally insulting adjectives—reflects more poorly on the user than on the person or persons designated. Unbiased language does not submit to stereotypes. It refers to people as they would wish to be referred to.

Among the most subtle and persistent biased language is that expressing narrow ideas about men's and women's roles, position, and value in society. This **sexist language** distinguishes needlessly between men and women in such matters as occupation, ability, behavior, temperament, and maturity. It can wound or irritate readers, and it indicates the writer's thoughtlessness or unfairness. The box on the next page suggests some ways of eliminating sexist language.

FILL IN THE BLANKS

Distribute copies of an essay with important words deleted, and ask students to fill in the blanks with the words they can find. Discuss the choices in class or in groups as a way of building students' vocabularies and of reaching consensus on questions of appropriateness and exactness.

appr
31a

ELIMINATING SEXIST LANGUAGE

1. Avoid demeaning and patronizing language.

SEXIST	Pushy broads are entering almost every occupation.
REVISED	*Women* are entering almost every occupation.
SEXIST	President Reagan came to Nancy's defense.
REVISED	President Reagan came to *Mrs. Reagan's* defense.

2. Avoid occupational or social stereotypes.

SEXIST	The caring doctor commends his nurse when she does a good job.
REVISED	Caring *doctors* commend *their nurses* on jobs well done.
SEXIST	Postmen are fairly well paid.
REVISED	*Letter carriers* are fairly well paid.
SEXIST	The grocery shopper should save her coupons.
REVISED	*Grocery shoppers* should save *their* coupons.

3. Avoid using *man* or words containing *man* to refer to all human beings.

SEXIST	Man has not reached the limits of social justice.
REVISED	*Humankind* (or *Humanity*) has not reached the limits of social justice.
SEXIST	The furniture consists entirely of man-made materials.
REVISED	The furniture consists entirely of *synthetic* materials.

4. Avoid using the generic *he* to refer to both genders. (See 8b-3, p. 248.)

SEXIST	The person who studies history knows his roots.
REVISED	The person who studies history knows *his or her* roots.
REVISED	*People* who study history know *their* roots.

appr
31a

EXERCISE 1

Replace words in the following sentences as needed for standard written English. Consult a dictionary to determine a word's appropriateness and to find suitable substitutes.

Example:

If negotiators get hyper during contract discussions, they may mess up chances for a settlement.

If negotiators *become excited or upset* during contract discussions, they may *harm* chances for a settlement.

1. The food shortages in some parts of Africa are so severe that tens of thousands of people have met their demise.
2. A few stockholders have been down on the company ever since it refused to stop conducting business in South Africa.
3. The most stubborn members of the administration still will not hearken to our pleas for a voice in college doings.
4. They bought a beaut of a Victorian house in a ritzy neighborhood.
5. A secretary often must support her boss even when she and he disagree.
6. During your first three months on the job, stifle your gripes and showcase your abilities for your boss.
7. Her arm often aches, but she says it doesn't bother her none.
8. Any candidate who understands the finest intricacies of democratic management and can thus covertly persuade the most recalcitrant legislators to do his every bidding could be elected governor of our fair state.
9. Too many Little League coaches know lots about baseball but not an awful lot about kids.
10. After every concert the cops hang around the parking lot until all the kids have taken off.

SAMPLE ANSWERS: EXERCISE 1

1. The food shortages in some parts of Africa are so severe that tens of thousands of people have <u>died</u>.
2. A few stockholders have been <u>critical of</u> the company ever since it refused to stop conducting business in South Africa.
3. The most stubborn members of the administration still will not <u>listen</u> to our <u>requests</u> for a voice in college <u>affairs</u>.
4. They bought a <u>beautiful</u> Victorian house in <u>an upper-class</u> neighborhood.
5. A secretary must support his or her boss even when they disagree.
6. During your first three months on the job, <u>refrain from complaining</u> and <u>demonstrate</u> your abilities to your <u>supervisor</u>.
7. Her arm often aches, but she says it doesn't both her.
8. Any candidate who understands politics well enough to persuade reluctant legislators without being obvious could be elected governor.
9. Too many Little League coaches know <u>a great deal</u> about baseball but <u>almost nothing</u> about <u>children</u>.
10. After every concert the police <u>remain in</u> the parking lot until all the <u>teenagers</u> have <u>left</u>.

31b Choosing the exact word

Good writers labor to find the words within the large vocabulary of standard English that fit their meaning exactly, with precisely the overtones they intend. Inexact words—wrong, vague, unspecific, or trite—weaken writing and often confuse readers.

1 Using the right word for your meaning

The precise expression of meaning requires understanding both the denotations and connotations of words. A word's **denotation** is the thing or idea it refers to, the meaning listed in the dic-

exact
31b

exact

31b

RESOURCES AND IDEAS

Theresa Ammirati and Ellen Strenski, "Using Astrology to Teach Connotation and Bias," *Exercise Exchange* 25 (1980): 9–11. The authors tell how to use the language in astrology books as a source of examples of connotation and bias.

PERSONAL RESPONSES

Give students a list of words and ask them to write out the personal connotations of each word. Asking students to share their responses with the class or a smaller group may further help them understand the potential richness of language.

---

tionary without reference to the emotional associations it may arouse in a reader. Using words according to their established denotations is essential if readers are to grasp your meaning. The person who writes *Older people must often endure infirmaries* has mistaken *infirmaries* for *infirmities*. In using the wrong word, the writer says something different from what he or she intended, thus either amusing or confusing the reader. The writer who says *The divergence between the estimate and the actual cost is surprising* has also missed the mark, though not as widely. The word needed is *discrepancy*, not *divergence*. The two words are second cousins, but they are not interchangeable. Some mistakes in diction occur because of confusion of **homonyms,** words such as *principle/principal* or *rain/reign/rein* that sound alike but have different spellings and meanings. (See 34a-1 for a list of commonly confused homonyms.) Whenever you are unsure of a word's exact meaning, consult your dictionary.

Writers miss the right word more often by misjudging its connotation than by mistaking its denotation. **Connotation** refers to the associations a word carries with it. Some connotations are personal, deriving from one's particular experiences. A person whose only experience with dogs was being bitten three times will have a different reaction to the word *dog* than will someone who lives with the warm memories of a childhood pet. Such personal associations aside, however, most people agree about the favorable or unfavorable connotations of words. To most readers, the connotations of *love, home,* and *peace* are favorable, whereas those of *lust, shack,* and *war* are unfavorable. Most of us prefer to hear our tastes described as *inexpensive* rather than *cheap.*

Understanding connotation is especially important in choosing among **synonyms,** words with approximately, but often not exactly, the same meanings. *Cry* and *weep* are similar, both denoting the shedding of tears; but *cry* more than *weep* connotes a sobbing sound accompanying the tears. *Sob* itself connotes broken, gasping crying, with tears, whereas *wail* connotes sustained sound, rising and falling in pitch, perhaps without tears. Used in the blank in the sentence *We were disturbed by his _____ing,* each of these words would evoke different sounds and images.

Tracking down the word whose connotation is exactly what you want can take time and effort. The most convenient resource is a dictionary, particularly the discussions of synonyms and their shades of meaning at the ends of many entries (see 32b-2 and 33c-2 for samples). Other useful resources are a thesaurus, which lists groups of synonyms, and a dictionary of synonyms, which both lists and defines them. (See 32a-3 for specific titles.)

EXERCISE 2

Revise the following sentences to replace any italicized word that is not used according to its established denotation. If the italicized word in a sentence is used correctly, circle the number preceding the sentence. Consult a dictionary if you are uncertain of a word's precise meaning.

Example:

Sam and Dave are going to Bermuda and Hauppauge, *respectfully*, for spring vacation.

Sam and Dave are going to Bermuda and Hauppauge, *respectively*, for spring vacation.

1. The *inference* of the report from the parents is that the school should care for their children in the afternoon.
2. Burning solid waste is not an *economic* way to generate power, but it eliminates the need for new dumping grounds.
3. The jury did not find the defendant's testimony *credible* and so convicted her.
4. Hospital personnel must wear protective clothing when tending a patient with a highly *communicative* disease.
5. I did not attend the lecture on artificial intelligence because I am *disinterested* in computers.
6. We've been without furniture for days, but now the movers are due to arrive *momentously*.
7. To support her argument she *sited* Mead's conclusion that schooling must challenge conventional views of the world.
8. After trying *continually* for two weeks to see my teacher, I finally complained to the dean.
9. One *affect* of the report is that doctors are less willing to order expensive tests for their patients.
10. Having been *deferred* from acting on impulse, she felt paralyzed by indecision.

EXERCISE 3

Describe how the connotation of each italicized word in the following sentences contributes to the writer's meaning. Give at least one synonym or related word that the writer could have used instead of the italicized word, and describe how the new word would alter the meaning. Consult a dictionary or thesaurus as necessary.

1. [The river] *slumbers* between broad prairies, *kissing* the long meadow grass, and *bathes* the overhanging boughs of elder bushes and willows or the roots of elms and ash trees and clumps of maples.　　　—NATHANIEL HAWTHORNE
2. The new earth, freshly *torn* from its parent sun, was a ball of *whirling* gases, *intensely* hot, *rushing* through the black

ANSWERS: EXERCISE 2

1. The <u>implication</u> of the report from the parents is that the school should care for their children in the afternoon.
2. Burning solid waste is not an <u>economical</u> way to generate power, but it eliminates the need for new dumping grounds.
3. Correct.
4. Hospital personnel must wear protective clothing when tending a patient with a highly <u>communicable</u> disease.
5. I did not attend the lecture on artificial intelligence because I am <u>uninterested</u> in computers.
6. We've been without furniture for days, but now the movers are due to arrive <u>momentarily</u>.
7. To support her argument, she <u>cited</u> Mead's conclusion that schooling must challenge conventional views of the world.
8. Correct.
9. One <u>effect</u> of the report has been that doctors are less willing to order expensive tests for their patients.
10. Having been <u>deterred</u> from acting on impulse, she felt paralyzed by indecision.

ANSWERS: EXERCISE 3

1. <u>Slumbered</u>, <u>kissing</u>, and <u>bathes</u> all connote gentle slowness in the movement of the river. Related words such as <u>lies</u>, <u>smacking</u>, and <u>showers</u> would connote the opposite.
2. <u>Torn</u>, <u>whirling</u>, <u>intensely</u>, <u>rushing</u>, and <u>immense</u> all connote great violence and magnitude. Weaker synonyms such as <u>separated</u>, <u>turning</u>, <u>very</u>, <u>moving</u>, and <u>large</u> would not convey the same extremes.
3. <u>Bluster</u>, <u>bravado</u>, and <u>flashing</u> connote the swagger of boys. Synonyms such as

exact

31b

noise, bravery, and glimmering would not convey the same strutting quality. Meadows connotes idyllic expanses in a way that fields, for instance, would not.

4. Modified connotes a lessening in the strength of principles—a meaning not specifically conveyed by the synonym changed. Pulverized connotes a more tangible sense of destruction than, say, demolish. Center—as opposed to say, middle or core—connotes a place around which competing forces might move.

5. Swoop connotes a bird's flight; a word like drive would not convey the same speed or ease of motion. Streaked connotes bright color, in contrast to the dark hills; words such as covered and dim would not convey the same contrast. Wheatstubble connotes a low, spiky landscape and intensifies the picture of harvested fields; even wheat stalks would not be so evocative.

spaces of the universe on a path and a speed controlled by *immense* forces.　　　–RACHEL CARSON

3. When the country loved it with a passion, baseball was boyhood eternal, all *bluster*, innocence, and *bravado flashing* across green *meadows* in the sunlight.　　–RUSSELL BAKER

4. I think all theories are suspect, that the finest principles may have to be *modified*, or may even be *pulverized* by the demands of life, and that one must find, therefore, one's own moral *center* and move through the world hoping that this center will guide one aright.　　–JAMES BALDWIN

5. After a long straight *swoop* across the pancakeflat prairies, hour after hour of harvested land *streaked* with yellow *wheat-stubble* to the horizon, it's exciting to see hills ahead, *dark* hills under clouds against the west.　–JOHN DOS PASSOS

2　Balancing the abstract and concrete, the general and specific

To understand a subject as you understand it, to experience it as you experience it, your readers need ample guidance from your words. When you describe a building as beautiful and nothing more, you force readers to provide their own conceptions of the features that make a building beautiful. If readers trouble to do the work you have assigned them—and they may not—they will call up diverse images of the many beautiful buildings they have seen, not a coherent image of the one you have seen. In evading your responsibility to be exact, you will have failed to communicate your meaning. Effective writing demands that abstract and general words like *beautiful* and *building*, which convey the broad outlines of ideas and objects, be balanced by concrete and specific words that make the ideas and objects sharp and firm. For instance, you might describe a *Victorian brick courthouse faced with stately arched windows and trimmed with ornate sandstone carvings.*

Abstract words name qualities and ideas: *beauty, inflation, depression, labor, management, truth, culture, network, liberal, conservative.* **Concrete words** name things we can know by our five senses of sight, hearing, touch, taste and smell: *brick, sandstone, arched, bacon, apple, sticky, crisp, hard.*

General words name classes or groups of things, such as *buildings, weather,* or *birds,* and include all the varieties of the class. **Specific words** limit a general class like *buildings* by naming one of its varieties, such as *Victorian courthouse, office tower,* or *hut. Weather* includes *sunshine, drought, rain, windstorm,* and *cyclone. Birds* include *sparrows, eagles, geese, parrots, bobolinks,* and *vultures.* But *general* and *specific* are relative terms. *Rain be-*

exact
31b

comes a general word in relation to *drizzle*, *sprinkle*, and *downpour*, and *downpours* can be *continuous* or *sudden*. You become more and more specific as you move from a general class to a unique item, from *bird* to *pet bird* to *parrot* to *my parrot Moyshe*. (See 1e on distinguishing between the general and specific in shaping ideas.)

Abstract and general words are useful in the broad statements that set the course for your writing.

The wild horse in America has a *romantic* history.

We must be *free* from *government interference* in our *affairs*.

Relations between the sexes today are only a *little* more *relaxed* than they were in the past.

But these statements must be developed with concrete and specific detail. Writing seldom fails because it lacks abstraction and generality. It often fails because it lacks concrete and specific words to nail down meaning and make the writing vivid, real, and clear. In your own writing choose the concrete and specific word over the general and abstract. Avoid words such as *interesting*, *nice*, *area*, and *nature* that are essentially meaningless (see also 31c-1). When your meaning does call for an abstract or general word, make sure you define it, explain it, and narrow it with the concrete and specific words that most precisely reflect your knowledge and experience. Look at how concrete and specific information turns vague sentences into exact ones in the examples below.

VAGUE	The size of his hands made his smallness real. [How big were his hands? How small was he?]
EXACT	Not until I saw his white, doll-like hands did I realize that he stood at least a full head shorter than most other men.
VAGUE	The long flood caused a lot of awful destruction in the town. [How long did the flood last? What destruction did it cause, and why was the destruction awful?]
EXACT	The flood waters, which rose swiftly and then stayed stubbornly high for days, killed at least six townspeople and made life a misery for the hundreds who had to evacuate their ruined homes and stores.

EXERCISE 4

Make the following paragraph vivid by expanding the sentences with appropriate details of your own choosing. Concentrate es-

ANSWERS: EXERCISE 4

Possible Revision

I remember <u>as if it were last week</u> how <u>frightened</u> I felt the first time I <u>neared</u> Mrs. Murphy's second-grade class. <u>Just three days before</u>, I had moved from a <u>rural one-street</u> town in Missouri to a suburb of Chicago <u>where the houses and the people were jammed together</u>. My new school looked <u>monstrous</u> from the outside and seemed <u>forbiddingly dim</u> inside as I walked haltingly down the <u>endless</u> corridor toward the classroom. The class was <u>clamorous</u> as I neared the door; but when I <u>slipped inside</u>, <u>twenty faces</u> became <u>still</u> and <u>gawked</u> at me. I felt <u>terrified</u> and <u>longed for</u> a place to hide. However, in a <u>booming</u> voice Mrs. Murphy <u>ordered</u> me to the front of the room to introduce myself.

exact
31b

pecially on substituting concrete and specific words for the abstract and general ones in italics.

I remember *clearly* how *awful* I felt the first time I *attended* Mrs. Murphy's second-grade class. I had *recently* moved from a *small* town in Missouri to a *crowded* suburb of Chicago. My new school looked *big* from the outside and seemed *dark* inside as I *walked* down the *long* corridor toward the classroom. The class was *noisy* as I neared the door; but when I *entered*, *everyone* became *quiet* and *looked* at me. I felt *uncomfortable* and *wanted* a place to hide. However, in a *loud* voice Mrs. Murphy *directed* me to the front of the room to introduce myself.

EXERCISE 5

For each abstract or general word below, give at least two other words or phrases that illustrate increasing specificity or concreteness. Consult a dictionary as needed. Use the most specific or concrete word from each group in a sentence of your own.

Example:

tired, *sleepy, droopy-eyed*

We stopped for the night when I became so *droopy-eyed* that the road blurred.

1. fabric	8. flower	15. crime
2. delicious	9. serious	16. smile (*verb*)
3. car	10. pretty	17. sick
4. narrow-minded	11. teacher	18. desire (*verb*)
5. reach (*verb*)	12. nice	19. candy
6. green	13. virtue	20. misfortune
7. walk (*verb*)	14. angry	

SAMPLE ANSWERS: EXERCISE 5

1. fabric, upholstery fabric, velvet
   She chose a wine-colored <u>velvet</u> for backing the pillow.
2. delicious, tart, lemony
   He made a meringue pie, <u>lemony</u> and delicately brown.
3. car, foreign car, Volvo station wagon
   He bought a 1973 <u>Volvo station wagon</u>.
4. narrow-minded, prejudiced, sexist
   My uncle's <u>sexist</u> attitudes cause many arguments in our family.
5. reach, stretch, lunge
   Each child <u>lunged</u> for the prize thrown by the clown.
6. green, dark green, bilious green
   The algae covered the surface with a <u>bilious green</u> scum.
7. walk, march, goose-step
   The soldiers <u>goose-stepped</u> menacingly.
8. flower, daisy, ox-eyed daisy
   Some people call the <u>ox-eyed daisy</u> a "brown-eyed Susan."
9. serious, solemn, grim
   His <u>grim</u> expression frightened us.
10. pretty; with small, regular features; with a button nose and a tiny, smiling mouth
    The infant, <u>with a button nose and a tiny, smiling mouth</u>, was a perfect model for baby products.
11. teacher, history teachers, American history teacher
    My <u>American history teacher</u> requires three research papers.

exact
31b

3 **Using Idioms**

Idioms are expressions in any language whose meanings cannot be determined simply from the words in them or whose component words cannot be predicted by any rule of grammar; often, they violate conventional grammar. Examples of English idioms include *put up with*, *plug away at*, and *make off with*. Because they are not governed by rules, idioms usually cause particular difficulty for people learning to speak and write a new language. For instance, those learning English as a second language find it easy to confuse certain prepositions such as *at/in/on* and *of/for*. But English prepositions can cause problems for native speakers of English, too, especially when a preposition is combined with an adjective or a verb. Some typical idioms with prepositions are listed on the next page for reference. Check a dictionary if you are unsure of what preposition to use with an idiom (see 32b-2).

abide *by* a rule
abide *in* a place or state

accords *with*
according *to*

accuse *of* a crime

adapt *from* a source
adapt *to* a situation

agree *with* a person
agree *to* a proposal
agree *on* a plan

angry *with*

capable *of*

charge *for* a purchase
charge *with* a crime

compare *to* something in a different class
compare *with* something in the same class

concur *with* a person
concur *in* an opinion

contend *with* a person
contend *for* a principle

differ *with* a person
differ *from* in appearance
differ *about* or *over* a question

identical *with* or *to*

impatient *at* her conduct
impatient *of* restraint
impatient *for* a raise
impatient *with* a person

independent *of*

inferior *to*

infer *from*

oblivious *of* something forgotten
oblivious *of* or *to* one's surroundings

occupied *by* a person
occupied *in* study
occupied *with* a thing

part *from* a person
part *with* a possession

prior *to*

rewarded *by* the judge
rewarded *for* something done
rewarded *with* a gift

superior *to*

wait *at* a place
wait *for* a train, a person
wait *on* a customer

12. nice, considerate, sympathetic
I need a <u>sympathetic</u> friend.
13. virtue, honesty, frankness
His <u>frankness</u> was refreshing after I had heard so much flattery.
14. angry, furious, raging
<u>Raging</u> uncontrollably, Andy insulted everyone around him.
15. crime, theft, armed robbery
Drug addicts sometimes commit <u>armed robbery</u> to pay for their habits.
16. smile, closed-lip smile, smirk
Her contemptuous <u>smirk</u> inflamed him even more.
17. sick, feverish, delirious
As her temperature rose above 104°, Ellen became <u>delirious</u>.
18. desire, long for, crave
When my mother discovered that she was diabetic, she <u>craved</u> sweets as she never had before.
19. candy, chocolate, Almond Joy
My little brother would be happy to subsist on <u>Almond Joys</u>.
20. misfortune, adversity, calamity
Losing his sister in the accident was a <u>calamity</u> that Jamie could not bear.

EXERCISE 6

Insert the preposition that correctly completes each idiom in the following sentences. Consult the preceding list or a dictionary as needed.

Example:

I disagree _____ many feminists who say women should not be homemakers.

I disagree *with* many feminists who say women should not be homemakers.

1. He had waited for years, growing impatient _____ her demands and _____ the money that she would leave to him.
2. The writer compared gorilla society _____ human society.
3. They agreed _____ most things, but they differed consistently _____ how to raise their child.
4. I was rewarded _____ my persistence _____ an opportunity to meet the senator.
5. He would sooner part _____ his friends than part _____ his Corvette.

ANSWERS: EXERCISE 6

1. He had waited for years, growing impatient <u>with</u> her demands and <u>for</u> the money that she would leave to him.
2. The writer compared gorilla society <u>to</u> human society.
3. They agreed <u>on</u> most things, but they differed consistently <u>about</u> (or <u>over</u>) how to raise their child.
4. I was rewarded <u>for</u> my persistence <u>with</u> an opportunity to meet the senator.
5. He would sooner part <u>from</u> his friends than part <u>with</u> his Corvette.

exact
31b

4 Using figurative language

Figurative language expresses or implies comparisons between different ideas or objects. The sentence *As I try to write, I can think of nothing to say* is literal. The sentence *As I try to write, my mind is a blank slab of black asphalt* is figurative. The abstract concept of having nothing to say has become concrete, something that readers can understand with their senses as bare, hard, and unyielding.

Figurative language is commonplace. We sprinkle our conversation with figures: having *slept like a log*, we get up to find it *raining cats and dogs*. The sports pages abound in figurative language: the Yankees *shell* the Royals, and the Cowboys *embark* on another season. Slang, too, is largely figurative: you may think chemistry *rots*, but you can *get into* physics.

The rapid exchange of speech leaves little time for inventiveness, and most figures of daily conversation, like hastily written news stories, are worn and hackneyed. But writing gives you time to reject the tired figure and to search out the fresh words and phrases that will carry meaning concretely and vividly.

RESOURCES AND IDEAS

Stephen Sossaman, "Detroit Designers: A Game to Teach Metaphors," *Exercise Exchange* 21 (1976): 2–3. Sossaman points out that car names provide good examples of metaphoric language.

The two most common figures of speech are the **simile** and the **metaphor.** Both compare two things of different classes, often one abstract and the other concrete. A simile makes the comparison explicit and usually begins with *like* or *as*.

> We force their [children's] growth as if they were chicks in a poultry factory. —ARNOLD TOYNBEE

> To hold America in one's thoughts is like holding a love letter in one's hand—it has so special a meaning. —E. B. WHITE

Instead of stating a comparison, the metaphor implies it, omitting such words as *like* or *as*.

> I refuse to accept the notion that nation after nation must spiral down a militaristic stairway into the hell of nuclear war.
> —MARTIN LUTHER KING, JR.

> A school is a hopper into which children are heaved while they are young and tender; therein they are pressed into certain standard shapes and covered from head to heels with official rubber stamps. —H. L. MENCKEN

**exact
31b**

Two other figures of speech, **personification** and **hyperbole,** are less common than metaphor and simile. Personification treats ideas and objects as if they were human.

> The economy consumes my money and gives me little in return.

> I could hear the whisper of snowflakes, nudging each other as they fell.

Hyperbole deliberately exaggerates.

> She appeared in a mile of billowing chiffon, flashing a rhinestone as big as an ostrich egg.

> I'm going to cut him up in small cubes and fry him in deep fat.

To be successful, figurative language must be fresh and unstrained, calling attention not to itself but to the writer's meaning. If readers reject your language as trite or overblown, they may reject your message. One kind of figurative language gone wrong is the **mixed metaphor,** in which the writer combines two or more incompatible figures.

> **MIXED**   He often hatched new ideas, using them to unlock the doors of opportunity.

Since metaphors often generate visual images in the mind of the reader, a mixed metaphor can create a ludicrous scene.

> **MIXED**   Various thorny problems that we try to sweep under the rug continue to bob up all the same.

To revise a mixed metaphor, follow through consistently with just one image.

> **IMPROVED**   Various thorny problems that we try to weed out continue to thrive all the same.

EXERCISE 7

Identify each figure of speech in the following sentences as a simile or a metaphor and analyze how it contributes to the writer's meaning.

1. All artists quiver under the lash of adverse criticism.
   —CATHERINE DRINKER BOWEN
2. Louisa spends the entire day in blue, limpid boredom. The caressing sting of it appears to be, for her, like the pleasure of lemon, or the coldness of salt water.
   —ELIZABETH HARDWICK
3. Every writer, in a roomful of writers, wants to be the best, and the judge, or umpire, or referee is soon overwhelmed and shouted down like a chickadee trying to take charge of a caucus of crows.   —JAMES THURBER
4. And meanwhile, like enormous, irresistible, gleaming and spinning toys, there are the missiles and their warheads, each one more destructive than one thousand Hiroshima bombs, loaded with magnificent navigational equipment more fun to play with than anything else on earth or in space.   —LEWIS THOMAS
5. At best today it [the railroad in America] resembles a fabled ruin, a vast fallen empire. More commonly it suggests a stodgy and even dirtier-looking subway; a sprawling anach-

ANSWERS: EXERCISE 7

1. Lash of adverse criticism is a metaphor that makes clear the words' power to hurt.
2. Blue, limpid boredom is a metaphor that gives boredom—an abstraction—some of the concrete qualities of water. The word like does not produce a simile, just a literal likeness: the pleasure of the state of boredom is like the pleasure of lemon or the coldness of salt water.
3. Here are similes: The judge is like a chickadee and the roomful of writers is like a caucus of crows.
4. The simile, comparing missiles and warheads to very amusing toys, belittles the people who play with such toys and, at the same time, makes the missiles more frightening because they are not toys.
5. Two similes describe the railroad as a vast fallen empire and as a stodgy and even dirtier-looking subway, stalled between stations.

exact
31b

ronism that conveys not ruin but mess, not age but senility, not something speeding across continents but stalled between stations. —LOUIS KRONENBERGER

ANSWERS: EXERCISE 8

Individual response.

EXERCISE 8

Invent appropriate figurative language of your own (simile, metaphor, hyperbole, or personification) to describe each scene or quality below, and use the figure effectively in a sentence.

Example:

the attraction of a lake on a hot day
The small waves *like fingers beckoned* us irresistibly.

1. the sound of a kindergarten classroom
2. people waiting in line to buy tickets to a rock concert
3. the politeness of strangers meeting for the first time
4. a streetlight seen through dense fog
5. the effect of watching television for ten hours straight

RESOURCES AND IDEAS

Don L. F. Nilsen, "Clichés, Trite Sayings, Dead Metaphors, and Stale Figures of Speech in Composition Instruction," *College Composition and Communication* 27 (1976): 278–82. Nilsen points out that reviving dead metaphors and clichés in class discussion can create an awareness of figurative language.

exact
31b

5 **Avoiding trite expressions**

Trite expressions, or **clichés,** are phrases so old and so often repeated that they become stale. They include worn figures of speech, such as *heavy as lead, thin as a rail, wise as an owl;* stale scraps from literature, such as *to be or not to be, trip the light fantastic, gone with the wind;* adjectives and nouns that have become inseparable, such as *acid test, crushing blow, ripe old age;* and simply overused phrases, such as *point with pride, easier said than done, better late than never.* Many of these expressions were probably once fresh and forceful, but constant use has dulled them. Using clichés will weaken your writing by suggesting that you have not thought about what you are saying and have resorted to the easiest phrase. To prevent clichés from sliding into your writing, be wary of any expression you have heard or used before.

The following list contains just a few of the dozens of trite expressions.

add insult to injury	ladder of success
beyond the shadow of a doubt	moving experience
brought back to reality	needle in a haystack
cool, calm, and collected	sadder but wiser
dyed in the wool	sneaking suspicion
face the music	sober as a judge
gentle as a lamb	stand in awe
hard as a rock	strong as an ox
hit the nail on the head	tired but happy
hour of need	tried and true

You can avoid such expressions by substituting fresh words of your own or by restating the idea in plain language.

TRITE
: A *motley crowd* of the singer's *ardent admirers* awaited her arrival in *breathless silence.*

REVISED
: *Dressed in wild, colorful costumes,* a crowd of the singer's *fans* awaited her arrival in *eager silence.*

EXERCISE 9

Revise the following sentences to eliminate trite expressions.

Example:

The basketball team had almost seized victory, but it faced the test of truth in the last quarter of the game.

The basketball team *seemed about to win,* but the *real test* came in the last quarter of the game.

1. These disastrous consequences of the war have shaken the small nation to its roots.
2. Some say that liberal arts majors face an uphill climb getting jobs in business; others observe that corporations have been looking high and low for liberal arts students.
3. When my father retired from the gas company after thirty long years, he was honored to receive a large clock in recognition of his valued service.
4. Sam shouldered his way through the crowd, hoping to catch a glimpse of the actress who had become the woman of his dreams.
5. My new car was supposed to be a technological triumph, but the catalytic converter started smelling to high heaven after only 500 miles.

SAMPLE ANSWERS: EXERCISE 9

1. These <u>disasters</u> of the war have shaken the small nation <u>severely.</u>
2. Some say that liberal arts majors face <u>difficulty</u> getting jobs in business; others observe that corporations <u>are</u> deliberately seeking liberal arts students.
3. When my father retired from the gas company after <u>thirty years</u>, he was honored <u>by a gift of</u> a large clock.
4. Sam shouldered his way through the crowd, <u>hoping to glimpse</u> the actress <u>he idolized.</u>
5. My new car was supposed to be <u>technologically flawless</u>, but the catalytic converter started smelling <u>terrible</u> after only 500 miles.

31c Avoiding wordiness

Avoiding wordiness means cutting whatever adds nothing to your meaning or the freshness of your writing. In editing your sentences, locate the forceful and exact words that are essential to your meaning. Cross out all the empty words; cut out repetition that neither clarifies nor emphasizes your meaning; and be sure you have used the most direct grammatical form to express your ideas. Don't sacrifice necessary detail or original expression for mere brevity, however. Concise writing does not waste words but still includes the concrete and specific details that make meaning clear. In concise writing the length of an expression is appropriate to the thought.

**w
31c**

WAYS TO ELIMINATE WORDINESS

1. Cut empty words and phrases (31c-1).

WORDY   The highly pressured nature of critical-care nursing is due to the patients' life-threatening illness.

REVISED   Critical-care nursing *is highly pressured because* the patients have life-threatening illnesses.

2. Cut unnecessary repetition (31c-2).

WORDY   Critical-care nurses must have steady nerves to care for patients who are critically ill.

REVISED   Critical-care nurses must have steady nerves to *help very sick* patients.

3. Simplify word groups and sentences (31c-3).

WORDY   The nurses must have possession of interpersonal skills and combine them with medical skills.

REVISED   The nurses must *possess* interpersonal *and medical* skills.

4. Avoid jargon (31c-4).

WORDY   It is considered by most health professionals that the critical-care nurse is an essential component in the improvement of the patient from the status of critical care to that of intermediate care or even that of home care.

REVISED   Most health professionals *consider* the critical-care nurse *essential to the patient's improvement* from *critical to intermediate or even home care.*

**W
31c**

CUTTING WORDS

Before your students hand in their essays, ask them to cut a specific number of words (ten to fifteen for a start) without harming the meaning. This approach can work with paragraphs as well and makes a good small-group activity.

1   **Cutting empty words and phrases**

Writers sometimes resort to empty words and phrases, either thinking that they sound authoritative or leaning on them when solid words will not come. But empty expressions simply fill space, and they should be eliminated in revision.

Filler phrases say in several words what a single word can say as well.

FOR	SUBSTITUTE
at all times	always
at the present time	now
at this point in time	now
in the nature of	like
for the purpose of	for
in order to	to
until such time as	until
for the reason that	because
due to the fact that	because
because of the fact that	because
by virtue of the fact that	because
in the event that	if
by means of	by
in the final analysis	finally

Some filler phrases—such as *all things considered*, *as far as I'm concerned*, and *for all intents and purposes*—can be cut entirely with no loss in meaning.

WORDY	*For all intents and purposes*, few women have yet achieved equal pay for equal work.
CONCISE	Few women have yet achieved equal pay for equal work.

All-purpose words, as their name implies, could mean almost anything. They include *angle, area, aspect, case, character, factor, field, kind, situation, thing,* and *type.* Because all-purpose words convey so little information, they almost always clutter and complicate the sentences they appear in.

WORDY	Because I chose the *field* of chemistry as my major, the whole *character* of my attitude toward the *area* of learning has changed.
CONCISE	Majoring in chemistry has changed my attitude toward learning.
WORDY	The *type* of large expenditures on advertising that manufacturers must make is a very important *aspect* of the cost of detergents.
CONCISE	Manufacturers' large advertising expenditures increase the cost of detergents.

EXERCISE 10

Revise the following sentences to achieve conciseness by cutting filler phrases and all-purpose words.

Example:

I came to college because of many factors, but most of all because of the fact that I want a career in medicine.

w

31c

SAMPLE ANSWERS: EXERCISE 10

1. Some lawyers still believe that <u>advertising will</u> damage their profession.
2. <u>Most people</u> are too absorbed in their own lives to care much <u>about others</u>.
3. <u>I like baseball best</u> when the game <u>seems almost over</u> and the home

team's slugger hits the winning run out of the park.

4. <u>Their athletic abilities rescue</u> a few unlucky teenagers <u>from</u> the pressures <u>of poverty</u>.

5. <u>One drawback</u> of majoring in Asian art <u>is that</u>, except for <u>rare</u> teaching and curatorial positions, jobs are <u>and probably will remain scarce</u>.

I came to college *primarily because* I want a career in medicine.

1. Some lawyers still believe that advertising is a thing that will damage their profession.

2. The fact is that most people are too absorbed in their own lives to care much about the situations of others.

3. The baseball situation I like best is when the game seems to be over, for all intents and purposes, and the home team's slugger hits the winning run out of the park.

4. By virtue of their athletic abilities, a few lucky teenagers are able to escape the types of pressures that living in a poverty situation can create.

5. One aspect of majoring in Asian art is a distinct drawback: except for a few rare teaching and curatorial positions, jobs are not available now and probably will not be available for some time to come.

2   Avoiding unnecessary repetition

Deliberately repeating words for parallelism or emphasis may clarify meaning and enhance coherence (see 17b and 18b). But unnecessary repetition weakens sentences. Avoid flabby repetition like that illustrated in the following example.

WORDY	The machine *crushes* the *ore* into fine bits and dumps the *crushed ore* into a bin.
CONCISE	The machine pulverizes the ore and dumps it into a bin.

Notice that using one word two different ways within a sentence is especially confusing.

CONFUSING	Preschool instructors play a *role* in the child's understanding of male and female *roles*.
CLEAR	Preschool instructors contribute to the child's understanding of male and female roles.

The simplest kind of useless repetition is the **redundant phrase,** a phrase that says the same thing twice, such as *few in number* and *large in size*. Some of the most common redundant phrases are listed below. (The unneeded words are italicized.)

biography *of his life*	*important* (*basic*) essentials
consensus *of opinion*	puzzling *in nature*
cooperate *together*	repeat *again*
final completion	return *again*
frank and honest exchange	square (round) *in shape*
habitual custom	*surrounding* circumstances

A related form of redundancy is repetition of the same idea in slightly different words. In the following sentences, the unneeded phrases are italicized.

WORDY	Theodore Fontane began his writing career late in life *at a relatively old age.*
WORDY	Many unskilled workers *without training in a particular job* are unemployed *and don't have any work.*

EXERCISE 11

Revise the following sentences to achieve conciseness. Concentrate on eliminating unnecessary or confusing repetition and redundancy.

> *Example:*
>
> Because the circumstances surrounding the cancellation of classes were murky and unclear, the editor of the student newspaper assigned a staff reporter to investigate and file a report on the circumstances.
>
> Because the circumstances leading to the cancellation of classes were unclear, the editor of the student newspaper assigned a staffer to investigate and report the story.

1. In today's world in the last quarter of the twentieth century, security has become a more compelling goal than social reform.
2. Deadly nightshade is aptly named. It has small white flowers and deep black fruit. The fruit looks like night, and it also looks like death. The fruit does happen to be poisonous, too.
3. As they embark on the beginning of an operation, all these specialists—the surgeon, the anesthetist, and the operating-room nurses—have specialized tasks to perform.
4. The disastrous drought was devastating to crops, but the farmers cooperated together to help each other out.
5. In deciding whether to choose a career in the field of dentistry, remember that some experts predict a future decline in the incomes of all health professionals.

SAMPLE ANSWERS: EXERCISE 11

1. <u>Today</u>, security has become a more compelling goal than social reform.
2. Deadly nightshade is aptly named: <u>its small white flowers become deep black, poisonous fruit the color of night and death.</u>
3. As they <u>begin</u> an operation, <u>the</u> surgeon, the anesthetist, and the operating-room <u>nurses all have</u> specialized tasks to perform.
4. The <u>drought devastated</u> crops, but the farmers <u>cooperated</u> to help each <u>other</u>.
5. In deciding whether to <u>become a dentist</u>, remember that some experts predict <u>a decline</u> in the incomes of all health professionals.

3 | **Simplifying word groups and sentences**

Choose the simplest and most direct grammatical construction that fits your meaning. Don't use a clause if a phrase will do; don't use a phrase if a word will do. *The strength that the panther has, the strength of the panther,* and *the panther's strength* mean the same thing. But the first takes six words, the last only three.

w
31c

Wordy	The figurine, which was carved from a piece of ivory, measured three inches.
Revised	The figurine, carved of ivory, measured three inches.
Concise	The carved ivory figurine measured three inches.
Wordy	People with jobs that are low in pay are more likely to develop problems in their health.
Concise	People with low-paying jobs are more likely to develop health problems.

REWRITE

Give students a particularly wordy sentence, and ask them to see who can rewrite it using the fewest words. This activity also works with whole paragraphs and can be used in small groups.

(See 16b for advice on the ways to subordinate information.)

You can streamline and strengthen sentences by choosing strong verbs that advance the action rather than weak verbs that merely mark time. Weak verbs and their baggage of extra words flatten sentences just where they should be liveliest and pad them needlessly.

Wordy	The painting *is a glorification of* Queen Victoria.
Concise	The painting *glorifies* Queen Victoria.

In the second sentence the direct, evocative verb *glorifies* substitutes for the colorless verb *is*, the long noun *glorification*, and the preposition *of*. Wordy constructions of a weak verb such as *is*, *has*, or *make* plus an adjective or noun commonly clutter writing.

Wordy	I *am desirous* of teaching music to children.
Concise	I *want* to teach music to children.
Wordy	He *had the sense* that she would die.
Concise	He *sensed* that she would die.
Wordy	Though they *made some advancement* in the next hours, they still failed to reach camp.
Concise	Though they *advanced* in the next hours, they still failed to reach camp.

Passive constructions usually contain more words (and much more indirectness) than active constructions. Revise passive constructions by shifting their verbs to the active voice and positioning the actor as the subject. (See also 7h and 18d.)

Wordy	*The building had been designed by the architects* six years earlier, and *the plans had been reviewed by no one* before *construction was begun*.
Concise	*The architects had designed the building* six years earlier, and *no one had reviewed the plans* before *construction began*.

w
31c

Whenever possible, avoid sentences beginning with the expletive constructions *there is* and *there are*. Revise such constructions by removing *there*, moving the subject to the beginning of the sentence, and substituting a strong verb for *is* or *are*. (See also 18e.)

WORDY	*There are several plots that are repeated* in television drama.
CONCISE	*Several plots occur repeatedly* in television drama.

EXERCISE 12

Make the following sentences as concise as possible. Simplify grammatical structures, replace weak verbs with strong ones, and eliminate passive and expletive constructions.

Example:

He was taking some exercise in the park when several thugs were suddenly ahead in his path.

He was *exercising* (or *jogging* or *strolling*) in the park when several thugs suddenly *loomed* in his path.

1. The new goal posts were torn down by vandals before the first game, and the science building windows were broken.
2. The house on Hedron Street that is brightly lighted belongs to a woman who was once a madam.
3. I am aware that most people of about my age are bored by politics, but I myself am becoming more and more interested in the subject.
4. When a social reform is taking root, such as affirmative action in education and business, it is followed by backlash from those for whom the reform is not directly beneficial.
5. The attendance at the conference was lower than we expected, but there is evidence that the results of the meeting have been spread by word of mouth.

SAMPLE ANSWERS: EXERCISE 12

1. <u>Vandals tore down</u> the new goal posts before the first game <u>and broke</u> windows in the science building.
2. The <u>brightly lighted</u> house on Hedron Street belongs to <u>an ex-madam</u>.
3. I know that <u>politics bores</u> most people <u>my age</u>, but <u>it interests me</u> more and more.
4. When a social reform such as affirmative action in education and business takes root, <u>a backlash follows</u> from those <u>not directly benefiting</u>.
5. The attendance at the conference was lower than we expected, but evidently the results of the meeting <u>have spread</u> by word of mouth.

4 Avoiding jargon

31c

Jargon is the special vocabulary of any discipline or profession—the terminology that permits doctors, economists, art historians, and others to communicate clearly and efficiently with their colleagues (see 31a-6). But *jargon* also commonly describes any vague, inflated language that states relatively simple ideas in unnecessarily complicated ways. The directions for using a shower head tell us that *this spray system will allow the user to reduce the mean diameter of the spray spectrum* instead of simply saying that *the nozzle will concentrate the spray*. Jargon often sounds as if the writer studied all the guidelines for being exact and concise and then set out to violate every one.

> **JARGON** The necessity for individuals to become separate entities in their own right may impel children to engage in open rebelliousness against parental authority or against sibling influence, with resultant confusion of those being rebelled against.
>
> **TRANSLATION** Children's natural desire to become themselves may make them rebel against bewildered parents or siblings.
>
> **JARGON** The weekly social gatherings stimulate networking among members of management from various divisions, with the aim of developing contacts and maximizing the flow of creative information.
>
> **TRANSLATION** The weekly parties give managers from different divisions a chance to meet and to share ideas.

ANSWER: EXERCISE 13

Possible Revision

After <u>much thought</u>, he <u>concluded</u> that carcinogens <u>could be treated like automobiles</u>. Rather than giving in <u>to a fear</u> of cancer, we <u>should balance the</u> benefits we receive from potential carcinogens (<u>such as</u> plastic and pesticides) against the damage <u>they do</u>. <u>Similarly</u>, rather than responding irrationally to <u>the pollution</u> caused by automobiles, we <u>have decided to live with them <u>and enjoy</u> their benefits <u>while simultaneously working to improve them</u>.

W
31c

REVISING STUDENT PARAGRAPHS

Choose three or four paragraphs from your students' essays that demonstrate imprecise language—wordiness, slang, colloquialisms, slanted language, and so on—and duplicate them for distribution in class. Have students work individually or in groups, first to define the problems in the writing and then to revise the paragraphs to improve them.

EXERCISE 13

Make the following passage as concise as possible. Eliminate wordiness by cutting unneeded or repeated words and by simplifying both words and grammatical structures. Consult a dictionary as needed. Be merciless.

Example:

The nursery school teacher education training sessions involve active interfacing with preschool children of the appropriate age as well as intensive peer interaction in the form of role plays.

Training for nursery school teachers involves *interaction* with *preschoolers* and *role playing with peers*.

At the end of a lengthy line of reasoning, he came to the conclusion that the situation with carcinogens [cancer-causing substances] should be regarded as analogous to the situation with the automobile. Rather than giving in to an irrational fear of cancer, we should consider all aspects of the problem in a balanced and dispassionate frame of mind, making a total of the benefits received from potential carcinogens (plastics, pesticides, and other similar products) and measuring said total against the damage done by such products. This is the nature of most discussions about the automobile. Rather than responding irrationally to the visual, aural, and air pollution caused by automobiles, we have decided to live with them (while simultaneously working to improve on them) for the benefits brought to society as a whole.

CHAPTER 32

Using the Dictionary

HIGHLIGHTS

Chapter 32 describes the information provided in a good dictionary, summarizes briefly the characteristics of several widely used desk dictionaries and some unabridged and specialized dictionaries, and explains typical entries from two abridged dictionaries to help students find information. Although the unavoidable accumulation of detail in such a brief chapter makes dense reading in places, the chapter is organized for easy reference so that you and your students can single out the most useful sections. Throughout the handbook, students are urged to consult a dictionary for answers to particular questions—the right preposition to use in an idiom, the usage status of a word, the forms of an irregular verb, and the like. No other supplementary reference will serve students as well as a good desk dictionary, as long as they know how to use it and do so. Students should be required, whenever practicable, to purchase one of the standard desk dictionaries.

Consulting a dictionary can strengthen your choice of words. It can show you what words fit your needs (see Chapter 31); it can help you build your vocabulary (see Chapter 33); and it can show you how to spell words (see Chapter 34). It can answer most of the questions about words you may ask. This chapter will show you how to choose a dictionary that suits your purpose, how to read a dictionary without difficulty, and how to work with a dictionary as a flexible, compact, and thorough word reference.

An ordinary dictionary records in an alphabetical list the current usage and meaning of the words of a language. To do this, it includes a word's spelling, syllables, pronunciation, origin, meanings, grammatical functions, and grammatical forms. For some words the dictionary may provide a label indicating the status of the word according to geography, time, style, or subject matter. It may also list other words closely related in meaning and explain the distinctions among them. Some dictionaries include quotations illustrating a word's history or special uses. Many dictionaries include additional reference information, such as an essay on the history of English, a vocabulary of rhymes, names and locations of colleges, and tables of weights and measures.

32a Choosing a dictionary

1 Abridged dictionaries

Abridged dictionaries are the most practical for everyday use. Often called desk dictionaries because of their convenient size, they usually list 100,000 to 150,000 words and concentrate on fairly common words and meanings. Though you may sometimes need to consult an unabridged or a more specialized dictionary, a good abridged dictionary will serve most reference needs for writing and reading. Any of the following abridged dictionaries, listed alphabetically, is dependable.

The American Heritage Dictionary, 2nd coll. ed. (1982). This dictionary's most obvious feature is its wealth of illustrations: more than 3000 photographs, drawings, and maps. The dictionary includes foreign words among the main entries and has separate sections on abbreviations and geographical and biographical names. The definitions are arranged in clusters of related meanings, with the most common meaning generally first. Usage labels (*slang*, *informal*, and so on) are applied liberally. Many words are followed by usage notes, which reflect the consensus of a panel of over 150 writers, editors, and teachers. The dictionary uses as few abbreviations and symbols as practicable. It includes guides to usage, grammar, spelling, and punctuation.

Oxford American Dictionary (1980). A descendant of the unabridged *Oxford English Dictionary* (see below), this abridged dictionary is somewhat briefer than any of the others listed here. Its pronunciation symbols are particularly straightforward and easy to use. Its word meanings, arranged according to the frequency of their use, are short and simple. The dictionary emphasizes correct American usage, applies usage labels frequently, and includes over 600 usage notes. Unlike most other abridged dictionaries, this one contains no special appendixes and no etymologies, or word histories.

The Random House College Dictionary, rev. ed. (1980). Based on the unabridged *Random House Dictionary* (see below), this dictionary includes abbreviations and biographical and geographical names in the main alphabetical listing. Its list of words is particularly up to date. Appendixes include a manual of style.

Webster's Ninth New Collegiate Dictionary (1987). This dictionary, based on the unabridged *Webster's Third New International Dictionary* (see below), concentrates on standard English and applies usage labels (such as *slang*) less frequently than do other dictionaries. Word definitions are listed in chronological order of their appearance in the language. The main alphabetical listing includes abbreviations. Geographical names and foreign words and phrases appear in appendixes, as does a manual of style.

Webster's New World Dictionary, coll. ed. (1988). This dictionary includes foreign words, abbreviations, and geographical and biographical names in the main alphabetical listing. The definitions of words are arranged in chronological order. Usage labels (*colloquial*, *slang*, and so on) are applied liberally, and words and

A BRIEF HISTORY OF DICTIONARIES

1721—Nathaniel Bailey's *Universal Etymological Dictionary of the English Language*, the first dictionary to resemble the dictionaries we have at present.

1755—Samuel Johnson's two-volume *Dictionary*.

1828—Noah Webster's *American Dictionary of the English Language*.

1857–1928—The compilation of the most comprehensive dictionary, the twelve-volume (now sixteen-volume) *Oxford English Dictionary*.

32a

phrases of American origin are starred. Appendixes on punctuation and mechanics and on manuscript form are included.

2 Unabridged dictionaries

Unabridged dictionaries are the most scholarly and comprehensive of all dictionaries, sometimes consisting of several volumes. They emphasize the history of words and the variety of their uses. An unabridged dictionary is useful when you are studying a word in depth, reading or writing about the literature of another century, or looking for a quotation containing a particular word. The following unabridged dictionaries are available at most libraries.

The Oxford English Dictionary, 16 volumes (1933–86). Also available in a compact, photographically reduced, three-volume edition (1971, 1987). This is the greatest dictionary of our language. Its purpose is to show the histories and current meanings of all words. Its entries illustrate the changes in a word's spelling, pronunciation, and meaning with quotations from writers of every century. Some entries span pages. The main dictionary focuses on British words and meanings, but the supplements include American words and meanings.

The Random House Dictionary of the English Language, 2nd ed. (1987). This dictionary is smaller (and less expensive) than many unabridged dictionaries (it has 315,000 entries compared with 450,000 in *Webster's Third New International*). Its entries and definitions are especially up to date, and it includes hundreds of usage notes. Among its appendixes are short dictionaries of French, Spanish, Italian, and German and a brief atlas with color maps.

Webster's Third New International Dictionary of the English Language (1986). This dictionary attempts to record our language more as it *is* used than as it *should be* used. Therefore, usage labels (such as *slang*) are minimal. Definitions are given in chronological order of their appearance in the language. Most acceptable spellings and pronunciations are provided. Plentiful illustrative quotations show variations in the uses of words. The dictionary is unusually strong in new scientific and technical terms.

3 Special dictionaries

Special dictionaries limit their attention to a single class of word (for example, slang, engineering terms, abbreviations), to a

CHOOSING A DICTIONARY

To unify the answers that students give to the exercises in this chapter, select a dictionary suitable to your class's needs and make it a required text for your course.

32a

ENGLISH AS A SECOND LANGUAGE

For ESL students, the most difficult part of learning English is learning idiomatic usage. The following sourcebooks may be particularly helpful to these students:

Freeman, William. *A Concise Dictionary of English Idioms*, 1976.

Whitford, Harold C., and Robert J. Dixson. *Handbook of American Idioms and Idiomatic Usage*, 1973.

single kind of information (synonyms, usage, word origins), or to a specific subject (black culture, biography, history). Thus special dictionaries provide more extensive and complete information about their topics than general dictionaries do.

Special dictionaries on slang or word origins not only can help you locate uncommon information but also can give you a sense of the great richness and variety of language. They often make entertaining reading.

FOR INFORMATION ON SLANG

Partridge, Eric. *A Dictionary of Slang and Unconventional English*. 8th ed. Ed. Paul Beale. 1984.

Wentworth, Harold, and Stuart Berg Flexner. *Dictionary of American Slang*. 2nd supp. ed. 1975.

FOR THE ORIGINS OF WORDS

Oxford Dictionary of English Etymology. Ed. Charles T. Onions et al. 1966.

Partridge, Eric. *Origins: A Short Etymological Dictionary of Modern English*. 4th ed. 1966.

Two kinds of special dictionaries—a usage dictionary and a dictionary of synonyms—are such useful references for everyday writing that you may want one of each on your own reference shelf. A dictionary of usage contains extensive entries for the words, phrases, and constructions that most frequently cause problems and controversy.

FOR GUIDANCE ON ENGLISH USAGE

Follett, Wilson. *Modern American Usage*. Ed. Jacques Barzun. 1966.

Fowler, H. W. *A Dictionary of Modern English Usage*. 2nd ed. Rev. and ed. Sir Ernest Gowers. 1965.

Morris, William, and Mary Morris. *Harper Dictionary of Contemporary Usage*. 2nd ed. 1985.

A dictionary of synonyms provides lists of words with closely related meanings. The lists are much more extensive than the usage notes in a general dictionary. Some dictionaries of synonyms contain extended discussions and illustrations of various shades of meaning.

FOR INFORMATION ABOUT SYNONYMS

Lewis, Norman. *The New Roget's Thesaurus of the English Language in Dictionary Form*. 1964.

Webster's New Dictionary of Synonyms. 1973.

See 35b for an extensive list of special dictionaries in fields such as literature, business, history, psychology, and science.

32a

32b Working with a dictionary's contents

1 Finding general information

The dictionary is a convenient reference for information of every sort. Most abridged dictionaries will tell you the atomic weight of oxygen, Napoleon's birth and death dates, the location of Fort Knox, the population of Gambia, what the Conestoga wagon of the Old West looked like, the origin and nature of surrealism, or the number of cups in a quart. Finding such information may require a little work—for instance, checking the entry *periodic table* or *element* as well as *oxygen*, or consulting an appendix of biographical names to find Napoleon. But a dictionary is often the quickest and most accessible reference for general information when an encyclopedia, textbook, or other reference book is unavailable or inconvenient to use.

2 Answering specific questions

Dictionaries use abbreviations and symbols to squeeze a lot of information into a relatively small book. This system of condensed information may at first seem difficult to read. But all dictionaries include in their opening pages detailed information on the arrangement of entries, pronunciation symbols, and abbreviations. And the format is quite similar from one dictionary to another, so becoming familiar with the abbreviations and symbols in one dictionary makes reading any dictionary an easy routine. The labeled parts of the two entries at the top of the next page—*conjecture* from the *American Heritage Dictionary* (referred to from now on as *AHD*) and *reckon* from *Webster's Ninth New Collegiate Dictionary*—are discussed in the following sections.

Spelling and word division

The small initial letters for both *conjecture* and *reckon* indicate that these words are not normally capitalized. (In contrast, *Franklin stove* is capitalized in both the *AHD* and *Webster's Collegiate* because *Franklin* is a proper noun.)

The centered periods in **con·jec·ture** and **reck·on** show the divisions of these words into syllables. If you are writing or typing a word of more than one syllable and need to break it at the end of a line, follow the dictionary's division of the word into syllables. (See also Chapter 30 for general rules about word division.)

32b

THE AMERICAN HERITAGE DICTIONARY

Spelling and word division | Pronunciation

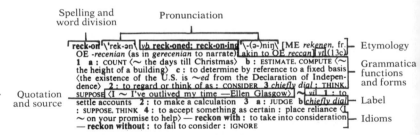

Meanings
Etymology
Synonyms

Grammatical functions and forms
Quotation

ADDITIONAL SAMPLE ENTRIES

From Webster's *New Universal Unabridged Dictionary*, 1983.

cŏn·jec'tūre, n. (L. *conjectura*, a putting together, a guess, an inference, from *conjectus*, pp. of *conjicere*, to throw or bring together, to guess.)
1. guesswork; inferring, theorizing, or predicting from incomplete or uncertain evidence; as, this critic is too fond of *conjecture*.
2. a guess; inference, theory, or prediction based on guesswork.

cŏn·jec'tūre, v.t.; conjectured, pt., pp.; conjecturing, ppr. to guess; to arrive at, propose, or predict by conjecture; as, he *conjectured* that some misfortune had happened.

cŏn·jec'tūre, v.i. to make a conjecture. *Syn.*—surmise, guess, suppose, imagine.

WEBSTER'S NINTH NEW COLLEGIATE DICTIONARY

Spelling and word division | Pronunciation

reck·on \'rek-ən\ *vb* **reck·oned; reck·on·ing** \-(ə-)niŋ\ [ME *rekenen*, fr. OE *-recenian* (as in *gerecenian* to narrate) akin to OE *reccan*] *vt*(13c)
1 a : COUNT ⟨~ the days till Christmas⟩ **b** : ESTIMATE. COMPUTE ⟨~ the height of a building⟩ **c** : to determine by reference to a fixed basis ⟨the existence of the U.S. is ~ed from the Declaration of Independence⟩ **2** : to regard or think of as : CONSIDER **3** *chiefly dial* : THINK, SUPPOSE ⟨I ~ I've outlived my time —Ellen Glasgow⟩ ~ *vi* **1** : to settle accounts **2** : to make a calculation **3 a** : JUDGE **b** *chiefly dial* : SUPPOSE. THINK **4** : to accept something as certain : place reliance ⟨I ~ on your promise to help⟩ — **reckon with** : to take into consideration — **reckon without** : to fail to consider : IGNORE

Quotation and source
Etymology
Grammatical functions and forms
Label
Idioms

If a word is a hyphenated compound word, such as *cross-question*, a dictionary shows the hyphen as part of the spelling: **cross-ques·tion.** The treatment of foreign words such as *joie de vivre* or *ex post facto*, which are normally italicized (or underlined) in writing, is more varied. *Webster's New World Dictionary* places a special symbol (‡) before each one. The *AHD* simply designates them as *French* and *Latin*, respectively, therefore indicating they should be italicized.

Dictionaries provide any variant spellings of a word at the beginning of an entry. Thus, for the word *dexterous*, *Webster's Collegiate* has "**dex·ter·ous** *or* **dex·trous,**" indicating that either spelling is acceptable.

32b

EXERCISE 1

Check the spelling of the following words in a dictionary. Correct any incorrect spellings, and divide all the words into syllables.

1. England
2. innoculate
3. reccommend
4. methodical
5. inheritence
6. over-estimate
7. depreciation
8. excruciating
9. grievance
10. secretery
11. trans-Atlantic
12. crossreference

Pronunciation

Dictionaries use symbols to indicate how to pronounce a word because the alphabet itself does not record all the sounds in the language. (Listen, for example, to the different sounds of *a* in only three words: *far, make,* and *answer.*) Most dictionaries provide a key to the pronunciation symbols at the foot of each page or every two facing pages.

The entries for *conjecture* and *reckon* show two slightly different pronunciation systems. In the *AHD*'s *conjecture* the pronunciation appears in parentheses; in *Webster's Collegiate* it appears in reversed slashes (\\). In both entries the stressed syllable is indicated by an accent mark (' and '); but in the *AHD* the mark follows the stressed syllable (kən-jĕk′chər), whereas in *Webster's Collegiate* it precedes the stressed syllable ('rek-ən).

Most unabridged and some abridged dictionaries provide variant pronunciations, including regional differences. The *AHD,* for example, provides two pronunciations for the last syllable of *licorice,* indicating that the word may be pronounced either of two ways: "lĭk′ər-ĭs, -ĭsh."

EXERCISE 2

Consult a dictionary for the correct pronunciation of the following words. Write out the pronunciation as given, using the dictionary's symbols. (If more than one pronunciation is given, write them all out.)

1. crucifixion
2. mnemonics
3. timorous
4. utilitarian
5. bathos
6. epitome
7. miserable
8. obelisk
9. polemic
10. yacht
11. promenade
12. insouciance

Grammatical functions and forms

Dictionaries give helpful information about a word's function and forms. The *Webster's Collegiate* entry for *reckon* shows the word to be a verb (*vb*), with the past tense and past participle *reck-*

**ANSWERS TO EXERCISES:
CHAPTER 32**

The answers to the exercises in Chapter 32 will depend on the dictionary being consulted. The recommended desk dictionaries disagree, for instance, over nearly half the syllable divisions in Exercise 1. Thus, no answers are provided for this chapter.

32b

SAMPLE ENTRY

reck'ŏn, v.t.; reckoned, pt., pp.; reckoning, ppr. (ME. *rekenen, reknen,* from AS. *gerecenian,* to explain. A derivative verb allied to AS. *gereccan,* to rule, direct, order, explain, tell; D. *rekenen;* Ice. *reikna,* to reckon.)

1. to count; to figure up; to compute; to calculate. I *reckoned* above two hundred and fifty on the outside of the church. —Addison
2. to consider as; to regard as being; to repute. He was *reckoned* among the transgressors. —Luke xxii. 37.
3. to make account or reckoning of. (Obs.) Faith was *reckoned* to Abraham for righteousness. —Rom. iv. 9.
4. to judge; to consider; to estimate.
5. to suppose, think, or believe; as, I *reckon* it will rain. (Colloq. or Dial.)

reck'ŏn, v.i.,

1. to count up; to figure
2. to depend; to rely (with *on*).
3. to settle an account
4. to pay a penalty; to be answerable (Obs.)

If they fail in their bounden duty, they shall reckon for it one day.   —Sanderson.

to reckon for; to be answerable or responsible for.

to reckon with; (a) to balance accounts and make a settlement with; (b) to take into consideration.

to reckon without one's host; to ignore, in a transaction, one whose cooperation is essential; hence, to reckon without considering some important factor or factors.

32b

oned and the present participle *reckoning,* and with both transitive (*vt*) and intransitive (*vi*) meanings. The *AHD* entry for *conjecture* shows it to be an even more versatile word. It is a noun (*n.*), with separate meanings in that function. And it is also a verb (*v.*): past tense and past participle *conjectured,* present participle *conjecturing,* and third-person singular present-tense *conjectures.* The verb has both transitive (*tr.*) and intransitive (*intr.*) meanings.

Most dictionaries provide not only the principal forms of regular and irregular verbs but also the plural forms of irregular nouns and the comparative and superlative forms of adjectives and adverbs that commonly show degree with *-er* and *-est.* An adjective or adverb without *-er* and *-est* forms in the dictionary requires the addition of *more* and *most* to show the comparative and superlative.

When other parts of speech are formed from the word being defined and have related meanings, those words are grouped at the end of the entry, where they are spelled, divided, accented, and identified by part of speech but not defined. Several of these so-called derivative forms are provided at the end of the *AHD* entry for *conjecture: conjecturable (adj.), conjecturably (adv.),* and *conjecturer (n.).*

The *Webster's Collegiate* entry for *reckon* ends with two uses of the word in idiomatic expressions (*reckon with* and *reckon without*). These phrases are defined (unlike the related parts of speech of *conjecture*) because, as with all idioms, their meanings cannot be inferred simply from the words they consist of (see 31b–3).

EXERCISE 3

Consult a dictionary to determine the part of speech of each of the following words. If the word functions as more than one part of speech, list them all. If the word is a verb, list its principal parts; if a noun, its plural form; if an adjective or adverb, its comparative and superlative.

1. little	5. machine	9. upset
2. that	6. orient	10. steal
3. study	7. roof	11. manifest
4. happen	8. ring	12. firm

Etymology

Dictionaries provide the **etymology** of a word (its history) to indicate its origin and the evolution of its meanings and forms. The dictionary can compress much information about a word into a small space through symbols, abbreviations, and different typefaces. An explanation of these systems appears in the dictionary's opening pages. The *AHD* traces *conjecture* first to Middle English (ME) (twelfth to fifteenth centuries) and then back to Latin (Lat.). As the entry in *Webster's Collegiate* shows, *reckon* came to English by a different route, arriving from Old English (OE) by way of Middle English (ME). The notation "(13c)" at the end of the second line indicates that the first recorded use of *reckon* to mean "count" occurred in the thirteenth century. (See 33a for a brief history of the English language.)

Sometimes dictionaries do not give the etymology for a word. Their practices differ (and are explained in their opening pages), but in general they omit etymology when it is obvious, unknown, or available elsewhere in the dictionary.

EXERCISE 4

Consult a dictionary for the etymologies of the following words. Use the dictionary's own explanations of abbreviations and symbols to get the fullest history of the word, and write out that history in your own words.

1. grammar	5. penetrate	9. calico
2. engage	6. promote	10. chauvinism
3. leaf	7. retrieve	11. assassin
4. moon	8. toxic	12. water

Meanings

Dictionaries divide the general meaning of a word into particular meanings on the basis of how the word is or has been actually used. They arrange a word's meanings differently, however, explaining the basis of their arrangement in their opening pages. *Webster's Collegiate* and *Webster's New World* list meanings in order of their appearance in the language, earliest first. The *AHD*, *Oxford American*, and abridged *Random House*, in contrast, usually place the word's most basic or common meaning first and follow it with the other meanings. These different policies will result in roughly the same arrangement of meanings only when the oldest meaning of a word is also the most common. Thus you should be sure you know the system of arrangement used by any dictionary you are consulting. Then read through the entire entry before settling on the meaning that most closely fits the context of what you're reading or writing.

Most dictionaries provide any special technical and scientific meanings of a word in separately numbered entries that are usually labeled. These labels are discussed on the next page.

REMINDER

For students: It is critical that you read the entire definition of a word before deciding its meaning for the context at hand. Careful reading of all the meanings of a word often reveals symbolism and intentions frequently missed by assumed understanding of a word's usage.

32b

ADDITIONAL REFERENCE

For more synonyms and antonyms, students can consult Norman Lewis, *The New Roget's Thesaurus of the English Language in Dictionary Form* (New York: Putnam's, 1978).

EXERCISE 5

Consult a dictionary for the meanings of the following words. How many distinct meanings does each word have? How does the dictionary list meanings, chronologically or in order of importance? If chronologically, is the oldest meaning also the most common? What changes have occurred in each word's use over time?

1. weight	5. order	9. prefer
2. recipe	6. apt	10. quit
3. color	7. astrology	11. spring
4. condition	8. offered	12. sue

Synonyms and antonyms

Synonyms are words whose meanings are approximately the same, such as *small* and *little*. **Antonyms** are words whose meanings are approximately opposite, such as *small* and *big*. When a word has many closely related synonyms that are hard to distinguish, an abridged dictionary may devote a separate paragraph to them. The *AHD* does so in distinguishing the verb *conjecture* from the verbs *surmise*, *guess*, *speculate*, *presume*, and *infer*, each of which can also be looked up in its alphabetical place. *Webster's Collegiate* defines *reckon* with some words in small capital letters (COUNT, ESTIMATE, COMPUTE, and so on). These are both synonyms and cross-references, in that each word may be looked up in its alphabetical place. Dictionaries specify antonyms less often than synonyms, usually with a boldface **ant** at the end of the entry.

Reading through the lists and discussions of synonyms and antonyms for a word can help you locate its meaning in a given context more exactly. (See 33c-2 for a discussion of how to use the synonyms provided by a dictionary to increase your vocabulary.)

EXERCISE 6

Consult a dictionary for the synonyms and antonyms of the following words. Use the word itself and each synonym and antonym appropriately in a sentence of your own.

1. suggest	4. discover	7. kind (*adj.*)
2. plain (*adj.*)	5. change (*v.*)	8. memory
3. high (*adj.*)	6. beautiful	9. serious

Labels

Dictionaries apply labels to words or to particular meanings that have a special status or use. The labels are usually of four kinds: subject, style, region, and time.

32b

Subject labels tell us that a word or one of its meanings has a special use in a field of knowledge or a profession. In its entry for *relaxation*, for instance, the *AHD* presents specialized meanings with the subject labels *physiology*, *physics*, and *mathematics*.

Style labels restrict a word or one of its meanings to a particular level of usage, such as *slang, colloquial* or *informal, nonstandard* or *substandard, vulgar*, and *poetic* or *literary*. The label *slang* indicates that a word should be used in writing only for a special effect. For example, all the abridged dictionaries label *crumb* as slang when it means "a worthless or despicable person." The label *informal* or *colloquial* is applied to words that are appropriate for conversation and informal writing but not for formal writing. For instance, the *AHD* labels as informal the use of *sure* in the sentence *We sure need that money* (the more formal word is *surely*). The label *nonstandard* or *substandard* is applied to words or their meanings that are considered inappropriate for standard speech and writing. The *AHD*, for instance, labels all uses of *ain't* as nonstandard. The label *vulgar*, or sometimes *vulgar slang*, is applied to words or their meanings that are normally considered offensive in speech and writing. The label *poetic* or *literary* designates words or their meanings (such as *eve* for *evening* and *o'er* for *over*) used only in poetry or the most formal writing.

Region labels indicate that a particular spelling, pronunciation, or meaning of a word is not national but limited to some area. A regional difference may be indicated by the label *dialect*. *Webster's Collegiate* labels as dialect (*dial*) the uses of *reckon* to mean "suppose" or "think" (as in *I reckon I'll do that*). More specific region labels may designate areas of the United States or other countries. The word *bloke* (meaning "fellow") is labeled as British by most dictionaries. And the *AHD* labels *arroyo*, "a deep gully" or "a dry gulch," as Southwestern U.S.

Time labels indicate words or their meanings that the language, in evolving, has discarded. These words and meanings are included in the dictionary primarily to help readers of some older texts that contain them. The label *obsolete* designates words or specific meanings that are no longer used, whereas the label *archaic* designates words or specific meanings that are out of date though still in occasional use.

See 31a for further discussion of levels of usage and their appropriateness in your writing.

EXERCISE 7

Consult at least two dictionaries to determine the status of each of the following words or any one of their meanings according to subject, style, region, or time.

ADDITIONAL EXAMPLES OF DICTIONARY LABELS

Slang—novel and colorful expressions that reflect a group's special experiences and set it off from others. Examples: *cool, into, funky, awesome*.

Colloquial—words and expressions appropriate to everyday spoken language and to informal writing. Example: Housework often takes a *bite* out of my weekend.

Regional—words and expressions used only in some geographical locations. For example, one kind of sandwich may be called a *hero*, a *hoagie*, a *submarine*, a *torpedo*, or a *grinder*, depending upon which region you are in.

Nonstandard or substandard—words and grammatical forms frequently used in speech but never acceptable in standard written English. Examples: *nowheres, hisself, throwed, could of*, and *hadn't ought*.

Obsolete or archaic—words or meanings of words that we never or rarely use but that appear in older documents and literature still read today. Examples: *enwheel* ("to encircle") and *belike* ("perhaps").

32b

A DICTIONARY WITH PLENTY OF SYNONYMS

Of the many dictionaries that include synonyms with their definitions of words, the *Funk & Wagnall's New Standard College Dictionary* gives more extensive coverage than most. The *Funk & Wagnall's* includes paragraphs on synonyms that define the various shades of meaning.

1. impulse	5. goof	9. mad
2. OK	6. goober	10. sing
3. irregardless	7. lift	11. brief (*n.*)
4. neath	8. potlatch	12. joint

Illustrative quotations

Dictionaries are made by collecting quotations showing actual uses of words in all kinds of speech and writing. Some of these quotations, or others that the dictionary makers invent, may appear in the dictionary's entries as illustrations of how a word may be used. Unabridged dictionaries usually provide many such examples, not only to illustrate a word's current uses but also to show the changes in its meanings over time. Abridged dictionaries use quotations more selectively: to illustrate an unusual meaning of the word, to help distinguish between two closely related meanings of the same word, or to show the differences between synonyms. The *AHD* entry for *conjecture* and the *Webster's Collegiate* entry for *reckon* both employ quotation.

EXERCISE 8

Consult a dictionary to find a quotation illustrating at least one meaning of each word below. Then write an illustrative sentence of your own for each word.

1. jolt	4. ceremonial	7. legitimate
2. articulate	5. sensuous	8. inquire
3. discreet	6. tremble	9. nether

32b

CHAPTER 33

Improving Your Vocabulary

A precise and versatile vocabulary is essential to effective communication. As you gain experience writing, you will want to improve the precision with which you use familiar words (see Chapter 31) and increase the number of words you can use appropriately. To a great extent, you can improve your vocabulary by frequent and inquisitive reading, by troubling to notice and learn the interesting or unfamiliar words used by other writers.

This chapter briefly describes the development of English and explains how words are formed. Then it offers some advice for learning to use new words. The chapter has a twofold purpose: to provide a sense of the potential of English by acquainting you with its history and range of words; and to help you increase the range, versatility, and precision of your own vocabulary.

HIGHLIGHTS

Most students can profit from systematic attention to improving their vocabulary; however, the course time available for such attention is often quite limited. Special workbooks are available, of course, for students with basic vocabulary problems. Chapter 33 provides a good introduction to vocabulary building for students who wish to enrich their vocabularies and suggests activities you may wish to assign. After glancing at the development of the English language and the variety of sources from which our rich vocabulary is drawn, the chapter looks at the roots, prefixes, and suffixes of words; it also looks at ways of learning new words from their context and the value of habitually consulting a dictionary—the best methods of gradually and continually expanding vocabulary while reading.

33a Understanding the sources of English

People change their language as they and their surroundings change. They revise spellings, pronunciation, and syntax, alter meanings, and even add or drop words to keep the language fresh and useful. English changes continuously, but its subtle and complex character stays the same.

English has over 500,000 words, probably more than any other language. This exceptional vocabulary and the power and range of expression that accompany it derive from its special mix of word sources. Unlike many other languages, English has borrowed a large number of words.

How English drew on its several sources and acquired its large vocabulary is the story of historical changes. The ancestor of

495

RESOURCES AND IDEAS

Journal of Basic Writing 2 (1979). This special issue on vocabulary includes general articles and notes on specific strategies.

English, Indo-European, was spoken (but not written) perhaps as far back as 5000 B.C., and it eventually spread to cover the area from India west to the British Isles. In what is now England, an Indo-European offshoot called Celtic was spoken extensively until the fifth century A.D. But over the next few centuries invaders from the European continent, speaking a dialect of another Indo-European language, Germanic, overran the native Britons. The Germanic dialect became the original source of English.

Old English, spoken from the eighth to the twelfth centuries, was a rugged, guttural language. It used a slightly different alphabet from ours (including the characters ð and þ for *th*), which has been transcribed in the sample below. The sample shows the opening lines of the Lord's Prayer: "Our Father, who art in heaven, hallowed be thy name. Thy kingdom come. Thy will be done on earth as it is in heaven."

> Fæder ure thu the eart on heofonum, si thin nama gehalgod. Tobecume thin rice. Gewurthe thin willa on eorthan swa swa on heofonum.

Many of our nouns, such as *stone, word, gift,* and *foot*, come from Old English. So do most of our pronouns, prepositions, and conjunctions, some (such as *he, under,* and *to*) without any change in spelling. Other Germanic tribes, using a similar dialect but settling on the European continent instead of in England, fostered two other languages, Dutch and German. As a result, Dutch, German, and English are related languages with some similar traits.

In 1066 the Normans, under William the Conqueror, invaded England. The Normans were originally Vikings who had settled in northern France and had forsaken Old Norse for their own dialect of Old French. They made Norman French the language of law, literature, and the ruling class in England. As a result, English acquired many French words, including many military and governmental words such as *authority, mayor, crime, army,* and *guard*. The common English people kept English alive during the Norman occupation, but they adopted many French words intact (*air, point, place, age*). Eventually, the French influence caused the language to shift from Old to Middle English, which lasted from the twelfth through the fifteenth centuries. During this time a great many Latin words also entered English, for Latin formed the background of Norman French and was the language of the Church and of scholars. English words that entered Middle English directly from Latin or from Latin through French include *language, luminous, memory, liberal,* and *sober*.

Middle English, as the following passage from Geoffrey Chaucer's *Canterbury Tales* shows, was much closer to our own language than to Old English.

33a

A clerk there was of Oxenford also,
That unto logyk hadde longe ygo.
As leene was his hors as is a rake,
And he nas nat right fat, I undertake,
But looked holwe, and therto sobrely.

Modern English evolved in the fourteenth and fifteenth centuries as the language's sound and spellings changed. This was the time of the Renaissance in Europe. Ancient Latin and Greek art, learning, and literature were revived, first in Italy and then throughout the continent. English vocabulary expanded rapidly, not only with more Latin and many Greek words (such as *democracy* and *physics*) but also with words from Italian and French. Advances in printing, beginning in the fifteenth century, made publications widely available to an increasingly literate audience. The Modern English of twentieth-century America is four centuries and an ocean removed from the Modern English of sixteenth-century England, but the two are fundamentally the same. The differences and the similarities are evident in this passage from the King James Bible, published in 1611:

And the Lord God commanded the man, saying, Of euery tree of the garden thou mayest freely eate. But of the tree of the knowledge of good and euill, thou shalt not eate of it: for in the day that thou eatest thereof, thou shalt surely die.

33b Learning the composition of words

Words can often be divided into meaningful parts. A *handbook*, for instance, is a book you keep at hand (for reference). A *shepherd* herds sheep (or other animals). Knowing what the parts of a word mean by themselves, as you do here, can often help you infer approximately what they mean when combined.

The following explanations of roots, prefixes, and suffixes provide information that can open up the meanings of words whose parts may not be familiar or easy to see. For more information, refer to a dictionary's etymologies, which provide the histories of words (see 32b).

1 Learning roots

A **root** is the unchanging component of words related in origin and usually in meaning. Both *illiterate* ("unable to read and write") and *literal* ("sticking to the facts or to the first and most obvious meaning of an idea") share the root *liter*, derived from *lit-*

HISTORY OF THE ENGLISH LANGUAGE

Prior to fifth century A.D.—Celtic-speaking peoples.

Fifth century—Anglo-Saxon invasion introduces Germanic dialects.

Eighth to twelfth century—In the Old English (OE) period the language combines Latin and Germanic dialects and contributes 183 of the 200 most frequently used words in Modern English. The Vikings arrive in A.D. 787 speaking Old Norse, which contributes hundreds of words to English.

A.D. 1066—The Normans invade and conquer England. Norman French, a dialect of Old French, replaces Old English as the official language of England, but English survives, continuing to evolve through the influence of French.

Twelfth century—English emerges in an altered form, Middle English (ME), which draws on both Old English and Norman French. Heavy borrowing of French words continues through the following centuries until the emergence of Modern English.

A.D. 1500 (approximately)—The language takes a form recognizable as Modern English.

33b

tera, a Latin word meaning "letter." A person who cannot understand the letters that make up writing is illiterate. A person who wants to understand the primary meaning of the letters (the words) in a contract is seeking the *literal* meaning of that contract.

At least half our words come from Latin and Greek. The list below includes some common Latin and Greek roots, their meanings, and examples of English words containing them.

Root (source)	Meaning	English words
aster, astr (G)	star	astronomy, astrology
audi (L)	to hear	audible, audience
bene (L)	good, well	benefit, benevolent
bio (G)	life	biology, autobiography
dic, dict (L)	to speak	dictator, dictionary
fer (L)	to carry	transfer, referral
fix (L)	to fasten	fix, suffix, prefix
geo (G)	earth	geography, geology
graph (G)	to write	geography, photography
jur, jus (L)	law	jury, justice
log, logue (G)	word, thought, speech	astrology, biology, neologism
luc (L)	light	lucid, translucent
manu (L)	hand	manual, manuscript
meter, metr (G)	measure	metric, thermometer
op, oper (L)	work	operation, operator
path (G)	feeling	pathetic, sympathy
ped (G)	child	pediatrics
phil (G)	love	philosophy, Anglophile
phys (G)	body, nature	physical, physics
psych (G)	soul	psychic, psychology
scrib, script (L)	to write	scribble, manuscript
tele (G)	far off	telephone, television
ter, terr (L)	earth	territory, extraterrestrial
vac (L)	empty	vacant, vacuum, evacuate
verb (L)	word	verbal, verbose
vid, vis (L)	to see	video, vision, television

33b

ANSWERS: EXERCISE 1

1. benefactor: The root bene means "good," and so the benefactor is or does good. The rest of the sentence hints that the benefactor provides aid.
2. vacuous: The root vac means "empty," which makes sense in the sentence. The heiress takes up volunteer work to avoid an empty life.
3. affixed: The root fix means "to fasten," and so affixed means fastened.

EXERCISE 1

Define the following italicized words, using the list of roots above and any clues given by the rest of the sentence. Check the accuracy of your meanings in a dictionary.

1. After guiding me through college, my *benefactor* will help me start a career.
2. Always afraid of leading a *vacuous* life, the heiress immersed herself in volunteer work.
3. The posters *affixed* to the construction wall advertised a pornographic movie.

4. After his *auditory* nerve was damaged, he had trouble catching people's words.
5. The child *empathized* so completely with his mother that he felt pain when she broke her arm.

4. auditory: The root audi means "to hear." The auditory nerve is the nerve producing hearing.
5. empathized: The root path means feeling, and the context completes the meaning. The child felt as his mother did.

2 Learning prefixes

Prefixes are standard syllables fastened to the front of a word to modify its meaning. For example, the word *prehistory* is a combination of the word *history*, meaning "based on a written record explaining past events," and the prefix *pre-*, meaning "before." Together, prefix and word mean "before a written record explaining past events," or before events were recorded. Learning standard prefixes can help you improve vocabulary and spelling just as learning word roots can. The following lists group prefixes according to sense so that they are easier to remember. When two or more prefixes have very different spellings but the same meaning, they usually derive from different languages, most often Latin and Greek.

Prefixes showing quantity

MEANING	PREFIXES IN ENGLISH WORDS
half	*semi*annual; *hemi*sphere
one	*uni*cycle; *mon*arch, *mono*rail
two	*bi*nary, *bi*monthly; *di*lemma, *dicho*tomy
three	*tri*angle, *tri*logy
four	*quad*rangle, *quar*tet
five	*quin*tet; *penta*gon
six	*sex*tuplets; *hexa*meter
seven	*sept*uagenarian; *hept*archy
eight	*oct*ave, *octo*pus
nine	*nona*genarian
ten	*dec*ade, *deca*thlon
hundred	*cent*ury; *hecto*liter
thousand	*milli*meter; *kilo*cycle

Prefixes showing negation

MEANING	PREFIXES IN ENGLISH WORDS
without, no, not	*a*sexual; *il*legal, *im*moral, *in*valid, *ir*reverent; *un*skilled
not, absence of, opposing, against	*non*breakable; *ant*acid, *anti*pathy; *contra*dict

33b

MEANING	PREFIXES IN ENGLISH WORDS
opposite to, complement to	*counter*clockwise, *counter*weight
do the opposite of, remove, reduce	*de*horn, *de*vitalize, *de*value
do the opposite of, deprive of	*dis*establish, *dis*arm
wrongly, bad	*mis*judge, *mis*deed

Prefixes showing time

MEANING	PREFIXES IN ENGLISH WORDS
before	*ante*cedent; *fore*cast; *pre*cede; *pro*logue
after	*post*war
again	*re*write

Prefixes showing direction or position

MEANING	PREFIXES IN ENGLISH WORDS
above, over	*super*vise
across, over	*trans*port
below, under	*infra*sonic; *sub*terranean; *hypo*dermic
in front of	*pro*ceed; *pre*fix
behind	*re*cede
out of	*e*rupt, *ex*plicit; *ec*stasy
into	*in*jection, *im*merse; *en*courage, *em*power
around	*circum*ference; *peri*meter
with	*co*exist, *col*loquial, *com*municate, *con*sequence, *cor*respond; *sym*pathy, *syn*chronize

EXERCISE 2

Provide meanings for the following italicized words, using the lists of prefixes and any clues given by the rest of the sentence. Check the accuracy of your meanings in a dictionary.

1. In the twenty-first century some of our oldest cities will celebrate their *quadricentennials.*
2. Most poems called sonnets consist of fourteen lines divided into an *octave* and a *sestet.*
3. When the Congress seemed ready to cut Social Security benefits again, some representatives proposed the *countermeasure* of increasing Medicare payments.
4. By increasing Medicare payments, the representatives hoped to *forestall* the inevitable financial squeeze on the elderly.
5. Ferdinand Magellan, a Portuguese sailor, commanded the first expedition to *circumnavigate* the globe.

ANSWERS: EXERCISE 2

1. Quadricentennial comes from quadri, meaning "four," cent, meaning "hundred," and annus, meaning "year." The cities will be celebrating their four-hundredth year.
2. Octave derives from oct, "eight"; sestet from sex, "six," The octave is eight lines, the sestet six.
3. The prefix counter means "opposite to"; a countermeasure is one opposed to another measure.
4. The prefix fore means "before"; in trying to forestall the squeeze, the representatives are, in effect, trying to stall it before it happens.
5. The prefix circum means "around"; to circumnavigate means to "navigate around."

33b

3 Learning suffixes

Suffixes are standard syllables fastened to the end of a word to modify its meaning and usually its part of speech. The word *popular* is an adjective. With different suffixes, it becomes a different adjective, an adverb, a noun, and two different verbs.

ADJECTIVE	popular	**NOUN**	popul*ation*
	popul*ous*	**VERB**	popul*ate*
ADVERB	popul*arly*		popul*arize*

Many words change suffixes in the same way. In fact, suffixes help us recognize what parts of speech many words are, as the following examples show.

Noun suffixes

mis*ery*	min*er*	intern*ship*	random*ness*
refer*ence*	base*ment*	presid*ency*	brother*hood*
relev*ance*	national*ist*	discus*sion*	king*dom*
operat*or*	national*ism*	agita*tion*	

Verb suffixes

hard*en*	pur*ify*
national*ize*	agit*ate*

Adjective suffixes

miser*able*	president*ial*	wonder*ful*	use*less*
ed*ible*	gigan*tic*	fibr*ous*	self*ish*
nation*al*	friend*ly*	adop*tive*	flatu*lent*

The only suffix regularly applied to adverbs is *-ly: openly, selfishly.*

NOTE: Inflectional endings—such as the plural *-s*, the possessive *-'s*, the past tense *-ed*, and the comparative *-er* or *-est*—appear at the ends of words but do not change a word's grammatical function.

EXERCISE 3

Identify the part of speech of each word below, and then change it to the part or parts of speech in parentheses by deleting, adding, or changing a suffix. Use the given word and each created word in a sentence. Check a dictionary, if necessary, to be sure suffixes and spellings are correct.

RESOURCES AND IDEAS

Sandra Stotsky, "Teaching the Vocabulary of Academic Discourse, *Journal of Basic Writing* 2 (1979): 15–39. Stotsky examines the language of textbooks and suggests using reading, dictating, précis writing, and affix study to develop vocabulary for academic reading and writing.

SAMPLE ANSWERS: EXERCISE 3

33b

1. magic, noun and adjective
   adjective: magical
   His success must be the result of magic. She performed magic tricks. Drawing everyone into a magical world, the movie charmed the audience.
2. durable, adjective
   noun: durability; adverb: durably
   The durable chair withstood many

years' wear. The <u>durability</u> of the old pitcher amazed the crowd. The pup tent was light but <u>durably</u> made.

3. <u>refrigerator</u>, noun
   verb: <u>refrigerate</u>
   Don't bother putting that in the <u>refrigerator</u>. I have already <u>refrigerated</u> it.

4. <u>self-critical</u>, adjective
   noun: <u>self-criticism</u>
   A <u>self-critical</u> stance is difficult to take. Her apparent <u>self-criticism</u> was really a plea for support.

5. <u>differ</u>, verb
   noun: <u>difference</u>; adjective: <u>different</u>
   We <u>differ</u> from each other. He was sure the campaign would not make any <u>difference</u>. The police found that she had committed a <u>different</u> crime.

6. <u>equal</u>, adjective
   noun: <u>equality</u>; adverb: <u>equally</u>
   <u>Equal</u> rights have not yet been achieved. <u>Equality</u> is the goal of a truly just society. The children were all punished, though all were not <u>equally</u> at fault.

7. <u>conversion</u>, noun
   verb: <u>convert</u>; adjective: <u>convertible</u>
   We expected her <u>conversion</u> to her new religion. To <u>convert</u> base metals into gold was the alchemists' dream. The <u>convertible</u> sofa comes in handy.

8. <u>strictly</u>, adverb
   adjective: <u>strict</u>; noun: <u>strictness</u>
   She was <u>strictly</u> raised. A <u>strict</u> parent need not be a tyrannical parent. The <u>strictness</u> of their morals makes the Victorians hard to understand today.

9. <u>assist</u>, verb
   noun: <u>assistance</u>
   Please <u>assist</u> us. Your <u>assistance</u> in this project will be greatly appreciated.

10. <u>qualification</u>, noun
    verb: <u>qualify</u>; adjective: <u>qualitative</u>
    The <u>qualification</u> he offered was important. To <u>qualify</u> for the Olympics, an athlete must be an amateur. The difference between the two tape decks is <u>qualitative</u>.

1. magic (*adjective*)
2. durable (*noun; adverb*)
3. refrigerator (*verb*)
4. self-critical (*noun*)
5. differ (*noun; adjective*)
6. equal (*noun; adverb*)
7. conversion (*verb; adjective*)
8. strictly (*adjective; noun*)
9. assist (*noun*)
10. qualification (*verb; adjective*)

33c Learning to use new words

You can learn a new word not only by understanding its composition but also by examining the context in which it appears and by looking it up in a dictionary—both ways to increase your vocabulary by multiplying and varying your experience with language.

1 Examining context

Most people guess the meaning of an unfamiliar word by looking at familiar words around it. Imagine, for example, that you read the following:

> I was so tired I didn't bother with a real bed. I just lay down on the liclac in the living room. As soon as my feet rested at one end and my head at the other, I fell asleep. In the morning I was cramped from pushing against the back of the liclac.

To guess what *liclac* means, you could examine all the familiar words and learn that (1) a liclac isn't a bed, but you can lie on it; (2) it's part of a living room; (3) it's the length of a person; (4) it's narrow and has a back. From these clues you might guess that the nonsense word *liclac* represents a piece of living room furniture similar to a couch or sofa.

Parallelism shows you which ideas line up or go together and can often suggest the meaning of a new word. Watch for parallel ideas in the following sentence.

> The kittens see their mother hunt and kill, and they in turn take up *predatory* behavior.

If you did not know the word *predatory*, you could put together clues from the context: parallel construction (*kittens see . . . and they . . . take up*); the tip-off phrase *in turn;* and the suggested idea of imitation (kittens watching their mother and taking up her behavior). These clues produce the correct assumption that predatory behavior consists of hunting and killing.

33c

The phrase *is called* or the word *is* often signals a definition.

> The point where the light rays come together is called the *focus* of the lens.

Sometimes definitions are enclosed in parentheses or set off by commas or dashes.

> In early childhood these tendencies lead to the development of *schemes* (organized patterns of behavior).

> Many Chinese practice *Tai Chi,* an ancient method of self-defense performed as exercise in slow, graceful motions.

> At *burnout*—the instant a rocket stops firing—the satellite's path is fixed.

> Noticing examples can also help you infer the meaning of a word. The expressions *such as, for example, for instance, to illustrate,* and *including* often precede examples.

> Society often has difficulty understanding *nonconformists* such as criminals, inventors, artists, saints, and political protesters.

The parallel examples help explain *nonconformist* because they all seem to be exceptions, people who go beyond the average or beyond the rules. This is close to an understanding of *nonconformists* as people who do not adapt themselves to the usual standards and customs of society.

> Sometimes an example that reveals the meaning of an unfamiliar word is not announced by a phrase.

> During the first weeks of *rehabilitation,* Brian exercised as best he could, took his medicine daily, and thought constantly about the physical condition he once possessed.

Guessing the meaning of *rehabilitation* requires considering what occurred during it: (1) exercising "as best he could," as if Brian had some kind of handicap; (2) taking medicine, as if Brian were ill; and (3) thinking about his past physical condition, as if Brian were wishing for the good shape he used to be in. Putting these examples together suggests that *rehabilitation* is returning to a healthy condition, which is one of its meanings. (The more precise definition is "restoring a former capacity"; and that idea includes reviving a skill as well as recuperation from a sickness.)

EXERCISE 4

Use context to determine the meanings of the words italicized below (not including titles). Check the accuracy of your guess by consulting a dictionary.

RESOURCES AND IDEAS

Regina M. Hoover, "In the Beginning: The Word," *Journal of Basic Writing* 2 (1979): 82–87. Copying sentences containing unfamiliar words can help build vocabulary and improve writing.

33c

ANSWERS: EXERCISE 4
Individual response.

1. Like America, Michael [Corleone, in *The Godfather*] began as a clean, brilliant young man *endowed* with incredible resources and believing in a humanistic idealism. Like America, Michael was an innocent who had tried to correct the ills and injustices of his *progenitors.* —Francis Ford Coppola

2. Everything about man is a *paradox.* The *magnanimous* man grown rich becomes mean. The creative artist for whom everything is made easy nods. Every doctrine swears that it will breed men, but none can tell us in advance what sort of men it will breed. —Antoine de Saint-Exupéry

3. "And this, too, shall pass away." How much [this sentence] expresses! How *chastening* in the hour of pride! How *consoling* in the depths of *affliction!* —Abraham Lincoln

4. As long as there is one upright man, as long as there is one compassionate woman, the *contagion* may spread and the scene is not *desolate.* Hope is the thing that is left to us in a bad time. —E. B. White

5. In a community where public services have failed to keep *abreast* of private consumption, . . . in an atmosphere of private *opulence* and public *squalor*, the private goods have full sway. —John Kenneth Galbraith

2   Using the dictionary

The dictionary is a quick reference for the meaning of words (see 32b). It can give the precise meaning of a word whose general meaning you have guessed by examining the word's context. It can also help you fix the word in your memory by showing its spelling, pronunciation, grammatical functions and forms, etymology, and synonyms and antonyms.

For example, suppose you did not understand the word *homogeneous* in the following sentence:

Its homogeneous population makes the town stable but dull.

The dictionary gives the meanings of the word: "of the same kind," "of similar composition throughout." Thus the town's population is made up of similar kinds of people. *Homogeneous* comes from the Greek words *hom,* meaning "same," and *genos,* meaning "kind, type." Obviously, the composition of the word reinforces its definitions. Looking down the dictionary's column after the entry for *homogeneous,* you would find a related word, *homogenize,* which might be more familiar because of the common phrase *homogenized milk.* To *homogenize* means "to blend into a smooth mixture" and "to break up the fat globules of milk by forcing them through minute openings." The relation between this familiar word and the other, less familiar one gives added meaning to both

33c

words. A similar expansion of meaning could come from examining an antonym of *homogeneous,* such as *heterogeneous,* meaning "consisting of dissimilar ingredients." Thinking of the two opposite words together might fix them both in your memory.

A dictionary of synonyms is the best source for the precise meanings of similar words (see 32a-3). But even an abridged dictionary will supply much information about synonyms (see 32a-1). Most abridged dictionaries list a word's common synonyms and either direct you to the entries for the synonyms or distinguish among them in one place. An example of the latter form is the paragraph below, which follows the main entry for the word *real* in *The American Heritage Dictionary of the English Language.* By drawing on this information as you write, you can avoid overreliance on the word *real* when a more precise word is appropriate.

Synonyms: *real, actual, true, authentic, concrete, existent, genuine, tangible, veritable. Real,* although frequently used interchangeably with the terms that follow, pertains basically to that which is not imaginary but is existent and identifiable as a thing, state, or quality. *Actual* connotes that which is demonstrable. *True* implies belief in that which conforms to fact. *Authentic* implies acceptance of historical or attributable reliability rather than visible proof. *Concrete* implies the reality of actual things. *Existent* applies to concepts or objects existing either in time or space: *existent tensions. Genuine* presupposes evidence or belief that a thing or object is what it is claimed to be. *Tangible* stresses the mind's acceptance of that which can be touched or seen. *Veritable,* which should be used sparingly, applies to persons and things having all the qualities claimed for them.

EXERCISE 5

The dictionary entry above lists the following words as synonyms for *real: actual, true, authentic, concrete, existent, genuine, tangible,* and *veritable.* Using this entry and consulting another dictionary if necessary, write nine sentences that make precise use of *real* and each of its eight synonyms.

ANSWERS: EXERCISE 5

Individual response.

33c

No quick formula exists for turning poor spellers into good ones. Students with serious spelling problems may need systematic instruction in spelling, which, like systematic instruction in vocabulary, is rarely allowed by course time. You may want to refer such students to a skills center on campus or, if there are no such services, to a good spelling workbook. There are, however, activities and assignments that can help. Most students can improve their spelling markedly by learning and actually applying the limited number of standard rules, by maintaining a record of words that repeatedly cause them trouble, and by faithfully practicing brief groups of words from a spelling list. Such advice, though uninspired and unoriginal, does produce real improvement if a student can be persuaded to follow it, perhaps with the added reminder that lack of confidence in spelling distracts the student from more important matters in writing.

CHAPTER REFERENCE LIST

The following is an outline of the chapter for quick reference.

CHAPTER 34

Spelling

Because of the history and complexity of English, spelling English words according to standard usage requires consistent attention. However, learning to spell well is worth the effort because misspelling can make writing seem incompetent or lazy. This chapter will show you how to recognize typical spelling problems, how to follow a handful of rules as a guide to spelling, and how to develop spelling skills through conscious effort.

34a Avoiding typical spelling problems

Spelling well involves recognizing situations that commonly lead to misspelling: pronunciation can mislead you in several ways; different forms of the same word may have different spellings; and some words have more than one acceptable spelling.

1 Avoiding excessive reliance on pronunciation

In English, unlike some languages, pronunciation of words is an unreliable guide to their spelling. The same letter or combination of letters may have different sounds in the pronunciation of different words. For an example, say aloud these different ways of pronouncing the letters *ough: tough, dough, cough, through, bough.* Another problem is that some words contain letters that are not pronounced clearly or at all, such as the *ed* in *asked,* the silent *e* in *swipe,* or the unpronounced *gh* in *tight.*

Pronunciation is a particularly unreliable guide to the spelling of **homonyms,** words pronounced the same though they have different spellings and meanings: for example, *great/grate, to/too/two, threw/through, horse/hoarse, board/bored, break/brake.* Some commonly confused homonyms and words with very similar pronunciations, such as *accept/except,* are listed below. (See 34c-4 for some tips on how to use spelling lists.)

WORDS COMMONLY CONFUSED

accept (to receive)
except (other than)

affect (to have an influence on)
effect (result)

all ready (prepared)
already (by this time)

allude (to refer to indirectly)
elude (to avoid)

allusion (indirect reference)
illusion (erroneous belief or
  perception)

ascent (a movement up)
assent (agreement)

bare (unclothed)
bear (to carry, or an animal)

board (a plane of wood)
bored (uninterested)

born (brought into life)
borne (carried)

brake (stop)
break (smash)

buy (purchase)
by (next to)

capital (the seat of a
  government)
capitol (the building where a
  legislature meets)

cite (to quote an authority)
sight (the ability to see)
site (a place)

desert (to abandon)
dessert (after-dinner course)

discreet (reserved, respectful)
discrete (individual or distinct)

elicit (to bring out)
illicit (illegal)

fair (average, or lovely)
fare (a fee for transportation)

forth (forward)
fourth (after *third*)

gorilla (a large primate)
guerrilla (a kind of soldier)

hear (to perceive by ear)
here (in this place)

heard (past tense of *hear*)
herd (a group of animals)

hole (an opening)
whole (complete)

its (possessive of *it*)
it's (contraction of *it is*)

lead (heavy metal)
led (past tense of *lead*)
lessen (to make less)
lesson (something learned)

meat (flesh)
meet (encounter)

no (the opposite of *yes*)
know (to be certain)

passed (past tense of *pass*)
past (after, or a time gone by)

patience (forbearance)
patients (persons under
  medical care)

(continued)

34d Using the Hyphen to Form Compound Words

1. Forming compound adjectives, p. 518.
2. Writing fractions and compound numbers, p. 519.
3. Forming coined compounds, p. 519.
4. Attaching some prefixes and suffixes, p. 519.
5. Avoiding confusion, p. 520.

HOMONYM HOMEWORK

Sometimes the quickest way to learn distinctions in spelling between words that sound the same is to memorize the words and their definitions. Have students learn the correct spellings and definitions of these words by writing each word and its definition ten times.

RESOURCES AND IDEAS

Roger Clark and I. Y. Hashimoto, "A Spelling Program for College Students," *Teaching English in the Two-Year College,* 11 (1984): 34–38. The authors present "a three-step program that emphasizes student participation in the diagnosis of spelling problems and practice in using an individualized reference dictionary created by students themselves from their own spelling errors."

sp
34a

WORDS COMMONLY CONFUSED (*continued*)

peace (the absence of war)
piece (a portion of something)

plain (clear)
plane (a carpenter's tool, or an airborne vehicle)

presence (the state of being at hand)
presents (gifts)

principal (most important, or the head of a school)
principle (a basic truth or law)

rain (precipitation)
reign (to rule)
rein (a strap for controlling an animal)

raise (to build up)
raze (to tear down)

right (correct)
rite (a religious ceremony)
write (to make letters)

road (a surface for driving)
rode (past tense of *ride*)

scene (where an action occurs)
seen (past participle of *see*)

stationary (unmoving)
stationery (writing paper)

straight (unbending)
strait (a water passageway)

their (possessive of *they*)
there (opposite of *here*)
they're (contraction of *they are*)

to (toward)
too (also)
two (following *one*)

waist (the middle of the body)
waste (discarded material)

weak (not strong)
week (Sunday through Saturday)

which (one of a group)
witch (a sorcerer)

who's (contraction of *who is*)
whose (possessive of *who*)

your (possessive of *you*)
you're (contraction of *you are*)

EXTRA EXAMPLES

In addition to the words listed here, words that can be expressed by different forms, depending on the intended meaning, might also give students trouble. For example, *already* is frequently confused with *all ready*, and *a while* is almost always written *awhile*. The two most frequently miswritten expressions, however, are *a lot* (commonly written "alot") and *all right* (commonly written "alright").

sp
34a

2 **Distinguishing between different forms of the same word**

Other spelling problems occur when the noun form and the verb form of the same word are spelled differently. For example:

VERB	NOUN	VERB	NOUN
advise	advice	enter	entrance
describe	description	marry	marriage
speak	speech	omit	omission

Sometimes the noun and the adjective forms of the same word differ.

NOUN	ADJECTIVE	NOUN	ADJECTIVE
comedy	comic	height	high
courtesy	courteous	Britain	British
generosity	generous		

The principal parts of irregular verbs are usually spelled differently.

begin, began, begun   know, knew, known
break, broke, broken   ring, rang, rung

Irregular nouns change spelling from singular to plural.

child, children   shelf, shelves
goose, geese   tooth, teeth
mouse, mice   woman, women

Notice, too, that the stem of a word may change its spelling in different forms.

four, forty   thief, theft

3   Using preferred spellings

Many words have variant spellings as well as preferred spellings (see 32b-2). Often the variant spellings listed in an American dictionary are British spellings.

AMERICAN	**BRITISH**
color, hum*o*r	col*our*, hum*our*
theater, cent*er*	thea*tre*, cen*tre*
cance*l*ed, trave*l*ed	cance*ll*ed, trave*ll*ed
judgment	judg*e*ment
reali*z*e	reali*s*e

CAREFUL PROOFREADING

Many of the errors made with spelling can be avoided through careful proofreading. Two proofreading techniques that force the writer to read more slowly and carefully are (1) reading the essay aloud and (2) reading the essay backward, from last to first paragraph.

34b   Following spelling rules

Misspelling is often a matter of misspelling a syllable rather than the whole word. The following general rules focus on troublesome syllables, with notes for the occasional exceptions.

1   Distinguishing between *ie* and *ei*

Words like *believe* and *receive* sound alike in the second syllable, but the syllable is spelled differently. How do you know which word should have *ie* and which one *ei*? Use the familiar jingle:

I before *e*, except after *c*, or when pronounced ''ay'' as in *neighbor* and *weigh*.

sp
34b

i BEFORE *e*	believe	bier	hygiene
	grief	thief	friend
	chief	fiend	
ei AFTER *c*	ceiling	conceive	perceive
	receive	deceit	conceit
ei SOUNDED AS "AY"	neighbor	freight	beige
	sleigh	eight	heinous
	weight	vein	

EXCEPTIONS: In some words an *ei* combination neither follows *c* nor is pronounced "ay." These words include *either, neither, foreign, forfeit, height, leisure, weird, seize,* and *seizure.* This sentence might help you remember some of them:

The weird foreigner neither seizes leisure nor forfeits height.

ANSWERS: EXERCISE 1

1. brief	9. leisurely
2. deceive	10. achieve
3. receipt	11. patience
4. seize	12. pierce
5. foreign	13. height
6. priest	14. freight
7. grievance	15. feint
8. fiend	

EXERCISE 1

Insert *ie* or *ei* in the words below. Check doubtful spellings in a dictionary.

1. br__f	6. pr__st	11. pat__nce
2. dec__ve	7. gr__vance	12. p__rce
3. rec__pt	8. f__nd	13. h__ght
4. s__ze	9. l__surely	14. fr__ght
5. for__gn	10. ach__ve	15. f__nt

2 Keeping or dropping a final *e*

Many words end with an unpronounced or silent *e:* for instance, *move, brave, late, rinse.* When adding endings like *-ing* or *-ly* to these words, do you keep the final *e* or drop it? You drop it if the ending begins with a vowel.

advise + able = advisable
force + ible = forcible
surprise + ing = surprising

You keep the final, silent *e* if the ending begins with a consonant.

advance + ment = advancement
accurate + ly = accurately
care + ful = careful

EXCEPTIONS: The silent *e* is sometimes retained before an ending beginning with a vowel. It is kept when *dye* becomes *dyeing,* to avoid confusion with *dying.* It is kept to prevent mispronunciation

sp
34b

of words like *shoeing* (not *shoing*) and *mileage* (not *milage*). And the final *e* is often retained after a soft *c* or *g*, to keep the sound of the consonant soft rather than hard.

courageous	changeable	noticeable
outrageous	manageable	embraceable

The silent *e* is also sometimes *dropped* before an ending beginning with a consonant, when the *e* is preceded by another vowel.

argue + ment = argument
true + ly = truly
due + ly = duly

EXERCISE 2

Combine the following words and endings, keeping or dropping final *e*'s as necessary to make correctly spelled words. Check doubtful spellings in a dictionary.

1. malice + ious
2. love + able
3. service + able
4. retire + ment
5. sue + ing
6. virtue + ous
7. note + able
8. battle + ing
9. suspense + ion

ANSWERS: EXERCISE 2

1. malicious
2. lovable *or* loveable
3. serviceable
4. retirement
5. suing
6. virtuous
7. notable
8. battling
9. suspension

3 Keeping or dropping a final *y*

Words ending in *y* often change their spelling when an ending is added to them. The basic rule is to change the *y* to *i* when it follows a consonant.

beauty, beauties	worry, worried	supply, supplier
folly, follies	merry, merrier	deputy, deputize

But keep the *y* when it follows a vowel; when the ending is *-ing;* or when it ends a proper name.

day, days	cry, crying	May, Mays
obey, obeyed	study, studying	Minsky, Minskys

sp
34b

EXERCISE 3

Combine the following words and endings, changing or keeping final *y*'s as necessary to make correctly spelled words. Check doubtful spellings in a dictionary.

1. imply + s
2. messy + er
3. apply + ing
4. delay + ing
5. defy + ance
6. say + s
7. solidify + s
8. Murphy + s
9. supply + ed

ANSWERS: EXERCISE 3

1. implies
2. messier
3. applying
4. delaying
5. defiance
6. says
7. solidifies
8. Murphys
9. supplied

4 Doubling consonants

Words ending in a consonant sometimes double the consonant when an ending is added. Whether to double the final consonant depends first on the number of syllables in the word.

In one-syllable words, double the final consonant when a single vowel precedes the final consonant.

slap, slapping flat, flatter
tip, tipped   pit, pitted

However, *don't* double the final consonant when two vowels or a vowel and another consonant precede the final consonant.

pair, paired   park, parking
real, realize   rent, rented

In words of more than one syllable, double the final consonant when a single vowel precedes the final consonant and the stress falls on the last syllable of the stem once the ending is added.

submit, submitted refer, referring
occur, occurred   begin, beginning

But *don't* double the final consonant when it is preceded by two vowels or by a vowel and another consonant, or when the stress falls on other than the stem's last syllable once the ending is added.

refer, reference   despair, despairing
relent, relented   beckon, beckoned

ANSWERS: EXERCISE 4

1. repairing
2. admittance
3. benefited
4. shopped
5. concealed
6. allotted
7. dripping
8. declaimed
9. paralleling

EXERCISE 4

Combine the following words and endings, doubling final consonants as necessary to make correctly spelled words. Check doubtful spellings in a dictionary.

1. repair + ing
2. admit + ance
3. benefit + ed
4. shop + ed
5. conceal + ed
6. allot + ed
7. drip + ing
8. declaim + ed
9. parallel + ing

5 Attaching prefixes

Adding prefixes such as *dis-*, *mis-*, and *un-* does not change the spelling of a word. When adding a prefix, do not drop a letter from or add a letter to the original word.

sp
34b

uneasy	disappoint	misinform
unnecessary	dissatisfied	misstate
antifreeze	defuse	misspell
anti-intellectual	de-emphasize	

(See also 34d-4 on when to use hyphens with prefixes.)

6 Forming plurals

Nouns

Most nouns form plurals by adding *-s* to the singular form.

boy, boys   table, tables   carnival, carnivals

Some nouns ending in *f* or *fe* form the plural by changing the ending to *ve* before adding *-s*.

leaf, leaves   wife, wives
life, lives   yourself, yourselves

Singular nouns ending in *-s*, *-sh*, *-ch*, or *-x* form the plural by adding *-es*.

kiss, kisses   church, churches
wish, wishes   fox, foxes

(Notice that verbs ending in *-s*, *-sh*, *-ch*, or *-x* form the third-person singular in the same way. *Taxes* and *lurches* are examples.)

Nouns ending in *o* preceded by a vowel usually form the plural by adding *-s*.

ratio, ratios   zoo, zoos

Nouns ending in *o* preceded by a consonant usually form the plural by adding *-es*.

hero, heroes   tomato, tomatoes

Some English nouns that were originally Italian, Greek, Latin, or French form the plural according to their original language: *piano, pianos; medium, media; datum, data; beau, beaux.*

Compound nouns

Compound nouns form plurals in two ways. An *-s* is added to the last word when the component words are roughly equal in importance, whether or not they are hyphenated.

MEMORY AID

Separating the *-sedes:*

Students may learn to distinguish which *-sede* (*-ceed*, *-cede*) should be planted at the end of a word by memorizing the words *proceed, exceed, succeed,* and *supersede. Proceed, exceed,* and *succeed* are the only words ending in *-ceed. Supersede* is the only word ending in *-sede.* All the remaining *-cede* words end in *-cede.*

sp
34b

| city-states | bucket seats | breakthroughs |
| painter-sculptors | booby traps | |

When the parts of the compound word are not equal—especially when a noun is combined with other parts of speech—then *-s* is added to the noun.

fathers-in-law   passersby

Note, however, that most modern dictionaries give the plural of *spoonful* as *spoonfuls*.

ANSWERS: EXERCISE 5

1. piles
2. donkeys
3. beaches
4. summaries
5. thieves
6. boxes
7. switches
8. rodeos
9. criteria
10. cupfuls
11. librettos *or* libretti
12. sisters-in-law
13. miles-per-hour
14. cargoes *or* cargos
15. hisses

EXERCISE 5

Make correct plurals of the following words. Check doubtful spellings in a dictionary.

1. pile
2. donkey
3. beach
4. summary
5. thief
6. box
7. switch
8. rodeo
9. criterion
10. cupful
11. libretto
12. sister-in-law
13. mile per hour
14. cargo
15. hiss

34c Developing spelling skills

The essential steps in improving spelling skills are to cultivate a general wariness about spelling and to make a habit of consulting a dictionary whenever you doubt a spelling. Start by looking up the word as you think it is spelled. Then try different variations based on the pronunciation of the word. Once you think you have found the correct spelling, check the definition to make sure you have the word you want. (Some word processors have built-in spelling checkers that can serve either as ready references or as active monitors of spelling. See Appendix B, p. 712.) In addition to regular use of a dictionary, you can improve spelling in several other ways discussed below.

1 Editing and proofreading carefully

If spelling is a problem for you, you will want to give it high priority while editing your writing (see 2c) and again while proofreading, your last chance to catch misspelled words (see 2d). Reading a draft backward, word by word, can help you spot mistakes such as switched or omitted letters in words you know. Because the procedure forces you to consider each word in isolation, it can also highlight spellings you may be less sure of. A sense of uncertainty is crucial in spotting and correcting spelling errors, even for good spellers who make relatively few errors. Listen to your own uncertainty, and let it lead you to the dictionary.

2   Pronouncing carefully

Careful pronunciation is not always a reliable guide to spelling (see 34a), but it can keep you from misspelling words that are often mispronounced. For example:

athletics (not ath*e*letics)	nuclear (not nuc*ular*)
disastrous (not disas*te*rous)	library (not libary)
recognize (not reconize)	mischievous (not mischie*vi*ous)
lightning (not light*e*ning)	stric*t*ly (not stricly)
height (not heigh*th*)	gover*n*ment (not goverment)
irrelevant (not irre*ve*lant)	hist*o*ry (not histry)
perform (not p*re*form)	represent*a*tive (not representive)

3   Using mnemonics

Mnemonics (pronounced with an initial "*n*" sound) are techniques for assisting your memory. The *er* in *letter* and *paper* can remind you that *stationery* (meaning "writing paper") has an *er* near the end; *stationary* with an *a* means "standing in place." Or the word *dome* with its long *o* sound can remind you that the building in which the legislature meets is spelled *capitol*, with an *o*. The *capital* city is spelled with *al* like *Albany*, the capital of New York. If you identify the words you have trouble spelling, you can take a few minutes to think of your own mnemonics, which may work better for you than someone else's.

4   Studying spelling lists

Learning to spell commonly misspelled words will reduce your spelling errors. Keep a list of all the words you misspell in your papers, and teach yourself tricks to remember their spellings. For general improvement in spelling, work with the following list of commonly misspelled words. Study only six or seven words at a time. If you are unsure of the meaning of a word, look it up in a dictionary and try using it in a sentence. Pronounce the word out loud, syllable by syllable, and write the word out. (The list of similar-

RESOURCES AND IDEAS

Muriel Harris, "The Big Five: Individualizing Improvement in Spelling," *Teaching the Basics—Really!* ed. Ouida H. Clapp (Urbana: NCTE, 1977): 104–7. Harris suggests making students aware of their habitual problems deriving from homophones, pronunciation, doubled consonants, word roots, and the schwa.

sp
34c

RESOURCES AND IDEAS

Jane McClellan, "A Clinic for Misspellers," *College English* 40 (1978): 324–29. McClellan suggests using several kinds of word lists and frequent drill to bring about improvement.

sounding words in 34a should be considered an extension of the one below.)

absence	attendance	conquer	discipline
abundance	audience	conscience	discriminate
acceptable	average	conscious	discussion
accessible		consistency	disease
accidentally	bargain	consistent	dissatisfied
accommodate	basically	continuous	distinction
accuracy	beginning	controlled	divide
accustomed	belief	controversial	divine
achieve	believe	convenience	division
acknowledge	beneficial	convenient	doctor
acquire	benefited	coolly	drawer
across	boundary	course	
actually	breath	courteous	easily
address	breathe	criticism	ecstasy
admission	Britain	criticize	efficiency
adolescent	bureaucracy	crowd	efficient
advice	business	cruelty	eighth
advising		curiosity	either
against	calculator	curious	eligible
aggravate	calendar		embarrass
aggressive	carrying	deceive	emphasize
all right	cede	deception	empty
all together	cemetery	decide	enemy
almost	certain	decision	entirely
although	changeable	definitely	environment
altogether	changing	degree	equipped
amateur	characteristic	dependent	especially
analysis	chief	descend	essential
analyze	chocolate	descendant	every
angel	choose	describe	exaggerate
annual	chose	description	exceed
answer	climbed	desirable	excellent
apology	coarse	despair	exercise
apparent	column	desperate	exhaust
appearance	coming	destroy	existence
appetite	commercial	determine	expense
appreciate	commitment	develop	experience
appropriate	committed	device	experiment
approximately	committee	devise	explanation
argument	competent	dictionary	extremely
arrest	competition	difference	
ascend	complement	dining	familiar
assassinate	compliment	disagree	fascinate
assistance	conceive	disappear	favorite
associate	concentrate	disappoint	February
atheist	concert	disapprove	finally
athlete	condemn	disastrous	forcibly

foreign
foresee
forty
forward
friend
frightening
fulfill

gauge
generally
government
grammar
grief
guarantee
guard
guidance

happily
harass
height
heroes
hideous
humorous
hungry
hurriedly
hurrying
hypocrisy
hypocrite

ideally
illogical
imaginary
imagine
imitation
immediately
immigrant
incidentally
incredible
independence
independent
individually
inevitably
influential
initiate
innocuous
inoculate
insistent
integrate
intelligence
interest

interference
interpret
irrelevant
irresistible
irritable
island

jealousy
judgment

knowledge

laboratory
leisure
length
library
license
lightning
likelihood
literally
livelihood
loneliness
loose
lose
luxury
lying

magazine
maintenance
manageable
marriage
mathematics
meant
medicine
miniature
minor
minutes
mirror
mischievous
missile
misspelled
morale
morals
mournful
muscle
mysterious

naturally
necessary
neighbor

neither
nickel
niece
ninety
ninth
noticeable
nuclear
nuisance
numerous

obstacle
occasion
occasionally
occur
occurrence
official
omission
omit
omitted
opponent
opportunity
opposite
ordinary
originally

paid
panicky
paralleled
particularly
peaceable
peculiar
pedal
perceive
perception
performance
permanent
permissible
persistence
personnel
perspiration
persuade
persuasion
petal
physical
pitiful
planning
pleasant
poison
politician
pollute

possession
possibly
practically
practice
prairie
precede
preference
preferred
prejudice
preparation
prevalent
primitive
privilege
probably
procedure
proceed
process
professor
prominent
pronunciation
psychology
purpose
pursue
pursuit

quandary
quantity
quiet
quizzes

realistically
realize
really
rebel
rebelled
recede
receipt
receive
recognize
recommend
reference
referred
relief
relieve
religious
remembrance
reminisce
renown
repetition
representative

RESOURCES AND IDEAS

Jean L. Buck, "A New Look at Teaching Spelling," *College English* 38 (1977): 703–6. Buck encourages the use of personal word lists dawn from students' writing as a basis for class activities, including an exchange of lists.

sp
34c

RESOURCES AND IDEAS

Ann Ruggles Gere, "Alternatives to Tradition in Teaching Spelling," *Teaching the Basics—Really!* ed. Ouida H. Clapp (Urbana: NCTE, 1977): 100–3. Gere proposes the use of individualized word lists and classroom games and also the teaching of phoneme-grapheme correspondences and word division.

resemblance	significance	surely	unconscious
resistance	similar	surprise	undoubtedly
restaurant	sincerely	suspicious	unnecessary
rhythm	sophomore		until
ridiculous	source	technical	usually
roommate	speak	technique	
	speech	temperature	vacuum
sacrifice	sponsor	tendency	vegetable
sacrilegious	stopping	than	vengeance
safety	strategy	then	vicious
satellite	strength	thorough	villain
scarcity	strenuous	though	visible
schedule	stretch	throughout	
science	strict	together	weather
secretary	studying	tomorrow	Wednesday
seize	succeed	tragedy	weird
separate	successful	transferred	wherever
sergeant	sufficient	truly	whether
several	summary	twelfth	wholly
sheriff	superintendent	tyranny	woman
shining	supersede		women
shoulder	suppress	unanimous	writing

34d Using the hyphen to form compound words

The hyphen (-) is a mark of punctuation used either to divide a word or to form a compound word. Always use a hyphen to divide a word at the end of a line and continue it on the next line as explained in Chapter 30 on word division. Using a hyphen to form compound words is somewhat more complicated.

Compound words express a combination of ideas. They may be written as a single word, like the noun *breakthrough;* as two words, like the noun *decision making;* or as a hyphenated word, like the noun *cave-in.* Sometimes compound words using the same element are spelled differently—for example, *cross-reference, cross section,* and *crosswalk.* Several reliable generalizations can be made about using the hyphen for compound words. But if you doubt the spelling of a compound word, consult a dictionary.

1 Forming compound adjectives

When two or more words serve together as a single modifier before a noun, a hyphen or hyphens form the modifying words clearly into a unit.

She is a *well-known* actor.
The conclusions are based on *out-of-date* statistics.
No *English-speaking* people were in the room.

When the same compound adjectives follow the noun, hyphens are unnecessary and are usually left out.

The actor is *well known*.
The statistics were *out of date*.
Those people are *English speaking*.

Hyphens are also unnecessary in compound modifiers containing an *-ly* adverb, even when these fall before the noun: *clearly defined terms; swiftly moving train.*

When part of a compound adjective appears only once in two or more parallel compound adjectives, hyphens indicate which words the reader should mentally join with the missing part.

School-age children should have eight- or nine-o'clock bedtimes.

2   Writing fractions and compound numbers

Hyphens join the numerator and denominator of fractions.

three-fourths
one-half

The whole numbers twenty-one to ninety-nine are always hyphenated.

Eighteen girls and twenty-four boys took the bus.
The total is eighty-seven.

3   Forming coined compounds

Writers sometimes create (coin) temporary compounds and join the words with hyphens.

Muhammad Ali gave his opponent a classic come-and-get-me look.

4   Attaching some prefixes and suffixes

Prefixes are usually attached to word stems without hyphens: *predetermine, unnatural, disengage.* However, when the prefix precedes a capitalized word or when a capital letter is combined with a word, a hyphen usually separates the two: *un-American, non-*

**sp
34d**

European, A-frame. And some prefixes, such as *self-*, *all-*, and *ex-* (meaning "formerly"), usually require hyphens no matter what follows: *self-control, all-inclusive, ex-student*. The only suffix that regularly requires a hyphen is *-elect*, as in *president-elect*.

A hyphen is sometimes necessary to prevent misreading, especially when a prefix and stem place the same two vowels together or when a stem and suffix place the same three consonants together.

> deemphasize, de-emphasize
> antiintellectual, anti-intellectual
> trilllike, trill-like

Check a recent dictionary for the current form, particularly for words that join two *e*'s or *i*'s. If the word you seek does not appear in the dictionary, assume that it should be hyphenated.

5   Avoiding confusion

If you wrote the sentence *Doonesbury is a comic strip character*, the reader might stumble briefly over your meaning. Is Doonesbury a character in a comic strip or a comic (funny) character who strips? Presumably you would mean the former, but a hyphen would prevent any possible confusion: *Doonesbury is a comic-strip character*.

Adding prefixes to words can sometimes create ambiguity. *Recreation* (*creation* with the prefix *re-*) could mean either "a new creation" or "diverting, pleasurable activity." Using a hyphen, *re-creation*, limits the word to the first meaning. Without a hyphen the word suggests the second meaning.

sp
34d

ANSWERS: EXERCISE 6

1. Correct.
2. de-escalate
3. forty-odd soldiers
4. little-known bar
5. seven-eighths
6. seventy-eight
7. happy-go-lucky
8. pre-existing
9. senator-elect
10. Correct.
11. two- and six-person cars
12. ex-songwriter
13. V-shaped
14. re-educate

EXERCISE 6

Insert hyphens as needed in the following compounds. Circle all compounds that are correct as given. Consult a dictionary as needed.

1. reimburse
2. deescalate
3. forty odd soldiers
4. little known bar
5. seven eighths
6. seventy eight
7. happy go lucky
8. preexisting
9. senator elect
10. postwar
11. two and six person cars
12. ex songwriter
13. V shaped
14. reeducate

PART VIII

Research Writing

The entire process of researching and writing—not simply the research paper itself—is the subject of this chapter and the two that follow (Chapter 35–37). Because working with sources can lead to several different kinds of writing—reporting, interpreting, or analyzing—these chapters provide two different examples of student papers-in-progress, one emphasizing interpretation, the other emphasizing analysis.

The present chapter looks at what are generally viewed as the earlier stages of the research/writing process. It acknowledges, however, that writing with sources, like writing in general, is often recursive and difficult to separate into discrete stages.

The chapter offers detailed and helpful advice about planning a research project and includes a planning form students may wish to adapt for their own projects. Following this, the chapter describes ways to find and limit a researchable topic as well as strategies for finding information and further refining a topic. Covered in detail are different research sources: reference books (and the library catalog), periodicals, general books, computerized data bases, and a writer's own sources (including interviews). The concluding section offers helpful advice on making a working bibliography and provides bibliographical models in accordance with the latest edition (3rd, 1988) of the *MLA Handbook*.

CHAPTER 35

Beginning a Research Project

Much of your writing in college will lead you to investigate and assess the work of others. So-called research or term papers serve an obvious practical function in training you to use the resources of a library—a valuable skill for many kinds of work and for life outside of work. But this is only one benefit. In research writing you learn to evaluate other people's work and draw on it to formulate, support, and extend your own opinions. You gain expertise as you study a topic in depth. You increase your control over your environment by uncovering, organizing, and contributing to information and ideas in a way that suits your needs and interests.

Your role in writing a research paper will depend on whether you are called upon mainly to report, to interpret, or to analyze sources. In **reporting,** you survey, organize, and present the available evidence about a topic (for instance, how lobbyists influence legislators' votes or how three mice responded to sleep deprivation). In **interpreting,** you examine a range of views on a topic in order to draw your own conclusions (for instance, the ethical dilemmas in using humans as experimental subjects), or you search in varied sources for facts and opinions relevant to your thesis (for instance, that adopted children should, or should not, have access to their birth records). In **analyzing,** you isolate an unsolved problem or unanswered question (for instance, the failure of an economics theory to explain a change in the economy or the significance of a repeated image in the work of a poet), and then you attempt to reach a solution or answer through critical evaluation (or analysis) of relevant scholarly sources or of texts such as literary works or historical documents. As the examples indicate, reporting generally serves an explanatory purpose, while interpreting and analyzing may serve either an explanatory or a persuasive purpose (see 1c).

The three operations are not exclusive: for instance, a paper analyzing a repeated image in a poet's work would also involve a survey of poems and an interpretation of their meaning. Because the three operations overlap, the research and writing process described in this and the next two chapters can generally serve any one of them. Throughout these chapters we will follow the development of research papers by two students, Mark Shannon and Ann Weiss. Shannon's work, emphasizing interpretation, receives somewhat more attention; Weiss's work, emphasizing analysis, enters the discussion whenever her process differed significantly from Shannon's. Both students followed the same basic process, however.

RESOURCES AND IDEAS

Robert A. Schwegler and Linda K. Shamoon, "The Aims and Process of the Research Paper," *College English* 44 (1982): 812–24. The authors suggest that the differences in how students and instructors view a research paper's aims and purposes are key in explaining why students' research papers often fail to meet requirements or expectations. They define the four basic patterns that research papers follow and provide an example of one pattern in use.

35a Planning a research project

Research writing is undeniably complex, and it can be daunting. Most experienced research writers have stories of blindly rushing around the library or spending weeks obsessed with a single source or, perhaps worst of all, freezing in panic before ever beginning work. And most have found the antidote in thoughtful plans and systematic procedures that help them anticipate and follow through on the diverse and overlapping activities of research writing.

As soon as you receive an assignment for a research project, you can begin developing a strategy for completing it. The first step should be making a schedule that apportions the available time to the necessary work. A possible schedule appears on the next page. In it, each item is a step in the process of research writing (discussed in the section given in parentheses). As you complete the schedule, take into account the deadline, the required length of the paper, your other commitments, and your own writing process. Since these factors vary widely, no general guide can tell you how long each step should take. You can, however, anticipate that each segment marked off by a rule will take *roughly* one-quarter of the total time—for example, a week in a four-week assignment or two weeks in an eight-week assignment. The most unpredictable segments are the first two, so it's wise to get started early enough to be able to accommodate the unexpected.

You can probably see that the research-writing process outlined in the box corresponds to the general writing process dis-

RESOURCES AND IDEAS

Michael Kleine, "What Is It We Do When We Write Papers Like This One—and How Can We Get Students to Join Us?" *The Writing Instructor* 6 (1987): 151–61. Kleine outlines a model of the research process based on his interviews with university scholars and suggests that instruction in the research paper (1) emphasize peers rather than teacher as audience and (2) encourage papers focusing on various areas of academic study.

35a

SCHEDULING STEPS IN RESEARCH WRITING

Complete
by:

_____ 1. Planning a research project (35a)

_____ 2. Finding and limiting a researchable topic (35b)

_____ 3. Finding information and refining the topic (35c)

_____ 4. Making a working bibliography (35d)

_____ 5. Scanning and evaluating sources (36a)

_____ 6. Developing a tentative thesis and outline (36b)

_____ 7. Taking notes using summary, paraphrase, and direct quotation (36c) and avoiding plagiarism (36d)

_____ 8. Revising the thesis sentence and writing a formal outline (36e)

_____ 9. Drafting the paper (36f)

_____ 10. Revising and editing the paper (36g)

_____ 11. Preparing the final list of works cited (36h)

_____ 12. Preparing final source citations (36i)

_____ 13. Preparing and proofreading the final manuscript (36j)

_____ Final paper due

cussed in Chapters 1–2, with the three stages of planning or developing (steps 1–8), drafting (step 9), and revising and editing (step 10), plus the additional important stage of documenting the sources you use (steps 11–12). Like any other essay, a research paper evolves gradually and recursively, the steps sometimes overlapping and repeating. For instance, while you do research, your reading leads you to organize ideas; and while you organize ideas, you discover where you need to do more research. You begin to limit your topic as soon as you have chosen it, and you continue to limit it as you progress. The working thesis and outline you develop must later be refined.

Allowing for such inevitable changes while continuing to forge ahead through the steps is one key to successful and rewarding research writing. Another is systematic procedures for locating, collecting, organizing, and using information—procedures that are the focus of this chapter and the next. These procedures will be easier to follow if you acquire some basic research equipment and carry it with you whenever you work on the project:

35a

1. A package of 3″ × 5″ index cards for source information (see 35d).
2. Several packages of 4″ × 6″ index cards for notes from sources (see 36c).
3. At least one pen plus a spare. Some researchers use several pens with different colors of ink to code their notes.
4. Paper clips and rubber bands for organizing notes.
5. Appropriate coins for operating the library's photocopiers.

In addition, carry index cards or a notebook with you at all times to use as a **research journal**, a place to record your activities and ideas. (See 1b-2 on journal keeping.) In the journal's dated entries, you can keep a record of sources you consult, the leads you want to pursue, any dead ends you reach, and, most important, your thoughts about sources, leads, dead ends, new directions, relationships, and anything else that strikes you. Notes on what your sources actually say should be taken and organized separately—for instance, on the note cards discussed in 36c. The research journal is the place for tracking and developing your own ideas. You will probably find that the very act of writing in it opens your mind and clarifies your thinking, making your research increasingly productive and rewarding.

35b Finding and limiting a researchable topic

Before reading this section, you may want to review the suggestions given in 1b (p. 6) for finding and limiting an essay topic. Generally, the same procedure applies to writing any kind of research paper: take a subject assigned to you, or think of one that interests you, and narrow it to manageable dimensions by making it specific. However, as this section will show, selecting and limiting a topic for a research paper do present special opportunities and problems.

Mark Shannon and Ann Weiss took slightly different approaches to finding and limiting their topics. For a composition course, Shannon's instructor assigned an interpretation with an argumentative purpose but left the selection of subject to the student. Since Shannon was currently enjoying a course in business management, he decided to take that broad subject as his starting point. Using clustering (see 1d-3), he pursued some implications of this subject as illustrated on the next page. An awareness of sex-role stereotyping, developed during a psychology course in high school, encouraged Shannon to give the most thought to the issue of women in management. He posed questions and more questions

35b

until he arrived at the one that seemed potentially most interesting and fruitful: "How far do women still have to go in management, and why?"

In developing a topic for an analysis paper assigned in a composition course, Ann Weiss followed a somewhat different procedure. Instead of starting with a general subject, as Shannon did, Weiss began by looking for an unresolved question, interesting problem, or disagreement among the experts in some field of study. She remembered a chapter on the evolution of the Declaration of Independence in an anthology used in her composition class (*Readings in the Arts and Sciences,* edited by Elaine P. Maimon et al.). The chapter mentioned disagreement among historians about the sources of Thomas Jefferson's ideas in his draft of the Declaration, and Weiss decided to pursue this dispute by consulting one of the recent books mentioned as a source in the chapter. Scanning this book, she discovered an additional disagreement over whether or not Jefferson's draft of the Declaration was improved as it underwent extensive revision in the Continental Congress before it was signed. This issue was more interesting to Weiss than the one about Jefferson's sources, in part because it gave her a chance to

35b

analyze the revisions of the Declaration in more detail than had been possible in her composition class. Like Shannon, Weiss framed the issue as a question that would guide her research: "Was Jefferson's Declaration improved by the Continental Congress?"

Though their approaches differed, both Shannon and Weiss arrived at topics that satisfied four main requirements of a topic for a research paper. First, both students could expect to find ample published sources of information. The topics were not too recent, as the latest medical breakthrough or yesterday's news item would be, so others would have had a chance to produce evidence, weigh it, and publish their conclusions. Nor were the topics so removed geographically that the sources on them would be inaccessible, as they might be for someone in Ohio writing about a minor event in California history.

Second, each topic promised to encourage research in the kinds and number of sources required by the assignment. Shannon could research his topic in a variety of sources to present the range of facts and opinions necessary for an interpretation. And Weiss could do the close reading of sources (historians' works as well as the Declaration itself) required for an analysis. In contrast, topics that require only personal opinion and experience, such as "How I see housewives being depicted in detergent commercials," might be suitable for a personal essay but not for any kind of research paper. Nor is a topic suitable if it requires research in only one source. For this reason straight factual biographies of well-known people and how-to topics such as "Making lenses for eyeglasses" generally make poor research subjects. (The only exception is the literary paper in which you analyze a single work such as a novel. But most literary *research* papers require consulting the published opinions of other critics as well. See 38b.)

The third requirement satisfied by Shannon's and Weiss's topics is that they promised to foster the objective assessment of sources that would lead to defensible conclusions. Even when a research paper is intended to be argumentative, the success of the argument will depend on the balanced presentation of all points of view. Controversial topics that rest on belief, dogma, or prejudice —such as "When human life begins" or "Why women (or men) are superior"—are certainly arguable, but they are risky because the writer's preconceptions can easily slant either the research itself or the conclusions.

Fourth, and finally, Shannon's and Weiss's topics suited the length of papers they were assigned (1800 to 2300 words, or about six to ten pages) and the amount of time they were given to prepare the papers (four weeks). In four weeks and ten pages, Shannon could not have given adequate coverage to one of his broader top-

RESOURCES AND IDEAS

Bruce T. Peterson and Jill N. Burkland, "Investigative Reading and Writing: Responding to Reading with Research," *College Composition and Communication* 37 (1986): 236–40. The authors believe that research, rather than being limited to the research paper, should be viewed as "a way of thinking about reading, writing, and our experience of all texts." They offer a method for showing students how to approach research through their personal responses to the text.

35b

QUALITIES OF A GOOD RESEARCH TOPIC

1. Published sources will be ample: the topic is neither too recent nor too removed.
2. Sources will be diverse: the topic is neither wholly personal nor wholly factual.
3. Sources can be assessed objectively: the topic is not solely a matter of belief, dogma, or prejudice.
4. Sources can be examined thoroughly in the assigned time and length: the topic is not too broad.

---

ics, such as "How much progress have women made in management?" For that, he would have had to canvass at least twenty years' data and opinions, and then in his paper he could have given no more than scant attention to the various measures of "progress" and how women have fared against them. The same would be true of the topic Weiss originally considered: the sources of Jefferson's ideas in his draft of the Declaration. To treat this topic, Weiss would have had to analyze not only the conflicting opinions of historians but also the actual works they named as Jefferson's sources.

ANSWERS: EXERCISE 1

Individual response.

EXERCISE 1

Choose three of the following subjects and narrow each one to at least one topic suitable for beginning library work on a research paper. Or list and then limit three subjects of your own that you would enjoy investigating. (This exercise can be the first step in a research paper project that continues through Exercises 2 and 5 in this chapter and Exercises 1, 5, 7, 9, 10, and 11 in Chapter 36.)

1. bilingual education
2. the Opium War
3. dance in America
4. the history of women's suffrage
5. food additives
6. illegal aliens in the United States
7. exploration of outer space
8. the nuclear protest movement
9. the effect of television on professional sports
10. child abuse
11. black Americans and civil rights
12. recent developments in cancer research
13. computer piracy
14. Social Security
15. the European exploration of North America before Columbus
16. hazardous substances in the workplace
17. television evangelism
18. science fiction
19. irrigation rights
20. water pollution
21. women writers
22. the history of child labor practices
23. comic film actors

35b

24. the best work of a prominent writer
25. genetic engineering
26. heroes and heroines in modern fiction
27. computers and the privacy of the individual
28. gothic or romance novels in the nineteenth and twentieth centuries
29. the social responsibility of business
30. trends in popular music

35c Finding information and refining the topic

When you investigate a topic, you have access to a wide variety of sources, many of them discussed in this section. (See the box on the next page for an index.) By far the most abundant are the reference books, periodicals, and general books in the library. Reference books are good sources for either a summary of a topic or information on where to find out about the topic (see below). Periodicals (magazines, journals, and newspapers) contain articles that usually provide detailed and current information on the topic (see p. 536). General books, which constitute the bulk of a library's collection and are usually available for circulation, include literary works, nonfiction surveys, and in-depth studies of a vast range of subjects (see p. 540). Your library may also provide computerized indexes that simplify the search for sources (see p. 542).

Much information for a brief research paper will appear in **secondary sources,** works that report and analyze information drawn from other sources. Whenever possible, however, you should also seek **primary sources,** which include works of literature as well as historical documents (letters, diaries, speeches, and the like) that provide eyewitness accounts of an issue, event, or period. Primary sources may also include your own interviews, experiments, observations, or correspondence, as discussed on page 543. (Both Ann Weiss and Mark Shannon were able to use primary sources in their research papers. Weiss used a paragraph of the

A TIP FOR RESEARCHERS

If you are unsure of how to locate or use your library's resources, ask a reference librarian. A reference librarian is very familiar with all the library's resources and with general and specialized research techniques, and it is his or her job to help you and others with research. Even very experienced researchers often consult reference librarians.

TAKING THE TOUR

Library tours, conducted by either the instructor or the librarian, are an effective way to introduce students to the library's research tools and materials. Have students, with topics in mind, take a library tour and then spend the remainder of the class time finding information that is pertinent to their topics.

35c

Declaration of Independence showing the editing of Jefferson's draft, which she found in Jefferson's notes on the proceedings in the Continental Congress. See p. 641. Shannon used his own interview with a woman manager. See p. 624.)

1 Using reference books

Reference books available in the library include encyclopedias, dictionaries, digests, bibliographies, indexes, atlases, almanacs, and handbooks. Your research *must* go beyond these sources, but they can help you decide whether your topic really interests you and whether it meets the requirements for a research paper (pp. 527–28). Preliminary research in reference books will also direct you to more detailed sources on your topic. For an analysis paper, a specialized encyclopedia or bibliography can identify the main debates in a field and the proponents of each side.

Mark Shannon's use of reference books illustrates how helpful such sources can be as a starting point. Shannon first consulted *The Encyclopedia of Management* (p. 532), whose section on women in industry summarized women's advances since the Civil Rights Act of 1964. The encyclopedia also listed several books and articles for Shannon to pursue.

The following list gives the types of reference works and suggests when each may be profitable. Once you have a topic, you can scan this list for a reference book with which to start. If you want a more comprehensive catalog and explanation of reference works, consult Eugene P. Sheehy, *Guide to Reference Books,* 10th ed. (1986).

General encyclopedias

General encyclopedias give brief overviews and brief bibliographies. Because they try to cover all fields, they are a convenient, but very limited, starting point. Be sure to consult the most recent edition.

Collier's Encyclopedia. 24 vols. 1981.
Encyclopedia Americana. 30 vols. 1983.
Encyclopedia International. 20 vols. 1982.
The New Columbia Encyclopedia. 1975.
The New Encyclopaedia Britannica. 30 vols. 1985.
Random House Encyclopedia. Rev. ed. 1983.

Specialized encyclopedias, dictionaries, bibliographies

A specialized encyclopedia, dictionary, or bibliography generally covers an entire field or subject. These works will give you more detailed and more technical information than a general reference book will, and many of them (especially bibliographies) will direct you to particular books and articles on your subject. One general reference work providing information on sources in many of the fields below is the *Essay and General Literature Index* (published since 1900 and now updated semiannually). It lists tens of thousands of articles and essays that appear in books (rather than periodicals) and that might not be listed elsewhere.

BUSINESS AND ECONOMICS

Buell, Victor P., ed. *Handbook of Modern Marketing.* 2nd ed. 1986.
Eatwell, John, Murray Milgate, and Peter Newman, eds. *The New Palgrave: A Dictionary of Economics.* 4 vols. 1988.
Graham, Irvin. *Encyclopedia of Advertising.* 2nd ed. 1969.
Greenwald, Douglas. *The McGraw-Hill Dictionary of Modern Economics.* 3rd ed. 1984.

35c

Heyel, Carl. *The Encyclopedia of Management*. 3rd ed. 1982.

Munn, Glenn G. *Encyclopedia of Banking and Finance*. 8th ed. Ed. Ferdinand L. Garcia. 1983.

Seidler, Lee L., and Douglas R. Carmichael. *Accountant's Handbook*. 6th ed. 2 vols. 1981.

Sloan, Harold S., and Arnold Zurcher. *A Dictionary of Economics*. 5th ed. 1970.

HISTORY

American Historical Association. *Guide to Historical Literature*. 1961.

Binder, Leonard, ed. *The Study of the Middle East: Research and Scholarship in the Humanities and Social Sciences*. 1976.

Cambridge Ancient History. 12 vols. 1923–39. Revision in progress.

Cambridge Mediaeval History. 9 vols. 1911–36. Revision in progress.

Fairbank, John K., and Denis Twitchett. *Cambridge History of China*. 14 vols. 1978–. In progress.

Freidel, Frank, and Richard K. Showman, eds. *Harvard Guide to American History*. Rev. ed. 2 vols. 1974.

Hammond, N. G. L., and H. H. Scullard. *Oxford Classical Dictionary*. 2nd ed. 1970.

Martin, Michael R., et al. *An Encyclopedia of Latin-American History*. Rev. ed. 1981.

Miller, Elizabeth W., and Mary Fisher, eds. *The Negro in America: A Bibliography. 1970.*

New Cambridge Modern History. 14 vols. 1957–80.

Prucha, Francis P. *A Bibliographical Guide to the History of Indian-White Relations in the United States. 1977.*

LITERATURE, THEATER, FILM, AND TELEVISION

Adelman, Irving, and R. Dworkin. *Modern Drama: A Checklist of Critical Literature on Twentieth Century Plays*. 1967.

Bukalski, Peter J. *Film Research: A Critical Bibliography with Annotations and Essays*. 1972.

Drabble, Margaret, ed. *The Oxford Companion to English Literature*. 5th ed. 1985.

Gerther, Richard, ed. *International Television Almanac*. Published annually since 1956.

Gohdes, Clarence L. F. *Bibliographical Guide to the Study of the Literature of the U.S.A*. 4th ed. 1976.

Hart, James D., ed. *The Oxford Companion to American Literature*. 5th ed. 1983.

Hartnoll, Phyllis, ed. *The Oxford Companion to the Theatre*. 4th ed. 1983.

Holman, C. Hugh, and William Harmon. *A Handbook to Literature*. 5th ed. 1986.

MLA International Bibliography of Books and Articles on the Modern Languages and Literatures. Published annually since 1922.

Schweik, Robert C., and Dieter Riesner. *Reference Sources in English and American Literature: An Annotated Bibliography.* 1977.

Spiller, Robert E. *Literary History of the United States: Bibliography.* 1974.

Ward, A. W., and A. R. Waller, eds. *The Cambridge History of English Literature,* 15 vols. 1907–33.

Watson, G., ed. *New Cambridge Bibliography of English Literature.* 4 vols. 1972–76.

MUSIC AND THE VISUAL ARTS

Apel, Willi. *The Harvard Dictionary of Music.* 2nd rev. ed. 1969.

Chujoy, Anatole, and P. W. Manchester. *The Dance Encyclopedia.* 1978.

Encyclopedia of World Art. 15 vols. 1959–68.

Maillard, Robert, ed. *New Dictionary of Modern Sculpture.* Trans. Bettina Wadia. 1971.

Moore, Frank L. *Crowell's Handbook of World Opera.* 1974.

Sadie, Stanley, ed. *The New Grove Dictionary of Music and Musicians.* 20 vols. 1980.

Stambler, Irwin. *Encyclopedia of Pop, Rock, and Soul.* 1977.

Thompson, Oscar. *International Cyclopedia of Music and Musicians.* 11th ed. 1985.

Trachtenberg, Marvin, and Isabelle Hyman. *Architecture: From Prehistory to Post-Modernism.* 1986.

PHILOSOPHY AND RELIGION

Broderick, Robert, ed. *The Catholic Encyclopedia.* Rev. ed. 1987.

Buttrick, George Arthur, and Keith R. Crim. *The Interpreter's Dictionary of the Bible.* 5 vols. 1976.

Cross, F. L., and Elizabeth A. Livingstone. *The Oxford Dictionary of the Christian Church.* 1974.

Edwards, Paul, ed. *The Encyclopedia of Philosophy.* 4 vols. 1973.

Ferm, Vergilius, ed. *An Encyclopedia of Religion.* 1976.

Rice, Edward. *Eastern Definitions: A Short Encyclopedia of Religions of the Orient.* 1978.

Roth, Cecil, ed. *The New Standard Jewish Encyclopedia.* 5th ed. Ed. Geoffrey Wigoder. 1977.

SCIENCES

Belzer, Jack, et al., eds. *Encyclopedia of Computer Science and Technology.* 14 vols. 1975–80.

Considine, Douglas, ed. *The Encyclopedia of Chemistry.* 4th ed. 1984.

Fairbridge, Rhodes W., ed. *The Encyclopedia of Oceanography.* 1966.

Gray, Peter. *The Encyclopedia of Biological Sciences.* 2nd ed. 1981.

Jobes, Gertrude, and James Jobes. *Outer Space: Myths, Name Meanings, Calendars from the Emergence of History to the Present Day.* 1980.

35c

The Larousse Encyclopedia of Animal Life. 1967.
The McGraw-Hill Encyclopedia of Science and Technology. 5th ed. 15 vols. 1982.
Sarton, George. *An Introduction to the History of Science.* 5 vols. 1927–75.
Thewlis, J., ed. *Encyclopaedic Dictionary of Physics.* 9 vols. plus supplements. 1961–75.

SOCIAL SCIENCES

Brock, Clifton. *The Literature of Political Science.* 1969.
Eysenck, Hans Jurgen, ed. *Encyclopedia of Psychology.* 2nd ed. 1979.
Foreign Affairs Bibliography. 5 vols. 1960–76.
Leach, Maria, and Jerome Fried, eds. *Funk and Wagnalls Standard Dictionary of Folklore, Mythology and Legend.* 2 vols. 1984.
Mitchell, G. Duncan, ed. *A New Dictionary of the Social Sciences.* 1979.
Mitzel, Harold, ed. *Encyclopedia of Educational Research.* 5th ed. 4 vols. 1982.
Sills, David L., ed. *International Encyclopedia of the Social Sciences.* 8 vols. plus supplement. 1977.
UNESCO International Committee for Social Science Documentation, ed. *International Bibliography of the Social Sciences.* 1960–86.
White, Carl M., et al. *Sources of Information in the Social Sciences: A Guide to the Literature.* 2nd ed. 1973.
Winick, Charles. *Dictionary of Anthropology.* 1977.

Unabridged dictionaries and special dictionaries on language

Unabridged dictionaries are more comprehensive than abridged or college dictionaries. Special dictionaries give authoritative information on individual aspects of language. (See Chapter 32 for more on the kinds of dictionaries and how to use them.)

UNABRIDGED DICTIONARIES

Craigie, Sir William, and James R. Hulbert. *A Dictionary of American English on Historical Principles.* 4 vols. 1938–44.
The Oxford English Dictionary. 16 vols. 1986. *The Compact Edition,* 3 vols., was issued in 1971 and 1987.
The Random House Dictionary of the English Language. 2nd ed. 1987.
Webster's Third New International Dictionary of the English Language. 1986.

SPECIAL DICTIONARIES

Follett, Wilson. *Modern American Usage.* Ed. Jacques Barzun. 1966.

35c

Fowler, H. W. *Dictionary of Modern English Usage.* 2nd ed. Rev. and ed. Sir Ernest Gowers. 1965.

Lewis, Norman. *The New Roget's Thesaurus in Dictionary Form.* 1986.

Morris, William, and Mary Morris. *Harper Dictionary of Contemporary Usage.* 2nd ed. 1985.

Onions, Charles T., et al., eds. *The Oxford Dictionary of English Etymology.* 1966.

Partridge, Eric. *A Dictionary of Slang and Unconventional English.* 8th ed. Ed. Paul Beale. 1984.

Partridge, Eric. *Origins: A Short Etymological Dictionary of Modern English.* 1977.

Webster's New Dictionary of Synonyms. 1984.

Wentworth, Harold, and Stuart Berg Flexner. *Dictionary of American Slang.* 2nd supp. ed. 1975.

Biographical reference works

If you want to learn about someone's life, achievements, credentials, or position, or if you want to learn the significance of a name you've come across, consult one of the reference works below. Note, in addition, that more specialized biographical sources are available in fields such as law, health care, and art.

American Men and Women of Science. 16th ed. 8 vols. 1986.

Contemporary Authors. 123 vols. Published since 1967 and updated regularly.

Current Biography. Published annually since 1940.

Dictionary of American Biography. 17 vols. plus supplements. 1927–81.

Dictionary of Literary Biography. 48 vols. plus supplements. Published since 1978 and frequently updated and enlarged.

Dictionary of National Biography (British). 22 vols. plus supplements. 1882–1986.

James, Edward T., and Janet W. James, eds. *Notable American Women.* 3 vols. 1971–80.

Webster's Biographical Dictionary. 1972.

Who's Who in America. 2 vols. Published biennially since 1899.

Atlases and gazetteers

Atlases are bound collections of maps; gazetteers are geographical dictionaries.

Columbia Lippincott Gazetteer of the World. 1962.

Cosmopolitan World Atlas. 1981.

Encyclopaedia Britannica World Atlas International. 1969.

National Geographic Atlas of the World. 5th ed. 1981.

The Times Atlas of the World. 2nd rev. ed. 1983.

35c

Almanacs and yearbooks

Both almanacs and yearbooks are annual compilations of facts. Yearbooks record information about the previous year. Almanacs give facts and statistics about a variety of fields.

Americana Annual. Published annually since 1923.
Britannica Book of the Year. Published annually since 1938.
Facts on File Yearbook. Published annually since 1940.
U.S. Bureau of the Census. *Statistical Abstract of the United States.* Published annually since 1878.
World Almanac and Book of Facts. Published annually since 1868.

RESOURCES AND IDEAS

James E. Ford, "The Research Loop: Helping Students Find Periodical Sources," *College Composition and Communication* 37 (1986): 223–27. Ford describes a "research loop" that leads students and their instructors through a systematic process for conducting research.

2 Using periodicals

Periodicals—journals, magazines, and newspapers—are invaluable sources of information in research. The difference between journals and magazines lies primarily in their content, readership, frequency of issue, and page numbering. Magazines, such as *Psychology Today, Newsweek,* and *Esquire,* are nonspecialist publications intended for diverse readers. Most magazines appear weekly or monthly. Journals, in contrast, often appear quarterly and contain specialized information intended for readers in a particular field. Examples include *American Anthropologist, Journal of Black Studies,* and *Journal of Chemical Education.* In most magazines the page numbering begins anew with each issue. Many journals also page each issue separately, but others do not. Instead, the issues for an entire year make up an annual volume, and the pages are numbered continuously throughout the volume, so that issue number 3 (the third issue of the year) may open on page 327. (The method of pagination determines how you cite a journal article in a list of works cited and, if you use them, in footnotes or endnotes; see pp. 553 and 599.)

Using indexes to periodicals

Several guides provide information on the articles in journals, magazines, and newspapers. The contents, formats, and systems of abbreviation in these guides vary widely, and they can be intimidating at first glance. But each one includes in its opening pages an introduction and explanation to aid the inexperienced user. (See also p. 542 on using computerized data bases for locating articles in periodicals.)

A typical and general periodical guide is the *Readers' Guide to Periodical Literature,* published since 1900 and updated semi-

35c

monthly. It lists—by author, title, and subject—articles published each year in more than a hundred popular magazines. For a paper on a current topic you should consult at least several years' *Readers' Guide* volumes. Mark Shannon, checking a quarterly cumulative volume from 1987, found these possible sources under "Women executives."

> **Women executives**
> *See also*
> Clothing and dress—Businesswomen
> Women entrepreneurs
> Assertiveness breeds contempt [male vs. female evaluations of assertive female managers; study by David L. Mathison] V. Bozzi. *Psychol Today* 21:15 S '87
> Like father, like daughter [father-daughter corporations] R. Rooney. il *Good Housekeep* 204:108-9+ Je '87
> Where women are succeeding. A. B. Fisher. il *Fortune* 116:78-80+ Ag 3 '87

Other general indexes to periodicals include the following:

The New York Times Index. Published annually since 1913. This index to the most complete U.S. newspaper can serve as a guide to national and international events and can indicate what issues of unindexed newspapers to consult for local reactions to such events.

Poole's Index to Periodical Literature. 1802–1907. An index by subject to British and American periodicals of the nineteenth century.

Popular Periodicals Index. Published annually since 1973. An index to about twenty-five contemporary, popular periodicals not listed in major indexes.

Wall Street Journal Index. An index to the leading business newspaper and to *Barron's*. Published monthly since 1958.

For scholarly journals, most libraries have a variety of specialized indexes. Shannon also consulted one of these, the *Social Sciences Index.* What follows is about one-third of its listings under "Leadership" for the year April 1984 through March 1985. At least five entries held some promise for Shannon.

> **Leadership**
> *See also*
> Authority
> Charisma
> Consensus (Social sciences)
> Cooptation
> Elite (Social sciences)
> Paternalism
> Political leadership
> Supervisors
> Are women invisible as leaders? N. Porter and others. bibl *Sex Roles* 9:1035-49 O '83
> Australian managers' leadership beliefs, 1970/82. B. W. Stening and P. S. K. Wong. *Psychol Rep* 53:274 Ag '83

35c

Cooperative and competitive relationships between leaders and subordinates. D. Tjosvold and others. bibl *Hum Relat* 36:1111-24 D '83

Determinants of management styles in business and nonbusiness organizations. G. Chitayat and I. Venezia. bibl *J Appl Psychol* 69:437-47 Ag '84

Effective leadership in geography: the role of the department chairperson. S. Khan and G. Vuicich. bibl *Prof Geogr* 36:158-64 My '84

The effects of competent behavior on interpersonal attraction and task leadership. J. W. Rhue and others. bibl *Sex Roles* 10:925-37 Je '84

Effects of leader warmth and directiveness on subordinate performance on a subsequent task. D. Tjosvold. bibl *J Appl Psychol* 69:422-7 Ag '84

Effects of psychological gender and sex-incongruent behavior on evaluations of leadership. M. Remland and others. bibl *Percept Mot Skills* 57 pt1:783-9 D '83

Emergent leadership as a function of sex and task type. D. K. Wentworth and L. R. Anderson. bibl *Sex Roles* 11:513-24 S '84

An estimate of variance due to traits in leadership. D. A. Kenny and S. J. Zaccaro. bibl *J Appl Psychol* 68:678-85 N '83

The factor structure of "most preferred co-worker", and "assumed similarity of opposites" scores. G. Shouksmith. *Psychol Rep* 53:255-8 Ag '83

Group process and sex differences. L. S. Kahn. bibl *Psychol Women Q* 8:261-81 Spr '84

Leader legitimacy, leader-follower interaction, and followers' ratings of the leader. O. Ben-Yoav and others. *J Soc Psychol* 121:111-15 O '83

Leader sex, leader success, and leadership process: two field studies. R. W. Rice and others. bibl *J Appl Psychol* 69:12-31 F '84

The following is a partial list of scholarly indexes:

America: History and Life. Published three times a year since 1955.

Applied Science and Technology Index. Published monthly since 1958. From 1913 to 1957 this work was combined with the *Business Periodicals Index* in the *Industrial Arts Index.*

Art Index. Published quarterly since 1929.

Biological and Agricultural Index. Published monthly since 1964. From 1916 to 1963 this work was called the *Agricultural Index.*

Business Periodicals Index. Published annually since 1958. From 1913 to 1957 this work was combined with the *Applied Science and Technology Index* in the *Industrial Arts Index.*

The Education Index. Published monthly since 1929.

ERIC (Education Resources Information Center). *Current Index to Journals in Education.* Published monthly since 1969.

General Sciences Index. Published monthly since 1978.

Humanities Index. Published quarterly since 1974. From 1965 to 1974 this author and subject index was combined with the *Social Sciences Index* in the *Social Sciences and Humanities Index.* From 1907 to 1965 the combined volume was called the *International Index.*

Index Medicus. Published monthly since 1960. From 1927 to 1959

35c

this work was called *Quarterly Cumulative Index Medicus.* From 1899 to 1926 it was *Index Medicus.*

MLA International Bibliography of Books and Articles in the Modern Languages and Literatures. Published annually since 1922.

Music Index. Published monthly since 1950.

Philosopher's Index. Published quarterly since 1967.

Social Sciences Index. Published quarterly since 1974. From 1965 to 1974 this author and subject index was combined with the *Humanities Index* in the *Social Sciences and Humanities Index.* From 1907 to 1965 the combined volume was called the *International Index.*

Using abstracts and citation indexes

Consulting a collection of article summaries—or **abstracts**—can tell you in advance whether you want to pursue a particular article further. Such collections are published in many academic disciplines. For example:

Abstracts of English Studies. Published quarterly since 1958.

America: History and Life (U.S. and Canadian history). Published three times a year since 1955.

Biological Abstracts. Published semimonthly since 1926.

Chemical Abstracts. Published weekly since 1907.

Communications Abstracts. Published quarterly since 1982.

Dissertation Abstracts International (doctoral dissertations). Published monthly since 1938. Before 1969, the title was *Dissertation Abstracts.*

Historical Abstracts (world history). Published since 1955.

Psychological Abstracts. Published monthly since 1927.

Sociological Abstracts. Published five times a year since 1952.

When you want to trace what has been written *about* an article or book you are consulting, use a **citation index.** This resource lists references to written works after they are published, as when one scientific article comments on an earlier article. The following is a partial list:

Arts and Humanities Citation Index. Published bimonthly since 1978.

Science Citation Index. Published bimonthly since 1955.

Social Science Citation Index. Published bimonthly since 1969.

Finding and using periodicals

Every library lists its complete periodical holdings either in the main catalog (see below) or in a separate catalog. The listing for each periodical tells how far back the issues go and where and

35c

in what form the issues are stored. The recent issues of a periodical are usually held in the library's periodical room. Back issues are usually stored elsewhere, in one of three forms: in bound volumes; on **microfilm,** a filmstrip showing pages side by side; or on **microfiche,** a sheet of film with pages arranged in rows and columns. Consulting periodicals stored on microfilm or microfiche requires using a special machine, or "reader," which locates and enlarges the page and projects it on a screen. Any member of the library's staff will show how to operate the reader.

HINT: TRACKING DOWN MATERIALS

Students should be prepared to face a few obstacles in tracking down library materials. One of the most common and frustrating obstacles is misplaced material. Remind students that they should plan to spend time looking around for their sources if these sources are not immediately apparent. Frequently, misplaced material will surface on unshelved bookracks, near photocopying machines, or on shelves adjacent to those on which the material is supposed to be.

3 **Using guides to books**

The library catalog

The library's catalog lists books alphabetically by authors' names, titles of books, and subjects. (In some catalogs authors and titles are alphabetized together and subjects are alphabetized separately.) If you are starting research on a subject you don't know very well, begin by looking under subject headings. If you know of an expert in the field and you want to find his or her books, look under the author's name. If you know the title of a relevant book but not the author's name, look for the title.

The library's catalog may be the familiar card file, cabinets of drawers containing 3″ × 5″ cards. But to save space and time, many libraries have converted their catalogs to other forms. A printed catalog in bound volumes contains small reproductions of the cards traditionally found in drawers. A catalog on microfilm or microfiche (see above) shows the library's collection on film viewed with a special reader. Increasingly, libraries are computerizing their catalogs: the user gains access to the computer's memory by typing a code onto a keyboard, and a screen displays the requested information. (With many computerized catalogs, the user can conduct a customized search through the library's holdings. See p. 542.) If you are uncertain about the location, form, or use of your library's catalog, seek help from a member of the library's staff.

Though the storage systems vary, all book catalogs contain similar information and follow a similar organization. By far the most widely used catalog format is that of the Library of Congress card. Samples of author, title, and subject cards appear on the opposite page.

The more systematically you approach the library's catalog, the more efficient and productive your search will be. The multivolume *Library of Congress Subject Headings* (*LCSH*) is a list of the various headings under which the Library of Congress catalogs

35c

Library call number —
HD 6054.3 .L63

AUTHOR CARD

Author's name — **Loden, Marilyn.**

Book title, subtitle, place of publication, publisher, date of publication — Feminine leadership, or, How to succeed in business without being one of the boys / Marilyn Loden. — New York: Times Books, © 1985.

xiii, 306 p. ; 22 cm.
Bibliography: p. 281–289.
Includes index.
ISBN 0-8129-1240-3

HD 6054.3 .L63

Feminine leadership

TITLE CARD

Book title —

Loden, Marilyn.
Feminine leadership, or, How to succeed in business without being one of the boys / Marilyn Loden. — New York: Times Books, © 1985.

Number of pages, height of book, additional material —
xiii, 306 p. ; 22 cm.
Bibliography: p. 281–289.
Includes index.
ISBN 0-8129-1240-3

HD 6054.3 .L63

WOMEN IN BUSINESS

SUBJECT CARD

Subject title —

Loden, Marilyn.
Feminine leadership, or, How to succeed in business without being one of the boys / Marilyn Loden. — New York: Times Books, © 1985.

xiii, 306 p. ; 22 cm.
Bibliography: p. 281–289.
Includes index.
ISBN 0-8129-1240-3

Other catalog listings for this title —
1. Women executives. 2. Women in business. 3. Leadership.
I. Title. II. Title: Feminine leadership. III. Title: How to succeed in business without being one of the boys.

21 MAY 87   12133597   MRKKdc

85-40283

Library of Congress

Card order number

books. Consulting this source and following its system of cross-references and headings at different levels of specificity, you will be able to discover the headings most likely to lead to appropriate sources. Mark Shannon, for instance, used *LCSH* to eliminate the heading of "Women—Employment," which was much too broad for his needs. He isolated the narrower "Women executives," with subcategories such as "Attitudes" and "Employment." Note that *LCSH* does not include most proper names of people, places, corporations, associations, government bodies, and the like.

References to books

Two types of reference books can help you identify general books that have information about your topic: publishing bibliographies and digests. Publishing bibliographies tell whether a book is still in print, whether a paperback edition is available, what books were published on a certain topic in a certain year, and so on. These bibliographies include the following:

Books in Print. Published and supplemented annually since 1873. Books indexed by author, title, and subject.

35c

Cumulative Book Index. Published monthly since 1898.
Paperbound Books in Print. Published semiannually since 1955.

You might, for example, want to know if the author of an encyclopedia article has published any relevant books since the date of the encyclopedia. You could look up the author's name in the latest *Books in Print* to find out.

If you want to evaluate a book's relevance to your topic before you search for it, a review index such as the following will direct you to published reviews of the book:

> *Book Review Digest.* Published annually since 1905. Summarizes *and* indexes reviews of books.
> *Book Review Index.* Published annually since 1965.
> *Index to Book Reviews in the Humanities.* Published since 1960.
> *Recent Publications in the Social and Behavioral Sciences.* Published annually.
> *Technical Book Review Index.* Published monthly since 1935.

4 Using computerized data bases

Libraries that use computers to store information about their holdings often provide researchers with a quick and effective way to find relevant sources. Either alone or with the aid of a staff member, the researcher gives the computer one or more key words about the topic, and the computer then consults its data base (its entire list of references) to produce a customized list of sources that have been indexed under the key word or words.

The kinds of computerized data bases and the specific search procedures vary widely from library to library. In some libraries only the catalog of general books can be used for a key-word search. The researcher can generally work unaided, following simple instructions on the computer screen. Other libraries have additional, more specialized data bases that index articles in periodicals, government documents, unpublished materials, and other resources. To search these data bases, the researcher often must enlist the help of a staff member, and the library may charge a fee for the service. Ask at your library to learn the resources available to you and the procedures you must follow.

The efficiency and reliability of a data-base search will be determined largely by the key word or words you give the computer. If a term is too general, it may turn up a long list of sources with only a tiny proportion relevant to your topic. If the term is too specific, it may turn up a too-short list or nothing at all. If Mark Shannon searched a computerized book catalog using the general word "women," the computer would show him every book in the library indexed under the word—a very long list. If, in contrast, he used the specific phrase "women executives," the computer would show him only the sources it could find that were indexed under both important words in the phrase.

A good source for appropriate key words is the *Library of Congress Subject Headings* (see p. 540). This reference can help with searches in other data bases besides a book catalog. Note, however, that some data bases have indexes of their own.

5 Generating your own sources

As noted on page 529, most of the sources you consult for a research project—and most of the resources of the library—are likely to be secondary sources in which the authors draw their information from other authors. However, academic writing will also require you to consult primary sources and to conduct primary research in which you generate information of your own. In many papers this primary research will be the sole basis for your writing, as when you analyze a poem or report on an experiment you conducted. In other papers you will be expected to use your research to support, extend, or refute the ideas of others.

Chapter 38 discusses the textual analyses, observations, experiments, and other primary sources you may use in writing for various academic disciplines. One primary source not covered there is the personal interview with an expert in the topic you are researching. Because of the give-and-take of an interview, you can obtain answers to questions precisely geared to your topic, and you can follow up instantly on points of confusion and unexpected leads. In addition, quotations and paraphrases from an interview can give your paper added immediacy and authority. Mark Shannon used just such an interview in his paper on women executives (see pp. 624–28).

A few precautions will help you get the maximum information from an interview with the minimum disruption to the person you are interviewing.

1. If you do not already know whom to consult for an interview, ask a teacher in the field or do some telephone or library research. Likely sources, depending on your topic, are those who have written about your topic or something closely related, officials in government, businesspeople, even your own aunt, if she is an expert in your topic because of experience, scholarship, or both.
2. In-person interviews are often easier and more productive than telephone interviews. But use the phone rather than forego a valuable source.
3. Call or write for an appointment. Tell the person exactly why

RESOURCES AND IDEAS

Thomas N. Tryzna, "Research Outside the Library: Learning a Field," *College Composition and Communication* 37 (1986): 217–23. The author suggests methods of finding sources outside the library and includes lists of organizations and their publications as possible sources.

35c

you are calling, what you want to discuss, and how long you expect the interview to take. Be true to your word on all points.

4. Prepare a list of open-ended questions to ask—perhaps ten or twelve for a one-hour interview. Listen to your subject's answers so that you can ask appropriate follow-up questions and pick up on unexpected but worthwhile points.

5. Take careful notes; or, if you have the equipment and your subject agrees, tape-record the interview. Before you quote your subject in your paper, check with him or her that the quotations are accurate.

6. Send a thank-you note immediately after the interview. Promise your subject a copy of your finished paper, and send the paper promptly.

ANSWERS: EXERCISE 2

Individual response.

> **EXERCISE 2**
>
> List at least five sources you can consult for further leads on each of the three topics you produced in Exercise 1 (p. 528) or for three other topics. Use the information provided in the preceding section and additional information at your library.

REMINDER FOR STUDENTS

Few things can be more frustrating than discovering, five pages into the writing of your paper, that you have forgotten to note key bibliographic information. Making detailed bibliography cards the first time you read your sources saves considerable time and footsteps. For detailed examples of bibliography cards and format, see pages 545–60.

 Making a working bibliography

1 Keeping systematic records of sources

Trying to pursue every source lead as you came across it would prove inefficient and probably ineffective. Instead, you'll want to find out what is available before deciding which leads to follow, and that requires systematically keeping track of where information is and what it is. You can keep track of sources by making a **working bibliography,** a file of the books, articles, and other sources you believe will help you. When you have a substantial file, you can decide which sources seem most promising and look them up first.

A working bibliography is your opportunity to record all the information you need to find your sources. You can use whatever system you like to keep track of information, but many experienced researchers find a card file safer and more flexible than, say, self-stick notes or pages of lists. Writing each source on an individual 3″ × 5″ card will allow you to arrange your sources alphabetically by author, to discard irrelevant sources without disrupting

bib
35d

your list, and later to transfer the information easily to your final list of sources.

Make a bibliography card for each source you think may be useful, whether you find it in the card catalog, in a reference book, or in an index to periodicals. Include all the information you will need for your final list of sources, using standard formats such as those discussed below. Getting all the information the first time will save you from having to retrace your steps later. For sources you find in the catalog of books, list every letter and number of the call number on the bibliography card to save time later. (However, you will not transfer the call number to the final list of sources.) Here are two examples of bibliography cards, the first for a book and the second for a periodical.

HD
6054.3
.L63

Loden, Marilyn. *Feminine Leadership, or, How to Succeed in Business Without Being One of the Boys.* New York: Times, 1985.

Bozzi, Vincent. "Assertiveness Breeds Contempt." *Psychology Today* Sept. 1987: 15.

When you turn in your paper, you will have to attach a list of the sources you have used (see 36h). So that readers can check or follow up on your sources, your list must include all the information needed to find the sources, in a format readers can understand. The following are two general guides to bibliographic formats that you can consult if your instructor does not specify a style to follow:

RESOURCES AND IDEAS

The resources and ideas presented on pages 545–61 are drawn from James E. Ford et al., "Research Paper Instruction: Comprehensive Bibliography of Periodical Sources, 1923–1980," *Bulletin of Bibliography* 39 (1982): 84–98.

RESOURCES AND IDEAS

Eleanor Blau, "The Forgotten Teacher," *The Independent School Bulletin* 31 (1972): 66–67. Blau argues that librarians can not only supervise a workshop but also provide instruction.

bib
35d

The Chicago Manual of Style. 13th ed. 1982.

Turabian, Kate L. *A Manual for Writers of Term Papers, Theses, and Dissertations.* 5th ed. Rev. and exp. Bonnie Birtwistle Honigsblum. 1987.

Editors and teachers in most academic disciplines require special formats in their scholarly journals and in student papers—formats that differ in the amount, arrangement, and punctuation of information. Chapter 38 lists the format guides published for psychology, biology, and several other disciplines; and the chapter illustrates some required formats. (See pp. 666 and 683.)

The following section discusses and illustrates the bibliographic formats of the *MLA Handbook for Writers of Research Papers*, 3rd ed. (1988). This book is published by the Modern Language Association and describes standard practice for courses and journals in composition, literature, foreign languages, and many other disciplines.

2 Using MLA bibliographic formats

The bibliographic models that follow are based on the *MLA Handbook*. Use the index opposite to find the page numbers of the models you need. Note that models may have to be combined; for example, in citing an article by four authors appearing in a biweekly periodical, you will need to draw on the models labeled "A book with more than three authors" and "A signed article in a weekly or biweekly periodical."

Books

The basic format for a book includes the following information:

Gilligan, Carol. In a Different Voice: Psychological Theory and Women's Development. Cambridge: Harvard UP, 1982.

1. The author's full name: the last name first, followed by a comma, and then the first name and any middle name or initial. Omit any title or degree attached to the author's name on the source, such as Dr. or Ph.D. End the name with a period and two spaces.

2. The full title of the book, including any subtitle. Underline the complete title, capitalize all important words (see 26b), separate the main title and the subtitle with a colon and one space, and end the title with a period and two spaces.

bib
35d

INDEX TO MLA BIBLIOGRAPHIC MODELS

3. The publication information: the city of publication, followed by a colon and one space; then the name of the publisher, followed by a comma; and finally the date of publication, ending with a period. All this information can be found
on the title page of the book or on the page after the title
page. Shorten most publishers' names—in many cases to a
single word. For instance, use "Knopf" for Alfred A. Knopf
and "Little" for Little, Brown. For university presses, use the
abbreviation "UP," as in the example above.

bib
35d

When other information is required for a reference, it is generally placed either between the author's name and the title or between the title and the publication information, as specified in the models below.

A BOOK WITH ONE AUTHOR

Gilligan, Carol. <u>In a Different Voice: Psychological Theory and Women's Development</u>. Cambridge: Harvard UP, 1982.

A BOOK WITH TWO OR THREE AUTHORS

Wimsatt, William K., and Cleanth Brooks. <u>Literary Criticism: A Short History</u>. Chicago: U of Chicago P, 1978.

Give the authors' names in the order provided on the title page. Reverse the first and last names of the first author *only,* and separate the authors' names with a comma.

A BOOK WITH MORE THAN THREE AUTHORS

Lopez, Robert S., et al. <u>Civilizations: Western and World</u>. Boston: Little, 1975.

You may, but need not, give all authors' names if the work has more than three authors. If you choose not to give all names, provide the name of the first author only, and follow the name with a comma and the abbreviation "et al." (for the Latin *et alii,* meaning "and others").

A BOOK WITH AN EDITOR

Ruitenbeek, Hendrick, ed. <u>Freud as We Knew Him</u>. Detroit: Wayne State UP, 1973.

The abbreviation "ed.," separated from the name by a comma, identifies Ruitenbeek as the editor of the work.

A BOOK WITH AN AUTHOR AND AN EDITOR

Melville, Herman. <u>The Confidence Man: His Masquer-</u>

ade. Ed. Hershel Parker. New York: Norton,

1971.

When citing the work of the author, give his or her name first, and give the editor's name after the title, preceded by "Ed." ("Edited by"). When citing the work of the editor, use the form above for a book with an editor, and give the author's name after the title preceded by "By": "Parker, Hershel, ed. *The Confidence Man: His Masquerade*. By Herman Melville."

A TRANSLATION

Alighieri, Dante.   The Inferno.   Trans. John Ciardi.

New York: NAL, 1971.

When citing the work of the author, give his or her name first, and give the translator's name after the title, preceded by "Trans." ("Translated by"). When citing the work of the translator, give his or her name first, followed by a comma and "trans.," and give the author's name after the title preceded by "By": "Ciardi, John, trans. *The Inferno*. By Dante Alighieri."

A BOOK WITH CORPORATE AUTHORSHIP

Editors of The Progressive.   The Crisis of Survival.

Glenview: Scott, 1970.

List the name of the corporation, institution, or other body as author.

AN ANONYMOUS BOOK

Webster's Seventh New Collegiate Dictionary.

Springfield: Merriam, 1963.

List the book under its title. Do not use "anonymous" or "anon."

A LATER EDITION

Bollinger, Dwight L.   Aspects of Language.   2nd ed.

New York: Harcourt, 1975.

For any edition after the first, place the edition number between the title and the publication information. Use the appropriate designation for editions that are named or dated rather than numbered—for instance, "Rev. ed." for "Revised edition."

bib
35d

A REPUBLISHED BOOK

James, Henry. The Golden Bowl. 1904. London: Pen-

guin, 1966.

Place the original date of publication (but not the place of publication or the publisher's name) after the title, and then provide the
full publication information for the source you are using.

A WORK IN MORE THAN ONE VOLUME

Lincoln, Abraham. The Collected Works of Abraham

Lincoln. Ed. Roy P. Basler. 8 vols. New

Brunswick: Rutgers UP, 1953.

Lincoln, Abraham. The Collected Works of Abraham

Lincoln. Ed. Roy P. Basler. 8 vols. New

Brunswick: Rutgers UP, 1953. Vol. 5.

For a work published in more than one volume, give the total number of volumes regardless of how many you are using. Use an Arabic numeral and the abbreviation "vols.," and place the information after the title (see "8 vols." in the first example). If you use only
one volume, add that information at the very end of the entry (see
"Vol. 5" in the second example).

A WORK IN A SERIES

Bergman, Ingmar. The Seventh Seal. Modern Film

Scripts Series. New York: Simon, 1968.

Place the name of the series (no quotation marks or underlining)
after the title.

A SELECTION FROM AN ANTHOLOGY

Herbert, George. "The Pilgrimage." The Norton An-

thology of English Literature. Ed. M. H.

Abrams et al. 2 vols. 5th ed. New York: Nor-

ton, 1986. Vol. I. 1348-49.

Give the author and the title of the selection you are citing, placing
the title in quotation marks and ending it with a period. Then give
the title of the anthology and the name of the editor(s) preceded by

"Ed." ("Edited by"). At the end of the entry give the inclusive page numbers for the entire selection, but do not include the abbreviation "pp." The entry above includes total number of volumes, edition number, and specific volume number as well.

TWO OR MORE SELECTIONS FROM THE SAME ANTHOLOGY

```
Grey, J. David, ed.   The Jane Austen Companion.   New

     York: Macmillan, 1986.

Southam, Brian.   "Janeites and Anti-Janeites."   Grey

     237-43.

---.   "Persuasion: The Cancelled Chapters."   Grey

     322-23.
```

When citing more than one selection from the same source, avoid unnecessary repetition by giving the source in full (as in the first entry) and then simply cross-referencing it in entries for the works you used. Thus, instead of full bibliographic information for the two Southam articles, give Grey's name and the appropriate pages in his book.

Note that the last two entries also illustrate how to handle two or more works by the same author when you are preparing your final list of works cited: in the second and subsequent entries, replace the author's name with three hyphens followed by a period. This format is discussed more fully on page 587.

AN ARTICLE OR ESSAY FROM A REPRINTED COLLECTION

```
Gibian, George.   "Traditional Symbolism in Crime and

     Punishment."   PMLA 70 (1955): 979-96.   Rpt. in

     Crime and Punishment.   By Feodor Dostoevsky.

     Ed. George Gibian.   Norton Critical Editions.

     New York: Norton, 1964.   575-92.
```

Provide the author and title of the article or essay you are using, placing the title in quotation marks and ending it with a period. Then, unless your instructor specifies otherwise, provide the complete information for the earlier publication of the piece, followed by "Rpt. in" ("Reprinted in") and the information for the source in which you found the piece. If you are not required to provide the earlier publication information, use the format above for a selection from an anthology.

bib

35d

RESOURCES AND IDEAS

AN INTRODUCTION, PREFACE, FOREWORD, OR AFTERWORD

```
Donaldson, Norman.  Introduction.  The Claverings.

    By Anthony Trollope.  New York: Dover, 1977.

    vii-xv.
```

An introduction, foreword, or afterword is often written by someone other than the book's author. When citing such a work, give its name without quotation marks or underlining. Follow the title of the book with its author's name preceded by "By." Give the inclusive page numbers of the part you cite. (In the example above, the small Roman numerals indicate that the cited work is in the front matter of the book, before page 1.)

When the author of a preface or introduction is the same as the author of the book, give only the last name after the title:

```
Gould, Stephen Jay.  Prologue.  The Flamingo's

    Smile: Reflections in Natural History.  By

    Gould.  New York: Norton, 1985.  13-20.
```

AN ENCYCLOPEDIA OR ALMANAC

```
"Mammoth."  The New Columbia Encyclopedia.  1975 ed.

Mark, Herman F.  "Polymers."  Encyclopaedia Britan-

    nica: Macropaedia.  1974.
```

Give the name of an author only when the article is signed; otherwise, give the title first. If the articles are alphabetized in the reference work, you needn't list the editors of the work itself or any page numbers. For familiar sources like those in the examples, provide only the edition number (if there is one) and the year of publication.

Periodicals: journals, magazines, and newspapers

The basic format for an article from a periodical includes the following information:

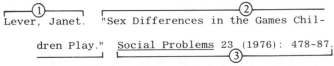

```
Lever, Janet.  "Sex Differences in the Games Chil-

    dren Play."  Social Problems 23 (1976): 478-87.
```

1. The author's full name: last name first, followed by a comma,

and then the first name and any middle name or initial. Omit any title or degree attached to the author's name on the source, such as Dr. or Ph.D. End the name with a period and two spaces.

2. The full title of the article, including any subtitle. Place the title in quotation marks, capitalize all important words in the title (see 26b), and end the title with a period (inside the final quotation mark) and two spaces.

3. The publication information: the underlined title of the periodical (minus any *A, An,* or *The* at the beginning); the volume or issue number (in Arabic numerals); the date of publication, followed by a colon and a space; and the inclusive page numbers of the article (without the abbreviation "pp."). The treatment of volume and issue numbers and publication dates varies depending on the kind of periodical being cited, as the following examples indicate.

A SIGNED ARTICLE IN A JOURNAL WITH CONTINUOUS PAGINATION THROUGHOUT THE ANNUAL VOLUME

```
Lever, Janet.   "Sex Differences in the Games Chil-

     dren Play."   Social Problems 23 (1976): 478-87.
```

Some journals number the pages of issues consecutively throughout a year, so that each issue after the first in a year begins numbering where the previous issue left off—say, at page 132 or 416. For that kind of journal, give the volume number after the title ("23" in the example above) and place the year of publication in parentheses. The page numbers will be enough to guide readers to the appropriate issue.

A SIGNED ARTICLE IN A JOURNAL THAT PAGES ISSUES SEPARATELY OR THAT NUMBERS ONLY ISSUES, NOT VOLUMES

```
Boyd, Sarah.   "Nuclear Terror."   Adaptation to Change

     7.4 (1981): 20-23.
```

Some journals page each issue separately (starting each issue at page 1). For these journals, use the same format as for the Lever article above, but give the volume number, a period, and the issue number (as in "7.4" in the Boyd entry). Then readers know which issue of the periodical to consult. When citing an article in a journal that numbers only issues, not annual volumes, treat the issue number as if it were a volume number, as in the Lever citation above.

bib
35d

A SIGNED ARTICLE IN A MONTHLY OR BIMONTHLY PERIODICAL

Stein, Harry. "Living with Lies." <u>Esquire</u> Dec.

1981: 23.

Follow the periodical title with the month (abbreviated) and the year of publication. Don't place the date in parentheses, and don't provide a volume or issue number.

A SIGNED ARTICLE IN A WEEKLY OR BIWEEKLY PERIODICAL

Whiteside, Thomas. "Onward and Upward with the Arts

(Cable Television--Part 1)." <u>New Yorker</u> 20 May

1985: 45-87.

Follow the periodical title with the day, the month (abbreviated), and the year of publication. Don't place the date in parentheses, and don't provide a volume or issue number.

A SIGNED ARTICLE IN A DAILY NEWSPAPER

Gargan, Edward A. "Buffalo Concern Gives Pop Sound

to Player Pianos." <u>New York Times</u> 16 Feb. 1984:

B1.

Give the name of the newspaper as it appears on the first page (but without *A*, *An*, or *The*). Then follow the same format as that above for a weekly or biweekly periodical, with one exception: if the newspaper is divided into lettered or numbered sections, with each section paged separately, provide the section designation before the page number when the newspaper does the same (as in "B1" above), or provide the section designation before the colon when the newspaper does not combine the two in its numbering (as in "sec. 1: 1 + " below).

AN UNSIGNED ARTICLE

"The Right to Die." <u>Time</u> 11 Oct. 1976: 101.

"Protests Greet Pope in Holland." <u>Boston Sunday</u>

<u>Globe</u> 12 May 1985, sec. 1: 1+.

Begin the entry for an unsigned article with the title of the article. The page number "1 + " indicates that the article does not run on consecutive pages but starts on page 1 and continues later in the issue (in this case, on page 21).

**bib
35d**

AN EDITORIAL, A LETTER TO THE EDITOR, OR A REVIEW

```
Ball, George W.   "Block That Vietnam Myth."   Edito-

     rial.  New York Times 19 May 1985: E21.
```

Don't use quotation marks or underlining for the word "Editorial." For an unsigned editorial, give the title first.

```
Dowding, Michael.   Letter.   Economist 5-11 Jan.

     1985: 4.
```

Don't use quotation marks or underlining for the word "Letter."

```
Dunne, John Gregory.   "The Secret of Danny Santiago."

     Rev. of Famous All over Town, by Danny San-

     tiago.  New York Review of Books 16 Aug. 1984:

     17-27.
```

"Rev." is an abbreviation for "Review." The name of the author of the work being reviewed follows the title of the work, a comma, and "by." If the review has no title of its own, then "Rev. of . . ." (without quotation marks) immediately follows the name of the reviewer.

AN ABSTRACT OF A DISSERTATION

```
Steciw, Steven K.   "Alterations to the Pessac Pro-

     ject of Le Corbusier."  DAI 46 (1986): 565C.

     Cambridge U, England.
```

For an abstract appearing in *Dissertation Abstracts* (*DA*) or *Dissertation Abstracts International* (*DAI*), give the author's name and the title as for any article. Then give publication information for the source and the name of the institution granting the author's degree.

Other sources

A PAMPHLET OR GOVERNMENT DOCUMENT

```
Resource Notebook.   Washington: Project on Institu-

     tional Renewal Through the Improvement of

     Teaching, 1976.
```

RESOURCES AND IDEAS

Robert Armour, "The Teaching of Research Methods Through Models," *Exercise Exchange* 20 (1976): 5–6. Armour's assignments "prepare the students for their own research by having them study widely known research projects in order to broaden their definition of research. . . ." *All the President's Men* and *Men of Aran* are given as examples. Instructors can probably supply more up-to-date examples.

bib
35d

Most pamphlets can be treated as books. In the example above, the pamphlet has no listed author, so the title comes first.

```
Hawaii.  Dept. of Education.  Kauai District

    Schools, Profile 1983-84.  Honolulu: Hawaii

    Dept. of Education, 1983.

United States.  Cong.  House.  Committee on Ways and

    Means.  Medicare Payment for Outpatient Occupa-

    tional Therapy Services.  98th Cong., 2nd sess.

    Washington: GPO, 1984.
```

Unless an author is listed for a government document, give the appropriate agency as author. Provide information in the order illustrated, separating elements with a period and two spaces: the name of the government, the name of the agency (which may be abbreviated), and the title and publication information. For a Congressional document (second example), the house and committee involved are given before the title, and the number and session of Congress are given after the title.

AN UNPUBLISHED DISSERTATION OR THESIS

```
Wilson, Stuart M.  "John Stuart Mill as a Literary

    Critic."  Diss.  U of Michigan, 1970.
```

The title is quoted rather than underlined. "Diss." stands for "Dissertation." "U of Michigan" is the degree-granting institution.

RESOURCES AND IDEAS

Dorothy McCoy, "Electrified Term Papers," *English Journal* 60 (1971): 107–10. McCoy argues for slides and movies with accompanying music growing out of the study of literature as an alternative to the traditional research projects.

A MUSICAL COMPOSITION OR WORK OF ART

```
Mozart, Wolfgang Amadeus.  Piano Concerto no. 20 in

    D Minor, K. 466.
```

Don't underline musical compositions identified only by form, number, and key. Do underline titled operas, ballets, and compositions (*Carmen*, *Sleeping Beauty*).

```
Sargent, John Singer.  Venetian Doorway.  Metropoli-

    tan Museum of Art, New York.
```

Underline the title of a work of art. Include the name and location of the institution housing the work.

A FILM OR TELEVISION PROGRAM

<u>King of America</u>. Writ. B. J. Merholz. Music Eliza-

beth Swados. With Larry Atlas, Andreas Katsulas,

Barry Miller, and Michael Walden. American

Playhouse. PBS. WNET, New York. 19 Jan. 1982.

Allen, Woody, dir. <u>Manhattan</u>. With Allen, Diane

Keaton, Michael Murphy, Meryl Streep, and Anne

Byrne. United Artists, 1979.

Generally, place the underlined title first (as in the first example), unless you are citing the work of an individual (second example). After the title, give additional information (writer, lead actors, and so on) as seems appropriate. For a television program, give the series title (if any), the network, and the local station, city, and date. For a film, give the distributor and the date.

A PERFORMANCE

<u>Ceremonies in Dark Old Men</u>. By Lonne Elder. Dir.

Douglas Turner Ward. Theater Four, New York.

15 May 1985.

Ozawa, Seiji, cond. Boston Symphony Orch. Concert.

Symphony Hall, Boston. 25 Apr. 1982.

As with films and television programs, the title generally comes first unless you are citing the work of an individual (second example). Provide additional information about participants after the title, as well as the theater, city, and date. Note that the orchestra concert in the second example is neither quoted nor underlined.

A RECORDING

Mitchell, Joni. <u>For the Roses</u>. Asylum, SD 5057,

1972.

Brahms, Johannes. Concerto no. 2 in B-flat, op.

83. Perf. Artur Rubinstein. Cond. Eugene Or-

mandy. Philadelphia Orch. RCA, RK-1243, 1972.

bib
35d

Begin with the name of the individual whose work you are citing. Then provide the title of the recording (first example) or the title of the work recorded (second example), the names of any artists not already listed, the manufacturer of the recording, the catalog number, and the date.

A LETTER

Buttolph, Mrs. Laura E.   Letter to Rev. and Mrs. C.

C. Jones.   20 June 1857.   In The Children of

Pride: A True Story of Georgia and the Civil

War.   Ed. Robert Manson Myers.   New Haven: Yale

UP, 1972.   334-35.

A published letter is listed under the writer's name. Specify that the source is a letter and to whom it was addressed, and give the date on which it was written. The remaining information is treated like that for an edited book. (See also p. 555 for the format of a letter to the editor of a periodical.)

James, Jonathan E.   Letter to his sister.   16 Apr.

1970.   Jonathan E. James Papers.   South Dakota

State Archive, Pierre.

For a letter in the collection of a library or archive, specify the writer, recipient, and date, as above, and give the name and location of the archive as well.

Packer, Ann E.   Letter to the author.   15 June 1988.

For a letter you receive, give the name of the writer, note the fact that the letter was sent to you, and provide the date of the letter.

A LECTURE OR ADDRESS

Carlone, Dennis J.   "Urban Design in the 1990s."

Sixth Symposium on Urban Issues.   City of Cam-

bridge.   Cambridge, 16 Oct. 1988.

Give the speaker's name, the title if known (in quotation marks), the title of the meeting, the name of the sponsoring organization, the location of the lecture, and the date. If you do not know the title, replace it with "Lecture" or "Address" but *not* in quotation marks.

AN INTERVIEW

Smithson, Councilman John.   Personal interview.   6

    Sept. 1985.

Martin, William.   Interview.   "Give Me That Big Time

    Religion." <u>Frontline</u>.   PBS.   WGBH, Boston.   13

    Feb. 1984.

Begin with the name of the person interviewed. Then specify "Personal interview" (if you conducted the interview in person), "Telephone interview" (if you conducted the interview over the phone), or "Interview" (if you did not conduct the interview)—without quotation marks or underlining. Finally, provide a date (first example) or other bibliographic information and then a date (second example).

AN INFORMATION OR COMPUTER SERVICE

Jolson, Maria K.   <u>Music Education for Preschoolers</u>.

    ERIC, 1981.   ED 264 488.

Palfry, Andrew.   "Choice of Mates in Identical

    Twins." <u>Modern Psychology</u> Jan. 1979: 16-27.

    Dialog file 261, item 5206341.

A source you get from an information or computer service should be treated like a book or a periodical article, as appropriate, with the author's name and then the title. If the source has not been published before, simply name the service (ERIC in the Jolson entry above), and give the year of release and the service's identifying number. If the source has been published before, give full publication information and then the name of the service and its identifying numbers, as in the Palfry entry.

COMPUTER SOFTWARE

<u>Project Scheduler 5000</u>.   Computer software.   Scitor,

    1988.   MS-DOS, 256 KB, disk.

Include the title of the software, the name of the writer (if known), the name of the distributor, and the date. As in this example, you may also provide information about the computer or operating system for which the software is designed, the amount of computer memory it requires, and its format.

RESOURCES AND IDEAS

Fredric J. Meystre, Jr., "Jobs from Term Papers!" *English Journal* 35 (1960): 198. Meystre describes term papers that draw on interviews with personnel managers and tells how the interviews have on occasion led to jobs.

bib

35d

RESOURCES AND IDEAS

Gwen Dungy et al., "Career Research: A Multi-Discipline Approach," *Community College Frontiers* 7 (1980): 15–19. The authors suggest teaching research skills by having students investigate possible careers in fields they find interesting.

3 **Abbreviations**

The bibliographic formats illustrated above eliminate many abbreviations. However, they still use some, and you may encounter many more in your reading. The most common abbreviations found in references and source citations appear below.

anon.	anonymous
bk., bks.	book(s)
c., ca.	*circa* ("about"), used with approximate dates
cf.	*confer* ("compare")
ch., chs.	chapter(s)
col., cols.	column(s)
comp., comps.	compiled by, compiler(s)
diss.	dissertation
ed., eds.	edited by, edition(s), editor(s)
et al.	*et alii* ("and others")
ff.	and the following pages, as in pages 17 ff.
ibid.	*ibidem* ("in the same place")
illus.	illustrated by, illustrator, illustration(s)
l., ll.	line(s)
loc. cit.	*loco citato* ("in the place cited")
ms., mss.	manuscript(s)
n., nn.	note(s), as in p. 24, n. 2
n.d.	no date (of publication)
no., nos.	number(s)
n.p.	no place (of publication), no publisher
n. pag.	no pagination
op. cit.	*opere citato* ("in the work cited")
P	Press (UP = University Press)
p., pp.	page(s)
passim	throughout
q.v.	*quod vide* ("which see")
rev.	revised, revision, revised by, review
rpt.	reprint, reprinted
sec.	section
supp., supps.	supplement(s)
trans.	translator, translated by
univ., U	university (UP = University Press)
vol., vols.	volume(s)

ANSWERS: EXERCISE 3

Individual response.

bib
35d

EXERCISE 3

Prepare bibliography entries from the following information. Follow the models of the *MLA Handbook* given on pages 546–59 unless your instructor specifies a different style.

1. A book called *Black Voices: An Anthology of Afro-American Literature*, published in 1968 by the New American Library in New York, edited by Abraham Clapham.

2. An article in *Southern Folklore Quarterly*, volume 24, published in 1960. The article is "The New Orleans Voodoo Ritual Dance and Its Twentieth-Century Survivals," written by John Q. Anderson, on pages 135–43. The journal is paged continuously throughout the annual volume.

3. The fifth volume of *The History of Technology*, published in 1958 in London by Oxford University Press, written by Charles Singer, E. J. Holmroyd, A. R. Hall, and Trevor I. Williams.

4. A pamphlet entitled *George Segal*, published in 1979 by the Whitney Museum of American Art in New York.

5. A book by John Bartlett called *Familiar Quotations*, in its fifteenth edition, which was edited by Emily Morison Beck, published in 1980 by Little, Brown and Company in Boston, Massachusetts.

RESOURCES AND IDEAS

Ellen Strenski, "A Worksheet Approach to the Research Paper," *Freshman English Resource Notes* 3 (1978): 11–12. Strenski presents sample worksheets designed to help students develop research skills.

EXERCISE 4

Prepare a working bibliography of at least ten sources for a research paper on one of the following people or on someone of your own choosing. Begin by limiting the subject to a manageable size, focusing on a particular characteristic or achievement of the person. Then consult reference books, periodical indexes, and the library's catalog of books. Record bibliographic information on note cards, using the models of the *MLA Handbook* unless your instructor specifies a different style.

1. John Lennon, or another performer
2. Sandra Day O'Connor, or another Supreme Court justice
3. Emily Dickinson, or another writer
4. Muhammad Ali, or another sports figure
5. Andrew Wyeth, or another artist

ANSWERS: EXERCISE 4

Individual response.

EXERCISE 5

Using one of the topics and the possible references for it from Exercise 2 (p. 544), or starting with a different topic and references, prepare a working bibliography of at least ten sources for your developing research paper. List on 3″ × 5″ cards the complete bibliographic information for each source. Use the formats of the *MLA Handbook* unless your instructor specifies a different style.

ANSWERS: EXERCISE 5

Individual response.

bib
35d

HIGHLIGHTS

In this chapter, the discussion of the research/writing process begun in Chapter 35 shifts focus to what are generally considered the later stages in the composition of a research paper: working with sources, focusing and shaping ideas, and drafting and revising a paper. Of particular interest is the emphasis on critical reading of sources and its role in note taking and summarizing. The links between critical reading as a part of the research process and Chapter 4's discussion of critical reading are made plain in the text through frequent cross references.

The essential but sometimes troublesome process of note taking (including paraphrasing and direct quotation) is also covered in practical detail. Section 36d ("Avoiding Plagiarism") provides a thorough treatment of this important matter.

Mark Shannon's and Amy Weiss's papers-in-progress provide examples throughout the chapter, including Sections 36e–36g, which cover the actual writing and revising of research papers. The advice in these sections presents strategies for introducing summaries, paraphrases, and quotations and for revising and editing.

The chapter also provides a detailed treatment of documentation that follows the latest edition (3rd, 1988) of the *MLA Handbook*. It concludes with advice about preparing the final manuscript.

CHAPTER 36

Working with Sources and Writing the Paper

The previous chapter led you through laying the groundwork for a research project. This chapter takes you into the most personal, most intensive, and most rewarding parts of research writing: reading, evaluating, and taking notes from sources; focusing and shaping your ideas; and drafting and revising the paper. In these stages you probe your topic deeply and make it your own.

As before, the work of Mark Shannon and Ann Weiss will illustrate the activity and thought that go into research writing.

36a Scanning and evaluating sources

When to stop looking *for* sources and start looking *at* them depends, of course, on the assigned length of the paper and on the complexity of your subject. You are probably ready to begin reading when your working bibliography suggests that you have explored most aspects of your topic and have found at least some sources that deal directly with your central concern. For a paper of 1800 to 2300 words, ten to fifteen promising titles should give you a good base.

1 Evaluating sources and reading for ideas

Once you have a satisfactory working bibliography, scan your cards for the sources that are most likely to give you an overview of your topic, and consult those sources first. Mark Shannon, for instance, began investigating titles that indicated a focus on the progress of women in upper corporate management. Ann Weiss, in contrast, began by looking at some of the sources referred to in the recent book she first consulted when she was searching for her topic. For an analysis paper like Weiss's that examines a disagreement among experts in a field, a recent work by one of the experts often lays out the disagreement and cites the works of others involved in it.

As you glance through your sources, your purpose is to evaluate their usefulness and to shape your thinking, not to collect information. A source is potentially useful to you if it is relevant to your topic and if it is reliable. Both relevance and reliability can be determined in part by consulting works *about* the source you are considering—that is, the works listed in citation indexes (p. 539) or book review indexes (p. 542). But unless you can dismiss the source on the basis of citations or reviews, you will also need to evaluate it yourself.

Scanning the introductions to books and articles and the tables of contents and indexes of books can help you determine whether a source is relevant. Reliability can be more difficult to judge. If you haven't already done so, read Chapter 4, which includes specific advice for evaluating the writing of others. When scanning potential sources, think critically, looking for sound reasoning, ample evidence, a fair presentation of opposing views, and other features discussed in Chapter 4. In addition, look for information about the author's background to satisfy yourself that the author has sufficient expertise in your subject. Then try to determine whether he or she might be biased. For instance, a book on parapsychology by someone identified as the president of the National Organization of Psychics may contain an authoritative explanation of psychic powers, but the author's view is likely to be biased. It should be balanced by research in other sources whose authors are more skeptical of psychic powers.

This balance or opposition is important. You probably will not find harmony among sources, for reasonable people often disagree in their opinions (see 4d-1). Thus you must deal honestly with the gaps and conflicts in sources. Old sources, superficial ones, slanted ones—these should be offset in your research and your writing by sources that are newer, more thorough, or more objective.

Read your sources quickly and selectively to obtain an overview of your topic so that your thesis encompasses the range of available information and represents your informed view. Don't allow yourself to get bogged down in taking very detailed notes at this stage. Without a sense of what information is pertinent, you may not leave time to cover all the potentially relevant sources.

RESOURCES AND IDEAS

The resources and ideas presented on pages 563–81 are drawn from James E. Ford et al., "Research Paper Instruction: Comprehensive Bibliography of Periodical Sources, 1923–1980," *Bulletin of Bibliography* 39 (1981): 84–98.

RESOURCES AND IDEAS

Lawrence F. Laban, "One Model for Teaching Research Skills," *Exercise Exchange* 21 (1977): 16–19. Laban describes a program that includes, among other activities, an evaluation of a book, a comparison of two different articles on the same subject, a comparison of points of view in several articles, and a research paper. The program helps develop skills in evaluating and analyzing sources.

36a

However, do write down general ideas that seem fundamental to your topic. Be especially careful to record ideas of your own, such as a connection between statements by two different writers, because these may not occur to you later. Use your research journal (see 35a).

RESOURCES AND IDEAS

Mary Ellen Grasso, "The Research Paper: Life Centered," *College English* 40 (1978): 83–89. Grasso begins the course with "trivia" presentations of her own, which move initially to student participation and ultimately to a "life-centered" research paper that answers the criticism that most research papers are simply school exercises.

36b Developing a tentative thesis and outline

1 Writing a tentative thesis sentence

When you have a fairly good grasp of the range of views on your topic, the information available, and your own opinion, try to develop a thesis in a tentative thesis sentence. (See 1g.) In your thesis sentence (or sentences, if you need two or three at this stage), you should state your general idea and the perspective you take. Although the sentence will undoubtedly need revising as you gather more information, drafting it early can help keep you focused as you do further research.

For his paper on women in management, Mark Shannon wrote the following tentative thesis sentence:

> Although women have come a long way in their journey to the top of the corporate ladder, they still have a number of obstacles to overcome before they can consider themselves to have arrived.

This thesis sentence stated Shannon's central idea that women still have not overcome all obstacles to upper management. As we will see, Shannon had to revise his thesis sentence later to reflect his further research and to ensure that it adequately communicated his topic and perspective to readers. But this tentative thesis gave him a focus and a way to organize his work.

To frame a tentative thesis sentence for her paper on the Declaration of Independence, Ann Weiss first had to draw a tentative conclusion about whether Jefferson's draft of the Declaration was improved by the Continental Congress. After skimming the works of the experts who disagreed on this question and closely reading the two versions of the Declaration, she came to believe that the Congress's version was generally more effective. Her tentative thesis sentence indicated that she disagreed with one of the experts:

> Despite one scholar's view that Jefferson's Declaration was damaged in revision, the changes made by the Congress actually improved the document.

Weiss's thesis sentence reflected the state of her knowledge at this stage: she preferred the Congress's version of the Declaration, but she did not have quite enough information to provide concrete reasons for her preference. Getting this information and refining her analysis would be her next goals.

2 Preparing an informal outline

Having written a tentative thesis for your paper, you will be ready to prepare an **informal outline** that will guide your subsequent research. Like the informal outline for an essay (see 1h-2), the outline should show the main divisions of your paper, in the order you think you will cover them, and it should include the important supporting ideas for each division. Shannon's informal outline, below, is probably sufficient. Notice that the organization corresponds to the arrangement of ideas in the thesis sentence: Shannon first covers women's progress to date and then explores the obstacles that remain.

How far women have come
    —Civil Rights Act of 1964
    —1970s workplace vs. present
Gains made since 1970s
    —Success: percentage of women in middle and upper management
    —Availability of mentors
    —Rise of high-tech and service industries
Obstacles
    —Statistics on women at the top
    —Breaking the "glass ceiling"
      —Last bastion for males
      —Conservatism at the top
      —"Queen bees" and male clones
    —Masculine management style

If you feel that you don't have enough information to complete an informal outline or that some of your ideas lack support, consult sources in your working bibliography that you skipped before, or reexamine the ones you skimmed. Even if you believe your information is adequate for an outline, you may need to experiment with several arrangements of material to produce one that seems satisfactory. But don't try to construct a detailed, final outline at this stage. Both your organization and your thesis will undoubtedly change as you do more research.

36b

EXERCISE 1

Read through the sources in the working bibliography you made in Chapter 35, Exercise 5 (p. 561). Jot down the main ideas re-

ANSWERS: EXERCISE 1
Individual response.

lated to your topic. Draft a thesis sentence based on those ideas that both states the topic and implies your perspective on it. Finally, construct an informal outline that contains your main divisions and several supporting ideas for each, returning to your sources as needed.

MATERIAL THAT NEED NOT BE CITED

1. Standard information (such as major acts of history).
2. Folk literature.
3. Commonsense observations.
4. Information that comes up repeatedly, without acknowledgment, in the student's reading.

36c Taking notes using summary, paraphrase, and direct quotation

After you have written a thesis sentence and prepared an informal outline, you are ready to gather, interpret, and analyze information. To begin this stage, take detailed notes from your sources to verify and expand your ideas and to record supporting evidence.

Keep a copy of your informal outline with you in the library as a guide to give order to your search. Try to research the headings and subheadings of your outline one at a time. But don't let the outline constrain your thinking. As you learn more about your topic, you will probably revise your outline by changing a heading, by dropping or adding one, or by rearranging headings. Revising is an inevitable, necessary, and beneficial part of research writing.

The most efficient method of reading secondary sources during research is skimming, reading quickly to look for pertinent information. (Primary sources usually need to be read more carefully, especially when they are the focus of your paper.) When skimming, you do not read randomly in hopes of hitting what you want. Rather, you read with a specific question in mind. Consult the table of contents or index to find what you want, and concentrate on headings and main ideas, skipping material unrelated to the specific question you are researching. Then, when you find something relevant, read slowly and carefully to achieve a clear understanding of what the author is saying and to interpret and evaluate the material in the context of your own and others' opinions.

If it is effective, your final paper will show that you have digested and interpreted the information in your sources—work that can be performed most efficiently in note taking. Taking notes is not a mechanical process of copying from books and periodicals. Rather, as you read and take notes you assess and organize the information in your sources according to your thesis and outline. Thus your notes both prompt and preserve your thoughts.

Using a system for taking notes helps simplify the process and later makes writing the paper easier. The most common method involves note cards: 4″ × 6″ cards allow more room than

$3'' \times 5''$. (Using photocopies from sources is discussed on p. 570.) Write only one fact or idea on a card so that you can easily rearrange information when you want to. (Such rearrangement is extremely difficult when notes are combined on sheets of paper.) If the same source gives you more than one idea or fact, make more than one card. At the top of every card, write the author's last name and the page number(s) of the source so that you will always know where the note came from. (Write a shortened form of the title as well if you are using two or more sources by the author.) In addition, write the outline heading that this note belongs under so that you can remember what you intended to do with it. This format is illustrated below by several note cards.

You can use four kinds of notes: summary, paraphrase, direct quotation, and a combination of these methods. When you **summarize,** you condense an extended idea or argument into a sentence or more in your own words. A full discussion of summary appears in 4a, and you should read that section if you have not already. Mark Shannon summarized the following quotation from one of his sources, Ann Hughey and Eric Gelman, ''Managing the Woman's Way,'' *Newsweek,* p. 47:

> Generalizing about male and female styles of management is a tricky business, because stereotypes have traditionally been used to keep women down. Not too long ago it was a widely accepted truth that women were unstable, indecisive, temperamental and manipulative and weren't good team members because they'd never played football. In fighting off these prejudices many women simply tried to adopt masculine traits in the office.

Compare this passage with Shannon's one-sentence summary, which picks out the kernel of Hughey and Gelman's idea:

Masc. and fem. management styles

Hughey and Gelman, p. 47

Rather than be labeled with the unflattering stereotypes that prevented their promotions, many women adopted masculine qualities.

36c

Summary is most useful when you want to record the gist of an author's idea without the background or supporting evidence.

When you **paraphrase,** you follow much more closely the author's original presentation, but you still restate it in your own words. Paraphrase is most useful when you want to reconstruct an author's line of reasoning but don't feel the original words merit direct quotation. The note card below shows how Shannon might have paraphrased the passage by Hughey and Gelman given above.

PARAPHRASING: GUIDELINES FOR STUDENTS

1. Read a source's material several times to be sure you understand what is being said. Avoid distorting the meaning of the material.
2. Restate the main ideas in your own words.
3. Do not change the emphasis or order of your source's material.
4. Write down all bibliographic information so that you may document your source.

> *Masc. and fem. management styles*
> *Hughey and Gelman, p. 47*
> *Because of the risk of stereotyping, which has served as a tool to keep women out of management, it is difficult to characterize a feminine management style. Women have been cited for their emotionality, instability, and lack of team spirit, among other qualities. Many women have defended themselves at work by adopting the qualities of men.*

Notice how the paraphrase uses different sentence structures and different words to express Hughey and Gelman's idea:

HUGHEY AND GELMAN'S WORDS	SHANNON'S PARAPHRASE
Generalizing about male and female styles of management is a tricky business, because stereotypes have traditionally been used to keep women down.	Because of the risk of stereotyping, which has served as a tool to keep women out of management, it is difficult to characterize a feminine management style.
Not too long ago it was a widely accepted truth that women were unstable, indecisive, temperamental and manipulative and weren't good team members because they'd never played football.	Women have been cited for their emotionality, instability, and lack of team spirit, among other qualities.
In fighting off these prejudices many women simply tried to adopt masculine traits in the office.	Many women defended themselves at work by adopting the qualities of men.

36c

As you summarize and paraphrase, be careful not to distort the author's meaning, but don't feel you have to put down in new words the whole passage or all the details. Select what is pertinent and restate only that. In this way you will be developing your thoughts about the topic as you read and take notes. (For more on paraphrasing and summarizing, see 36d.)

Summary and paraphrase may be the methods you use most often in taking notes from secondary sources. But you will also want to use **direct quotation** from secondary sources when you feel an author's words give a special effect you want to include, when you want to give impact to an expert's opinion, or when you plan to use a graph, table, or diagram from a source. And in a paper analyzing primary sources such as literary works, you will use direct quotation extensively to illustrate and support your analysis. (Ann Weiss used many quotations from her primary source, the Declaration of Independence; see her final paper, pp. 638–48.)

When taking a quotation from a source, copy the material *carefully*. Take down the author's exact wording, spelling, capitalization, and punctuation. Proofread every direct quotation *at least twice*, and be sure you have supplied big quotation marks so that later you won't confuse the direct quotation with a paraphrase or summary. If you want to add words for clarity, use brackets (see 25d). If you want to omit irrelevant words or sentences, use ellipsis marks, usually three spaced periods (see 25e). The note card below shows how Shannon might have quoted rather than summarized Hughey and Gelman, using ellipses and brackets to make the quotation more concise and specific.

> <u>Masc. and fem. management styles</u>
>
> Hughey and Gelman, p. 47
>
> "Generalizing about male and female styles of management is a tricky business . . . . Not too long ago it was a widely accepted truth that women were unstable, indecisive, temperamental and manipulative and weren't good team members because they'd never played football. In fighting off these prejudices many women simply tried to adopt masculine traits [such as steadiness and sportsmanship] in the office."

Using quotation in combination with summary or paraphrase can help you shape the material to suit your purposes (al-

DIRECT QUOTATIONS: GUIDELINES FOR STUDENTS

1. When to use direct quotations:
   a. When you feel an author's words give a special effect that you want to include.
   b. When you want to give impact to an expert's opinion.
   c. When you plan to use a graph, table, or diagram from a source.
   d. To illustrate and support your analysis.
2. Set off a quotation with quotation marks if the quotation is less than three typed lines. Use an indented paragraph if the quotation extends beyond three typed lines.
3. Use brackets to show additional words needed for understanding.
4. Use ellipsis marks (three spaced periods) to show omissions of irrelevant words or sentences.
5. Make sure to copy your source accurately. Proofread every direct quotation at least twice. Check for exact wording and for proper spelling, capitalization, and punctuation.
6. Document your sources.

36c

though you must be careful not to distort the author's meaning). The card below shows how Shannon might have used a combination of quotation and paraphrase to record the statement by Hughey and Gelman. Notice that the quotation marks are clearly visible and that the quotations are absolutely exact.

Masc. and fem. management styles
Hughey and Gelman, p. 47

It is difficult to characterize a feminine style of management "because stereotypes have traditionally been used to keep women down." Women have been cited as "unstable, indecisive, temperamental and manipulative" and have been accused of not being "good team members." Many women defended themselves at work by adopting the qualities of men.

If the material you are quoting, summarizing, or paraphrasing runs from one page to the next in the source, make a mark (such as a check mark or a slash) at the exact spot where one page ends and the next begins. When writing your paper, you may want to use only a part of the material (say, the first or second half). The mark will save you from having to go back to your source to find which page the material actually appeared on.

A note on photocopying

To ensure accuracy of quotations and also to save time, researchers often photocopy sources. (All libraries provide one or more copying machines for this purpose.) But just running pages through a copier does not generate the creative, interpretive, and analytical thinking about sources that is so crucial in taking notes. If you do use a copier, turn to the photocopy soon after you make it, when you still have your hand on the original source and your thoughts about it are still fresh in your mind. At the top of the copy, write a heading from your outline, the author's name, the source title, and the page number as you would on a note card. Then circle or underline the relevant passages and make notes in the margin about their significance to your topic. To make it possible to integrate photocopied notes with your notes on cards, you might want to paste or tape the copy on a notecard of the same size you are us-

36c

ing for your handwritten notes. If the photocopy won't fit on one card, cut it apart and paste it on two or more cards. Be sure to write the appropriate source information at the top of each card so that you don't lose track of where the copy, or a part of it, came from.

EXERCISE 2

Prepare two note cards, one containing a summary of the entire paragraph below and the other containing a paraphrase of the first four sentences (ending with the word *autonomy*). Use the format for a note card provided in the preceding section, omitting only the outline heading.

> Federal organization [of the United States] has made it possible for the different states to deal with the same problems in many different ways. One consequence of federalism, then, has been that people are treated differently, by law, from state to state. The great strength of this system is that differences from state to state in cultural preferences, moral standards, and levels of wealth can be accommodated. In contrast to a unitary system in which the central government makes all important decisions (as in France), federalism is a powerful arrangement for maximizing regional freedom and autonomy. The great weakness of our federal system, however, is that people in some states receive less than the best or the most advanced or the least expensive services and policies that government can offer. The federal dilemma does not invite easy solutions, for the costs and benefits of the arrangement have tended to balance out.
> —PETER K. EISINGER ET AL., *American Politics*, p. 44

EXERCISE 3

Prepare a note card containing a combination of paraphrase or summary and direct quotation that states the major idea of the passage below. Use the format for a note card provided in the preceding section, omitting only the outline heading.

> Most speakers unconsciously duel even during seemingly casual conversations, as can often be observed at social gatherings where they show less concern for exchanging information with other guests than for asserting their own dominance. Their verbal dueling often employs very subtle weapons like mumbling, a hostile act which defeats the listener's desire to understand what the speaker claims he is trying to say (but is really not saying because he is mumbling!). Or the verbal dueler may keep talking after someone has passed out of hearing range—which is often an aggressive challenge to the listener to return and acknowledge the dominance of the speaker.
> —PETER K. FARB, *Word Play*, p. 107

ANSWERS: EXERCISE 2

Possible Summary

Eisinger et al., *American Politics*, p. 44

Federalism, unlike a unitary system, allows the states autonomy. Its strength and its weakness—which are in balance—lie in the regional differences it permits.

ANSWERS: EXERCISE 3

Possible Paraphrase

Eisinger et al., *American Politics*, p. 44

Under federalism, each state can devise its own ways of handling problems and its own laws. The system's advantage is that a state can operate according to its people's culture, morals, and wealth. A unitary system like that in France does not permit such diversity.

36c

36d **Avoiding plagiarism**

Plagiarism (from a Latin word for "kidnapper") is the presentation of someone else's ideas or words as your own. You plagiarize deliberately if you copy a sentence from a book and pass it off as your writing, if you summarize or paraphrase someone else's ideas without acknowledging your debt, or if you buy a term paper to hand in as your own. You plagiarize accidentally if you carelessly forget quotation marks around another writer's words or mistakenly omit a source citation for another's idea because you are unaware of the need to acknowledge the idea. Whether deliberate or accidental, plagiarism is a serious and often punishable offense.

You do not plagiarize, however, when you draw on other writers' material and acknowledge your sources. That procedure is a crucial part of honest research writing, as we have seen. This section shows you how to avoid plagiarism by acknowledging sources when necessary and by using them accurately and fairly.

1 **Knowing what to acknowledge**

When you write a research paper, you coordinate information from three kinds of sources: (1) your independent thoughts and experiences; (2) common knowledge, the basic knowledge people share; and (3) other people's independent thoughts and experiences. Of the three, you *must* acknowledge the third, the work of others.

Your independent material

You need not acknowledge your own independent material—your thoughts, compilations of facts, or experimental results, expressed in your words or format—to avoid plagiarism. Such material includes observations from your experience (for example, a conclusion you draw about crowd behavior by watching crowds at concerts) as well as diagrams you construct from information you gather yourself. Though you generally should describe the basis for your conclusions so that readers can evaluate your thinking, you need not cite sources for them. However, someone else's ideas and facts are not yours; even when you express them entirely in your words and format, they require acknowledgment.

Common knowledge

Common knowledge consists of the standard information of a field of study as well as folk literature and commonsense observa-

---

CHECKLIST FOR AVOIDING PLAGIARISM

1. What type of source are you using: your own independent material, common knowledge, or someone else's independent material? You must acknowledge someone else's material.
2. If you are quoting someone else's material, is the quotation exact? Have you inserted quotation marks around quotations run into the text? Have you shown omissions with ellipses and additions with brackets?
3. If you are paraphrasing or summarizing someone else's material, have you used your own words and sentence structures? Does your paraphrase or summary employ quotation marks when you resort to the author's exact language? Have you represented the author's meaning without distortion?
4. Is each use of someone else's material acknowledged in your text? Are all your source citations complete and accurate? (See 36i.)
5. Does your list of works cited include all the sources you have drawn from in writing your paper? (See 36h.)

---

tions. Standard information includes, for instance, the major facts of history. The dates of Charlemagne's rule as emperor of Rome (800–814) and the fact that his reign was accompanied by a revival of learning—both facts available in many reference books—do not need to be acknowledged, even if you have to look up the information. However, an interpretation of facts (for instance, a theory of how writing began) or a specialist's observation (for instance, an Asian historian's opinion of the effects of Chinese wall posters) is considered independent, not common, knowledge and must be documented.

Folk literature, which is popularly known and cannot be traced to particular writers, is considered common knowledge. Mother Goose nursery rhymes and fairy tales like "Snow White" are examples. However, all literature traceable to a particular writer should be acknowledged. Even a familiar phrase like "miles to go before I sleep" (from Robert Frost's poem "Stopping by Woods on a Snowy Evening") is literature, not folk literature, and requires acknowledgment.

Commonsense observations, such as the idea that weather affects people's spirits or that inflation is most troublesome for people with low and fixed incomes, are considered common knowledge and do not require acknowledgment, even when they also appear in someone else's writing. But a scientist's findings about the effects of high humidity on people with high blood pressure, or an economist's argument about the effects of inflation on immigrants from China, will require acknowledgment.

36d

You may treat common knowledge as your own, even if you have to look it up in a reference book. You may not know, for example, the dates of the French Revolution or the standard definition of *photosynthesis*, although these are considered common knowledge. If you do not know a subject well enough to determine whether a piece of information is common knowledge, make a record of the source as you would for any other quotation, paraphrase, or summary. As you read more about the subject, the information may come up repeatedly without acknowledgment, in which case it is probably common knowledge. But if you are still in doubt when you finish your research, always acknowledge the source.

Someone else's independent material

You must always acknowledge other people's independent material—that is, any facts or ideas that are not common knowledge or your own. The source may be anything, including a book, an article, a movie, an interview, a microfilmed document, or a computer program. You must acknowledge not only ideas or facts themselves but also the language and format in which the ideas or facts appear, if you use them. That is, the wording, sentence structures, arrangement of thoughts, and special graphic format (such as a table or diagram) created by another writer belong to that writer just as his or her ideas do. The following example baldly plagiarizes the original quotation from Jessica Mitford's *Kind and Usual Punishment*, p. 9.

ORIGINAL	The character and mentality of the keepers may be of more importance in understanding prisons than the character and mentality of the kept.
PLAGIARISM	But the character and mentality of prison officials (the keepers) is of more importance in understanding prisons than the character and mentality of prisoners (the kept).

Though the writer has made some changes in Mitford's original and even altered the meaning slightly (by changing *may be* to *is*), she has plagiarized on several counts. She has copied key words (*character, mentality, keepers, kept*), duplicated the entire sentence structure, and lifted the idea—all without acknowledging the source. As illustrated in the following section, the writer must either enclose the exact quotation in quotation marks or state the idea in her own words and in her own sentence. Whichever she does, she *must* acknowledge Mitford as the source.

You need to acknowledge another's material no matter how

RESOURCES AND IDEAS

Michael T. O'Neill, "Plagiarism: (1) Writing Responsibility," *ABCA Bulletin* 43 (1980): 34–36. O'Neill argues that by clarifying the meaning of plagiarism, by teaching conventions, and by teaching paraphrasing that pays attention to ideas as well as words, instructors can help reduce unintentional plagiarism.

36d

you use it, how much of it you use, or how often you use it. Whether you are quoting a single important word, paraphrasing a single sentence, or summarizing three paragraphs, and whether you are using the source only once or a dozen times, you must acknowledge the original author every time. See 36i for discussion and examples of how to acknowledge sources in your text.

If you read someone else's material during your research but do not include any of that material in your final draft, you need not acknowledge the source with a note because you have not actually used the material. However, your instructor may ask you to include such sources in your list of works cited (see 36h).

2 Quoting, summarizing, and paraphrasing honestly

When using direct quotation, be sure to copy the material from the source accurately and with clear quotation marks. Use the quotation marks in the running text of your paper even if you are only quoting a single word that the original author used in a special or central way. (See 24c for the style to use with poetry and long quotations, which are set off from the text and not enclosed in quotation marks.) Acknowledge the source in the manner appropriate for the documentation style you are using. (See 36i for the MLA citation style.)

To correct the plagiarism of Mitford's sentence above, the writer would place Mitford's exact words in quotation marks and cite the source properly (in this case, in MLA style).

> QUOTATION   According to one critic of the penal system, "The character and mentality of the keepers may be of more importance in understanding prisons than the character and mentality of the kept" (Mitford 9).

When you summarize or paraphrase, you do not use quotation marks, because the words are your own. However, you must acknowledge the author of the idea. Here is a paraphrase of the Mitford quotation above (with the source citation again in MLA style).

> PARAPHRASE   One critic of the penal system maintains that we may be able to learn more about prisons from the psychology of the prison officials than from that of the prisoners (Mitford 9).

If you adopt the source's sentence pattern and simply substitute synonyms for key words, or if you use the original words and

RESOURCES AND IDEAS

R. G. Martin, "Plagiarism and Originality: Some Remedies," *English Journal* 60 (1971): 621–28. Martin argues that requiring synthesis rather than regurgitation will forestall plagiarism.

36d

merely change the sentence pattern, you are not paraphrasing but plagiarizing, even if you acknowledge the source, because both methods use someone else's expression without quotation marks. The inadequate paraphrase below plagiarizes the original source, Frederick C. Crews's *The Tragedy of Manners: Moral Drama in the Later Novels of Henry James*, page 8.

ORIGINAL   In each case I have tried to show that all the action in a "Jamesian novel" may be taken as a result of philosophical differences of opinion among the principal characters, and that these differences in turn are explainable by reference to the characters' differing social backgrounds.

PLAGIARISM   According to Crews, the action in a "Jamesian novel" comes from philosophical differences of opinion between characters, differences that can be explained by examining the characters' differing social backgrounds (8).

The plagiarized passage lifts several expressions verbatim from the source, without change and without quotation marks: *action in a "Jamesian novel"; philosophical differences of opinion; the characters' differing social backgrounds.* Thus, even though the writer acknowledges the author's work (by giving Crews's name and the parenthetical page number, 8), he plagiarizes because he does not also acknowledge the author's words with quotation marks. The paraphrase below both conveys and acknowledges the author's meaning without stealing his manner of expression.

PARAPHRASE   According to Crews, the characters in Henry James's novels live out philosophies acquired from their upbringing and their place in society (8).

In this paraphrase, although the writer retains Crews's essential meaning, he restates that meaning in a sentence that he himself has clearly constructed and designed to fit his larger purpose.

    In paraphrasing or summarizing you must not only devise your own form of expression (or place quotation marks around the author's expressions) but also represent the author's meaning exactly, without distorting it. In the following inaccurate summary the writer has avoided plagiarism but has stated a meaning exactly opposite that of the original. The original quotation, from the artist Henri Matisse, appears in Jack D. Flam, *Matisse on Art*, page 148.

ORIGINAL   For the artist creation begins with vision. To see is itself a creative operation, requiring an effort. Everything that we see in our daily life

36d

is more or less distorted by acquired habits, and this is perhaps more evident in an age like ours when cinema posters and magazines present us every day with a flood of ready-made images which are to the eye what prejudices are to the mind.

INACCURATE SUMMARY

Matisse said that the artist can learn how to see by looking at posters and magazines (qtd. in Flam 148).

The revision below combines summary and quotation to represent the author's meaning exactly.

IMPROVED SUMMARY

Matisse said that the artist must overcome visual "habits" and "prejudices," particularly those developed in response to popular cultural images (qtd. in Flam 148).

To be sure you acknowledge sources fairly and do not plagiarize, review the checklist on page 573 both before beginning to write your paper and again after you have completed your first draft.

EXERCISE 4

The numbered items below show various attempts to quote or paraphrase the following passage. Carefully compare each attempt with the original passage. Which are plagiarized, inaccurate, or both, and which are acceptable? Why?

I would agree with the sociologists that psychiatric labeling is dangerous. Society can inflict terrible wounds by discrimination, and by confusing health with disease and disease with badness.
—GEORGE E. VAILLANT, *Adaptation to Life*, p. 361

1. According to George Vaillant, society often inflicts wounds by using psychiatric labeling, confusing health, disease, and badness (361).
2. According to George Vaillant, "psychiatric labeling [such as 'homosexual' or 'schizophrenic'] is dangerous. Society can inflict terrible wounds by . . . confusing health with disease and disease with badness" (361).
3. According to George Vaillant, when psychiatric labeling discriminates between health and disease or between disease and badness, it can inflict wounds on those labeled (361).
4. Psychiatric labels can badly hurt those labeled, says George Vaillant, because they fail to distinguish among health, illness, and immorality (361).
5. Labels such as "homosexual" and "schizophrenic" can be hurtful when they fail to distinguish among health, illness, and immorality.

ANSWERS: EXERCISE 4

1. Plagiarized. Takes phrases directly from the original without quotation marks.
2. Acceptable.
3. Inaccurate and plagiarized. The passage uses phrases from the original without quotation marks and distorts its meaning.
4. Acceptable. Puts the original into the author's own words and correctly conveys its meaning.
5. Inaccurate and plagiarized. Fails to acknowledge the source and fails to convey accurately the concepts of "discrimination" and "confusing" outlined in the original.

36d

I. First main idea
  A. First subordinate idea
    1. First evidence for subordinate idea
      a. First detail of evidence
      b. Second detail of evidence
    2. Second evidence for subordinate idea
  B. Second subordinate idea
II. Second main idea

In this model main ideas are labeled with Roman numerals, the first sublevel with capital letters, the second with Arabic numerals, and the third with small letters. (A fourth sublevel, if needed, is labeled with Arabic numerals enclosed in parentheses.) Each level of the outline is indented farther than the one it supports.

To be an effective organizer for your thoughts, a formal outline should be detailed and should adhere to several principles of logical arrangement, clarity, balance, and completeness. These are discussed in detail and illustrated in Chapter 1, pages 46–48. Briefly: (1) The outline should divide material into groups that indicate which ideas are primary and, under them, which subordinate. A long, undivided list of parallel items probably needs to be subdivided. (2) Parallel headings should represent ideas of parallel importance and should not overlap one another. (3) Single sublevels should be avoided because they illogically imply that something is divided into only one part.

If you compare Mark Shannon's sentence outline on pages 608–09 with his informal outline on page 565, you can see that the formal outline has more information and a tighter, more logical arrangement of ideas and details.

ANSWERS: EXERCISE 6

Possible Revision

I. Processing, preserving, and improving the appearance of foods
  A. Processing
    1. Leavening
    2. Preventing foaming
    3. Binding ingredients together
  B. Preserving
    1. Protecting from internal destruction by enzymes
      a. Discoloration
      b. Overripening
    2. Protecting from external destruction
      a. Bacteria
      b. Fungi

36e

EXERCISE 6

Identify the flaws in the following partial outline for a research paper. Check especially for departures from formal outline form, including illogical subdivision of topics, inconsistent wording of items, and nonparallel placement of ideas of parallel importance.

THESIS SENTENCE

Food additives, which aid in processing foods and in preserving them or improving their appearance, are more useful to us than they are dangerous.

FORMAL OUTLINE

I. Processing, preservation, appearance
  A. Processing
    1. Leavening agents
    2. Antifoaming agents

3. Emulsifiers
   a. Bind ingredients together
B. Preservation
  1. Protect from internal destruction
    a. Natural enzymes can cause discoloration or over-ripening
    b. Must remove or disable enzymes
  2. External destruction
    a. Bacteria
    b. Fungus
  3. Environment
    a. Heat, moisture, humidity
    b. Humectants protect foods from excess moisture
C. Appearance
  1. Glazing agents
  2. Foaming agents cause bubbles to appear in hot chocolate
  3. Firming agents
    a. Keep fruits and vegetables firm in cans
    b. Thickeners
      1. Prevent ice crystal formation, as in ice cream
      2. Improve texture
  4. Sequestrants prevent discoloration

    c. Heat
    d. Moisture
    e. Humidity
C. Improving appearance
  1. Glazing
  2. Causing foaming in hot chocolate
  3. Firming canned fruits and vegetables
  4. Thickening texture
  5. Preventing discoloration

EXERCISE 7

Consulting your research journal and using the note cards you prepared in Exercise 5 (p. 578), revise the thesis sentence from Exercise 1 (p. 565) and construct a formal sentence or topic outline (as specified by your instructor) from which to write a paper.

ANSWERS: EXERCISE 7

Individual response.

36f Drafting the paper

    Many writers begin drafting a research paper early, even before they have finished reading, as a means of testing their ideas and finding direction for further research. If you have not yet begun drafting, however, you should be ready to do so after you have taken notes from your sources, revised your thesis as necessary, and written a formal outline for your paper. Take time to organize your notes carefully according to your formal outline. Once you have arranged your notes, go through them slowly, considering which of your ideas each note supports, how you will link the evidence in one note with that in others, and how you will move from one idea and block of evidence to the next. Unless you have done so already, consult your research journal for insights and connections that can help you get started and keep moving.

RESOURCES AND IDEAS

Robert M. Esch, "Research Paper Paranoia," *College Composition and Communication* 26 (1975): 42–43. Esch offers a humorous account of a student's nightmare about her teacher and her research paper, as a way of presenting the student's outlook.

36f

1   Writing the first draft

Beginning a draft of what will be a relatively long and complicated paper can be difficult, so it may help to remember that you do not have to proceed methodically from beginning to end. To get your juices flowing and give yourself a sense of direction, try writing a quick two- or three-paragraph summary of what the paper will be about. (Pretend you're writing to a friend if that will help loosen you up.) Then, when you turn to the paper itself, skip any parts that scare you or give you undue trouble, even the introduction. Try starting with the section that you feel most confident about. Move from there to other sections of the paper, attempting to fit the sections together only after you begin to see the draft take shape.

In writing sections of your draft, remember that a primary reason for doing a research paper is learning how to evaluate and interpret the evidence in sources, draw your own conclusions from the evidence, and weave the two together in a convincing whole. The weaving will be easier if you view each principal idea in your outline as a unit. Depending on the importance of the idea to your scheme, on its complexity, and on the amount of evidence needed to support it, a unit may require a single paragraph or a block of two or three paragraphs.

Begin each unit by stating the idea, which should be a conclusion you have drawn from reading and taking notes. Follow the statement with specific support from your notes: facts and examples; summaries, paraphrases, or quotations of secondary sources; quotations of passages from primary sources with your analysis; and so on. If your research focuses on or has uncovered a disagreement among experts, present the disagreement fairly and give the evidence that leads you to side with one expert or another. As much as possible, try to remain open to new interpretations or new arrangements of ideas that occur to you.

As you draft your paper, insert the source of each summary, paraphrase, and quotation in parentheses in the text—for instance, "(Hughey and Gelman 47)," referring to page 47 in a work

---

TIPS FOR DRAFTING A RESEARCH PAPER

1. As a warm-up, write a quick, brief summary of the paper.
2. Start wherever you like.
3. Work in chunks, one unit or principal idea at a time.
4. Insert source information (author's name and page number) into the draft as you quote, paraphrase, or summarize.

by Hughey and Gelman. If you are conscientious about inserting these notes and carrying them through successive drafts, you will be less likely to plagiarize accidentally and you will have little difficulty citing your sources in the final paper. (Citing sources is discussed on pp. 588–604.)

2 Introducing summaries, paraphrases, and quotations

One of your challenges in writing a research paper will be deciding when, where, and how to introduce summaries, paraphrases, and quotations from your sources into your text. Whether you summarize, paraphrase, or quote, make others' facts and opinions serve your ideas; don't allow them to overwhelm your own point of view. Except when you are analyzing literature or other primary sources, favor paraphrases and summaries over quotations. Quote secondary sources only when the original wording is essential to understanding the exact meaning or is particularly succinct, forceful, or otherwise interesting (for instance, a bold statement from an acknowledged authority or an inventive comparison). Keep quotations short by eliminating sentences and phrases that are not essential to the intended meaning and that do not contribute to your purpose. Most papers of six to ten pages should not need more than two to four quotations that are longer than a few lines. More than that may bury rather than enhance your argument.

When using summaries, paraphrases, and quotations, be careful to integrate them into your own sentences and at the same time explain why you are using them. A quotation, summary, or paraphrase that is dumped in readers' laps is unlikely to achieve what you intend it to, as the following example illustrates:

A DUMPED QUOTATION

In short, many news editors and reporters maintain that it is impossible and perhaps not even desirable to keep personal opinions from influencing the selection and presentation of facts. "True, news reporters, like everyone else, form impressions of what they see and hear. However, a good reporter does not fail to separate his opinions from his facts" (Lyman 52).

The writer of this passage provides no clues that the quotation contradicts the first sentence; instead, she forces us to figure that out for ourselves. In addition, she loses an opportunity to explain who Lyman is and why his opinion is worthwhile; consequently, we aren't likely to see the quotation as very strong evidence.

With some rewriting, the quotation above can be smoothly

36f

integrated into the writer's sentences so that the contradiction and the reason for quoting Lyman are both clear:

> **AN INTEGRATED QUOTATION**
>
> In short, many news editors and reporters maintain that it is impossible and perhaps not even desirable to keep personal opinions from influencing the selection and presentation of facts. Yet not all authorities agree with this view. Harold Lyman, a newspaper editor for more than forty years, grants that "news reporters, like everyone else, form impressions of what they see and hear." But, Lyman insists, "a good reporter does not fail to separate his opinions from his facts" (52).

In this passage the second sentence and the writer's words *grants*, *But*, and *insists* tell us what to expect in the quotation. (A list of verbs for introducing borrowed material appears below.) And the phrase identifying Lyman, *a newspaper editor for more than forty years*, tells us why Lyman is quoted and why we should value his opinion.

It is not always necessary to name your sources and indicate their credentials in your running text. In fact, such introductions

---

VERBS FOR INTRODUCING SUMMARIES, PARAPHRASES, AND QUOTATIONS

Introduce borrowed material with a verb that conveys information about the source author's attitude or approach to what he or she is saying. In the sentence *King _____ that the flood might have been disastrous*, filling the blank with *observes*, *finds*, or *insists* would create different meanings.

AUTHOR IS NEUTRAL	AUTHOR INFERS OR SUGGESTS	AUTHOR ARGUES	AUTHOR IS UNEASY OR DISPARAGING
comments	analyzes	alleges	belittles
describes	asks	claims	bemoans
explains	assesses	contends	complains
illustrates	concludes	defends	condemns
notes	considers	disagrees	deplores
observes	finds	holds	deprecates
points out	predicts	insists	derides
records	proposes	maintains	laments
relates	reveals		warns
reports	shows	**AUTHOR AGREES**	
says	speculates	admits	
sees	suggests	agrees	
thinks	supposes	concedes	
writes		concurs	
		grants	

may get in the way when you are simply establishing facts or weaving together facts and opinions from varied sources. In the following passage from Ann Weiss's paper, the information is more important than the source, so the name of the source is confined to a parenthetical acknowledgment:

> To end the abuses of the British, many colonists were urging three actions: forming a united front, seceding from Britain, and taking control of their own international trade and diplomacy (Wills 325–36).

(See pp. 589–95 for an explanation of the parenthetical form of citation used in this passage and the ones above.)

In papers analyzing literature, historical documents, and other sources, quotations will often be both the target of your analysis and the chief support for your ideas. You may need to quote many brief passages, integrated into your sentences, and then comment on the quotations to clarify your analysis and win readers' agreement with it. An example of such extensive quotation can be seen in Ann Weiss's analysis of the Declaration of Independence (pp. 643–44) and in the literary analysis in Chapter 38 (pp. 657–59).

If you need guidance in the mechanics of quotation, see 21h (punctuating explanatory words such as *he insists*), 24c (quoting poetry and long prose passages), and 25d and 25e (using brackets and ellipsis marks for additions to and deletions from quotations).

EXERCISE 8

Drawing on the ideas in the following paragraph and using examples from your own observations and experiences, write a paragraph about anxiety. Integrate at least one direct quotation and one paraphrase from the following paragraph into your own sentences. In your paragraph identify the author by name and give his credentials: he is a professor of psychiatry and a practicing psychoanalyst.

> There are so many ways in which man is unique from all the lower forms of animals, and almost all of them make us uniquely susceptible to feelings of anxiousness. Our imagination and reasoning powers facilitate anxiety; the anxious feeling is precipitated not by an absolute impending threat—such as the worry about an examination, a speech, travel—but rather by the symbolic and often unconscious representations. We do not have to be experiencing a potential danger. We can experience something related to it. We can recall, through our incredible memories, the original symbolic sense of vulnerability in childhood and suffer the feeling attached to that. We can even forget the original memory and still be stuck with the emotion—which is

ANSWERS: EXERCISE 8

Sample Paragraph

Why does a woman who is otherwise happy regularly suffer anxiety attacks at the first sign of spring? Why does a man who is otherwise a competent, relaxed driver feel panic whenever he approaches a traffic rotary? According to Willard Gaylin, a professor of psychiatry and a practicing psychoanalyst, such feelings of anxiety are attributable to the uniquely human capacities for remembering, imagining, and forming "symbolic and often unconscious representations" of experiences (23). The feeling of anxiety, Gaylin says, "is . . . compounded by its seemingly irrational quality," its appearance despite the absence of an immediate source of worry or pain (23). The anxious woman is not aware of it, but her father's death twenty years before in April has caused her to equate spring with death. Similarly, the man has forgotten that a terrible accident he witnessed as a child occurred at a rotary. For both people, the anxious feelings are not reduced but heightened because they seem to be unfounded.

36f

then compounded by its seemingly irrational quality at this time. It is not just the fear of death which pains us, but the anticipation of it; or the anniversary of a specific death; or a street, a hospital, a time of day, a color, a flower, a symbol associated with a death. —WILLARD GAYLIN, "Feeling Anxious," p. 23

36g Revising and editing the paper

When you have written a first draft, take a break for at least a day so that you can gain some objectivity about your work and read the draft critically when you begin to revise. Then evaluate your first draft according to the advice and revision checklist in 2b (p. 56). Be especially attentive to the following:

1. Ensure that your thesis sentence accurately describes your topic and your perspective as they emerged during drafting, so that the paper is unified and coherent.
2. Be alert for major structural problems that may not have been apparent in your outline:

   —illogical arrangements of ideas;
   —inadequate emphasis of important points and overemphasis of minor points;
   —imbalance between the views of others (support) and your own views (interpretation or analysis).

3. Hunt out irrelevant ideas and facts that crept in just because you had notes on them.
4. Look for places where supporting evidence is weak.
5. Examine your explanations to be sure your readers will understand them. Define terms and clarify concepts that readers may be unfamiliar with.

When you complete your revision, retype the new draft if possible so that you have a clean copy to edit. For editing, consult the advice and checklist in 2c (p. 63). Try to read the paper from the point of view of someone who has not spent hours planning and researching but instead has come fresh to the paper. Look for lapses in sense, awkward passages, poor transitions between ideas and evidence, unnecessary repetitions, wrong or misspelled words, errors in grammar, punctuation, or mechanics—in short, anything that is likely to interfere with a reader's understanding of your meaning.

When you finish editing your paper, but before you prepare and proofread the final draft, you need to prepare your list of sources and insert the final source citations into the text. Prepar-

36g

ing the list and citing sources are the subjects of the next two sections.

EXERCISE 9

Write the research paper you have been preparing in Chapter 35, Exercises 1, 2, and 5, and this chapter, Exercises 1, 5, and 7. Before beginning the first draft, study your research journal and your notes. While writing, follow your note cards (Exercise 5) and formal outline (Exercise 7) as closely as you need to, but stay open to new ideas, associations, and arrangements. Then revise and edit thoroughly and carefully, working to improve not only your presentation of ideas but also, if necessary, the ideas themselves.

ANSWERS: EXERCISE 9
Individual response.

36h Preparing the final list of works cited

When you finish editing your paper, prepare a final list of the sources you used in it. Include in your list all the sources you quoted, paraphrased, or summarized. Unless your instructor requests it, don't include sources you examined but did not actually use in your paper.

If you are following the guidelines of the *MLA Handbook*, title your list of sources "Works Cited." (Use the title "Works Consulted" if your instructor asks you to include all the sources you examined as well as those you actually used.) Type the information about sources in the formats given on pages 546–59, and arrange them in alphabetical order by the last name of the author or, if an author is not given, by the first main word of the title (excluding *A, An,* or *The*). Double-space the entire list (within and between entries), and indent the second and subsequent lines of each entry five spaces from the left. Place the list at the end of your paper. See the lists of works cited in the papers by Mark Shannon (pp. 634, 636) and Ann Weiss (p. 648) and the comments opposite Shannon's list (pp. 635, 637) for the form to follow in typing this section.

The *MLA Handbook* gives a special format for listing two or more works by the same author:

```
Gardner, Howard.  The Arts and Human Development.

    New York: Wiley, 1973.

---. The Quest for Mind: Piaget, Lévi-Strauss, and

    the Structuralist Movement.  New York: Knopf,

    1973.
```

36h

The author's name is given only in the first entry. For the second and any subsequent works by the same author, substitute three hyphens for the author's name, followed by a period. Arrange the sources alphabetically by the first main word of the title. Note that the three hyphens stand for *exactly* the same name or names. If the second source above were by Gardner and somebody else, both names would have to be given in full.

Guidelines for source lists in other disciplines are given in Chapter 38 (pp. 666 and 683).

EXERCISE 10

Prepare the final list of works cited for the research paper you wrote and revised in Exercise 9 (p. 587). Follow the *MLA Handbook* models on pages 546–59 unless your instructor specifies a different format.

36i Preparing final source citations

Every time you borrow the words, facts, or ideas of others, you must acknowledge the source in your text so that readers know you borrowed the material and know where you borrowed it from. You do not need to acknowledge your own ideas or ideas that are considered common knowledge when you express these in your own words. But you must acknowledge direct quotations, illustrations, and summaries or paraphrases of others' ideas, facts that aren't common knowledge, and associations between them—no matter what their length or how often you have already cited the source. (See 36d for a full discussion of what to acknowledge.)

As you drafted your paper, you should have inserted the sources for all your quotations, summaries, and paraphrases. (See p. 582.) Now, as you read through your paper, recheck these inserts against your note cards. Make sure each summary, paraphrase, and quotation has a citation, proofread every quotation a final time, and then locate the corresponding entry in your list of works cited. The page numbers recorded in your draft and the information on your list of works cited give you everything you need to write final source citations.

The format of source acknowledgments differs from discipline to discipline. The next two sections explain and illustrate the parenthetical style recommended by the *MLA Handbook* (below) and footnotes or endnotes (p. 595). Chapter 38 explains and illustrates the systems in other disciplines. Your instructor will tell you which format to follow.

1 Using the MLA style of parenthetical reference

The documentation system of the *MLA Handbook* employs brief parenthetical references within the text that direct readers to the list of works cited. For example:

```
Only one article mentions this discrepancy (Wolfe 62).
```

The name Wolfe directs readers to the article by Wolfe in the list of works cited, and the page number 62 specifies the page in the article on which the cited material appears.

The following pages describe this documentation system: what must be included in a reference (below), where to place references (p. 593), and when to use footnotes or endnotes in addition to parenthetical references (p. 594).

What to include in a parenthetical reference

The in-text references to sources must include (1) just enough information for the reader to locate the appropriate source in your list of works cited and (2) just enough information for the reader to locate the place in the source where the borrowed material appears. Usually, you can meet these requirements by providing the author's last name and the page(s) in the source on which the material appears. The reader can find the source in your list of works cited and find the borrowed material in the source itself. Refer to the index on the next page to find the form of reference for the kind of source and citation you are using.

AUTHOR NOT NAMED IN THE TEXT

When you have not already named the author in your sentence, provide the author's last name and the page number(s), with no punctuation between them, in parentheses.

```
One researcher concludes that "women impose a dis-

tinctive construction on moral problems, seeing

moral dilemmas in terms of conflicting responsibili-

ties" (Gilligan 105).
```

AUTHOR NAMED IN THE TEXT

If the author's name is already given in your text, you need not repeat it in the parenthetical reference. The reference just gives the page number(s).

```
One researcher, Carol Gilligan, concludes that

"women impose a distinctive construction on moral
```

RESOURCES AND IDEAS

For more detailed information on documentation, see Joseph Gibaldi and Walter S. Achtert, *MLA Handbook for Writers of Research Papers*, 3rd ed. (New York: Modern Language Association, 1988).

cit
36i

INDEX TO MLA PARENTHETICAL REFERENCES

---

problems, seeing moral dilemmas in terms of con-

flicting responsibilities" (105).

A WORK WITH TWO OR THREE AUTHORS

If the source has two or three authors, give all their names in the text or in the reference:

Wimsatt and Brooks note the power of Tolstoy's "wal-

loping caricatures of metropolitan fashionable cul-

ture" (464).

Tolstoy wrote "walloping caricatures of metropolitan

fashionable culture" (Wimsatt and Brooks 464).

A WORK WITH MORE THAN THREE AUTHORS

If the source has more than three authors, you may list all their last names or use only the first author's name followed by "et al." (the abbreviation for the Latin "and others"). The choice depends on what you do in your list of works cited (see p. 548).

It took the combined forces of the Americans, Euro-

peans, and Japanese to break the rebel siege of Pe-

king in 1900 (Lopez et al. 362).

It took the combined forces of the Americans, Euro-

peans, and Japanese to break the rebel siege of Pe-

king in 1900 (Lopez, Blum, Cameron, and Barnes 362).

cit
36i

AN ENTIRE WORK (NO PAGE NUMBERS)

When you cite an entire work rather than a part of it, the reference will not include any page number. If the author's name appears in the text, no parenthetical reference is needed. But remember that the source must appear in the list of works cited.

```
Boyd deals with the need to acknowledge and come to

terms with our fear of nuclear technology.
```

A MULTIVOLUME WORK

If you used only one volume of a multivolume work, your list of works cited can indicate that by giving the appropriate volume in the entry (see the second entry for Lincoln on p. 550). However, if you used and listed all the volumes, your parenthetical reference must specify which volume you are referring to.

```
After issuing the Emancipation Proclamation, Lincoln

said, "What I did, I did after very full delibera-

tion, and under a very heavy and solemn sense of re-

sponsibility" (5: 438).
```

The number 5 indicates the volume from which the quotation was taken; the number 438 indicates the page number in that volume. If you are referring generally to an entire volume of a multivolume work and are not citing specific page numbers, add the abbreviation "vol." before the volume number, as in "(vol. 5)." Then readers will not misinterpret the volume number as a page number.

A WORK BY AN AUTHOR OF TWO OR MORE WORKS

If your list of works cited includes two or more works by the same author, then your reference must tell the reader which of the author's works you are citing. Use the appropriate title or a shortened version of it in the parenthetical reference.

```
At about age seven, most children begin to tell sto-

ries accurately, describe scenes realistically, and

use appropriate gestures to reinforce their story

(Gardner, Arts 144-45).
```

The title *Arts* is shortened from Gardner's full title, *The Arts and Human Development* (see the entry for this book on p. 587). Often, as here, the first main word in the title is enough to direct the reader to the appropriate source.

cit
36i

AN UNSIGNED WORK

Anonymous works are alphabetized by title in the list of works cited. In the text they are referred to by full or shortened title.

```
One article notes that a death-row inmate may demand

his own execution to achieve a fleeting notoriety

("Right").
```

This reference is to an unsigned article titled "The Right to Die." A page reference is unnecessary because the article is no longer than a page (see the entry for the article on p. 554).

A GOVERNMENT DOCUMENT OR A WORK WITH A CORPORATE AUTHOR

If the author of the work is listed as a government body or a corporation, cite the work by the name given as the author's. If the name is long, work it into the text to avoid an intrusive reference.

```
A 1983 report by the Hawaii Department of Education

predicts a gradual increase in enrollments (6).
```

AN INDIRECT SOURCE

When you quote or paraphrase one source's quotation of another source, your reference must indicate as much. In the following reference "qtd. in" ("quoted in") says that Davino was quoted by Boyd.

```
George Davino maintains that children as young as

three "are experiencing nightmares about nuclear

war" (qtd. in Boyd 22).
```

A LITERARY WORK

Novels, plays, and poems are often available in many editions, so your instructor may ask you to provide information that will help readers find the passage you cite no matter what edition they consult. For novels, the page number comes first, followed by a semicolon and then information on the appropriate part or chapter of the work.

```
Toward the end of James's novel, Maggie suddenly

feels "the thick breath of the definite--which was

the intimate, the immediate, the familiar, as she

hadn't had them for so long" (535; pt. 6, ch. 41).
```

cit
36i

For verse plays and poems, you can omit the page number and instead cite the appropriate part or act (and scene, if any) plus the line number(s). Use Arabic numerals for acts and scenes ("3.4") unless your instructor specifies Roman numerals ("III.iv").

```
Later in King Lear Shakespeare has the disguised

Edgar say, "The prince of darkness is a gentleman"

(3.4.147).
```

For prose plays, provide the page number followed by the act and scene, if any (see the reference to *Death of a Salesman* on the next page).

MORE THAN ONE WORK

If you use a parenthetical reference to cite more than a single work, separate the citations by a semicolon.

```
Two recent articles urge small businesses not to

rush to buy a personal computer, even an inexpensive

one, on the grounds that a computer badly used is

less efficient than no computer at all (Richards

162; Gough and Hall 201).
```

Since long references in the text can distract the reader, you may choose to cite several or more works in an endnote or footnote rather than in the text. See page 594.

Where to place parenthetical references

Generally, place a parenthetical reference at the end of the sentence in which you summarize, paraphrase, or quote a work. The reference should follow a closing quotation mark but precede the sentence punctuation. (See the examples in the previous section.) When a reference pertains to only part of a sentence, place the reference after the material being cited and at the least intrusive point—usually at the end of a clause.

```
Though Spelling argues that American automobile man-

ufacturers "have done the best that could be ex-

pected" in meeting consumer needs (26), not everyone

agrees with him.
```

When a reference appears at the end of a quotation set off

from the text, place it two spaces *after* the punctuation ending the quotation.

```
In Arthur Miller's Death of a Salesman, the most

poignant defense of Willie Loman comes from his

wife, Linda:

            He's not the finest character that ever

            lived.  But he's a human being, and a

            terrible thing is happening to him.  So

            attention must be paid.  He's not to be

            allowed to fall into his grave like an old

            dog.  Attention, attention must finally be

            paid to such a person.  (56; act 1)
```

(The reference includes the act number as well as the page number. See "A literary work" on the preceding page.)

See the two sample research papers starting on pages 606 and 638 for further examples of placing parenthetical references.

Using footnotes or endnotes in special circumstances

Occasionally, you may want to use footnotes or endnotes in place of parenthetical references. If you need to cite several sources at once, listing them in a long parenthetical reference could be intrusive. In that case, signal the citation with a numeral raised above the appropriate line of text and write a note with the same numeral to cite the sources:

```
TEXT        At least five subsequent studies have

            confirmed these results.[1]

NOTE        [1] Abbott and Winger 266-68; Casner

            27; Hoyenga 78-79; Marino 36; Tripp,

            Tripp, and Walk 179-83.
```

You may also use a footnote or endnote to comment on a source or provide information that does not fit easily in the text:

```
TEXT        So far, no one has succeeded in con-

            firming these results.[2]
```

NOTE
> [2] Manter reports spending nearly a
> year trying to replicate the experi-
> ment, but he was never able to produce
> the high temperatures reported by the
> original experimenters (616).

In a note the raised numeral is indented five spaces and followed by a space. If the note appears as a footnote, place it at the bottom of the page on which the citation appears, set it off from the text with quadruple spacing, and single-space the note itself. If the note appears as an endnote, place it in numerical order with the other endnotes on a page between the text and the list of works cited; double-space all the endnotes. (See pp. 632–33 for examples of endnotes and the format to use in typing a page of endnotes.)

2 Using footnotes or endnotes to document sources

Until 1984, the *MLA Handbook* recommended using footnotes and endnotes to cite sources, and the current edition continues to provide an explanation and illustrations of this reference system for those who want or are required to use it.

When you document sources with notes (either footnotes or endnotes), you place a raised numeral ([1]) in the text at the end of the material you are acknowledging, and you number the citations consecutively throughout the paper. The notes themselves then fall in the same order. Footnotes are placed at the bottoms of appropriate pages; endnotes are collected on separate pages between the end of the paper and the list of works cited.

Here is a passage from Mark Shannon's paper showing the use of note numbers in the text.

> In a 1983 test of people's reactions to videotapes
> of male and female leaders, the psychologists
> Virginia Brown and Florence Geis found that
> "[a]lthough both leaders used the same script, the
> woman was faulted more than the man for being too
> dominating, cold, and insensitive."[6] Such results
> reveal that while sex-role stereotyping may not be

as obvious as it was in a 1971 study,[7] it remains

pervasive in our society.

For footnotes, begin the first entry four lines below the last line of text (two double spaces), single-space each footnote, and double-space between notes. For endnotes, double-space within and between notes, as in the following sample:

[6] Virginia Brown and Florence Geis, "Turning

Lead into Gold: Evaluations of Women and Men Leaders

and the Alchemy of Social Consensus," Journal of

Personality and Social Psychology 46 (1984): 822.

[7] I. K. Broverman et al., "Sex-Role

Stereotypes: A Current Appraisal," Journal of Social

Issues 28.2 (1971): 59-78.

See pages 632–33 for the heading, spacing, and other elements of a page of endnotes.

The format for a note differs from that for an entry in the list of works cited.

LIST OF WORKS CITED

Wimsatt, William K., and Cleanth Brooks. Literary

Criticism: A Short History. Chicago: U of Chi-

cago P, 1978.

NOTE

[2] William K. Wimsatt and Cleanth Brooks,

Literary Criticism: A Short History (Chicago: U of

Chicago P, 1978) 312.

In the works cited entry you start the first line at the left margin and indent the second and subsequent lines five spaces; but in the note you indent the first line and not the others. The note is intended to be read as a sentence, so a period appears only at the end while the body of the note is punctuated with commas and colons. In the note, unlike the works cited entry, you enclose the publication information (place of publication, publisher, date of publication) in parentheses. Whereas you start the works cited entry with the first author's last name, to make it easier to find the name in an alphabetical listing, in the note you give the author's name in normal order. And in the note you include the specific page number(s) in the source from which the summary, paraphrase, or quotation is taken (but without "p." or "pp.").

The note models below use the same sources as those in the bibliographic models on pages 548–59, and the explanations on those pages point out the special information that must be included for each kind of source. Like bibliographic models, note models may be combined if necessary; for example, the model for a book with an editor may be combined with that for a multivolume book if your source is a multivolume edited work. The following note models are for first reference to a source. When you acknowledge the same source more than once in the same paper, you should use the shortened form of reference given on pages 603–04.

Books

A BOOK WITH ONE AUTHOR

 ¹ Carol Gilligan, <u>In a Different Voice:</u> <u>Psychological Theory and Women's Development</u> (Cambridge: Harvard UP, 1982) 27.

A BOOK WITH TWO OR THREE AUTHORS

² William K. Wimsatt and Cleanth Brooks, <u>Literary Criticism: A Short History</u> (Chicago: U of Chicago P, 1978), 312.

A BOOK WITH MORE THAN THREE AUTHORS

³ Robert S. Lopez et al., <u>Civilizations:</u> <u>Western and World</u> (Boston: Little, 1975) 281-82.

A BOOK WITH AN EDITOR

⁴ Hendrick Ruitenbeek, ed., <u>Freud as We Knew</u> <u>Him</u> (Detroit: Wayne State UP, 1973) 64.

A BOOK WITH AN AUTHOR AND AN EDITOR

⁵ Herman Melville, <u>The Confidence Man: His</u> <u>Masquerade</u>, ed. Hershel Parker (New York: Norton, 1971) 49.

fn
36i

A TRANSLATION

    [6] Dante Alighieri, <u>The Inferno</u>, trans. John Ciardi (New York: NAL, 1971) 73-74.

A BOOK WITH CORPORATE AUTHORSHIP

    [7] Editors of <u>The Progressive</u>, <u>The Crisis of Survival</u> (Glenview: Scott, 1970) 61.

AN ANONYMOUS BOOK

    [8] <u>Webster's Seventh New Collegiate Dictionary</u> (Springfield: Merriam, 1963) 824.

A LATER EDITION

    [9] Dwight L. Bollinger, <u>Aspects of Language</u>, 2nd ed. (New York: Harcourt, 1975) 20.

A REPUBLISHED BOOK

    [10] Henry James, <u>The Golden Bowl</u> (1904; London: Penguin, 1966) 163.

A WORK IN MORE THAN ONE VOLUME

    [11] Abraham Lincoln, <u>The Collected Works of Abraham Lincoln</u>, ed. Roy P. Basler, 8 vols. (New Brunswick: Rutgers UP, 1953) 5: 426-28.

A WORK IN A SERIES

    [12] Ingmar Bergman, <u>The Seventh Seal</u>, Modern Film Scripts Series (New York: Simon, 1968) 6.

A SELECTION FROM AN ANTHOLOGY

    [13] George Herbert, "The Pilgrimage," <u>The Norton Anthology of English Literature</u>, ed. M. H. Abrams et al., 2 vols., 5th ed. (New York: Norton, 1986) 1: 1348.

fn
36i

AN ARTICLE OR ESSAY FROM A REPRINTED COLLECTION

[14] George Gibian, "Traditional Symbolism in Crime and Punishment," PMLA 70 (1955): 979-96, rpt. in Crime and Punishment, by Feodor Dostoevsky, ed. George Gibian, Norton Critical Editions (New York: Norton, 1964) 577.

AN INTRODUCTION, PREFACE, FOREWORD, OR AFTERWORD

[15] Norman Donaldson, introduction, The Claverings, by Anthony Trollope (New York: Dover, 1977) viii.

[16] Stephen Jay Gould, prologue, The Flamingo's Smile: Reflections in Natural History, by Gould (New York: Norton, 1985) 16.

AN ENCYCLOPEDIA OR ALMANAC

[17] "Mammoth," The New Columbia Encyclopedia, 1975 ed.

[18] Herman F. Mark, "Polymers," Encyclopaedia Britannica: Macropaedia, 1974.

Periodicals: journals, magazines, and newspapers

A SIGNED ARTICLE IN A JOURNAL WITH CONTINUOUS PAGINATION THROUGHOUT THE ANNUAL VOLUME

[19] Janet Lever, "Sex Differences in the Games Children Play," Social Problems 23 (1976): 482.

A SIGNED ARTICLE IN A JOURNAL THAT PAGES ISSUES SEPARATELY OR THAT NUMBERS ONLY ISSUES, NOT VOLUMES

[20] Sarah Boyd, "Nuclear Terror," Adaptation to Change 7.4 (1981): 20-21.

fn
36i

A SIGNED ARTICLE IN A MONTHLY OR BIMONTHLY PERIODICAL

21 Harry Stein, "Living with Lies," <u>Esquire</u> Dec. 1981: 23.

A SIGNED ARTICLE IN A WEEKLY OR BIWEEKLY PERIODICAL

22 Thomas Whiteside, "Onward and Upward with the Arts (Cable Television--Part 1)," <u>New Yorker</u> 20 May 1985: 49.

A SIGNED ARTICLE IN A DAILY NEWSPAPER

23 Edward A. Gargan, "Buffalo Concern Gives Pop Sound to Player Pianos," <u>New York Times</u> 16 Feb. 1984: B1.

AN UNSIGNED ARTICLE

24 "The Right to Die," <u>Time</u> 11 Oct. 1976: 101.

25 "Protests Greet Pope in Holland," <u>Boston Sunday Globe</u> 12 May 1985, sec. 1: 21.

AN EDITORIAL, A LETTER TO THE EDITOR, OR A REVIEW

26 George W. Ball, "Block That Vietnam Myth," editorial, <u>New York Times</u> 19 May 1985: E21.

27 Michael Dowding, letter, <u>Economist</u> 5-11 Jan. 1985: 4.

28 John Gregory Dunne, "The Secret of Danny Santiago," rev. of <u>Famous All over Town</u>, by Danny Santiago, <u>New York Review of Books</u> 16 Aug. 1984: 20.

AN ABSTRACT OF A DISSERTATION

29 Steven K. Steciw, "Alterations to the Pessac Project of Le Corbusier," <u>DAI</u> 46 (1986): 565C (Cambridge U, England).

fn
36i

Other sources

A PAMPHLET OR GOVERNMENT DOCUMENT

³⁰ <u>Resource Notebook</u> (Washington: Project on Institutional Renewal Through the Improvement of Teaching, 1976) 17.

³¹ Hawaii, Dept. of Education, <u>Kauai District Schools, Profile 1983-84</u> (Honolulu: Hawaii Dept. of Education, 1983) 2.

³² United States, Cong., House, Committee on Ways and Means, <u>Medicare Payment for Outpatient Occupational Therapy Services</u>, 98th Cong., 2nd sess. (Washington: GPO, 1984) 3.

AN UNPUBLISHED DISSERTATION OR THESIS

³³ Stuart M. Wilson, "John Stuart Mill as a Literary Critic," diss., U of Michigan, 1970, 7.

A MUSICAL COMPOSITION OR WORK OF ART

³⁴ Wolfgang Amadeus Mozart, Piano Concerto no. 21 in D Minor, K. 466.

³⁵ John Singer Sargent, <u>Venetian Doorway</u>, Metropolitan Museum of Art, New York.

A FILM OR TELEVISION PROGRAM

³⁶ <u>King of America</u>, writ. B. J. Merholz, music Elizabeth Swados, with Larry Atlas, Andreas Katsulas, Barry Miller, and Michael Walden, American Playhouse, PBS, WNET, New York, 19 Jan. 1982.

³⁷ Woody Allen, dir., <u>Manhattan</u>, with Allen,

fn
36i

Diane Keaton, Michael Murphy, Meryl Streep, and Anne Byrne, United Artists, 1979.

A PERFORMANCE

38 <u>Ceremonies in Dark Old Men</u>, by Lonne Elder, dir. Douglas Turner Ward, Theater Four, New York, 15 May 1985.

39 Seiji Ozawa, cond., Boston Symphony Orch. Concert, Symphony Hall, Boston, 25 Apr. 1982.

A RECORDING

40 Joni Mitchell, <u>For the Roses</u>, Asylum, SD 5057, 1972.

41 Johannes Brahms, Concerto no. 2 in B-flat, op. 83, perf. Artur Rubinstein, cond. Eugene Ormandy, Philadelphia Orch., RCA, RK-1243, 1972.

A LETTER

42 Mrs. Laura E. Buttolph, letter to Rev. and Mrs. C. C. Jones, 20 June 1857, in <u>The Children of Pride: A True Story of Georgia and the Civil War</u>, ed. Robert Manson Myers (New Haven: Yale UP, 1972) 334.

43 Jonathan E. James, letter to his sister, 16 Apr. 1970, Jonathan E. James Papers, South Dakota State Archive, Pierre.

44 Ann E. Packer, letter to the author, 15 June 1988.

A LECTURE OR ADDRESS

45 Dennis J. Carlone, "Urban Design in the 1990s," Sixth Symposium on Urban Issues, City of Cambridge, Cambridge, 16 Oct. 1988.

fn
36i

AN INTERVIEW

⁴⁶ Councilman John Smithson, personal interview, 6 Sept. 1985.

⁴⁷ William Martin, interview, "Give Me That Big Time Religion," Frontline, PBS, WGBH, Boston, 13 Feb. 1984.

AN INFORMATION OR COMPUTER SERVICE

⁴⁸ Maria K. Jolson, Music Education for Preschoolers (ERIC, 1981) 16 (ED 264 488).

⁴⁹ Andrew Palfry, "Choice of Mates in Identical Twins," Modern Psychology Jan. 1979: 19 (Dialog file 261, item 5206341).

COMPUTER SOFTWARE

⁵⁰ Project Scheduler 5000, computer software, Scitor, 1988, MS-DOS, 256 KB, disk.

Subsequent references to the same source

To minimize clutter in notes and to give readers a quick sense of how often you acknowledge a source, you should use a shortened form for subsequent references to a source you have already cited fully. When you refer to only one source by the author cited (or only one source bearing the title cited if there is no author), the *MLA Handbook* recommends that subsequent references carry only the author's name (or a short form of the title) and the page reference appropriate for the later citation. Here are two examples, preceded by the full citations.

⁵ Herman Melville, The Confidence Man: His Masquerade, ed. Hershel Parker (New York: Norton, 1971) 49.

⁵¹ Melville 62.

²⁴ "The Right to Die," Time 11 Oct. 1976: 101.

⁵² "Right" 101.

fn
36i

However, if two of your sources are by the same author, give a shortened form of the appropriate title so there can be no confusion about which work you are citing. For example:

1 Carol Gilligan, In a Different Voice:

Psychological Theory and Women's Development

(Cambridge: Harvard UP, 1982) 27.

53 Carol Gilligan, "Moral Development in the

College Years," The Modern American College, ed. A.

Chickering (San Francisco: Jossey-Bass, 1981) 286.

54 Gilligan, "Moral" 288.

NOTE: The *MLA Handbook* discourages use of the Latin abbreviation "ibid." (in the same place") as a means of indicating that a citation refers to the source in the preceding note.

EXERCISE 11

Add the final source citations to the research paper you wrote and revised in Exercise 9 (p. 587), using the list of works cited you prepared in Exercise 10 (p. 588). Use the style of parenthetical reference recommended by the *MLA Handbook* (pp. 589–95) unless your instructor specifies a different style.

36j Preparing and proofreading the final manuscript

Most instructors expect research papers to be neatly typed with clear titling, double spacing, standard margins, and minimal handwritten corrections. The *MLA Handbook* recommends a format for manuscripts that is spelled out in Appendix A of this book and illustrated in the research papers of Mark Shannon and Ann Weiss, starting on page 606. The format is not difficult to follow, and it will make your paper professional looking and easy to read.

Before you submit your paper, proofread it carefully for typographical errors, misspellings, and other slight errors. (See 2d for proofreading tips.) Unless the errors are very numerous (more than several on a page), you can correct them by whiting out or crossing out (neatly) and inserting the correction (neatly) in ink. (See Appendix A, p. 706, for an example.) Don't let the pressure of a deadline prevent you from proofreading, for even minor errors can impair clarity or annoy readers and thus negate some of the hard work you have put into your project.

36j

CHAPTER 37

Two Sample Research Papers

HIGHLIGHTS

This chapter contains the finished research papers of Mark Shannon and Ann Weiss, presented as papers-in-progress throughout the preceding two chapters (35 and 36). Though the papers and the marginal comments on them are largely self-explanatory, you may wish to (1) discuss them at length in class or (2) use parts of them as examples to reinforce a lesson or to set a goal for your students' writing.

The following pages show the research papers of Mark Shannon and Ann Weiss, whose work we followed in the last two chapters. (Shannon's paper begins on the next page, Weiss's on p. 638.) Both students used the bibliographic formats and the style of parenthetical reference recommended by the *MLA Handbook*, and both typed their papers following the advice on manuscript format in Appendix A of this handbook. Facing each page of Shannon's paper are comments, keyed by number, that explain the format of his manuscript and some of the decisions he made in moving from research to writing. Comments in the margins of Weiss's paper note the distinctive features of her analysis.

Breaking the Glass Ceiling   1

By

Mark Shannon

English 101, Section B

Ms. C. Mahoney

May 28, 1988

37

1. **Title page format.** Provide a separate title page if your instructor requests it or if you are required to submit an outline with your paper. On his title page Shannon includes the title of his paper about a third of the way down the page, his own name (preceded by "By") about an inch below the title, and, starting about an inch below his name, some identifying information requested by his instructor (course number, section label, and instructor's name) and the date. He centers all lines in the width of the page and separates them from each other with at least one line of space. If your instructor does not require a title page for your paper, place your name, the identifying information, and the date on the first page of the paper. See Ann Weiss's paper (p. 638) for this alternative format.

Next two pages

2. **Outline format.** If your instructor asks you to include your final outline, place it between the title page and the text, as Shannon does on the following pages. Number the pages with small Roman numerals (i, ii), and place your name just before the page numbers in case the pages of your paper become separated. Place the heading "Outline" an inch from the top of the first page, and double-space under the heading.

3. **Outline content.** Shannon includes his final thesis sentence as part of his outline so that his instructor can see how the parts relate to the whole.

4. Shannon casts his final outline in full sentences. Some instructors request topic outlines, in which ideas appear in phrases instead of in sentences and do not end with periods.

5. Notice that each main division (numbered with Roman numerals) relates to the thesis sentence and that all the subdivisions relate to their main division.

37

Shannon i

Outline

2

<u>Thesis sentence</u>: If women are ever to break

3

through the glass ceiling in significant numbers, business attitudes will have to change,
particularly the definition of successful
management styles.

I. Women face resistance from both men and

4

women in top management.

A. Women are in a double bind: they are
expected to act like men, but are
criticized when they do.

B. Women also face resistance from
"queen bees," other women who are already executives.

1. Queen bees feel that younger women
should not have it any easier than
they did.

2. Queen bees interfere with working
conditions, morale, and promotions.

II. Business favors a masculine management

5

style over a feminine style.

A. A masculine management style is characterized by a militaristic atmosphere that fosters competition.

Shannon ii

B. Women are not given the option to exercise their own style.

C. When women imitate men, they are subject to sex-role stereotyping and alienation.

   1. Brown and Geis found stereotyping in their study.

   2. Woman executives pass around a humorous list of characteristics of businessmen versus businesswomen.

   3. Loden says that women are less effective when they imitate men.

III. A feminine management style must be accepted in business if women are to make it into top management.

A. An interview with a female manager illustrates a feminine style of cooperation and participation.

B. Loden and others emphasize that a feminine management style takes account of people's emotions, an important part of their lives.

C. A feminine style of management will help not only women but business itself.

37

Shannon 1

Breaking the Glass Ceiling   6

"You've come a long way, baby." Most   7
people will recognize this slogan from popular cigarette advertisements, but its meaning
goes beyond women's freedom to smoke in public. Nowhere are women's gains more clear
than in the business world. The Civil Rights   8
Act of 1964 made it illegal to discriminate
against women in employment. Twenty years
later, women had established themselves firmly
in corporations on a number of management
levels. Their progress can be measured by
what is expected of companies with regard to
their treatment of women employees. Accord-   9
ing to <u>Business Week</u>'s Irene Pave:

> Back in 1966 the mark of a good   10
> company [for women to work in] was   11
> women in at least entry-level man-
> agement and other non-clerical
> jobs. In 1976 it was women in mid-
> dle management. Today a good com-
> pany has women above that level or
> in jobs that have remained male
> turf in most companies. (75)   12

37

6. **Title.** Shannon has chosen an intriguing title, just ambiguous enough to make his audience want to read further. A more descriptive title, such as "Why Women Are Still Rare in Top Corporate Management," would also have been appropriate but less interesting. **Paper format.** the margins of the paper are one inch all around. The title appears on the first page of the paper even if a title page is used. The title is typed an inch from the top of the page, and it is neither placed in quotation marks nor underlined. The first line of text is typed two lines (double space) below the title. (See Ann Weiss's paper, p. 638, for the format of the first page when a title page is not required.)

7. **Introduction.** Shannon begins with a familiar sentence that calls to mind the strides women have made in the past century. He delays presenting his thesis (next page of paper) in order to establish some background: women have indeed made inroads into some levels of management (this paragraph), yet not into the highest levels (next paragraph). The question opening the second paragraph (next page) sets up the thesis at the end of the paragraph.

8. **Common knowledge.** Shannon did not know about the Civil Rights Act before he began his research, but he found it referred to without documentation in a number of sources. When he realized that it was considered common knowledge, he chose, correctly, not to document it. (See 36d for further discussion of common knowledge.)

9. **Introducing quotations.** Here and elsewhere, Shannon effectively introduces his quotations: he establishes the credentials of each source in an identifying phrase; and he summarizes each source's point of view. (For additional examples, see p. 3 of the paper. See 36f-2 for a discussion of introducing quotations.)

10. **Format of long quotations.** The Pave quotation exceeds four typed lines, so Shannon sets it off from the text. Such a displayed quotation is set off by double-spacing above and below, is itself double-spaced, and is indented ten spaces from the left margin.

11. **Adding to quotations.** Shannon inserts a clarifying phrase so that readers will understand what Pave means by a "good company." The brackets tell the reader that the phrase is added (see 25d).

12. **Reference when the author is named in the text.** Shannon has already mentioned Pave's name in the text, so he does not repeat it in the reference. **Reference with displayed quotation.** The parenthetical reference after the quotation falls *outside* the sentence period and is separated from the period by two spaces.

37

Shannon 2

Clearly, women have come far in business. But have they come far enough? The fact is, women are still rare in the highest executive positions, representing only about 3 percent of all corporate directors in 1984 (Lewin). Pave notes that "no one cites 'equal numbers of men and women in top management positions' as the mark of a good company for women. No company would qualify" (76). Despite women's persistence, a "glass ceiling," or invisible barrier, continues to separate women in middle and upper management from positions in top management.[1] If women are ever to break through the glass ceiling in significant numbers, business attitudes will have to change, particularly the definition of successful management styles.

Most experts agree that the main reason women have not broken through the glass ceiling is, quite simply, that they are women. Often these women find themselves in a double bind. On the one hand, they face resistance from male executives who want their successors to be just like themselves and who therefore will not consider women for top-

13. **Paraphrasing.** Shannon paraphrases Lewin because it is the statistic rather than the author's presentation of it that is important. For other instances of paraphrasing, see the bottom of this page and pages 6 and 7–8 of the paper. **Reference when the author is not named in the text.** Because Shannon has not used Lewin's name in the text, he provides it in the reference. **Reference to a one-page article.** Lewin's article appears on only one page of the newspaper it is in, and Shannon gives that page number in the list of works cited (see p. 634). Thus he does not need to repeat the page number in the reference.

14. **Quotation within a quotation.** Since he must enclose Pave's words in double quotation marks, Shannon encloses her quotation in single quotation marks (see 24b).

15. **Using an endnote for supplementary information.** Here Shannon helps his readers by briefly defining a key term, "glass ceiling." He provides additional information about the term in a note at the end of the paper. (See p. 632.)

16. **Relation to outline.** This paragraph begins part I of Shannon's outline (see p. 608). Part II begins on page 5 of the paper and part III on page 8.

17. **Paraphrase.** Shannon paraphrases part of a quotation from Pave. His notecard follows.

> <u>Sexual stereotypes</u>
>
> Pave, p. 78
>
> "Male chauvinism is most crippling to women at the great divide between upper and top management. Senior managers who always pick men for top spots want clones... — so women always get locked out."

Citing a paraphrase. Shannon includes Pave's name in the reference (next page) because it is not used in the text. In contrast, the reference later in the paragraph to Schwartz does *not* include the name because the text *does*.

37

Shannon 3

management positions (Pave 78). On the other
hand, resistance sometimes comes from men who
do not want to see women acting the role of
executive. According to Felice Schwartz, the
founder and president of Catalyst, a firm that
conducts research on corporate women, "It
goes against the grain of most senior executives to encourage and welcome the women, so
unlike their wives, who put career before
marriage and rearing children" (185). Thus   18
some women are held back if they behave too
much like women, while others are held back
because they behave too much like men.

As if these two problems were not
enough, women also encounter resistance from
the few women who have made it to the top.
These successful women should be acting as
mentors for those coming up behind them,
serving as role models and providing guid-   19
ance. Instead, many do just the opposite.
David Mathison, an associate professor of
business administration at Loyola Marymount
University, identifies the "queen bee syndrome": a successful woman feels threatened
by the success of other women and resists

18. **Interpreting sources.** In this summary sentence Shannon pulls together information from the two sources cited earlier in the paragraph and shows how the information relates to his point about the double bind women are in. Thus he does not force his readers to guess why he paraphrases and quotes sources, and he clears the way for the next point.

19. **Defining terms.** Shannon slips in a definition of "mentors" after the comma in this sentence. Since his audience would consist of his classmates as well as his instructor, he thought it likely that at least a few readers would not know the term. Yet he opted to abbreviate and downplay the definition in order not to offend any readers who already understood the term. Here is Shannon's edited draft of this passage:

These successful women should be acting as
mentors, *for those coming up behind them, serving as* ~~A mentor is usually an older and pro-~~

~~fessionally more advanced person who acts as a~~

role model*s*, and provid~~es~~ *ing* guidance. *Instead,* ~~to a younger~~
many do just the opposite.
~~colleague who is usually younger and subordinate.~~

~~Yet often these successful women are the opposite~~

~~of mentors.~~

Shannon 4

them as "intrusions" into her territory (qtd.
in Bozzi).   20

   In a 1986 survey of executive women,
Edith Gilson, with Susan Kane, found that   21
the "queen bee" was thriving in American
business: 68 percent of those responding
to a questionnaire felt that "their female
colleagues were 'unnecessarily competitive'
with one another." Some of the respondents
exhibited signs of the "queen bee syndrome."
One woman declared, "I managed to climb to my
position without any special help. . . . It   22
was tough, but if I did it, why can't other
women?" (184-86).   23

   Gilson and Kane emphatically warn
against the dangers of this attitude among
women:

> Women's undue competitiveness is a
> major stumbling block to their suc-
> cess. It keeps them awash in anger
> and fear when their energies could
> be used more constructively; sets a
> negative example for lower-level
> women; creates difficult working
> conditions for the women who are

37

20. **Reference to an indirect source.** With the use of "qtd. in," Shannon indicates correctly that he obtained the information on Mathison from the article by Bozzi. **Indirect sources.** The Mathison study is important for Shannon's paper, and the information in Bozzi's article clearly indicated that it had been published in a readily available journal. Instead of relying on a brief summary in a magazine, Shannon should have gone directly to Mathison's article. Use indirect sources (and "qtd. in") only when the original material is not available for you to consult. See, for example, page 7 of the paper and comment 32, page 623.

21. **Reference to a book written with an assistant.** The word "with" appears before Kane's name on the cover and title page of the Gilson and Kane book. It indicates that Kane assisted Gilson, the researcher and principal author, probably by helping with the writing. Shannon makes this clear to his readers by using "with" as well. (See also the list of works cited, p. 13 of the paper, and comment 49, p. 635.) **Introducing and citing a discussion of one work.** By mentioning the names of Gilson and Kane at the beginning of the discussion, Shannon makes it clear that what follows is from their work. The page reference at the very end of the paragraph announces that the citation covers all the intervening material. If, instead, Shannon had placed both parts of the citation together (the page reference in the first sentence or the authors' names in the last sentence), readers might be unsure of how much material the citation covered. **Mixing summary, paraphrase, and quotation.** In the rest of this paragraph, Shannon summarizes, paraphrases, and quotes from several pages of Gilson and Kane's book to give the reader a good sense of one of Gilson's findings.

22. **Editing quotations.** Shannon uses an ellipsis mark to show that he has eliminated irrelevant material from the quotation (see 25e). The ellipsis itself consists of three spaced periods. It is preceded by a sentence period closed up to the last word in the sentence, and it is followed by two spaces.

23. **Placing and punctuating parenthetical references.** The page reference for all the Gilson and Kane material in this paragraph falls at the end of the paragraph (see comment 21). Since the final quotation ends in a question mark, the reference is followed by a separate period.

37

Shannon 5

its targets; diminishes the effec-

tiveness of teamwork; and, in some

cases, <u>actively inhibits career</u>

<u>progress</u>. (186-87; emphasis added)   24

Like the male executive's reluctance to pro-   25

mote women, the "queen bee syndrome" must

change before women can make serious inroads

into top management.

Even more significant than the attitudes   26

described above, however, is the preference

for a masculine rather than feminine manage-

ment style. The feminine management styles

seem to have succeeded quite well at the

middle-management level. But the continued

prevalence of the masculine style of manage-

ment at top levels, along with the apparent

resistance of top managers to changing that

style, is the single most significant obstacle

to women seeking executive positions.

Characterizing the managerial style of   27

most American industrial corporations, Ann

Hughey and Eric Gelman of <u>Newsweek</u> refer to a

"paramilitary form of organization" enforced

by "rigid, drill-sergeant managers" (46).

Marilyn Loden, the author of <u>Feminine Leader-</u>

37

24. **Adding emphasis to quotations.** Shannon underlines certain words in the quotation that reinforce his thesis especially clearly. He acknowledges this change inside the parenthetical reference, separated by a semicolon from the page number.

25. **Summary statement.** For three paragraphs Shannon has been discussing the single idea of how sex discrimination by both sexes holds women back. This concluding statement ties the paragraphs together in preparation for a new section of the paper.

26. **Relation to outline.** With this paragraph Shannon begins part II of his outline (see p. 608). **Transitional paragraph.** Shannon devotes a whole paragraph to the shift in direction, briefly summing up the preceding section and then introducing his final and most important point.

27. **Using sources effectively.** In this paragraph Shannon combines material from two sources to support a single point about corporate managerial style. The two sources reinforce each other and strengthen Shannon's conclusion at the end of the paragraph.

37

Shannon 6

ship, or, How to Succeed in Business Without
Being One of the Boys, borrows a term from
the feminist writer Betty Friedan in noting
the "masculinism" of the traditional managerial style (23). Its basic premise, Loden
says, is competition: the successful manager
must conquer his corporate enemies, just as
he was trained for victory on the football
field or the battlefield; and strategic
thinking must take precedence over emotion
(24-26). It is no wonder that women--who
have been reared to be emotional, cooperative, and generous--encounter difficulties
when attempting to adapt to this style.

Despite the difficulties, women are encouraged to imitate men if they want to succeed. Loden surveyed "how to" books written
during the 1970s and discovered that virtually all of them gave women exactly that
advice (28). Yet women who acquire more masculine traits are then subject to stereotyping. In a 1983 test of people's reactions to
videotapes of male and female leaders, the
psychologists Virginia Brown and Florence
Geis found that "[a]lthough both leaders used

28. **Drawing conclusions.** Shannon correctly places the page reference for Loden after the paraphrase but before the conclusion he draws from the evidence. His conclusion not only spells out the significance of the preceding paragraph but also prepares for the next paragraph. However, Shannon should have found and offered evidence for his understanding that women are "reared to be emotional, cooperative, and generous." The statement may seem self-evident, but many readers would justly criticize it as just the kind of stereotype that Shannon himself is criticizing (see 4b-4).

29. **Altering capitalization in quotations.** In the source the word "although" began a sentence and was capitalized. To fit the quotation smoothly into his own sentence, Shannon wanted to use a small letter. The brackets indicate that he altered the capitalization. (See 26a.)

37

Shannon 7

the same script, the woman was faulted more
than the man for being too dominating, cold,
and insensitive" (822). Such results reveal
that while sex-role stereotyping may not be
as obvious as it was in a 1971 study (Broverman et al.), it remains pervasive. 30

The dilemma of women is also illustrated
in a list comparing businessmen and businesswomen that made the round of women executives
several years ago.

> *A businessman is aggressive; a 31
> businesswoman is pushy.
> *A businessman is good on details;
> she's picky.
> *He loses his temper at times be-
> cause he's so involved in his
> work; she's temperamental.
> *He knows how to follow through; 32
> she doesn't know when to quit.
> (qtd. in Loden 38)

The humor here underlines a serious
problem. Loden observes that if a woman 33
tries to adapt to male business culture without retaining any of her feminine traits, she
will end up feeling more rather than less

30. **Reference to a work with more than three authors.** Here and in the list of works cited (see p. 13 of the paper), Shannon uses "et al." ("and others") to indicate that the work had at least three other authors besides the one named. Shannon could have given all authors' names, too. Either form is correct as long as the list of works cited and the text references are consistent.

31. **Reproduction of list.** By indenting the list ten spaces like any other long quotation, Shannon indicates that it is indeed a quotation.

32. **Reference to an indirect source.** Shannon's use of "qtd. in" indicates that Loden herself quoted the list. In this case, unlike on pages 3–4 of the paper, the use of an indirect source is appropriate because the list was available only in Loden's book, not also in another readily available source. (See comment 20, p. 617.)

33. **Selective quotation.** Throughout this paragraph, Shannon chooses quotations carefully. Since he is relying heavily on Loden in this section, he does not simply report what she says but rather uses her ideas and words selectively to support his thesis.

37

Shannon 8

alienated (22). But this is precisely what
many woman have been expected to do--and in
fact have done--in order to succeed. Loden
explains that "fraternity pledging"--the
term she uses for the first stage of the adaptation process--"causes women to gradually
deny what they truly think and feel" (32).
Thus rigid insistence on a masculine managerial style is not only detrimental in preventing many women from making it to the top
but also harmful in causing those women who
do make it to manage less effectively than
they might.

It seems clear that if business is going   34
to benefit from women's talents, it must accommodate a feminine managerial style. As
Hughey and Gelman observe, "the very qualities that men have traditionally denigrated
as feminine--sympathy, sensitivity, a lack
of the killer instinct--may often be advantages when it comes to getting the best out
of people" (46).

A case in point is a story from a woman   35
I interviewed, Nora Crisi, who is a manager
responsible for several departments in a re-

37

34. **Relation to outline.** At this paragraph Shannon begins part III of his outline (see p. 609).

35. **Primary source: personal interview.** Shannon has tested his ideas by interviewing a woman in a management position. He weaves together paraphrases and quotations from the interview, which he tape-recorded after obtaining Crisi's permission. He does not use a parenthetical reference because all the necessary information (Crisi's name) appears in the text.

37

Shannon 9

tail organization. A subordinate of hers, Susan, refused to use the guidelines in the company manual to train her own subordinates. In debating how to handle the situation, Crisi says,

> my only real role model was my own
> boss, a man who kept everyone in
> line like a drill instructor. He
> would have called Susan in and
> given her a stern lecture, complete
> with threats. I knew I couldn't
> pull that off; it wasn't my nature.

Instead, Crisi explained to Susan the necessity for common training practices and encouraged the young supervisor to offer suggestions for revising the manual if she found problems with it. Then Crisi emphasized that she would not tolerate any refusal to adhere to company policy. The result was surprising: "You know what? She <u>thanked</u> me! I'd been expecting a fight, but I think Susan saw that I respected her, and she appreciated not being treated like a schoolgirl." Crisi's reliance on her sensitivity, coupled with some of the firmness she had learned from her own boss,

37

36

36. **Drawing conclusions.** Again, Shannon does not force readers to figure out the significance of his evidence but states plainly what he got from the interview (and what he wants readers to get).

37

Shannon 10

served her well in a conflict that is common between managers and subordinates.

Crisi's encouragement of feedback on the company's policy illustrates another advantage of a feminine management style: such "participative management," as it is commonly called, permits both emotional and rational assessments of and responses to business situations.[2] Acknowledgment of the importance of emotion has long been absent from traditional management styles. But, in the words of Antonia Shusta, an executive with Citibank, "Business is all people and people in large degree are very emotional. . . . If you don't understand emotion, you're missing out on a lot" (qtd. in Hughey and Gelman 47).

According to Marilyn Loden, "Feminine leaders see the world through two different lenses concurrently and, as a result, respond to situations on both the thinking and the feeling levels" (61). Loden does not advocate substituting the feminine management style for the masculine style (5). Rather, she argues that business must adopt both styles. Only then, she claims, will women

37

38

39

37

37. **Using an endnote for supplementary information.** Shannon did not want to do more than mention the term "participative management," whose meaning he thought clear enough from the words themselves. For readers who might want more information, he provides an endnote with a source to consult.

38. **Selecting supporting evidence.** Shannon uses two separate sources here to develop his point, mixing the views of a practitioner and an expert.

39. **From note cards to paper.** Shannon wanted to use material from two widely separated passages in Loden's book, both of which he had quoted on his note cards (see below). In the paper, however, he opted for paraphrases of the quotations because he did not want to quote excessively and because he could fit the paraphrases together more smoothly than he could the quotations.

<u>Adapting management styles</u>

Loden, p. 5

"[T]he feminine style of leadership is not a replacement of the traditional style."

<u>Adapting management styles</u>

Loden, p. 277

"Equality will be achieved only when organizations acknowledge feminine leadership as an acceptable alternative to the traditional style of management."

Shannon 11

achieve true equality in the top levels of
management (277).

American business has been operating on
a masculine model since the industrial revolution. But times have changed, and so has
the business population. Now women as well
as men must be encouraged to break through
into top management. In order for that to
happen, the "old-boy network" must be pene-
trated, the "queen bee syndrome" must be
cured, and old prejudices--women's as well
as men's--must be abandoned. Even more important, for women and for business itself,
is the adaptation to a more flexible, feminine
style of management. Only when these changes
are made will that glass ceiling finally be
broken.

40

40. **Conclusion.** In his final paragraph Shannon summarizes the main points of his argument in a way that reminds readers of both what holds women back and what he thinks needs to change. The last sentence—by referring to the title and providing a vivid image—gives the paper a dramatic finish.

37

Shannon 12

Notes

41

[1] "Glass ceiling" is commonly used in articles and books about women in management. Although I was unable to find any information on the origins of the term, it appears to have been coined just to describe the situation of women (not men).

42

[2] For further information on women and participative management, see "Special Talents."

43

37

41. **Format of notes.** the word "Notes" is centered one inch from the top of the page. (The heading would be singular—"Note"—if Shannon had not had more than one note.) The notes begin two lines (one double space) below the heading. The notes themselves are double-spaced. The first line of each is indented five spaces and preceded by a raised number corresponding to the number used in the text. A space separates the number and the note.

42. **Endnotes for additional relevant information.** Shannon's first note provides readers with background information on a definition. His second note refers interested readers to an article on participative management.

43. **Reference to an unsigned article.** Since Shannon is referring to an unsigned article, he uses a shortened form of the title for his citation. Since the article is only one page, he does not include the page number. See the entry for this work in the list of works cited, page 14 of the paper.

37

Shannon 13

Works Cited   44

Bozzi, Vincent. "Assertiveness Breeds Con-   45
    tempt." Psychology Today Sept. 1987: 15.

Broverman, I. K., et al. "Sex-Role Stereo-   46
    types: A Current Appraisal." Journal of
    Social Issues 28.2 (1972): 59-78.

Brown, Virginia, and Florence Geis. "Turning   47
    Lead into Gold: Evaluations of Women and
    Men Leaders and the Alchemy of Social
    Consensus." Journal of Personality and
    Social Psychology 46 (1984): 811-24.

Crisi, Nora. Personal interview. 17 May   48
    1988.

Gilson, Edith, with Susan Kane. Unnecessary   49
    Choices: The Hidden Life of the Execu-
    tive Woman. New York: Morrow, 1987.

Hughey, Ann, and Eric Gelman. "Managing the   50
    Woman's Way." Newsweek 17 Mar. 1986:
    46-47.

Lewin, Tamar. "Women in Board Rooms Are   51
    Still the Exceptions." New York Times
    5 July 1984: C1.

Loden, Marilyn. Feminine Leadership, or, How   52
    to Succeed in Business Without Being One
    of the Boys. New York: Times, 1985.

37

44. **Format of list of works cited.** The heading "Works Cited" is centered one inch from the top of the page. The first entry is typed two lines (one double space) below the heading, and the entire list is double-spaced. The first line of each entry begins at the left margin; subsequent lines of the same entry are indented five spaces. The entries are alphabetized.
45. Entry for a **signed article in a monthly periodical.**
46. Entry for an **article with more than three authors.** A source with more than three authors may be listed with all authors' names or just with the first author's name followed by "et al." ("and others"). As his bibliography card indicates, Shannon had all the names but opted not to use them. His text reference to the Broverman et al. article is consistent with this decision (see p. 7 of the paper).

Broverman, I. K., S. R. Vogel, D. M. Broverman, F. E. Clarkson, and P. S. Rosenkrantz. "Sex-Role Stereotypes: A Current Appraisal." Journal of Social Issues 28.2 (1972): 59-78.

The Broverman entry also illustrates a **signed article in a journal that pages issues separately** (see p. 553).
47. Entry for a **signed article in a journal with continuous pagination throughout an annual volume** (see p. 553).
48. Entry for a **personal interview.**
49. Entry for a **book written with an assistant.** See the discussion of this source in comment 21, p. 617. Note that this entry differs from one for a source with two authors, such as the Hughey and Gelman, below.
50. Entry for a **signed article in a weekly periodical.**
51. Entry for a **signed article in a daily newspaper.**
52. Entry for a **book with one author.**

37

Shannon 14

Pave, Irene. "A Woman's Place Is at GE, Federal Express, P&G. . . ." <u>Business Week</u>
   23 June 1986: 75+.   53

Schwartz, Felice N. "Don't Write Women Off
   as Leaders." <u>Fortune</u> 8 June 1987: 185+.

"The Special Talents Women Bring to Partici-   54
   pative Management." <u>International Man-
   agement</u> Aug. 1986: 60.

53. Entry for an **article in which pagination is not consecutive.** The "+" indicates that the article does not continue on page 76 but farther back in the issue.
54. Entry for an **unsigned article.** The source is alphabetized in the list of works cited by the first main word of its title, "Special." Here is Shannon's bibliography card for this source:

"The Special Talents Women Bring to
Participative Management."
<u>International Management</u> Aug.
1986: 60.

Weiss 1

Ann Weiss

Ms. Seaver

April 29, 1985

Format of heading and title when no title page is required

The Editing of the

Declaration of Independence:

Better or Worse?

The Declaration of Independence is so widely regarded as a statement of American ideals that its origins in practical politics tend to be forgotten. The document drafted by Thomas Jefferson was intensely debated in the Continental Congress and then substantially revised before being signed. Since then, most historians have agreed that Jefferson's Declaration was improved in the process. But Jefferson himself was disappointed with the result (Boyd 37); and recently his view has received scholarly support. Thus it is an open question whether the Congress improved a flawed document or damaged an inspired one. An answer to the question requires understanding the context in which the Declaration was conceived and examining the document itself.

Statement of topic

Focus on the disagreement to be resolved

Statement of how the disagreement will be resolved

37

Weiss 2

The Continental Congress in 1776 was attended by representatives of all thirteen colonies. The colonies were ruled more or less separately by Great Britain and had suffered repeated abuses at the hands of King George III, the British parliament, and local appointed governors. To end the abuses of the British, many colonists were urging three actions: forming a united front, seceding from Britain, and taking control of their own international trade and diplomacy (Wills 325-26). They saw the three actions as dependent on each other, and all three were spelled out in a resolution that was proposed in the Congress on June 7, 1776 (Wills 326-27).

The Congress named a five-man committee to prepare a defense of this resolution in order to win the support of reluctant colonists and also to justify secession to potential foreign allies (Malone 219; Wills 330-31). Jefferson, the best writer on the committee, was assigned to draft the document. The other committee members made a few minor

Historical background: the context in which the Declaration was conceived (next two paragraphs)

37

Weiss 3

changes in his draft before submitting it to the Congress. The Congress made many small and some quite large alterations before approving the document on July 4 (Becker 171).

The most interesting major change, because of the controversy it ultimately generated, was made in Jefferson's next-to-last paragraph. (See Figure 1 on the next page for Jefferson's version with the Congress's editing.) Jefferson made several points in the paragraph: the colonists had freely submitted to the British king but not to the British parliament; they had tried repeatedly and unsuccessfully to gain the support of the British people for their cause; yet the British ("unfeeling brethren") had not only ignored the colonists' pleas but also worsened their difficulties by supporting the parliament. These actions, Jefferson concluded, gave the colonists no choice but to separate from England. The Congress cut Jefferson's paragraph by almost two-thirds, leaving only the points about the colonists' appeals to the British, the refusal of the British to listen, and the need for separation.

Isolation and summary of the material to be analyzed

Weiss 4

Photocopy of
the material
to be analyzed
(a primary
source)

Nor have we been wanting in attentions to our British brethren.
we have warned them from time to time of attempts by their legislature to extend ∧ [a] jurisdiction over ∧ [these our states.] we have
reminded them of the circumstances of our emigration & settlement
here, [no one of which could warrant so strange a pretension: that
these were effected at the expence of our own blood & treasure, un-
assisted by the wealth or the strength of Great Britain: that in
constituting indeed our several forms of government, we had
adopted one common king, thereby laying a foundation for per-
petual league & amity with them: but that submission to their
parliament was no part of our constitution, nor ever in idea, if
history may be credited: and,] we ∧ appealed to their native justice
and magnanimity ∧ [as well as to] the ties of our common kindred
to disavow these usurpations which ∧ [were likely to] interrupt our
connection and correspondence. they too have been deaf to the
voice of justice & of consanguinity, [and when occasions have been
given them, by the regular course of their laws, of removing from
their councils the disturbers of our harmony, they have, by their
free election, re-established them in power. at this very time too
they are permitting their chief magistrate to send over not only
souldiers of our common blood, but Scotch &   foreign mercenaries
to invade & destroy us. these facts have given the last stab to ago-
nizing affection, and manly spirit bids us to renounce for ever these
unfeeling brethren. we must endeavor to forget our former love
for them, and to hold them as we hold the rest of mankind enemies
in war, in peace friends. we might have been a free and a great
people together; but a communication of grandeur & of freedom it
seems is below their dignity. be it so, since they will have it. the
road to happiness & to glory is open to us too. we will tread[19] it apart
from them, and] ∧ acquiesce in the necessity which denounces our
[eternal] separation ∧ !

Marginal annotations (left):
∧ an un-
warrantable
∧ us
∧ have
∧ and we
have con-
jured them
by
∧ would
inevitably

Marginal annotations (right):
∧ we must
therefore

∧ and hold
them as we
hold the rest
of mankind,
enemies in
war, in peace
friends.

Fig. 1. Next-to-last paragraph of the Declaration of Independence, photocopied from
Jefferson (318-19). The text is Jefferson's
as submitted by the five-man committee to the
Continental Congress. The Congress deleted
the passages that are underlined and added
the passages in the margin.

Figure
caption and
source

37

Weiss 5

Until recently, most historians accepted all the Congress's changes in the
Declaration as clear improvements. Dumas
Malone, author of the most respected biography of Jefferson, expresses "little
doubt that the critics strengthened" the Declaration, "primarily by deletion" (222). Julian Boyd, a historian of the period and the
editor of Jefferson's papers, observes that
"it is difficult to point out a passage in
the Declaration, great as it was, that was
not improved by their [the delegates'] attention" (36). Carl Becker, considered an expert on the evolution of the Declaration,
agrees that "Congress left the Declaration
better than it found it" (209). These scholars make few specific comments about the
next-to-last paragraph. Becker, however,
does say that Jefferson's emphasis on the
British parliament is an allusion to a theory
of government that is assumed in the rest of
the document, so that the paragraph "leaves
one with the feeling that the author, not
quite aware that he is done, is beginning
over again" (211-12).

Quotation and
paraphrase
of three
important
scholars on
one side of the
disagreement

Weiss 6

The agreement in favor of the Congress's changes was broken in 1978 when the journalist and humanities scholar Garry Wills published a detailed defense of Jefferson's original, particularly his next-to-last paragraph. According to Wills, "Jefferson's declaration of independence is a renunciation of unfeeling brethren. His whole document was shaped to make that clear" (319). The British people had betrayed the colonists both politically (by supporting the intrusive parliament) and emotionally (by ignoring the colonists' appeals), and that dual betrayal was central to Jefferson's argument for secession (303). Wills contends that in drastically cutting the next-to-last paragraph, "Congress removed the heart of his argument, at its climax" (319).

Quotation and paraphrase of the scholar on the other side of the disagreement

As an explanation of Jefferson's intentions, Wills's presentation is convincing. However, a close examination of the original and edited versions of the next-to-last paragraph supports the opinions of earlier historians rather than Wills's argument that the Declaration was damaged by the Con-

Weiss's resolution of the disagreement

37

Weiss 7

gress. The paragraph may have expressed Jefferson's intentions, but it was neither successful in its tone nor appropriate for the purposes of the Congress as a whole.

> Thesis sentence

    Part of Jefferson's assignment "was to impart the proper tone and spirit" to the Declaration (Malone 221). He did this throughout most of the document by expressing strong feelings in a solemn and reasonable manner. But in the next-to-last paragraph Jefferson's tone is sometimes overheated, as in the phrases "invade & destroy us," "last stab to agonizing affection," and "road to happiness & to glory." At other times Jefferson sounds as if he is pouting, as in "we must endeavor to forget our former love for them" and "a communication of grandeur & of freedom it seems is below their dignity." Wills comments that critics have viewed this paragraph as resembling "the recollections of a jilted lover" (313). Wills himself does not agree with this interpretation of the tone, but it seems accurate. All the quoted passages were deleted by the Congress.

> Supporting analysis of the Declaration, including quotations and comment (next three paragraphs)
>
> Analysis of tone

37

Weiss 8

More important than the problem in tone is the paragraph's inappropriateness for the purposes of the Declaration as the Congress saw them. Specifically, the paragraph probably would not have convinced reluctant colonists and potential foreign allies of the justice and logical necessity of secession. The Congress needed the support of as many colonists as possible, but many colonists still felt strong ties to their friends and relatives in England (Becker 127-28; Boyd 31-32). They would probably have been unhappy with phrases such as "renounce forever" and "eternal separation" that threatened a permanent break in those ties. The Congress deleted those phrases, and it also gave greater stress to Jefferson's one hint of a possible reconciliation with the British: "We must . . . hold them as we hold the rest of mankind enemies in war, in peace friends." This thought was moved by the Congress from inside the paragraph to the very end, where it strikes a final note of hope.

The Congress also strengthened the appeal of the Declaration to potential al-

Analysis of appropriateness for purposes of Congress (next two paragraphs)

First purpose of Congress

Second purpose of Congress

37

lies, who would have needed assurance that the colonists were acting reasonably and cautiously. Both Jefferson's and the Congress's versions note that the colonists often "warned" and "reminded" the British and "appealed to their native justice & magnanimity," but that the British were "deaf to the voice of justice & consanguinity" and left the colonists no choice besides "separation." However, Jefferson buried these statements in lengthy charges against the British, while the Congress stripped away the charges to emphasize the colonists' patience in exploring all avenues of redress and their reluctance in seceding. Instead of "beginning over again," as Becker says Jefferson's version seems to do, the revised paragraph clearly provides the final rational justification for the action of the colonists. At the same time, it keeps enough of Jefferson's original to remind the audience that the colonists are feeling people, motivated by their hearts as well as by their minds. They do not secede enthusiastically but "acquiesce in the necessity" of separation.

37

Weiss 10

Though the Declaration has come to be
a statement of this nation's political
philosophy, that was not its purpose in 1776.
Jefferson's intentions had to bow to the
goals of the Congress as a whole to forge
unity among the colonies and to win the support of foreign nations. As Boyd observes,
the Declaration of Independence "was the result not just of Jefferson's lonely struggle
for the right phrase and the telling point,
but also of the focussing of many minds--
among them the best that America ever produced" (38).

Summary,
and restate-
ment of thesis

37

Works Cited

Becker, Carl. <u>The Declaration of Independence: A Study in the History of Political Ideas</u>. New York: Knopf, 1956.

Boyd, Julian P. <u>The Declaration of Independence: The Evolution of a Text</u>. Princeton: Princeton UP, 1945.

Jefferson, Thomas. "Notes of the Proceedings in the Continental Congress." <u>The Papers of Thomas Jefferson</u>. Ed. Julian P. Boyd et al. 21 vols. Princeton: Princeton UP, 1950-74. 1: 309-27.

Malone, Dumas. <u>Jefferson the Virginian</u>. Vol. 1 of <u>Jefferson and His Time</u>. 6 vols. Boston: Little, 1948.

Wills, Garry. <u>Inventing America: Jefferson's Declaration of Independence</u>. Garden City: Doubleday, 1978.

37

CHAPTER 38

Writing in the Disciplines

Writing in the academic disciplines you study in college helps you learn concepts, focus ideas, reflect on assumptions, answer questions, interpret patterns, and analyze data. Learning is thus an important reason for writing: when you write a paper for a course in history, anthropology, or biology, you demonstrate your understanding of concepts and explain how you arrived at that understanding.

This chapter explains how to adapt the writing strategies explained in Chapters 1–2 on the writing process and Chapters 35–37 on research writing to academic writing in general (38a) and, more specifically, to the writing situations you will encounter in the humanities (38b), the social sciences (38c), and the natural and applied sciences (38d). For each field or group of related disciplines, the chapter introduces the basic information needed to follow the guidelines below.

HIGHLIGHTS

Most composition instructors would agree that writing is an activity too important to be left to composition classes alone. Many colleges have recently developed writing-across-the-curriculum programs in recognition of the importance of writing (and the thinking that accompanies it) in all academic disciplines. Some of these programs consist of composition courses focusing on academic writing in general or on writing in a particular area, such as writing in the social sciences. Others consist of courses in a content area (such as biology or history) that are designed to be writing intensive.

This chapter provides both a reference guide for students in content area courses and a framework for a writing course focusing on the varieties of academic discourse. It looks in turn at the aims, methods, and forms of writing in the humanities, the social sciences, and the natural and applied sciences. Each section also reviews the preferred forms of documentation in the various disciplinary areas and provides two sample student papers that can serve as both models and subjects for discussion.

GUIDELINES FOR ACADEMIC WRITERS

1. For the discipline you are writing in, understand the methodology and the kinds of evidence considered appropriate and valid.
2. Analyze the special demands of the assignment—the kind of research and sources you need. The questions you set out to answer, the assertions you wish to support, will govern how you choose your sources and evidence.
3. Know the specialized tools and language of the discipline.
4. Use the style of documentation and the manuscript format customarily used by writers in the discipline.

RESOURCES AND IDEAS

David Bartholomae, "Inventing the University," in *When a Writer Can't Write*, ed. Mike Rose (New York: Guilford, 1985), 134–65. For Bartholomae, mastering the various specialized discourses of the academic community is an essential part of being a college student but is also a gradual process that is likely to pass through several stages, each more closely approximating the work of thinking and writing that characterizes a discipline.

38a

38a Understanding the goals and requirements of the disciplines

1 Methods and evidence

The **methodology** of a discipline is the way its practitioners study their subjects—that is, how they proceed when investigating the answers to questions. Academic or scholarly writers do not compose directly out of their personal experience. Rather, they collect and organize the kinds of evidence appropriate to the discipline, and they base any opinions on that evidence. The evidence comes from research like that described in the last three chapters: it may come from the researcher's own close observations and analysis of a text or experiment; or it may come from sources, most likely those located in a library.

When you conduct original research, you generate your own evidence. You might analyze the images in a poem and then use examples as evidence for your interpretation of the poem. Or you might conduct a survey of fellow students and then use data from the survey to support your conclusions about students' attitudes. Either of these kinds of evidence would be a **primary source,** a firsthand or original account that does not rely on others' sources. Additional examples of primary sources include historical documents such as letters and diaries, works of art such as paintings or photographs, and reports on experiments that the writer has conducted. The research papers in the preceding chapter both use primary sources: Mark Shannon's paper includes the results of an interview he conducted (see p. 624), and Ann Weiss's includes her own analysis of changes made in the Declaration of Independence (see p. 644). The sample papers in this chapter also depend on primary sources.

As the examples of primary sources indicate, many are to be found in the library. But more prevalent among a library's holdings are **secondary sources,** books and articles written *about* primary sources. Much academic writing requires that you use such sources to spark, extend, or support your own ideas, as when you review the published opinions and information on your subject before contributing conclusions from your original research.

2 Assignments

For most academic writing, your primary purpose will be either to explain something to your readers or to persuade them to accept your conclusions. (See 1c on purpose.) To achieve your purpose, you will adapt your writing process to the writing situation, particularly to the kinds of evidence required by the assignment and to the kinds of thinking you are expected to do. Most assignments will contain key words that tell you what these expectations are—words such as *compare, define, analyze,* and *illustrate* that express customary ways of thinking about and organizing a vast range of subjects. Sections 1d-6 and 3c-2 explore these so-called patterns of development. You should be aware of them and alert to the wording in assignments that directs you to use them. In addition, if you have not already done so, you should read Chapter 4 on critical reading and writing, skills fundamental to completing almost any academic writing assignment.

3   Tools and language

When you write in an academic discipline, you use the scholarly tools of that discipline, including specialized references such as periodical indexes, abstracts, and computerized data bases. (See 35c for helpful lists of references.) In addition, you may use the aids developed by practitioners of the discipline for efficiently and effectively approaching research, conducting it, and recording the findings. Many of these aids, such as a system of note cards for recording evidence from sources, are discussed in Chapters 35 and 36 and can be adapted to any discipline. Other aids are discussed in later sections of this chapter.

Pay close attention to the texts assigned in a course and any materials given out in class, for these items may introduce you to valuable references and other research aids, and they will use the specialized language of the discipline. This specialized language allows practitioners to write to each other both efficiently and precisely. It also furthers certain concerns of the discipline, such as accuracy and objectivity. Scientists, for example, prefer the verb *indicate* rather than *prove* in discussing their conclusions, because all results are provisional. Some of the language conventions like this one are discussed in the following sections. As you gain experience in a particular discipline, keep alert for such conventions and train yourself to follow them.

4   Documentation and format

Most disciplines publish journals that require authors to use a certain documentation style and manuscript format. In turn, most instructors in a discipline require the same of students writing papers for their courses.

RESOURCES AND IDEAS

C. W. Griffin, ed., *New Directions for Teaching and Learning: Teaching Writing in All Disciplines* (San Francisco: Jossey-Bass, 1982). The essays in this collection look at ways to use writing as a tool for learning and at ways of helping students master the kinds of writing required by different disciplines.

38a

When you document your sources, you tell readers which ideas and information you borrowed and where they can find your sources. Thus documentation indicates how much knowledge you have and how broad and deep your research was. It also helps you avoid **plagiarism,** the serious offense of presenting the words, ideas, and data of others as if they were your own. (See 36d on avoiding plagiarism.)

Manuscript format includes such features as margins and the placement of the title. But it also extends to special elements of the manuscript, such as tables or an abstract, that may be required by the discipline.

The following sections direct you to the style guides published by different disciplines and outline the basic requirements of the ones used most often. If your instructor does not require a particular style, consult one of the general guides listed on page 546, or use the style of the Modern Language Association, which is described and illustrated at length in 35d-2 (p. 546), 36i-1 (p. 589), and Appendix A (p. 702).

38b Writing in the humanities

The humanities, sometimes known as the reconstructive and speculative disciplines, include the arts, film, literature, history, and philosophy. The texts in these disciplines record and speculate about the growth, ideas, and emotions of human beings. Writing in the humanities explains, interprets, analyzes, and reconstructs, based on the evidence in both primary and secondary sources.

This section concentrates on writing about literature and about history and concludes with two sample literary papers (see p. 658). The other disciplines mentioned have their own concerns, of course, but share many important goals and methods with literature and history.

1 Methods and evidence in the humanities

Literature

As a reader and a student of literature, you read a work and interpret and analyze its implications. You make inferences or draw conclusions from the writer's written words (the text).

A literary analysis is often based only on the text or texts themselves, without recourse to secondary sources. Your assignment may, however, ask you to augment your own inferences with

RESOURCES AND IDEAS

Sylvan Barnet, *A Short Guide to Writing About Literature* (Glenview: Scott, 1985). This text provides helpful advice about strategies for analytical reading and writing that students can use when preparing papers for a literature course or for a composition course built around literary texts.

those of other critics who have written about the work(s). (See pp. 658 and 660 for examples of both kinds of literary analysis.)

When analyzing a literary work, you can use the list on the next page to track the elements of the work and ask questions about them.

History

History as a discipline attempts to reconstruct the past. In Greek the word for history means "to inquire": historians inquire into the past to understand the events of the past. Then they report, explain, analyze, and evaluate those events in their context, asking such questions as what happened before or after the events or how the events were related to the existing political and social structures.

Historians' reconstructions of the past—their conclusions about what happened and why—are always supported with reference to the written record. The evidence of history is mainly primary sources, such as eyewitness accounts and contemporary documents, letters, commercial records, and the like. For history papers, you might also be asked to support your conclusions with those in secondary sources.

In reading historical sources, you need to weigh and evaluate their evidence. If, for example, you find conflicting accounts of the same event, you need to consider the possible biases of the authors or their sources so that you can reject unreliable sources or balance opposing evidence. In general, the more a historian's conclusions are supported by public records such as deeds, marriage licenses, and newspaper accounts, the more reliable the conclusions are likely to be.

RESOURCES AND IDEAS

Mark A. Schlesinger, "The Road to Teaching Thinking," *JGE: The Journal of General Education* 36 (1984): 182–96. Schlesinger surveys four contemporary approaches to teaching students to think, including those that address global skills like analysis and synthesis; those that focus on strategies for problem solving; those that rely on developmental models like those of Piaget and Perry; and those that stress generic thinking skills such as selective attention or identifying components. He points out the overlapping among these approaches and identifies both their strengths and weaknesses.

2   Assignments in the humanities

Papers in the humanities generally perform one or more of the following operations: analysis, explanation, interpretation, evaluation, and synthesis. Using **analysis,** you might examine the elements of a story or painting or break down the causes and effects of a historical event. Using **explanation,** you might show how a film director created a particular sequence, or you might clarify a general's role in a battle. Using **interpretation,** you might infer the meaning of a poem from its images. Using **evaluation,** you might weigh the merits of a historian's conclusions or of an architect's design. Using **synthesis,** you might create a sense of a historical period based on an archive of contemporary letters. Most likely, you will use these operations in combination—say, inter-

38b

QUESTIONS FOR A LITERARY ANALYSIS

Plot: the relationships and patterns of events in a short story, novel, or play.

> What actions happen?
> How are the events connected?
> How do the actions begin or end?

Character: the people the author creates.

> Who are the principal people in the story, play, or poem?
> How do they stay the same? Why?
> How do they change? Why?

Point of view: the perspective or attitude of the speaker in a poem or the voice who tells a story. The point of view of a narrator may be **first person** (*I*) or **third person** (*he, she, it, they*). If third person, it may be **omniscient** (able to see and hear everything both inside and outside all characters), **limited** (able to see and hear what is inside only the main character), or **objective** (able only to see and hear what is external to the characters— what they do and say).

> Who is the narrator? Is he or she identified?
> What are the significance and effect of the author's choice of narrator and point of view?
> Is the narrator subjective or objective? Is he or she trustworthy?

Tone: the feelings conveyed; the predominant attitude.

> Do the words sound sad? happy? something else?
> Does the narrator have an ironic tone, saying one thing and meaning another?
> What does the tone say about the author's attitudes and intentions?

Images: word pictures or visual details.

> What images does the writer use? What pictures do they evoke?
> What is the significance of images in conveying the author's meaning?

Setting: the place where the action happens.

> What is the principal setting, and what does it contribute to the author's meaning?
> When the scene shifts, why does it?

Theme: the main idea or general meaning of the work

> What do all the other elements point to as the author's intended meaning?

38b

preting and explaining the meaning of a painting before evaluating the merits of the work.

3 Tools and language in the humanities

Literature

Analyzing a work of literature (or any work of art) requires looking closely at its elements. As you read, pose questions about the text, such as why a character speaks with a lisp or why images of water recur in a poem. One helpful way of staying sharp and curious while reading is to make notes in a **reading journal,** a log of questions, reactions, and insights in any form you can reread and use later for writing. (It's a good idea to note page numbers of the text in your journal so that you can always find the appropriate passages.) If you own your copy of the text, you can also underline key passages and use the margins for comments and questions. The point is to interact with the text—talk back to it, ask questions of it, analyze it.

When you write about a literary work, you explicate or unfold its meaning or the meaning of devices employed by the author. Your evidence is mainly direct quotations from the work, although you will occasionally use paraphrase and summary as well (see 36c). When using quotations, keep the following guidelines in mind.

GUIDELINES FOR USING QUOTATIONS IN LITERARY ANALYSIS

1. Choose quotations that clearly support your assertions. Don't use your own words merely to explain quotations, and don't use quotations just to use quotations. Instead, make quotations serve your ideas.
2. When you use a quotation, specify how it relates to your idea. Introduce it, and draw a conclusion from it.
3. Work quotations into your own prose. Avoid dumping quotations in readers' laps. (See 36f-2.)
4. Reproduce spelling, punctuation, capitalization, and all other features exactly as they appear in the source. (See 25d for the use of brackets when you need to add something to a quotation; and see 25e for the use of an ellipsis mark when you need to omit something from a quotation.)
5. Document your sources. (See p. 656.)

38b

Generally, literary analysts avoid claiming absolute certainty about an author's meaning, saying that the author *suggests* or *implies* (rather than *means* or *intends*) to convey that they are making inferences. Note also that it is conventional in writing about literature to use the present tense of verbs in describing both the author's work and the action in the work. For example:

> On the surface, the poet *addresses* a young child, Margaret, who *mourns* the falling of the gold-colored leaves in a grove.

> Margaret *represents* the stage of childhood in which we first become aware that "nature imitates man's mortality."

These passages come from the literary papers on pages 658 and 660, which also illustrate the other features discussed here.

History

The historian's tools are those of any thorough and efficient researcher, as discussed in Chapters 35 and 36: a system for finding and tracking sources (35c, 35d); methodical examination of sources, including evaluation of their biases (36a); a system for taking notes from sources (36c); and a separate system, such as a research journal, for tracking one's own evolving thoughts (35a).

When writing about history, it's important to remain as objective as possible. Historians strive for precision and logic; they do not guess about what happened or speculate about "what if." They avoid trying to influence readers' opinions with words having strongly negative or positive connotations, such as *stupid* or *brilliant* (see 31b-1). Instead, they show the evidence and draw conclusions from that. Generally, they avoid using *I:* it tends to draw attention away from the evidence and toward the writer, and it may imply a bias even when there is none.

Writing about history demands some attention to the tenses of verbs to maintain consistency. (See also 13b.) Generally, historians use the past tense to refer to events that occurred in the past. They reserve the present tense only for statements about the present or statements of general truths (see 7e-1). For example:

> Franklin Delano Roosevelt *died* in 1945. Many of Roosevelt's economic reforms *persist* in programs such as social security, unemployment compensation, and farm subsidies.

38b

4 Documentation and format

Most writers in the humanities follow the guidelines for documentation and manuscript format established by the Modern Language Association (MLA) and set forth in the *MLA Handbook* for *Writers of Research Papers*, 3rd ed. (1988). In the MLA documentation style, parenthetical citations in the text of a paper refer to a list of works cited at the end. The system is thoroughly explained and illustrated in Chapters 35 and 36: bibliographic formats in 35d (p. 546), the list of works cited in 36h (p. 587), and parenthetical citations in 36i-1 (p. 589).

You should be aware that some literature instructors and practitioners of other disciplines in the humanities prefer an earlier MLA style of endnotes or footnotes rather than parenthetical references. This earlier style is explained and illustrated in 36i-2 (p. 595). Some historians and philosophers may prefer a different style of endnotes or footnotes or a different style of parenthetical references (such as that of the American Psychological Association; see pp. 666–74). Clearly, your first move in deciding what documentation style to use is to ask your instructor.

The MLA guidelines for manuscript format are given in Appendix A of this book (p. 702) and illustrated in the two sample research papers in Chapter 37 (pp. 606 and 638). Consult Appendix A if you are in doubt about matters of format, and ask your instructor if he or she has any special requirements not mentioned there.

5 Two sample literary papers

The following sample papers illustrate two kinds of literary analysis, one based solely on the literary work itself (below), and one drawing as well on secondary sources (p. 660). Both papers are by the same student and take as their subject the following poem.

GERARD MANLEY HOPKINS

Spring and Fall

To a Young Child

Margaret, are you grieving	1
Over Goldengrove unleaving?	
Leaves, like the things of man, you	
With your fresh thoughts care for, can you?	
Ah! as the heart grows older	5
It will come to such sights colder	
By and by, nor spare a sigh	
Though worlds of wanwood leafmeal lie;	
And yet you will weep and know why.	
Now no matter, child, the name:	10
Sorrow's springs are the same.	
Nor mouth had, no nor mind, expressed	
What heart heard of, ghost guessed:	
It is the blight man was born for,	
It is Margaret you mourn for.	15

38b

A literary analysis (no secondary sources)

John D. Teehan

Professor Roche

English 203

October 29, 1988

Death and Resurrection in Hopkins's

"Spring and Fall"

In Gerard Manley Hopkins's poem "Spring and Fall: To a Young Child," a duality presents itself through the poet's address to a young child: namely, death and resurrection.

On the surface, the poet addresses a young child, Margaret, who mourns the falling of the gold-colored leaves in a grove. As a child, the poet implies, Margaret may not yet understand that mortal things such as leaves or "things of man" (line 3) all eventually come to an end. They are born, they live, and they die. The poet then goes on to explain that as one grows older, one becomes accustomed to such routine cycles as the falling of leaves or decaying trees and even comes "to such sights colder / By and by" (5-6). This cycle of death, decomposition, rebirth, life, and back to death is inevitable.

Humans, too, as part of this natural process, are born to die. Margaret has no conception of this fact, but the poet, being older and less innocent, recognizes that she mourns the leaves in anticipation of her own death: "It [death] is the blight man was born for, / It is Margaret you mourn for" (14-15). Eventually she "will weep and know why" (9). She can escape neither her own death nor an awareness of it. And that awareness will always form "Sorrow's springs" (11).

But death can also lead to resurrection. For Hopkins as a Christian and more especially as a priest, all humans and human-born Christ inevitably come to death, just as the leaves on a tree must inevitably fall; but then they are reborn. Hopkins omits any explicit reference to resurrection in this rather bleak poem. Yet it permeates the whole because of the person to whom this bleakness is addressed: the innocent Margaret. It may be, as Hopkins says, that the aging heart grows increasingly cold to death and does not "spare a sigh / Though worlds of wanwood leafmeal lie" (7-8). Margaret, however, with her "fresh thoughts" (4), is proof that innocence may be reborn. And, in that, she is proof of the rebirth of all living things. Even as Margaret comes to the realization of the inevitability of death and her part in it, other innocents will take her place to prove the equal inevitability of new life.

Thus this poem about death also seems to be about life. The young child heads unaware to her own end, but briefly, at least, she signifies immortality.

[New page.]

Work Cited

Hopkins, Gerard Manley. "Spring and Fall: To a Young
     Child." The Poems of Gerard Manley Hopkins. Ed. W.
     H. Gardner and N. H. Mackenzie. 4th ed. London:
     Oxford UP, 1967.

38b

A literary analysis with secondary sources

John D. Teehan

Professor Roche

English 203

November 16, 1988

Death and Resurrection in Hopkins's

"Spring and Fall"

In Gerard Manley Hopkins's poem "Spring and Fall: To a Young Child," a duality presents itself through the poet's address to a young child: namely, death and resurrection.

On the surface, the poet addresses a young child, Margaret, who mourns the falling of the gold-colored leaves in a grove. As a child, the poet implies, Margaret may not yet understand that mortal things such as leaves or "things of man" (line 3) all eventually come to an end. They are born, they live, and they die. The poet then goes on to explain that as one grows older, one becomes accustomed to such routine cycles as the falling of leaves or decaying trees and even comes "to such sights colder / By and by" (5-6). This cycle of death, decomposition, rebirth, life, and back to death is inevitable.

Margaret represents the stage of childhood in which we first become aware that "nature imitates man's mortality" (Mackenzie 143). Humans, too, are born to die. Margaret has no conception of this fact, but the poet, being older and less innocent, recognizes that she mourns the leaves in anticipation of her own death: "It [death] is the blight man was born for, / It is Margaret you

mourn for" (14-15). Eventually she "will weep and know

why" (9). She can escape neither her own death nor an

awareness of it. And that awareness will always form

"Sorrow's springs" (11).

But death can also lead to resurrection. According

to his biographer, W. H. Gardner, Hopkins destroyed all

the poems he had written before becoming a Jesuit novi-

tiate (68). Once a priest, he imbued his poetry with a

religious faith, so it is reasonable to seek evidence of

such faith even in this rather bleak poem.

For Hopkins as a Christian, and more especially as a

priest, all humans and human-born Christ inevitably come

to death, just as the leaves on a tree must inevitably

fall; but then they are reborn. Though Hopkins omits any

explicit reference to resurrection, it permeates the

whole because of the person to whom he addresses his

seemingly bleak view: the innocent Margaret.

The word "Spring" in the title of the poem "has the

reader see the young girl as a representative of that

fresh season" (Mackenzie 142)--a representative not

only of spring's newness but also of its sinlessness,

its purity (Gardner 161). It may be, as Hopkins says,

that the aging heart grows increasingly cold to death and

does not "spare a sigh / Though worlds of wanwood leaf-

meal lie" (7-8). As Norman Weyand points out, Hopkins

seems to be expressing the human longing for lasting,

unspoiled beauty, a state before the original sin

(64). Margaret, with her "fresh thoughts" (4), is proof

38b

that such a state of innocence may be reborn. And, in that, she is proof of the rebirth of all living things. Even as Margaret comes to the realization of the inevitability of death and her part in it, other innocents will take her place to prove the equal inevitability of life.

Thus this poem about decay and death also seems to be about purity and life. The young child heads unaware to her own end, but briefly, at least, she signifies immortality.

[New page.]

Works Cited

Gardner, W. H. <u>Gerard Manley Hopkins (1844-1889)</u>. New Haven: Yale UP, 1948.

Hopkins, Gerard Manley. "Spring and Fall: To a Young Child." <u>The Poems of Gerard Manley Hopkins</u>. Ed. W. H. Gardner and N. H. Mackenzie. London: Oxford UP, 1967.

Mackenzie, Norman H. <u>A Reader's Guide to Gerard Manley Hopkins</u>. Ithaca: Cornell UP, 1981.

Weyand, Norman, ed. <u>Immortal Diamond: Studies in Gerard Manley Hopkins</u>. New York: Octagon, 1969.

RESOURCES AND IDEAS

Art Young and Toby Fulwiler, eds., *Writing Across the Disciplines: Research into Practice* (Upper Montclair: Boynton/ Cook, 1986). The essays in this collection describe and evaluate a universitywide writing-across-the-curriculum program. Included are essays on writing in the social sciences, the humanities, and the natural and applied sciences.

38c

38c Writing in the social sciences

The social sciences—including anthropology, economics, education, management, political science, psychology, and sociology—focus on the study of human behavior. As the name implies, the social sciences examine the way human beings relate to themselves, to their environment, and to each other.

1 Methods and evidence in the social sciences

Researchers in the social sciences systematically pose a question, formulate a **hypothesis** (a generalization that can be tested), collect data, analyze those data, and draw conclusions to support or disprove their hypothesis. This is the scientific method developed in the natural sciences (see p. 681). Social scientists gather data in several ways. They make firsthand observations of human behavior and record the observations in writing or on audio- or videotape. They interview subjects about their attitudes and behavior, recording responses in writing or on tape. (See 35c-5, p. 543, for guidelines on conducting an interview.) They conduct broader surveys using questionnaires that ask people about their attitudes and behavior. (See the box on the next page.) And they conduct controlled experiments, structuring an environment in which to encourage and measure a specific behavior. In their writing, social scientists explain their own research or analyze and evaluate others' research.

The research methods of social science generate two kinds of data, quantitative and qualitative. **Quantitative data** are numerical, such as statistical evidence based on survey, polls, tests, and experiments. When public-opinion pollsters announce that 47 percent of Americans polled approve of the President's leadership, they are offering quantitative data gained from a survey. Social science writers present quantitative data in graphs, charts, and other illustrations that accompany their text. (See pp. 674–75.)

Qualitative data are not numerical but more subjective: they are based on interviews, firsthand observations, and inferences, taking into account the subjective nature of human experience. An example is the work of the anthropologist Margaret Mead, whose experiences among the people of Samoa led to an important description of how adolescent Samoans become aware of adult concerns and rituals. Mead's book, *Comimg of Age in Samoa*, contains few numbers; the data are qualitative.

2 Assignments in the social sciences

Depending on what social science courses you take, you may be asked to complete a variety of assignments. The **summary or review of research** reports on the available research literature on a subject such as infant perception of color. The **case analysis** explains the components of a phenomenon such as a factory closing. The **problem-solving analysis** explains the components of a problem, such as unreported child abuse, and suggests ways to solve it. The **research paper** interprets and sometimes analyzes the writings

38c

CONDUCTING A SURVEY

1. Decide what you want to find out—what your hypothesis is. The questions you ask should be dictated by your purpose.
2. Define your population. Think about the kinds of people your hypothesis is about—for instance, college men, or five-year-old children. Plan to sample this population so that your findings will be representative.
3. Write your questions. Surveys may contain closed questions that direct the respondent's answers (check lists and multiple-choice, true/false, or yes/no questions) or open-ended questions allowing brief, descriptive answers. Avoid loaded questions that reveal your own biases or make assumptions about subjects' answers, such as "Do you want the United States to support democracy in Nicaragua?" or "How much more money does your father make than your mother?"
4. Test your questions on a few respondents with whom you can discuss the answers. Eliminate or recast questions that respondents find unclear, discomforting, or unanswerable.
5. Tally the results in actual numbers of answers, including any nonanswers.
6. Seek patterns in the raw data that confirm or conflict with your hypothesis. Revise the hypothesis or conduct additional research if necessary.

RESOURCES AND IDEAS

Linda K. Shamoon and Robert A. Schwegler, "Sociologists Reading Student Texts: Expectations and Perceptions," *The Writing Instructor* 7 (1988): 71–81. The authors argue that the way sociologists perceive the features of a student paper differ considerably from the way composition instructors often perceive the features. Sociologists look first of all for a line of sociological reasoning carried throughout a paper, supported by evidence acceptable to sociologists and made clear by indicators such as topic sentences.

38c

of other social scientists about a subject such as the effect of national appeals in advertising. The **research report** explains the author's own original research or attempt to replicate someone else's research. A research paper appears in Chapter 37, page 606. Excerpts from a problem-solving analysis appear at the end of this section, on page 675.

Most social science disciplines have special requirements for the content and organization of each kind of paper. The requirements appear in the style guides of the disciplines, such as the *Publication Manual of the American Psychological Association* (APA), 3rd ed. (1983). (Guides for other disciplines are listed on p. 666.) The APA manual specifies the following outline for the text of a research report.

1. *Abstract:* a summary (about 100 words) of the subject, the research method, the findings, and the conclusions.
2. *Introduction:* a presentation of the problem researched, the research method used, the background (such as other relevant studies), the purpose of the research, and the hypothesis tested.
3. *Method:* a detailed discussion of how the research was con-

ducted, including a description of the research subjects, any
materials or tools used (such as questionnaires), and the procedure followed.

4. *Results:* a summary of the data collected and how they were
   statistically analyzed, along with a detailed presentation of
   the data, often in tables, graphs, or charts.

5. *Discussion:* an interpretation of the data and presentation of
   conclusions, related to the original hypothesis. (When the
   discussion is brief, it may be combined with the previous section under the heading "Results and Discussion.")

To this basic text are added a title page and a list of references (the
latter described on pp. 666–67).

Because of the differences among disciplines and even among
different kinds of papers in the same discipline, you should always
ask your instructor what he or she requires for an assignment.

<hr>

3   **Tools and language in the social sciences**

Although a research journal or log may not be required in undergraduate courses, such a notebook can be very helpful. Use it to
pose preliminary questions as you begin formulating a hypothesis.
In the field (that is, when conducting research), use the journal to
react to the evidence you are collecting, to record changes in your
perceptions and ideas, and to assess your progress. To avoid confusing reflections on evidence with the evidence itself, keep records
of actual data—notes from interviews, observations, surveys, and
experiments—separately from the field journal.

Each social science discipline has specialized terminology
for concepts basic to the discipline. In sociology, for example, the
words *mechanism, identity,* and *deviance* have specific meanings
different from those of everyday usage. And *identity* means something different in sociology, where it applies to groups of people,
than in psychology, where it applies to the individual. Social scientists also use precise terms to describe or interpret research. For
instance, they say *The subject expressed a feeling of* rather than *The
subject felt* because human feelings and intentions are not know-
able for certain; or they say *These studies indicate* rather than
These studies prove because conclusions are only tentative.

Just as in their research social scientists strive for objectivity, so in their writing they strive to demonstrate their objectivity
through language. They avoid expressions such as *I think* in order
to focus attention on what the evidence shows rather than on the
researcher's opinions. (However, many social scientists prefer *I* to
the artificial *the researcher* when they refer to their own actions, as

38c

in *I then interviewed the subjects.* Ask your instructor for his or her preferences.) Social scientists also avoid direct or indirect expression of their personal biases or emotions, either in discussions of other researchers' work or in descriptions of research subjects. Thus, one social scientist does not call another's work *sloppy* or *immaculate* and does not refer to his or her own subjects as *drunks* or *innocent victims.* Instead, the writer uses neutral language and ties conclusions strictly to the data.

4 Documentation and format

As mentioned earlier, many of the social sciences publish style guides that advise practitioners how to organize, document, and type papers. The following is a partial list:

American Psychological Association. *Publication Manual of the American Psychological Association.* 3rd ed. 1983.

American Sociological Association. "Editorial Guidelines." Inside front cover of each issue of *American Sociological Review.*

American Anthropological Association. "Style Guide and Information for Authors." *American Anthropologist* (1977): 774–79.

By far the most detailed and often-used guide in the social sciences is the *Publication Manual of the American Psychological Association* (APA). Its documentation system of in-text parenthetical references and a reference list and its manuscript format are observed in many disciplines besides psychology, and they are similar to the styles in anthropology, sociology, economics, and other disciplines. By all means, ask your instructor in any discipline what style you should use. If, as is likely, the preferred style is the APA's, then you can use the following explanation and models.

The APA reference list

The APA documentation style is like that of the Modern Language Association in that in-text parenthetical citations (see p. 671) refer the reader to a list of sources at the end of the paper. The list of sources is titled "References" and includes full publication information on every source cited in the paper. The sources are arranged alphabetically by the author's last name or, if there is no author, by the first main word of the title. In the models that follow for various sources, observe these features:

1. Double-space all entries. Type the first line of each entry at the left margin, and indent all subsequent lines three spaces.
2. List all authors last-name first, separating names and parts

of names with commas. Use initials for first and middle names. Use an ampersand (&) rather than "and" before the last author's name.

3. In titles of books and articles, capitalize only the first word of the title, the first word of the subtitle, and proper names; all other words begin with small letters. In titles of journals, capitalize all significant words. Underline the titles of books and journals. Do not underline or use quotation marks around the titles of articles.

4. Give full names of publishers, excluding "Co.," "Inc.," and the like.

5. Use the abbreviation "p." or "pp." before page numbers in books, magazines, and newspapers, but *not* for scholarly journals.

Additional features are noted below.

A BOOK WITH A SINGLE AUTHOR

Rodriguez, R. (1982). <u>A hunger of memory: The education of Richard Rodriguez</u>. Boston: David R. Godine.

A BOOK WITH TWO OR MORE AUTHORS

Nesselroade, J. R., & Baltes, P. B. (1979). <u>Longitudinal research in the study of behavioral development</u>. New York: Academic Press.

A BOOK WITH AN EDITOR

Dohrenwend, B. S., & Dohrenwend, B. P. (Eds.). (1974). <u>Stressful life events: Their nature and effects</u>. New York: John Wiley.

List the editors' names as if they were authors, but follow the last name with "(Eds.)."—or "(Ed.)." with only one editor. Note the periods inside and outside the final parenthesis.

A BOOK WITH A TRANSLATOR

Trajan, P. D. (1927). <u>Psychology of animals</u>. (H. Simone, Trans.). Washington, DC: Halperin & Bros.

38c

The name of the translator appears in parentheses after the title, followed by a comma, "Trans.," a closing parenthesis, and a final period. Note also the absence of periods in "DC."

A BOOK WITH A CORPORATE AUTHOR

Editors of <u>The Progressive</u>. (1970). <u>The crisis of</u>

<u>survival</u>. Glenview: Scott, Foresman.

For works without named individuals as authors—such as a book with a corporate or group author (above) or an anonymous book (below)—begin the entry with the corporate or group name or the work's title, respectively. In the references list, alphabetize the work as if the first main word (excluding *The*, *A*, and *An*) were an author's last name.

AN ANONYMOUS BOOK

<u>Webster's seventh new collegiate dictionary</u>.

(1963). Springfield: G. & C. Merriam.

TWO OR MORE WORKS BY THE SAME AUTHOR(S)

Gardner, H. (1973a). <u>The arts and human develop-</u>

<u>ment</u>. New York: John Wiley.

Gardner, H. (1973b). <u>The quest for mind: Piaget,</u>

<u>Lévi-Strauss, and the structuralist movement</u>.

New York: Alfred A. Knopf.

When citing two or more works by exactly the same author(s), arrange the sources in order of their publication dates, earliest first. When citing two or more works by exactly the same author(s), published in the same year—as in the examples above—arrange them alphabetically by the first main word of the title and distinguish the sources by adding a letter to the date. Both the date *and* the letter are used in citing the source in the text (see p. 673).

A LATER EDITION

Bollinger, D. L. (1975). <u>Aspects of language</u> (2nd

ed.). New York: Harcourt Brace Jovanovich.

The edition number in parentheses follows the title and is followed by a period.

A WORK IN MORE THAN ONE VOLUME

Lincoln, A.   (1953).   <u>The collected works of Abraham

   Lincoln</u> (R. P. Basler, Ed.).   (Vol. 5).   New

   Brunswick: Rutgers University Press.

Lincoln, A.   (1953).   <u>The collected works of Abraham

   Lincoln</u> (R. P. Basler, Ed.).   (Vols. 1-8).   New

   Brunswick: Rutgers University Press.

The first entry cites a single volume (5) in the eight-volume set. The second cites all eight volumes. Use the abbreviation "Vol." within parentheses, and follow the closing parenthesis with a period. (In the absence of an editor's name, the description of volumes would follow the title without intervening punctuation.)

AN ARTICLE OR CHAPTER IN AN EDITED BOOK

Paykel, E. S.   (1974).   Life stress and psychiatric

   disorder: Applications of the clinical approach.

   In B. S. Dohrenwend & B. P. Dohrenwend (Eds.),

   <u>Stressful life events: Their nature and effects</u>

   (pp. 239-264). New York: John Wiley.

The publication date of the collection (1974) is given as the publication date of the article or chapter. Following the article or chapter title and a period, information on the collection begins with "In," then the editors' names (in normal order), then "(Eds.)" and a comma, and then the title of the collection and the page numbers of the article in parentheses.

AN ARTICLE IN A JOURNAL WITH CONTINUOUS PAGINATION THROUGHOUT THE ANNUAL VOLUME

Emery, R. E.   (1982).   Marital turmoil: Interper-

   sonal conflict and the children of discord and

   divorce.   <u>Psychological Bulletin</u>, <u>92</u>, 310-330.

See page 553 for an explanation of journal pagination. Note that the article title is not placed in quotation marks and that only the first words of the title and subtitle are capitalized. The journal title, in contrast, is underlined, and all significant words are capital-

38c

ized. The volume number is separated from the title by a comma and is underlined. No "pp." precedes the page numbers.

AN ARTICLE IN A JOURNAL THAT PAGES ISSUES SEPARATELY

Boyd, S.   (1981).   Nuclear Terror.   Adaptation to

Change, 7(4), 20-23.

Again, consult page 553 for an explanation of journal pagination. In this case, the issue number in parentheses follows the volume number without intervening space. The issue number is *not* underlined.

AN ARTICLE IN A MAGAZINE

Van Gelder, L.   (1986, December).   Countdown to

motherhood: When should you have a baby?   Ms.,

pp. 37-39, 74.

In the absence of a volume number, give the month of publication after the year, separating them with a comma. Give all page numbers even when the article appears on discontinuous pages. Use "pp." before the page numbers.

AN ARTICLE IN A NEWSPAPER

Herbers, J.   (1988, March 6).   A different Dixie:

Few but sturdy threads tie new South to old.   The

New York Times, sec. 4, p. 1.

Give month *and* date along with year of publication. Use *The* in the newspaper name if the paper itself does.

AN UNSIGNED ARTICLE

The right to die.   (1976, October 11).   Time, p. 101.

A REVIEW

Dinnage, R.   (1987, November 29).   Against the mas-

ter and his men.   [Review of A mind of her own:

The life of Karen Horney].   The New York Times

Book Review, pp. 10-11.

38c

If the review is not titled, use the bracketed information as the title, keeping the brackets.

A VIDEOTAPE OR OTHER NONPRINT SOURCE

```
Heeley, D. (Director), & Kramer, J. (Producer).

    (1988). Bacall on Bogart [Videotape]. New York:

    WNET Films.
```

The names of major contributors are followed by parenthetical designation of their function. The medium is specified in brackets after the title, with no intervening punctuation. Other nonprint sources include films, slides, art works, and musical performances.

COMPUTER SOFTWARE

```
Microsoft word: Version IV. (1987). [Computer pro-

    gram]. Bellevue, WA: Microsoft.
```

APA parenthetical citations

In the APA style parenthetical citations within the text of a paper direct readers to the list of references. The citations contain a minimum of information: the author's last name, the date of publication (a key difference from MLA style), and the page number from which material is borrowed.

AUTHOR NOT NAMED IN THE TEXT

```
One critic of Milgram's experiments insisted that

the subjects should have been fully informed of the

possible effects on them (Baumrind, 1968, p. 34).
```

When you do not name the author in your text, place in parentheses the author's name, the date of the source, and the page number(s) preceded by "p." or "pp." Separate the elements with commas. Position the reference so that it is clear what material is being documented *and* so that the reference fits as smoothly as possible into your sentence structure. The following would also be correct:

```
In the view of one critic of Milgram's experiments

(Baumrind, 1968, p. 34), the subjects should have

been fully informed of the possible effects on them.
```

38c

AUTHOR NAMED IN THE TEXT

Baumrind (1968, p. 34) insisted that the subjects in

Milgram's study should have been fully informed of

the possible effects on them.

When you use the author's name in the text, do not repeat it in the reference. Position the reference next to the author's name. If you cite the same source again in the paragraph, you need not repeat the reference as long as the page number (if any) is the same and it is clear that you are using the same source. Here is a later sentence from the paragraph in which the preceding example appears:

Baumrind also criticized the experimenters' rationale.

A WORK WITH TWO AUTHORS

Pepinsky and DeStefano (1977) demonstrate that a

teacher's language often reveals hidden biases.

One study (Pepinsky & DeStefano, 1977) demonstrated

the hidden biases often revealed in a teacher's lan-

guage.

When given in the text, two authors' names are connected by "and." In a parenthetical reference, they are connected by an ampersand, "&."

A WORK WITH THREE TO SIX AUTHORS

Pepinsky, Dunn, Rentl, and Corson (1973) further

demonstrated the biases evident in gestures.

In the first citation of a work with three to six authors, name all the authors, as in the example above. In the second and subsequent references to a work with three to six authors, give only the first author's name, followed by "et al." (Latin for "and others"):

In the work of Pepinsky et al. (1973), the loaded

gestures included head shakes and eye contact.

A WORK WITH MORE THAN SIX AUTHORS

One study (Rutter et al., 1976) attempts to explain

38c

these geographical differences in adolescent experi-

ence.

For more than six authors, even in the first citation of the work, give only the first author's name, followed by "et al."

A CORPORATE AUTHOR

An earlier prediction was even more somber (Editors

of The Progressive, 1970).

AN ANONYMOUS WORK

One article ("Right to Die," 1976) noted that a

death-row inmate may crave notoriety.

For an anonymous or unsigned work, use the first two or three words of the title in place of an author's name, excluding an initial *The, A,* or *An.* Unlike in the reference list, the title of an article is placed in quotation marks. (Compare the citation above with the reference on p. 670.) Book and journal titles are underlined, as in the reference list. In all titles cited in the text—not just journal titles, as in the reference list—the significant words are capitalized.

ONE OF TWO OR MORE WORKS BY THE SAME AUTHOR(S)

At about age seven, most children begin to use ap-

propriate gestures to reinforce their stories (Gard-

ner, 1973a. pp. 144-145).

When you cite one of two or more works by the same author(s), the date will tell readers which source you mean—as long as your reference list includes only one source published by the author(s) in that year. If your reference list includes two or more works published by the same author(s) in the same year, the works should be lettered as explained on page 668. Then your parenthetical citation should include the appropriate letter, as in the example above.

TWO OR MORE WORKS BY DIFFERENT AUTHORS

Two studies (Herskowitz, 1974; Marconi & Hamblen,

1980) found that periodic safety instruction can

dramatically reduce employees' accidents.

38c

List the sources in alphabetical order by the first author's name. Insert a semicolon between sources.

APA manuscript format

In general, the guidelines of the APA for manuscript format coincide with those of the MLA, explained in Appendix A of this book (p. 702). There are, however, some important differences and additions:

1. Use a 1½-inch margin on the left and 1-inch margins on the other three sides.
2. Number pages consecutively, starting with the title page. Identify each page (including the title page) with a shortened version of the title as well as a page number. For instance:

```
                                    Dating Violence

                                                  5


66 males) at a large state university in the north-

east United States.  The sample consisted of stu-

dents enrolled
```

3. Put the abstract (if there is one) on a page by itself immediately after the title page, with the heading "Abstract" centered at the top of the page.
4. Run into your text all quotations of fewer than forty words, and enclose them in quotation marks. For quotations of more than forty words, set them off from your text by indenting all lines five spaces, double-spacing above and below, and double-spacing the quotation itself. Do not use quotation marks around a quotation displayed in this way.
5. Do not label the introduction with a heading. For other main sections of your paper, such as "Method" and "Results," center the heading, type it in capital and small letters, do not underline it, and double-space above and below it. (Do not start new pages for these sections.) If you use another level of heading below the main level, begin at the left margin, use capital and small letters, and underline the heading. See page 676 for examples of both headings.
6. Present data in tables and figures (graphs or charts), as appropriate. (See the sample on p. 678 for a clear format to follow.) Begin each illustration on a separate page. Number each kind of illustration consecutively and separately from the other (Table 1, Table 2, etc., and Figure 1, Figure 2, etc.). Refer to all illustrations in your text—for instance, "(See Figure 3.)." Either place illustrations immediately after the text

38c

references to them, or, if there are many illustrations, collect them at the end of the paper, after the reference list. (See p. 685 for more information on illustrations.)

7. The reference list starts a new page after the last page of the text, with the heading "References" centered at the top of the page and the entire list typed double-space. (See also p. 680.)

Because many departments and instructors have their own preferences for manuscript format, you should ask your instructor for his or her wishes before preparing your final draft.

5   A sample social science paper

On the following pages are excerpts from a sociology paper. The student followed the organization described on pages 664–65 in both establishing the background for her study and explaining her own research. She also followed the APA style of documentation and manuscript format, although page borders, most page breaks, and other features have been omitted here.

Excerpts from a problem-solving analysis (sociology)

[Title page: center vertically and horizontally.]

An Assessment of

Dating Violence on Campus

Karen M. Tarczyk

Sociology 213

Dr. Durkan

May 6, 1987

[New page.]

Abstract

Little research has examined the patterns of abuse and violence occurring within couples during courtship. With a questionnaire administered to a sample of college students, the extent and nature of such abuse and violence were investigated. The results, some interpretations, and implications for further research are discussed.

RESOURCES AND IDEAS

Carol Berkenkotter, "Writing and Problem Solving," *Journal of Basic Writing* 5 (1988).

38c

An Assessment of

Dating Violence on Campus

In recent years, a great deal of attention has been devoted to family violence. Numerous studies have been done on spouse and child abuse. However, violent behavior occurs in dating relationships as well. The problem of dating violence has been relatively ignored by sociological research. It should be examined further since the premarital relationship is one context in which individuals learn and adopt behaviors that surface later in marriage.

The sociologist James Makepeace (1979) contends that courtship violence is a "potential mediating link" between violence in one's family of orientation and violence in one's later family of procreation. His provocative study examining dating behaviors at Bemidji State University in Minnesota caused a controversy. Makepeace reported that one-fifth of the respondents had had at least one encounter with dating violence. He concluded by extending these percentages to students nationwide, suggesting the existence of a major hidden social problem. [The introduction continues.]

All these studies indicate a problem that is being neglected. The present study's objective was to gather information on the extent and nature of premarital violence and to discuss some possible interpretations.

Method

Sample

I conducted a survey of 200 students (134 females,

66 males) at a large state university in the northeast United States. The sample consisted of students enrolled in an introductory sociology course. The mean age of the respondents was 19.35 years, ranging from 18 to 31. Predominantly, most students (87.8%) resided in campus dormitories, not at home or in their own apartments. Moreover, the majority of the sample (93.5%) were single and not self-supporting.

The Questionnaire

A questionnaire exploring the personal dynamics of relationships was distributed during regularly scheduled class. Questions were answered anonymously in a 30-minute time period. The survey consisted of three sections: section 1 and section 2 were filled out by all respondents; section 3 was filled out only by students currently dating someone (123 of 200 students).

[The explanation of method continues.]

Section 3 required participants to provide information about their current dating relationships. Levels of stress and frustration, communication between partners, and patterns of decision making were examined. These variables were expected to influence the amount of violence in a relationship. The next part of the survey was adopted from Murray Strauss's Conflict Tactics Scales (1982). These scales contain 19 items designed to measure conflict and the means of conflict resolution, including reasoning, verbal aggression, and actual violence. The final page of the questionnaire contained general

38c

questions on the couple's use of alcohol, sexual activity, and overall satisfaction with the relationship.

Results

The incidence of verbal aggression and threatened and actual dating violence was examined. A high prevalence of students, 53% (76 of 123 subjects), reported that they had been the victim of verbal abuse, either being insulted or sworn at. In addition, 15% (18 of 123) of respondents admitted being threatened with some type of violence. Low percentages were reported for the various types of actual physical violence. (See Table 1.)

[The explanation of results continues.]

[Table on a page by itself.]

Table 1

Incidence of Courtship Violence

Type of violence	Number of students reporting	Percentage of sample
Insulted or swore	62	53.0
Threatened to hit or throw something	17	14.0
Threw something	8	6.6
Pushed, grabbed, or shoved	18	14.9
Slapped	8	6.6
Kicked, bit, or hit with fist	7	6.0
Hit or tried to hit with something	2	1.6
Threatened with a knife or gun	1	0.8
Used a knife or gun	1	0.8

38c

Discussion

Violence within premarital relationships has been relatively ignored. The results of the present study indicate that abuse and force do occur in dating relationships. Although the percentages are small, so was the sample. Extending them to the entire campus population would mean significant numbers. For example, if the 6% incidence of being kicked, bitten, or hit with a fist is typical, then 300 students of a 5,000-member student body might have experienced this type of violence.

[The discussion continues.]

If the courtship period is characterized by abuse and violence, what accounts for it? The other sections of the survey examined some variables that appear to influence the nature of the relationship. Level of stress and frustration, both within the relationship and in the respondent's life, was one such variable. The communication level between partners, both the frequency of discussion and the frequency of agreement, was also seen to have an influence on the nature of the relationship.

[The discussion continues.]

The method of analyzing the data in this study, utilizing frequency distributions, provided a clear overview. However, more tests of significance and correlation need to be done. A closer look at the social and individual variables affecting the relationship is warranted. The courtship period may set the stage for patterns of married life. It merits more attention.

38c

[New page.]

References

Cates, R. L., Rutter, C. H., Karl, J., Linton, M., & Smith, K. (1982). Premarital abuse: A social psychological perspective. Journal of Family Issues, 3(1), 79-90.

Glaser, R., and Rutter, C. H. (Eds.). (1984). Familial violence [Special issue]. Family Relations, 33(3).

Laner, M. (1983). Recent increases in dating violence. Social Problems, 22, 152-166.

Makepeace, J. M. (1981). Courtship violence among college students. Family Relations, 30, 97-102.

Socko performance on campus. (1981, June 7). Time, 66-67.

Strauss, M. L. (1982). Conflict tactics scales. New York: Sociological Tests.

RESOURCES AND IDEAS

David Hamilton, "Writing Science," *College English* (1978): 32–40. Hamilton argues that instruction in science writing should emphasize writing not simply as a tool for scientists but as an essential and creative part of the scientific act.

RESOURCES AND IDEAS

Marjorie Fink Vargas, "Writing Skills for Science Labs," *The Science Teacher* (November 1986): 29–33. The author describes a fifty-minute class activity that helps students understand choices of person and voice dictated by the stylistic conventions of lab reports.

38d ## Writing in the natural and applied sciences

The natural and applied sciences include biology, chemistry, physics, mathematics, engineering, computer science, and their branches. Their purpose is to understand natural and technological phenomena. (A *phenomenon* is a fact or event that can be known by the senses.) Scientists conduct experiments and write to explain the step-by-step processes in their methods of inquiry and discovery.

1 ### Methods and evidence in the sciences

Scientists investigate phenomena by the **scientific method,** a process of continual testing and refinement. (See the box opposite.) Scientific evidence is almost always quantitative—that is, it consists of numerical data obtained from the measurement of phenomena. These data are called **empirical** (from a Greek word for "experience"): they result from observation and experience, gen-

THE SCIENTIFIC METHOD

1. Observe carefully. Accurately note all details of the phenomenon being researched.
2. Ask questions about the observations.
3. Formulate a **hypothesis,** or preliminary generalization, that explains the observed facts.
4. Test the hypothesis with additional observation or controlled experiments.
5. If the hypothesis proves accurate, formulate a **theory,** or unified model, that explains *why*. If the hypothesis is disproved, revise it or start anew.

erally in a controlled laboratory setting but also (as sometimes in astronomy or biology) in the natural world. Often the empirical evidence for scientific writing comes from library research into other people's reports of their investigations. Surveys of known data or existing literature are common in scientific writing.

2 Assignments in the sciences

No matter what your assignment, you will be expected to document and explain your evidence carefully so that anyone reading can check your sources and replicate your research. It is important for your reader to know the context of your research—both the previous experimentation and research on your particular subject (acknowledged in the survey of the literature) and the physical conditions and other variables surrounding your own work.

Assignments in the natural and applied sciences include a **summary,** which distills the essence of a research article in brief, concise form; a **critique,** which summarizes and critically evaluates a scientific report; a **laboratory report,** which explains the procedure and results of an experiment conducted by the writer; a **research report,** which reports on the experimental research of other scientists and reports the writer's own methods, findings, and conclusions; and a **research proposal,** which reviews the relevant literature and explains a plan for further research. Summary is discussed at length in 4a (p. 125). A laboratory report in biology begins on page 686.

A laboratory report has four or five major sections:

1. *Abstract:* a summary of the report. (See p. 686.)
2. *Introduction* or *Objective:* a review of why the study was undertaken, a summary of the background of the study, and a statement of the problem being studied.

38d

3. *Method* or *Procedure:* a detailed explanation of how the study was conducted, including any statistical analysis.
4. *Results:* an explanation of the major findings (including unexpected results) and a summary of the data presented in graphs and tables.
5. *Discussion:* an interpretation of the results and an explanation of how they relate to the goals of the experiment. This section also describes new hypotheses that might be tested as a result of the experiment. If the section is brief, it may be combined with the previous section in a single section of *Conclusions.*

In addition, laboratory or research reports may include a list of references (if other sources were consulted). They almost always include tables and figures (graphs and charts) containing the data from the research (see p. 687).

3 Tools and language in the sciences

Keeping a journal or notebook can help you reflect on and rethink your ideas for writing, pose and answer questions, or explore your changing attitudes about a subject. In the sciences, a **lab notebook** or **scientific journal** is almost indispensable for accurately recording the empirical data from observations and experiments. Use such a notebook or journal for these purposes:

1. Record observations from reading, from class, or from the lab.
2. Ask questions and refine hypotheses.
3. Record procedures.
4. Record results.
5. Keep an ongoing record of ideas and findings and how they change as data accumulate.
6. Sequence and organize your material as you compile your findings and write your report.

When writing in your notebook, try to observe as well the special conventions of language in the sciences. The main convention is the use of objective language that removes the writer as a character in the situation and events being explained, except as the impersonal agent of change, the experimenter. Accordingly, scientists rarely use *I* in their reports and evaluations, and they often resort to the passive voice of verbs, as in *The mixture <u>was</u> then <u>subjected</u> to centrifugal force.* This conscious objectivity focuses attention (including the writer's) on the empirical data and what they show. It discourages the writer from, say, ascribing motives and will to animals and plants. For instance, instead of asserting that the sea tortoise *evolved* its hard shell *to protect* its body, a sci-

RESOURCES AND IDEAS

John Olmsted III, "Teaching Varied Technical Writing Styles in the Upper Division Laboratory," *Journal of Chemical Education* 61 (1984): 798–800. Olmsted describes a course that asks students to prepare reports in a variety of styles on experiments they have conducted. He describes in detail the twelve different kinds of reports students must submit during the course.

38d

entist would write only what could be observed: that the hard shell *covers and thus protects* the tortoise's body.

As in the social sciences, each discipline in the natural and applied sciences has a specialized vocabulary that permits precise, accurate, and efficient communication. Some of these terms, such as *pressure* in physics, have different meanings in the common language and must be handled carefully in science writing. Others, such as *enthalpy* in chemistry, have no meanings in the common language and must simply be learned and used correctly.

4 Documentation and format in the sciences

Within the natural and applied sciences, the scholars and teachers of each discipline use a slightly different style of documentation and manuscript format. Following are some of the style guides most often consulted:

American Chemical Society. *Handbook for Authors of Papers in American Chemical Society Publications.* 1978.

American Institute of Physics. *Style Manual for Guidance in the Preparation of Papers.* 3rd ed. 1978.

American Mathematical Society. *A Manual for Authors of Mathematical Papers.* 8th ed. 1980.

Council of Biology Editors. *CBE Style Manual: A Guide for Authors, Editors, and Publishers in the Biological Sciences.* 5th ed. 1983.

Documentation

Some documentation styles in the sciences closely resemble other styles discussed in this chapter and Chapter 36: the APA system of in-text parenthetical citations and a separate reference list (see pp. 666–74) and the system of in-text raised numerals referring to separate footnotes or endnotes described in the *MLA Handbook* (see pp. 575–604). In a third style (described briefly below), in-text numbers in parentheses or brackets refer to a list of correspondingly numbered references. Obviously, you must ask your instructor's preference for style and consult the appropriate style guide before preparing a final manuscript.

In a style recommended by the Council of Biology Editors (CBE), the list of references (titled "References") arranges and numbers sources in the order in which they were cited in the text of the paper. For example:

```
1. Hepburn, P. X.; Tatin, J. M. Human physiology.

New York: Columbia University Press; 1975.
```

RESOURCES AND IDEAS

W. Daniel Goodman and John C. Bean, "A Chemistry Laboratory Project to Develop Thinking and Writing Skills," *Journal of Chemical Education* 60 (1983): 483–84. The authors outline "a method for conducting an undergraduate chemistry laboratory, in this case sophomore organic chemistry, that integrates a project laboratory with a writing task involving peer group interaction." The method requires "students to carry out an independent investigation of the synthesis of one or more aliphatic esters and to present their research in the form of professional papers."

38d

```
2. Jonson, P., editor. Anatomy yearbook. Los Ange-
   les: Anatco; 1987.
3. Ancino, R.; Carter, K. V.; Elwin, D. J. Factors
   contributing to viral immunity: a review of the
   research. Developmental Biology 30:156-169; 1983.
```

Note that since the sources are arranged in order of citation, they are not in alphabetical order. Also note the key features of the bibliographic formats as outlined below. (Compare these formats with those of the APA, pp. 667–71, which differ especially in punctuation and the handling of titles.)

1. Each entry begins a new line and is numbered. The number is followed by a period and two spaces. Subsequent lines of each entry then begin directly under the first word of the first line.
2. Authors' first and middle names are represented by initials.
3. Authors' names are separated by semicolons (references 1 and 3).
4. No titles are underlined or placed in quotation marks.
5. Only in journal titles (reference 3) is any but the first word of a title capitalized. In book and article titles and subtitles, all words after the first word begin with small letters (references 1–3).
6. The name of the publisher is separated from the date of publication by a semicolon (references 1 and 2).
7. No punctuation falls between a journal's title and volume number (reference 3). Page numbers are connected to the volume number with an unspaced colon. The date of publication then follows a semicolon and a space.

When citing sources in the text, use only the numbers from the reference list, plus any page number(s). For example:

```
These forms of immunity have been extensively re-
searched (3).
```

```
Two standard references (1, 2) use this term.
```

```
According to one report (3, p. 160), research into
some forms of viral immunity is almost nonexistent.
```

```
Hepburn and Tatin (1) do not discuss this project.
```

Manuscript format

As with documentation style, the science disciplines each have their own preferred manuscript formats with subtle differences among them. The CBE format closely resembles that of the APA (see pp. 674–75). Again, ask your instructor for his or her preferences.

Undoubtedly, the most troublesome aspects of manuscript preparation in the sciences are equations or formulas and illustrations (tables and figures). When typing equations or formulas, be careful to reproduce alignments, indentions, underlining, and characters accurately. If your typewriter or word processor lacks special characters, write them in by hand. (Stationery and art-supply stores also have sheets of transfer type special characters in different sizes that can be applied to your manuscript by rubbing.)

Because you will be expected to share your data with your readers, most of your writing for the sciences is likely to require illustrations to present the data in concise, readable form. Tables usually summarize raw data (see p. 687 for an example), whereas figures (mainly charts and graphs) recast the data to show noteworthy comparisons or changes. Follow these guidelines in preparing and positioning illustrations:

1. Give each illustration a clear label. Number tables and figures separately (Table 1, Table 2, etc.; Figure 1, Figure 2, etc.).
2. Give each illustration a clear title so that readers know what to look for in it. (Generally, a table's label and title are placed above the illustration, whereas a figure's label and title are placed under the illustration.)
3. Provide clear labels for all the parts of illustrations, such as columns in a table and bars in a bar graph. Unless your instructor specifically requests abbreviations, avoid them in the interest of clarity.
4. If you borrow the data or the whole illustration from another source, provide a source note under the illustration. For instance:

```
Source: Ann Menaker.   Spectroscopy of plasmas.   New

York: Van Nostrand, 1981.
```

5. Refer to each illustration ("See Figure 6") at the point(s) in the text where readers will benefit by consulting it.
6. If your paper includes many illustrations, collect them at the end of the paper, after the reference list. If it includes only a few illustrations, place each one on a page by itself immediately after the page that refers to it.

38d

5 A sample science paper

The following excerpts from a laboratory report in genetics, a branch of biology, illustrate many of the features described in the preceding pages. Some elements, such as page borders and identifiers, have been omitted, but otherwise the format illustrates that recommended by the Council of Biology Editors (CBE). (The paper is based entirely on the student's own laboratory experiment and thus does not include text citations or a reference list.)

Excerpts from a laboratory report (biology)

[Title page: center title vertically and horizontally.]

Demonstration:

Genetic Engineering

Lynn Treacy
Genetics
Dr. Smith
March 29, 1988

[New page.]

Abstract

The transfer of the conjugative plasmid for chloraphenicol resistance from the donor, E. coli HT-99, to a suitable recipient, E. coli J-53R, was demonstrated using in vitro techniques.

[New page.]

Demonstration: Genetic Engineering

Objective

The purpose of this experiment was to illustrate the basic goal of genetic engineering through a demonstration/experiment. In this experiment, a donor, E. coli HT-99, which is resistant to chloraphenicol and sensitive to

38d

rifampicin, and a host cell, E. coli J-53R, which is resistant to rifampicin and sensitive to chloraphenicol,
were mated. The donor cell contained a chimera, a plasmid
of the E. coli donor that had the gene for resistance to
the antibody, chloraphenicol, that would serve as a
marker for the detection of a successful conjugation.

Procedure

The results of the experiment were gathered from the
observance of growth or of lack of growth of the donor,
host, and suspected exconjugant on nutrient agar plates
containing (1) rifampicin; (2) chloraphenicol; and (3)
both rifampicin and chloraphenicol.

[The explanation of procedure continues.]

[Table on a page by itself.]

Table 1. Growth (+) or nongrowth (−) of donor, host, and
exconjugant

	Growth on plates containing		
Organism	Rifampicin	Chloraphenicol	Rifampicin and chloraphenicol
Donor	−	+	−
Host	+	−	−
Exconjugant, 4 hrs	NA	NA	−
Exconjugant, 18 hrs	NA	NA	+

NA = not applicable because not tested for.

38d

Conclusions

The HT-99 cells will grow in the presence of chloraphenicol, because they contain the genes to make them resistant to chloraphenicol, whereas they will not grow in the presence of rifampicin (either alone or containing chloraphenicol). After successful conjugation the exconjugant cells should grow on both plates since the cells possess the genes coding for resistance to rifampicin, and they also have the genes for resistance to chloraphenicol contained in a plasmid. The first test of the exconjugant was negative because the constant agitation of the shaker did not allow conjugation to occur (interrupted the mating between the cells). After the mixture sat overnight, the exconjugant cells were found, since successful conjugation had occurred.

[The conclusions continue.]

Successful conjugation is easily detected by the use of nutrient agar plates containing the antibiotics chloraphenicol and rifampicin; the simple observation of growth and of no growth is all that is needed to signal a successful or unsuccessful mating.

38d

Practical Writing

CHAPTER 39

Essay Examinations

In writing an essay for an examination, you summarize or analyze a topic, usually in several paragraphs or more and usually within a time limit. An essay question not only tests your knowledge of a subject (as short-answer and objective questions do) but also tests your control and synthesis of that knowledge and helps you see it in a new way (as other kinds of questions usually cannot do).

39a Preparing for an essay examination

Taking lecture notes, thoughtfully reading the assigned texts or articles, and reviewing regularly will help you prepare for any kind of examination. In addition, for an essay examination you can practice synthesizing what you know by creating summaries that help you recast others' ideas in your own words and extract the meaning from notes and texts (see the extensive discussion of summary in 4a). And you can prepare outlines that reorganize the course material. For instance, in a business course you could evaluate the advantages and disadvantages of several approaches to management. In a short-story course you could look for a theme running through all the stories you have read by a certain author or from a certain period. In a psychology course you could contrast various theorists' views of what causes a disorder like schizophrenia. Any one of these is a likely topic for an essay question. Thinking of such categories not only can help you anticipate the kinds of questions you may be asked but also can increase your mastery of the material.

39b Planning your time and your answer

When you first look at your examination, always read it all the way through at least once before you start answering any questions. As you scan the examination, determine which questions seem most important, which ones are going to be most difficult for you, and approximately how much time you'll need for each question. (Your instructor may help by assigning a point value to each question as a guide to its importance or by suggesting an amount of time for you to spend on each question.) You will want to provide your best answer for every question, so this initial planning is important.

To avoid straying from an essay question or answering only part of it, read it at least twice. Examine the words and consider their implications. Look especially for words like *describe*, *define*, *explain*, *summarize*, *analyze*, *evaluate*, and *interpret*, each of which requires a different kind of response. For instance, the instruction *Define dyslexia and compare and contrast it with two other learning disabilities* contains important clues for how an essay should be written. *Define dyslexia* tells you to specify the meaning of the term. A description of how children with dyslexia feel about their disability, however well done, would be irrelevant. Instead, you should say what dyslexia is—a perceptual impairment causing a reader to reverse or scramble letters—and extend the definition by providing distinctive characteristics, ways the impairment seems to work, examples of its effects, and so on. The words *compare and contrast it with two other learning disabilities* tell you to analyze not only its similarities to but also its differences from the other disabilities. Answering this part of the question thus involves thinking of categories for comparison, such as causes, treatments, frequency of occurrence, and severity of effect. An essay that described only similarities or only differences would not answer the question completely.

After you're sure you understand the question, make a brief outline of the main ideas you want to include in your essay. Use the back of the test sheet or exam booklet for scratch paper. Write a brief thesis sentence for your essay that responds directly to the question and represents your view of the topic. (If you are unsure of how to write a thesis sentence, see 1g.) Include key phrases that you can expand with supporting evidence for your view. This stage is much like the planning of an essay or a research paper. Though you don't have as much time to refine and rearrange your ideas, planning will help make your essay unified, coherent, well supported, and concise.

EXAMS OF THEIR OWN

Discussions of essay exams and writing strategies for them are likely to be most practical and most memorable when directed toward questions from classes students have taken or are likely to take in the future. Ask students to bring in questions from exams they have taken; choose several that make good examples, and write them on the board or distribute them to the class. Discussion can focus on the best ways to go about preparing, planning, starting, developing, and rereading an exam essay.

39c

39c Starting the essay

A well-constructed thesis sentence will contribute much to an examination essay. Drawing on the brief thesis you devised during planning, you can begin an essay effectively by stating your thesis immediately and including in it an overview of the rest of your essay. Such a capsule version of your answer tells your reader (and grader) generally how much command you have and also how you plan to develop your answer. It also gets you off to a good start.

The opening statement should address the question directly and exactly. The following thesis sentence, in response to the question below, does *not* meet these criteria.

QUESTION

Given humans' natural and historical curiosity about themselves, why did a scientific discipline of anthropology not arise until the twentieth century? Explain, citing specific details.

TENTATIVE THESIS SENTENCE

The discipline of anthropology, the study of humans, actually began in the early nineteenth century and was strengthened by the Darwinian revolution, but the discipline did not begin to take shape until people like Franz Boas and Alfred Kroeber began doing scientific research among nonindustrialized cultures.

This tentative thesis sentence says nothing about *why* anthropology did not arise as a scientific discipline until the twentieth century. Instead, it supplies an unspecific (and unrequested) definition of anthropology, vaguely reasserts the truth implied by the question, and adds irrelevant details about the history of anthropology. The following thesis sentence—revised to address the question directly, to state the writer's view, and to preview the essay—begins the answer more effectively.

REVISED THESIS SENTENCE

Anthropology did not emerge as a scientific discipline until the twentieth century because nineteenth-century Westerners' limited contact with remote peoples and the corresponding failure to see those other people as human combined to overcome natural curiosity and to prevent objective study of different cultures.

This thesis sentence specifies the writer's view of the two main causes of the slow emergence of anthropology—limited contact with remote peoples and, related to that, a narrow definition of humanity—that she will analyze in her essay.

AN EXAM OF YOURS

If you are teaching a course that employs essay exams, bring in one of the essay questions you have used, discuss your expectations and grading standards, and give some indication of the successful and unsuccessful ways students answered the question. Your students will probably appreciate what you can reveal to them about the expectations of academic readers, particularly if your course is similar to others they may take in future semesters.

39d Developing the essay

You develop your essay by supporting your thesis sentence with sound generalizations, which you support in turn with *specific* evidence. (See 4e.) Avoid filling out your essay by repetition. Avoid substituting purely subjective feelings about the topic for real analysis of it. (It may help to abolish the word *I* from your essay.)

The student answering the anthropology question must show that contact between Western and non-Western cultures was limited and must specify how the limitations dulled curiosity, prevented objective study, and hampered the development of anthropology. She also needs to demonstrate how a consequently narrow definition of humanity had the same results. And she *must* support her assertions with concrete evidence. For instance, she might cite nineteenth-century writings that illustrate feelings of superiority toward distant peoples.

The student would not be providing effective evidence if she introduced unsupported generalizations or substituted her subjective feelings for an objective analysis of the problem. For instance, a blanket statement that all nineteenth-century Westerners were narrow-minded or a paragraph condemning their narrowness would only pad the essay.

39e Rereading the essay

The time limit on an essay examination does not allow for the careful rethinking and revision you would give an essay or research paper. You need to write clearly and concisely the first time. If you do have a few minutes after you have finished the entire exam, reread the essay (or essays) to correct illegible passages, misspellings, grammatical mistakes, and accidental omissions. Verify that your thesis is accurate—that it does, in fact, introduce what you ended up writing about. Check to ensure that you have supported all your generalizations thoroughly. Cross out irrelevant ideas and details, and add any information that now seems important. (Write on another page, if necessary, keying the addition to the page on which it belongs.)

HIGHLIGHTS

Chapter 40 is more than a reference guide students can consult when writing one of the kinds of documents covered in the discussion: business letters, job applications and résumés, letters of request or complaint, and business memos. It offers instructors an opportunity to design writing assignments that incorporate these forms of writing, knowing that they will not have to spend valuable class time on matters of format and can direct attention to more substantive issues.

CHAPTER 40

Business Writing

When you write a letter to request information, to complain about a product or bill, or to apply for a job, or when you write a memo or report to someone you work with, you are addressing busy people who want to see quickly why you are writing and how they should respond to you. A wordy, incoherent letter or memo full of errors in grammar and spelling may prevent you from getting what you want, either because the reader cannot understand your wish or because you present yourself so poorly. In business writing, state your purpose at the very start. Be straightforward, clear, objective, and courteous, and don't hesitate to be insistent if the situation warrants it. Observe conventions of grammar and usage, for these not only make your writing clear but also impress a reader with your care.

40a Writing business letters and job applications

1 Using a standard form

Business correspondence customarily adheres to one of several acceptable forms. Use either unlined white paper measuring at least 5½″ × 8½″ or what is called letterhead stationery with your address printed at the top of the sheet. Type the letter if possible, single-spaced, on only one side of a sheet. Follow a standard form for each of the letter's parts. (The form described below and illustrated in the sample letter on the facing page is one common model.)

Return
address   —   17A Revere St.
heading   Boston, MA 02106
                January 1, 1989

Ms. Ann Herzog
Circulation Supervisor
<u>Sporting Life</u>   — Inside
25 W. 43rd St.   address
New York, NY 10036

Dear Ms. Herzog:———— Salutation

Thank you for your letter of December 20,
which notifies me that <u>Sporting Life</u> will resume my subscription after stopping it in error after I had received the July issue.
Since I missed at least five months' issues because of the magazine's error, I expected my
subscription to be extended for five months after it would have lapsed--that is, through June
1989. Instead, you tell me that the magazine
will send me the back issues that it failed to
send and that the January issue (which I have
not received) will complete my current subscription.   Body

I have no interest in receiving the back issues of <u>Sporting Life</u> because the magazine is
not useful or interesting unless it is current. Since <u>Sporting Life</u> erred in stopping
my subscription prematurely, I still expect it
to make up the difference on the other end of
my subscription.

Unless I hear otherwise from you, I will count
on your extending my subscription at least
through June 1989. If <u>Sporting Life</u> cannot
compensate for its error in this way, I will
cancel my subscription and request a refund.

Close ———— Sincerely,

Signature ——— *Janet M. Marley*
                Janet M. Marley

The return-address heading of the letter gives your address (but not your name) and the date. (If you're using letterhead stationery, you need add only the date.) Align the lines of the heading on the left, and place the whole heading on the right of the page, allowing enough space above it to center the entire letter vertically on the page.

The inside address shows the name, title, and complete address of the person you are writing to, just as this information will appear on the envelope. Begin the address a few lines below the heading at the left side of the page.

The salutation greets the addressee. Place it two lines below the address and two lines above the body of the letter. Always follow it with a colon, not a comma or dash. If you are not addressing a particular person, use a general salutation such as *Dear Sir or Madam* or *Dear Smythe Shoes* (the company name). Use *Ms.* as the title for a woman when she has no other title, when you don't know how she prefers to be addressed, or when you know that she prefers to be addressed as *Ms.* If you know a woman prefers to be addressed as *Mrs.* or *Miss*, use the appropriate title.

The body of the letter, containing its substance, begins at the left margin. Instead of indenting paragraphs, you may place an extra line of space between them so that they are readily visible.

The letter's close begins two lines below the last line of the body and aligns at the left with the heading at the top of the page. Typical closes include *Yours truly* and *Sincerely.* Only the first word is capitalized, and the close is followed by a comma.

The signature of a business letter has two parts: a typed one, four lines below the close, and a handwritten one filling in the space. The signature should consist only of your name, as you sign checks and school documents.

Below the signature, at the left margin, you may want to include additional information such as *Enc.* (something is enclosed with the letter); *cc: Margaret Newton* (a carbon copy is being sent to the person named); or *CHC/enp* (the initials of the author/the initials of the typist).

The envelope for the letter (see facing page) should show your name and address in the upper left corner and the addressee's name, title, and address in the center. Use an envelope that is the same width as your stationery and about a third the height. Fold the letter horizontally, in thirds.

2   Writing requests and complaints

Letters requesting something—for instance, a pamphlet, information about a product, a T-shirt advertised in a magazine—

```
Janet M. Marley
17A Revere St.
Boston, MA 02106


              Ms. Ann Herzog
              Circulation Supervisor
              Sporting Life
              25 W. 43rd St.
              New York, NY 10036
```

40a

must be specific and accurate about the item you are requesting. The letter should describe the item completely and, if applicable, include a copy or description of the advertisement or other source that prompted your request.

Letters complaining about a product or a service (such as a wrong billing from the telephone company) should be written in a reasonable but firm tone. (See the sample letter on p. 695.) Assume that the addressee is willing to resolve the problem when he or she has the relevant information. In the first sentence of the letter, say what you are writing about. Then provide as much background as needed, including any relevant details from past correspondence (as in the sample letter). Describe exactly what you see as the problem, sticking to facts and avoiding discourses on the company's social responsibility or your low opinion of its management. In the clearest possible words and sentences, proceed directly from one point to the next without repeating yourself. Always include your opinion of how the problem can be solved. Many companies are required by law to establish a specific procedure for complaints about products and services. If you know of such a procedure, be sure to follow it.

SOME SUGGESTIONS FOR ASSIGNMENTS

Students who have chosen business or public administration as a field may sense the usefulness of an assignment like "Prepare a résumé for yourself." For other students (and for some business students as well) the best approach is to design an assignment in which a memo or letter grows out of a specific situation. Providing students with the details of a social situation in which the writing meets a specific need and within which they as writers have a number of rhetorical and value judgments to make (sometimes called a *case approach* to writing instruction) often leads to better writing and thinking.

3   **Writing a job application and résumé**

In writing to apply for a job or to request a job interview, you should announce at the outset what job you desire and how you heard about it. (See the sample letter on the next page.) Then summarize your qualifications for the job, including facts about your education and employment history. Include only the relevant facts, mentioning that additional information appears in an accompanying résumé. Include any special reason you have for applying, such as a specific career goal. At the end of the letter, mention that you are available for an interview at the convenience of the addressee, or specify when you will be available (for instance, when your current job or classes leave you free, or when you could travel to the employer's city).

The résumé that you enclose with your letter of application should contain, in table form, your education, your employment history, and information about how to obtain your references. (See the sample résumé on the facing page.) In preparing your résumé,

---

3712 Swiss Ave.
Dallas, TX 75204
March 2, 1988

Personnel Manager
Dallas News
Communications Center
Dallas, TX 75222

Dear Sir or Madam:

In response to your posting in the English department of Southern Methodist University, I am applying for the summer job of part-time editorial assistant for the Dallas News.

I am now enrolled at Southern Methodist University as a sophomore, with a dual major in English literature and journalism. As the enclosed résumé shows, I have worked on the university newspaper for nearly two years, I have published articles in my hometown newspaper, and I worked a summer there as a copy aid. My goal is a career in journalism. I believe my educational background and my work experience . qualify me for the opening you have.

I am available for an interview at any time and would be happy to show samples of my newspaper work. My telephone number is 744-3816.

Sincerely,

Ian M. Irvine

Ian M. Irvine

Enc.

RÉSUMÉ

Ian M. Irvine
3712 Swiss Ave.
Dallas, TX 75204
(214) 744-3816

Position desired

Part-time editorial assistant.

Education

1986 to present
Southern Methodist University.
Current standing: sophomore.
Major: English literature and journalism.

1982-1986
Abilene (Texas) Senior High School.
Graduated with academic degree.

Experience

1986 to present
Reporter on the Daily Campus, student newspaper of Southern Methodist University.
Responsibilities include writing feature
stories and sports coverage.

Summer 1987
House painter and free-lance writer. Pub-
lished two articles in the Abilene (Texas)
Reporter-News.

Summer 1986
Copy aid at Abilene Reporter-News. Responsible for copy routing. Watched over tele-
printer, ran errands, assisted reporters.

References

Academic: Placement Office
               Southern Methodist University
               Dallas, TX 75275.

Employment: Ms. Millie Stevens
               Abilene Reporter-News
               Abilene, TX 79604

Personal: Ms. Sheryl Gipstein
               26 Overland Dr.
               Abilene, TX 79604

40b

you may wish to consult one of the many books devoted to application letters, résumés, and other elements of a job search. Two helpful guides are Richard N. Bolles, *What Color Is Your Parachute? A Practical Manual for Job-Hunters and Career Changers* (1988), and Tom Jackson, *The Perfect Résumé* (1981).

40b Writing business memos

Unlike business letters, which address people in other organizations, business memorandums (memos, for short) address people within the same organization. A memo can be quite long, but more often it reports briefly and directly on a very specific topic: an answer to a question, a progress report, an evaluation. Both the form and the structure of a memo are designed to get to the point and dispose of it quickly.

The memo has no return address, inside address, salutation, or close. Instead, as shown in the sample memo on the facing page, the heading typically consists of the date, the addressee's name, the writer's name, and a subject description or title. (If you are sending copies of the memo to someone besides the addressee, give his or her name after *cc,* meaning "carbon copy." See the sample.) Type the body of the memo as you would the body of a business letter: single-spaced, double-spaced between paragraphs, and no paragraph indentions. Never sign a business memo, though you may initial your name in the heading.

Immerse your reader in your subject at the very beginning of the memo. State your reason for writing in the first sentence, but do not waste words with expressions like "The purpose of this memo is. . . ." Devote the first paragraph to a succinct presentation of your answer, conclusion, or evaluation. In the rest of the memo explain how you arrived at your answer, the facts on which you base your conclusion, and your method of evaluation. The paragraphs may be numbered so that the main divisions of your message are easy to see.

A business memo can be more informal in tone than a business letter, particularly if you know the addressee; but it should not be wordy. Use technical terms if your reader will understand them, but otherwise keep language simple and use short sentences. Provide only the information that your reader needs to know.

The following sample memo, from a sales representative to her district manager, illustrates these guidelines. Notice especially the form of the memo, the writer's immediate statement of her purpose, the clear structure provided by the three numbered paragraphs, and the direct tone of the whole.

December 20, 1988

To: Chuck Tufts
cc: Jim Burch
From: Becky Gough
Subject: 1988 sales of Quick Wax in territory 12

Since it was introduced in January of this
year, Quick Wax has been unsuccessful in my
territory and has not affected sales of our
Easy Shine. Discussions with customers and my
own analysis of Quick Wax suggest three reasons for its failure to compete with our product.

1. Quick Wax has not received the promotion
    necessary for a new product. Advertising
    --primarily on radio--has been sporadic and
    has not developed a clear, consistent im-
    age for the product. In addition, the
    Quick Wax sales rep in this territory is
    new and inexperienced; he is not known to
    customers, and his sales pitch (which I
    once overheard) is weak. As far as I can
    tell, his efforts are not supported by
    phone calls or mailings from his home
    office.

2. When Quick Wax does make it to the store
    shelves, buyers do not choose it over our
    product. Though priced competitively with
    our product, Quick Wax is poorly packaged.
    The container seems smaller than ours,
    though in fact it holds the same eight
    ounces. The lettering on the Quick Wax
    package (red on blue) is difficult to
    read, in contrast to the white-on-green
    lettering on our package.

3. Our special-purchase offers and my in-
    creased efforts to serve existing custom-
    ers have had the intended effect of keep-
    ing customers satisfied with our product
    and reducing their inclination to stock
    something new.

Preparing a Manuscript

A legible, consistent, and attractive manuscript is a service to readers because it makes reading easier. This appendix discusses the materials necessary for manuscript preparation and some conventions of format adapted from the *MLA Handbook*, 3rd. ed. (Most of these guidelines are standard, but your instructor may request that you follow different conventions in some matters.)

A1 Choosing the appropriate materials

a Handwritten papers

For handwritten papers, you can use regular white paper, 8½″ × 11″, with horizontal lines spaced between one-quarter and three-eighths of an inch apart. Don't use paper torn from a notebook, unlined paper, paper with narrow lines, colored paper, or paper other than 8½″ × 11″ (such as legal or stenographer's pads). Use the same type of paper throughout a project. Write on only one side of a sheet.

Use black or blue ink, not pencil. If possible, use an ink eraser or eradicator to correct mistakes. If you must cross out material, draw a single line through it. Don't scribble over or black out a mistake, and don't write corrections on top of mistakes.

b Typewritten papers

For typewritten papers, use 8½″ × 11″ white bond paper of sixteen- or twenty-pound weight. Some instructors also accept the same size surface-coated bond paper (called "erasable" or "corrasable"), but ink smears easily on such paper. Onionskin sheets, paper torn from notebooks, colored paper, and paper smaller or larger than 8½″ × 11″ are unacceptable. Use the same type of paper throughout a project. Type on only one side of a sheet.

Use a black typewriter ribbon that is fresh enough to make a dark impression, and make sure the keys of the typewriter are clean. To avoid smudging the page when correcting mistakes, use a liquid correction fluid or a correction tape. Don't use hyphens or *x*'s to cross out mistakes, and don't type corrections (strikeovers) on top of mistakes.

c   Papers produced on a word processor

Two kinds of printers are used with most computerized word processors. Letter-quality printers (including daisywheel and laser printers), like a regular typewriter, produce characters with solid lines. Dot-matrix printers form characters out of tiny dots, and the legibility of their type varies considerably. If you use a word processor with a dot-matrix printer, make sure the dots are close enough together to produce legible characters. In addition, make sure the tails on letters such as *j*, *p*, and *y* descend below the line of type, as they do in the typeface used here. Resist the temptation to use any of the unusual type sizes or styles that your printer may be capable of producing, for such embellishments can clutter your manuscript and distract readers from what you are saying. Before you submit a paper printed on a dot-matrix printer, show your instructor a sample of the type to be sure it is acceptable.

Be sure the printer ribbon is fresh so that it leaves a dark impression. Use standard-sized (8½″ × 11″) white bond paper of sixteen- or twenty-pound weight, not the lightweight green-striped paper associated with computer print-outs. If you use continuous paper folded like a fan at perforations, it will also come with a row of holes along each side for feeding the paper into the printer. Before submitting your paper, remove these strips of holes along the perforations and separate the pages at the folds.

A2   Following a standard format

A consistent physical format makes the script, margins, paging, title, and identification visually effective and avoids the illegibility and the confusion of inconsistencies. See the sample research papers in Chapter 37 (pp. 606 and 638) for examples of the items below. (For the special formats of source citations and a list of works cited, which are not discussed here, see 36h and 36i.)

ms
A2

a ■ Script

Handwritten script should be reasonably uniform and clear. Be sure letters are easily distinguishable. Cross all *t*'s; dot all *i*'s with dots, not circles; form the loops of letters carefully. Make capital letters and small letters clearly different. Space consistently between words and between sentences. If your handwriting is difficult to read, submit a typed paper if possible. If you don't have access to a typewriter and your handwriting is illegible or unusual in size, decoration, or slant, make it more legible or conventional when writing the final manuscript. Indent the first line of every paragraph about an inch. Write on every line or every other line as specified by your instructor.

In script produced on a typewriter or word processor, indent the first line of every paragraph five spaces and double-space throughout. Leave one space between words. Type punctuation as indicated in the box on the facing page. Use handwriting to make any symbols that are not on your keyboard, leaving three or four spaces and then inserting the symbol in ink.

For both typed and handwritten script, try to avoid breaking words at the ends of lines. If you must break a word, follow the guidelines provided in Chapter 30. Don't start a line with any mark of punctuation other than a dash, an opening parenthesis, an opening quotation mark, or an ellipsis mark when one of these is called for.

Set off quotations of more than four lines of prose or three lines of poetry; two- or three-line poetry quotations may be set off or placed in the text (see 24c). In handwritten copy, indent all lines of a displayed quotation an inch from the left margin. In typewritten copy, indent all lines ten spaces. Double-space above and below each quotation, and double-space the quotation itself. (See 24c.)

b ■ Margins

Use one-inch margins on all sides of each page. The top margin will contain the page numbers (see below). If the right margin is uneven, it should be no narrower than an inch. If you have a word processor or electronic typewriter that produces an even (or justified) right margin, use the feature only if it does not leave wide spaces between words and thus interfere with readability. When using a word processor, be sure to instruct the computer to set appropriate margins. Don't let the lines of type run across the perforations on continuous fanfold paper.

c ■ Paging

Whether or not you provide a separate title page, begin numbering your paper on the first text page, and number consecutively

FORMING AND SPACING PUNCTUATION

ONE SPACE AFTER

Comma	dog, and
Semicolon	dog; and
Colon	dog: its
Apostrophe ending word	dogs' toys
Closing quotation mark	
Double	"dog" and
Single	'dog' and (use apostrophe)
Closing parenthesis	(dog) and
Closing bracket	[dog] and (or leave space and handwrite: ⌈dog⌉)

TWO SPACES AFTER

Sentence period	dog. The
Question mark	dog? The
Exclamation point	dog! The (or type an apostrophe over a period)

NO SPACE EITHER SIDE

Dash (two hyphens)	dog--its
Hyphen	one-half
Apostrophe within word	dog's

ONE SPACE BEFORE AND AFTER

Ellipsis mark within sentence	dog . . . in

EXCEPTIONS

Two spaces after closing quotation mark, parenthesis, or bracket after the end of a sentence:

   dog." The
   dog.) The
   dog.] The

When an ellipsis mark ends a sentence, one space after the sentence period and two spaces after the ellipsis mark:

   dog. . . . The

No space between two or more adjacent punctuation marks:

   "Who knows the word 'anoxia'?"
   (The dog finally came home.)

through the end. Use Arabic numerals (1, 2, 3), and do not add periods, parentheses, hyphens, or the abbreviation "p." However, for every page after the first, place your last name before the page number in case the pages become separated after you submit your paper. (See p. 608 for an example.) Align the page number with the right margin, and position it about half an inch from the top of the page, at least two lines above the first line of text.

d Title and identification

If you do not use a separate title page for an essay, provide your name and the date, plus any other information requested by your instructor, on the first text page. Place this identification an inch from the top of the page, aligned with the left margin and double-spaced. Double-space again, and center the title. Don't underline the title or place quotation marks around it, and capitalize the words in the title according to the guidelines in 26b. Double-space between the title and the first line of text. (See p. 638 for an example of this format.)

For a research paper, your instructor may ask you to provide a separate title page. If so, follow the guidelines and example on pages 606–07. On page 1 of the paper repeat the title, centered an inch from the top of the page, and double-space between the title and the first line of text. (See p. 610 for an example.)

A3 Proofreading, correcting, and submitting the final manuscript

Proofread each page of your paper carefully, concentrating on spelling, punctuation, mechanics, grammar, and manuscript format. (See 2d for proofreading tips and a proofreading exercise.) If a page has several errors, retype or rewrite the page. If it has one or two errors and you can't eradicate them, correct them in ink. Draw a single line through a word you want to delete. Don't try to correct a misspelled word without crossing out and rewriting the whole word. To replace a word or mark of punctuation, draw a line through the item, place a caret ($\wedge$) underneath it, and write the new word or mark in the space above the old one. To add words or marks of punctuation, place a caret underneath the line at the point where you wish to insert the word or mark; then center the word or mark over the caret in the space above the line.

> An ecosystem is a community of ~~organisms~~ *organisms* interacting
>
> with each other and with *the* environment.

If you have to add more words than will fit between the lines of text, rewrite or retype the page.

When you submit your final paper, be sure the pages will stay together when the paper is shuffled in with others. Depending on the wishes of your instructor, you may fold the paper in half lengthwise, paperclip or staple the pages in the upper left corner, or place the paper in a special binder.

APPENDIX B

Writing with a Word Processor

Writing with a word processor can save time and make writing easier. The advantage of word processing is that you can perform such operations as adding to notes, rearranging outlines, and rewriting first drafts without having to cut pages apart or retype entire pages. The machine will not think for you, but it may leave you more time for the important work of thinking, exploring ideas, focusing and organizing material, and improving content and clarity. This appendix explains how you can incorporate a word processor into your writing process, following the stages of development, drafting, and revising discussed in Chapters 1 and 2.

Using a word processor does not require an understanding of computers or expert typing skills. All it takes is a little perseverance and a few hours of practice. If you do not have your own word processor, find out what's available at your school, for many colleges have computers available for student use. When you begin using a word processor, carefully read the system's **documentation**—the materials that explain the system, such as a user's manual, tutorial, and reference manual. Study the keyboard carefully, and make a list of the basic keystrokes you need in order to perform important commands, such as inserting, deleting, saving, and printing text. Be adventurous: experiment with commands, and learn by trial and error. Your play will not hurt the machine, and it will help you.

You may have heard of writers losing all their work because their word processor somehow failed or "crashed." It is possible to lose text accidentally, but a few precautions will prevent permanent loss of your work. These are spelled out in the box on the next page.

707

B1

TIPS FOR SUCCESSFUL WORD PROCESSING

1. Save your work frequently by using the **save** or **file** command. Then your text will be permanently stored—usually on a magnetic disk that you can remove from the computer for safekeeping.
2. Think of each computer disk as a separate file drawer containing electronic copies of your papers. Label each paper with its own **file** or **document name** for easy retrieval.
3. Make a **back-up** or duplicate disk of your work at the end of each word-processing session as insurance against the loss or damage of your working disk.
4. Keep your disks in dust covers, and store them safely away from heat, cold, or sources of magnetism such as the computer itself or a stereo or television.
5. Regularly print paper copies of your work. They serve as second back-up copies and, more important, they give you something to work on when you revise and edit.

B1 Using a word processor for development

All word processors can aid the initial steps of the writing process (see Chapter 1). You can generate ideas on the computer, expand and reorganize them, and then transfer usable material directly into your draft or revision.

a Finding a topic and generating ideas

A word processor is an excellent medium for freewriting (see 1b-5 and 1d-1). Most computer monitors, or screens, have a dial that controls the brightness of the images on the screen. While freewriting, you can turn the brightness all the way down so that the screen appears blank. The computer will record what you write but keep it from you and thus prevent you from tinkering with your prose. This **invisible writing** can free the mind for very creative results. When you're finished freewriting, simply turn up the brightness control to read what you've written and then save or revise it as you see fit. Later, you can transfer some or all of your freewriting into your draft.

The computer is also useful for listing ideas or brainstorming (see 1d-2). You may actually find that you can generate more ideas faster with a computer than with a pen or a typewriter. When you're finished, delete weak ideas and expand strong ones. As you exhaust your topic, save your list and print it for further consideration. Later, you can develop it further by adding, deleting, and rearranging. You can also freewrite from the list, exploring items that seem promising.

b Making notes

Keeping an electronic journal is a good way to build a file of ideas. Write and save regular entries, just as you would in a paper journal (see 1b-2). Then you can move blocks of it into another discovery exercise or a draft.

The computer can also help you take notes from your reading or create notes according to your own structure. For example, you can type passages underlined or marked in your reading into the computer—as long as you are careful to protect against plagiarism by using quotation marks and keeping a record of the author, source, and page number(s) (see 36d). When you are ready to do so, you can transfer the best quotations (and the citations for them) into your draft.

To develop your own notes, try using the journalist's questions (see 1d-5) or the questions derived from the patterns of development (1d-6). Type either list of questions into the computer and save it. Then for each writing project, duplicate the list in a new file and insert possible answers. Print out your notes so that you can select material from them for future drafts.

c Considering audience and organizing ideas

You can create a standard file of questions for considering audience by typing the "Questions About Audience" from page 27 into your computer and saving them. For each assignment, duplicate the file and insert appropriate answers between the questions. Save the answers under a new file name, and print a copy for future reference.

The ease of adding, deleting, and rearranging on a word processor makes it the ideal tool for shaping and organizing material (see 1h). Beginning with just a list of ideas, you can isolate the more general points and then use the computer's tab settings to indent the more specific material. Unusable ideas can be deleted; redundant ideas can be merged. Print out each version of your outline to work on or use as a guide to planning, drafting, or revising. The outline in memory can be called up and revised as needed to reflect changes in your thinking and writing.

Many word processors can display two separate files on the screen at the same time, one on the top of the screen and one on the bottom. (The two slots are sometimes called **windows**.) To organize notes with this feature, start with a blank screen on the top, retrieve a file of notes at the bottom, and transfer selected copy (such as a thesis statement and general ideas) to the top. Or convert an informal outline to a formal one by transferring details from notes at the bottom of the screen to an informal outline at the top, inserting appropriate indentions, numbers, and letters for different levels of generality.

B1

B2

B2 Using a word processor for drafting

Many writers find that a word processor eases the transition from developing ideas to drafting. You can retrieve notes to the screen and rewrite, delete, or insert as needed. You can expand your outline into a draft by composing paragraphs directly under headings, deleting the remnants of the outline and adding transitions as you go along. Or you can freewrite a first draft, starting with a blank screen and letting the words flow until you're ready to consult your notes or outline for new material. If you're borrowing material from other writers, be sure to transfer source information as well as quotations from your notes to your draft so that you don't plagiarize, even accidentally. (The split-screen capability can help with documentation if you write your draft on one half and retrieve quotations and source citations from notes on the other half.)

Whatever your drafting style, take advantage of the word processor's speed and flexibility. Don't stop to correct errors or rewrite—both of which the computer will help you handle easily in a later draft. Put alternative ideas or phrasings in brackets so that you can consider them later without getting sidetracked now. Use an asterisk (*) or some other symbol to mark places where you feel blocked or very uncertain. Later, you can find these places quickly by instructing the computer to search for the symbol. If it helps, use invisible writing just to keep moving through a draft (see p. 708).

Frequently save or file the text you're drafting—at least once every twenty minutes or every few pages and every time you take a break or leave the computer for any reason. When you finish a drafting session, save your work, make a back-up copy on a separate disk, and print a paper copy in case anything happens to your disks. You will need the paper copy for revising and editing.

B3 Using a word processor for revising and editing

The convenience of extensive revision and editing is the greatest advantage of word processing. The machine eliminates the tedious, often messy labor of typing or writing out successive drafts or pieces of drafts. Instead, working on a copy of the most recent draft stored in the computer, you can add, delete, and move words, lines, and whole passages with a few keystrokes. If you want to compare, say, two different organizations or ways of explaining an important point, you can work on two duplicates of the latest draft, print both, and read them side by side. (A split-screen word processor allows this function on the screen as long as the passages are fairly short.)

Like most writers, you may find that you revise and edit more on a word processor than you do on a typewriter or in handwriting. It's important, though, that you not let the ease of revision lure you into obsessive rewriting—a kind of wheel-spinning in which changes cease to have a marked effect on meaning or clarity and may in fact sap the writing of energy. In addition, you need to think beyond the confines of the screen so that larger issues of meaning and structure are not lost to superficial matters such as word choice and sentence arrangement.

Here are some guidelines for using a word processor as an effective revision tool.

1. Deal with major revisions first: see the revision checklist on page 58. Save editing, formatting the manuscript, and proofreading for later drafts.
2. Use commands for deleting and moving blocks of copy as you would cut and paste a handwritten draft.
3. Save earlier drafts under their own file names in case you need to consult them for ideas or phrasings. Make a duplicate of any draft you want to revise, and work on the duplicate.
4. If you tend to rewrite excessively when working on the computer or have trouble finding your focus or organizing your paper, print a copy of your draft and work on it. Many writers prefer to work on paper copy (also called **hard copy**) because it is easier to read and allows a view of the whole not permitted on the computer screen. It is an easy matter to transfer changes from printed copy to computer.

The word processor is also an excellent tool for editing and proofreading—tightening, clarifying, refining, and correcting. (See the editing checklist on p. 64.) The following guidelines will help you make the most of the machine.

1. Save your drafts on the computer, print your work, and do your editing on a paper copy. Almost everyone finds it much harder to spot errors on the computer screen than on paper. And paper copy may discourage you from overediting to the point where you say less with less life. You can easily transfer the editing changes from paper to the computer.
2. After editing, return to the draft in the computer. Either work through the draft line by line or use the **search command** to find the places you want to change. The search command directs the computer to locate any words or phrases you specify.
3. Use the search command as well to find misused words or stylistic problems that tend to crop up in your writing. Such problems might include *there are, it is,* and other expletive constructions (see 5e-4); *the fact that* and other wordy phrases (31c-1); and *is, are,* and other forms of *be,* which often occur in wordy constructions (31c-3) and passive sentences (7h).
4. Make sure that you neither omit needed words nor leave in unneeded words when deleting or inserting text on the computer.
5. Resist the temptation to view the final draft coming out of the printer as perfect simply because the copy is clean. Always proofread your final draft *carefully.* (See 2d for proofreading tips.)

B3

A note on manuscript format

Most word processors provide automatic settings for margins, tabs, indentions, and other features of manuscript format. Use these settings to produce a manuscript that coincides with the format described in Appendix A or any format requested by your instructor. Appendix A also contains advice about print styles, paper, and other aspects of word processing. See especially A1-c and A2-b.

B4 Using optional programs on a word processor

Many word processors either come with optional programs such as spelling checkers or are compatible with other packages that provide these programs. The following list describes the kinds of programs you're most likely to see.

1. *Invention or discovery programs* help you develop a topic by prompting you with a structured set of questions or by providing creative analogies that help you think imaginatively. These programs can help you get started and develop new insights.
2. *Outlining programs* help you organize your work by providing automatic indentions, easy resequencing, and other features.
3. *Style-checking programs* help you find and correct wordy and awkward phrases and faulty grammar and punctuation. These programs are usually limited because they cannot identify the context of a possible flaw or error. Consult this book whenever you are unsure of a style checker's advice.
4. *Thesaurus programs* help with word choices by responding to your word with a display of several synonyms (words with similar meanings) and sometimes antonyms (words with opposite meanings). A single keystroke allows you to replace your word with a displayed word. (However, you should always consult a dictionary for the meaning of any word you are not sure of.)
5. *Spell-checking programs* help you find typographical errors and misspelled words, and they display correct spellings on the screen. They can be valuable proofreading aids. However, they are limited because they cannot store every possible word and thus may identify a word you use as misspelled even though it is correct. In addition, they are unreliable because they cannot identify errors such as a confusion among *there, their,* and *they're.* Maintain a file of your frequent misspellings and use the search command to check them yourself.

Glossary of Usage

This glossary provides notes on words or phrases that often cause problems for writers. The recommendations for standard written English are based on current dictionaries and usage guides like the ones listed in 32a. Items labeled **nonstandard** should be avoided in speech and especially in writing. Those labeled **colloquial** and **slang** occur in speech and in some informal writing but are best avoided in the more formal writing usually expected in college and business. (Words and phrases labeled *colloquial* include those labeled by many dictionaries with the equivalent term *informal*.) See Chapter 31 for further discussion of word choice and for exercises in usage. See 32b-2 for a description of dictionary labels. Also see 34a-1 for a list of commonly confused words that are pronounced the same or similarly. The words and definitions provided there supplement this glossary.

The glossary is necessarily brief. Keep a dictionary handy for all your writing, and make a habit of referring to it whenever you doubt the appropriateness of a word or phrase.

a, an Use *a* before words beginning with consonant sounds, including those spelled with an initial pronounced *h* and those spelled with vowels that are sounded as consonants: *a historian, a one-o'clock class, a university.* Use *an* before words that begin with vowel sounds, including those spelled with an initial silent *h: an orgy, an L, an honor.*

When you use an abbreviation or acronym in writing (see 28b), the article that precedes it depends on how the abbreviation is to be read: *She was once an HEW undersecretary.* (*HEW* is to be read as three separate letters, and *h* is pronounced "aitch.") *Many Americans opposed a SALT treaty.* (*SALT* is to be read as one word, *salt.*)

See also *article* in the Glossary of Grammatical Terms (p. 732).

accept, except *Accept* is a verb meaning "receive." *Except* is usually a preposition or conjunction meaning "but for" or "other than"; when it is used as a verb, it means "leave out." *I can accept all your suggestions except the last one. I'm sorry you excepted my last suggestion from your list.*

adverse, averse *Adverse* and *averse* are both adjectives, and both mean "opposed" or "hostile." But *averse* describes the subject's opposition to something, whereas *adverse* describes something opposed to the subject: *The president was averse to adverse criticism.*

advice, advise *Advice* is a noun, and *advise* is a verb: *Take my advice; do as I advise you.*

affect, effect Usually *affect* is a verb, meaning "to influence," and *effect* is a noun, meaning "result": *The drug did not affect his driving; in fact, it seemed to have no effect at all.* But *effect* occasionally is used as a verb meaning "to bring about": *Her efforts effected a change.* And *affect* is used in psychology as a noun meaning "feeling or emotion": *One can infer much about affect from behavior.*

aggravate *Aggravate* should not be used in its colloquial meaning of "irritate" or "exasperate" (for example, *We were aggravated by her constant arguing*). *Aggravate* means "make worse": *The President was irritated by the Senate's stubbornness because he feared any delay might aggravate the unrest in the Middle East.*

agree to, agree with *Agree to* means "consent to," and *agree with* means "be in accord with": *How can they agree to a treaty when they don't agree with each other about the terms?*

ain't Nonstandard for *am not, isn't,* or *aren't.*

all, all of Usually *all* is sufficient to modify a noun: *all my loving, all the things you are.* Before a pronoun or proper noun, *all of* is usually appropriate: *all of me, in all of France.*

all ready, already *All ready* means "completely prepared," and *already* means "by now" or "before now": *We were all ready to go to the movie, but it had already started.*

all right *All right* is always two words. *Alright* is a common misspelling.

all together, altogether *All together* means "in unison," or "gathered in one place." *Altogether* means "entirely." *It's not altogether true that our family never spends vacations all together.*

allusion, illusion An *allusion* is an indirect reference, and an *illusion* is a deceptive appearance: *Paul's constant allusions to Shakespeare created the illusion that he was an intellectual.*

almost, most *Almost* is an adverb meaning "nearly"; *most* is an adjective meaning "the greater number (or part) of." In formal writing, *most* should not be used as a substitute for *almost: We see each other almost (not most) every day.*

a lot *A lot* is always two words, used informally to mean "many." *Alot* is a common misspelling.

among, between In general, *among* is used for relationships involving more than two people or things. *Between* is used for relationships involving only two or for comparing one thing to a group to which it belongs. *The four of them agreed among themselves that the choice was between New York and Los Angeles.* Increasingly, though, *between* is used for relationships involving three or more comparable people or things: *Let's keep this just between the three of us, shall we?*

amongst Although common in British English, in American English *amongst* is an overrefined substitute for *among.*

amount, number *Amount* refers to a quantity of something (a singular noun) that cannot be counted. *Number* refers to countable items (a plural noun). *The <u>amount</u> of leftover ice we can save depends on the <u>number</u> of containers we have to put it in.*

an, and *An* is an article (see *a, an*). *And* is a coordinating conjunction. Do not carelessly omit the *d* from *and*.

and etc. *Et cetera* (*etc.*) means "and the rest"; *and etc.* therefore is redundant. See also *et al., etc.*

and/or *And/or* is awkward and often confusing. A sentence such as *The decision is made by the mayor <u>and/or</u> the council* implies that one or the other or both make the decision. If you mean both, use *and;* if you mean either, use *or.* Use *and/or* only when you mean three options.

and which, and who When *which* or *who* is used to introduce a relative clause, *and* is superfluous: *WCAS is my favorite AM radio station, <u>which</u>* (not *<u>and which</u>*) *I listen to every morning. And which* or *and who* is correct only when used to introduce a second clause beginning with the same relative pronoun: *Jill is my cousin <u>who</u> goes to school here <u>and who</u> always calls me at seven in the morning.*

ante-, anti- The prefix *ante-* means "before" (*antedate, antebellum*); *anti-* means "against" (*antiwar, antinuclear*). Before a capital letter or *i, anti-* takes a hyphen: *anti-Freudian, anti-isolationist.*

anxious, eager *Anxious* means "nervous" or "worried" and is usually followed by *about. Eager* means "looking forward" and is usually followed by *to. I've been <u>anxious about</u> getting blisters. I'm <u>eager</u>* (not *<u>anxious</u>*) *<u>to</u> get new running shoes.*

anybody, any body; anyone, any one *Anybody* and *anyone* are indefinite pronouns; *any body* is a noun modified by an adjective; *any one* is a pronoun or adjective modified by *any. How can <u>anybody</u> communicate with <u>any body</u> of government? Can <u>anyone</u> help Amy? She has more work than <u>any one</u> person can handle.*

any more, anymore *Any more* is used in negative constructions to mean "no more." *Anymore*, an adverb meaning "now," is also used in negative constructions. *He doesn't want <u>any more</u>. She doesn't live here <u>anymore</u>.*

anyplace Colloquial for *anywhere.*

anyways, anywheres Nonstandard for *anyway* and *anywhere.*

apt, liable, likely *Apt* and *likely* are interchangeable. Strictly speaking, though, *apt* means "having a tendency to": *Horace is <u>apt</u> to forget his lunch in the morning. Likely* means "probably going to": *Horace is leaving so early today that he's <u>likely</u> to catch the first bus.*
    Liable is normally used to mean "in danger of" and should be confined to situations with undesirable consequences: *If Horace doesn't watch out, he is <u>liable</u> to trip over that lawn sprinkler.* In the strictest sense, *liable* means "responsible" or "exposed to": *If Horace trips over that lawn sprinkler, the owner will be <u>liable</u> for damages.*

gl/us

as   *As* is often used to mean *because, since, while, whether,* or *who.* It may be vague or ambiguous in these senses: *As we were stopping to rest, we decided to eat lunch.* (Does *as* mean "while" or "because"?) Usually a more precise word is preferable. See also 16c.

   As never should be used as a substitute for *whether* or *who. I'm not sure whether* (not *as*) *we can make it. That's the man who* (not *as*) *gave me directions.*

as, like   In formal speech and writing, *as* may be either a preposition or a conjunction; *like* functions as a preposition only. Thus, if the construction being introduced is a full clause rather than a word or phrase, the preferred choice is *as* or *as if* (see 16c): *The plan succeeded as* (not *like*) *we hoped. It seemed as if* (not *like*) *it might fail. Other plans like it have failed.*

   When *as* serves as a preposition, the distinction between *as* and *like* depends on meaning. *As* suggests that the subject is equivalent or identical to the description: *She was hired as an engineer. Like* suggests resemblance but not identity: *People like her do well in such jobs.* See also *like, such as.*

as, than   In comparisons, *as* and *than* may be followed by either subjective- or objective-case pronouns: *You are as tall as he* (subjective). *They treated you better than him* (objective). The case depends on whether the pronoun is the subject or object of a verb: *I love you more than he* (*loves you*) (*he* is the subject of the missing verb *loves*). *I love you more than* (*I love*) *him* (*him* is the object of the missing verb *love*). See also 6e.

assure, ensure, insure   *Assure* means "to promise": *He assured us that if we left early, we would miss the traffic. Ensure* and *insure* often are used interchangeably to mean "make certain," but some reserve *insure* for matters of legal and financial protection and use *ensure* for more general meanings: *We left early to ensure that we would miss the traffic. It's expensive to insure yourself against floods.*

as to   A stuffy substitute for *about: The suspect was questioned about* (not *as to*) *her actions.*

at   The use of *at* after *where* is wordy and should be avoided: *Where are you meeting him?* is preferable to *Where are you meeting him at?*

at this point in time   Wordy for *now, at this point,* or *at this time.*

averse, adverse   See *adverse, averse.*

awful, awfully   Strictly speaking, *awful* means "awe-inspiring." As intensifiers meaning "very" or "extremely" (*He tried awfully hard*), *awful* and *awfully* are colloquial and should not be used in formal speech or writing.

a while, awhile   *Awhile* is an adverb; *a while* is an article and a noun. Thus *awhile* can modify a verb but cannot serve as the object of a preposition, and *a while* is just the opposite: *I will be gone awhile* (not *a while*). *I will be gone for a while* (not *awhile*).

bad, badly   In formal speech and writing, *bad* should be used only as an adjective; the adverb is *badly. He felt bad because his tooth ached*

gl/us

badly. In *He felt bad*, the verb *felt* is a linking verb and the adjective *bad* is a subject complement. See also 9b.

being as, being that   Colloquial for *because*, the preferable word in formal speech or writing: *Because* (not *Being as*) *the world is round, Columbus never did fall off the edge.*

beside, besides   *Beside* is a preposition meaning "next to." *Besides* is a preposition meaning "except" or "in addition to" as well as an adverb meaning "in addition." *Besides, several other people besides you want to sit beside Dr. Christensen.*

better, had better   *Had better* (meaning "ought to") is a verb modified by an adverb. The verb is necessary and should not be omitted: *You had better* (not *better*) *go.*

between, among   See *among, between.*

bring, take   Use *bring* only for movement from a farther place to a nearer one and *take* for any other movement. *First, take these books to the library for renewal, then take them to Mr. Daniels. Bring them back to me when he's finished.*

bunch   In formal speech and writing, *bunch* (as a noun) should be used only to refer to clusters of things growing or fastened together, such as bananas and grapes. Its use to mean a group of items or people is colloquial: *crowd* or *group* is preferable.

burst, bursted; bust, busted   *Burst* is a standard verb form meaning "to fly apart suddenly" (principal parts *burst, burst, burst*). The past-tense form *bursted* is nonstandard. The verb *bust* (*busted*) is slang.

but, hardly, scarcely   These words are negative in their own right; using *not* with any of them produces a double negative (see 9f). *We have but an hour* (not *We haven't got but an hour*) *before our plane leaves. I could hardly* (not *I couldn't hardly*) *make out her face in the dark.*

but however, but yet   These and similar expressions, in which *but* is combined with another conjunction, are redundant and should be avoided: *He said he had finished, yet* (not *but yet*) *he continued.*

but that, but what   These wordy substitutes for *that* and *what* should be avoided: *I don't doubt that* (not *but that*) *you are right.*

calculate, figure, reckon   As substitutes for *expect* or *imagine* (*I figure I'll go*), these words are colloquial.

can, may   Strictly, *can* indicates capacity or ability, and *may* indicates permission: *If I may talk with you a moment, I believe I can solve your problem.*

can't help but   This idiom is common but redundant. Either *I can't help wishing* or the more formal *I cannot but wish* is preferable to *I can't help but wish.*

case, instance, line   Expressions such as *in the case of, in the instance of*, and *along the lines of* are usually unnecessary padding in a sentence and should be avoided.

gl/us

gl/us

censor, censure To *censor* is to edit or remove from public view on moral or some other grounds; to *censure* is to give a formal scolding. *The lieutenant was censured by Major Taylor for censoring the letters his men wrote home from boot camp.*

center around *Center on* is generally considered more logical than, and preferable to, *center around.*

climatic, climactic *Climatic* comes from *climate* and refers to weather: *Last winter's low temperatures may indicate a climatic change. Climactic* comes from *climax* and refers to a dramatic high point: *During the climactic duel between Hamlet and Laertes, Gertrude drinks poisoned wine.*

complement, compliment To *complement* something is to add to, complete, or reinforce it: *Her yellow blouse complemented her black hair.* To *compliment* something is to make a flattering remark about it: *He complimented her hair. Complimentary* can also mean "free": *a complimentary sample of our new product; complimentary tickets.*

conscience, conscious *Conscience* is a noun meaning "a sense of right and wrong"; *conscious* is an adjective meaning "aware" or "awake." *Though I was barely conscious, my conscience told me to confess.*

contact Often used imprecisely as a verb when a more exact word such as *consult, talk with, telephone,* or *write to* would be appropriate.

continual, continuous *Continual* means "constantly recurring": *Most movies on television are continually interrupted by commercials. Continuous* means "unceasing": *Cable television often presents movies continuously without commercials.*

convince, persuade In the strictest sense, to *convince* someone means to change his or her opinion; to *persuade* someone means to move him or her to action. *Convince* thus is properly followed by *of* or *that,* whereas *persuade* is followed by *to: Once he convinced Othello of Desdemona's infidelity, Iago easily persuaded him to kill her.*

could of See *have, of.*

couple of Used colloquially to mean "a few" or "several."

credible, creditable, credulous *Credible* means "believable": *It's a strange story, but it seems credible to me. Creditable* means "deserving of credit" or "worthy": *Asked to play "Red River Valley," Steve gave a creditable performance. Credulous* means "gullible": *The credulous Claire believed Tim's statement that he was quitting school.* See also *incredible, incredulous.*

criteria The plural of *criterion* (meaning "standard for judgment"): *Of all our criteria for picking a roommate, the most important criterion is a sense of humor.*

data The plural of *datum* (meaning "fact"): *Out of all the data generated by these experiments, not one datum supports our hypothesis.* Usually, a more common term like *fact, result,* or *figure* is preferred to *datum.* Though *data* is very often used as a singular noun, it is still treated as plural in much formal speech and writing: *The data fail* (not *fails*) *to support the hypothesis.*

device, devise *Device* is the noun, and *devise* is the verb: *Can you devise some device for getting his attention?*

differ from, differ with To *differ from* is to be unlike: *The twins differ from each other only in their hairstyles.* To *differ with* is to disagree with: *I have to differ with you on that point.*

different from, different than *Different from* is preferred: *His purpose is different from mine.* But *different than* is widely accepted when a clause follows, particularly when a construction using *from* would be wordy: *I'm a different person now than I used to be* is preferable to *I'm a different person now from the person I used to be.*

discreet, discrete *Discreet* (noun form *discretion*) means "tactful": *What's a discreet way of telling Maud to be quiet? Discrete* (noun form *discreteness*) means "separate and distinct": *Within a computer's memory are millions of discrete bits of information.*

disinterested, uninterested *Disinterested* means "impartial": *We chose Pete, as a disinterested third party, to decide who was right. Uninterested* means "bored" or "lacking interest": *Unfortunately, Pete was completely uninterested in the question.*

don't *Don't* is the contraction for *do not,* not for *does not: I don't care, you don't care,* but *he doesn't* (not *don't*) *care.*

due to *Due* is an adjective or noun; thus *due to* is always acceptable as a subject complement: *His gray hairs were due to age.* Many object to *due to* as a preposition meaning "because of" (*Due to the holiday, class was canceled*). A rule of thumb is that *due to* is always correct after a form of the verb *be* but questionable otherwise.

due to the fact that Wordy for *because.*

each and every Wordy for *each* or *every.* Write *each one of us* or *every one of us,* not *each and every one of us.*

eager, anxious See *anxious, eager.*

effect See *affect, effect.*

elicit, illicit *Elicit* is a verb meaning "bring out" or "call forth." *Illicit* is an adjective meaning "unlawful." *The crime elicited an outcry against illicit drugs.*

ensure See *assure, ensure, insure.*

enthused Used colloquially as an adjective meaning "showing enthusiasm." The preferred adjective is *enthusiastic: The coach was enthusiastic* (not *enthused*) *about the team's victory.*

especially, specially *Especially* means "particularly" or "more than other things"; specially means "for a specific reason." *I especially treasure my boots. They were made specially for me.*

gl/us

et al., etc. *Et al.*, the Latin abbreviation for "and other people," is often used in source references for works with more than three authors: *Jones et al.* (see 35d-2, 36i-1). *Etc.*, the Latin abbreviation for "and other things," should not be used to refer to people. *Etc.* should be avoided in formal writing. When used, it should not substitute for precision, as in *The government provides health care, etc.* See also *and etc.*

everybody, every body; everyone, every one *Everybody* and *everyone* are indefinite pronouns: *Everybody* (*everyone*) *knows Tom steals. Every one* is a pronoun modified by *every, every body* a noun modified by *every.* Both refer to each thing or person of a specific group and are typically followed by *of: The game commissioner has stocked every body of fresh water in the state with fish, and now every one of our rivers is a potential trout stream.*

everyday, every day *Every day* is a noun modified by *every; everyday* is an adjective meaning "used daily" or "common": *Every day she had to cope with everyday problems.*

everywheres Nonstandard for *everywhere.*

except See *accept, except.*

except for the fact that Wordy for *except that.*

explicit, implicit *Explicit* means "stated outright": *I left explicit instructions. The movie contains explicit sex. Implicit* means "implied, unstated": *We had an implicit understanding. I trust Marcia implicitly.*

farther, further *Farther* refers to additional distance (*How much farther is it to the beach?*), and *further* refers to additional time, amount, or other abstract matters (*I don't want to discuss this any further*).

fewer, less *Fewer* refers to individual countable items (a plural noun), *less* to general amounts (a singular noun): *Skim milk has fewer calories than whole milk. We have less milk left than I thought.*

field The phrase *the field of* is wordy and generally unnecessary: *Margaret plans to specialize in* (not *in the field of*) *family medicine.*

figure See *calculate, figure, reckon.*

fixing to Avoid this colloquial substitute for "intend to": *The school intends* (not *is fixing*) *to build a new library.*

flaunt, flout *Flaunt* means "show off": *If you have style, flaunt it. Flout* means "scorn" or "defy": *Hester Prynne flouted convention and paid the price.*

flunk A colloquial substitute for *fail.*

former, latter *Former* refers to the first-named of two things, *latter* to the second-named: *I like both skiing and swimming, the former in the winter and the latter all year round.* To refer to the first- or last-named of three or more things, say *first* or *last: I like jogging, swimming, and hang gliding, but the last is inconvenient in the city.*

fun An an adjective, *fun* is colloquial and should be avoided in most writing: *It was a pleasurable* (not *fun*) *evening.*

further See *farther, further.*

get This common verb is used in many slang and colloquial expressions: *get lost, get with it, get your act together, that really gets me, getting on. Get* is easy to overuse; watch out for it in expressions like *it's getting better* (substitute *it's improving*) and *we got done* (substitute *we finished*).

good, well *Good* is an adjective, and *well* is nearly always an adverb: *Larry's a good dancer. He and Linda dance well together. Well* is properly used as an adjective only to refer to health: *You don't look well. Aren't you feeling well? (You look good,* in contrast, means "Your appearance is pleasing.")

good and Colloquial for "very": *I was very* (not *good and*) *tired.*

had better See *better, had better.*

had ought The *had* is unnecessary and should be omitted: *He ought* (not *had ought*) *to listen to his mother.*

half Either *half a* or *a half* is appropriate usage, but *a half a* is redundant: *Half a loaf* (not *A half a loaf*) *is better than none. I'd like a half-gallon* (not *a half a gallon*) *of mineral water, please.*

hanged, hung Though both are past-tense forms of *hang, hanged* is used to refer to executions and *hung* is used for all other meanings: *Tom Dooley was hanged* (not *hung*) *from a white oak tree. I hung* (not *hanged*) *the picture you gave me.*

hardly See *but, hardly, scarcely.*

have, of Use *have,* not *of,* after helping verbs such as *could, should, would, may,* and *might: You should have* (not *should of*) *told me.*

he, she; he/she The pronouns *he* and *she* refer to male and female antecedents, respectively. When the antecedent could be either male or female, convention has allowed the use of *he* to mean "he or she": *After the infant learns to crawl, he progresses to creeping.* However, many people today object to this use of *he* because readers tend to think of *he* as male, whether or not that is the writer's intention. The construction *he/she,* one substitute for *he,* is awkward and objectionable to most readers. The better choice is to use *he or she,* to make the pronoun plural, or to rephrase. For instance: *After the infant learns to crawl, he or she progresses to creeping. After infants learn to crawl, they progress to creeping. After learning to crawl, the infant progresses to creeping.* See also 8b-3 and 31a-8.

herself, himself See *myself, herself, himself, yourself.*

hisself Nonstandard for *himself.*

hopefully *Hopefully* means "with hope": *Freddy waited hopefully for a glimpse of Eliza.* The use of *hopefully* to mean "it is to be hoped," "I hope," or "let's hope" is now very common; but since many readers continue to object strongly to the usage, you should avoid it. *I hope* (not *Hopefully*) *Eliza will be here soon.*

idea, ideal An *idea* is a thought or conception. An *ideal* (noun) is a model of perfection or a goal. *Ideal* should not be used in place of *idea*: *The idea (not ideal) of the play is that our ideals often sustain us.*

if, whether For clarity, begin a subordinate clause with *whether* rather than *if* when the clause expresses an alternative: *If I laugh hard, people can't tell whether I'm crying.*

illicit See *elicit, illicit.*

illusion See *allusion, illusion.*

impact Careful writers use both the noun and the verb *impact* to connote forceful or even violent collision. Avoid the increasingly common diluted meanings of *impact:* "an effect" (noun) or "to have an effect on" (verb). The diluted verb (*The budget cuts impacted social science research*) is bureaucratic jargon.

implicit See *explicit, implicit.*

imply, infer Writers or speakers *imply*, meaning "suggest": *Jim's letter implies he's having too good a time to miss us.* Readers or listeners *infer*, meaning "conclude": *From Jim's letter I infer he's having too good a time to miss us.*

in, into *In* indicates location or condition: *He was in the garage. She was in a coma. Into* indicates movement or a change in condition: *He went into the garage. She fell into a coma. Into* is also slang for "interested in" or "involved in": *I am into Zen.*

in . . . A number of phrases beginning with *in* are unnecessarily wordy and should be avoided: *in the event that* (for *if*); *in the neighborhood of* (for *approximately* or *about*); *in this day and age* (for *now* or *nowadays*); *in spite of the fact that* (for *although* or *even though*); and *in view of the fact that* (for *because* or *considering that*). Certain other *in* phrases are nothing but padding and can be omitted entirely: *in the case of, in nature, in number, in reality, in terms of*, and *in a very real sense.* See also 31c.

incredible, incredulous *Incredible* means "unbelievable"; *incredulous* means "unbelieving": *When Nancy heard Dennis's incredible story, she was frankly incredulous.* See also *credible, creditable, credulous.*

individual, person, party *Individual* should refer to a single human being in contrast to a group or should stress uniqueness: *The U.S. Constitution places strong emphasis on the rights of the individual.* For other meanings *person* is preferable: *What person (not individual) wouldn't want the security promised in that advertisement? Party* means "group" (*Can you seat a party of four for dinner?*) and should not be used to refer to an individual except in legal documents.

infer See *imply.*

in regards to Nonstandard for *in regard to* (or *as regards* or *regarding*). See also *regarding.*

inside of, outside of The *of* is unnecessary when *inside* and *outside* are used as prepositions: *Stay inside* (not *inside of*) *the house. The decision is outside* (not *outside of*) *my authority. Inside of* may refer colloquially to time, though in formal English *within* is preferred: *The law was passed within* (not *inside of*) *a year.*

instance See *case, instance, line.*

insure See *assure, ensure, insure.*

irregardless Nonstandard for *regardless.*

is because See *reason is because.*

is when, is where These are mixed constructions (faulty predication; see 15b) in sentences that define: *Adolescence is a stage* (not *is when a person is*) *between childhood and adulthood. Socialism is a system in which* (not *is where*) *government owns the means of production.*

its, it's *Its* is a possessive pronoun: *That plant is losing its leaves. It's* is a contraction for *it is: It's likely to die if you don't water it.* Many people confuse *it's* and *its* because possessives are most often formed with-'s; but the possessive *its*, like *his* and *hers*, never takes an apostrophe.

-ize, -wise The suffix *-ize* is frequently used to change a noun or adjective into a verb: *revolutionize, immunize.* The suffix *-wise* commonly changes a noun or adjective into an adverb: *clockwise, otherwise, likewise.* But the two suffixes are used excessively and often unnecessarily, especially in bureaucratic writing. Avoid their use except in established words: *The two nations are ready to settle on* (not *finalize*) *an agreement. I'm highly sensitive* (not *sensitized*) *to that kind of criticism. From a financial standpoint* (not *Moneywise*), *it's a good time to buy real estate.*

kind of, sort of, type of In formal speech and writing, avoid using *kind of* or *sort of* to mean "somewhat": *He was rather* (not *kind of*) *tall.*
　　Kind, sort, and *type* are singular and take singular modifiers and verbs: *This kind of dog is easily trained.* Agreement errors often occur when these singular nouns are combined with the plural demonstrative adjectives *these* and *those: These kinds* (not *kind*) *of dogs are easily trained. Kind, sort,* and *type* should be followed by *of* but not by *a: I don't know what type of* (not *type* or *type of a*) *dog that is.*
　　Use *kind of, sort of,* or *type of* only when the word *kind, sort,* or *type* is important: *That was a strange* (not *strange sort of*) *statement. He's a funny* (not *funny kind of*) *guy.*

later, latter *Later* refers to time; *latter* refers to the second-named of two items. See also *former, latter.*

lay, lie *Lay* is a transitive verb (principal parts *lay, laid, laid*) that means "put" or "place" and takes a direct object. *If we lay this tablecloth in the sun next to the shirt Sandy laid out there this morning, it should dry quickly. Lie* is an intransitive verb (principal parts *lie, lay, lain*) that means "recline" or "be situated": *I lay awake all night last* *night, just as I had* <u>*lain*</u> *the night before. The town* <u>*lies*</u> *east of the river.* See also 7b.

leave, let *Leave* and *let* are interchangeable only when followed by *alone; leave me alone* is the same as *let me alone.* Otherwise, *leave* means "depart" and *let* means "allow": *Julia would not* <u>*let*</u> *Susan* <u>*leave.*</u>

less See *fewer, less.*

let See *leave, let.*

liable See *apt, liable, likely.*

lie, lay See *lay, lie.*

like, as See *as, like.*

like, such as When you are giving an example of something, use *such as* to indicate that the example is a representative of the thing mentioned, and use *like* to compare the example to the thing mentioned: *Steve has recordings of many great saxophonists* <u>*such as*</u> *Ben Webster, Coleman Hawkins, and Lee Konitz. Steve wants to be a great jazz saxophonist* <u>*like*</u> *Ben Webster, Coleman Hawkins, and Lee Konitz.*

　　Most writers prefer to keep *such* and *as* together: *Steve admires saxophonists* <u>*such as*</u> rather than *Steve admires* <u>*such*</u> *saxophonists* <u>*as.*</u>

likely See *apt, liable, likely.*

line See *case, instance, line.*

literally This adverb means "actually" or "just as the words say," and it should not be used to qualify or intensify expressions whose words are not to be taken at face value. The sentence *He was* <u>*literally climbing the walls*</u> describes a person behaving like an insect, not a person who is restless or anxious. For the latter meaning, *literally* should be omitted.

lose, loose *Lose* is a verb meaning "mislay": *Did you* <u>*lose*</u> *a brown glove? Loose* is an adjective meaning "unrestrained" or "not tight": *Don't open the door; Ann's canary got* <u>*loose.*</u> *Loose* also can function as a verb meaning "let loose": *They* <u>*loose*</u> *the dogs as soon as they spot the bear.*

lots, lots of Colloquial substitutes for *very many, a great many,* or *much.* Avoid *lots* and *lots of* in college or business writing. When you use either one informally, be careful to maintain subject-verb agreement: *There* <u>*are*</u> (not <u>*is*</u>) *lots of fish in the pond.*

may, can See *can, may.*

may be, maybe *May be* is a verb, and *maybe* is an adverb meaning "perhaps": *Tuesday* <u>*may be*</u> *a legal holiday.* <u>*Maybe*</u> *we won't have classes.*

may of See *have, of.*

media *Media* is the plural of *medium* and takes a plural verb: *All the news* <u>*media are,*</u> *increasingly visual.*

might of See *have, of.*

moral, morale   As a noun, *moral* means "ethical conclusion" or "lesson": *The moral of the story escapes me. Morale* means "spirit" or "state of mind": *Victory improved the team's morale.*

most, almost   See *almost, most.*

must of   See *have, of.*

myself, herself, himself, yourself   The *-self* pronouns are reflexive or intensive, which means they refer to or intensify an antecedent (see 5a-2): *Paul and I did it ourselves; Jill herself said so.* Though the *-self* pronouns often are used colloquially in place of personal pronouns, especially as objects of prepositions, they should be avoided in formal speech and writing unless the noun or pronoun they refer to is also present: *No one except me* (not *myself*) *saw the accident. Our delegates will be Susan and you* (not *yourself*).

nohow   Nonstandard for *in no way* or *in any way.*

nothing like, nowhere near   As colloquial substitutes for *not nearly*, these idioms are best avoided in formal speech and writing: *The human bones found in Europe are not nearly* (not *nowhere near*) *as old as those found in Africa.*

nowheres   Nonstandard for *nowhere.*

number   See *amount, number.*

of, have   See *have, of.*

off of   *Of* is unnecessary. Use *off* or *from* rather than *off of: He jumped off* (or *from*, not *off of*) *the roof.*

OK, O.K., okay   All three spellings are acceptable, but avoid this colloquial term in formal speech and writing.

on, upon   In modern English, *upon* is usually just a stuffy way of saying *on.* Unless you need a formal effect, use *on: We decided on* (not *upon*) *a location for our next meeting.*

on account of   Wordy for *because of.*

on the other hand   This transitional expression of contrast should be preceded by its mate, *on the one hand: On the one hand, we hoped for snow. On the other hand, we feared that it would harm the animals.* However, the two combined can be unwieldy, and a simple *but, however, yet,* or *in contrast* often suffices: *We hoped for snow. Yet we feared that it would harm the animals.*

outside of   See *inside of, outside of.*

owing to the fact that   Wordy for *because.*

party   See *individual, person, party.*

people, persons   In formal usage, *people* refers to a general group: *We the people of the United States. . . . Persons* refers to a collection of individuals: *Will the person or persons who saw the accident please notify. . . .* Except when emphasizing individuals, prefer *people* to *persons.*

gl/us

per Except in technical writing, an English equivalent is usually preferable to the Latin *per*: *$10 an* (not *per*) *hour; sent by* (not *per*) *parcel post; requested in* (not *per* or *as per*) *your letter.*

percent (per cent), percentage Both these terms refer to fractions of one hundred and should be avoided except when specifying actual statistics. Use an expression such as *part of, a number of,* or *a large* (or *small*) *proportion of* when you mean simply "part."

    Percent always follows a numeral (*40 percent of the voters*), and the word should be used instead of the symbol (%) in general writing. *Percentage* usually follows an adjective (*a high percentage*).

person See *individual, person, party.*

persons See *people, persons.*

persuade See *convince, persuade.*

phenomena The plural of *phenomenon* (meaning "perceivable fact" or "unusual occurrence"): *The Center for Short-Lived Phenomena judged that the phenomenon we had witnessed was not a flying saucer.*

plenty A colloquial substitute for *very*: *He was going very* (not *plenty*) *fast when he hit that tree.*

plus *Plus* is standard as a preposition meaning *in addition to: His income plus mine is sufficient.* But *plus* is colloquial as a conjunctive adverb: *Our organization is larger than theirs; moreover* (not *plus*), *we have more money.*

practicable, practical *Practicable* means "capable of being put into practice"; *practical* means "useful" or "sensible": *We figured out a practical new design for our kitchen, but it was too expensive to be practicable.*

precede, proceed The verb *precede* means "come before": *My name precedes yours in the alphabet.* The verb *proceed* means "move on": *We were told to proceed to the waiting room.*

prejudice, prejudiced *Prejudice* is a noun; *prejudiced* is an adjective. Do not drop the *-d* from *prejudiced: I was fortunate my parents were not prejudiced* (not *prejudice*).

pretty Overworked as an adverb meaning "rather" or "somewhat": *He was somewhat* (not *pretty*) *irked at the suggestion.*

previous to, prior to Wordy for *before.*

principal, principle *Principal* is a noun meaning "chief official" or, in finance, "capital sum." As an adjective, *principal* means "foremost" or "major." *Principle* is a noun only, meaning "rule" or "axiom." *Her principal reasons for confessing were her principles of right and wrong.*

proceed, precede See *precede, proceed.*

provided, providing *Provided* may serve as a subordinating conjunction meaning "on the condition (that)"; *providing* may not. *The grocer will begin providing food for the soup kitchen provided* (not *providing*) *we find a suitable space.*

question of whether, question as to whether   Wordy for *whether*.

raise, rise   *Raise* is a transitive verb that takes a direct object, and *rise* is an intransitive verb that does not take an object: *The Kirks have to rise at dawn because they raise cows.*

real, really   In formal speech and writing, *real* should not be used as an adverb; *really* is the adverb and *real* an adjective. *Popular reaction to the announcement was really (not real) enthusiastic.*

reason is because   Mixed construction (faulty predication; see 15b). Although the expression is colloquially common, formal speech and writing require a *that* clause after *reason is: The reason he is absent is that* (not *is because*) *he is sick.* Or: *He is absent because he is sick.*

reckon   See *calculate, figure, reckon.*

regarding, in regard to, with regard to, relating to, relative to, with respect to, respecting   Stuffy substitutes for *on, about,* or *concerning: Mr. McGee spoke about* (not *with regard to*) *the plans for the merger.*

respectful, respective   *Respectful* means "full of (or showing) respect": *If you want respect, be respectful of other people. Respective* means "separate": *After a joint Christmas celebration, the French and the Germans returned to their respective trenches.*

rise, raise   See *raise, rise.*

scarcely   See *but, hardly, scarcely.*

sensual, sensuous   *Sensual* suggests sexuality; *sensuous* means "pleasing to the senses." *Stirred by the sensuous scent of meadow grass and flowers, Cheryl and Paul found their thoughts growing increasingly sensual.*

set, sit   *Set* is a transitive verb (principal parts *set, set, set*) that describes something a person does to an object: *He set the pitcher down. Sit* is an intransitive verb (principal parts *sit, sat, sat*) that describes something done by a person who is tired of standing: *She sits on the sofa.* See also 7b.

shall, will   *Will,* originally reserved for the second and third persons, is now generally accepted as the future-tense helping verb for all three persons: *I will go, you will go, they will go.* The main use of *Shall* is for first-person questions requesting an opinion or consent: *Shall I order a pizza? Shall we dance?* (Questions that merely inquire about the future use *will: When will I see you again?*) *Shall* can also be used for the first person when a formal effect is desired (I *shall expect you around three*), and it is occasionally used with the second or third person to express the speaker's determination (*You shall do as I say*).

should, would   *Should* expresses obligation for first, second, and third persons: *I should fix dinner. You should set the table. Jack should wash the dishes. Would* expresses a wish or hypothetical condition for all three persons: *I would do it. Wouldn't you? Wouldn't anybody?* When the context is formal, however, *should* is sometimes used instead of *would* in the first person: *We should be delighted to accept your kind invitation.*

should of See *have, of.*

since *Since* is often used to mean "because": *Since you ask, I'll tell you.* Its primary meaning, however, relates to time: *I've been waiting since noon.* To avoid confusion, some writers prefer to use *since* only in contexts involving time. If you do use *since* in both senses, watch out for ambiguous constructions, such as *Since you left, my life is empty,* where *since* could mean either "because" or "ever since."

sit, set See *set, sit.*

situation Often unnecessary, as in *The situation is that we have to get some help* (revise to *We have to get some help*) or *The team was faced with a punting situation* (revise to *The team was faced with punting* or *The team had to punt*).

so Avoid using *so* alone as a vague intensifier: *He was so late. So* needs to be followed by *that* and a clause that states a result: *He was so late that I left without him.*

some *Some* is colloquial as an adverb meaning "somewhat" or "to some extent" and as an adjective meaning "remarkable": *We'll have to hurry somewhat* (not *some*) *to get there in time. Those are remarkable* (not *some*) *photographs.*

somebody, some body; someone, some one *Somebody* and *someone* are indefinite pronouns; *some body* is a noun modified by an adjective; and *some one* is a pronoun or an adjective modified by *some. Somebody ought to invent a shampoo that will give hair some body. Someone told Janine she should choose some one plan and stick with it.*

someplace Informal for *somewhere.*

sometime, sometimes, some time *Sometime* means "at an indefinite time in the future": *Why don't you come up and see me sometime? Sometimes* means "now and then": *I still see my old friend Joe sometimes. Some time* means "span of time": *I need some time to make the payments.*

somewheres Nonstandard for *somewhere.*

sort of, sort of a See *kind of, sort of, type of.*

specially See *especially, specially.*

such Avoid using *such* as a vague intensifier: *It was such a cold winter. Such* should be followed by *that* and a clause that states a result: *It was such a cold winter that Napoleon's troops had to turn back.*

such as See *like, such as.*

supposed to, used to In both these expressions, the *-d* is essential: *I used to* (not *use to*) *think so. He's supposed to* (not *suppose to*) *meet us.*

sure Colloquial when used as an adverb meaning *surely: James Madison sure was right about the need for the Bill of Rights.* If you merely want to be emphatic, use *certainly: Madison certainly was right.* If your goal is to convince a possibly reluctant reader, use *surely: Madison surely was right. Surely Madison was right.*

sure and, sure to; try and, try to *Sure to* and *try to* are the preferred forms: *Be sure to* (not *sure and*) *buy milk. Try to* (not *Try and*) *find some decent tomatoes.*

take, bring See *bring, take.*

than, as See *as, than.*

than, then *Than* is a conjunction used in comparisons, *then* an adverb indicating time: *Holmes knew then that Moriarty was wilier than he had thought.*

that, which *That* always introduces restrictive clauses: *We should use the lettuce that Susan bought* (*that Susan bought* identifies the specific lettuce being referred to). *Which* can introduce both restrictive and nonrestrictive clauses, but many writers reserve *which* only for nonrestrictive clauses: *The leftover lettuce, which is in the refrigerator, would make a good salad* (*which is in the refrigerator* simply provides more information about the lettuce). See also 21c.

their, there, they're *Their* is the possessive form of *they: Give them their money. There* indicates place (*I saw her standing there*) or functions as an expletive (*There is a hole behind you*). *They're* is a contraction for *they are: They're going fast.*

theirselves Nonstandard for *themselves.*

then, than See *than, then.*

these kind, these sort, these type, those kind See *kind of, sort of, type of.*

this here, these here, that there, them there Nonstandard for *this, these, that,* or *those.*

thru A colloquial spelling of *through* that should be avoided in all academic and business writing.

thusly A mistaken form of *thus.*

till, until, 'til *Till* and *until* have the same meaning; both are acceptable. *'Til,* a contraction of *until,* is an old form that has been replaced by *till.*

time period Since a *period* is an interval of time, this expression is redundant: *They did not see each other for a long time* (not *time period*). *Six accidents occurred in a three-week period* (not *time period*).

to, too, two *To* is a preposition; *too* is an adverb meaning "also" or "excessively"; and *two* is a number. *I too have been to Europe two times.*

too Avoid using *too* as an intensifier meaning "very": *Monkeys are too mean.* If you do use *too,* explain the consequences of the excessive quality: *Monkeys are too mean to make good pets.*

toward, towards Both are acceptable, though *toward* is preferred. Use one or the other consistently.

try and, try to See *sure and, sure to; try and, try to.*

type of See *kind of, sort of, type of.* Don't use *type* without *of*: *It was a family type of* (not *type*) *restaurant.* Or, better: *It was a family restaurant.*

uninterested See *disinterested, uninterested.*

unique As an absolute adjective (see 9e-5), *unique* cannot sensibly be modified with words such as *very* or *most*: *That was a unique* (not *a very* or *the most unique*) *movie.*

until See *till, until, 'til.*

upon, on See *on, upon.*

usage, use *Usage* refers to conventions, most often those of a language: *Is "hadn't ought" proper usage? Usage* is often misused in place of the noun *use: Wise use* (not *usage*) *of insulation can save fuel.*

use, utilize *Utilize* means "make use of": *We should utilize John's talent for mimicry in our play.* In most contexts, *use* is equally or more acceptable and much less stuffy.

used to See *supposed to, used to.*

wait for, wait on In formal speech and writing, *wait for* means "await" (*I'm waiting for Paul*), and *wait on* means "serve" (*The owner of the store herself waited on us*).

ways Colloquial as a substitute for *way: We have only a little way* (not *ways*) *to go.*

well See *good, well.*

whether, if See *if, whether.*

which See *that, which.*

which, who *Which* never refers to people. Use *who* or sometimes *that* for a person or persons and *which* or *that* for a thing or things: *The baby, who was left behind, opened the door, which we had closed.* See also 12f.

who's, whose *Who's* is the contraction of *who is: Who's at the door? Whose* is the possessive form of *who: Whose book is that?*

will, shall See *shall, will.*

-wise See *-ize, -wise.*

with regard to, with respect to See *regarding.*

would See *should, would.*

would have Avoid this construction in place of *had* in clauses that begin *if* and state a condition contrary to fact: *If the tree had* (not *would have*) *withstood the fire, it would have been the oldest in town.* (See also 7g-2.)

would of See *have, of.*

your, you're *Your* is the possessive form of *you: Your dinner is ready. You're* is the contraction of *you are: You're bound to be late.*

yourself See *myself, herself, himself, yourself.*

gl/us

Glossary of Grammatical Terms

absolute phrase A phrase that consists of a noun or pronoun and a participle, modifies a whole clause or sentence (rather than a single word), and is not joined to the rest of the sentence by a connector: *Our accommodations arranged, we set out on our trip. They will hire a local person, other things being equal.* When the participle in an absolute phrase is a form of the verb *be* (*being, been*). the participle is often omitted: *They will hire a local person, other things equal.* See also 5c-3 and 21d.

abstract noun See *noun*.

acronym A pronounceable word formed from the initial letter or letters of each word in an organization's title: NATO (North Atlantic Treaty Organization). See also 20b and 28b.

active voice See *verb*.

adjectival A term sometimes used to describe any word or word group, other than an adjective, that is used to modify a noun. Common adjectivals include nouns (*wagon train, railroad ties*), phrases (*fool on the hill*). and clauses (*the man that I used to be*). See *clause* and *phrase*. See also 5c.

adjective A word used to modify a noun or a word or word group used as a noun.

> **Descriptive adjectives** name some quality of the noun: *beautiful morning; dark horse.*
>
> **Limiting adjectives** narrow the scope of a noun. They include **possessives** (*my, their*); words that show number (*eight, several*); **demonstrative adjectives** (*this train, these days*); **interrogative adjectives** (*what time? whose body?*); and **numbers** (*two boys*).
>
> **Proper adjectives** are derived from proper nouns: *French language, Machiavellian scheme.*

Adjectives also can be classified according to position.

> **Attributive adjectives** appear next to the nouns they modify: *full moon.*
>
> **Predicate adjectives** are connected to their nouns by linking verbs: *The moon is full.* See also *complement*.

See also *comparison*, 5b-1, and Chapter 9.

adjective clause See *clause*.

adjective phrase See *phrase*.

adverb   A word used to modify a verb, an adjective, another adverb, or a whole sentence. Any one-word modifier that is not an adjective, a word used as an adjective, or an article is an adverb: *If you go south you'll hit a more heavily traveled road.* (*South* modifies the verb *go; heavily* modifies the adjective *traveled;* and *more* modifies the adverb *heavily.*) See also *comparison,* 5b-1, and Chapter 9.

adverb clause   See *clause.*

adverbial   A term sometimes used to describe any word or word group, other than an adverb, that is used to modify a verb, an adjective, another adverb, or a whole sentence. Common adverbials include nouns (*This little piggy stayed home*), phrases (*This little piggy went to market*), and clauses (*This little piggy went wherever he wanted*). See *clause* and *phrase.* See also 5c.

adverbial conjunction   See *conjunctive adverb.*

adverb phrase   See *phrase.*

agreement   The correspondence of one word to another in person, number, or gender. A verb must agree with its subject; a pronoun must agree with its antecedent; and a demonstrative adjective must agree with its noun. *Every week the commander orders these kinds of sandwiches for his troops.* (The verb *orders* and the pronoun *his* both agree with the noun *commander.* The demonstrative adjective *these* agrees with the noun *kinds.*) See Chapter 8.
    Logical agreement requires consistency in number between other related words, usually nouns: *The students brought their books* (not *book*). See also 13a.

antecedent   The noun, or word or word group acting as a noun, to which a pronoun refers: *Jonah, who is not yet ten, has already chosen the college he will attend.* (*Jonah* is the antecedent of the pronouns *who* and *he.*) See also 8b.

appositive   A word or phrase appearing next to a noun or pronoun, or to a word or word group acting as a noun, that explains or identifies it and is equivalent to it: *My brother Michael, the best horn player in town, won the state competition.* (*Michael* is a restrictive appositive that identifies which brother is being referred to. *The best horn player in town* is a nonrestrictive appositive that adds information about *My brother Michael.*) See also 5c-5 and 21c-2.

article   The word *a, an,* or *the.* Articles are usually classed as adjectives; they are sometimes called **determiners** because they always signal that a noun follows. See the Glossary of Usage (p. 713) for a discussion of choosing between *a* and *an* before a noun or abbreviation.
    Articles often present problems for those whose native language is not English, because many languages use articles differently or less frequently than English does. The main conventions for using articles in English can be summarized as follows:

1. *The* is a **definite article:** it precedes a noun when the thing named is already known to the reader (*Visitors may tour the house*). *A* and *an* are **indefinite articles:** they precede a noun when the thing named is not already known to the reader (*They share a house*).

2. Use *a, an,* or *the* with a singular count noun—that is, a singular noun that names something countable: *a glass, an apple, the mirror.* Count nouns can form plurals with the addition of *-s* or *-es* (*glass, glasses*) or in some irregular way (*child, children*).

3. Do not use *a* or *an* with a plural noun: *apples* (not *an apples*). And do not use *a* or *an* with a mass noun—that is, a singular noun that names something not normally countable: *mail* (not *a mail*), *supervision* (not *a supervision*). Unlike count nouns, mass nouns do not form plurals. Note, however, that many nouns are sometimes count nouns and sometimes mass nouns: in *We have a room for you, room* is a mass noun meaning "space"; in *We have room for you, room* is a count noun meaning "walled area."

4. Do not use *the* with a plural noun or a mass noun when the noun refers generally to all representatives of what it names: *Men* (not *The men*) *and women* (not *the women*) *are different. Democracy* (not *The democracy*) *fosters freedom* (not *the freedom*) *of expression* (not *the expression*). Use *the* when referring to one or more specific representatives of what the noun names: *The women came and went.*

This summary omits many special uses of articles. Fuller discussions can be found in many composition textbooks designed for students using English as a second language.

auxiliary verb   See *helping verb.*

cardinal number   The type of number that shows amount: *two, sixty, ninety-seven.* Contrast *ordinal number* (such as *second, ninety-seventh*).

case   The form of a noun or pronoun that indicates its function in the sentence. Nouns have two cases: the **plain case** (*John, ambassador*), for all uses except to show possession; and the **possessive** (or **genitive**) **case** (*John's, ambassador's*). Pronouns have three cases: the **subjective** (or **nominative**) **case** (*I, she*), denoting the subject of a verb or a subject complement; the **possessive case,** for use as either an adjective (*my, her*) or a noun (*mine, hers*); and the **objective case** (*me, her*), denoting the object of a verb, verbal, or preposition. See page 208 for a complete list of the forms of personal and relative pronouns.

clause   A group of related words containing a subject and predicate. **A main (independent) clause** can stand by itself as a sentence; a **subordinate (dependent) clause** cannot.

> **MAIN CLAUSE**   *We can go to the movies.*
>
> **SUBORDINATE CLAUSE**   *We can go if Julie gets back on time.*

Subordinate clauses may function as adjectives, adverbs, or nouns.

> **Adjective clauses** modify nouns or pronouns: *The car that hit Fred was running a red light* (clause modifies *car*).
>
> **Adverb clauses** modify verbs, adjectives, other adverbs, or whole clauses or sentences: *The car hit Fred when it ran a red light* (clause modifies *The car hit Fred*).
>
> **Noun clauses,** like nouns, function as subjects, objects, or complements: *Whoever was driving should be arrested* (clause is sentence subject).

See also 5c-4.

collective noun   See *noun.*

comma splice   A sentence error in which two main clauses are separated by a comma with no coordinating conjunction.

> COMMA SPLICE   The book was long, it contained useful information.
>
> REVISED   The book was long; it contained useful information.
>
> REVISED   The book was long, *but* it contained useful information.

See 11a and 11b.

common noun   See *noun.*

comparative   See *comparison.*

comparison   The inflection of an adverb or adjective that shows its relative intensity. The **positive degree** is the simple, uncompared form: *gross, clumsily.* The **comparative degree** compares the thing modified to at least one other thing: *grosser, more clumsily.* The **superlative degree** indicates that the thing modified exceeds all other things to which it is being compared: *grossest, most clumsily.* The comparative and superlative degrees are formed either by adding the endings *-er* and *-est* or by preceding the modifier with the words *more* and *most, less* and *least.* See also 5b-1 and 9e.

complement   A word or word group that completes the sense of a subject, an object, or a verb.

> **Subject complements** follow a linking verb and modify or refer to the subject. They may be adjectives, nouns or pronouns, or words or word groups acting as adjectives or nouns: *I am a lion tamer, but I am not yet experienced.* (The noun *lion tamer* and the adjective *experienced* complement the subject *I.*) Adjective complements are also called **predicate adjectives.** Noun complements are also called **predicate nouns** or **predicate nominatives.**
>
> **Object complements** follow and modify or refer to direct objects. The complement can be an adjective, a noun, or a word or word group acting as an adjective or noun: *If you elect me president, I'll*

keep the unions satisfied. (The noun *president* complements the direct object *me,* and the adjective *satisfied* complements the direct object *unions.*)

Verb complements are direct and indirect objects of verbs. They may be nouns, pronouns, or words or word groups acting as nouns: *Don't give the chimp that peanut.* (*Chimp* is the indirect object and *peanut* is the direct object of the verb *give.* Both objects are verb complements.)

See also *object* and 5a-3.

complete predicate   See *predicate.*

complete subject   See *subject.*

complex sentence   See *sentence.*

compound   Consisting of two or more words that function as a unit. **Compound words** include **compound nouns** (*milestone, featherbrain*); **compound adjectives** (*two-year-old, downtrodden*); and **compound prepositions** (*in addition to, on account of*). **Compound constructions** include **compound subjects** (*Harriet and Peter poled their barge down the river*); **compound predicates** (*The scout watched and waited*) or parts of predicates (*He grew tired and hungry*); and **compound sentences** (*He smiled, and I laughed*). See also 5d.

compound-complex sentence   See *sentence.*

compound predicate   See *compound.*

compound sentence   See *sentence.*

compound subject   See *compound.*

concrete noun   See *noun.*

conjugation   A list of the forms of a verb showing tense, voice, mood, person, and number. The conjugation of the verb *know* in present tense, active voice, indicative mood is *I know, you know, he/she/it knows, we know, you know, they know.* See also Chapter 7.

conjunction   A word that links and relates parts of a sentence. **Coordinating conjunctions** (*and, but, or, nor, for, so, yet*) connect words or word groups of equal grammatical rank: *The lights went out, but the doctors and nurses cared for their patients as if nothing were wrong.* See also 5d-1. **Correlative conjunctions** or **correlatives** (such as *either . . . or, not only . . . but also*) are pairs of coordinating conjunctions that work together: *He was certain that either his parents or his brother would help him.* See also 5d-1. **Subordinating conjunctions** (*after, although, as if, because, if, when, while,* and so on) begin a subordinate clause and link it to a main clause: *The seven dwarfs whistle while they work.* See also 5c-4.

conjunctive adverb (adverbial conjunction)   An adverb (such as *besides, consequently, however, indeed,* and *therefore*) that relates two main clauses in a sentence: *We had hoped to own a house by now; however, housing costs have risen too fast.* See also 5d-2.

connector (connective)   Any word or phrase that links words, phrases, clauses, or sentences. Common connectors include coordinating, correlative, and subordinating conjunctions; conjunctive adverbs; and prepositions.

connotation   An association called up by a word, beyond its dictionary definition. See 31b-1. Contrast *denotation.*

construction   Any group of grammatically related words, such as a phrase, a clause, or a sentence.

contraction   A condensation of an expression, with an apostrophe replacing the missing letters: for example, *doesn't* (for *does not*), *we'll* (for *we will*). See also 23c.

coordinating conjunction   See *conjunction.*

coordination   The linking of words, phrases, or clauses that are of equal importance, usually with a coordinating conjunction: *He and I laughed, but she was not amused.* See also 16a. Contrast *subordination.*

correlative conjunction (correlative)   See *conjunction.*

count noun   See *noun.*

dangling modifier   A word or phrase modifying a term that has been omitted or to which it cannot easily be linked.

DANGLING	*Having arrived late,* the concert had already begun.
REVISED	Having arrived late, *we* found that the concert had already begun.
REVISED	*Because we arrived late,* we missed the beginning of the concert.

See also 14f.

declension   A list of the forms of a noun or pronoun, showing inflections for person (for pronouns), number, and case. See Chapter 6, page 208, for a complete declension of the personal and relative pronouns.

degree   See *comparison.*

demonstrative adjective   See *adjective.*

demonstrative pronoun   See *pronoun.*

denotation   The main or dictionary definition of a word. See 31b-1. Contrast *connotation.*

dependent clause   See *clause.*

derivational suffix   See *suffix.*

descriptive adjective   See *adjective.*

determiner   A word such as *a, an, the, my,* and *your* which indicates that a noun follows. See also *article.*

diagramming   A visual method of identifying and showing the relations among various parts of a sentence.

direct address   A construction in which a word or phrase indicates the person or group spoken to: *Have you finished, John? Farmers, unite.*

direct object   See *object.*

direct quotation (direct discourse)   See *quotation.*

double negative   A nonstandard form consisting of two negative words used in the same construction so that they effectively cancel each other: *I don't have no money.* Rephrase as *I have no money* or *I don't have any money.* See 9f.

double possessive   A possessive using both the ending *-'s* and the preposition *of: That is a favorite expression of Mark's.*

ellipsis   The omission of a word or words from a quotation, indicated by the three spaced periods of an **ellipsis mark:** *"that all . . . are created equal."* See also 25e.

elliptical clause   A clause omitting a word or words whose meaning is understood from the rest of the clause: *David likes Minneapolis better than (he likes) Chicago.* See also 5c-4.

expletive   A sentence construction that postpones the subject by beginning with *there* or *it* followed by a form of the verb *be: It is impossible to get a ticket; I don't know why there aren't more seats available.* (*To get a ticket* is the subject of *is; seats* is the subject of *aren't.*) See also 5e-4.

finite verb   A term used to describe any verb that makes an assertion or expresses a state of being and can stand as the main verb of a sentence or clause: *The moose eats the leaves.* See also 5c-2. Contrast *gerund, participle,* and *infinitive*—all formed from finite verbs but unable to stand alone as the main verb of a sentence: *I saw the moose eating the leaves* (participle). Contrast also *verbal* (*nonfinite verb*).

fragment   See *sentence fragment.*

function word   A word, such as an article, conjunction, or preposition, that serves primarily to clarify the roles of and relations between other words in a sentence: *We chased the goat for an hour but finally caught it.* Contrast *lexical word.*

fused sentence (run-on sentence)   A sentence error in which two main clauses are joined with no punctuation or connecting word between them.

FUSED	I heard his lecture it was dull.
REVISED	I heard his lecture; it was dull.

See 11c.

future perfect tense   See *tense.*

gl/gr

future tense See *tense*.

gender The classification of nouns or pronouns as masculine (*he, boy, handyman*), feminine (*she, woman, actress*), or neuter (*it, typewriter, dog*).

genitive case Another term for possessive case. See *case*.

gerund A verbal that ends in *-ing* and functions as a noun. The form of the gerund is the same as that of the present participle. Gerunds may have subjects, objects, complements, and modifiers: *Working is all right for killing time.* (*Working* is the subject of the verb *is; killing* is the object of the preposition *for* and takes the object *time*.) See also 5c-2, *verbal*, and *participle*.

helping verb A verb (also called an **auxiliary verb**) used with a main verb in a verb phrase: *will give, has been seeing, could depend.* Helping verbs indicate tense and sometimes also indicate voice, person, number, or mood. **Modal auxiliaries** include *can, could, may, might, must, ought, shall, should, will,* and *would.* They indicate a necessity, possibility, capability, willingness, or the like: *He can lift 250 pounds. You should write to your grandmother.* See also 5a-2 and Chapter 7, pages 218 and 224.

idiom An expression that is peculiar to a language and that may not make sense if taken literally: for example, *dark horse, bide your time,* and *by and large.* See 31b-3 for a list of idioms involving prepositions, such as *agree with them* and *agree to the contract.*

imperative See *mood*.

indefinite pronoun See *pronoun*.

independent clause See *clause*.

indicative See *mood*.

indirect object See *object*.

indirect quotation (indirect discourse) See *quotation*.

infinitive The plain form of a verb, the form listed in the dictionary: *buy, sharpen, rinse.* Usually in combination with the **infinitive marker** *to*, infinitives form verbals and verbal phrases that function as nouns, adjectives, or adverbs. They may have objects, complements, or modifiers: *Alex's goals are to make money and to live well.* (*To make* and *to live,* following a linking verb, are complements of the subject *goals. To make* takes the object *money* and *to live* is modified by the adverb *well.*) See also 5c-2 and *verbal*.

infinitive marker See *infinitive*.

infinitive phrase See *phrase*.

inflection The variation in the form of a word that indicates its function in a particular context. See *declension*, the inflection of nouns and pronouns; *conjugation*, the inflection of verbs; and *comparison*, the inflection of adjectives and adverbs.

gl/gr

inflectional suffix   See *suffix*.

intensifier   A modifier that adds emphasis to the word(s) it modifies: for example, *very slow, so angry*.

intensive pronoun   See *pronoun*.

interjection   A word standing by itself or inserted in a construction to exclaim or command attention: *Hey! Ouch! What the heck did you do that for?*

interrogative   Functioning as or involving a question.

interrogative adjective   See *adjective*.

interrogative pronoun   See *pronoun*.

intransitive verb   See *verb*.

inversion   A reversal of usual word order in a sentence, as when a verb precedes its subject or an object precedes its verb: *Down swooped the hawk. Our aims we stated clearly.*

irregular verb   A verb that forms its past tense and past participle in some other way than by the addition of *-d* or *-ed* to the plain form: for example, *go, went, gone; give, gave, given*. See also 5a; and see 7a for a list of irregular verbs. Contrast *regular verb*.

lexical word   A word, such as a noun, verb, or modifier, that carries part of the meaning of language. Contrast *function word*.

linking verb   A verb that relates a subject to its complement: *Julie is a Democrat. He looks harmless. Those flowers smell heavenly.* Common linking verbs are the forms of *be;* the verbs relating to the senses, such as *feel* and *smell;* and the verbs *become, appear,* and *seem*. See also 5a-3 and *verb*.

logical agreement   See *agreement*.

main clause   See *clause*.

mass noun   See *noun*.

misplaced modifier   A modifier so far from the term it modifies or so close to another term it could modify that its relation to the rest of the sentence is unclear.

MISPLACED	The boys played with firecrackers that they bought illegally *in the field*.
REVISED	The boys played *in the field* with firecrackers that they bought illegally.

A misplaced modifier that could modify the words on either side of it is called a **squinting modifier.**

SQUINTING	The plan we considered *seriously* worries me.
REVISED	The plan we *seriously* considered worries me.
REVISED	The plan we considered worries me *seriously*.

See also 14a to 14e.

mixed construction A sentence containing two or more parts that do not fit together in grammar or in meaning.

> MIXED Of those who show up will not all be able to get in.
>
> REVISED Not all those who show up will be able to get in.

See also 15a and 15b.

modal auxiliary See *helping verb*.

modifier Any word or word group that limits or qualifies the meaning of another word or word group. Modifiers include adjectives and adverbs as well as words, phrases, and clauses that act as adjectives and adverbs. See also "Guide to Modifiers," pages 205–06.

mood The form of a verb that shows how the speaker views the action. The **indicative mood**, the most common, is used to make statements or ask questions: *The play will be performed Saturday. Did you get us tickets?* The **imperative mood** gives a command: *Please get good seats. Don't let them put us in the top balcony.* The **subjunctive mood** expresses a wish, a condition contrary to fact, a recommendation, or a request: *I wish George were coming with us. Did you suggest that he join us?* See also 7g.

nominal A noun, a pronoun, or a word or group of words used as a noun: *Joan and I talked. The rich owe a debt to the poor* (adjectives acting as subject and object). *Baby sitting can be exhausting* (gerund acting as subject). *I like to play with children* (infinitive phrase acting as object).

nominative See *case*.

nonfinite verb See *verbal*.

nonrestrictive element A word, phrase, or clause that does not limit the term or construction it refers to and that is not essential to the meaning of the sentence's main clause. Nonrestrictive elements are usually set off by commas: *This electric mixer, on sale for one week only, can be plugged directly into your kitchen counter* (nonrestrictive adjective phrase). *Sleep, which we all need, occupies a third of our lives* (nonrestrictive adjective clause). *His wife, Patricia, is a chemist.* (nonrestrictive appositive). See also 21c. Contrast *restrictive element*.

noun A word that names a person, place, thing, quality, or idea: *Maggie, Alabama, clarinet, satisfaction, socialism.* Nouns normally form the possessive case by adding -'s (*Maggie's*) and the plural by adding -s or -es (*clarinets, messes*), although there are exceptions (*men, women, children*).

> **Common nouns** refer to general classes: *book, government, music.*
>
> **Proper nouns** name specific people or places: *Susan, Athens, Candlestick Park.*

Collective nouns name groups: *team, class, jury, family.*

Count nouns name things that can be counted: *ounce, camera, pencil, person, cat.*

Mass nouns name things that are not normally counted: *jewelry, milk, music, information.*

Concrete nouns name tangible things: *ink, porch, bird.*

Abstract nouns name ideas or qualities: *equality, greed, capitalism.*

See "Guide to Nouns" (p. 201) and also 5a-2.

noun clause   See *clause.*

number   The form of a noun, pronoun, demonstrative adjective, or verb that indicates whether it is singular or plural: *woman, women; I, we; this, these; runs, run.* See also Chapter 8.

object   A noun, a pronoun, or a word or word group acting as a noun that receives the action of or is influenced by a transitive verb, a verbal, or a preposition.

Direct objects receive the action of verbs and verbals and frequently follow them in a sentence: *We sat watching the <u>stars</u>. Emily caught <u>whatever it was you had</u>.*

Indirect objects tell for or to whom or what something is done: *I lent <u>Stan</u> my car. Reiner bought <u>us all</u> champagne.*

Objects of prepositions usually follow prepositions and are linked by them to the rest of the sentence: *They are going to <u>New Orleans</u> for the <u>jazz festival</u>.*

See also 5a-3, and 5c-1.

object complement   See *complement.*

objective   See *case.*

ordinal number   The type of number that shows order: *first, eleventh, twenty-fifth.* Contrast *cardinal number* (such as *one, twenty-five*).

parenthetical element   A word or construction that interrupts a sentence and is not part of its main structure, called *parenthetical* because it could (or does) appear in parentheses: *Childe Hassam (1859–1935) was an American painter and etcher. The book, <u>incidentally</u>, is terrible.* See 21c-3.

participial phrase   See *phrase.*

participle   A verbal showing continuing or completed action, used as an adjective or part of a verb phrase but never as the main verb of a sentence or clause.

Present participles end in *-ing: My heart is <u>breaking</u>* (participle as part of verb phrase). *I like to watch the <u>rolling</u> waves* (participle as adjective).

gl/gr

Past participles most commonly end in *-d, -ed, -n* or *-en* (*wished, shown, given*) but often change the spelling of the verb (*sung, done, slept*): *Jeff has* <u>*broken*</u> *his own record* (participle as part of verb phrase). *The meeting occurred behind a* <u>*closed*</u> *door* (participle as adjective).

See also *gerund*, 5b-2, and 5c-2.

parts of speech   The classes into which words are commonly grouped according to their form, function, and meaning: nouns, pronouns, verbs, adjectives, adverbs, conjunctions, prepositions, and interjections. See separate entries for each part of speech. See also 5a to 5d.

passive voice   See *verb*.

past participle   See *participle*.

past perfect tense   See *tense*.

past tense   See *tense*.

perfect tenses   See *tense*.

person   The form of a verb or pronoun that indicates whether the subject is speaking, spoken to, or spoken about. In English only personal pronouns and verbs change form to indicate difference in person. In the **first person,** the subject is speaking: *I* <u>*am*</u> (or *We* <u>*are*</u>) *planning to go to the party tonight.* In the **second person,** the subject is being spoken to: <u>*Are you*</u> *coming?* In the **third person,** the subject is being spoken about: <u>*She was*</u> (or <u>*They were*</u>) *going.* See also Chapter 8.

personal pronoun   See *pronoun*.

phrase   A group of related words that lacks a subject or a predicate or both and that acts as a single part of speech. There are several common types of phrases:

> **Verb phrases** are verb forms of more than one word that serve as predicates of sentences or clauses: *He says the movie* <u>*has started*</u>.
>
> **Prepositional phrases** consist of a preposition and its object, plus any modifiers. They function as adjectives, as adverbs, and occasionally as nouns: *We could come back* <u>*for the second show*</u> (adverb). See also *preposition*.
>
> **Absolute phrases** consist of a noun or pronoun and usually a participle. They modify whole clauses or sentences: <u>*Our seats being reserved*</u>, *we probably should stay.* See also *absolute phrase*.
>
> **Verbal phrases** are formed from verbals (see 5c-2). **Infinitive phrases** consist of an infinitive and its object, plus any modifiers, and they sometimes also include a subject. They function as nouns, adjectives, and adverbs: *I'd hate* <u>*to go all the way home*</u> (noun). (See also *infinitive*.) **Participial phrases** consist of a participle and its object, plus any modifiers. They function as adjectives: *The man* <u>*collecting tickets*</u> *says we may not be too late.* (See also *participle*.) **Gerund phrases** consist of a gerund (the *-ing* form of a verb used as a noun) and its object, plus any modifiers, and

they sometimes also include a subject. They function as nouns: *Missing the beginning is no good, though.* (See also *gerund.*)

plain case See *case.*

plain form The infinitive or dictionary form of a verb. See *infinitive.*

positive degree See *comparison.*

possessive See *case.*

predicate The part of a sentence other than the subject and its modifiers. A predicate must contain a finite verb and may contain modifiers and objects of the verb as well as object and subject complements. The **simple predicate** consists of the verb and its auxiliaries: *A wiser person would have made a different decision.* The **complete predicate** includes the simple predicate and any modifiers, objects, and complements: *A wiser person would have made a different decision.* See also 5a and 5b.

predicate adjective See *complement.*

predicate noun (predicate nominative) See *complement.*

prefix A letter or group of letters (such as *sub-, in-, dis-, pre-*) that can be added at the beginning of a root or word to create a new word: *sub- + marine = submarine; dis- + grace = disgrace.* See also 33b-2. Contrast *suffix.*

preposition A word that links a noun, a pronoun, or a word or word group acting as a noun (the object of the preposition) to the rest of a sentence: *If Tim doesn't hear from that plumber by four, he'll call someone else before dinner.* Common prepositions include those in the preceding example as well as *about, after, beside, between, for, in,* and *to.* See 5c-1 for a fuller list. See also *object* and *phrase.*

prepositional phrase See *phrase.*

present participle See *participle*

present perfect tense See *tense.*

present tense See *tense.*

principal clause A main or independent clause. See *clause.*

principal parts The three forms of a verb from which its various tenses are formed: the **plain form** or **infinitive** (*stop, go*); the **past tense** (*stopped, went*); and the **past participle** (*stopped, gone*). See *infinitive, participle,* and *tense.* See also 5a-2 and Chapter 7.

progressive tense See *tense.*

pronoun A word used in place of a noun or noun phrase (its antecedent). There are eight types of pronouns, many of which differ only in function, not in form:

> **Personal pronouns** (*I, you, he, she, it, we, they*): *They want you to come with us.*

Reflexive pronouns (*myself, themselves*): *Can't you help your-selves?*

Intensive pronouns (*myself, themselves*): *I myself saw it. She her-self said so.*

Interrogative pronouns (*who, which, what*): *What was that? Which is mine?*

Relative pronouns (*who, which, that*): *The noise that scared you was made by the boy who lives next door.*

Demonstrative pronouns (*this, that, these, those*): *These are fresher than those.*

Indefinite pronouns (*each, one, anybody, all*): *One would think somebody must have seen it.*

Reciprocal pronouns (*each other, one another*): *I hope we'll see each other again.*

See also 5a-2, "Guide to Pronouns" (p. 202), and Chapter 6.

proper adjective   See *adjective.*

proper noun   See *noun.*

quotation   Repetition of what someone has written or spoken. In **direct quotation (direct discourse),** the person's words are duplicated exactly and enclosed in quotation marks: *Polonius told his son, Laertes, "Neither a borrower nor a lender be."* An **indirect quotation (indirect discourse)** reports what someone said or wrote but not in the exact words and not in quotation marks: *Polonius advised his son, Laertes, not to borrow or lend.* See also 13d and Chapter 24.

reciprocal pronoun   See *pronoun.*

reflexive pronoun   See *pronoun.*

regular verb   A verb that forms its past tense and past participle by adding *-d* or *-ed* to the plain form: *dip, dipped, dipped; open, opened, opened.* See also 5a and Chapter 7. Contrast *irregular verb.*

relative pronoun   See *pronoun.*

restrictive element   A word, phrase, or clause that is essential to the meaning of a sentence because it limits the thing it refers to. Restrictive elements are not set off by commas: *The keys to the car are on the table. That man who called about the apartment said he'd try to call you tonight.* See also 21c. Contrast *nonrestrictive element.*

rhetoric   The principles for finding and arranging ideas and for using language in speech or writing so as to achieve the writer's purpose in addressing his or her audience.

rhetorical question   A question asked for effect, with no answer expected. The person asking the question either intends to provide the answer or assumes it is obvious: *If we let one factory pollute the river, what does that say to other factories that want to dump wastes there?*

run-on sentence   See *fused sentence.*

sentence A complete unit of thought, consisting of at least a subject and a predicate that are not introduced by a subordinating word. Sentences can be classed on the basis of their structure in one of four ways: *simple, compound, complex,* or *compound-complex.*

> **Simple sentences** contain one main clause: *I'm leaving.*

> **Compound sentences** contain at least two main clauses: *I'd like to stay, but I'm leaving.*

> **Complex sentences** contain one main clause and at least one subordinate clause: *If you let me go now, you'll be sorry.*

> **Compound-complex sentences** contain at least two main clauses and at least one subordinate clause: *I'm leaving because you want me to, but I'd rather stay.*

See also *clause* and 5f.

sentence fragment A sentence error in which a group of words is set off as a sentence even though it begins with a subordinating word or lacks either a subject or a predicate or both. See also Chapter 10.

FRAGMENT	She wasn't in shape for the race. *Which she had hoped to win.* [*Which,* a relative pronoun, makes the italicized clause subordinate.]
REVISED	She wasn't in shape for the race, which she had hoped to win.
FRAGMENT	He could not light a fire. *And thus could not warm the room.* [The italicized word group lacks a subject.]
REVISED	He could not light a fire. Thus he could not warm the room.

sentence modifier An adverb or a word or word group acting as an adverb that modifies the idea of the whole sentence in which it appears rather than any specific word: *In fact, people will always complain.*

simple predicate See *predicate.*

simple sentence See *sentence.*

simple subject See *subject.*

simple tense See *tense.*

split infinitive The often awkward interruption of an infinitive and its marker *to* by an adverb: *The mission is to boldly go where no one has gone before.* See also *infinitive,* and see 14e.

squinting modifier See *misplaced modifier.*

subject The noun, or word or word group acting as a noun, that is the agent or topic of the action or state expressed in the predicate of a sentence or clause. The **simple subject** consists of the noun alone: *The quick brown fox jumps over the lazy dog.* The **complete subject** includes the simple subject and its modifiers: *The quick brown fox jumps over the lazy dog*. See also 5a.

subject complement   See *complement*.

subjective   See *case*.

subjunctive   See *mood*.

subordinate clause   See *clause*.

subordinating conjunction (subordinator)   See *conjunction*.

subordination   The use of grammatical constructions to make one element in a sentence dependent on rather than equal to another and thus to convey the writer's sense that the dependent element is less important to the whole: *Although I left six messages for him, the doctor failed to call me back*. See also 16b. Contrast *coordination*.

substantive   A word or word group used as a noun.

suffix   A **derivational suffix** is a letter or group of letters that can be added to the end of a root word to make a new word, often a different part of speech: *child, childish; shrewd, shrewdly; visual, visualize*. See also 33b-3. **Inflectional suffixes** adapt words to different grammatical relations: *boy, boys; fast, faster; tack, tacked*. See also 5a and 5b.

superlative   See *comparison*.

syntax   The division of grammar that is concerned with the relations among words and the means by which those relations are indicated.

tag question   A question attached to the end of a statement and consisting of a pronoun, a helping verb, and sometimes the word *not: It isn't raining, is it? It is sunny, isn't it?*

tense   The form of a verb that expresses the time of its action, usually indicated by the verb's inflection and by helping verbs.

> The **simple tenses** include the **present** (*I race, you go*); the **past** (*I raced, you went*); and the **future,** formed with the helping verb *will* (*I will race, you will go*).

> The **perfect tenses,** formed with the helping verbs *have* and *had,* indicate completed action. They include the present perfect (*I have raced, you have gone*); the **past perfect** (*I had raced, you had gone*); and the **future perfect** (*I will have raced, you will have gone*).

> The **progressive tense,** formed with the helping verb *be* plus the present participle, indicates continuing action (*I am racing, you are going*).

See also Chapter 7, especially pages 225–27.

transitive verb   See *verb*.

verb   A word or group of words indicating the action or state of being of a subject. A **transitive verb** conveys action that has an object: *He shot the sheriff*. An **intransitive verb** does not have an object: *The* *sheriff died.* A **linking verb** connects the subject and a complement that describes or renames the subject: *The sheriff was brave.* Often the same verb may be transitive, intransitive, or linking, depending on its use in the sentence: *The dog smelled the bone* (transitive). *The dog smelled* (intransitive). *The dog smelled bad* (linking).

Transitive verbs also may be either in the **active voice,** when the subject is the agent of the action, or in the **passive voice,** when the subject is the recipient of the action. Active: *We all made the decision together.* Passive: *The decision was made by all of us.*

The inflection of a verb and the use of helping verbs with it indicate its tense, mood, number, and sometimes person: *shall go, were going, have gone.*

See also "Guide to Verbs and Verbals" (pp. 203–04), Chapter 7, *tense,* and *mood.*

verbal (nonfinite verb) A verb form used as a noun (*Swimming is good exercise*), an adjective (*Blocked passes don't make touchdowns*), or an adverb (*We were prepared to run*). A verbal can never function as the main verb in a sentence. Verbals may have subjects, objects, complements, and modifiers. See *participle, gerund, infinitive,* and *phrase.* Contrast *finite verb.* See also 5c-2 and "Guide to Verbs and Verbals" (pp. 203–04).

verbal phrase See *phrase.*

verb phrase See *phrase.*

voice The active or passive aspect of a transitive verb. See *verb.* See also 5e-3.

word order The arrangement of the words in a sentence, which plays a large part in determining the grammatical relation among words in English.

gl/gr

Lawrence A. Mayer, from "The Confounding Enemy of Sleep," *Fortune* (June 1974). Reprinted by permission.

Jan Morris, from *Destinations: Essays from Rolling Stone* by Jan Morris. Copyright © 1980 by Rolling Stone Press and Jan Morris. Reprinted by permission of Oxford University Press, Inc.

Newsweek, 7 July 1980, from "The New Immigrants." Copyright 1980, by Newsweek, Inc. All rights reserved. Reprinted by permission.

Robert Ornstein, from "A Letter from the Director," *Human Nature* (August 1978). Copyright © 1978 by Human Nature, Inc. Reprinted by permission of the publisher.

William G. Ouchi, Ph.D., from *Theory Z: How American Business Can Meet the Japanese Challenge*, copyright © 1981. Reprinted by permission of Addison-Wesley Publishing Company.

Laurence Perrine, from "Fifteen Ways to Write Five Hundred Words," *The CEA Critic* (November 1962). Copyright by The College English Association, Inc., 1962. Reprinted by permission.

Francine Prose, from "Therapy Cliches," *The New York Times*, 9 May 1988. Copyright © 1985 by The New York Times Company. Reprinted by permission.

Readers' Guide to Periodical Literature, July–October 1987, p. 710, from entries under "Women Executives." Copyright © 1987 by The H. W. Wilson Company. Material reproduced by permission of the publisher.

Frank Rich, excerpt from Review by Frank Rich "Stage: A Rock Reprise in 'Leader of the Pack,' " *The New York Times*, 9 April 1985. Copyright © 1985 by The New York Times Company. Reprinted by permission.

Roger Rosenblatt, from "Consistency as a Minor Virtue," *Time*, 7 February 1983. Copyright 1983 Time, Inc. Reprinted by permission from *Time*.

Social Science Index, April 1984–March 1985, p. 662, from entries under "Leadership." Copyright © 1984, 1985 by The H. W. Wilson Company. Material reproduced by permission of the publisher.

Karen M. Tarczyk, excerpts from "An Assessment of Dating Violence on Campus," student research paper, July 12, 1988.

John D. Teehan, "Death and Resurrection in Hopkins' 'Spring and Fall,' " student research paper, July 30, 1988.

Lewis Thomas, from "The Art of Teaching Science," *The New York Times Magazine*. Copyright © 1982 by The New York Times Company. Reprinted by permission.

Lynn Treacy, excerpts from "Demonstration: Genetic Engineering," student research paper, August 12, 1988.

Barbara Tuchman, from "The Decline of Quality," *The New York Times Magazine*, 2 November 1980. Copyright © 1980 by The New York Times Company. Reprinted by permission.

Stewart L. Udall, from *The Quiet Crisis*. Copyright © 1963 by Stewart L. Udall. Reprinted by permission of Holt, Rinehart and Winston, Publishers.

Michael Walzer, from "The Community," *The New Republic*, 1 March 1982. Reprinted by permission of The New Republic. © 1982 The New Republic, Inc.

Judith Wax, from *Starting in the Middle* by Judith Wax. Copyright © 1979 by Judith Wax. Reprinted by permission of Holt, Rinehart and Winston, Publishers.

Bayard Webster, from "Should Vivisection Be Abolished?" *The New York Times*, 27 September 1983. Copyright © 1983 by The New York Times Company. Reprinted by permission.

Diane White, from "At Large," *The Boston Globe*, 27 January 1979. Reprinted courtesy of *The Boston Globe*.

E. B. White, in "Poetry" from *One Man's Meat* by E. B. White. Copyright 1944 by E. B. White. Reprinted by permission of Harper & Row, Publishers, Inc.

E. B. White, from *The Wild Flag* (Houghton Mifflin). © 1943, 1971 E. B. White. Originally in *The New Yorker*. Reprinted by permission.

George F. Will, from *Statecraft as Soulcraft: What Government Does* by George F. Will. Copyright © 1983 by G.F.W., Inc., A Maryland Corporation. Reprinted by permission of Simon & Schuster, Inc.

Kenneth L. Woodward, from "Life After Death?" *Newsweek*, 12 July 1976. Copyright 1976 by Newsweek, Inc. All rights reserved. Reprinted by permission.

Richard Wright, excerpt from *Black Boy* by Richard Wright. Copyright 1937, 1942, 1944, 1945 by Richard Wright. Reprinted by permission of Harper & Row, Publishers, Inc., and Mrs. Ellen Wright.

William Zinsser, from *The Lunacy Boom* by William Zinsser. Copyright © 1966, 1968, 1969, 1970 by William Zinsser. Reprinted by permission.

Index

Index

Index

Index

Index

PLAN OF THE BOOK AND GUIDE TO CORRECTION CODE AND SYMBOLS